American Academic Cultures

American Academic Cultures

A History of Higher Education

PAUL H. MATTINGLY

The University of Chicago Press

CHICAGO AND LONDON

The University of Chicago Press, Chicago 60637
The University of Chicago Press, Ltd., London

Published 2017
Printed in the United States of America

26 25 24 23 22 21 20 19 18 17 1 2 3 4 5

ISBN-13: 978-0-226-50512-1 (cloth)
ISBN-13: 978-0-226-50526-8 (paper)
ISBN-13: 978-0-226-50543-5 (e-book)
DOI: 10.7208/chicago/9780226505435.001.0001

Library of Congress Cataloging-in-Publication Data

Names: Mattingly, Paul H., author.
Title: American academic cultures : a history of higher education / Paul H. Mattingly.
Description: Chicago ; London : The University of Chicago, 2017. |
Includes bibliographical references and index.
Identifiers: LCCN 2017011375 | ISBN 9780226505121 (cloth : alk. paper) |
ISBN 9780226505268 (pbk. : alk. paper) | ISBN 9780226505435 (e-book)
Subjects: LCSH: Education, Higher—United States—History. |
Education—United States—Philosophy.
Classification: LCC LA226 .M388 2017 | DDC 378.00973—dc23
LC record available at https://lccn.loc.gov/2017011375

♾ This paper meets the requirements of ANSI/NISO Z39.48-1992 (Permanence of Paper).

To the truly distinguished, life-enhancing teachers and colleagues—intellectually adventurous, pedagogically sensitive, and interpretively thrilling—whom I had the good fortune to encounter along the way:

DOM STEPHEN REID, OSB
St. Anselm's Abbey School, Washington, DC
REV. WILLIAM V. DYCH, SJ
Georgetown University, Washington, DC
REV. JOHN R. DONAHUE, SJ
Georgetown University, Washington, DC
LOUIS DUPRE
Georgetown University, Washington, DC
HISHAM SHARABI
Georgetown University, Washington, DC
WILLIAM R. TAYLOR
University of Wisconsin, Madison
HARVEY GOLDBERG
University of Wisconsin, Madison
KARL KROEBER
University of Wisconsin, Madison
BARBARA ABRASH
New York University, New York City
RACHEL BERNSTEIN
New York University, New York City
MILLARD CLEMENTS
New York University, New York City
DAVID A. HARNETT
last on this list but in a category all his own is my lifelong friend, whose conversations over the years were the equivalent of another university education

Contents

Acknowledgments

This book had its origins in a request by my distinguished New York University colleague Frederick L. Redefer (1905–76) in 1970 to teach a course in the history of American higher education. At the time Professor Redefer was a member of the graduate Program in Higher Education at NYU and had earlier served as executive secretary of the Progressive Education Association (1932–40) and as its director from 1940 to 1943. I have always appreciated Fred's understanding of the power of history in shaping a professional perspective. Every two years thereafter, I taught the course happily and attended to the discourse on the subject. The present study represents the culmination of the research over these years. I owe substantive thanks to readers of the manuscript, especially to David F. Allmendinger and, for especially close commentaries, David A. Harnett and Colin Burke. For comments on particular chapters, I should like to thank my colleagues Roger Geiger, Peter D. Hall, Ellen Lagemann, James McLachlan, James E. Scanlon, and Peter Wosh and two astute readers for the University of Chicago Press. I would be remiss if I did not also acknowledge the high professionalism of University of Chicago Press's editors, Elizabeth Branch Dyson and Mark Reschke, particularly their commitment to fine bookmanship.

INTRODUCTION

Why has it become so difficult to assess America's tradition of higher learning and to reimagine different approaches to the subject? This question underlies so much of the criticism and commentary about America's touted university system. Critics explore policies of admission, concentrations of gender and race in both faculty and student bodies, vast investments by state governments and foundations, and extraordinary indebtedness by gifted students who submit themselves to the promise of career and economic rewards, not to mention naysayers who deplore the privileges of the American colleges and universities and the impracticality of humanistic study. Does historical analysis offer any insights into the present-day conundrums of American academia? The answer is yes, but only if history itself is presented as something more than earlier factual examples, something more than a linear progress through time. In this book American higher learning becomes the product of varied generational cultures, each grounded in their special moment in time, each driven by historically distinct values that produce a special cadre of leaders, problems, and organized responses. History is something less than a discernable continuity; rather, I am assuming, the past affords the present an opportunity to study how different sets of assumptions condition social assumptions and expectations that are both inherently unique and yet passed on to later generations. The study of higher learning at distinct moments in time provides us with the great luxury of rethinking how our present issues played out earlier in different circumstances. That rethinking is the indispensable prerequisite that history offers to reconstruction and innovation.

In the 1970s scholars began experimenting with new approaches to American higher education. Influenced by the creative surge in social history, which itself was stimulated by an international discourse on the subject,[1] scholars began to examine a range of postsecondary schools as germane to the scholarship. No longer was higher education interpreted through the screen of its most prestigious institutions or through the defensive hagiography of centennial celebrations. Scholars scrutinized the official rhetoric of colleges and universities and found ways to explore less obvious meanings. Once institutions of higher learning became part of larger political and cultural discussions, the official purposes of these schools took on different connotations. New methodologies led, for example, to an examination of students themselves, so often omitted from house histories or centennial studies of higher education. The demography of students raised issues about, not only official rhetoric, but also permitted explorations of actual achievement and specifications of how colleges and universities served as sorting devices in American society. The central aim of the present study is to synthesize this scholarship and rework some of the still prevalent misconceptions about the achievement of American academic cultures.

The notion of culture itself, thankfully imprecise, becomes here an integrating notion of many factors documenting the larger social impact of American colleges and universities. These institutions embody singular assumptions about their social environment at any given moment in time. Colleges and universities thereby become windows into the latent assumptions about larger American social priorities. It will be axiomatic here that colleges and universities must be studied both inside and "outside the walls," probing values and influences that put pressure on many institutions, not just educational ones. Still, the colleges and universities were always products of their historical moment, and that historical moment regularly received challenges and countercurrents that affected the reigning standard. Colleges and universities embodied values and language that their public recognized and sought to impart to succeeding generations. They also sheltered assumptions that could not have meant the same thing a generation earlier or later. What passed as a college at seventeenth-century Harvard was nothing like Harvard College in the early eighteenth century. Or again, the early nineteenth-century precollegiate academy had very little in common with the post–Civil War public high school or the private boarding school that fed higher education institutions. Land-grant institutions of the Civil War era had nothing in common with state universities after World War I. The different cultures of these educational moments produced specific institutions and resonant individuals that differ from our own time but are connected to the issues we face.

The intellectual debates and rationales associated with distinctive colleges and universities play a central role in this analysis. Some readers may judge the intellectual emphasis too prolonged. But I want to suggest that historically laden ideas are always social forces, equal to or more powerful and shaping than many political agencies or economic trends. My concern, like the treatment of "the inculcation of moral character," an early nineteenth-century educational mantra, is to explore this value as seen by its users and without the benefit of later hindsight. The point is to begin with their distinctive notions and work down to their basic assumptions. One astute commentator argues that the most important thing to know about an individual or a society is what they take for granted. The time spent on their arguments reconstructs their cultural mind-set, often clarifying not only their actual accomplishments but also illuminating the issues they left for their successors. I consider this methodology to be deeply historical. If successful, one grasps the normative priories of a period, particularizing it so that it cannot apply to an earlier or later circumstance. But vicariously it becomes a bridge to our own problems of higher learning.

On another level, this study has assumed that there never was one American culture but several at any given moment in time, usually contending with each other. But in every generation, there have been influential ideas that gained a special educational power and shaped a "culture" of distinctive assumptions. For example, in the eighteenth century, where the study begins, there is a pronounced emphasis on evangelical and denominational values. The few colleges that existed believed that their indoctrinating messages benefited the society at large. So long as a single denomination prevailed in the relevant social region, their assumptions were true and established a cultural mind-set. But soon other denominations appeared, and other notions of social good. During the early and middle thirds of the eighteenth century, every denomination, stimulated by the dynamics of the Great Awakening, created its own college, primarily in the New England and Middle Colonies. The ferment and competitions of the Great Awakening produced the first actual collegiate culture, and I use the example of eighteenth-century Yale College as a kind of prototype and exemplar of this first generational culture (generational culture #1; chapter 1).

Similar denominational energy in the Southern Colonies produced a very different outcome due to distinct cultural forces. The patrician hierarchy of Virginia, especially, created an educational design that sought to thwart denominational indoctrination. Thomas Jefferson, in particular, tried first to reform his alma mater, William and Mary College, and failing that, to create an entirely new paradigm of schooling that peaked in a reconfigured school of higher education, the University of Virginia. His idea of a publicly supported school, grounded in indigenous mores, produced an educational alternative to the denominational model, which vigorously resisted the idea of a "godless" state university. But the form of the Virginia alternative became such an ongoing rhetorical (more than an effective) counter to its nemesis that "Mr. Jefferson's university" needs to be viewed as both a part of the eighteenth century's complex assumptions and an expression of a distinct cultural outlook (generational culture #2; chapter 2).

By the early nineteenth century, evangelical schooling for all the denominations gave way to a new, post-Revolutionary republicanism and caused a reorganization of both schooling and purpose. A new generation of denominational schools had to fashion outreaches to larger, heterogeneous publics in order to be seen as cohesive rather than divisive, hence the rise of official nondenominational aspirations for schools with sectarian roots. Nineteenth-century schooling, public and private, sought officially to produce upright citizens—they called it "moral character"—rather than true believers with a special theology. The nineteenth-century nondenominational college was thus different than its eighteenth-century predecessors and offered a distinct cultural mentalité (generational culture #3; chapter 3).

After the Civil War, another generation of colleges began to appreciate the new power of organization and technical ingenuity in reshaping American society. Schools enlisted in this cause began, even in the antebellum years, to give "science" (rather than "moral character") a new pride of place and created within their enclaves many instructional models that formerly had operated out of the workplace. By the end of the nineteenth century, colleges had added a new professional layer of instruction, a postgraduate experience, affecting many different kinds of work and producing the earliest university models. But both colleges and universities also required different, larger financial investments, each with their self-interested viewpoints. New philanthropic institutions contributed to the emerging organizational matrix of late nineteenth-century higher education. The organizational novelty of the late nineteenth-century university initially seemed to marginalize the older colleges and normal schools until those institutions staged a comeback in the late nineteenth and early twentieth century. In the process a new sense of higher learning expressed itself in a distinct space known as a "campus" cultivated unprecedented forms of philanthropic support, and produced special layers of organization that purported to serve a large, industrializing public. The upshot, epitomized by the work of Charles Eliot at Harvard, was a university that embodied a new bundle of late nineteenth-century cultural values (generational culture #4; chaps. 4–8).

Even before the turn of the century, the rise of the city and a new Progressive activism (generational culture #5; chapter 9) had begun to change both the old college and the relatively new state universities and worked to redefine the meaning of democracy and higher education for this generation. The effort to demonstrate the service of higher learning to an (demographically different) American public enlisted the support and encouragement of multiple groups and, in return, required the university to reconcentrate its energies, not only in particular departments and schools, but also to reach out into the society itself with adult programs, training institutes, after-hours classes, and extracurricular lectures that realized the university as a resource for a larger democratic public.

A later generation after World War I sought a distinct legitimation of higher learning in scientific inquiry, which had roots in the eighteenth century but which now assumed very different social and reformist connotations. The dominant pragmatic ideology (generational culture #5; chapters 10–11) of the interwar period created alliances with federal and state governments but continued to insist on its academic independence. Its emphasis on scientific research, however, faced a substantive countercurrent from components within the university and outside in the liberal arts (often once denominational) colleges to provide a new commitment to teaching on a par with empirical scientific research.

The internal tension of the university—scientific research versus liberal arts instruction—during the interwar period experienced the unexpected influx of German Jewish scholars fleeing Nazism. Though many of these researchers with different academic and ideological priorities found work difficult in America, their presence on teaching faculties in small colleges and midwestern state universities gave them initial shelter until such time (the postwar period) that their academic distinction became better known in their host country. As their work moved into the American academic mainstream and created an influential culture of their own (generational culture #6; chapter 12), their publications and reputations bolstered the indigenous resistance to the pragmatic hegemony of prominent American universities.

A final post–World War II generation filtered many of these inherited dynamics into a cohesive ideology of pragmatism, which insisted on fostering a new power of prediction and risk reduction for a modern world. The upshot, driven by federal government preferences for applied scientific solutions to problems of national security, expanded the earlier pragmatic inheritance so forcefully as to create a new academic culture entirely (generational culture #7; chapters 13–15). This latest American academic culture took many of its initiatives from "outside its walls," from federal government as well as satellite technical, engineering, and scientific corporations, often located nearby or on the institution's own campus. The late twentieth- and early twenty-first-century university had merged seamlessly into America's corporate culture.

These seven broadly sketched generational cultures—(1) evangelical, (2) Jeffersonian, (3) republican/nondenominational, (4) industrially driven postgraduate/professional organization, (5) a Progressive (urban-driven) pragmatism with a substantive liberal arts/teaching countercurrent, (6) an international academic discourse that critically probed America's pragmatic mentalité, and finally (7) a federally driven set of initiatives that both activated pro- and antipragmatic stances—continually reworked values and features of earlier and later eras but realized a corporate model that compromised the university's once cherished research and teaching independence.

The essays that follow intend to complement but deepen the existing overview histories of the subject. In their way, the chapters here are each self-contained analyses of a historical subject that bears on and refines a generational progression. The overarching theme of this study is that cultures drive politics and societies. The distinctive historical assumptions of a period condition the choices of educators and students and become the shapers of a given institution's structure. In this way, a historical habit of thought, weaned on episodes from the past with seemingly different issues, becomes a powerful resource in reconsidering and thus better comprehending higher education issues in our present time. A social history of American higher education must set a framework that goes well beyond educational institutions; it must use advanced schooling as an integrating device for subject matter beyond students, curriculum, school presidents, and faculty. One cannot understand any school by studying data on that school alone.

The significance of the study directly relates to current issues of educational values and administrative expectations. Increasingly in the twentieth and twenty-first century, college and university leaders rarely arise out of the school's ranks; they assume authority with very little knowledge of their institution's history or the patterns of particular generic models of advanced educational practice. The consequences can often be tumultuous and costly in wasted time and resources. In addition, parents guiding their sons and daughters to higher education employ experts and guidebooks with anecdotal information of the past rather than informed historical knowledge of institutional achievement. Students navigate their schools experientially, often unmindful of structural barriers and opportunities that shape their undergraduate and graduate experiences. Historical knowledge would significantly enhance all three experiences—those of institutional leaders, parents, and students—by clarifying the probabilities and expectations of particular forms of higher education, now largely inchoate and intuitional.

The significance is larger still, since America's institutions of higher education are highly selective devices for producing not only trained minds but also a social leadership class. The history and fate of American higher education developed within central national debates over the production of powerful individuals in a society formally committed to democratic equality. The contentious and highly contingent responses to this dilemma have literally shaped both the politics and the culture of America. An insightful history of the subject would clearly establish how little actual consensus there has been over time but also, however knotty the problem, how rooted our present response to the issue must be in the elements and configurations of previous decision making. History does not produce facile clarity or overarching themes, but it does orchestrate the ingredients and the past cases of policy making that informed citizens' needs to make new and ideally improved departures for the future. Its value lies in the force of context rather than of prediction.[2]

In addition, the reconstruction of the past in areas of high debate and varied opinion sets the context for new knowledge, of new perceptions that refuse to replicate the limits of past educational and political practice. What sorts of educational priorities did colleges set before "science" became the preeminent goal for higher education? Did denominational practice or ethical standards in higher education "lose authority" with the rise of science and research? Have there been examples where religion and science or other seemingly contentious priorities nevertheless functioned side by side within the same institution? Did philanthropic benefactions redirect a university's orientation in ways that benefited the donor self-interestedly or diverged from an institution's espoused priorities? Exactly how and when have political agendas undermined or enhanced a college or university's established goals? Have the graduates of America's colleges and universities, with their disproportionate power and rewards, created an ironic oligarchy within the democratic framework, or have they produced a modern variation on democratic leadership, efficacious in spite of the ironies?

The methodology of *American Academic Cultures* will be distinctly historical rather than descriptively chronological. It will attempt to interpret generational moments over time that involved the changing "politics," the competing elements of higher education, both inside and outside institutional walls. One of the distinctive features of this approach is the effort to resist the dominance of hindsight, to "stand in the shoes" of key protagonists, to acknowledge the peculiar configuration of time-bound assumptions and behaviors accepted familiarly by earlier cultures. The use of textual analysis will not simply report the arguments of distinctive generations but will probe the distinctive meanings of key ideas—democracy, education, intellect, science, character, career, and so on—that most generations use but which each redefines for itself. The competition for meaning becomes a key component of the competition for power and cultural preeminence. Of course, reliable statistical (both economic and demographic) configurations will extend the dimension and reach of intellectual patterns and provide a complex and layered landscape for every targeted institution. But the emphasis on singular individuals and resonant ideas will illuminate, I am assuming, the humanizing and causal dimensions that differentiate generations and cultures.

CHAPTER ONE

The Great Awakening and the Eighteenth-Century Colleges

The history of the eighteenth-century college in America began in the second half of that century. Before 1740, there were three institutions that aspired to college status in the American colonies: Harvard (1636), Yale (1702), and William and Mary College in Virginia (1693). For the most part, these institutions rooted themselves locally, attracted students in the English sense of "college," that is, a preparatory stage of instruction, and operated on a curriculum of rudiments. All proselytized the denominational tenets of their region: Calvinism and Congregationalism at Harvard and Yale, Anglicanism at William and Mary. Their students were predominantly adolescents, and their teachers were often trained ministers, resulting in a curriculum that was undifferentiated from the prevailing Protestant denomination of their region. Between 1641 and 1750, the three earliest schools—they were not instructing in ways comparable to the colleges and universities in Europe—graduated 2,282 individuals, a miniscule proportion of the colonial population. An additional 321 persons attended but failed to take a degree. The total number of "collegians" in this period amounted to 2,603. College classes were small in numbers, and the roles colonial college graduates later filled permit one to argue that the American college before the Great Awakening (roughly the 1730s and early 1740s) contained more an aspiring than an actual social and political power.[1]

Between 1750 and 1780, the colonies' multiple denominations produced a new generation of schools and its first collegiate culture. They more than doubled the output of college degrees (2,989 in the post-1750 period alone with an additional 935 students attending but failing to take a degree). The total

TABLE 1. Chartering of colleges by region in the United States through 1800

Decade chartered	*LS*	*MA*	*MW*	*NE*	*ONW*	*OSE*	*PC*	*SW*	*US*	*Total*
1631–40	0	0	0	1	0	0	0	0	0	1
1691–00	0	0	0	0	0	0	0	0	1	1
1701–10	0	0	0	1	0	0	0	0	0	1
1741–50	0	1	0	0	0	0	0	0	0	1
1751–60	0	2	0	0	0	0	0	0	0	2
1761–70	0	1	0	2	0	0	0	0	0	3
1781–90	4	2	0	0	0	0	0	0	5	11
1791–00	1	1	0	4	0	0	0	0	4	10

LS = Lower South (NC, SC, GA)

MA = Middle Atlantic (DE, NJ, NY, PA)

MW = Middle West (AR, IA, KS, MN, MO, WI)

NE = New England

ONW = Old Northwest (OH, IL, IN, MI)

OSE = Old Southeast (AL, LA, MO, MS)

PC = Pacific (CA, OR)

SW = Texas

US = Upper South (DC, KY, MD, TN, VA)

number of collegians immediately benefiting from the colleges of the Great Awakening (founded between 1750 and 1800) amounted to 3,924. Furthermore, as college graduates began to opt for nonministerial careers in unprecedented numbers, the role of the college changed in levels of instruction and the ages of the students as well as in actual nation building and in the public consciousness.

By the end of the eighteenth century, the American college had become a strategic cultural force in ways that it was not before, and that produced a precedent-setting collegiate culture. This new model of higher learning requires a historical explanation.[2] The Great Awakening matured and peaked as a widespread religious event that arose without initial leadership or organization and substantively sharpened differences within and between the colonies and their denominations. For the first time, the colleges gravitated from their strictly religious didactics and began to use the language of theology to probe issues beyond religion. The Awakening's spread surprised America's Protestant leadership, but retrospectively its social and economic precedents make the event more comprehensible. In the 1730s, the American population had expanded nearly tenfold from the last decades of the seventeenth century. Desirable property in the eastern colonies compelled many new immigrants to move west, opening tensions between the less cultivated areas and the older settled sections.[3] The strains of expansion and settlement exacerbated the problems of economic and political cohesion. Many colonial cities in the 1730s experienced a damaging diphtheria epidemic with an estimated twenty thousand deaths, and that underscored the fragility of existence. The epidemic made colonial thinking receptive to the larger shapers of their life chances. In addition, the epidemic coincided with the first major trade imbalance of the eighteenth century and the loss of fortunes that, in turn, made credible dire interpretations of divine judgment about human behavior. Similarly colonial leaders worried about the rise in premarital sexual behavior that signaled the loss of parental control of marriage. Such breaches disrupted not only family decorum but also the usual merger of property holdings that eighteenth-century marriages often connoted. Physical contagion, economic downturns, and aberrant social behavior all contributed a special import to Puritan sermons that chastised citizens for their religious insensibilities. The special economic tensions of the period set the context for the religious upheaval we have come to call the Great Awakening. Suddenly individual revival meetings crossed denominational lines and confused traditional roles of established ministers and familiar religious authorities. By the mid-1730s the religious turmoil had spread widely by word of mouth, spread from Georgia to Massachusetts by a new type of minister, who possessed no permanent institutional home and who might have had little formal education. These events would have a transformative effect on the colonies and would introduce an invigoration of and challenge to Protestant orthodoxy. Not the least of affected institutions were the colonial colleges, traditionally assigned to intellectual training and the production of God-fearing leaders.[4]

It is impossible then to understand the eighteenth-century college in America without understanding the broader dilemmas presented by itinerant preachers. Their criticism of religious orthodoxy and ultimately *their defense of multidenominational worship* went to the heart of the Great Awakening. The most remarkable of all the itinerant preachers in this period was the Reverend George Whitefield (1714–70), a native of Gloucestershire, England, and an ordained Anglican priest, who visited America on six notable occasions and ultimately died there in 1770.[5] His preaching has generally been credited as the strategic spark that accelerated the powerful cultural crisis, now called the Great Awakening. This movement produced the first serious intercolonial network of correspondence and travel of the eighteenth century. In a key communication to the students of both Harvard and Yale Colleges (July 1741), Whitefield enunciated the controversial message that would be seen both as bedrock common sense for some and for others dangerously disruptive heresy. "Learning without piety," Whitefield cautioned the collegians, "will only make you more capable of promoting the kingdom of Satan. Henceforward, therefore, I hope you will enter into your studies not to get a parish, nor to be polite preachers, but to be great saints. This, indeed, is the most compendious way to true learning: for an understanding enlightened by the spirit of GOD, is more susceptible of divine truths, and I am certain will prove most useful to mankind."[6] How did such a message give rise to such social and intellectual turmoil for learned and unlearned alike? Why would it be especially disruptive to the three established colleges of Yale, Harvard, and William and Mary?

Whitefield set the pace for all subsequent itinerants, and in his own journals strove to translate a newly minted Methodist didactic into graphic, material terms that anyone could understand. In one German community, a woman heard Whitefield preach and claimed never to have been so edified, though she understood no English.[7] His journals meticulously recorded the numerous daily sermons he delivered; they also underscored the frequency with which he preached in the open air to crowds too large to be contained in colonial assemblies; they offered frequent estimates of the hundreds or, at times, thousands who listened to his words. And, not long after the journals were written, they were published for widespread consumption, serving too as additional dissemination devices to converted and unconverted communities alike.

The very idioms of his language—the sensational, much-repeated "sweetness"—reflected a harmony of minds between preacher and listener. Movement toward such "sweetness," the force of the gospel upon the unconverted, he often called a "melting" or a "quickening," and the words matched the physical experience he described. Whitefield's favorite metaphor for engaging Scripture and probing his spiritual life was a "wrestling" with God. His extraordinarily physical itinerary, favoring the seaport towns and detailing all the impediments to travel, nevertheless covered all the colonies between Boston and Georgia, by foot, by horse, by boat. Even astute skeptics like Benjamin Franklin felt obliged to listen and engage when confronted by the experience of Whitefield. First, there was the standard of willpower. Franklin resolved to make no donation to Whitfield's cause but, as he listened, gradually lowered his resistance to the coppers in his pocket, then to the silver, then to the gold, capitulating in the end, to his own amusement, to all his pocket resources. "His delivery of the latter [the much practiced, much traveled sermon]," Franklin shrewdly observed, "was so improved by frequent repetitions that every accent, every emphasis, every modulation of voice was so perfectly well turned and well placed that, without being interested in the subject, one could not help being pleased with the discourse, a pleasure of much the same kind with that received from an excellent piece of music." Beyond this performance standard, Franklin then turned to mathematics and acoustics. On one occasion in Philadelphia, at the edge of the crowd, he could still hear Whitefield clearly. He then backed up to the point where the preacher's voice could not be heard, then imagining "a semicircle, of which my distance by should be the radius, and that it were filled with auditors, I computed that he might well be heard more than thirty thousand."[8] In an instant Franklin believed once suspect stories of generals haranguing armies of thousands before a battle. Whitefield represented a phenomenon that challenged all manner of familiar eighteenth-century habits.

In England and America, Whitefield's preaching initially received enthusiastic endorsement. But gradually the power of his message and its manifest effectiveness in amassing unprecedented concentrations of people made all scrutinize his actual arguments in the light of established orthodoxy. These skeptics, especially the founder of Methodism itself, the Reverend John Wesley, found cause to reexamine the power of evangelism. But before these countercurrents began, exemplars of an old theocratic Calvinist inheritance, both governors and ministers welcomed Whitefield as an energizing presence. At Yale College in New Haven, he dined with the new rector, just appointed in 1740, Rev. Thomas Clap (Harvard 1722), only days before an enthusiastic Sunday reception with Connecticut's colonial governor. Neither seemed worried about Whitefield's recognizable theme of "the dreadful Ill-consequences of an unconverted Ministry" or fretted about anything more than an aggressive application of Calvinist orthodoxy.[9] But rumblings had already begun about the itinerant having crossed the fine line between encouraging a constant spiritual discipline and criticizing specific ministerial authorities. Whitefield's Oxford training, his urbanity, and, even to Franklin, his manifest honesty protected him early on. His American counterparts were less fortunate, and by 1745 Yale's official attitude had changed dramatically. Upon his return to New Haven, Yale officially rejected Whitefield's preaching and no longer welcomed him to their ranks.

In part, Whitefield's successors were less nuanced in their intellectual arguments. Within the Calvinist frame, the will of God was inscrutable, yet all were obliged, upon pain of the loss of their souls, to accommodate implicitly the divine will. This pressing dilemma would be mitigated, never settled, only by close scrutiny of God's will reflected in Scripture, hence the importance of intellectual training and of gospel instruction, mediated by the authority of the congregation. In any literal theological sense, no one was saved, except by divine judgment, by God's grace, always elusive and imprecise in human terms. Historically, however, Calvinism could accommodate considerable shifts in social and political arrangements with very modest adjustments in theological emphasis; it stressed at different times literal adherence to Scripture, to the collective judgment of the congregation, and to the most learned congregant, usually the minister. All those views could make education a priority, but the nature and place of education made all the difference in the social and political latitude that followed.[10] Both sides could defend "education"; each side stressed different mixes of formal and pious "learning."

In the case of Whitefield's precursors as well as followers, the suspicion of "learning" as a self-delusion, a sense of understanding divine intent better than others, sent believers down very destructive paths. Whitefield's thematic attack on "learning without piety" began to shift in the hands of his followers to a broad-brush attack on a learned ministry. After all, in a literal Protestant sense, education afforded no more spiritual achievement than the work of the illiterate. Whitefield was not above reprimanding college-trained ministers in both England and America, but he left the criticisms sufficiently muted to cause only a general and healthy discomfort, a disciplinary check upon the intellectual hubris of ministers. On the one hand, the Calvinist congregation in eighteenth-century New England channeled an orthodox theological dilemma directly into the halls of Yale and Harvard Colleges: learning could never achieve salvation on its own, and yet an untrained ministry ignored God's gift of intellect to decipher the meaning of Scripture. Within the eighteenth-century frame, the Calvinist colleges of Harvard and Yale were thought to be essential to the social and political fabric of the colony and yet, on another level, the college graduate was not more spiritually distinct than any member of the congregation. Such itinerant theology made denominational orthodoxy distinctly problematic, and seemed to discount the work of established educational institutions.

Whitefield's preaching served to disseminate this dilemma and opened the way for an itinerant preacher different from himself, one who possessed little or no collegiate training to interpret the Bible or who disparaged learning in preaching God's truth. In Whitefield's exact wake came a string of native preachers, like Rev. Gilbert Tennent (Yale 1725), Rev. James Davenport (Yale

1732), Rev. Samuel Buell (Yale 1741), and Rev. Ebenezer Pemberton (Harvard 1721), all of whom sought to model themselves after Whitefield.[11] They corresponded with him, accompanied him on portions of his travels, defended him to his critics, and initially did not treat the three existing college communities—Harvard in Massachusetts, Yale in Connecticut, and William and Mary in Virginia—as special targets. His 1739 visit to William and Mary College prompted Whitefield's observation that students there "are under about the same regulation and discipline as in our Universities at home. The present masters came from Oxford. . . . I rejoiced in seeing such a place in America." Whitefield, however, introduced a small caveat: unlike the "seminaries of paganism" at home, William and Mary College held promise of "learning Christ . . . as one end of their studies, and arts and sciences only introduced and pursued as subservient to that."[12] By the early 1740s, the itinerants pressured colleges and congregations both to keep piety foremost in any spiritual and intellectual training.[13]

For the first half of the eighteenth century, the college presidents of the three colonial colleges were all college-trained, ordained ministers. Rev. Thomas Clap, who assumed the rectorship of Yale in 1739 at age thirty-six, had graduated from Harvard College (1722) and after his ordination had ministered to Connecticut congregations. Once appointed rector of Yale, he worked closely with the Reverend Joseph Noyes, minister of New Haven and spiritual leader of Yale students.[14] The Clap-Noyes relationship underscored the absence of strict divisions between town and gown; the college was thought to be part of a homogeneous community rather than itself a separate autonomous entity. Still, the tight community of New Haven and Yale produced some distinctive historical features. During the 1740s, the entering classes at Yale ranged from twelve to thirty-six students, with an average class size of twenty-two individuals. The majority came from Connecticut, while a quarter to a third consisted of natives of adjacent colonies. Collegians experienced a division between poorer, older students who disproportionately entered the ministry and younger, more affluent and systematically prepared students who entered the professions, business, or lives of quiet retirement. Several tutors, usually recent graduates of the college with ministerial ambitions, assisted the president in a course of study that consisted of both lectures and tutorials.[15]

In the 1740s, this small but strategic collegiate world fragmented over the dilemma posed by itinerants. The Reverend Thomas Clap had worried privately and in consultation with his associate, the Reverend Noyes, over slack student attendance at Noyes's Sunday services. Whatever steps had been taken failed to correct this pattern. Then during the spring break (1742), two Yale students from Canterbury, Connecticut, attended the sermons of a lay exhorter. It happened that this particular exhorter, an uncle of the Yale students, preached without the permission of the established church. As often happened with Whitefield, itinerants attracted listeners of all persuasions, even church members of established parishes. The power of their preaching was graphic and forceful, affecting some to the point of physical contortions, open public confessions of sinfulness, awakened resolutions, and conversions. But as they fomented breakaway, separated congregations, and posed stark contrasts to the erudite exegesis of ministers like Rev. Joseph Noyes, lay exhorters shifted from saving souls to attacking ministers in their churches. In 1742 such rebellious student behavior worried the college faculty, put unchurched spiritual activity in a suspicious light, and forced the closing of Yale College.[16]

Once the college reopened, Clap's own response was unequivocal. He kept a sharp eye on pro-itinerant, New Light aberrations and maintained an explicit collegiate discipline. In 1745, he expelled two students, John and Ebenezer Cleaveland, when months, after the Canterbury exhortation, Clap learned of their summer attendance at this unofficial spiritual gathering from an unidentified informant. The students' protests of the expulsion order had far-reaching implications for the place and function of the eighteenth-century college. They objected, first, that they had their parents' permission to attend their uncle's preaching and, as "moral agents, capable of trying things (in religion) for ourselves." Second, they insisted that the episode occurred well beyond the aegis of the college's grounds. Third, they protested that they had violated no college strictures. To these objections, Clap retorted that his many lectures and sermons to the students had made the Cleavelands fully cognizant of the "Rector's Mind." He had been adamantly opposed to groups separating arbitrarily from congregations and affronting the moral authority of a church, always a moral entity that was more than the sum of its parts. Their attendance challenged the rector's authority, which implicitly overrode the authority of parent and family or even, in this case, the evident learning of the lay exhorter. The "Rector's Mind" did not need to be explicitly codified into collegiate laws for it to be a commanding standard of the collegian's thought and behavior. Clap's defense not only had extended the former authority of the college; it made clear that the rector's spiritual role, now equivalent to that of Noyes's insofar as students were concerned, went beyond the traditional, educational leadership of a college president. The college henceforth would be its own moral community within the established New Haven congregation.[17]

Clap's dramatic and novel intervention had its parallels in most congregations throughout the colonies. The resistance of established churches and colleges to self-appointed preachers and itinerants led to a public specification of new laws and authorities. "The laws of God and the laws of College," Clap pronounced to the Cleavelands, "are one." Even before the Cleavelands' expulsion, the governor of Connecticut had arranged with the assembly the passage of laws narrowing the terms of "sober dissent" and formally restricting itinerants to sermons invited by established parishes. Similarly, the college passed a new set of bylaws, which made explicit the "Rector's Mind." The ensuing episode of the Cleavelands brought home the inadequacy of these strictures in stemming the force of the Great Awakening. In short, the consequences of evangelical itinerancy threatened the moral authority of existing community (New Haven, in this case) arrangements and required the college to become a more forceful social and intellectual presence than it had hitherto been.

Most important and often lost in accounts of this spiritual and civic crisis was the latitude that remained within New England orthodoxy.[18] Even as Yale College sought to retrench and defend its orthodoxy, Clap actually arrogated greater authority to the college's (and the minister's) place within the religious congregations of Connecticut and New England. He also overstated the place of intellect in the Calvinist armament. In these extensions of doctrine, Clap echoed in surprisingly similar ways the very different overstatements of the revivalists. When evangelizers like the Reverend Ebenezer Pemberton preached at Yale early in 1741, they emphasized the force of piety and the consuming experience of grace, which they termed "the experimental knowledge of Christ." This knowledge was "most useful and necessary" and dramatically different from "the wisdom of this world," which allegedly served to gratify present inclination and temporal advantage. Imitating Whitefield's criticism of unconverted ministers, Pemberton also chastised learned individuals who prided themselves on their informed and elegant discourses. "All their knowledge," Pemberton warned, "is but specious ignorance, and is esteemed by God no better than foolishness."[19] As forcefully as itinerants attacked the piety of ministers, just as forcefully did college leaders, like Clap, reaffirm the power of instruction and intellectual discipline at the heart of a moral community.

Whatever the official instruction of the college in humane learning, many students clearly subordinated formal instruction to spiritual regimens outside the classroom. Students who took Pemberton's teaching to heart confided to their diaries their worries that studies interfered with their spiritual progress.[20]

In addition, they were likely among their classmates to spread suspicions about their own and others' spiritual status. In one notable instance, one student, David Brainerd, offered a private opinion that one Yale instructor had no more spirituality than a chair. This private confidence actually made its way to Rector Clap, who challenged Brainerd to admit his characterization, and then expelled Brainerd for refusing a public renunciation in the College's Hall. The difficulty in recognizing when behavior was spiritually informed and when spiritual propriety had been breached permeated student-to-student relations as well. Brainerd, while still a new student, though age twenty-three, challenged a fellow student, his senior in class rank, though aged twenty-one, to look more carefully to the state of his soul. Thus, Clap's college witnessed a fluidity of "collegiate status,"[21] a confusion of rector-student roles, and heightened perceptions of social and spiritual dangers. This spiritual crisis unleashed an anti-intellectualism that often hovered just below the surface of Calvinist denominationalism but which the college sought to keep in check.

Clap's reassertion of order at the college began with mundane restrictions to lower the age of admission of incoming students and with a less mundane reexamination of the relations between learning and piety. For the college's part, Pemberton's implicit attack on formal instruction and doctrinal exegesis needed a reply, which had begun earlier with Whitefield's critics, the so-called Old Lights. All these tensions and criticisms paved the way for the 1744 Yale commencement address, delivered by one of Clap's young tutors, Chauncey Whittelsey (1717–87). His discourse, "A Faithful Improvement of Talents," anchored his remarks in the gospel parable of the talents, the admonition to improve the different powers and advantages awarded to each individual. One of the great powers that all have been given, he argued, was the means of acquiring knowledge. By gradual study one cultivates the habit of acquiring first basic knowledge, then more complex forms, with its attendant obligations and implications for behavior. Only by a habituation, by a discipline of mind, "early and in earnest," can one approach wisdom and thus improve one's talent usefully and thus dispose oneself to whatever rewards God bestows. Implicitly intellectual awakening did not come with a sudden and dramatic conversion. Whittelsey took care to avoid any intimation that intellectual training guaranteed spiritual advantage, but equally strong was his insistence that such advantage would be improbable without a long-term discipline of natural talents. Deftly he asked his graduating audience, "are not these sufficient to fire our Breasts with a holy Ambition, to animate our Zeal, to strengthen our Resolution, that we will make this the incessant

Pursuit of our Lives?" Whittelsey strove here to reverse Pemberton's "experiential knowledge of Christ" that put piety ahead of intellect but without denying the force of intellect altogether. Prudence, diligence, and intelligence, Whittelsey repeated variously, led the way to personal happiness and social service; all were based on carefully constructed habits and scriptural reflection rather than mercurial indulgence that left men like "the door on its Hinges . . . easily moved backwards and forwards."[22] Whittelsey's forceful admonition and articulation of the college's broad commitments preceded by one month Clap's expulsion of the Cleavelands.

Both Pemberton's and Whittelsey's exploration of piety and intellect represented two variations of each concept within Calvinist orthodoxy and demonstrated two typological approaches to conversion. In no small way, the furor of contention and zeal that marked the Great Awakening was a function of the diversity within the orthodox framework, a historical feature that has often been oversimplified. The possible legitimate interpretations also guaranteed that the question of different viewpoints posed a permanent challenge to the meaning of orthodoxy. Pemberton and Whittelsey established but one set of polarities, but other variations played themselves out in virtually all eighteenth-century colleges and congregations. In retrospect, it is this lack of doctrinal homogeneity within Calvinist orthodoxy that sustained a relentless point/counterpoint in many Calvinist debates, reinforcing the denomination's intellectual commitments. In one illuminating episode, a stellar representative of the New Light faction, the Reverend Eleazar Wheelock (Yale 1733), corresponded with Rector Clap, his doctrinal nemesis. Wheelock sought to commit his own son "to your Care under God." Not only was Wheelock sending his son to Yale and the aegis of the Old Lights, he begged Clap's favor in specifying his roommate, in allowing his son to defray some collegiate expenses by waiting on tables (a select privilege), and in permitting him to ride horses to strengthen his weak constitution. Wheelock also took this opportunity to apprise Clap of "Religious Affairs of this part of ye country," assuring him that "Dreadful Religion which consists so much in fire, Bitterness and Censoriousness, I think is Dying, and People seem generally convinc'd it is not true Religion." Of course, it had been precisely these doctrinal dynamics that caused the disruptions at New Haven and elsewhere and to which Wheelock was not only associated as a New Light spokesman himself but on account of which he had lost his congregation at Lebanon, Connecticut. Though Clap and Wheelock differed over the Awakening and itinerancy, Wheelock minimized their differences as if communing with an old friend and spiritual colleague.

Clap's reply showed the important range of diversity tolerated within an Old Light orthodoxy. He granted Wheelock's son admission, the selection of roommate, and horse-riding permission. The waiting on tables was not permitted, only because it had been already promised to another. Somewhat disingenuously, Clap then proceeded to describe "religious Affairs" at Yale, specifying the public repudiation of errors among New Light–leaning students and the absence of interests in itinerants and revivals. He disabused Wheelock of any hints that Yale instructors tolerated the heresy of Arminianism, so often attributed to revivalists.[23] This heresy attempted to soften the hard edge of predestination and suggested that certain good acts of humankind might be considered spiritually efficacious. To the Old Lights, spiritual efficacy was a function only of grace, dispensed by God's arbitrary will. In no way could man earn heaven; rather, all good works and spiritual habits only disposed men to grace, paved the way for grace to be received, were it fortunately bestowed.[24] Clap kept his remarks theologically focused but implicitly posed a warning to Wheelock were he to be further tinged with charges of heresy. Clap dug in his heels, both for Yale and orthodoxy, but hesitated to burn his bridges to preachers like Wheelock, without the most explicit proof of aberration. There were a range of differences tolerated within Old Light orthodoxy.

Eighteenth-century colleges—five in number to 1750—represent more than formal charters, political arrangements, and presidential tenures. They were containment areas for ideological debate, intellectual discourses that then and later embodied the essence of the educational institutions. These discourses were more than intellectual exercises but rather became the spiritual essence and heart of both the organization and instruction. The next generation of colleges that followed from the debates of the Great Awakening—the College of Philadelphia (1755), later the University Pennsylvania; the College of New Jersey (1746), later Princeton University; King's College (1754), later Columbia University; the College of Rhode Island (1764), later Brown University; Queen's College (1766), later Rutgers University; and Dartmouth College (1769)—became heirs of the foregoing discussions of piety and intellect. The colleges that were influenced by both Old and New Light ministers initially were denominationally distinct but embodied many eighteenth-century assumptions about the role and nature of higher education. Every denomination, Calvinist and non-Calvinist alike, understood its ideological contingency and the experimental risks of its enterprises. However mutually competitive, these colleges shared a common experience, namely, their minority presence in a sea of social uncertainty. However, they also subscribed, as an earlier generation did not, to the power of intellectual exchange, a classical vernacular drawn from their collegiate curricula, and a conscious allocation of social and personal resources that fortified their aspirations for the future.

Out of this range of institutional experiences came one of the most creative minds of the eighteenth century: Rev. Jonathan Edwards (1703–58), soon to be president of the new College of New Jersey. Before the full implications of the religious revivals had been manifest but clearly after Whitefield and his itinerants had initiated the Great Awakening, Edwards traveled to Yale, his alma mater (1720), and delivered an address, shortly after Yale's commencement in September 1741, "Distinguishing Marks of a Work of the Spirit of God." His sermon addressed the ongoing dilemma of Calvinism that the revivals of the 1730s and 1740s had exacerbated: exactly how does one recognize signs of the divine will, and what merit attaches to human responses to that will? It was a particularly pressing question for the college's recent graduating classes, which generally sent almost half into the ministry.[25] But the question rapidly affected the nonministerial graduates as well, since, as Connecticut's sitting governor, Jonathan Law, had put it, civic and ecclesiastical authority form "One Body Corporate."[26] In a theocratic state, any events like revivals, which were thought to disrupt the spiritual order in the collective minds of its ministers, directly affected the civil order. Edwards's response manifested not only the new collegiate role in matters of central import. He would also dramatize the ingenuity and promise of the college's intellectual discipline. His sermon offered nothing less than a third alternative approach to conversion, one that respected not just instinct (Pemberton) and intellect (Whittlesey) but which elevated natural observation into the realm of divine guidance.

Edwards's remarks both synthesized and transcended existing theological differences between Old and New Lights; they provided a highly imaginative rationale for the denominational college within an increasingly challenged orthodoxy. Edwards's argument laid the foundation for a transition to enlightened learning associated with the second half of eighteenth century in America and for the new genre of colleges to be founded between the Great Awakening and the American Revolution. Initially his sermon attempted to address the surprising dynamics of religious revivals but also underscored the changing assumptions about civil and ecclesiastical relations, about their mixed authority in the production of a social leadership. The college implicitly became a civic resource for a highly diverse community rather than a legitimating organ of denominational orthodoxy. Edwards opened his sermon with the simple but fundamental question, what are the signs by which men distinguish between true and false spirits? At the heart of the problem of knowledge lay, not man's salvation, which, in the eighteenth-century theological vernacular, was wholly determined by God's grace, but rather in the relative worth of man's trying to understand a divine will, which by definition was inscrutable. To the human intellect, limited and sinful, one might easily confuse some signs as true that in fact were false. Edwards reminded his listeners that in the apostolic age, no less than in the present Awakening, Christ's message had multiple manifestations. To keep the message of the gospels "plain and safe, and well accommodated to use and practice," certain clear marks of interpreting Scripture were set and followed. Scripture then was to be man's guide and contained many "rules or marks" that inquirers ignored at their peril. If he proceeded no further, Edwards might well have seemed to be articulating an exclusive defense of Old Light orthodoxy.

However, the entire next section of his sermon underscored the expectation that divine revelation would hardly be the same for every age. The Holy Spirit, Edwards declared, "uses a great variety" of signs, as vast and unknowable as the divine will. Hence, many things could possibly be divine signs that did not have their exact equivalent in Scripture but at the same time did not do violence to it. Implicitly many of the strange and often incomprehensible consequences of the revivals—physical contortions, noisy shouting, contentious disputations, and emotional outpourings—need not be taken on their face as diabolic. Edwards's sermon proceeded to offer numerous considerations about the feebleness of human discretion to differentiate extraordinary behavior and religious ecstasies from signs "not from God." Ingeniously he turned the basic caveat of Calvinism, an intellect sinful and myopic, to erode the facile polarizations of Old and New Lights. If one cannot know God's will, on what grounds can one play God and damn unfamiliar behavior as unorthodox?

Edwards's argument opened a substantial tolerance for unprecedented and awakening behavior, but then he went still further. Scripture presented, he insisted, good examples, which in turn would become a device for teaching one's fellows. "There is," he inferred, "a language in actions; and in some cases, much more clear and convincing than in words."[27] He conceded that often scriptural exegesis in sermons had very superficial impact, thereby at least associating himself with some of Whitefield's old cautions about an unconverted ministry. Some people's behaviors (that is, itinerant preachers'), however strange and extraordinary, are the very means by which scriptural truth and a "real zeal for God" are made manifest to others. In most instances where a group or region was spiritually energized, confusion and irregularity followed as a consequence of good works, as in the New Testament accounts of early Corinth, the overzealousness of Constantine, or the censorings of Calvin himself. Vile practices and gross heresies coexist alongside the work of the Spirit, just as Judas dwelt among the original twelve apostles. The existence of evil was not evidence that God's work is not "gloriously carried on."

With his litany of "negative signs," unprecedented signs that were not necessarily hostile to the Spirit of God, Edwards exploited a traditional, exegetical style to pull the exceptional features of revivalism within the orthodox fold. Then he turned to the ostensibly more difficult task of "positive signs," more difficult because of the risk of identifying with some degree of certainty which worldly clues illuminated God's inscrutable will. Anything, Edwards continued, that compels men to put away the things of the world and worldly lusts and to attend to Holy Scripture "must needs be the Spirit of God." From the gospel of Matthew, he forced the logic that "Satan would not cast out Satan." If the early sections of his sermon attacked reflexive and narrow rejections of religious awakening, the middle sections seemed to strike a remarkably ecumenical tone. The last portion of his sermon expansively embraced a dangerously nondenominational scope. Here Edwards recorded his personal witness of revival emotions in the hopes that his testimony would join others of "sound mind, good understanding and known integrity," to establish a new version of these extraordinary signs. He assured his listeners that in all his experience revivals did not deprive the affected of their reason, or in rare cases of distress, only momentarily. Their distress, he reported, was not a function of deception but of a newly conscious recognition of their sinfulness, the waste of their past lives. Erratic behavior and emotional outbursts in these cases ultimately were signs of transformation, which ultimately supported spiritual righteousness and social discipline. To interfere with the work of itinerant preachers or to wait for definitive signs was to risk a parallel with the Jews' incomprehension of and hostility to Christ himself. "A work of God without stumbling blocks," Edwards warned, "is never to be expected." The standard for a "distinguishing mark" of God's spirit was not established practice but rather receptivity to unprecedented and problematic behavior.

However supportive of the revivalists his sermon was, however much it was intended to sway Old Light anxieties, Edwards was not offering an uncritical apologia for the Awakening. He cautioned itinerants not to indulge the unprecedented, emotional features of the Awakening, to avoid unnecessarily confusing the cautious and doubtful. He insisted that God's grace was more often manifest in "sweet communion with God" than in miraculous experiences. Commonplace experiences were far more likely than miracles to achieve the true meaning of grace. Moreover, he chastised those who rejected slow learning and methodical study of Scripture as a fundamental human approach, if not to grace itself, than to the "preparation for publicly instructing others."[28] Such study of scriptural rules at the very least should caution men against making God-like judgments about the spirituality of others, against prideful distinctions between saints and hypocrites. A disciplined mind, though ineffective in actually producing grace or salvation (God-given benefits), nevertheless kept sinners focused on self-discipline and self-control; it could, in effect, engineer a profound sense of contingency and adaptability in their own spiritual and indeed physical state. The inscrutability of God's grace led, in Edwards's distinctive eighteenth-century sense, to a focus upon what man's intellect could control, the discipline of self, the scrutiny of human behavior, the patterns of the God-created natural world.

Edwards's New Haven sermon was calculated to legitimate revivalists while offering criticism of both revivalists and their critics. It was also a spirited defense of Yale's intellectual enterprise, though at times his use of men's behavior—action as a language—seemed to be as powerful a "spiritual sign" as scriptural testimony. The most important thrust of Edwards's preaching focused upon the human uncertainties associated with both the laws of God and laws of men. His newly contingent brand of learning neither eschewed formal learning nor relied on it more than the rituals of piety, as some revivalists urged. His learning was no more efficacious than learning had ever been within the Calvinist framework. However, for him the conditioning of the mind was within human power and represented something man could control, the preparation for salvation, were it ever to come.[29] Edwards's expansive and complex brand of revivalism extracted major portions from both the arguments of the Old and New Lights.

For his part, Edwards, like many itinerants before him, began to redefine his legitimate congregation in very expansive, nondenominational terms. His protégé, David Brainerd, became a missionary to the Indians, and Rev. Eleazar Wheelock opened an Indian school, later to be removed to New Hampshire, where it laid the foundation for a new college altogether, eventually called Dartmouth (founded 1769). Edwards followed suit in his own way and in 1758 assumed the presidency of the College of New Jersey (founded 1746 in Elizabeth, New Jersey). Not long after, the college became itself an itinerant institution, shifting to Newark, then later (1756) to the town of Princeton.[30] This receptivity to new collegiate populations was one feature of Edwards's muting of Calvinist orthodoxy and its adaptation to a distinctively American context. Though Yale and Princeton and the post–Great Awakening colleges all continued to be led by minister-presidents, they all found different modes of tolerance toward other Protestant creeds. The sectarian debate out of Yale in the 1740s led in one observer's words to a distinctively American consequence in collegiate instruction: "Morality over theology; prudence over absolute norms of behavior; the combination of humane, scientific, and practical subjects over traditional classical learning; preparation for public life rather than for the ministry."[31]

Several graduates of Clap's Yale students—William Livingston (1723–90), William Peartree Smith (1723–1801), William Smith Jr. (1728–93), and John Morin Scott (1730–84)—had taken their college instruction to heart as they moved to read law in New York City. There Anglican efforts to create a college institution for their denomination (to be led by their fellow Yale grad, Rev. Samuel Johnson [1696–1772]) led to a public debate over the nature of such a school. Livingston and his friends produced a short-lived weekly journal, the *Independent Reflector*, to argue against sectarian instruction. Their defense of intellectual freedom (with Lockean overtones) did not stop the 1754 creation of King's College (later Columbia).[32] Their publication argued for sectarian equality and religious toleration, which followed easily from the implications of Jonathan Edwards's sermon. In particular, they argued the need for the state to favor no one church denomination and government impartiality to all sects. If it favored a close adherence to Anglican theology, King's College nevertheless arose within a new and expansive sectarian debate, one that shifted priorities from theological to practical, political applications. Originally King's College was to be Anglican, but the pressure from other denominations resulted in an Anglican president and a board with non-Anglican representatives, a political consequence of the ethnic diversity of New York City.

Within the intellectual dynamics of Edwards's expansive revivalism, a new generation of colonial colleges emerged by the time of the American Revolution and conditioned the debate into the early years of the nineteenth century. In part, some new institutions proposed to create a special protective space for their denominations, while others probed the possibilities of a training ground for a distinct public statesman. Baptists created their own school in Rhode Island in 1764, a college eventually to become Brown University.[33] Queen's College (chartered 1766, rechartered 1770), later Rutgers, was founded in New Jersey by the Dutch Reformed and experienced a sequence of openings and closings until the school stabilized in the nineteenth century.[34] A Philadelphia charity school and a building for Rev. George Whitefield's preaching became the focal points for fund-raising that eventually mutated into the College of Philadelphia, which hoped to privilege English and practical subjects over classical or religious instruction and promised a nondenominational board of trustees, a rationale advanced by Benjamin Franklin but modified over time.[35] These urban-based initiatives continued for over a decade before the college received a charter in 1750 and eventually became the University of Pennsylvania (chartered 1755).

The Great Awakening at Yale had begun as a defense of orthodox Congregationalism but ended with the college president as a public figure in an increasingly nontheocratic state. The intracollegiate discourse, which had originally focused on the dynamics of individual salvation and its pious suspicions of unconverted ministers, ended with the creation of multiple, competitive colleges in more heterogeneous societies.[36] The example of Yale, once again, demonstrates the progression. Rector Thomas Clap of Yale joined Harvard in a formal attack on itinerants and George Whitefield, when the great preacher proposed to return to these college communities. For a time thereafter, Clap continued to defend Old Light leaders, like Rev. Joseph Noyes in New Haven, but also began to redefine his rectorship and arrogate to himself the spiritual guidance of Yale students. He lobbied successfully to the civil authorities to prohibit itinerants and to grant the college a formal charter of the state in 1745. Not only, in his eyes, did such maneuvers give a legal imprimatur to the college's colonial standing, state support gave a new legitimacy to his fund-raising plans. In the decade after the Awakening, Yale would double its size and become the largest producer of college graduates in the colonies. Within the college hall, Clap proceeded to exclude older students whom he saw as fomenters of "Separation." In the process the college rector assumed considerably greater autonomy, more the imperious authority of a parent in a family than that of a minister to his congregation.[37] A defense of the status quo had propelled the college president and his institution into unprecedented territory.

All of these defensive innovations intended to forestall any subsequent challenges like itinerancy, but in a curious way they began to replicate some of the revivals' own consequences. Clap's protective strategies functionally effected a peculiar separation of town and gown, of a Yale congregation within the congregation of New Haven. His increased stature as a defender of orthodoxy initially pitted Yale in the 1740s against the New Light revivalists. But this Old Light opposition, as Edwards's sermon demonstrated, still shared much common ground with the New Light teaching. Gradually Clap's use of Yale as an instrument of Calvinist orthodoxy led in 1753 to the creation of a new professorship of divinity, and, to the consternation of Old Lights, the appointment went to a recent Yale graduate, Naphtali Daggett (1727–80).[38] In part, Daggett's appointment represented Clap's increasing fears of Old Light gravitation toward the heresy of Arminianism, an overstatement about the saving efficacy of human activity but also loosely associated with censorious moralizing in place of evangelization.[39] Clap's intentions to sever ties with New Haven's Old Light First Church and solidify his own spiritual leadership of the college were sealed with the construction of a brick college chapel in 1761, adjacent to the main college building on New Haven's green.[40]

The new religious autonomy actually was won at a sacrifice of the college's civil power. The influence of the New Lights in the colonial assembly behooved Clap to attend to his common ground with them. Clap's problem was to resist civil interference with college operations but at the same time to lobby for increases in government subsidy. Ultimately Clap's outreach to civil authorities made Yale a formal corporation and enhanced its self-sufficiency but also admitted nonministerial officials to the college's board of trustees and to scrutiny that led to his own ouster in 1766.[41] Both Old and New Lights contributed to a new tradition about scrutiny of spiritual and civil authority that pressured the fundamental assumptions of old and new colleges alike.

Internal changes parallel the external shifts. The older curriculum had devoted substantive time both to traditional classical learning as well as to secular studies of astronomy, natural philosophy, and mathematics, not to mention the rector's chapel commentaries that concentrated on current affairs rather than theological points of Scripture.[42] If there was a historical shift away from denominationalism without abandoning its Calvinist religious commitments, the Great Awakening turned theological discussion away from Milton's seventeenth-century study of the ways of God to man and toward an examination of human behavior and the physical world as distinguishing marks of divine will. Edwards's important sermon had indulged human behavior and natural observations as equivalent evidence to that of Scripture. It would be a small step from Edwards's appreciation of nonscriptural evidence to an investigation of the practical matters of commerce and government. Within a generation of the new colleges of the Great Awakening, public discussion would focus as avidly on the political authority of Britain as it once had on the spiritual authority of God's spirit.

Both old and new colleges generally insisted that the president of a college serve the school as a member of the founding denomination. However, in the very practical matter of fund-raising and student recruitment, most eighteenth-century colleges practically saw new merits in defining expansively the "community of saints." Most colleges favored newspaper broadsides, followed by hired itinerants, a variation on a basic pattern of evangelical itinerancy. Their fund-raising rhetoric tended to soften the denominational but not the evangelical argument. Every college thus walked the narrow line between a guarantee of effective religious instruction and a tolerance of other denominations. "People may be the better satisfied in sending their children for education to this college," Samuel Johnson declared for the new (1754) Anglican-led King's College in New York, "it is to be understood that as to religion, there is no intention to impose on the scholars the peculiar tenets of any particular sect of Christians, but to inculcate upon their tender minds, the great principles of Christianity and morality . . . and to train them up in all virtuous habits."[43] Colleges aimed their public pronouncements less against other specific denominations and more on bolder secular targets, like barbarism and British dependency. These arguments were tailored to specific audiences, and clearly "British dependency" played little role in the raising of £43,000 for American colleges in the thirty years before the American Revolution. Half of that figure came from England.[44] In England the "conversion of the Indians," rarely used in the colonies, proved an effective substitute appeal.

Evangelical itinerants, ranging well beyond their college's traditional boundaries, contributed a basic economic component to the construction of America's eighteenth-century college, equal in importance to their religious and cultural significance. They were the principal agents of the Great Awakening that permeated colonial eighteenth-century society at midcentury. No significant religious or governmental institution escaped its impact, and the established colleges were no exception. In reaction, new denominational colleges were formed, and older colleges eventually accommodated the revivalists' influences. The changes for the most part remained within the framework of predominantly Calvinist culture but nevertheless exacerbated values that many Protestant leaders sought to leave latent. What exactly constituted the means for transmitting an upright social and individual virtue? Once "converted," how formalized should the rules of thought and behavior become to sustain the gains? Exactly what were the long-term consequences for society and government, if the itinerants' enthusiasms led to separated and fractured communities?

The debates over these issues transformed the eighteenth-century college and turned its distinctly religious discussions into wholesale reexaminations of social routines and of political behavior. The momentary effect was to appreciate the advantages of nondenominationalism and a broad interpretation of God's community in America. In its wake the Great Awakening introduced a new collegiate tradition, evangelical but accommodating to scientific discoveries, scripturally based but cognizant of the Bible's "practical applications." Part of these changes too was increasing differentiations between collegiate training and ministerial instruction, recognition that increasingly the majority of collegians would not enter religious life.[45] The sensual language and prosaic examples of the early itinerants, like George Whitefield, represented the seedpods of a new evangelical learning that boasted a broader civic virtue for the New World. One of the ironies of the Great Awakening as a whole was the very presence of enthusiastic itinerants, fomenting separation and thereby proving the absence of cultural homogeneity, at the very moment they perpetrated the colonies' ubiquitous fears of social declension.

The multiple confusing turns of theological debate raised the question of social and spiritual authority in a perplexing world. Equally pressing was the power of individual conscience and the knotty problem of when individuals might challenge and replace both ministerial and political leaders. Were colonial governors to fail in supporting resistance to often unlettered itinerants, did they not thereby forfeit their authority in preserving an established social order? But similarly too great a defense of one denomination in a society of multiple religious beliefs could easily appear tyrannical, not to mention discouraging to much needed immigrant labor. The role of the college ascended during the Great Awakening from a seventeenth-century mechanism to produce ministers into prominence as a strategic and selective institution in the shaping of both church and state roles in eighteenth-century America.[46]

The most singular consequence of the Great Awakening was not the emotional gyrations of the newly converted or the preoccupations with social disintegration that the itinerants engendered. Rather, a new brand of knowledge, so central to Edwards's own philosophical awakening[47]—contingent, morally informed, materially engaged—replicated itself in the proliferation of colleges for every major American denomination. The eighteenth-century college would henceforth be used not only to stabilize a religious presence in secularized societies; they were to become the hubs of an impressive, though still voluntary, network of intercolonial schools that would regularly feed the central college community.[48] The college's intellectual training, no less than its aspiration for spiritual salvation, made college leaders particularly disposed to their own school's survival in a new competition for souls and citizens. In their various ways, they all mirrored the organizational and cultural innovations of Yale in the 1740s—a strong presidential presence, a legitimating charter from the colonial government, delineations between college and town life, the cultivated image of nondenominational outreach, a public commencement spectacle, and a self-perpetuating board of trustees who were no longer residents of the college community. This two-way development of local rootedness and expansive outreach not only made the college a public power beyond its geographical size, but, by the Revolutionary period, it actually formalized and transformed the original itinerant paths into a formidable intercolonial culture.[49] Thus the Great Awakening and the ensuing colleges continued an intellectual movement in America away from the stringent theology of early Calvinism.[50] It also compelled all denominational colleges to consider their competitors a permanent part of the new American landscape.

By 1800 a new generation of colleges initiated aspirations in a colonial culture that remained substantially religious and never completely shed the educational goal of conversion. These aspirations reshaped a narrow denominational outlook into a broader, colonial culture. It set in motion a new intellectual authority for civic behavior and political leadership. The colleges' impact, though small in graduates, faculty members, and educational buildings, nevertheless had an influence well beyond their resources. Over half of the signers of the Declaration of Independence were college graduates in 1776. This disproportionate influence of college-educated leaders could not be called a "cultural phenomenon" until well into the nineteenth century. But its taproot, originating in the religious culture of the eighteenth century, would become a substantive presence in American society from the days of the Great Awakening. The morally laden inheritance of that foundational experience would remain with college instruction for generations, compelling successive schools to work out the problematic relationship between indoctrination and instruction.

CHAPTER TWO

Enlightenment and Denominationalism in Jefferson's Virginia

The relatively small size of all American colleges at the end of the eighteenth century underscored the absence of an intellectual class in America. The emergence of any concentration of college-educated individuals had to respond to the distinctive features of colonial settlement. For the most part, New England had fewer groups of well-educated citizens but had the distinctive advantage of lower mortality rates. Certainly, by the late seventeenth century, New England no longer depended for growth on immigration, but rather had begun to repopulate itself by natural increase. Early on, most of its education leadership, like John Winthrop (1588–1649), Massachusetts Bay Colony's first governor, had been trained at Cambridge University, and, though few in number, these educated individuals were comparatively long-lived, many living into their seventies.[1] Early New England society experienced less disruption and discontinuity in both leadership and personal inheritance because of the longevity of its educated, immigrant leaders. With relative speed New England colonists ceased sending their sons to England and Ireland to complete their education and relied, as the examples of Increase (1639–1723) and Cotton (1663–1728) Mather showed, on the intellectual resources of Harvard College, founded in 1636, and later Yale College in New Haven.[2] The theological differences with Anglicanism, a stimulus for Calvinists' emigration from the outset, also played a part in New England's effort to create their own colleges and avoid reliance on Oxford and Cambridge.

By contrast, the Chesapeake Colonies were racked by high mortality and the constant mobility and transiency of immigrant labor, disrupting many essential routines. The educated classes were not an exception. The Virginia and Maryland Colonies' early college-trained settlers outnumbered their New England counterparts substantially but experienced a dramatically different lifespan, barely surviving on the average into their fifties.[3] The Southerner's shortened years were largely due to dependency on tidal river commerce and bad-water diseases like cholera and typhoid. In addition, the early educated immigrants in the Southern Colonies received their education at Oxford University but later in Scotland due to the predominance of the tobacco trade in Glasgow and that city's university's reputation for medical training.[4] Select individual university graduates tended to live longer than the average of the educated cohort, and achieved distinction as much through their longevity as through their actual work.

Some groups of college students provided a distinct counterpoint precisely because of efforts to impose British mores on the colonies. Generally unnoticed in this transatlantic educational traffic is the number of Catholic students, usually from Maryland, like Charles (1737–1832) and John (1735–1815) Carroll who went to Europe in the eighteenth century for their advanced study. More Americans went to Saint Omer's College in eighteenth-century Flanders than attended Oxford or Cambridge combined,[5] a direct result of the English Penal Laws that restricted Catholic behaviors including office-holding, bearing of arms, and religious education. Historian James McLachlan has claimed that the English-Catholic minority in Maryland was probably the most highly educated group of colonials outside New England, an exception created by application of British laws in the South.[6] For the most part, the Chesapeake began with a deference to Britain for both training and supply of educated personnel from the seventeenth into the eighteenth century. Robert Beverley's *History and Present State of Virginia* (1705), the first history of the colony, has demonstrated this baseline aspiration.[7] But from the outset, American circumstances constricted and modified inherited British values, and the Catholic resistance represented but one of many difficulties in applying British standards of the mother country. Exactly how did these cultural and demographic differentiations between Southern and New England Colonies shape a distinctive culture for Southern higher education?

Early British models of educational privilege, coupled with their agricultural and trade economies, helped produce a distinct Southern leadership model, centering largely on estates with river access. They also complemented the highly varied, British-influenced class arrangements and educational outlooks.[8] The Chesapeake mode of settlement contributed to its chronic labor shortage, immigrant mobility, and the absence of towns. Large landholdings of coveted tidewater properties had virtually ensured that by the 1760s aspirant settlers would necessarily move west toward the mountains, were they to take advantage of the powerful attraction of self-sufficient land ownership, an opportunity few could ever have had in England. The availability of frontier homesteads was too tempting to individuals whose lives until then had been dominated by a tradition of British tenantry. As soon as indentures were complete (and often before), immigrants in the Southern Colonies gravitated west. Indenture, early mortality, and unsettled land assured late marriages, shorter fertility periods, and a consequent reduction of natural propagation. These special social features ensured that Southern Colonies would experience shorter tenures of land ownership and leadership than their New England counterparts, upsetting both their citizens and social stability.[9] Again the educated classes were no exception and found these colonial arrangements before the American Revolution disruptive of any intellectual or cultural concentration, apart from a few select plantations.[10] Parishes and schools were in constant need of resupply from Britain, and shortages of university men became a constant in the colonial period.

There were also basic structural features that impeded the emergence of a Southern intellectual stratum. Southern towns were seasonal and largely political units of colonial society, which materialized late in the seventeenth century; the economic business of the colonies operated from plantation wharves.[11] The intellectual and religious life of Chesapeake culture concentrated on the plantations, where select owners prided themselves on their libraries and their chapels, on whom Southern clergymen were economically and socially dependent.[12] For most of the colonial period, there were never enough ministers, mostly émigrés, for the established parishes. In learning situations without university men, instruction gravitated away from the denominational study. Unlike their New England counterparts, Southern plantation libraries favored the practical knowledge of agricultural tracts and medical manuals over theological books. History and literature outnumbered religious sermons. William Byrd, whose fellowship in the Royal Society (founded 1662) and whose inherited wealth made him an exceptional Virginian, nevertheless exemplified the style of learning that mixed an extraordinarily physical management of his own plantations with regular reading in the classics, confidence in his practical medical knowledge, recreational skimming of the British periodical, the *Tattler*, and enormous pride in his voluminous library of over three thousand books and pamphlets.[13] Byrd's library was not only the largest in Virginia; it bore comparison with libraries anywhere in the colonies during the same period. In 1723, for example, the Harvard College library catalog numbered about 3,500 volumes, having started in 1638 with John

Harvard's donation of four hundred books.[14] Similarly, most educated men in the Southern Colonies were not primarily religiously oriented, and were comparatively short-lived. Their ministers necessarily relied on the good graces of plantation owners and their society, and deferred to their hosts' priorities to ensure their own positions and well-being.

The fluidity and instability of social arrangements in the Southern Colonies effectively postponed the creation and operation of a college until well into the eighteenth century. The 1693 founding of William and Mary College by the Anglican commissary, Rev. James Blair (1656–1743), seems far more propitious in retrospect than it did in seventeenth-century Williamsburg. Its royal charter of 1693 and the construction of an imposing building based on designs by Sir Christopher Wren represented only a modest groundswell of support from the landed gentry. Financial strains alone assured that Blair's rational "Scottish" design of grammar school, philosophy school, and divinity school would take several decades to be realized.[15] William and Mary's first president, Scottish-born James Blair, was a 1673 graduate of Scotland's Marischal College and the University of Edinburgh. In actual fact, only the grammar school level of William and Mary's Scottish plan characterized the "college" until well into the 1720s. But the emergence of the school began to draw attention to the Chesapeake's "seasoning," the gradual emergence of a native-born and native-educated group. Still, few students completed a full course of study until well into the eighteenth century.

The instabilities of Chesapeake society into the eighteenth century made learning an erratic affair, associated with library holdings of varied quality and the occasional itinerant tutor. When a traveling teacher or minister in search of extra funds could be found, a school generally set up within the aegis of a plantation. The only organizational arrangement with educational independence in the Southern Colonies was the British-financed and London-directed network called the Society for the Propagation of Christian Knowledge (SPCK), later the Society for the Propagation of the Gospel in Foreign Parts. For the most part, this organization, founded in 1701 by the Anglican commissary in Maryland, Rev. Thomas Bray (1658–1730), created a loose chain of "stations" that consisted of schools and libraries from Nova Scotia to Georgia. The SPCK paralleled the more informal patterns of itinerant evangelists in New England. However, the South's special missionary task sought to stem the tide of "barbarism," initially by targeting Pennsylvania Quakers and the Jesuit-led Papists of southern Maryland. Unlike the plan for William and Mary College, the SPCK stations reflected the library values of plantation owners, mixing practical medical and craft knowledge with doctrinal learning. However, instead of drawing their missionaries from Oxford graduates, the SPCK initially sought to draw more roughly tutored men from outside the cultural mainstream, from Scotland, Ireland, and Wales, but especially from the colonies themselves.[16] This combination of organizational recruitment and the Southern mortality of university men who arrived early resulted in a vacuum later filled by an influx of Scottish-trained individuals, like the Reverend James Blair. Historian James McLachlan has documented that between 1681 and 1780 some 443 college or university men had migrated to the Chesapeake, 39 percent of whom were Scottish trained and 31 percent of whom were clergymen.[17] Still, the SPCK's British expectations, mainly disdain for colonial practices and insistence on highly formal, even military deference and organizational discipline, contrasted markedly with American realities, especially early death and instable work and residential patterns.[18] In its earliest years, the new college at Williamsburg was little more than an ephemeral "station" of the SPCK missionary network with few graduates of a multiyear curriculum. The Scottish influence further shifted American educational values away from the British models of Oxford and Cambridge.

The early instruction at the College of William and Mary and the missionary imperialism of the SPCK ensured that whatever passed as "collegiate learning" in the Southern Colonies depended largely on the intellectual aspirations of scattered Chesapeake gentry.[19] Large landholders comprised the vestries of the churches, and similar individuals controlled the assembly, the House of Burgesses, which created church parishes. Also the absence of a British commissary or bishop to oversee college operations and appointments meant there was no real authority to enforce a British college model.[20] If educators' achievements were erratic and difficult to document, there is little question that the plantation libraries more than the schools contained any vestiges of Anglican culture in the South. In spite of men like William Byrd who sought to imitate inherited Georgian manners of style and dress, American circumstances compelled substantive modifications of English styles. Byrd's appreciation for the experimental learning of the Royal Society, which, like the writings of John Locke, sought a counterweight to the speculative, Tory standards of Oxford, meant that, even among educated planters, American intellectual values would not follow the college norms of Oxford and Cambridge.[21] The values of the Virginia gentry contributed substantively to alternative forms of learning, especially by the teaching in the more practical and empirically oriented public lectures of London's Gresham College (founded 1597).[22]

In addition, America's Southern college model had some decidedly interdenominational features. Shifting religious tendencies and the practical, competitive need to attract students, whatever their religious persuasions, disposed educational leaders to reconsider the connections between their sectarian goals and the needs of a wider public. The Scottish influence of Rev. James Blair, William and Mary College's rector-president from 1693 to 1743, reflected the Southern Colonies' general, provincial asperity against British snobbery as well as hopes for provincial autonomy and respect. Blair's Scottish education would set its own standard for a cohort of Scottish-trained ministers throughout the South.[23] Among these transmitters of Scottish culture, one must include a transcolonial cohort that included, in addition to Blair, William Small (1734–75), Rev. William Smith (1727–1803), Francis Allison (1705–79), John Morgan (1735–89), John Witherspoon (1723–89), Robert Harpur (1731–95), Samuel Bard (1742–1821), and Peter Middleton (1752–81).[24] Their teaching would be a powerful influence later in bridging the educational gap between a classical British education and Enlightenment experimentalism (without risking the taint of atheism), in reconciling Calvinist Presbyterianism with an Americanized Anglican tradition.[25] The Scottish influence was also aided by the eastward migration of Americans to Europe for education: of the estimated colonial total of 321 individuals who left the colonies, 44 percent of the non-Catholic (84) colonists studied at Scottish universities. The majority of these, like virtually all of their Catholic counterparts, who represented 41 percent of the total (132), were from the Chesapeake.[26] This influence also had a substantive influence in Virginia's Rappahannock and Shenandoah valleys, west of the large coastal estates, where late arriving emigrants (1720–50), German, Scotch-Irish, and formerly repulsed religious like the Quakers, found shelter and arable land. In this context, a distinct counter-British enclave not only flourished but also influenced late eighteenth-century Virginia in substantive (antislavery) ways.[27]

Not only should one be cautious about the exact influence of Oxford and Cambridge on the American college model, but also one needs to avoid an overly neat and homogenized image of Britain's own university tradition, which itself was undergoing fundamental shifts in this same period. Critical colonists often consciously oversimplified the British model for both educational praise and blame. American commentators and later American historians, for example, have indulged the example of the dissenting academies in Britain that questioned British divine right rule, deductive scholastic disputation, and student ranking according to inherited social status.[28] Americans have celebrated the learning of dissenting academy persons like Daniel

Defoe (1661–1731), Thomas Malthus (1766–1834), and Joseph Priestley (1733–1804). In these academies, some Americans thought they had found the "liberalizing" source of America's own educational resistance to its mother country. However, as historian David Humphrey has convincingly argued, the dissenting academies actually reflect the constructive ferment of eighteenth-century educational debate in Britain itself rather than any model for the eighteenth-century American colleges. These debates over education and science in the academies were driven by the larger, international currents of the Enlightenment, which left their mark on all extant Western institutions of higher learning. Many early colonial divines and college presidents, including Rev. Thomas Clap (1703–67) and Rev. Jonathan Edwards (1703–58), read and admired John Locke (1632–1704), Francis Bacon (1561–1626), and Isaac Newton (1642–1727).[29] Edwards's own conversion model created space for natural observations that comported with biblical narrative to discern the divine will.[30] One of the central issues of all colonial institutions of learning was the exploration and interpretation of how an older brand of religious instruction actually connected with the newest discoveries of natural philosophy and political economy.[31]

This broader intercontinental ferment manifested itself also in the governmental structure of eighteenth-century colleges. The actual governance of both New England and Southern colleges followed a Reformationist or Calvinist model, which favored civil supervision of college appointments and academic service over Oxbridge models of royal sponsorship and academic corporate autonomy.[32] The very designation of "college" in the American colonies did not accept the English version of the word, a residential concentration of tutors and scholars with no degree-granting authority. In the British tradition, degrees were granted by a university corporation, formally chartered by royal decree, and supervised by nonresident (i.e., nonacademic) royal appointees.[33] Even though William and Mary College had the imprimatur of a royal charter, until well into the eighteenth century classes were composed of young men in need of basic grammar-level instruction and tailored their "colleges" to available work opportunities. The college's Board of Visitors consisted of local civil servants and lay government officials (with the Bishop of London as its titular chancellor) rather than an incorporated and autonomous board of scholarly peers or ministers. The examples of Harvard and Yale especially, but also William and Mary College, followed a religiously oriented but civically controlled model, quite familiar in Reformation Europe in places like Leiden and Geneva.[34] This trusteeship model bypassed the incorporated standard established by Oxford and Cambridge and introduced a civic as opposed to a royal or religious authority for collegiate governance. To the extent that they followed the British example at all, American models of collegiate government did so by imitating English preparatory schools, like Rugby (founded 1567), rather than an Oxbridge example.[35]

The adaptive governance structures of the early colleges necessarily reflected the mercurial social and demographic arrangements of the colonies. The Reformationist structures implicitly acknowledged the need for some organizational focus and autonomy but refrained from distancing themselves too far from the public they hoped to serve. Rev. James Blair is generally thought to have abrogated for too many years his collegiate leadership in political battles with the Virginia governor. Some colleges, like Harvard, opted for a divided governing authority: a Corporation of Fellows composed of teachers and president and a Board of Overseers composed of nonresident representatives of the colony, both lay and ministerial.

The relatively basic modes of "college" instruction, until the middle decades of the eighteenth century, make it plain how fragmented the educated classes were in spite of considerable travel and communication among themselves. In the colonies, classical instruction, thought to be so necessary for a gentlemanly style, was sufficiently routinized and restricted to a canon that prepared rudimentarily trained students to recognize shopworn Latin phrases in public discourse.[36] The very denominational presence and ministerial leadership of all the pre-Revolutionary colleges prevented the expansive, intellectual discourse reflected by the European Enlightenment and carried out in coffeehouses, salons, and learned societies rather than within the halls of colleges and universities.

In addition, the role of the city itself cannot be underestimated in both the shaping of a comparable collegiate instruction and the emergence of a truly educated class.[37] Most of the nine colonial colleges before the Revolution situated themselves in major coastal ports that would become cities by the late eighteenth century—Providence, New Haven, New York, and Philadelphia—and produced a disproportionate number of colonial statesmen and professionals. But until the Revolution, the collegiate experience of the colonial colleges remained provincial, and neither measured nor encompassed all the opportunities for learning in eighteenth-century society. The very looseness of collegiate structures—governmental and curricular—attest to a fluid socialization process, one as picaresque and voluntary as a London coffeehouse, a planter's library, or a group of ambitious tradesmen, like Benjamin Franklin's Junto, a club for workingmen's mutual improvement.[38]

By the middle of the eighteenth century, colleges, like other public institutions in the Chesapeake South, achieved a "seasoning," represented by both non-foreign-born college students and a concomitant empathy to increasingly anti-Anglican forces. These pressures reflected not merely a burgeoning colonial ambivalence toward the British Empire but also powerful Anglican competition with the Baptists and Methodists.[39] In spite of the presence at William and Mary College of professors trained at Oxford's Queen's College, the operation of the school underscored the dilemma of most colonial institutions: they bore minimal resemblance to their British models and trained students primarily at the grammar school level. The force of adaptation to colonial circumstance was too obvious in college instruction, no less than in the law, politics, arts, and domestic economy. The Virginia gentry strained to imitate an aristocratic British society but by midcentury conceded, by their oversensitivity to the comments of British visitors, that Americans were approaching a cultural crisis as severe as the looming economic and political crisis of the American Revolution. To what extent was this widening cultural gap between British colonies and the mother country an opportunity for higher learning and the shaping of an educated leadership?

This pervasive problem represented less a choice for the Revolutionary generation than an emerging American outlook: how might an ambitious young man acquire the skills and connections to make his way in a fluid colonial world? In 1821, not long before his death, Thomas Jefferson began an autobiographical account of his Revolutionary trajectory and identified a sequence of social and educational developments that would shape his colonial generation. His cultivation of Enlightenment ideas emerged from his efforts to reform his alma mater, then to create not only a university but, more important, a rationale for both a Southern and an American higher learning. This transformation arose out of the historical patterns distinctive to his native colony and helps clarify why his ideas, so enduring in his nation's educational history, were so imperfectly realized in his own time.

Jefferson's grandfather arrived in Virginia too late to acquire coastal property and hence headed inland to seek his agricultural life chances. Jefferson's lineage was a patchwork of the British provinces—Wales and Scotland. Before Thomas no Jefferson had been formally educated, but, he claimed, his father "read much and improved himself" so effectively he was chosen with the William and Mary professor of mathematics to survey the boundary between Virginia and North Carolina, a significant political responsibility. The value of self-constructed education motivated the family to send young Thomas to another Scottish-trained clergyman for Latin and Greek, William

Douglas (1708–98), and to another, "a correct classical scholar," the Anglican clergyman James Maury (1718–69), for two years.[40] In 1760 at age seventeen, he entered William and Mary College where he came under professor of mathematics William Small's influence, "my great good fortune and what probably fixed the destinies of my life." Small's pedagogy contrasted markedly with the educational benchmark set at Harvard and Yale in these same years: Small, himself Scottish trained, was first and foremost, "a man profound in the most useful branches of science, with a happy talent of communication, correct and gentlemanly manners, and an enlarged and liberal mind." Small went on to fill the college's chair of philosophy and "was the first who ever gave, in that college, regular lectures in Ethics, Rhetoric and Belle Lettres."[41]

Beyond Small's seminal lectures, however, was the educational force of Williamsburg's political milieu and the informal conversations with Virginia politicians and planters. Small's closest friend was the native-born and wholly self-taught lawyer, George Wythe (1726–1806), with whom Jefferson spent five years of legal study in the 1760s and formed a lifetime friendship. In turn, Small and Wythe shared the confidence and the regular society of Lieutenant Governor Francis Fauquier (1703–68), "the ablest man," Jefferson claimed, "whoever filled that office." "To the habitual conversations on these occasions," Jefferson adds with considerable understatement, "I owed much instruction."[42] The informal counsel of these *amici omnium horarum* stayed on his mind throughout his life, especially late in life when making educational recommendations to others.[43] It was the influence of this informally structured group rather than his classroom instruction that Jefferson used to characterize his "college years."

Jefferson summarized the force of this learning by recounting his short-lived legal career (1767–76) and his failed efforts to have passed a bill emancipating slaves. "During the royal government, nothing liberal could expect success. Our minds were circumscribed within narrow limits, by a habitual belief that it was our duty to be subordinate to the mother country in all matters of government, to direct all our labors in subservience to her interests, and even to observe a bigoted intolerance for all religions but hers." In Jefferson's retrospective account, the rising prominence of self-taught men and those outside the Oxford collegiate standard illuminated the tension of the Virginia Colony. He felt the force of reason that arose from indigenous experiences was equal to any advantage of William and Mary's British model of formal education or political behavior. Jefferson's hindsight actually obscured a number of things that were clearer in 1821 than in the 1760s, not the least of which was the problematic nature of slavery itself. However, his remarks cannot obscure the emphatic 1760s sense of experimentation that the American experience necessitated. While at college, he happened upon a select group of individuals for whom experimentation, detailed observation of society and nature, and the powers of critical discourse were seminal educational values. Fortuitously Jefferson learned these skills of observation during his college years but not as a function of the William and Mary College curriculum. Implicitly he made two resolutions out of this experience: 1) the constructive feature of his experience must be systematized, and 2) the college's educational governance must be aligned with the indigenous features of the colonial environment.

However orderly and rationalized was Jefferson's response, his effort to use reason to move action beyond the status quo, struck an important chord in his life's work. It was also a conscious departure from the uses of reason applied by the legal instruction of Blackstone, whose interpretation of the English common law and defense of the status quo was the benchmark of the legal profession in England and America.[44] In his explicit educational advice to others, Jefferson made central the socializing force of a distinctive environment, precisely because to his generation what was most distinctive was the rise to prominence of backcountry landowners outside the Anglican aegis. In 1785 Jefferson replied to an inquiry about European education, noting advantages to studying in Geneva and Rome. But the authoritative portion of his reply was a broadside against Americans studying in Europe because the customs of any foreign country ineluctably accompanied the instruction. "If he goes to England," Jefferson observed, "he learns drinking, horse-racing and boxing. These are the peculiarities of English education." In Europe a student cannot avoid a "fondness for European luxury and dissipation and contempt for the simplicity of his own country."[45] "Cast your eye over America," the statesman concluded sweepingly, "who are the men of most learning, of most eloquence, most beloved by their country and most trusted and promoted by them? They are those who have been educated among them, and whose manners, morals, and habits are perfectly homogeneous with those of the country."[46] In the extraordinarily rich detail of Jefferson's sermon, his emphasis rested upon the shaping power of social context rather than curriculum. The constructive force of education was to align and adapt basic instruction to the culture of one's lifework. But if nature and social arrangements played so predictable a role in human socialization, could man-made laws and institutional reorganization engineer any significant transformation of eighteenth-century cultural practice?

In his work as a member of the House of Burgesses, the elected assembly of colonial governance and in his governorship of Revolutionary Virginia in the 1770s, Jefferson was working through his basic ideas about the necessity of college training for a newly republican leadership. He sought to institutionalize in law a systematic plan of statewide education, but in his 1779 Bill for the More General Diffusion of Knowledge the emphasis was on the collegiate ideal. In these same years, he capitalized on public antipathy to the college faculty's Tory bias and offered a bill to amend the charter of his alma mater, William and Mary College.[47] The educational innovation of these proposals was not pronounced, since many of the ideas had been in circulation for some years. Jefferson's own classical teacher, Rev. James Maury, for example, can be found arguing against too great a "Virginia Gentleman's" time commitment to the study of Greek and Latin. But rather, since few planters had the resources or inclination to educate their sons for the professions, a gentleman's education should include, Maury explained, after completing the basics of English grammar and arithmetic, some history, some geography, some law and literature. These latter subjects ideally should be completed by age fourteen or fifteen, since at such time prospective gentlemen must be tutored by someone in the business he hopes to engage himself as a livelihood.[48] Not only did the clergyman Maury neglect the place of religious or moral training in his gentlemanly proposal, the role of college was decidedly given short shrift. Jefferson's long-term conceptions would have to convince both his foes and his friends about the merits of formal higher learning.

Jefferson himself seems not to have concurred with the reduction of classical instruction but decidedly turned higher study toward science, history, and letters, more the mainstay of his informal learning than collegiate instruction. While Jefferson's own experience was rather singular, enough fellow Virginians had mirrored his trajectory of spare preparation, some college training, and administrative and political responsibility to make his proposals recognizable but not necessarily "popular" or supportable. The history of the House of Burgesses in these same years suggests that Jefferson's political colleagues would experience careers that were self-taught or where privately tutored individuals rose to power as readily as the college educated. Only forty of the some 110 leading eighteenth-century Burgesses were graduates of William and Mary, while a few others studied in English academies and the Inns of Court.[49] Far more significant than formal schooling was the political apprenticeship of planter-politicians in county and local office, that is, vestryman, sheriff, surveyor, or justice of the peace—the socializing offices for a potential leadership pool.[50]

Still, the connection in Jefferson's mind between republican virtue and education became fixed early on, during or shortly after his own collegiate study. When he returned from Philadelphia and his authorship of the Declaration of Independence, he set himself to the task of refashioning with his old mentor, George Wythe, the Virginia Statutes, tailoring them to Virginia but retaining a traditional English common law base. During this same period he submitted four bills that he considered seminal to the shaping of republican virtue: 1) the elimination of primogeniture and 2) the repeal of entail, two central statutes of British land control; 3) the elimination of the Anglican Church as the state-established religion; and 4) the creation of a bill for the general diffusion of knowledge. The education bill was distinguished from the others for its failure to pass the Virginia legislature. His subsequent efforts to convert his alma mater into a state university and to create a special library for the research needs of the republican leadership also failed.

The failures are important for their documentation of late eighteenth-century social and cultural priorities that made an educational system appear a luxury. Jefferson's innovation was a statewide system of education with three tiers: one, at county level, to instruct, for three years and tuition free, all youth in the basics of reading, writing and ciphering, and the history of Greek, Roman, English, and American civilizations (no Bible study); two, "to rake from the rubbish annually," as his *Notes on the State of Virginia* explained, the poor but talented among them (the affluent must pay tuition) for a "brick or stone" grammar school, which would board them and train them for up to six years in Latin and Greek languages, English grammar, geography, and advanced arithmetic; and three, "only the best in genius and disposition" to study at William and Mary College for three years at public expense.[51] With a single student from each of the twenty grammar schools, he tried to ensure a culling of the "natural aristocracy" of talent, so lacking in the mother country. Jefferson's structure was to ensure that the people would always remain the "safe depositories" of the government and its leadership.[52]

The peculiar feature of this state-governed structure was its focus on "diffusion" of general knowledge. However, the very educational goal of mere "diffusion" obscured the deeper intent of Jefferson's preoccupation with republican virtue. Exactly how could any state create an educational system that would, by the traditional process of lecture and drill, produce individuals of probity and insight for the commonweal? In retrospect, "diffusion" seemed to pale by comparison with New England's eighteenth-century collegiate goal of forceful "inculcation" or transforming "conversion." In part, diffusion of general knowledge connoted to Jefferson an unobtrusive dissemination of information; it responded to his own compulsory penchant for the orderly implementation of ideas, his enumeration of priorities, and his lawyerly bias for procedure. In part, too, diffusion followed from his political efforts to disestablish the Anglican Church and other trappings of British imperial rule that disrupted the special features of Virginian republicanism. He had cause to worry about these competitive, denominational values, for in the very years when his political career was getting under way itinerant preachers began to pour into the Chesapeake in unprecedented numbers and exacerbated the already complicated competitions of Chesapeake life. Not the least of these features was the ubiquitous influx after 1765 of itinerant evangelists, especially the Baptists and Methodists, hostile to the Anglican Church.[53] In retrospect, these evangelists were thought to have exceeded the tumultuous and emotional extremes of the Great Awakening revivals.[54]

Few of Jefferson's educational schemes became institutionalized in his lifetime and did not represent the prevailing wisdom of his fellow Virginians. However, his proposals became part of an ongoing political debate that went beyond the colony and state itself. It was Jefferson's considerable contribution to pose the issues that his own and subsequent generations confronted concerning the relationships between education and republican virtue. For all his compulsive cataloging of subjects and books, as he catechized his correspondents with his curricular schemes, there were two preoccupations that stayed on all of Jefferson's systemic college proposals, in the reform of William and Mary, then in the establishment of the University of Virginia in 1819. (The university's first classes occurred in 1825.) First was the defense of reason against the force of the individual passions and against the incursions of didactic evangelization. His advice to his nephew, Peter Carr (from Paris, August 10, 1787), illuminates Jefferson conundrum. He advises against the study of moral philosophy as if it were a science: "He who made us would have been a pitiful bungler if he had made the rules of our moral conduct a matter of science." And yet Man did have an innate sense of right and wrong: "The moral sense, or conscience, is as much a part of man as his leg or arm.... It may be strengthened by exercise, as may any particular limb of the body."[55] "State a moral case to a ploughman or a professor. The former will decide it as well, and often better than the latter, because he has not been led astray by artificial rules." The real task of education, especially in religious and political instruction, was to keep deliberation, interpretation, and opinion as close to unfettered nature as possible. "Read the bible then, as you would read Livy or Tacitus. The facts which are within the ordinary course of nature you will believe on the authority of the writer." Again and again Jefferson reworked his thematic refrain, "keep your reason firmly on the watch," deferring to the Lockean assumption that sense knowledge operated independent of human bias and judgment. He assumed that the information of the eye was more authoritative for being yet uncorrupted by ideological manipulation. To see Jefferson's overconfidence in the "self-evident" facts of ordinary nature, in his assumption that ordinary and unobstructed common sense was sufficient check against dogmatism, is to understand a good deal about his eighteenth-century meaning of "diffusion."

Jefferson's bill to disestablish Anglicanism from its status as a state church followed from similar assumptions to leave religion out of the formal instruction of a college, especially one that received state sponsorship. When it finally opened in 1819, his University of Virginia would have no religious requirements on faculty or students and no professorship of theology. Jefferson had to acquiesce, however, on a complete distancing from denominational instruction. In 1822 Jefferson invited the different denominations to establish their own theological schools nearby, so that ministerial students would have the opportunity of university instruction.[56] He thus justified the omission of a divinity professor, while checking criticism of irreligion and hoping in a sense to avoid any dominant sectarianism. His point was not one of fomenting irreligion but the use of reason as a check against the disruptive polarizations of denominational belief.

Denominational leaders were clear about Jefferson's antisectarianism; it is less clear whether they grasped his new, substitute dogma of procedure. Jefferson's instruction to Peter Carr was to follow his reason in either believing in the existence of God or not. "Your own reason," Jefferson admonished, "is the only oracle given you by heaven, and you are answerable not for the rightness but uprightness of the decision."[57] Whatever else his argument achieved, Jefferson thereby sought to constrict sectarian religious belief and didactic morality to the realm of the private rather than to the public sectors of education and politics. In its stead he hoped to insert a different methodology, one of scientific and rational rather than doctrinal conversion. Of course, his political opponents had a field day with charges of atheism and godlessness at "Mr. Jefferson's University," erroneously charging Jefferson with the suppression of religion altogether.[58]

The ease with which Jefferson's argument could be countered by spirited evangelical preaching underscored the near impossibility in proposing "diffusion" of general knowledge as sufficient for engendering republican virtue. In working out the details of a "state University," Jefferson insisted that professors have no restrictions upon their choice of texts and of lecture development, and students would have choice in the selection of their studies.

In comparison to the fixed curricula of other colleges, the new Virginia institution might have appeared too "diffuse," as in having no focus or core, tolerating electives. How could the expected fifteen-year-old students of the early classes shape a course of study without predetermined guidance?[59] In 1818 Jefferson specified fifteen years of age as the probable level of admitted student; however, in 1824 the University Visitors had enacted rules that no student under sixteen be admitted. However, in the earliest class only three were sixteen years old, with the average age being over nineteen (six of sixty-one were over twenty-one years old).[60]

The structured course of studies, of course, limited what students could actually choose. Though his thinking went through several mutations, Jefferson settled at the last (1824) for eight "schools" of study. First, the ancient languages, which included both Hebrew, history, and belles lettres as well as Latin and Greek (though he argued vigorously for the classics to have been mastered upon admission); second, the modern languages, which stressed German and included modern history and geography; third, higher mathematics, from algebra to civil architecture; fourth, mechanics, which focused on the laws of physics including astronomy; fifth, the physical sciences; sixth, medicine, including anatomy, surgery, and pharmacy; seventh, philosophy, especially logic and ethics; and eighth, law, government, and political economy.[61] Though he resisted preconditions to his professors' reading, Jefferson was not above making strong recommendations, particularly and expectedly, in the matter of law, government, and political economy. A student who successfully completed the work of a "school" was to be known as a university graduate.[62]

In Jefferson's mind, however, the actual pedagogical force of the university lodged in the regimented design of his campus, his "Academical Village." He created parallel pavilions, which contained masters' quarters above and classrooms below. Student quarters filled the space between faculty pavilions like guest cottages. Two lines of these pavilions provided both rational balance and orderly environment with familial atmosphere. The living and teaching quarters framed a village green or mall that led to the library rotunda, influenced profoundly by Andrea Palladio's (1508–80) *The Four Books of Architecture* and by Benjamin Latrobe's (1764–1820) Americanization of the classical dome and pavilion.[63] Jefferson had invested his educational values intensively in his university design, consciously shaping in his own mind a new intellectual and cultural authority for post-Revolutionary America. In the process he respected the force of history while continually tinkering with adaptive innovations. He had imposed his reason upon nature, while, in his mind, enhancing both. The effect was to shape students indirectly but didactically and with no sense of contradiction in this mixture of purposes and persons.

Exactly what did Jefferson's university guarantee with this apparent transformation of eighteenth-century institutional control? Undaunted, Jefferson proposed a curriculum that encompassed not only the classics but also "all the branches of science deemed useful at this day and in this country."[64] Alone such curricular goals had three important consequences in all parts of the country that appreciated Jefferson's lead: 1) a new accessibility of all denominations to the halls of higher learning; 2) less paternalistic attitudes toward student behavior; and 3) a competitive proliferation of separate theological seminaries for groups consciously seeking a learned and orthodox ministry.[65] All Jefferson's discussions of education have a peculiar antipedagogical, antipsychological dimension. He never worries about the techniques of disseminating information and interlards his letters with imperatives to tolerance and uncoerced reflection. Much of his educational discourse concerns its administration and supervision features. Jefferson employed a constitutional quality of specifying the process of subject selection and supervision of teachers. His effort was to control and defuse subjective judgment. All procedures needed to follow a minutely attuned set of procedures, which respected contextual arrangements. In his case, of course, such respect meant a constant inclusion of the Chesapeake's elitist, landholding tradition without ignoring the needs of a wider public. It was this constant but gradual attuning that fixed Jefferson's focus and made the value of reason almost one of slowing down the decision-making process to ensure no easy, self-perpetuating political dominance by any of the participating groups. His educational system was a constitutional construct, more "for the public" than it was the prototype of a system "of" or "by" the people. "Education," he offered summarily in his blueprint for the University of Virginia, ". . . engrafts a new man on the native stock, and improves what in his nature was vicious and perverse into qualities of virtue and social worth."[66] This engrafting captured much of what he thought to be "scientific" and "useful" in the educational process; its abject dependence on the forces of nature argued for human designs that paralleled rather than overcame experience, that argued patience and watchfulness rather than introspection and submission.

Jefferson had engrafted a more public scheme on the inherited stock of English colleges, sponsored by royal charter. Emphatically he had introduced an educational alternative to the evangelical prototypes of the Great Awakening colleges. But his achievement, even at his Academical Village in

Charlottesville, was powerfully affected by the aggressive sectarianism of the proliferating Protestant denominations. Between 1782 and 1800, twenty-one new colleges were chartered in the American colonies, creating, in effect, another generation of primarily denominational colleges in both the North and the South: Dickinson (1783) and Franklin (1787) (later Franklin and Marshall in Pennsylvania); Washington College (1783) and St. John's (1784) in Maryland; Bowdoin (1794) in Maine; Union (1795) in New York; and Middlebury (1800) in Vermont; among others.[67] Even the Catholics, though a small minority, created Georgetown in 1789 to claim their own collegiate space and a distinctive endorsement of church-state separation.[68] The multiplication of competitive religious schools plagued Jefferson's University of Virginia, forcing him continually to make careful distinctions between moral training and denominational dogmatism. Jefferson's arguments were often repeated in those other Southern states that attempted their own post-Revolutionary state educational systems: Maryland, 1784; Georgia, 1785; North Carolina, 1789; Tennessee, 1794; and South Carolina, 1801.[69] All of these efforts attempted modifications of the English government's sponsorship of higher learning, but all of them, too, contained caveats about the degrees of political control and the limits upon religious dogmatism.

The post-Revolutionary period witnessed expansive college founding, tripling the existing number of colleges by 1800. These newer colleges, although primarily evangelical, continued to be driven by nationalist, anti-British dynamics that were changing all institutions. Like their older counterparts, the newer colleges accepted the fact that the higher education was intimately connected to the purposes of the new republic. King's College in New York City made the point explicit with a name change to Columbia College, as did Queen's College in New Jersey to Rutgers. Even some of the older bastions of evangelical orthodoxy, like Yale, recognized they too would be affected by the rise of new leadership. Their scientific-minded president, Rev. Ezra Stiles, invited Jefferson himself (and George Washington) to accept an honorary degree, which he did with full academic ceremony.[70] And most of the schools founded in the Northeast—Williams College, Union College, Dickinson, Bowdoin, and others—propounded primarily the Federalist version of historical and political events in faculty classes and presidential sermons.

The political identifications of colleges in the Northern states contrasted with the general, political ambivalence of Southern colleges after the Revolutionary War. Ironically William and Mary, which had been the most formally political, government-sponsored college, reflected the least pointed political commentaries in its commencement exercises, probably because of its Tory associations and its royal charter in the pre-Revolutionary years. After the Revolution, the school tended to reflect the denominational competitions in the South and to soften its overt partisanships or else espouse an untraditional tolerance of religious and political views. Transylvania, founded in 1799 in Kentucky, and the University of Georgia, founded in 1785, and for a time the University of North Carolina, founded in 1789, followed this nonsectarian model and Jeffersonian Republican sentiments.[71] Elsewhere, during the Revolution, especially at Harvard, at the College of Rhode Island and at the College of Philadelphia (where students attended nearby debates of the Continental Congress), the patriot cause was explicitly endorsed.[72] The long-term impact of this conscious political attuning was the introduction of both new subjects, especially history, geography, and belles lettres plus modern language (especially French in the years just after the Revolution). But even within older courses, like moral philosophy, emergent political party debates outside the college classes made their impact on the increasingly partisan biases of the colonial colleges.[73] Few colleges could keep their presidents' and their faculty's politics completely private or neutral. Under President Timothy Dwight, Jefferson and the French Revolution became special whipping posts of Yale's emphatic Federalist didacticism, sentiments sustained by many of the old and new colleges of New England and the Middle Colonies. For new colleges in the West, evangelism and sheer survival on the frontier tended to eclipse the conscious political preoccupations of the older, coastal schools.[74]

In the short-term, the American Revolution disrupted America's older collegiate tradition. Some schools—like Princeton and William and Mary—were literally occupied by opposing British and American armies by turns. Others, like Harvard, temporarily relocated to other locales, and several denominational colleges, like Columbia, Pennsylvania, and Dartmouth, were temporarily taken over by their state governments. In the longer term, after the Revolution, republican values were ritually endorsed by all. However, all developed structures and ideologies that varied according to earlier colonial traditions and regional dynamics, and all made problematic the very meaning of an American college.[75] The central issue for both government and college concerned the degrees of civil control and "republican" indoctrination. Out of the Southern tradition, well illuminated by Jefferson's example and ideas, a less denominational countertradition emerged. Its espousal of science and a pronounced role for state government in college development posed a challenge to the Northern model of the denominational college, even in its less emotional and more gradual institutional form. Neither cultural tradition—inculcation or diffusion—would escape the post-Revolutionary factionalism of American society in general and the aggressive sectarian competition for youth and resources. Ultimately both alternatives would proselytize their different modes of indoctrination: the evangelicals' self-conscious effort to meld conversion with a sense of republican duty; the Enlightenment partisans' forging an awakened sense of scientific process and imposing it in the name of the principle of nonindoctrination.[76] In 1800 the evangelicals held numerical sway but keenly felt the force of the Enlightenment innovations and its distinct cultural assumptions (generational culture #2).

Both Northern and Southern cultures in the eighteenth century produced conceptually distinct rationales for their more advanced schools. The very meaning of college was sufficiently varied in the eighteenth and early nineteenth century to ensure it was not yet a generic designation. For both sections of the postcolonial period, the institutional variations of the "college" were shaped by preexisting cultural dynamics that disrupted education no less than basic social arrangements. However much American higher learning differed geographically, the Northern and Southern cultural paradigms greatly influenced all subsequent discussions of higher learning. It would, however, be well into the nineteenth century before these educational arguments developed into distinctly generic institutional models. Until then the arguments about higher learning were themselves the primary legacies of college founding rather than eighteenth-century curricular proposals, organizational design, or architectural planning.

CHAPTER THREE

Antebellum Colleges and the Inculcation of Moral Character

In early nineteenth-century America, schooling, especially beyond the district or common school, assumed an increasingly important role in both the moral and the commercial life of the nation.[1] Numerically colleges increased from about thirty in 1800 to 169 in 1860, a greater than fivefold expansion into every state and territory. Much historical scholarship has examined these antebellum colleges, in particular, with twentieth-century assumptions of their importance, their place in a calibrated educational ladder, and their necessity in the training of social leaders and professionals.[2] However, the college in the early American Republic was the product of vigorous nineteenth-century competitions, which often shared little of the meaning and conceptions that later generations would attribute to college instruction. During the antebellum period, the need for the largely denominational college by the Republic was not obvious. Had not the majority of Americans achieved literacy with minimal or no formal schooling?[3] What service could any advanced instruction provide when work and experience offered basic learning skills to every citizen? For the American college to become a pivotal institution in the American Republic, it had to prove its value. Its spokesmen could not do so by advancing a religious or political indoctrination, shared by a minority group. Denominations had to engage and retool inherited practice without seeming to indulge parochialism and to convince a skeptical public that unencumbered study was a necessity rather than a privilege. In the early nineteenth century, the American college shifted from an uncertain commodity in the American marketplace to a constructive resource of republican civic virtue. Most colleges did not agonize overly in adopting a purportedly nondenominational goal, the inculcation of moral character.

TABLE 2. Chartering of colleges by region in the United States, 1800 through 1860

Decade chartered	*LS*	*MA*	*MW*	*NE*	*ONW*	*OSE*	*PC*	*SW*	*US*	*Total*
1801–10	1	2	0	0	2	1	0	0	4	10
1811–20	0	3	0	1	2	0	0	0	4	10
1821–30	0	2	0	2	3	3	0	0	4	14
1831–40	7	3	1	2	14	5	0	0	5	38
1841–50	3	7	7	0	13	4	0	2	5	41
1851–60	5	10	13	1	13	4	6	0	4	56
Total	16	27	21	6	47	17	6	2	26	169

Note: James McLachlan Database. This data, developed independent of Burke's, nevertheless provides a powerful confirmation of the equally definitive statistics in Burke's *American Collegiate Populations*.

LS = Lower South (NC, SC, GA)

MA = Middle Atlantic (DE, NJ, NY, PA)

MW = Middle West (AR, IA, KS, MN, MO, WI)

NE = New England

ONW = Old Northwest (OH, IL, IN, MI)

OSE = Old Southeast (AL, LA, MO, MS)

PC = Pacific (CA, OR)

SW = Texas

US = Upper South (DC, KY, MD, TN, VA)

The American college in the early nineteenth century developed its collegiate culture before the creation of a distinct institutional model. The 169 colleges created between 1800 and the Civil War were nominally denominational and energized by the boosterism of newfound communities.[4] Religious missionaries and new settlers ensured that new colleges were created along lines of settlements and away from the eastern seaboard and away from cities in the first half of the century. By 1860 the Midwest had produced 28 percent of all colleges, though in 1800 they had none.[5] These institutions were often created by individuals with no college experience and headed by trustees without college degrees.[6]

Town promoters projected and plotted on paper more colleges than actually taught students or sustained operations over time. Many colleges that actually received students remained preparatory and eclectic in their offerings, although often labeling themselves "colleges." The formal affiliation of a college with a denomination also masked the number of attending students from other denominations. Religious sects made many compromises for the sake of survival and tolerated a collegiate interdenominationalism that they had not in the eighteenth century and did not in their new, nineteenth-century seminaries for their sect's ministers. This pattern of founding meant that institutional distinctions between college, academy, seminary, and institute remained very fluid and imprecise throughout the period. In addition, the educational goals of colleges, however denominationally oriented they were in practice, gravitated toward a common *voluntary* esprit that softened the sharp edges of sectarianism.[7] In its way nineteenth-century voluntarism in collegiate life sought to internalize a civic order that hitherto had been imposed and monitored by denominational authority. "Inculcation" became an alternative to indoctrination but no less effective in shaping an internal gyroscope, making individual choice compatible with external civic boundaries. The colleges of the antebellum period, still rooted in traditional denominational patterns, attempted through inculcation a conversion experience without specific denominational demarcations. This voluntary tradition both respected an inherited Protestant tradition of conversion and a new republican ideal that avoided narrow sectarian self-interest.

The aim of antebellum colleges and other organizations to enhance Christian behavior concentrated on instilling in every citizen an inner drive to reshape and improve civic society through self-discipline.[8] Both formal and informal organizations—schools as well as religious revivals—kept this goal prominent. In spite of their own didactic traditions, schoolmen increasingly professed to be wary of any education or social discipline that controlled behavior externally. The "voluntary principle" was especially energized by a collective Protestant hostility to Roman Catholicism and its expanding membership from the 1830s onward. The hierarchy and ritualism of the Catholic Church—the perceived imposition of their credo through censure and punishment—was thought to be offset by the Protestant "inculcation of moral character," which could not be imposed or externally enforced.[9] But, of course, Presbyterian educators would hardly complain if their schools graduated a majority of civic-minded Presbyterians.

In spite of its diverse institutional forms, the nineteenth-century college contributed to a major cultural shift, the preference for a republican rather than a denominationally religious outcome. Colleges sought to yoke together two disparate traditions, one religious, the other political, to find a common ground by which existing colleges could contribute to something larger than sectarian competition. First, its spokesmen reformulated a defensive evangelical tradition into a proposive, "educational" ideology that muted denominational tenants and focused on "moral character."[10] In addition, Whiggish political commentators included the college in their ideological matrix. Whig values favored organization, legalistic compromise, and a gradual constitutional process of change. The career of Horace Mann (1796–1859), who moved from public schooling into Whig politics as a US congressman, concluded with the presidency of Antioch College and illuminated the blend of traditional religion and political reconstruction in the American college. In his published writings and reports, there was a new commitment to produce a morally upright citizen, able to think both independently yet responsibly for the social good. In the proceedings of major voluntary associations of the period, like the American Institute of Instruction (founded 1830), to which Mann and most other nineteenth-century educational leaders belonged, schoolmen like Horace Mann fashioned an educational goal that applied to public schools while also contributing to the public weal.[11] Mann's generation sought to "inculcate" habits of thought that would mature and function without overt, external monitoring. It became a cliché of the period that the college president embodied the mission of his school. The college president became one example of Ralph Waldo Emerson's (1803–82) assertion in "Self-Reliance" that "an institution is the lengthened shadow of one man." In spite of diverse regional variations, the antebellum college drew from both of these traditions to promote an idealized educated citizen, inspired by national republican values yet locally grounded. The new tradition was thought to be distinctively voluntary, adaptive in subject matter yet disciplined, factually informed yet inquiring, and socially engaged without demagogy.[12] The new collegiate ideal both arose out of and promoted this American "voluntary principle," while resisting any sharp generic or sectarian prescriptions about antebellum colleges or college life.

To explore this transition, this essay will examine several episodes involving "collegiate values" in the antebellum period. First, the essay establishes a broad, economic context within which any college, denominational or otherwise, necessarily had to compete. Next, the peculiar nondenominational pressures of the antebellum period, I am assuming, arose more clearly in the cases of newly founded institutions rather than in those with explicit eighteenth-century, denominational inheritances. These newer institutions help explain the force of the new civic pressures that all schools had to engage. Hence the case of Girard College with its novel rationale of civic production and individual transformation absent denominational attachments becomes particularly germane, because Girard adopted the quasi-evangelical ideal of inculcating moral character. Like most of the other institutions of the period, the college sought to avoid any association with a rigid, ideological standard of instruction but attempted a kind of conversion experience that produced an upright citizen, ideally independent of social origins or social class. Girard's targeting of male orphans made this claim especially poignant, but not significantly different from other colleges with students of varied backgrounds.[13] How the prevalent denominational colleges dealt with such an alternative can be explored by examining resonant episodes of the period but from a newly critical stance, in particular, the often-studied (1816–19) Dartmouth College case. Finally the equally familiar Yale Report (1828) played an important role in demonstrating how the denominational college began its own reconstruction and accommodation to new, institutional ideology about advanced instruction. Out of this antebellum competition among colleges arose a transformed sense of American higher learning and its republican dividends by midcentury.[14]

I

Alongside official addresses by the nation's leadership and in the US Congress, the *National Intelligencer,* which became Washington, DC's self-proclaimed newspaper of record, also filled its pages with random advertisements of equal importance to the antebellum national readership: steamship schedules and rates, rewards for runaway slaves, legal notices of land transfers and equity actions, obituaries, special cargoes (plows, fodder, etc.), lottery announcements, and of course, especially in August and September, before classes began, advertisements for seminaries, medical departments, academies, tutorials, and colleges. Georgetown College (founded 1789) in the nation's capital, for example, boasted its "university" status, under boldface headings, like "Georgetown College," with no sense of incongruity.[15] Roman Catholic Georgetown underscored its advertising pitch by trumpeting its 1815 charter from the US Congress and its receptivity to non-Catholic students. By the 1830s the American college had claimed an attractive, though imprecise, commercial value—its strategic location in the nation's capital and its welcome to students of all denominations—aggressively competing for a special foothold among American consumers.[16] The antebellum "college" in America had not yet achieved a distinctive generic meaning and consequently cultivated multiple, even contradictory, claims.

The founding rationale of Girard College illuminates one of the original strands of this emerging collegiate identity. The Girard case demonstrates not only the problematic meaning of "college" itself but also the conceptual pressures on such institutions to broaden their appeal beyond a traditional, sectarian clientele.[17] On July 4, 1833, the *National Intelligencer* published Nicholas Biddle's (1786–1844) address at the dedication of Girard College in Philadelphia. Out of the beneficence of Stephen Girard (1750–1831), self-described Philadelphia "Merchant and Mariner," would arise, Biddle assured his listeners, "the spirit which may more influence the destiny of ourselves and our children than all else the world now contains. . . . It is that knowledge, which trampling down in its progress the dominion of brutal force and giving to intellect its just ascendancy, has at length become the master power of the world." Biddle associated the multiplying example of Girard's philanthropy and moral discipline with the "safety" of the Republic and "the public spirit of community at once enlightened and generous."[18] The inaugural speech was nationally propitious not only for its timing and association with the origins of the American Republic but also for other associations made explicit in Biddle's address. Biddle articulated values that would embed themselves in the ubiquitous voluntary associations of the period and that would dramatically affect all institutions shaped by American Whig culture, most especially colleges.[19]

Several features of Girard's benevolence made it both extraordinary and problematic for a democratic republic. The sheer amount of money involved—$2 million—provided in a stroke an endowment that exceeded the sum of all other American colleges.[20] The beneficence projected a cultural and architectural image of enduring influence commensurate with the values of Greek culture and polity. The school would be spatially as well as fiscally autonomous. All activities of schooling and residence were to be contained, according to Girard's will, within a single institution. If further guarantees of endurance were required, Nicholas Biddle, the chairman of the college's board of trustees, currently served as the president of the Bank of the United States. Many American citizens would have viewed such antebellum associations as guaranteeing the school's endurance via its uncommon fiscal backing. Biddle's stewardship of the new college would have also suggested to the bank's Jacksonian critics a major expansion of Whig elitism in the nation's commerce and republican values.[21] Even in Girard College, designed for orphans, crucial choices emerged by the late 1850s and early 1860s that privileged some by permitting a small elite in the collegiate department and sent the majority off into apprenticeship and the world of work.[22] At issue was the basic public benefit to the Republic of a new institution—a "college"—that did not directly serve all of the people. These connotations of power and endurance—its endorsement by the head of the nation's central bank—set Girard College apart from many collegiate institutions of the time.[23]

Its own endowment and implicit durability as well as its sponsoring elite made Girard's school singular, but its actual operations illuminated historic features common to a range of different schools. Least remarkable at the time—but surprising from a twentieth-century viewpoint—was its appropriation of the term "college" for the instruction of orphans of district school age. Girard's will had specified poor white male orphans between the ages of six and ten. The school, Girard had insisted, was neither to be an almshouse nor a charity school but a "college"; it would thus provide the various branches of sound education in reading; writing; grammar; arithmetic; geography; navigation; surveying; practical mathematics; astronomy; natural, chemical, and experimental philosophy; and the French and Spanish languages. The founder's only caveats opposed uniform dress and excessive stress on Greek and Latin. Girard also incorporated in his will the stipulation that "no ecclesiastic, missionary or minister of any sect whatsoever" should have any capacity in his institution.[24] The result would embrace "everything necessary to form a well-educated man," producing in the process an institution that will be "the civil West Point of the country."[25] If his sentiment expressed a more extreme secular penchant than many contemporary colleges, Girard nevertheless articulated the goal of a distinctly republican educational ideal.

Significantly, Biddle professed an admiration, not for Girard's pedagogical specifications, but for his enlarged spirit of benevolent, public stewardship, the centerpiece of antebellum Whig republicanism.[26] Prominent college supporters underscored this notion of stewardship, which defined both the conceptual breadth of collegiate expectation and the elasticity of the word "college" for the antebellum period. For Girard the term contained no implications for subject sorting or institutional rank; it connoted nothing of the historic British meanings of college, namely, a collection of youthful students studying beyond basic levels or even a residence hall where such students lived; it implied no official or legal degree-granting authority. Its practical aims were to have fatherless youth trained for employment by ages fourteen to eighteen, converting them into responsible citizens. However, its profound ("irradiating") social impact followed from the example-setting philanthropy of Girard and the consequences of a morally informed educational purpose.[27] This dynamic of voluntarism yoked to an expansive Whig Republicanism formed the common ground that Girard College shared with other social and cultural institutions of the antebellum period. Whig Republican institutions, like most antebellum colleges, stressed the benevolent esprit—they called it "character"—which ideally softened the sharp, self-interested edges of privilege and selectivity associated with older antebellum institutions.[28]

This voluntary standard, so rooted in denominational didactics and practice, nevertheless had shed many of its pointedly sectarian aspects during the antebellum period. Still, antebellum voluntarism retained a secularized missionary fervor but with a didactic "nondenominational" message; it continued an espoused preference for the indirect persuasion of example and a substitution of civic benevolence for sectarian piety. Antebellum voluntarism thus retained older features of religious evangelism in its basic structure and in its increasingly widespread educational and political expressions.[29] Girard's stipulation against direct denominational proselytizing did not belie a new didacticism: his effort to internalize the moral compass of civic behavior was but a variant on an older process of evangelical conversion. His Girard College demonstrated the degree to which a diluted evangelism had become a part of America's cultural fabric by the 1830s. The novelty of antebellum voluntarism like Girard's lay with the effort to disseminate a new republican civility through schools to ground the political order in its citizens rather than through demagoguery, which to some Whigs was represented by the narrow didacticism of the pulpit. The historic achievement of this new voluntarism was the substitution of a "nondenominational" moral code for an older dogmatic sectarianism and its formal adoption even by consciously denominational colleges.

Girard College represented a bold form of this new Whig republicanism by proposing a public service unallied with any denomination. Since most previous education and especially antebellum colleges had been driven by a denominational élan, how representative was Girard's school? Girard College was historically important for its clear insistence upon republican values in its college fabric without also eclipsing completely the moral ideals of its denominational competitors. Several denominations made a post-Revolutionary effort to broaden the aegis of the Christian religion to the new Republic as a whole. The peculiar antebellum organizations that followed—"the Voluntary System"—even when they resulted in a less broad denominational consciousness, approached nonsectarian outreaches like Girard's.[30] Both denominational and nondenominational colleges evidenced a new voluntarism like Girard's that would appear to accommodate the competitive spirit of America's antebellum republic.

II

Girard College's example may have exemplified a clarification of college goals, but antebellum collegiate practice remained varied and problematic. The antebellum "college" encompassed schools instructing youth from ages anywhere between six and thirty. Its curricular offerings varied substantively, depending on region and local priorities, from the sacred to the profane. Many were consciously and aggressively denominational, while others, like both Girard College and the University of Virginia, explicitly distanced themselves from religious association. Nearly all had fiscal problems that sometimes compelled them to close their doors prematurely, sometimes reopening, often under new names. These mercurial economics forced more than one, like Transylvania University in Kentucky, to be transferred successively to distinct and competing Protestant denominations or, in a word, to suffer the tenuousness or failure of many American businesses.[31] Between 1800 and 1860, their student bodies fluctuated from several dozen to several hundred. Few schools could afford to be so selective that they achieved associations with definable elites; most adopted ringing statements of standards and purpose, then sought to fill their classrooms with students of widely different preparations.[32]

The heterogeneity of the antebellum student body has not appeared as a significant feature of this subject until recently. Instead, historians have focused on a few dramatic figures and special episodes to impose a thematic but decontextualized order to American collegiate history. The historical variety of collegiate "models" has led to judgments of inadequacy and failure to characterize the pre–Civil War patterns.[33] Both legal and denominational history has given most scholars of the American college an overly precise, that is, oversimplified, categorical framework for the antebellum period. The most powerful definition of the early republican college in America emanated from the Supreme Court decision known as the Dartmouth College case (1819), which supposedly distinguished between a "public" and a "private" corporation. However, the court decision, like Girard's legacy, tells us more about the problematic transition of an eighteenth-century denominational college into its nineteenth-century mode of nondenominational voluntarism than it tells us about a self-consciously "private" tradition of collegiate operation. From the perspective of American higher education, the Dartmouth College case showed the need for a practical blueprint to achieve the American colleges' newfound, republican ideal.

The Dartmouth College case arose in 1816 when William Plumer (1759–1850), the New Hampshire governor and political associate of Thomas Jefferson, called for a revision of Dartmouth's collegiate charter. That document had been awarded originally by the British king by means of his colonial assembly in 1769. The college president, John Wheelock (1754–1817), son of the school's founder, had clashed with his trustees over several staff appointments and curricular changes. The trustees' opposition implicitly raised questions about how responsive and adaptable a college should be to the public. Direct accountability to politically elected leaders struck both the governor and Dartmouth's president as particularly desirable and civic in America's post-Revolutionary period. But the royal charter, the college's trustees retorted, represented a special brand of public autonomy, attuned to but not whiplashed by the political whims of party and faction. From the trustees' viewpoint, a college was a privately held charity, influential in its community but not directly answerable to its local constituency.

In actual fact, the antebellum fears of any institution, educational, commercial, or otherwise, becoming distinctly "private," that is, a self-perpetuating monopoly, raised the specter of monarchical exploitation that the Revolution was thought to have redressed. Jefferson himself had taken great pains to specify how "public" universities in a democracy must remain subordinate and politically accountable to the elected representatives of the people.[34] Similarly concerned, the New Hampshire legislature passed a formal revision of the colonial charter giving the governor special powers of trustee appointment and of creating overseers for the college, which was thus construed as a state and civic rather than an eleemosynary institution. The new law also changed the name of the school to a university and gave it legal authority over the management of Dartmouth's property holdings and resources. For a time, the trustees resisting, Dartmouth College and Dartmouth University operated side by side.[35]

The Dartmouth trustees, who were Congregationalist in religion and Federalist in politics, appealed to the New Hampshire Supreme Court, which upheld the new charter's revision. This new decision considered Dartmouth the only college in the state and hence a state institution. The trustees appealed to the US Supreme Court to recover their property and hired the eminent Dartmouth alumnus and future Whig statesman Daniel Webster (1782–1852) to defend them. The Supreme Court's decision reversed the state's legislative and judicial judgment; it upheld the original trustees and the colonial charter on the grounds that "no state shall pass any . . . law impairing the obligation of contracts." By this precedent, the chartered American college thus became a private, charitable corporation. Corporate contracts were held inviolate from direct state or public interference, a distancing from Jeffersonian institutional assumptions about public accountability.[36] The ownership of the college was firmly set with the trustees. The US Supreme Court's decision also presaged a new relationship between colleges and the state. However, the Court decision left the "public" responsibility for such "private" institutions an unsettled issue.

The ultimate importance of *Dartmouth v. Woodward* rested with later interpretations of a legal charter for American business. When promulgated, the Dartmouth case only affected the integrity of the original charter and left the college's organization to its trustees. In their minds the public service of the college would support their educational priorities rather than those of the state's elected leadership. The case did not, as Frederick Rudolph has suggested, lead to the founding of additional private colleges, nor did it subordinate state power to communal rights nor put the college beyond public passions.[37] The case had little impact on neighboring institutions or the newer schools of the antebellum period. A few subsequent colleges, most with eighteenth-century roots, for example, at Harvard, Union College, University of Maryland, and Bowdoin College, explicitly used the Dartmouth precedent in analogous struggles, but many newer nineteenth-century college founders evinced little knowledge or explicit encouragement from the Dartmouth legal precedent.[38] Historian Colin Burke has persuasively argued that some states continued to restrict the role and place of private colleges and charitable institutions, and, on their part, private colleges like Bowdoin, University of Pennsylvania, Amherst, Williams, and Columbia continued to petition states for funds, though with declining success.[39] More important, the case had little import for the Southern states and some Northern ones, like New York, which sustained restrictive statutes against private endowments like colleges. New England's distinctive cultural and economic dynamics, by contrast, gave rise to private corporations, private endowments, and private colleges, creating Boston as a regional hub. That city thus added a new institutional autonomy—the integrity of the corporate charter—to its fiscal and cultural powers, which put Boston in a singularly advantageous position at the end of the nineteenth century.[40] Individual entrepreneurs and their institutions could be seen as public or republican resources without close state monitoring.

In essence, the Dartmouth College case prevented state political interests from interfering with and reinterpreting the social contribution of a college. It legitimated the rights of such institutions to serve as a public resource, even though they were not extensions of the state political system. The intellectual fears that sectarian organizations would inevitably produce more narrow and self-interested entities were momentarily shelved. As the only college in the state, Dartmouth could be recognized as a public resource in spite of its denominational origins. In the context of the Dartmouth decision, however, colleges, which sought a new republican legitimacy, needed to take care about how they acknowledged their historical priorities. The nineteenth-century tension between national and sectarian allegiances played through the Dartmouth case without necessarily resolving the problem for one side or the other. To be sure, the respect of the college charter provided as much legal protection for the denominational college as it did for the state university. The Supreme Court's decision offered no incentive to prefer one model over the other, and the case would not have its full legal implications—for the protection of corporate contracts—until much later in the nineteenth century. Its importance for the history of American higher education was actually quite modest: individuals and institutions were free to contribute to the body politic as they saw fit, and government's role was to protect their private property. Antebellum colleges advanced their public usefulness via a special idealized integrity in their students, namely, moral character. From the collegiate viewpoint, the crucial instrument of power had to be internalized, variously called moral or pietistic in the nineteenth century, not externalized through paternalist monitors, like the state or its representatives.[41] The Dartmouth College case did not modify the college as a voluntary organization but rather enabled the colleges' implicit social promise—to create self-reliant citizens rather than self-serving interested parties. This distinctive antebellum ideal was the fundamental goal of Girard's model of civic stewardship for Protestant and non-Protestant schools alike, and without great fanfare many denominational colleges approached this standard before the Civil War.[42]

The immediate, historic significance of the Dartmouth College case was not its distinction between public and private colleges but rather its contribution to the ongoing exploration of public worth that affected many antebellum institutions. The court actually engineered a translation of the Dartmouth trustees' Congregational tradition into Daniel Webster's nascent Whig values; it also permitted Webster's trustee defense to triumph over elected state politicians. But even more, the Dartmouth College case sustained the problematic nature of the college by publicizing two legitimate but competing "public" traditions—the college as a charitable creation or the college as politically attuned service—for understanding the larger social and historical force of America's collegiate culture in the antebellum period. The court decision did little to settle how colleges could guarantee a different brand of leadership while avoiding the divisive partisanship of denominations and political factions. The decision did not formalize Whig biases in behalf of property owners and a weakened governing executive, so much as it continued the conundrum about the kind of education that a republic needed. The decision left untouched the knotty issue of how college training benefited a republic and its leaders.

Subsequently state governments would assume a more detached role in the face of citizens' legitimate organizational ventures, but these new processes emerged slowly, largely out of economic considerations, not with the thunderclap of a courtroom decision. States willingly chartered new schools and colleges but regularly resisted any responsibility for financial support. As historian John Whitehead has noted, Dartmouth's trustees requested that the state legislature pay their legal costs, after supposedly winning a clear distinction between the public and private sectors. Like many other financially strapped "private" colleges, Dartmouth continued to appeal for state support throughout the antebellum period, sometimes offering the state representation on the trustee board in exchange.[43] Few legal scholars relied on the public/private distinction in subsequent pre–Civil War arguments, precisely because the intent of those arguments was to distinguish two brands of "public" organization, one charitable, dominated by citizens' voluntary associations, and the other civil, dominated by state organizations, like Jefferson's conception of a state university.[44] Neither connoted "private" in any twentieth-century sense.

III

Not only did antebellum colleges resist easy categorization as "public" or "private," most colleges emphatically resisted identification as local or sectarian (while cultivating both and becoming denominationally affiliated). For instance, Wesleyan University's charter prohibited restrictions against any other denomination in spite of its explicitly Methodist identity. Initially various denominations were represented on any number of trustee boards and in their student populations. Similarly Georgetown College, the oldest Roman Catholic college in the United States (founded 1789), admitted into their earliest classes all denominations and advertised the point boastfully through the 1830s. For the first three decades of the nineteenth century, one-quarter to one-third of Georgetown's student body were non-Catholic. While Wesleyan and Georgetown relied substantively in their early years on local benefactors, both schools worked from the outset to reach interdenominational, regional, national, and even international audiences.[45]

Economic realities compelled old and new nineteenth-century colleges alike to resist the defensiveness that characterized their eighteenth-century counterparts. Antebellum colleges did not become isolated communities in spite of their varied efforts to cultivate a new nineteenth-century college conception. This period saw public images of institutions with fences and walls separating town and gown, and later residential dorms, refectories, and collegiate chapels on a definable "campus."[46] Despite such physical autonomy, a college at times connected itself organizationally with broader, translocal, denominational networks. Early on, it became clear that local resources were insufficient to sustain not only colleges but also many other educational levels beyond the common school: academies, female seminaries, normal schools, or literary institutes.[47] Financial stability necessitated continual outreach, and the success of such enterprises often resulted in spawning intensive competition. Wesleyan, for example, cultivated Methodist donors in Boston, until one of these benefactors decided to found Boston University in 1869. This Boston competitor, even among Methodists, siphoned off Wesleyan's New England donations and forced it to shift its focus to New York City friends and alumni.[48] Similarly Randolph-Macon College in Virginia originally anticipated wide support from several Methodist conferences, but the competition from Pennsylvania's Dickinson College (founded 1783) eroded its earlier support from the Baltimore Conference. Further, the creation of Emory (founded 1836) in Georgia narrowed Randolph-Macon's geographical base to central and southern Virginia and parts of North Carolina.[49] Ironically the necessary network outreach for funds and students often resulted in a geographical constriction of the college's physical aegis, forcing such schools to consider solicitations beyond their denominational base.

The tension between grand vision and local realities during the antebellum period became clearly expressed in the oil portrait of New York University, founded in 1831 in the heart of the nation's emergent commercial metropolis. One of the first members of the faculty, artist-inventor Samuel F. B. Morse (1791–1872), depicted his newborn university as an ancient Gothic oasis in an idyllic Tuscan landscape. The overstated historic roots of his conception projected the image of autonomy, stability, and safety in a natural countryside that fit easily into many national or cultural canons. The connotations of composure and isolated self-sufficiency required standards of conception and technique that transcended not only local but also American boundaries. And in spite of ambitious national and international advertisements, New York University within a few short years was scrambling for its financial life and sharing the mercurial history of its antebellum collegiate counterparts.[50]

The history of most antebellum colleges reflected regular fluctuations in financial support and student enrollment. The universal fact of collegiate life was competition for a modest pool of basically trained youth that required active solicitation and constant cultivation.[51] Virtually all schools of "collegiate" level consciously imitated the recruitment and endowment campaigns pioneered in the early nineteenth century—if not before—by itinerant college agents. The Congregational network, which eventually formed itself into the

American Education Society, operated out of Andover Theological Seminary (founded 1808) and included members of college and universities in the South and west as far as the Mississippi by the 1830s.[52] Few of its ministers rode circuit, only preaching the gospel of Christ. Most were empowered to solicit funds for various institutions, award scholarship-appointing authority to substantial donors, discount or waive tuition to promising but impoverished youth, and to advertise the distinctive merits of "nondenominational" schools without abrogating their continuing denominational ties.[53] These recruiting efforts differentiated eighteenth- from nineteenth-century colleges, the difference between "surprising," that is, spontaneous Great Awakening revivals versus engineered evangelical events of the antebellum period.

However calculated these collegiate solicitations, their public appeals made them appear in retrospect as encompassing to all rather than as exclusive overtures to coreligionists. In actual practice, many schools seemed to offer a wide range of subjects that their smaller faculties could never teach. For those fortunate enough to experience student increases, the public pretense implied a general recognition of educational excellence. Princeton, for example, sustained its operations on an active network well beyond New Jersey. The college cultivated an expanding network of schools in a number of Southern states and made minor distinctions between its supporting academies and sister colleges. Not only did these institutions serve as feeder schools, however loosely affiliated with Princeton, but also these networks served to energize contact between Presbyterian congregations and at times enhance the salaries and stature of both aspirant and established ministers.[54] The traffic within such networks was not closely monitored as Presbyterian and participating students of different persuasions took advantage of nearby schools whatever their denominational or secular origins. Historian Colin Burke has noted that schools in the loose "academy" genre increased from 3,200 in 1840 to over 6,700 by 1860, increases commensurate with primary school expansion.[55] The enduring precollegiate schools were often not self-contained, educational institutions but links in larger, regional organizations.

The career of Robert Baird (1798–1863) illuminates the trajectory of such loosely connected but efficient voluntary networks. Born in western Pennsylvania, Baird attended first a local Uniontown (Pennsylvania) academy, then for several terms Washington and (1818) Jefferson colleges. Though degreeless, he had sufficient preparation for entering and graduating from Princeton Theological Seminary (founded 1812)[56] in 1822. His subsequent ministerial work included the principalship of the Princeton Academy while tutoring at Princeton College. His concomitant civic work in the 1820s with the American Bible Society enabled him to assess educational deficiencies. His effort to redress them led to public addresses and political lobbying to propose a New Jersey public school system. He then assumed a revivalist service as general agent for the American Sunday School Union and later (1835) international agent in Paris and Rome for the American and Foreign Christian Union, which promoted temperance and educational reforms worldwide. Virtually none of these revivalist positions were distinctly specialized, and all proceeded from his denominational base to broader public endeavors. His writing and preaching were considered informational and public-spirited rather than acquisitive or self-promoting. Throughout an entire career of instruction and benevolent voluntarism, Baird sought to mix charitable and civic work, a harmonizing standard of antebellum stewardship, common to both local and national organizational leadership.[57]

One of the corollary features of such pre–Civil War voluntarism was its distinctive organizational structure, particularly its overlapping informal networks. Given the informality of the varied networks Baird went through, one has difficulty in retrospect understanding the institutional relationships except through biography. In the organizational shifts of Baird's career, one glimpses the loose overlap of organizations and their interactions. Any specific history of one of these institutions fails to illuminate how they were used over time, except by viewing individual careers. The short periods of time Baird spent in a number of these organizations testified to their loose boundaries, but together they document the constant reliance of Baird on his evangelical skills, public speaking and written accounts of travel and experiences. His Presbyterian base never seems to have been as pronounced as his larger public goals, the distinguishing feature of his nineteenth-century revivalism over those of his eighteenth-century predecessors.

Baird's moral purposes remained primary through his career. In spite of the particular goals of his endeavors—precollege and college instruction at the same time, Bible distribution, analysis of district schools (before the existence of a public school system), and overseas fieldwork to advance a moral and civic order together. These sequential career moves implied no hierarchy of purpose or career advancement. Promoting temperance in a particular locale did not suggest it ranked ahead of collegiate solicitation. Like newspaper advertisements, local priorities grounded his reform enterprises, but the end point was always beyond local parameters. Increasingly, a particular college's interests shared the social saddlebag of the American evangelist with other worthy causes. But emphatically regional concerns mixed kaleidoscopically with other issues that worthily sought to construct a republican, Christian commonwealth.[58] Increasingly colleges played a strategic role in this larger organizational enterprise.

Within the 1801 Plan of Union forged by the Presbyterian and Congregational denominations, churchmen created voluntary organizations of a national scope. Their intention was to project their special brand of Protestantism and make it coincident with the malleable, local voluntary associations still developing in the East and, more important, about to develop in the West. In 1843 the Society for the Promotion of Collegiate and Theological Education at the West (SPCTEW) began its work, funneling small-donor support and didactic, revivalist-oriented printed matter all across the trans-Appalachian West. What resources this East Coast network generated would soon be channeled to select western colleges. By 1874, when the organization dissolved, the SPCTEW had supported twenty-six colleges and provided a model for competing Baptist and Methodist organizations.[59] The basic voluntary mode of organization extended to kindred associations, like the American Tract Society, the Sunday School Union, and the American Bible Society, which made their mark powerfully, though indirectly, on the collegiate enterprise.[60] Officials of these interdenominational organizations were generally themselves college graduates and were sought out, not only by college presidents for collegiate donations but also for advice and for arbitrating knotty interdenominational collegiate disputes. One of the crucial attractions of this voluntary tradition was the mixture of moral coercion and persuasion within a personalized, informal style, as if knotty issues could still be settled short of contentious, political confrontations.

Antebellum colleges may have originated from select denominational roots, local resources, and merchant capitalists, but, in the decades before the Civil War, they participated in broader, voluntary networks that clarified a common reality of collegiate culture: collegiate survival could not depend for long on local resources alone.[61] Some denominations had come to this insight early, like the Congregationalists and the Presbyterians. Among other denominations, like the Baptists, the Methodists, and the Disciples of Christ, who came late to the value of advanced instruction, the college's moral leadership experienced substantial strains between a college's denominational goals and the practical, worldly concerns of the college's business patrons. Randolph-Macon College (founded 1830) was one of some 229 colleges, academies, and lower schools founded by the Methodists before 1860, all but ten after 1830. Randolph-Macon avoided creating a theology professorship and a wholly Methodist trustee board in order to obtain a charter from the Virginia state legislature.[62] Still, the school sought to privilege its denominational base by gradually drawing in individuals with regional and business connections.[63] But most of all early funding and stability were a function of the circuit of select evangelical ministers, in this case rides to the Carolinas and Georgia (rather than north to Baltimore or West over the Appalachians).[64] While they concentrated on fellow religionists, ministerial solicitors were not fussy about the sources of their funds. In the effort to modify their denominational roots, the college took its namesakes—Nathaniel Macon and John Randolph—from statewide worthies who were not Methodists. In the effort to accommodate a nondenominational aura, colleges necessarily made choices that signaled local and nonlocal affiliations. In a similar way, Stephen Girard, whose "local" college contributed to Philadelphia pride, had not only drawn upon his own international experience but projected with his philanthropy a less politically contentious American Republic. In these features Girard provided a two-way, local-national trajectory for antebellum collegiate voluntarism, imitated even by his nemesis, the ubiquitous denominational college.

Unmistakably regional rather than local or national boundaries became the forceful parameters of the antebellum college in America.[65] Early on New England began to develop highly restrictive admissions standards, whereas in the South and Midwest before the Civil War institutional survival necessitated fairly unrestrictive policies with respect to age or previous schooling. Oberlin College (founded 1831) in Ohio, for example, admitted literally hundreds of students and was noted for its earliest admission of both women and blacks to collegiate instruction. However, within Oberlin's aegis there were multiple departments, accommodating students in primary and "normal" (i.e., teacher-preparatory) instructional groupings as well as in collegiate and theological seminary levels. Most institutions outside the Northeast, as Colin Burke has compellingly demonstrated, were scaled-down versions of Oberlin.[66] High tuitions in the East reinforced the expense of city residence, permitting coastal urban colleges to charge at times three times the costs of instruction outside New England.[67] In the Midwest and South, the functioning patterns of fiscal anxiety, student accessibility, and evangelical piety kept tuition low.[68] In large part, colleges with large preparatory and collegiate departments appeared in the Midwest and South in sparsely or recently settled areas, particularly where the New England model of the state-supported common school had not yet penetrated. Varied levels of "collegiate instruction" responded to all comers, averaging about twenty students in their highest collegiate level, when their eastern counterparts could field two or three times as many, a few admitting up to four hundred students. With such a student pool, eastern colleges early on could eliminate their preparatory classes, a shaping moment toward a distinctive collegiate identity.

Those communities that could not raise sufficient funds, even using a particular denominational network, responded with an adaptive, multipurpose academy, the ubiquitous college preparatory school before the Civil War.[69] Such schools were often the taproot of a later college.[70] Amherst Academy, for example, founded in 1814 as a coeducational school, led within a decade to the founding of an exclusively male college with a state charter and a consciously classical focus. Still, Amherst's early curriculum resembled the collegiate aspirations of many academies, and one of its early presidents, Edward Hitchcock (1793–1864), assumed the collegiate leadership with theological rather than regular collegiate training. Probably more important than any degree was Hitchcock's experience as principal of nearby Deerfield Academy and as a self-taught geologist.[71]

The distinction between academy and college became sharper as the nineteenth century wore on, a function, first of age grouping, then curricular organization, and ultimately sociocultural distinctions. In the *National Intelligencer* (November 2, 1833), the flourishing Brookville (Maryland) Academy publicized its refusal to admit students over seventeen, while a month earlier the same newspaper printed the University of Virginia announcement of a cutoff age of no younger than sixteen. Though academies and colleges often offered complementary studies, their curricular subjects in science, mathematics, language, and philosophy had begun to receive greater specification at institutions striving for a higher status in these years.

Until the sharpening of sectional division and North-South barriers after the 1830s, college leaders strove to reach out beyond their regional boundaries. Physical traffic moved constantly between the two regions, in many ways heightening rather than breaking down regional consciousness of distinctive cultures. By midcentury, however, the South had forgone an earlier aspiration to create expansive state-supported public school systems modeled on Massachusetts's example. The rising dichotomy between Cavalier and Yankee compelled the South to rely more heavily upon elitist support for private academies and denominational colleges as well as their public universities, subordinating earlier Southern commitments to tax-supported public education.[72]

In the first half of the nineteenth century and later, the American college had a clear conceptual goal—the inculcation of moral character—but lacked any single, formal standard of structure or operation to implement it; rather, it fluctuated problematically between curricular and administration offerings driven by local dynamics and regional pressures, often influenced by its denominational origins. In the competition for students and donors, exaggerated goals and ambitions abounded, masking the strategic force of local elites and sectarian priorities. In the process of survival, schools depended on localities and denominations, in spite of lofty republican, even national, aspirations. At any given point, a college could strum multiple chords to woo students, trustees, or financial resources. And at times, with minimal regard to educational theory, different institutions transformed themselves, from academy to college, from local to regional, from sectarian to functioning nondenominational institutions, all within Girard's original "college" conception of an agency converting youth to responsible citizenship, a voluntary venture in civic evangelism.

IV

In this erratic and fluctuating context, Yale College emerged as distinct, not simply for amassing the largest student body before the Civil War,[73] but also for sharpening the meaning and practice of the antebellum college itself. In the justly touted Yale Report of 1828 three college faculty members—the president, Rev. Jeremiah Day (1773–1867); its distinguished scientist, Benjamin Silliman (1779–1864); and its classicist, James L. Kingsley (1778–1852)—posed an argument that consciously refashioned a merger of the school's inherited evangelical values with the demands of the day. Like virtually all other antebellum colleges, the coiners of the Yale argument had to explain to their several constituencies how the moral mantle handed down to them from their Congregational founders would survive in a world that was incompletely Congregational. In addition, they needed to explain why anyone should bother to apply himself from two to four years of costly study, when the jobs and careers of America's economy could be had and exploited with little more than the basic instruction of the district school. The Yale Report advanced an operational model of inculcating moral character.

The Yale Report can be read as an effort to synthesize the contextual factors previously discussed—mixed student ages, irregular pupil attendance, varied economic backgrounds, faculty with different skills and resources, indifferent funding and wage scales, large preparatory populations, minimal systematic study over time—and as a plan for an integration of these features into a coherent curricular plan. The report addressed the dilemmas of their community's moral and secular culture with an argument and a practical model that won the allegiances of many colleges in vastly different circumstances. Their apologia for collegiate instruction began with a disarming admission that colleges must not offer a "blind opposition to salutary reform" but rather must be adaptable "to the spirit and wants of the age." Their commitment needed to avoid rigid defensiveness and to adhere "to some of its original features . . . from a higher principle." Every institution, it suggested expansively, should reexamine its original purpose and should entertain the possibility of breaking up its older organization. Most important, they implicitly asked, how much of an inherited brand of eighteenth-century instruction could antebellum Yale condone in the nineteenth?

The Yale Report also confronted charges that antebellum Yale housed elitist pretensions, incompatible with republican values. Its argument took the high road and insisted no college could gear itself to those whose ambitions concentrated on political leadership or specific vocational skills. "In this country, where offices are accessible to all who are qualified for them, superior intellectual attainments ought not to be confined to any description of persons." In actual fact, like most New England colleges, Yale graduates throughout the first half of the nineteenth century were not all wealthy. One-third to nearly one-half of its students graduated at age twenty-three or older.[74] Many of these "mature" students, originating from New England's poorer hill country villages, completed their college study only after delays and disruptions of their educations and earlier ministerial aspirations. Many left college to teach common schools or academies and required outside charitable contributions to finish their schooling, while others pursued a string of cul-de-sac jobs before returning to college and study among substantially younger males. The Yale Report thus made a civic virtue out of the widely shared age mix of college students rather than probing its implied pedagogical problems.[75]

Yale's defensive protestations against atavism and elitist preferences only heightened the problematic character of collegiate service and worth. If it were so completely adaptable to the spirit of the age, how could anyone discern whether or not the college was actually meeting its obligations for advancement and enlightenment? Who or what locale would determine the adjudicating "spirit of the age?" In response, Yale established two priorities for its collegiate mission: first, everyone must receive a "thorough education" through the cultivation of a discipline and "furniture of the mind." Education would be "inculcated" by "daily and vigorous exercise," and subjects would be taught that would best "fix attention, directing the train of thought, analyzing a subject proposed for investigation." Both these claims and their institutional applications resisted any sharp prediction of behavioral or vocational results; their conceptual authority, like that of evangelism itself, lay primarily within each individual's disposition.[76]

The diffusion of knowledge, so central to Jefferson's eighteenth-century educational values, had been consciously replaced with "inculcation," which assumed an internalization of both method and information, in its way, the production of a civic conversion. The Yale Report stressed the outcomes of order and stability in training the faculties with words like "arranging," "balancing," "guiding," "controlling," "directing," "fixing the attention," and "establishing the tone." Further analysis of the report revealed, perhaps unconsciously, a concern about the actual turmoil and riot that characterized so much of student life in the antebellum college, exacerbated by the mélange of youth and young adults.[77] Ultimately collegiate education would throw the individual, so the report argued, on the resources of his own mind, resulting ideally in the "sublimest efforts of genius."

The college continued its role as a quasi-moral institution without adopting any distinct sectarianism (whatever its Congregational inheritances) and, in the process, laid claim to education more basic than training in law, medicine, ministry, public school teaching, or business.[78] If "inculcation" represented a nondenominational modification of Yale's eighteenth-century support of revivalism, the Yale Report went on to claim a new nineteenth-century evangelical space. Collegiate knowledge, it argued, was unlike professional learning; it was transferable and ultimately realized only later in specific local communities. Professional knowledge and occupational training, which so many colleges were pressured to adopt, belonged to training in precise locations, a special vocational apprenticeship adapted exclusively to a geographical place; it was a finished education, whereas the conclusion of a college education resulted in a "commencement," a beginning of long-term work prospects based on principles. A college education concerned itself with foundations and discipline, was local without becoming parochial, and, most important, should precede professional instruction, lest learning result in rigidity, self-serving myopia, or "extravagance."

But of course such assertions were meaningless without some specification about how Yale would achieve its goals. The heart of collegiate discipline, as many educators had already insisted, was the classics. "Should the time come," classics' antebellum defenders intoned, "when Latin and Greek should be banished from our Universities, and the study of Cicero and Demosthenes, of Homer and Virgil, should be considered unnecessary for the formation of a scholar, we should regard mankind as fast sinking into absolute barbarism, and the gloom of mental darkness as likely to increase until it should become universal."[79] Educational backsliding followed a perilously similar course to moral backsliding. The kinds of control that colleges produced were ideally not dogmatically imposed. The actual impact of a collegiate community was thought to be most beneficial when natural, informal, and indirect, in a word, voluntary rather than externally coerced.

The Yale Report synthesized much of an inherited educational wisdom by reaffirming the classics not only as foundational but also as the concrete means for inculcating moral character without resort to any denominational or sectarian interpretation of piety. The deference to the classics was not an uncritical deference to tradition or conservative biases; it reflected rather a cultural anxiety about guaranteeing constructive changes that educators could not assess precisely or technically. The classics substituted for an older biblical lingua franca and became the educational and linguistic code of a new republican, educated elite before the Civil War. The emerging importance of the classics did not connote a relaxation of denominational fervor but rather a reformulation of it into a wider republican sphere.[80]

Of course, the promulgation of the Yale Report did not substantively interfere with rising importance of mathematics, science, literature, philosophy, or even consciously vocational training, which had already reduced the doctrinal orientation of Yale's eighteenth-century curriculum.[81] Colleges continued to fluctuate between harsh times and flush times throughout the period, while the Yale Report offered a curricular and organizational priority that would not have been possible a generation earlier and was indeed aggressively new in 1828. At Yale itself, the report did not result in a dogged entrenchment of the classics. The college gradually modified its classical requirements to make way for advanced mathematics, experimental science, and history. These curricular emphases seemed to reflect the particular abilities of the well-trained individuals whom President Jeremiah Day and his nineteenth-century successors hired rather than any curricular or "market" demands.[82]

The intellectual influence of the report spread through the work of Yale's graduates, whose missionary pattern continued in an evangelical vein, whether carried by ministerial alumni or not. At the time of the report's publication, Yale had the largest enrollment in the country (ca. 250), when large colleges averaged 150. Yale also had the largest living and most geographically dispersed alumni, giving it a legitimate claim to a national constituency. In addition, many of its faculty produced widely used textbooks, codifying subjects and methodologies, and associated Yale with their disseminated reputations.

In 1840 Yale and Princeton graduates filled many of the presidencies of American colleges.[83] The so-called Yale Band founded colleges across the Midwest, like Beloit College in Wisconsin, Illinois College in Illinois, DePauw in Indiana, Berea College in Kentucky, Miami in Ohio, and Hobart in New York. Some of these satellite schools explicitly cited the Yale Report in their college brochures.[84] The ingenuity of the report's argument about a basic, principled discipline and (classical) furniture of the mind was widely disseminated and had much to do with the reinterpretation of the college's place in American society; it was hardly the conservative impediment to reform that has often been claimed.[85]

The strength of the Yale Report's argument drew upon its respect for its own traditional values, while advancing a novel conception of the college. Given the range of options, Yale's insistence that the college must be viewed as a family with the president and teachers as substitute parents took risks by using an established Congregational metaphor. In most Calvinistic denominations, the congregation, the ultimate device for probing spiritual matters, was always more than the sum of its parts; it was, rather, a special moral entity, and Calvinist ministers used familial metaphors to explain the organic relationship of members to church. However, given the character of the antebellum college, the usurpation of the familial mantle, not only as metaphor but as practice, had to be an exercise in risk taking. Such familial authority must have come more easily to colleges like Girard with students not yet in their teens. For Yale, admitting students ages fourteen through twenty-three, familial deference had to be not only jarring but inappropriate to Yale's espoused goals of training self-possessed and morally informed citizens. The report thus acknowledged the need to reduce the number of students younger than sixteen and older than twenty-one from the college family, an effort that would be largely complete shortly after the Civil War.

The very diversity, diffuseness, and fragmentation of the antebellum collegiate experience have distracted scholars from the cohering sense that an inculcated voluntarism provided to the shapers and practitioners of the nineteenth-century collegiate tradition.[86] The thread that links most antebellum collegiate institutions in spite of their variation was the supra-denominational energy, which sought to influence, if not control, a new republican spirit in America. It was impossible to insist on dogmatic, denominational correctness in such a competition, especially among and between many Protestant sects. The coerced embrace of a modified doctrinal evangelism, which ministers themselves depicted as the "voluntary principle," served to extend many conceptual and traditional features of an older missionary fervor. After the

American Revolution, many denominations engineered a crucial sharing of power between churches and schools in an effort to "train up the character" of the next generation.

The competition for students and resources led many colleges to reach beyond their original geographical locales when their rhetoric and energies became centrifugal. The powerful image of the autonomous, local college sought a new educational leadership that was, like Stephen Girard's, more stewardly than ministerial. His civic example seemed to make his money secondary; it illuminated the central instructional standard of the nineteenth century: the power of persuasion, rhetoric, and example that accepted ubiquitous differences of opinion and behavior but idealized a society of self-disciplined citizens, harmonized by their distinctly (Whiggish) republican commitments. This new civic religion became coincident with a collegiate voluntarism that simultaneously (and often contradictorily) promised both individualized morality and its institutionalized dissemination. Before the model of tax-based public schooling, the antebellum college carried the burden of a higher learning for a new republic. Its antebellum years can be best understood as a spirited episode in promoting education as a special republican power before Americans had the institutional apparatus for achieving it.

The antebellum culture that succeeded its eighteenth-century denominational model crafted a blend of inherited evangelical traditions onto a new republican ideal. The transition also accommodated the economic and demographic turmoil of the early nineteenth century, which constantly compromised any formal organizational model of higher instruction. The very terminology of the period—college and university especially—remained imprecise. Local and regional variations abounded and pressured higher education leaders to keep very fluid conceptions of their work. Their "voluntary" assumptions did not necessarily imply a legitimation of subjective choice or individual whim, so much as they connoted a socialized behavior of "self-discipline" and "moral character" that required minimal external monitoring. The cultural assumptions of the antebellum period thus pioneered a new "republican" standard beyond any inherited denominational pedagogy. It did nevertheless build upon that inheritance to produce a distinctive nineteenth-century argument about higher learning.

CHAPTER FOUR

Science and System in Nineteenth-Century Collegiate Culture

Historians have understandably regarded the antebellum college as an anomaly. Upon the collegiate experience they have imposed distinct trajectories from denominationalism to secularism, from classical to scientific curricula, from local booster entities to nascent universities. However, in reality, both denominational inheritances and new nondenominational appeals continued to influence collegiate operations throughout the middle decades of nineteenth century. So long as they remained in their earlier religiously denominational orientations, colleges have been seen as retrospectively narrow and dogmatic, even intellectually retrograde and inhospitable to the academically curious.[1] The scholarship of the 1970s and 1980s redressed some of these antebellum characterizations by examining the historical nature of the student body (often surprisingly neither elite nor affluent) and the gradual expansion of curricular choice.[2] This new scholarship revealed many new elements in the midst of older denominational practices.

The pedagogical proposals engineered by protagonists, like Francis Wayland (1796–1865), who served Brown University as president from 1827 to 1855, showed that the significance of the antebellum college lay also in its experimentation with a formal organization to match its educational rhetoric. Wayland has retrospectively received warm praise for his work in collegiate "reform," a man ahead of his time. He anticipated the reduction of the classics and the rise of the sciences in his school and in his speeches.[3] But his supporters made little of his service as a Baptist minister, as a proselytizer of denominationalism,[4] or as an advocate of his state's public school system or indeed of other social reforms in the temperance, prison, and peace movements. His commentators have reduced this array of social enterprises to a focus upon his "failure" to revitalize his college. His writings on the advanced social science of "political economy"[5] plus his college experiments revealed the mixture of both traditions, old and new, leading to a novel sense of organization, his planned curriculum of study to match the social aspirations of antebellum collegiate institutions. Such a change could not be the achievement of a single leader but rather was the result of a broader discovery of an institutional matrix that would blend the best of older classical and newer scientific learning.[6] Wayland's experience and career illuminated these new, historical features of America's collegiate culture in the years before the Civil War.

The range and sometimes contradictory character of Wayland's views have promoted judgments that he was both religiously conservative and educationally liberal. But his own trajectory into the presidency of Brown University at age thirty-one clarified his peculiar priorities as an antebellum educator, and his career also illuminated the place of college in the lives of aspiring and ambitious young men of the period. Wayland attended Union College (founded 1795, purportedly the first nondenominational college in America) under the long-term presidency of Rev. Eliphalet Nott (1804–66), a Presbyterian divine and himself a patented inventor. There the introduction of courses in science (as well as military and physical training, engineering, agriculture, modern languages, and history) complemented the traditional offering in the classics and religion.[7] Much the same could be said of experimental practices of many aspiring, denominational colleges of the period. For example, Henry Barnard, recently graduated from Yale in 1830, was shocked to find a more advanced scientific laboratory at Roman Catholic Georgetown during a visit to the nation's capital.[8]

Industrializing Schenectady (New York) with its early cotton mills backed Union College's systematic science instruction comprehensively and was receptive to innovative subjects. Wayland graduated from Union in 1813 and went first to Troy, New York, then to New York City itself seeking lectures and instruction in medicine. In 1816 he shifted career ambitions and went to Andover Theological Seminary and the tutelage of Moses Stuart (1780–1852), one of the country's eminent biblical scholars. Lack of finances cut short his seminary training, and he returned to Union as an instructor (and local Baptist pastor), then professor of mathematics and natural philosophy before assuming the presidency of the sorely stressed Brown University in 1827. At both Union and Brown, Wayland experienced the ease with which ambitious students could move between religion and science. All his life he treated the two as compatible disciplines.[9] He also experienced the distinctive career disruptions of the period and, well before his presidential office, determined to address the importance of inexpensive but high quality instruction.[10] A college, he later argued in his widely read *Thoughts on the Present Collegiate System in the United States* (1842), must "furnish means for the most perfect development of the intellectual treasures of the country. . . . This talent is very equally distributed among the various orders of society, least of all is it limited to the rich."[11] If multiple options enhanced individual careers, worldly circumstance restricted the resources to pursue them. How far beyond obvious educational priorities should the college go? Should colleges be responsible for funding tuition of needy but deserving students?

Wayland's impressive career and extensive writings cumulatively pressed for a resolution of the inherited antebellum tension between denominational persuasion and nondenominational Republican service. In his pulpit sermons and public addresses, he made clear that neither religion nor politics could have the dominant presence in America's "collegiate system." Nondenominational claims seemed to soften the indoctrinating role of the numerous evangelical colleges and represented decidedly a shift of America's institutional heritage. To give graphic force to his argument, Wayland turned again and again to the limited roles for collegiate personnel. One of the keys to his thinking lay with the word "system" itself, even if implicitly he acknowledged that system was belied by the variety of collegiate practices and quality. "A system," Wayland would argue, "in order to work well, must be pervaded in every member by a vital energy, each part performing in its own appropriate functions in harmony with the rest, but yet not interfered with by them."[12] A second key lay in the scope of the system, one that encompassed not just a college's own immediate community but rather the "intellectual treasures of the country." Like most of his fellow Whig sympathizers,[13] Wayland's eye was always on comprehensive organization without ever overtly sacrificing the interests of Providence (Rhode Island), his school's host city. In 1830 he served as the first president of the American Institute of Instruction, which sought to be, and irregularly was throughout the century, the national forum for exploring and debating educational issues.[14]

The heart of his own collegiate thinking lay less with overblown statements of moral or educational purpose or fending off college critics but rather with an organizational system. Wayland structured his *Thoughts* according to the structural components of the university: the trustees, the visitors, the faculty, the students. His operative word throughout was "system," by which he connoted more than just orderly relationships but also the simplification of complex processes, necessary to a producing and manufacturing culture.[15] It is not too much to say that his self-conscious promotion of organization provided the civil counterpart to deep shifts in America's political tradition. The French commentator Alexis de Tocqueville has argued in this very period, that the ubiquitous voluntary associations of American life explained much about the successful consequences of the American Revolution. These pervasive, voluntary structures in everyday life—from camp meetings to fraternal societies—at once cultivated individual judgment and also a proclivity for centralized government to ensure and protect individual rights. This contradictory tension proved to be one of the French political theorist's most powerful insights. The resulting associational matrices—informal, loosely configured, and democratically accessible—created a system, functional in spite of contradictions, which in Europe only fostered faction and tyranny.[16] Wayland's reworking of this voluntary dynamic into a more formal organization used his institutional arrangements to implement his reforms. In the process, he blended the potential dichotomies of science and religion into a coherent curriculum.

At the end of the 1830s, Wayland had served as Brown's president for over a decade and clearly grounded his "system" upon his operational grasp of his institution. He also had spent a portion of 1840 in Europe, especially England, and returned more conscious of the connection between the British educational system and their educated graduates. He openly discussed his sensitivity to social and collegiate interrelationships, the way that graduates confirmed the value of their education with respected careers in the professions and civil service. He was determined to retool Brown to produce something more than a practiced dilettante, able to evince knowledge of multiple disciplines but really master of none. Implicitly he needed a reconfiguring of the college's place in both Providence and in American careers. Clearly he had inherited the older problems of mere institutional survival, competition, and funding, but now he tried to produce an educational experience that incontestably advanced individual and social life chances and garnered the fiscal support of industrial beneficiaries.

This expansive perspective he set in the context of multiple "reforms"—classical and scientific curricula, stronger preparatory work in high schools and academies, manual labor colleges, tuition reductions, upgrading salaries for college faculty, and so on—all of which together challenged existing public and trustee perceptions. Still, Wayland drew the inference that the public wanted quality education and would be willing to pay for it, as they would pay for the furniture, carpets, and piano in an attractive parlor, as they would pay for the stock and acres of a farmland. Wayland sought a wider swath for the collegiate net, the middle-class consumer of town and city, the productive farmer and mechanic classes. He pushed hard for his priorities, stressing the rationality of practical organization, while eschewing the evils of overt indoctrination. Without attacking the evangelical tradition of which he was a part, Wayland attempted to move the college into a more socially central role in Providence's diverse economy.

Wayland opened his *Thoughts on the Present Collegiate System in the United States* with a discussion of the board of trustees, who held the primary power of the institution and, as he noted almost as an afterthought, awarded degrees. They generally combined powers separated in England, the power of visitation and the power of appointment of faculty, of future plans and present commitments. They were the final arbiter to whom even the executive officer of the college deferred. Could one then expect their tenure to be prescient as well as fair-minded? Could one expect them to administer the corporation according to the founding purpose as well as forecast adaptations to forces no one ever anticipated? Wayland thought not and began to redesign the trustees' role, in effect, getting them out of the educational process and the college's day-to-day operation. Henceforth, while retaining their legal oversight duties, he sought the end of any trustee examination of students for degrees, any quotas for certain professions among the faculty; rather, he relegated trustees to non-self-perpetuating, nonpolitical roles; reduced their numbers; limited their periods of service; and directed them to goals beyond collegiate pedagogy, namely, the "intellectual cultivation of the community."[17] Wayland sought to invest a trustee's role with a new public accountability, to work for the college in their own business milieu. His differentiation of educational and trustee roles created a formal rather than an implicit linkage to the extramural society of Providence and beyond.

Through much of the first third of the nineteenth century, the Brown trustees' leadership had concentrated on achieving a basic stability in the college's financing. The central figure here was Nicholas Brown (1769–1841), a Brown University graduate from the namesake family and a longtime merchant in the China and India trade. Often singlehandedly he and his merchant partners ensured the endurance and occasionally the expansion of the institution. He had been the prime benefactor of the main classroom building and chapel in 1835, the 1840 library—land, building, and books—and sundry donations across the years plus a final legacy in his will.[18] The rest of the trustees were chosen from Providence's merchant, banking, and professional classes and included several Brown graduates and Brown family relatives.

Oddly, Wayland felt, "after men have bestowed money, they seem utterly indifferent as to the manner in which it is to be employed."[19] For the first four decades of the nineteenth century, the trustees had the authority but rarely presided over the quality and design of a traditional curriculum of classics and math (including algebra, geometry, navigation, and astronomy) for the early years, and for the later years more classics, modern languages, science (including mechanics, physiology, pneumatics, hydrostatics, optics, and chemistry), and philosophy. Every student took every subject for tuition of thirty-six dollars per year.[20] At no point did the trustees make formal suggestions for change or acquit their supervisory roles of visitation. "In no other country," Wayland concluded, "is the whole plan for the instruction of the young so entirely dissevered from connexion [*sic*] with the business of subsequent life."[21] Wayland's proposed changes did little more than reflect actual trustee practice, but he used the changes to rationalize a new place and resource for the college in the larger community.

Trustees, above all, Wayland explained, should recognize that they serve "in the place of the public" and, if they could not serve responsibly, then the office should be abolished.[22] In part, no trustee could acquit his responsibility if the public itself was indifferent. However, with public support the trustee role became clear: they should be learned, above reproach, especially distant from party and faction, and appointed for tenure rather than for life (which invites somnolence, i.e., "ineffective"); they should be few in number (to avoid intrigue), no more than twelve, elected "out of themselves" (not self-perpetuating); and they should at least report to some supervisory public. If all these conditions applied, the trustees should use their visitorial power especially "to construct a system, so to arrange its various stimulants and so to bring them to bear upon every department, that the machine would go of itself without perpetual tinkering."[23]

Wayland's thoughts about faculty roles in the American collegiate system argued for an intellectual process that operated competitively but impartially and resulted in appointments of merit. The attendant honor of academic appointment would, in turn, provide the proper stimulus for attracting individuals of superior talent. Such a system would avoid European alternatives of appointment by family or religious status, rather than by extensive state-operated examination. It would also avoid the alternative of American Southern colleges of appointment by mere "testimonial," that is, recommendation from some influential authority. In addition, Wayland hoped to provide a small guaranteed salary but to leave a professor's actual remuneration to the number of attending students. His assumption was that recompense would be contingent upon meritorious exertion, as if, after appointment, academics functioned without guile or political ambition. Wayland worked to create a new faculty organization, beginning immediately upon his appointment as president, by eliminating nonresident faculty. Residential faculty, he thought, ensured his organization with ongoing supervision of students' moral as well as intellectual education and provided a necessary "parental" role to the collegiate "family."[24]

Wayland's proposed reforms at Brown made him cognizant of the need for appointing first-rate faculty. But he faced great hurdles. Unlike in England, his university had no means of creating a pool of fellows or a young ministerial class from which new faculty might be drawn. Instead, existing faculty more often than not arose from recent graduates or even present tutors with only a few years' experience, and a perfunctory approval by the trustees. Salaries below those of other professionals could not expect to draw distinguished scholars with large reputations. Wayland's Brown had the benefit of the president, three to four professors, two tutors, a librarian, and the school registrar/steward. This staff of nine to ten in the 1830s and 1840s served a university student population that fluctuated between 150 and 225. When enrolment fell, so did the number of tutors and faculty salaries.[25]

Wayland's systemic reforms of control and curriculum rested on their integration with his existing social environment. He was a minister himself and did not wish to sacrifice classical and theological instruction at Brown that laid the foundation for the profession of ministry. He may well have realized that New England had become magisterially saturated early in the century and that for his region the ministry was not a growth profession.[26] He was known to have developed a refrain to "go west," an admonition that proved fortuitous in more than one case.[27] In part, it also may have been his early medical training and affinity with science that made him very receptive—even more than his own trustees—to an expansion of scientific study in a manufacturing city.[28] Equally important was his effort to keep Brown attractive to students outside Rhode Island, students who had always composed 50 to 75 percent of the school's population.[29] Increasingly into the 1840s, when overall student enrollments precipitously declined (and made the trustees more open to Wayland's recommended "reforms"), Brown's percentage of students from outside New England (which had only reached 6–8 percent of its student body until the 1830s) climbed to 28 percent in 1855, the year of Wayland's resignation.[30] Many of these were from the mercantile and manufacturing areas of the Middle States, with a sprinkling of cotton-growing Southerners, probably connected to Providence's textile industries. Brown's declining enrollments in traditional areas plus the technical interests of his mercantile city may have prodded his natural inclination to create a more substantive education in science and applied subjects.

These contingencies were factors in Wayland's effort at reorganization. His *Thoughts on the Present Collegiate System in the United States* not only described a role for trusteeship, but he also specifically argued an alternative curriculum from the traditional, mandated emphasis upon designated classical and scientific textbooks. Merely adding subjects into the existing curriculum only invited superficiality. Why not, he asked, permit students to elect their courses and exhaust a subject, which would give them emphatic mastery and connect them to future employment? Why not let the market determine faculty remuneration? If students could be reasonably certain of honorable and lucrative work because of their training, colleges need develop no artificial stimuli or supervisory regimens to field popular and worthy courses. His plan, however, did not intend to abandon undergraduate education, but rather Wayland sought to make the honorific MA, usually an "unearned" degree taken a year after a BA with the payment of a fee, an actual reflection of advanced work. He had developed an impressive reputation himself as a moral philosopher and political economist and was the author of widely read books on these topics. Through the 1840s, as student enrollments declined at Brown, he argued the need to experiment with a more flexible collegiate organization.

Wayland's competitive spirit and his awareness of the dozen or so other New England colleges probably clouded the realization that New England's entire collegiate population was in decline in these years. Brown's enrollment problems were not directly a function of its economic interaction with Rhode Island's market forces but were a result of a broader based phenomenon. The putative "collegiate system" did not operate systematically, was highly varied from place to place, and could not control the many other schools, like normal schools, female seminaries, academies, and institutes of varied grades, which provided advanced instruction that once was the exclusive purview of colleges. The available youth pool, roughly 2 percent of the college-age population in the antebellum period, was already attending some form of advanced instruction.[31] In addition, the eastern collegiate youth pool in the late 1840s and 1850s was increasingly composed of foreign-born in need of basic instruction. Curricular experiments and even new buildings and facilities would not actually solve the problem of declining enrollments and economic crisis for colleges like Brown. America's market forces were more complicated than Wayland's assumptions about collegiate interaction with mercantile priorities, about matching scientific study with manufacturing expansion.[32]

In 1850, frustrated with his slow progress toward reform, Wayland submitted his resignation as president of Brown and almost immediately a public hue and cry demanded that he remain. In response to a trustees' overture, Wayland wrote out a formal address describing his "new system." Instead of diluting the proscribed college curriculum, students should be permitted to focus their concentrations. They should not be mandated to subscribe to the full four years of study but rather spend the time pursuing subjects that engaged them profoundly. Thus the university would become an arena for multiple subjects, a great resource of knowledge, rather than a regimen for subjects whose power is lost in routinized pedagogy. He argued for a "partial" course for those not yet ready for college-level study, conceding that he sought students who probably never thought of college. In addition, he argued the need for faculty salaries to depend in part on the success of their instruction. Student fees plus a fixed (and reduced) amount would put new zest into a tired recycling of old lectures. Wayland sought a curricular reorganization that would serve the new technical needs of Providence and the nation.[33] In all his proposals, Wayland never considered fiscal sources other than tuition and trustee donation.

Brown's new system of 1850 was in effect an "elective" system that Wayland meant to attract larger numbers of students and to tailor offerings to desirable careers. He was no reflexive critic of the classics, conceding their power when well taught. But his concern was intellectual mastery, which he felt had atrophied, especially by comparison with his European and British observations. Initially the university's student body rose to a high of 283 in 1854 but almost immediately began a precipitous fall to 203 by 1856–57. Wayland's successor tried to explain diplomatically that the elective system had resulted in attracting not only inferior students but also rejected applicants from its fellow New England colleges. Brown's effort to treat students as adults, capable of shaping their own life chances, had made the institution little more than a degree mill, indifferent to the monitoring and examination process of their competitors. As receptive as the trustees had been to Wayland's experimental new system, they turned back quickly to a traditional, classically weighted curriculum and to older images of traditional pedagogies of memorization and recitation.[34] Historically Wayland's reforms were more than mere trial-and-error experiments but rather opened an important discussion that implicitly elevated practical science and broke the antebellum college from its preoccupation with classics.[35] Even though many colleges would adhere to the dicta of the Yale Report (which itself included an appreciation of the sciences), the classics no longer were seen as a clear guarantee of a basic discipline and "furniture of the mind." Their staying power, however, documents the depths of conviction to provide an established, educational order in the midst of unprecedented economic change.

Both the traditional and the nontraditional arrangements of American colleges in these years attest to the contingency of the antebellum college's structure and purpose.[36] That contingency challenged the widely held assumptions of faculty psychology that informed both nineteenth-century pedagogy and institutional organization. These assumptions about the mind posited a natural order of distinct faculties for separate applications: memory, emotion, reasoning, and so on. The basic faculty of sensation and empirical recognition could be trained by drill and repetition. Gradually the more disciplined mind eased into the interpretive faculties that were reserved for more mature students. There the emotions and faculties of will ideally would submit to powers of reason. The process of education thus followed from pyramidal laws of natural and intellectual development: objective knowledge or sense perception at the first stages of learning; at the next, intermediate knowledge or generalization from specific facts; and finally abstract knowledge and spiritual apprehension for mature college students, which Wayland candidly noted, were often absent from American colleges.[37] In 1854 Wayland asserted that "graded schools" from common schools to colleges, incorporating these basic laws of knowledge and organization, represented the greatest educational advance in the last quarter century.

Wayland's blueprint argument, *Thoughts on the Present Collegiate System in the United States*, described his priorities and his hopes rather than any realistic model he had created in his years at Brown. His ideas did reveal importantly that college leaders of the 1840s and 1850s, unlike their predecessors, had begun to think along curricular trajectories, had begun to weigh the balance of one subject upon another, and had, in fact, *to think organizationally*. Unlike the schools of the early nineteenth century, colleges like Brown had begun to consider their place in the larger society. They now had a record of graduates going into the world, representing the actual product of their overstated collegiate assertions, namely, that a college graduate was thereby prepared for a life of upright behavior. In Wayland's generation, colleges were also now clear about the limits of funding from tuition as well as local, even city, resources and from denominational support.[38] For colleges like Brown, the 1840s and 1850s were a period of considering an organizational reach that delivered upon rather than just boasted about civic ideals of national scope and republican virtue.[39]

Wayland's own commitment to science illuminated a broader change, not only in the culture of many colleges, but also in the national culture itself. What passed as science for much of the eighteenth and early nineteenth century represented a "mental discipline" arguing the distinctive features of flora and fauna and especially their placement within a larger Linnaean matrix. Science was first descriptive, then philosophical. By midcentury scientific faculty at times sought practical applications of their scientific knowledge as well as ingenious and entertaining devices for disseminating science. Notable academics like Harvard's Louis Agassiz (1807–73) stumped the lecture circuit to demonstrate known scientific principles. The fine line between genuine science and entertainment was often breached as in P. T. Barnum's (1810–91) New York City museum. But the baseline commitment to a serviceable science as a resource to one's community began in the antebellum period to give way to a more professional science, beyond the public's ken. In the popular agricultural societies, where issues of fertilization and soil improvement became pressing, scientists worked in increasingly arcane areas that were less obviously beneficial to current communal needs. Most colleges developed some brand of laboratory work to foster such advances and to train students with a demonstrable mastery rather than for mere showmanship. It was this transition that set the context for Wayland's "reforms" and the next generation's idea of "new knowledge" that would refashion the meaning of science.[40] Wayland's initial hires of professionally trained scientists, William A. Norton (1810–83) as professor of civil engineering and John A. Porter (1822–66) as professor of chemistry in 1852, quickly left Brown to become the core faculty of Yale's new Sheffield Scientific School. If this collegiate competition between Brown and Yale impaired Brown, it also guaranteed the influence of Wayland's scientific values into the second half of the century.[41]

At Dartmouth, Brown, and elsewhere, the inability of the colleges to control their own world, neighborhood, or "family" can be seen in the rise of college literary societies. These voluntary organizations had begun earlier as the result of student initiatives. Out of students' own private funds came money for books and periodicals unavailable in the college or university library. Their selections, centered on literature, scientific and political tracts, and overseas journals, often reached a size equal to that of the college library itself.[42] In addition, some societies fielded their own publications, staged mock debates over current issues (particularly of foreign policy concerning Hispanic America and Britain in the 1840s and early 1850s after which "slavery" became a central preoccupation), fraternized in ways that made students sad to leave the school at graduation. For many graduates who went on to careers in the law, the ministry, and indeed into teaching, the literary societies rather than their actual college subjects became their fondest memories of college days.[43]

Until the 1840s and 1850s, these college literary societies operated with virtual autonomy and were accepted as attractive resources of college life. College faculty paid little heed to the forensic discipline or even subject matter the societies' students cultivated. They hardly noticed how the goals of liberal education—independent thought, extempore speech, authoritative references to literature, philosophy, and history, not to mention public eloquence in an age of oratory—were served by these organizations. At times they would collectively protest college policies that interfered with their activities. The self-imposed collective discipline of the literary societies emanated from their student-designed constitutions, which proscribed behaviors and fined aberrants. Their committee structure actually immersed their members into the experience of a constitutional order, far more than the theoretical injunctions of classes in political economy or even the culminating course in moral philosophy of their senior classes.[44] These societies were more serious and intellectually concerned than the fraternities that would succeed them late in the century.

The ferment, experimentation, and at times the polarized voices defending either religion or science have obscured the driving force of the antebellum college, its straining to create an organizational fit in a larger system that served republican values. Of course, sheer service was a prerequisite for survival at the local level;[45] and some public appreciation of moral character as a collegiate goal was essential for both denominational and nominally nondenominational schools; but the sheer ubiquity of experimentation with intramural and extramural organization attested to a more compelling priority, a practical education that did not sacrifice educational quality.[46] Most colleges had the first two dimensions—communal adaptation and moral inculcation. But the third, where science and "system" became a frequent source of debate, occurred on major commercial thoroughfares rather than in backcountry schools. For example, even before becoming the eastern gate to the Erie Canal, Union College in Schenectady operated as the strategic entrepot connecting New York City with the state's western interior. Similar strategic locations fostered other "scientific" institutions, like West Point on the Hudson River above New York City (stressing engineering over military strategy in these years) or Brown University in Providence along the eastern coastal traffic.[47]

Organizational preoccupation registered itself least successfully outside the urban orbit, in the country towns where colleges were often indistinguishable from academies and seminaries. By contrast, this new ferment about applied science appeared quickly in specialized schools like normal schools for training professional teachers, mechanics' institutes, or distinctive urban establishments like Philadelphia's Franklin Institute, New York University in the 1850s, and Washington's Smithsonian Institution.[48] Analogous developments had occurred elsewhere in Europe in the previous century, where many large commercial cities, like London or Saint Petersburg, flourished without a major college or university. However, literary, scientific, and professional societies served well the needs of the city's elite for high quality information about instruction in new discoveries.[49] Often the most innovative training occurred outside the traditional classical college in separate or loosely affiliated schools like Harvard's Lawrence Scientific School (founded 1846), Yale's Sheffield Scientific School (founded 1847), or Dartmouth's Chandler Scientific School (1852), all disparaged by many overly complacent fellow collegians.[50] While shallow-rooted antipathies arose over these experiments, pitting science against the classics, for example, collectively these scientific establishments became resources that somehow had to be tethered to an American collegiate system for which no one had a precedent.[51] The debates over classics and science represented important dimensions of the reshaping of the college as a generic organization, initially expressed in curricular terms.[52] In this debate, the humanities received important support from a select group of individuals who studied them in Germany before the Civil War.[53]

The other antebellum calls for collegiate reform generally had less systematic proposals than Wayland's 1850 plan for reorganization. They often were narrow, single-issue proposals that added ingredients to the academic pot rather than ranked or reconfigured the multiple, disparate elements. The Reverend Noah Porter (1811–92), Yale graduate (class of 1831), longtime faculty member, philosopher, and ultimately president of Yale College (1871–85), has been used by later historians as an exponent of nineteenth-century resistance to modernism, offering a traditional, moral vision of regenerating a largely immature student body.[54] But his actual public pronouncements and achievements represent continuing probes of pressing issues in the light of older college traditions. His work at Yale demonstrates the postwar consequences of Wayland's antebellum reforms.

Porter's doughty Congregational model for the college—a self-contained moral entity more than the sum of its parts—was but a thinly veiled analogy to an orthodox Protestant community, and it had served him well for much of his life. What portions need be changed, he seemed to ask (putting the burden more on demands for change than on his model), to keep the mechanism attuned? As Yale's leader, he would oversee the construction of ten new buildings and the first stage of creating an architecturally self-contained quadrangle, a structural expression of the college's autonomous presence in the heart of the larger New Haven community. He resisted, then relented modestly to, elective studies, fostered both theological libraries and scientific laboratories, especially the Peabody Museum, expanded both the student body (755 in 1871 to 1,076 in 1886) and the faculty while substantially increasing the value of the college plant. He reorganized the board of trustees to include six representatives elected by the graduates, the first voices of the alumni in official policy councils. He continued his academic teaching throughout his presidency and, after his resignation from that post, continued to teach until his death in 1892.[55]

Porter and many of his ilk represented the resilience of the older collegiate tradition as well as their receptivity to alternative arguments about science and organization. His contribution was the articulation of practical values and systemic changes that had manifestly succeeded and required no radical revision, only sensitive adaptation. In his mind and those of his college community, he had thereby maintained the continuous stewardship of his predecessor, Rev. Theodore Woolsey (1801–89), longtime faculty member and president from 1846 to 1871. Porter dedicated his 1870 book on American colleges to him. Collegiate stability and order were no mean values in the light of social and moral upheavals of American society. The college would remain the oasis and resource for upright citizens and a new republican leadership. But it was not enough to reaffirm successful models of moral inculcation, particularly when they constantly needed attuning, when they manifestly did not encompass and integrate emergent brands of "useful knowledge,"[56] that is, the mastery of technical learning associated with shop, trade, and profession.

This problem of integrating moral with scientific and technical subjects pervaded antebellum colleges at midcentury, and the lack of a distinct pattern of response documented the varied mix of local and translocal forces within their college bounds. However, one can still get a general perspective on these continuing collegiate changes by examining a classic pastoral college, like Dartmouth, significantly different than city-rooted Brown or Yale. In the

1850s Dartmouth's denominational orientation still reflected its Congregational origins, its holistic sense of collegiate community, the rural orientation of its graduates' careers. In short, its history reflected the cultural impact of the community-oriented colleges with its mix of republican rhetoric and evangelizing pedagogy. In spite of the stark differences of their locale, Dartmouth, on the upper Connecticut River, nearly two hundred miles from the coast, shared with Brown and Yale a mix of science and classics in its formal offerings. The New Hampshire school established the Chandler Scientific School in 1852, one of the few such schools in the country. It also could boast an early medical college, when most medical practitioners still acquired their skills, apart from formal lectures on anatomy, via an apprenticeship to a practicing physician. The college also harbored extracurricular literary societies, the Social Friends and the United Fraternity, each with their very different cultures.[57] Its president for many years, a contemporary of Francis Wayland, was Rev. Nathan Lord (1792–1870), who had served as local pastor and college trustee before assuming the presidency in 1828. But for his antiabolitionist views, he would likely have served past 1863, but, excepting his personal politics, his successors continued his collegiate practices.

One of these successors, a contemporary of Yale's Noah Porter, was the Reverend Samuel C. Bartlett (1817–98). Bartlett had multiple pastoral and professional experiences beyond those of Lord. He had taught in a college (1846–52) in Cleveland and at a theological seminary (1858–77) in Chicago. He retained an interest and lifelong commitment to domestic and foreign missionary organizations, ultimately authoring an 1872 book of missionary lives and organizations. Like Lord, Bartlett was raised in rural New England, had advanced theological training at Andover Theological Seminary, the oldest in the country, and had mixed his college appointments with local pastorates. Like most of his fellow faculty members, Bartlett was a graduate of Dartmouth (class of 1836) and a native of New Hampshire. He viewed the college paternalistically, as a moral teaching machine for individual consciences. Like Noah Porter at Yale, Bartlett's defensive public image as an antebellum college president would assure that the college's evangelical tradition received a privileged hearing in any contest with the pressures of modern life.[58]

Bartlett did not have long to wait, facing postwar challenges. In 1881, four years after becoming Dartmouth's president, he confronted the major threat to his academic career, a challenge not only to his authority but also implicitly to his entire view of collegiate culture. The precipitating event was the appointment to the Greek professorship. His candidate, privately vetted with select confidants and trustees, had been a college teacher of Greek but was better known for his pastoral ministries. His faculty, many of whom were recently hired and considerably younger than Bartlett, expressed dismay at the lack of faculty consultation and felt impugned by a candidate with no scholarly publications or reputation. From Bartlett's view, the "rebellion" ignored the ministerial privilege of the president, the moral mission of the college, and the allegiance to its evangelical purposes expected of faculty.

The faculty had dramatically introduced a different agenda of faculty autonomy and peer review, professional research over teaching values and implicitly dual allegiances to both the college classroom and the newly emerging national professional organizations. Only a minority of the rebels were New Hampshire born, and most had demonstrable scientific commitments rather than ministerial training or aspiration in their pasts.[59] The rebels' generational differences also matched the shifting profile of the Dartmouth student body. At midcentury Dartmouth's student body was one of the largest in the United States, producing graduating classes averaging fifty to sixty students annually. In 1851 the backgrounds and aspirations of the graduating class reflected their families restricted farming origins and New England birthplace. Only 20 percent of graduates had fathers with professional occupations, and an additional 8 percent fathers with business occupations. Most of the students came from families with limited means, and many had taught during winter vacation (fourteen weeks for about ten dollars per month) to pay their college tuition, a common practice among all New England colleges. Such teaching permitted students to "board round" in the communities they served, affording detailed knowledge of their students' lives. Seventeen percent of the 1851 graduates would make teaching their lifelong career, and the majority of their fellows would enter the more established professions of law (52 percent) and ministry and medicine (9 percent each). Eleven percent entered business.[60] Forty-five percent went west for their careers, possibly due to gold rush euphoria, while 39 percent remained in New England, usually away from cities like Boston or New York.

One generation later the profile of Dartmouth graduates had changed considerably. Its earlier rural orientation had substantially declined. Now a new and significant minority of students (26 percent) came from residences outside New England entirely; only 16 percent came from farming families, while students from professional (11 percent) and business (25 percent) families represented a marked sociological shift. Only a minority of parents (12 percent) represented families of definably limited means (mechanics and laborers). Students clearly were coming from families of a different social class, were more affluent, were less rooted in rural culture of New Hampshire or New England, and expected to have careers in not only the established professions (26 percent) but also the rising occupations of education (25 percent) and business (20 percent). In addition, they expected their careers to be associated with major cities like Boston and New York rather than the rural country towns.[61]

This shifting sociological pattern was due in part to college policies. Many schools had eliminated the long winter vacation, which hitherto had enabled some students to earn their tuition by teaching. But more importantly, the economic power of the American cities, especially as a source of both students and financing, provided shifts beyond the college's control. These changes tended to weaken the antebellum college's image as an evangelical entity separating town and gown. The postbellum college not only harbored a more pluralistic student body; it cultivated a self-conscious sense of difference between college students and Hanover residents, whose lives had once been routinely intertwined via boarding students, public entertainments, and services. By the 1880s the students viewed Hanover townsmen as "townies," uncouth bumpkins rather than as mutually advantageous resources.

More than the dilution of the antebellum goals of collegiate inculcation was with the postbellum demography of students. Students now felt sufficiently self-possessed not only to offer criticism of faculty and the president but also to call for an active alumni voice on the board of trustees. The appointment of a Greek professor with minimal scholarly credentials galvanized the alliance of students with rebellious younger faculty. Unthinkable in the antebellum period, the 1881 rebels publicized the event in metropolitan newspapers, characterizing Dartmouth's "deplorable management" and policies leading to "impending disaster." It was no small advantage and a powerful symbol of the changing collegiate culture to have as an activist alumnus the editor of the *New York Times*. If the rhetoric was overblown, rural Dartmouth College had swirled into an unfamiliar urban vortex. Though other colleges closer to cities and mercantile hubs may have experienced Dartmouth's "trial" earlier and in more muted forms, variations on this transformation permeated the nineteenth-century college as it was becoming a distinctive institutional genre for the first time, both conceptually and organizationally.[62]

The ensuing "trial" of Samuel C. Bartlett in 1881 was not a legal procedure but rather a public airing of collective differences; even more important, it signaled a qualitative reorganization of the antebellum college. The older moral paradigm of the antebellum college as an organic, moral community had experienced tinkering and multiple adaptations for all of its history;

however, by the 1880s the older, evangelical paradigm received only a rhetorical defense and a substantive loss of support from trustees, faculty, and students. Still, the rhetoric and the tradition were not sufficient to force the president's resignation. Bartlett continued in office for another decade, documenting the ongoing power of the older evangelical tradition as well as a widespread impetus to change.

But the essential roles in college life had changed substantively, even if the president and his rhetoric tried to stanch the tide. In most colleges of the 1880s, the trustees had relinquished powers over course revision, over student admissions and final course examinations. Faculty now juggled a greater voice about teaching duties with professional, scholarly activities, increasingly in national organizations of their subject discipline. Organizations like the American Historical Association (1884), American Economic Association (1885), American Psychological Association (1897), American Political Science Association (1904), and the American Sociological Association (1905) helped academics set their own standards for new professional practice, proving a base for resisting some college and university policies as well as shaping new academic discourses.[63] Students, whose ages began to bunch into a narrow cohort of seventeen-to-twenty-one-year-old youth, considered more self-consciously the connection between instruction and subsequent careers. The alternative notions of college governance by younger faculty and students registered new dynamics that the older college could only ignore at its peril. In retrospect, student criticism at Dartmouth and elsewhere[64] translated into a different collegiate culture, one that embraced urban dynamics and translocal resources as a part of Dartmouth's "community." The new role of alumni extended the college's organization to the distant city, making possible eventually new financial resources and a more sympathetic president to replace Bartlett and an older tradition. The late nineteenth-century college looked to metropolitan values, scholarly reputation for faculty, and higher intellectual standards for students. These new dynamics led to a self-conscious sense of "campus" as a cohesive locus more than a cohesive community, at once set apart from local but not national values. The American college had become the hub of an extensive geographical and multilayered organizational wheel, sketchily conceived as early as the 1840s by Francis Wayland at Brown but operationally impossible until the 1890s. Those same historical forces would also create a formidable, new competitor in the form of the American university.[65]

Earlier scholars of the nineteenth-century college have stressed the undeniable force of evangelism and denominational values. But virtually every college also contained counterforces, research-oriented academics, student resistance, external economic pressures, and larger national aspirations that served to qualify the continuity of moral instruction. At times, as the example of Rev. Francis Wayland made clear, the primary agent of this qualification was its own religious leader. From small beginnings the tiny teaching faculty of the early nineteenth-century college—which thereby could overindulge the metaphors of "college family"—became a complex organization well beyond its "voluntary" roots. The novel features of mid- and late nineteenth-century colleges were their discovery and implementation of an organization that merged the college with some definable larger society. Its introduction of curricular options, the sifting out of both younger (under sixteen) and older (over twenty-two) students, the investiture in career faculty with explicit ties to national professional associations, the admission of alumni representation to trustee decision making, and a reduction of the trustees' aegis to noneducational matters effectively produced a different educational culture by the end of the nineteenth century. So conditioned to the fact of twentieth- and twenty-first-century organizations' environments, scholars have been slow to grasp the institutional innovation of the nineteenth century, the discovery of system as a reform and its formidable mediation of conflicting, or at least competitive, values. Wayland is but one of a core of collegiate leaders whose labors for educational reform have been adumbrated by their inability to realize their visions in their own time. Nevertheless, their work and their writings, many of which contain insights realized before the end of the century, help clarify the significance of the nineteenth-century college. Their histories also illuminate dynamic, educational experiments that led to the formation of the American university. These generic forms were never as separate as their narrators have often made them, and together their stories illuminate the educational contribution both have made to American academic cultures.

CHAPTER FIVE

Land-Grant Colleges and the Emergence of an Academic Space

After the Civil War, Americans added many additional pressures to higher education, including the need for colleges and universities to join in the shaping of the leadership class and public stability. A heightened consciousness of higher learning as a social resource led to a number of organizational changes and educational priorities, initiated especially by their own presidents and alumni. Americans began to channel their thinking into the creation of a specially designed place for advanced instruction, in particular, a campus for higher learning. The word "campus," originally the Latin word for "field," described the rural siting of many small colleges and academies. By mid-nineteenth century, the word had become a referent not only for the cluster of buildings associated with a school but for the special esprit they embodied and ideally imparted to their students.[1] Without much rhetorical fanfare, a new collegiate environment arose out of explicit designs for a new learning environment. Gone were the hilltop colleges with a central building, often resembling a steepleless church with its supporting rectories and serviceable buildings. In places, like Oberlin, the transition was softer, since the early buildings arranged themselves around the town's village green.[2] Initially the effect of building collages was a visible mix of college and community purposes. Gradually as towns expanded and grew beyond the original boundaries of a school, colleges seemed abandoned to their own devices, left, like Yale, with its central buildings in a row on the town green, the remains of a once projected quadrangle. A new sensibility differentiated itself from commercially oriented schools as well as from inherited, even idealized, European models.[3] The campus as a distinct entity became a part of a self-conscious sense of the power of organization.

The notion of campus responded to the antebellum college's often serendipitous construction. Once a school's foundations were no longer tied to adjacent towns or single denominations, colleges pursued loftier, even national goals, which gradually influenced school building and planning. The new artifact—campus—produced a design in the nineteenth century for a college, all too cognizant of its place within a larger educational enterprise. Post–Civil War collegiate institutions continued to deal with multifaceted goals; and they always raised a stone-and-mortar argument about coherence. The creation of a designed landscape and environment brought to the fore the need for a less varied external appearance than the postwar college inherited from its earlier models.[4] Most of all, new designs attempted to complement the central feature of the postwar college, that learning required a distinctive, conducive environment, one that recognized the mutually reinforcing exchange of mind and nature.

The central figure of campus design was the same individual responsible for the promotion of nineteenth-century urban landscapes, Frederick Law Olmsted (1822–1903), best known for his designs (with his partner Calvert Vaux [1824–95]) of Central Park in New York City and Prospect Park in Brooklyn.[5] The earliest campus designs of, say, Thomas Jefferson and his early nineteenth-century "Academical Village" influenced few collegiate physical plants before the end of the nineteenth century. Until the surge of reorganization after the Civil War, collegiate environments reflected the insufficiency of funding that most schools experienced. They built what they could when they could, without a good deal of attention to common architectural (or educational) inheritances. Olmsted came to campus design serendipitously, winding his ways through problems of Southern agriculture and slavery, scientific farming in the British tradition, and war work for Civil War wounded, and finally addressing the city as a tension between civic survival and expanding population density.[6] Tempering nature's unpredictable patterns, disciplining the Southern plantation's exploitation of slavery, responding to wartime's degeneracy of humanizing values, all underscored for Olmsted the seeming ubiquity and institutionalization of force, coercion, and even violence in congested modern life. All of these problems intensified in the city, he believed, where rampant development, if left uncontrolled, exacerbated the problem and made incivility a daily experience and a barometer of worse things to come. An indifference to manners, which had once characterized country town civility, became an early measure of city liabilities. Olmsted's animus was not only to conceptualize the problem of the city but to address it in some practical way. His concern for urban and college landscape arose from his observations of the dangers and incivility of city life rather than from any formal training or collegiate study.

His masterpiece, New York City's Central Park, drove his thinking about civic space in other venues, in idyllic cemeteries, in winding, landscaped parkways, in designed suburbs, and finally in campus spaces. Although he prided himself on his unromanticized journalistic reportage, Olmsted's narrations and landscape designs necessarily incorporated elements of a neo-romantic quality. His fascination with English villages with their tidy, comfortable inns, his regular remarks on hospitable British or country manners, and the role of natural environment in checking any sense of social isolation, loneliness, or dislocation were values he attached to older cultures. He refused to sacrifice these natural qualities in his adaptive, architectural designs. His preoccupation with privacy and a genteel context for voluntary interaction clearly clashed with his perception of a postwar society, increasingly deferent to the impersonal survival of the fittest. The novelty of Olmsted's views was his concession that an older civility would no longer emerge naturally, as it was once thought to have done; it had to be created and protected by calculation, by ingenuity, even by illusion.[7]

Olmsted's notion of landscape incorporated, in part, the English landscape tradition of concealment and humor as well as varied and extensive perspectives. His contribution was to tailor the aristocratic tradition of Capability Brown (1716–83) and other landscapists into a democratic framework. Instead of expansive estates and the long view, Olmsted managed nature to protect privacy as well as social class mixing, to provide varied and surprising natural perspectives, and to ensure the endurance of a routine civility as cultivated as his terrains. His engineered nature was a Whiggish cultural haven as much as it was a preserve of the original environment. In Central Park he buried the transverse roads carrying commercial traffic and preserved the serenity of walkways; along park borders he planted trees that would obscure the rising office buildings to preserve the sense of removal from the city's hard rationalities; he introduced lagoons and lakes where none had been and emphatically razed the shanties of the poor. Virtually no square footage of Central Park had remained in its natural state upon its completion in 1867. He worked hard to prevent low leisure activities like cockfighting, boxing, beer drinking, and so on, in the park to ensure special strata for "recreation" and a special and restricted social class interaction. Olmsted's organized environment, originally considered a means of preserving privacy and individual discretion, became ironically a quasi-naturalistic device, privileging some social class behaviors like the social display of the promenade and carriage trails while eliminating others.[8] His designs for land-grant university campuses would bear strong analogies to his many park landscapes. His "uplifting" environment became an educational force in its own right.

Fortuitously Olmsted became an acquaintance of first congressman and later senator from Vermont Justin Morrill (1810–98).[9] Morrill's legislative proposals for a different kind of state-supported public institution for higher learning had been frustrated since 1856, when he first began to shape his land-grant college proposal, namely, a publicly supported institution of higher learning in every state.[10] But in the heat of the Civil War, he combined his concern for disseminating a science of agriculture and mechanics with an expedient proposal for military instruction. His bill passed in 1862 due to the absence of Southern opponents and became the precedent for the American state university. Ultimately sixty-nine universities would effectively be created in the nineteenth century out of the 1862 law and a later 1890 companion piece (for schools in new states and for formerly excluded African Americans), underscoring both the strategic role of public support and for a democratic access to higher learning.[11]

Once the 1862 bill passed and states considered the creation of a university, sometimes de novo, sometimes reorganizing existing colleges, they turned to Morrill for advice. There is no direct evidence of Morrill referring such requests to Frederick Law Olmsted's published writings, but particularly in the early 1870s when he arranged for Olmsted to redesign the grounds of the national Capitol, he had to have had knowledge of Olmsted's published work on collegiate landscaping.[12] Precisely in Olmsted's years of work on the Capitol grounds, Morrill labored hard to increase federal support for his land-grant institutions. Olmsted's new work of landscape design dramatically altered the natural landscape to produce a cultivated imitation of nature (always severely controlled parkland). His reconstruction of nature began with his travels through England, his own experiments with scientific agriculture on Staten Island, and his energizing sense of the indirect force of environment upon individual values and attitudes. Olmsted's fascination with the nineteenth-century city shaped an innovative argument about the educational force of urban spaces. His postwar career would focus imaginatively upon the blending of beauty and utility in crafted city spaces: cemeteries, parks, boulevards, suburbs, and school campuses, which would tolerate neither nature uncontrolled nor wholly rationalized schemas, like the rectangular grid designs of New York and other cities.[13] Olmsted gave considerable thought to the impact of this reorganization of nature. He had, after all, served during the Civil War, as executive secretary of the US Sanitation Commission, which began as a voluntary organization and ended as a major corporate structure delivering health services ("scientific benevolence") to wounded military nationwide.[14] Olmsted's fascination with organization and design matched the experience of so many military men, like Thomas Scott (1823–81), whose postwar career rocketed into the Pennsylvania Railroad, the largest corporation in America at the time and one of the driving engines of the American economy. The very emergence of the corporate organization, particularly in the Union Army's Quartermaster Corps, some attributed to the Union victory in the Civil War.[15] Whatever the truth of the claim, Americans generally took two major educational inferences from the war: first, a new order of technical and industrial production and knowledge to match should distinguish the postwar era; and second, the stratified line of command, so essential to military organization, posed a new organizational possibility beyond the paradigm of the ubiquitous, antebellum voluntary association.

These two important insights took some time to register in the educational fabric of the nation, now (1865) 31 million strong, 80 percent of whom resided on farms. Perhaps in recognition of these fundamental realities, Lincoln had also created in 1862 the Department of Agriculture and signed the Homestead Act. But the war had a way of galvanizing the nation's collective attention, and few could be indifferent to a key statistic, especially once the war began for the North in a string of failures. In 1860 the military strength of the Union Army consisted of fifteen thousand soldiers. By the war's end, the drafts and subscription expanded that same army to 2.5 million men. Clothing, arming, feeding, transporting, and sustaining soldiers in battle required more than an unprecedented manufacturing output and technical knowledge; it required a generically different transformation of attitudes about organization itself.[16] Both Morrill and Olmsted had observed firsthand the danger and waste of farmers without science and the military without organizationally minded leaders, and both turned their heads to a new postwar educational discipline that would follow and disseminate new managerial forms.[17] Morrill and Olmsted shaped their earlier Whig social and educational foundations into a new notion of higher education, at once socially useful but distinctively self-contained. Their views would be guaranteed and projected publicly by a picturesque landscape design, a campus.

Morrill's vision had been shaped by more than the emerging managerial revolution and Olmstead's romanticism. His Vermont hometown of Sheffield was not far from Norwich University (founded 1819), whose leading spirit,

Alden Partridge (1785–1854), had once taught at West Point. At both schools engineering knowledge formed the basis of the military training and curricula.[18] Morrill's early proposals drew on his familiarity with Norwich, and he copied into his land-grant proposals essential components of both West Point and Annapolis, especially in recruitment. For example, early on he proposed that scholarships be awarded for his proposed schools like the army and navy academies, one student nomination for every congressman and two statewide nominees for every state. His land-grant schools would teach the science and technical skills necessary to check the flagging state of agricultural production in the East.[19] He orchestrated depressing statistical formulas to show that especially in the eastern states, wheat, tobacco, cotton, and so on, had fallen sharply in the preceding decade. The same was not true of European countries, like Belgium and England, with much smaller land parcels than the United States. Moreover, the impending collapse of the East's agricultural economy not only jeopardized the US Treasury, but it tended to siphon farmers off the land. The land-grant colleges, Morrill argued, would shore up national finance as well as invigorate the social fabric of a predominately agricultural nation.[20] "College students," Morrill argued, "obliterate state lines."[21]

In the same year—1862—that he established a renewed national commitment to agriculture with a cabinet-level voice and territorial expansion via a homestead formula, Lincoln signed the Morrill Land Grant Act. This precedent-setting legislation activated features of the Northwest Ordinance of 1787. That precedent gave the federal government authority to distribute public lands and to convert the territories into states. This democratic instrument of power distribution also contained stipulations to fund a new educational establishment, a public college or university in every state.[22] The 1862 law also amended the general educational support from taxes to stress agricultural and mechanical studies. Importantly this legislation specified the integration of these new studies with existing liberal and classical instruction. Morrill himself saw the law as a device to strengthen the farmer in particular, encouraging his professional status and giving the farmer abilities to offer a political defense of agriculture's interests.[23] The pretense in both law and education was one of reasonable adaptation to new circumstances; the reality would ultimately transform American higher education, though not functionally until the twentieth century.

The Morrill Land Grant Act of 1862 awarded thirty thousand acres of land for every congressman and senator, to be used to finance at least one public institution in every state. The law included even states in rebellion, in spite of the South's vigorous opposition to Morrill's earliest proposals. After the war the Reconstruction legislatures would ensure that the funds supported the first black land-grant institutions, Alcorn State University (founded 1871) in Mississippi and Lincoln University in Missouri (founded 1866).[24] The land grants were, however, susceptible to a real estate economy that was saturated with land grants. Railroad entrepreneurs building the first transcontinental railroad had received 130 million acres for its construction; veterans of the Mexican War and other military episodes had been paid in land script backed by an additional 61 million acres; and the Homestead Act had already begun to sell public lands in the amount of 70 million acres. Morrill's land-grant allocation of 17,430,000 acres had to compete in an inflated market and generally resulted in returns of little more than one dollar an acre.

For expectant colleges, the insufficiency of funds led Morrill immediately to launch a long campaign to buttress the state institutions. Even under the most fortuitous circumstances—the cases of Cornell and the University of California—land-grant funds never amassed the estimated $47,000 required to operate a university for a year.[25] After seven formal proposals, Morrill finally won passage in 1890 for a second federal law, awarding $15,000 per year, later raised to $25,000, for every land-grant school. In addition, the 1890 law provided for state institutions in the territories that had become states since 1862. Notably the 1890 law attacked racial discrimination and specified no distinction in support for race or color. Though the reigning Jim Crow sentiment of "separate but equal" ensured separate facilities for blacks and whites, several new black state schools arose, like the Colored Normal, Industrial, Agricultural and Mechanical College of South Carolina (later South Carolina State University) in 1896 and the State Normal School for Colored Persons (later Kentucky State University) in 1897.[26] These exceptions were not immediately popular. The majority of black collegians still preferred the smaller and supportive black liberal arts colleges until well into the twentieth century.

Immediately the passage of the 1862 law had a multifaceted effect in its organizational and curricular ramifications. In the older sections of the country, like New Jersey and New Hampshire, existing schools—Rutgers University and Dartmouth College—became the state land-grant recipient.[27] In Massachusetts legislators channeled funds to two institutions, the Agricultural State College in the western Berkshires and in the eastern part of the state the Massachusetts Institute of Technology (MIT), which had been incorporated in 1861 and opened in 1865. In other states, like New York and Indiana, lawmakers used the public money to buttress portions of already existing, privately funded institutions: Cornell and Purdue Universities. In the trans-Mississippi west, the land-grant money generally fostered entirely new schools. By the end of 1862, Iowa became the first school to accept the new law's conditions to become the first land-grant university. But by 1865 eighteen more joined the new genre, and sixteen additional by 1870. But for much of the nineteenth century, few of these new "public" institutions were larger than the traditional, denominationally rooted colleges that commanded the relevant youth pool. Initially the commitment of public lands was a promissory note for future stability; it was also a recognition that the American public had accepted the early nineteenth-century college's broader civic claims, namely, that their graduates would provide the core of stability and leadership for the Republic's welfare.[28]

The curricular priorities of the land-grant colleges varied from place to place. If agriculture received little shrift—the University of Wisconsin would not graduate an agricultural major until 1878[29]—the reason lay less with the land-grant colleges and more with the usual pattern by which Americans garnered their agricultural expertise. Generally that knowledge came from magazines, county fairs, seasonal lectures, and the occasional large town museum, all of which could be integrated into the farmers' demanding seasonal schedule.[30] The land-grant college would not become the center of American agricultural knowledge until after the federal government passed additional legislation. The Hatch Act in 1887 created agricultural stations in every state to provide a formal, clearinghouse of farming data. The station agents began to ride circuit, like earlier religious missionaries, creating highly effective, informal networks that gradually embraced and activated the agricultural mission of the land-grant institutions. It was actually this network of stations, more than the college or university teaching positions that formally undergirded the first, lifelong careers in American science at the end of the nineteenth century.[31]

The absence of a federal collegiate blueprint and the competition of varied state interests for land-grant support ensured a vigorous discussion over the shape of land-grant institutions. This intellectual ferment helped galvanize and focus several strands of Olmsted's prewar and wartime experiences. Frederick Law Olmsted, age forty-three in 1865, was little more than an astute, amateur scientist as he began to fashion the science of landscape architecture. His serendipitous employments thus far—reporter, administrator, and more recently California speculator and mining manager—mirrored the path of his generation, the first to consider lines of employment building into "careers." His generation had found formal education was not a necessary step to a profession, traditional or emergent. Olmsted's own college instruction consisted of less than a year auditing Yale lectures while his brother studied there. By 1865 he had spent half a lifetime on the borders of science, experimenting, reading, lecturing, proselytizing. From his own point of view, his first campus design—the College of California in the new San Francisco suburb of Berkeley—was neither an afterthought nor a full-time preoccupation. Olmsted was in California to manage a Sierra gold-mining firm; to evaluate the possibility of a western branch of the *Nation* for its editor, E. L. Godkin (1831–1902), and to manage his own speculative investments. In retrospect, the most important duty of these years was informal, an examination of Yosemite valley and a proposal for its possible preservation as a national resource. The broad swath of these endeavors were fundamentally educational but in a new key; Olmsted was working to restructure and design new civilizing creations. To Godkin, he lamented, "Do recollect that except at a very few points there is no cultivated *society* in America, but a great many intelligent men and women to whom a newspaper may well be the only substitute for whatever, in a society more elaborately civilized, keeps a man's commonplace civilization alive."[32] Though speaking specifically of newspapers, he was within this same year to make an analogous case for choice scenery (Yosemite), for a second great urban park (Prospect Park in Brooklyn), for well-organized communities (Berkeley, California), and not least for an attractive and inspiring campus for learning (College of California).[33] Each of these designs in their way advanced the element of planning and organization to a new level in the postbellum era: a conscious separation of city and country, a consciously designed organization to connect them technically and aesthetically, and a sequestered, "natural" space for both, the prerequisite for an orderly and efficient response to the challenges of modern life.

At the time of Olmsted's 1866 design, the College of California was a private institution, soon to be the recipient of Morrill's Land Grant Act and to become in 1868 a state university.[34] Olmsted began his report by presenting both the public's role and the force of the environment as educational agents.[35] He offered to the board of the college a special insistence: a college should be located neither in the country nor in the city. A country location would divorce students from domestic life and civilization and be a throwback to monastic seclusion. The city's distractions, however, were equally debilitating. A planned suburb like Berkeley was ideal, having the advantages of both country and city without their liabilities. Olmsted explicitly declared his intention to lay out the college's property "on the Llewellyn plan," invoking the early planned New Jersey suburb of the 1850s designed by his friend Alexander Jackson Davis (1803–92). The design modeled itself on the plan of a naturalistic park, where both campus and domestic values shared boundaries that were permeable, accessible, pleasant, and refining to experience. The walks and roadways meandered, accessible by both suburbanites and students, for relaxation, for exercise, and strategically for spectacular vistas of the Golden Gate and the Pacific.[36] The college enhanced the community, took advantage of it and its domesticating values but operated as a physically distinct entity.

The term "campus" shifted in its postwar meaning from its Latin root for "field" to indicate both a locus and a socializing agent. Olmsted's California plan put the two main buildings at the eastern end of the property rather than squarely in the center of an open field, which seemed to be the preference of most college boards. His design for student dorms broke with the prevailing barracks traditions and created an enlarged domestic design to accommodate twenty to forty lodgers. These accommodations should include drawing rooms and dining rooms, private rooms, and eventually gardens. He specifically argued to the trustees for a picturesque rather than symmetrical environment. He reasoned that the choice would blend with the local community, would allow for expansion were that required, and most of all would blend practical and moral values: the campus would instill refining and civilizing values without the faculty monitoring of earlier colleges, which presumed underage and ill-trained youth. The campus would literally prepare young students for subsequent lives of responsibility and gentility.[37]

In 1866 Olmsted published his views as *Report upon a Projected Improvement of the Estate of the College of California at Berkeley, near Oakland*, which, in addition to his editorials in the *Nation*, gave him exposure to new land-grant leaders casting about for design advice. While he was still working on the California campus, the new Massachusetts Agricultural College (founded 1863 and later the University of Massachusetts, Amherst)—his first land-grant client—approached him. Here his communal designs adopted a rural structure, siting buildings along a rural road like a scattered New England village. The military obligation of the Land Grant Act enabled him to focus the campus upon a drill ground that functioned like a village common, with one border the meandering rural road.[38] Academic buildings with classrooms helped define the green, while again student dormitories were designed as large domestic residences, each for no more than thirty students. Additional houses with similar design could be added as required, avoiding the overbuilding so characteristic of other ambitious, start-up colleges and universities. Though the trustees balked initially, Olmsted's thinking achieved a wider circulation with an unsigned *Nation* article, "How Not to Establish a College,"[39] probably authored by the designer. By the following year, Olmsted received invitations to design and consult for the Maine Agricultural College (later University of Maine at Orono), the national Deaf-Mute Institute in Washington, DC (later Gallaudet College), the Pennsylvania Agricultural College, Hampton Institute in Virginia, and Cornell University. Even for schools that did not consult him, his ideas were clearly influential at land-grant colleges in Michigan, Iowa, and Kansas.[40]

Olmsted's ideas may also have spurred other land-grant recipients away from notions of campus as parkland. Several major recipients, like the University of Wisconsin and the University of Illinois, attempted variations on Jefferson's older model: centrally sited main building containing administrative offices and library with some classroom space, facing down a central mall bordered by student dormitories and chapel. It was a model, often open-ended on a fourth side (hence not really a quadrangle), that was adopted, too, by schools like the University of Notre Dame, which achieved a finished form in the later years of the nineteenth century.[41] However divergent from Olmsted's debated views (which were not often followed by his clients), the postwar college and university had experienced a new sense of possibility and autonomy that required a new physical plant. The message of that construction reflected aspirations for internal cohesiveness while accepting different talents and career aspirations among students. The long-term impact of the land-grant college was a closer articulation between education and career occupations. This coordination also implied—as did the language of the 1862 act itself—that beyond the classics there were additional worthy studies that an industrializing American would surely prize. Morrill himself had explicitly asserted in arguing for his land-grant idea that "the design is not to lower even the highest rank of scholarship, but to raise up more scholars; not to depress the altitude of mountain peaks, but to elevate the great plains."[42]

However, postwar dynamics ensured that the land-grant college design would not sweep the nation with an ambitious new model of higher learning. A money crisis, inflation, greenback debates, and several economic panics meant that universities should move cautiously in building construction, lest they overextend themselves and guarantee the failure of the institution. Land-grant colleges and their trustees thus devoted a great deal of attention to the economic pitfalls of bricks and mortar, to design and long-term finance. The economics of the era and the lack of a visible curricula meant that the more utilitarian courses in land-grant colleges had to wait for at least a generation before they could fulfill the promise of disciplined careers. The land grant, cheapened by a market flooded with land scrip, did not achieve an immediate stability, a clear higher education alternative, or a sought opportunity for able youth. Generically the land-grant institutions functioned as schools of comparable size with existing liberal arts colleges. Until sufficient new courses were offered, and in fact were shortened due to pressure from the organized farmers via the Grange, the Farmers' Alliance, and later the Populists, even the most advanced of state institutions could not really deliver on the "agricultural and mechanic" language in the 1862 law.[43]

The Morrill legislation did not specify a curricular model, any more than it did an architectural or landscape design. The clear intention, however, of legitimating agricultural and mechanical courses alongside the regular classical curriculum aimed at some formalization of the scientific experiments of the past several decades. However, it would be several decades more before any satisfactory course of studies would materialize. Many scholars have their champion for "the first democratic American university." Usually the specific college or university selected depended on an articulate leader—Andrew White (1832–1918) in Cornell's case—and a well-funded institution that preserved its own archival history. Cornell had both, and that led later historians to give it a special nod. However the variety of "agricultural and mechanical course of study" depended sharply on local and regional resources, and all of them had to contend with the ongoing national preeminence of the classical curriculum.[44]

A typical land-grant institution, like the University of Illinois under the presidency of John Gregory (1867–80), struggled with inadequate financing, a lack of curricular guidance in the Morrill Acts, and a student body often lacking college preparation. In spite of pressures from trade school proponents and denominationally oriented liberal arts advocates, Gregory steered a different course, but even then the University of Illinois faced years of uncertainty. Emphatically he sought a "university" that was more than the familiar alternatives, and he also sought (not very successfully) to take the advice he had solicited for campus design from Frederick Law Olmsted.[45] Gregory proposed six departments, which clearly addressed the Morrill mandate: agriculture, polytechnics, military, chemistry and natural science, trade and commerce, and general science and literature. The last would serve as a prerequisite for the other departments and greatly resembled an idealized liberal arts curriculum at Kalamazoo College, where he had recently served as president (1864–67). Gregory's own ordination as a Baptist minister provided more of a target for his critics than his professional experience as superintendent of schools in Michigan, not to mention his scientific proclivities, rooted in his own college days at Eliphalet Nott's Union College.[46] Gregory's pragmatic support of a manual labor option for self-supporting students also seemed to associate him with antebellum schools with low academic prospects. The first class at Illinois Industrial University in 1867 admitted fifty students and reached seventy-seven by the end of the semester. Forty-five of these had resided close to the school's town of Champaign, and hence were local youth, and the majority were poorly prepared. Gregory had ambitions no less lofty than Cornell's Andrew White but, like most of the land-grant presidents, had dramatically different resources.[47]

This new emphasis of land-grant schools on "practical" subjects would eventually become a powerful new alternative in American higher education. Its early years, however, involved much experimentation and debate, much having to do with a new national demography and the creation of distinct and fewer stages in Americans' careers.[48] A new type of schoolmen had emerged, individuals, like Andrew White and his friend Daniel Coit Gilman (1831–1908), both thoughtful about a new higher learning, widely traveled and in regular communication with a coterie of like-minded educators. This new generation had emphasized educational leadership as a distinct career and gradually reconfigured the role of college leadership with these new state institutions. They shunned the antebellum priority of biblical and religious instruction in colleges and crafted study so that multiple occupations had the cache of the older professions.[49] These background dynamics nevertheless carried great respect for the older classical instruction. Even at Cornell, White expanded the college courses into "practical" arenas, while leavening his novelty with a deference to the classics. Gilman would do the same as first president of the University of California. So would his associate John Gregory (1822–98) at the University of Illinois and John Bascom (1827–1911) at the University of Wisconsin in the 1870s and 1880s. They saw their work as democratizing but rarely referred to their universities or their ideals as democratic.[50]

The real novelty of the land-grant institutions was this new practical dimension, giving a special authority to applied work to satisfy the demands of a practical, democratic education.[51] But even more was its contribution to the sense of higher education organization as self-possessed, a kind of intellectual autonomy, an integrated campus that included multiple talents and interests, mutually at work, faculty and students, to connect education to the subsequent occupations of life. The land-grant leaders inflated these goals as they lobbied for political support. They knew that the land-grant alternative was their initiative far more than it was one of a demand from state legislatures. Andrew White was one of the first of the new university leaders to clarify his goals by attacking the competitive "little American college" as "sordid" and worse. In part, this strategy was to bid for the available student population, to concentrate the federal money into a single, new institution, and to project a "university" of modern literary, historical studies and practical subjects. His design, of course, was beyond the means of most American colleges and most existing American universities as well. Equally important, in spite of the dissonance between reality and conception, White promoted Cornell at every opportunity. He did, however, concede in his autobiography that his "great university" with its library, professorial chairs, and dignified towers and quadrangles was a "[castle] in the air." "This dream," he would retrospectively admit, "became an obsession."[52] To realize the obsession he had to expand the curriculum, incorporate women (first in 1872), add on physical education and military drill as optional subjects, and accept without apology some courses of study entirely without classics.[53] The notion of a campus became increasingly complex but a necessary ingredient in maintaining the pretense of cohesion.

None of the new land-grant schools had sufficient resources to build programs of academic respectability or attract already celebrated scholars as faculty. Most of them quietly followed Cornell's lead in contacting such scholars in established private universities in order to hire their young students who would grow into their own academic celebrities. Thus, the federal policy of forming public institutions depended on the prestige and benefit of established private universities. At the University of Wisconsin, two students of Harvard's Alexander Agassiz (1835–1910), the noted Swiss naturalist, arrived to create niches for biology (Addison E. Verrill [1839–1926] in 1868) and zoology (Edwin A. Birge [1851–1950] in 1875). Outside the sciences, scholars like William Allen (1830–89) came to Wisconsin in 1867 after work in German universities to teach the first courses in history (incorporating geographic, economic, and social components in his notions of significant change) and began training native youth, like Frederick Jackson Turner (1861–1932), who already served on the faculty as instructor of elocution.[54] New scientific specializations, new personnel, new avenues to professional careers, all followed from the expansive academic rush to "practicality."

The money from the Morrill grants, however, returned too little for the majority of schools that desired to become true centers of learning. Some schools received as little as fifty cents an acre, and most returned less than

$10,000 annually when four or five times that amount was thought minimal for a starting college.[55] In addition, the public's and students' expectations many times played a negative role. They saw the land-grant institutions as service centers, like the modern community colleges. Many citizens thought they could come for a single course of study in a subject of interest. One farmer who sought basic reading skills at Cornell became indignant with Andrew White, who suggested he go to his local public school. Still more, in 1860 there were only 243 high schools nationwide, or sixteen for every million Americans, too few to graduate a prepared pool for higher education.[56] Consequently, most land-grant schools put all faculty (averaging ten to twenty teachers) and resources in single buildings and had them face classes with students barely beyond elementary study. By contrast, the Cornell campus stood out for its fiscal perspicacity and its opening (1868) admission of 412 students, the largest student body in US history at the time.[57]

The land-grant alternative set in motion a major discussion about higher education that only marginally focused on the strategic role of the federal government. Since the federal government had left the implementation of the Morrill Acts to the state discretion, the notable early feature of the land grants was the diverse uses states made of their limited money. The economic fluctuation after the Civil War and especially after the Panic of 1873 led to instability in higher education for years thereafter. By the 1880s, however, not only had the economy tempered, driven heavily by extraordinary railroad and industrial expansion, but the land-grant institutions had begun to win substantive state recognition. In Wisconsin, Robert M. La Follette (1855–1925), an 1879 graduate of his state university, would be an elected district attorney for Dane County and would become an emergent power broker. Not only did he attribute his successful political campaigns to his university network of alumni, his argument for a strong binding relation between university research and Progressive legislation would become nationally influential as the "Wisconsin Idea." As state university graduates worked in state and national assemblies, the groundwork was laid for state subsidy to the state university, even before the passage of the 1890 Second Morrill Act of the US Congress.[58]

In the last two decades of the nineteenth century, land-grant schools began to be taken over by a succeeding generation of leaders. These individuals had generally not fought in the Civil War but had to take advantage of the rapid expansion of wealth and corporate organization that characterized the period. Their influence began to be felt in new admission policies; in the elimination of the preparatory departments; in the continued cultivation of literary societies and student cultures, particularly in the Midwest; in the early inclusion of alumni on the boards of trustees; in the cultivation of political allies in their state legislatures; and finally in their scientific, agricultural, and mechanical priorities in education. These transitions, many of them far from dramatic, became in their way as transformational and as revolutionary as the analogous shifts of the 1840s for an expansive liberal arts college like Francis Wayland envisioned in the antebellum period.

Politics at the federal level began to play a part in the land-grant redesign of the 1880s. Through individuals like George Atherton (1837–1906), president of Pennsylvania State University, the land-grant schools received not only a coherent voice but also an organization, the Association of American Agricultural Colleges and Experimental Stations (founded 1887). It was Atherton who behind the scenes had actually authored the Hatch Act in 1887 and the Second Morrill Act of 1890.[59] These two landmark laws provided the rush of money and moral support that made the agency a potent political lobby and gave land-grant institutions another set of opportunities. The laws led to formal linkages with the state and federal governments, especially the Department of Agriculture, via their extension programs. These public services paralleled linkages backward into the public school system, where the universities took responsibility for training personnel, monitoring the articulation of subjects, and gradually positioning themselves at the head of the public school system. In addition, in spite of teaching and research analogies with many private colleges and universities, the land-grant schools rose in the national mind as a distinctive genre. Their heterogeneous student body and low tuition, allowed by tax subsidies denied to private colleges, went far to modify any elitist connotations. University of Michigan president James Angell (1829–1916) explained his public strategy: "First, I have endeavored to induce every citizen to regard himself as a stockholder in the institution, who had a real interest in making it of the greatest service to his children. Secondly, I have sought to make all the schools and teachers in the State understand that they and the university are parts of one united system, and that therefore the youngest pupils in the most secluded schoolhouse should be encouraged to see that the path was open from his home up and through the university."[60] Their cultivation of a distinctive image, now more explicitly "democratic," was part and parcel of the shaping of architecture and landscape into seemingly self-contained campuses.

However awkward and tentative its beginnings, the land-grant model created a new educational ideology with a compelling sense of place, a campus, and projected the ideal into successive generic models of educational institutions.[61] In reality these schools were the hubs of far larger regional and national networks. In their projection of more coherence than they actually possessed, their leaders were wont to invoke the ringing prose of John Henry Newman's *The Idea of a University* (in spite of Newman's teaching instead of scientific, or even "democratic," priorities), particularly his insistence on a *genius loci*, a distinctly supportive place for higher learning in America.[62]

The emergence of a distinctive spatial ideal for higher learning could not have arisen in the mid-nineteenth century and have been realized without the concomitant development of an industrial economy and new corporate organizations fostered by Civil War dynamics. The antebellum diversity of educational institutions and curricula continued into the later decades of the nineteenth century but now, an important cultural shift, the possibility of orchestrating people, education, and technologies for qualitatively demonstrable advances, was manifest in every town and city. Publicly supported land-grant colleges began as varied in facilities and services as their antebellum college competitors, but, after the Civil War, such universities pioneered new chains of command, lines of authority in policy making, curricular distinctions between basic and advanced courses of subjects, and patterned responses to both alumni and fiscal benefactors. They soon became their own growth industries for their states and regions, and with their alumni in the state legislatures, they began to receive regular public fiscal support. The same cultural forces (generational culture #4) that favored these changes also increasingly emphasized the practical applications of science in the college curriculum, receptivity to alternative funding mechanisms like the general purpose foundation, and its outreach to national professional organizations. This new organizational sensibility received its graphic counterpart in the design of collegiate space. If there were still differences of architectural styles and debates over the center and periphery of the campuses, there was incontestably a penchant for a new institutional order encapsulated by its collegiate landscape, the academic campus, a distinctive cultural icon.

CHAPTER SIX

The Generic University

Charles William Eliot (1834–1926) at age thirty-five became president of Harvard College in 1869 and led that institution for forty years. Most scholars credit him not only with the transformation of a sleepy little college on the Charles River into a generic university, one that viewed higher education as the epitome of an educational system and distinctively integrated a collegiate with a professional and graduate research experience. Historians also have used his record to illuminate the issues and measures for assessing American higher education in the late nineteenth and early twentieth century. However, the new American university was not solely Eliot's at Harvard or indeed in America. Eliot was but one of a cohort of individuals who came into educational leadership positions after the Civil War and with extraordinary self-consciousness and personal determination redesigned higher learning in this country.[1] It is, however, Eliot's prominence, even in this singular cohort that included Andrew White of Cornell and Daniel Coit Gilman of Johns Hopkins, among others, that gives his views and achievement a special resonance and through his experience permits a retrospective understanding of American academic culture (generational culture #4) in his time.[2]

Eliot embodied, though he did not create, the metaphor of the Boston Brahmin. It was of course advantageous to have a wealthy merchant father, who served as Boston's mayor and among many other offices, and act as a member of the Harvard Corporation. His mother belonged to the wealthy and influential Lyman family, also at various times contributing one of its members as an officer of Harvard College. Eliot himself would marry into the prominent Peabody family and on strategic occasions would remind himself and others of this fortunate family network. However, as the historian Ronald Story well reminds us, these networks and the hallowed Brahmin stature were a nineteenth-century novelty.[3] Their most remarkable feature was not their range and cohesiveness but rather their ability to create a historical aura, to award themselves a historical legitimacy, and to integrate at times individuals and ideas not exactly coincident with the circle's social and political conservatism. This aura also shielded Eliot's many academic changes from being criticized as hostile to Harvard's best interests.

During the period between 1820 and 1840, industrialists and merchants, particularly those from Salem and its region, gravitated to Boston, to Beacon Hill residences and to officerships in the city's increasingly selective network of charitable organizations, notably Massachusetts General Hospital, the Boston Athenaeum, the Massachusetts Historical Society, Mount Auburn Cemetery, and the Lowell Institute.[4] But most of all, these businessmen assumed control of the Harvard Corporation and shifted the source of school funding from the state and from many individuals to a small cadre of wealthy philanthropists. These individuals replaced the largely ministerial and scholarly members without eliminating them entirely. Their secular habits of close observation, accounting, and above all administration began indirectly to influence the subject matter of the college curriculum. The traditional classical subjects of Latin and Greek plus mathematics and rhetoric found themselves joined by courses in science, history, and modern language and literature. This transformation at Harvard was rapid compared with colleges whose funding and sponsorship would not reflect such entrepreneurial values for another two generations. Still, the challenges to evangelical didacticism, the classics, and quasi-parental mentorship signaled a movement in many American colleges that the old-time curriculum was giving way to technical subjects and organizational skills more reflective of an industrializing society.

The transformation of Boston society and Harvard's governing structure occurred in the very years of Eliot's youth. His enlarged family participated in and benefited from these organizational changes. Eliot himself found greater fascination in the science of chemistry than in many other traditional school subjects, and, it should be noted early on, he cultivated all his life an appreciation for organization that accommodated individualized proclivities. By his own account, his extracurricular work with a Harvard faculty member and a few select associates energized him intellectually more than his formal course of studies. He would reinforce the pattern in his extraordinarily sensitive biography of his son and namesake, Charles Eliot Jr. His son, he readily admitted, struggled with the classics and with formal schooling, though clearly could drive himself with energy and discipline once his interests in nature and the outdoors became primary. His son would first study with the landscape architect Frederick Law Olmsted, then become his partner, in the then nonuniversity study of landscape architecture. But more importantly, his son reinforced Eliot's lifelong assumption that individual talents must be given their head rather than be subordinated by formal regimens.[5]

This firm commitment to individual ingenuity as a force of nature strangely never posed a contradiction to Eliot's renowned achievement of institution building. One might say, following the insight of historian Hugh Hawkins, that these two values—individuality and system—provided the distinctive nineteenth-century bedrock of Eliot's educational ideology.[6] These values registered themselves in Eliot's reputation for his best-known educational promotion, the elective system. However, the actual elective system, that is, choice among courses for seniors and gradually for well-schooled underclassmen, could be found at Harvard and other colleges by the 1830s. Unlike later schoolmen, Eliot did not invoke electives as a wedge against the classics but rather in behalf of a deep-seated belief in lifelong learning. Eliot appreciated a wide range of subjects, many never entertained as university worthy, if only students' engagement with them could be intensively engineered. Precisely how could such engineering occur and be individualized within the standardized process of formal and systematic schooling?

Election alone for Eliot was no panacea and decidedly choice was not realized by a student's subjective options; Eliot's "choice" was the conscious product of an organization that offered curricular alternatives. Students elected courses of study, not merely subjects that took their fancy. In 1869 Eliot inherited a college organization that would take a generation for him to reshape, develop, and mature. The Corporation of Fellows and Overseers had put Harvard at the center of an interlocking urban network and reflected the values of businessmen who distanced themselves in their policy councils from both politicians and clergymen. They also had excluded themselves from an older practice of incorporating faculty members on their board. In 1828 an effort by the faculty to gain such positions was turned back by a legal defense, advanced by Harvard law faculty member Joseph Story (1779–1845) who shortly would be the highest paid member of the university faculty. Since that time faculty acquiesced in their subordinate role to the non-academic corporation and Board of Overseers. Subsequently these bodies selected faculty after close scrutiny of their politics and their reputation for religion (Unitarian) and gentility. One-third of the faculty developed ties by blood or marriage to the board members and experienced the benefits of the urban elite. The upshot was a tacit compatibility of outlook between the board and the faculty, who in turn received salaries considerably higher than most competitive institutions.[7]

By mid-century Harvard had achieved a cohesive institutional culture. The trustees need not fret over the introduction of new subjects or the shift of pedagogy away from recitation to lecture. In a period before mass textbook publication, lecture became the preferred method for widespread dissemination of basic subject material. Even students not formally enrolled in a course could attend. The lecture became a convenient device for organizing a subject and preparing a textbook for use in other colleges. The resources available to Harvard faculty enabled them to produce such books and thereby attach the ensuing authority on the subject to their college. In addition, few worried that the overseers' traditional duty of public examination began to wane as faculty submitted students to written examinations on lecture material (to which overseers were not necessarily privy). The carefully vetted faculty could be entrusted with an increasing educational autonomy and assumption of the examination duty once reserved for the overseers.

The relative lack of controversy over elective courses exemplified the narrow range of diversity within the Harvard culture. Before Eliot became president, freshmen courses were prescribed, as were many of the sophomore offerings. A few electives for juniors and seniors could be chosen from only a short list. Faculty teaching required courses feared the loss of clientele if the elective alternative were introduced. They feared also the hiring of inexperienced teachers and faddish subjects that might dilute the intellectual authority previously accorded to the classics. After 1869 the new president presided over these debates with an easy hand. His own training in chemistry sustained a bias for scientific work, which he associated with fieldwork experience and close laboratory observation. Eliot never denied the pedagogical force of the classics and prided himself on students, like his son, who mastered these subjects, even with difficulty. Eliot began to hire and support scientists who shared his confidence that scientific method equaled the classics in its disciplinary power. The strategic difference for Eliot and his colleagues was that the scientific method was not coincident with specific subjects—as was the argument about the classics with Latin and Greek—but was an intellectual process transmitted by a number of different subjects.

The debates over scientific method remained within a specific pedagogical frame but nevertheless had important organizational and theoretical consequences. The argument that science was a valid educational method legitimated the introduction of many new subjects, at least at Cambridge. By 1884 Eliot had achieved the first completely elective system in the United States, applicable to all classes from freshmen to senior level.[8] Outside of Harvard, electives invited remark and fears of educational anarchy. As this public debate about the classics and science spread, one important dividend was the formation of another generation of educational associations or the energizing of older organizations, like the American Institute of Instruction. More important, the elective system opened a budding national debate that would result in a general expansion of curricular offerings and specializations, including internally the new organization of college instruction by departmental units.

But the central question of the moment, only clear in retrospect, was the nature of the new system that would support both the scientific method and student election of subjects. Historically scholars have attributed Eliot's published essay in the *Atlantic Monthly* as the prescient views of the quintessential educational spokesman of the moment. Actually, Eliot's writings on these subjects were little more than explanations to the Boston public, which, he knew, needed a new clarity about their educational priorities. They were not so much declarations of educational principles as they were probes into the new business consciousness, an experimental bridge between the entrepreneurs and the educators. In his published essays, he was explicit: "No men have greater need of the power of expressing their ideas with clearness, conciseness and vigor than those whose avocations require them to describe and discuss material resources, industrial processes, public works, mining enterprises and the complicated problems of trade and finance. In such writings embellishments may be dispensed with, but the chief merits of style—precision, simplicity, perspicuity and force—are never more necessary."[9] The new industrial complex needed reconciliation with the skills of collegiate culture. Eliot recognized these needs not only from his family's investments and his Harvard network, but also from his experience in teaching both mathematics and chemistry at Harvard. His failure to gain a permanent faculty appointment from Harvard opened him to a European tour of school systems and universities that would offer an alternative to his alma mater's organization and values. He accepted a professorial appointment at the new and innovative school in Cambridge, the land-grant beneficiary known as the Massachusetts Institute of Technology. This offer came to him in Venice as he toured different European school systems and universities, an opportunity to observe both models of organization and alternative scientific apparatus. During this European tour, he met a number of individuals who would become companions in his new university-shaping career.[10]

In the context of his European travels and his work at the new experimental MIT, Eliot offered his nation and his Boston audience the distillation of his insights in two *Atlantic Monthly* articles (February–March 1869), entitled "The New Education: Its Organization," the year he accepted the presidency of Harvard College. The thrust of these writings unmistakably was a call for a new process of scientific training: "What the country needs is a steady supply of men well trained in recognized principles of science and art, and well informed about established practice. . . . Americans must not sit down contented with their position among industrial nations. We have inherited civil liberty, social mobility and immense native resources. The advantages we thus hold over the European nations is inestimable. The question is, not how much our freedom can do for us unaided but how much we can help freedom by judicious education."[11] Eliot added to this conclusion a series of practical suggestions: avoid early theorizing in science but rather begin with commonsense observation before the age seventeen; rely on Latin more than Greek in classical training; recognize that polytechnic training—more urban, more manual, in close proximity to industry and manufactures—differs from collegiate instruction—more bookish, literary, and in need of seclusion from everyday bustle.

Not only did Eliot's essays modify an inherited collegiate tradition—training for the ministry uniquely prepared one for collegiate administration—he opened an argument not only on behalf of science but also for a more complex higher education curriculum and institutional culture.[12] His essays laid the foundation for a more sophisticated generic version of the American university. Surprisingly they actually did not discuss higher learning so much as preparatory training, schooling before age seventeen. Eliot was conscious that American youth differed from European in zest and energy but not so in actual training in multiple subjects. Eliot invested considerable space in his essay to argue the principle of differentiating fact and inference, accumulating a body of experience before organizing the factual mass into a comprehensible theory, clearly a task for higher learning. In the process Eliot embarked on a lifelong career of differentiating precollegiate and collegiate education, of creating for the first time in American education a distinctive *organizational ladder* of instruction, with specified subjects, time frames, and alternative courses of study.

Eliot did not set out to design a generic American university; he began, once offered the Harvard presidency a few months after the appearance of his

Atlantic Monthly essays, only to improve his alma mater, Harvard College. Other scholars understandably have studied Eliot's own scientific proclivities, his failed efforts to merge MIT and Harvard College, and ultimately his university achievements: more students, more faculty, more professional schools, an enlarged plant and endowment (from $325,000 in 1869 to $1 million in 1899).[13] But even more significantly, as his early published essays forecast, Eliot simultaneously cultivated individuals he could trust in the work of preparatory education. One such person was Edwin P. Seaver (1838–1904), whose origins in rural Northboro, Massachusetts, contrasted with Eliot's Brahmin upbringing. Earlier on, Seaver evidenced some precocity toward the teaching profession, and he graduated from the early normal school prototype, Bridgewater (Massachusetts) State Normal School and two years later (1857) from Harvard College with honors. He then taught in a number of rural public schools while participating in the premier professional association of that time, the American Institute of Instruction. He then traveled to Europe, observing educational practice in England, France, and Germany. Upon his return Harvard offered him first a tutorship, then an assistant professorship in mathematics, which he taught for several years (1865–74). Seaver then traveled once again to Europe in 1871–72 and upon his return accepted in 1874 the principalship of Boston's English High School. From this position he wrote and lectured on the need to reorganize the American public high school to ensure an effective, collegiate preparation. Seaver's election to Harvard Board of Overseers in 1879 and again in 1885 signaled Charles Eliot's imprimatur. In 1880 Seaver became superintendent of Boston schools and until his death in 1904 one of New England's preeminent schoolmen.[14]

Seaver was professionally active not only in the American Institute of Instruction since 1858, but he was also a visible presence in the Massachusetts Association of Classical and High School Teachers. There he found himself in a cohort of kindred spirits that included John Tetlow (1843–1911), a graduate of Brown University and Civil War veteran. Tetlow may have first encountered Seaver at the New Bedford Friends' Academy where they both had taught. Tetlow had also traveled in Europe (1868–69), had returned to the principalship of the New Bedford Academy, and had become the son-in-law of the well-reputed New Bedford superintendent of schools, Henry F. Harrington. Tetlow's professional peers expected his next professional promotion to be a college presidency. Instead, he accepted the first headmastership of Boston's Girls' Latin School in 1878, where he proceeded to create the functional model of a high school for collegiate preparation, especially after its merger with Boston's Girls' High School in 1885. After soliciting successfully

Charles W. Eliot's support, Tetlow, Seaver, and others created the New England Association for Colleges and Preparatory Schools in 1885, a major forum for gaining professional schoolmen's support for Eliot's educational ideology. The upshot was an organizational network committed to generic linkages between both preparatory and university institutions.[15]

Initially Eliot's concerns for a new elective system and for fostering student choice concentrated on a "fundamental proposition," especially for the preparatory level: "a man will be productive and happy in his lifework just in proportion to his natural fitness for it. The teacher, mother or father can do nothing better for a boy than to find out, or help him to find out, this innate aptitude."[16] In part, Eliot's endorsement of the elective principle attempted to shift the shaping of aptitude away from the institution and onto the learner himself. So also did the school's diversification of subjects available for study. The organization merely offered opportunities for instruction and was not thought to be an interference with the process of intellectual discovery. At times Eliot would make specific suggestions like shortening grammar or preparatory instruction or of reducing the number of women in teaching (since the work was a temporary respite before their true domestic calling), but the impact of the organization was treated as entirely benign. In Eliot's eyes, school organization, like the social structure afterward, was a neutral force into which intelligent beings "fit" (Eliot's characterization) themselves. The student's option for a course of study became more important than any accommodation of the institution to the student.

Eliot's assumptions about curricular organization gave his proposals for reform both a practical and nonrevolutionary connotation. One of the reasons for proposing changes in the preparatory system was not in any way to adopt an inclusive and democratic admissions system, such as that proposed for the land-grant colleges of the 1860s. Eliot's first concern was to attract students fully prepared in training and commitment for collegiate work. He had to have known, as a graduate of the class of 1853, that Harvard students increasingly came (or should come) from the more affluent class of Bostonians, unlike their earlier counterparts in the 1800s who came from the surrounding counties and other parts of New England. He had to have known that the tuition costs of a Harvard education had risen from roughly $20 per year in 1810 to $104 in 1860. Actual costs were higher, at $225 in 1810 to $700 on average in 1860, more than the annual salary of a respectable workingman's income. Admissions tests had risen, requiring now disciplined training in mathematics and preparatory study of Latin for a year and a half. Such training was often not available except in private boarding schools, like Phillips Andover and Phillips Exeter, competitive schools like Boston Latin, which were unavailable to rural populations or else from private tutors. Not only had the expenses of Harvard risen—without much of an expansion in the average class size (forty-five to fifty-five between 1810 and 1860)—but increasingly only those with privileged preparation stood a chance with the traditional admission testing, which had become by 1850 eight hours long.[17] Eliot had become concerned about the preparatory institutions, since there were not enough of them to ensure Harvard's traditional academic standards, were Harvard to expand. Eliot turned his eye quickly in the 1870s to the relatively few public high schools in the larger New England towns as well as private schools that traditionally had not sent students in critical masses to college.

In 1869 the Harvard Corporation sent Charles W. Eliot's name to their Board of Overseers to become president of the college. The message in effect offered him the presidency of the institution at age thirty-five, which would have been very remarkable had not his essays on "The New Education" made his priorities clear and convincing to the now very cohesive Corporation of Fellows and Board of Overseers. It didn't hurt that several of Eliot's relatives by blood and by marriage served in these bodies. Eliot himself had sat on the Board of Overseers since 1868 and had to be very conscious that the present Harvard Board reflected recent Massachusetts laws that eliminated the ex officio representations of state elected officials. Since 1866 Massachusetts law (by a very narrow majority) put the election of overseers in the hands of Harvard alumni, making the school distinctly private at the every moment when Eliot was about to argue its public responsibilities. The new legislation had ensured that the Corporation of Fellows and the Board of Overseers were more homogeneous in wealth and class than ever before. Yet the boards had taken many months to agree to the selection of Eliot, only after considering others and offering it first to the US ambassador to Britain, Charles Francis Adams. The final vote for Eliot, sixteen to eight, reflected less social or cultural differences and more a generational split, one favoring literary and ministerial individuals, the other favoring a new scientific bent, as Eliot himself had argued in his *Atlantic Monthly* articles.[18] But once he had been voted in and had some time to forge alliances, the differences did little to impede his reforms.

In his inaugural address to his Harvard constituency, Eliot had shifted away from his defense of science in college as well as his sense of the systemic relations between higher and secondary education. Rather, he had to articulate notions about the presidency, the faculty, the curriculum, and higher learning's public responsibility. Eliot had thought about these issues in his two European trips, visiting especially French and German universities, not to mention during debates while on the Harvard faculty in the early 1860s and on the Board of Overseers in 1868. But now his inaugural speech needed to focus and abbreviate a decade of observation and reflection. He began expansively by naming classics and mathematics, science and metaphysics as equally important contributors to intellectual discipline. "We would," he intoned expansively, "have them all, and at their best. . . . There is room for them all in a sound scheme."[19] He noted training in all these subjects paled by comparison to Europe, implicitly signaling early his tacit desire to hire his faculty from European or European-trained scholars. Eventually, he predicted, the preparatory system would permit American colleges to focus on the completion of general education and then to begin the shift to practical applications that characterized the university's professional schools, an area where substantive expansion would distinguish Eliot's tenure. Eliot's speech adeptly placated traditionalists, encouraged experimentation, and idealized an educational system that peaked in collegiate work plus advanced training.

The vehicle for realizing these goals for Eliot was the elective system. Eliot was quick to point out that electives went back several decades at Harvard and elsewhere. It was not a revolutionary or risky development, but it had not been a characteristic throughout the college culture, because in the past Harvard and other colleges necessarily had to compensate for the inadequate training in precollegiate instruction. Eliot made the case for the possibility and public worth of a truly "higher" learning. Near the end of his speech, he began to raise the standard of scholarship to one of new research, that is, beyond mere dissemination of existing knowledge. He was mindful of two impediments that prevented him from insisting on the public benefit of new knowledge. First, Harvard was very selective, expensive, and Boston oriented, which newspapers regularly characterized as "aristocratic." He also faced practical barriers. Expanding the elective system meant many more faculty members and smaller classes. Both translated into an increased need for revenues, which Eliot feared he would have difficulty extracting from the new Boston industrial elite that dominated the Harvard Corporation. Harvard's scholarship system, Eliot knew, was small, the product only of the last fifteen years. The corporation was now about to be called upon to open its doors to students or faculty who would strive to change its long-cultivated priorities.

Eliot's inaugural address had to make a highly selective, indeed privileged, education seem a widespread public benefit. "The community," he argued, "does not owe superior education to all children, but only to the elite—to those who, having the capacity, prove by hard work that they have also the necessary perseverance and endurance."[20] Rich and poor were welcome at Harvard once that capacity was demonstrated. He conceded the poor would encounter difficulties, but such trials were the proof of educational capacity. A community suffered also when its rich were "ignorant and unrefined." These criticisms of both rich and poor students became less important in the face of the one "aristocracy" that Harvard did embrace: "the aristocracy which excels in manly sports, carries off the honors and prizes of the learned professions, and bears itself with distinction in all fields of intellectual labor and combat." Eliot's somewhat disingenuous dismissal of rich and poor pre-college circumstances underscored the institution's claimed indifference to students' origins before entering Harvard. Once in college, Eliot averred, any student's life chances only improved if he sustained his resolve and discipline, gradually clarifying his career objectives. Eliot's Harvard peeled away environmental or inherited impediments to learning by focusing on its central goal: "This University aspires to serve the nation by training men to intellectual honesty and independence of mind. . . . A university is built, not by a sect, but by a nation."[21] Though indirectly, the community and the nation shaped its intellectual resources and talent via its university organization and measured success by their graduates' future careers.

To some extent Eliot had begun the construction of a powerful argument about higher education by focusing not on the university but rather on the learner and the community and nation outside its walls. In one respect, he had broadened the university's aegis; on the other hand, he obscured the post–Civil War configuration of the institution by concentrating on intellectual discipline rather than subject matter. Particularly by avoiding any privileged attitude toward science over classics, Eliot distanced himself from an existing faculty division. By concentrating on a broadly conceived general education based on electives, Eliot reduced the university's obligation to course offerings and a class-neutral admission process. Eliot in a sense had pressured preparatory institutions to upgrade and measure their success by college entrance and had positioned Harvard as a mature environment in which intellectually grounded students could make choices on their own behalf. He then added another litmus test for a prestige university. The real test of the university, research and new knowledge, would rest on the professional schools, which took their cues from the nation's industrial complex. In these programs the new president expected and realized his ambitions on behalf of "practical" subjects. There the university could bestow prestige and legitimacy on advanced work that hitherto had not been associated with higher education. With his elective system, new admissions policies, and new graduate research programs, Eliot's Harvard embarked on the generic development of the American university.

In his first decade as president, Eliot concentrated on the older, professional schools of divinity, law, and medicine. He was supremely conscious of the absence of "general education" backgrounds among the faculty of these schools. Other university leaders tended not to support Eliot's effort to make a full course of college study the prerequisite for admission to professional schools. James McCosh of Princeton thought the professional schools already offered some of the courses that entering collegians needed. Even at the turn of the century, William Rainey Harper of Chicago and Arthur Hadley of Yale thought professional training could begin before the regular collegiate course was completed.[22] Until the twentieth century, many professional schools admitted students directly from high school, and, it should be noted, were not high-paying professions in obvious need of increased schooling. Eliot succeeded in making a bachelor's degree a prerequisite first in the divinity school and lastly in 1901 in the medical school. This college standard remained problematic until the 1920s.[23]

Even more problematic was the emergence of new industrial careers for which there was no actual professional training. Eliot had himself served on the faculty of the Lawrence Scientific School at Harvard in its early years. He had been mindful of the animus against such practical training in the sciences and the intimations of "vocationalism" that some literary traditions associated with hands-on instruction. Eliot had also served on the early faculty of MIT and did his utmost to design there a model curriculum, based on his earlier experience in Harvard's science labs. At times Eliot gathered support by arguing new technical schools left literary and classical training to their special niche. Still, in his 1869 inaugural address, he emphasized the power of the traditional subjects but insistently equated the study of the sciences among the building blocks of the new university. His appointment of Christopher C. Langdell (1826–1906) as law school dean helped usher in a more scientific preparation for the law via the case-study method.[24] Langdell introduced a method based on the pattern of decision making in actual cases rather than designing a law school on the model of law office. His more "scientific" standard of the "case-study" law powerfully influenced law schools nationwide by the turn of the century.

Eliot also took on the challenge of responding to the demands on new fields of study to become more scientific. To some extent the success of the case-study method of the law school put indirect pressure on subjects that had not been based on scientific methods, like educational pedagogy or humanistic study. Eliot tried to respond to those issues. Early in his presidency, he began to speak to and participate in educational meetings in the Boston environs. His work in founding the New England Association of Colleges and Preparatory Schools in 1885 associated him with educational reformers. Eliot had many practical suggestions enthusiastically supported by teachers, especially the argument for teacher tenure based on successful practice and for teacher pensions. However, on two points Eliot began to face an educational countercurrent: first, his reluctance to accord women teachers professional status and, second, his sense that pedagogy could be readily mastered via lectures, since it was not a science. The increasing success of the Massachusetts model of normal school training, first introduced in 1838 at the Bridgewater State Normal School, had by the 1880s given rise to a second generation of state-supported institutions for teacher training. These schools had succeeded in culling many talented youth who might have gone on to colleges like Harvard. For all these reasons, Eliot opposed the expansion of state-supported normal schools, and in 1891—in the face of public money creating in Boston a normal college with postgraduate courses—he proposed to experiment at Harvard with teacher training as a university subject.[25]

The "Harvard Normal" offered lectures in all the basic subjects of public school instruction and also arranged internships in local Cambridge schools. One long-term dividend of this exercise was William James's (1842–1910) lectures and subsequent book, *Talks to Teachers*. In addition, Prussian-born Paul Hanus (1855–1941) (with a bachelor's degree from the University of Michigan but no professional training) lectured on the theory of education and provided a presence for professional university training throughout his career. However, the practical, hands-on experience that Eliot associated with science was never part of Harvard's teacher-training agenda. Its absence incensed the professional teachers' associations and Bridgewater graduate Albert E. Winship (1845–1933), who edited the influential *Journal of Education* from 1886 to his death. In 1891, the very year of Harvard's experiment, Winship urged Harvard to follow the normal school model, as had Johns Hopkins, the University of Pennsylvania, the University of Michigan, and recently Columbia's new Teachers College. "We say unhesitatingly," Winship editorialized, "that unless the whole philosophy upon which normal school work in Germany, France and America has rested is radically wrong, this Harvard course cannot meet the demand for high normal school training in Massachusetts. It is not information about methods but training in methods that has been demanded."[26] Eliot actually never seemed to want these educational lectures to train teachers but rather to offer Harvard's imprimatur to school supervisors and educational experts.[27] Education never reached the status of university-based profession at Harvard during his tenure.

The situation was very different in another area where Eliot approached the possibilities with great personal investment and indeed imagination. His eldest son, Charles Eliot Jr. (1859–97), had reacted against the formal instruction of schooling from his elementary days. An able enough student in most subjects, the younger Eliot experienced great difficulties in classical training, still for his era necessary for college admission. His true love was the outdoors, especially at the family retreat on Mount Desert Island. Sailing and hiking were young Charles's natural element, and he organized in college an amateur expedition to document the flora and fauna of the island. He negotiated Harvard's entrance exams but received two conditions on his Greek test. Through diligence and coursework, he had the conditions removed within a year. His métier was science, where he thrived on the detail and the hands-on examination, skills his father inherently appreciated. Upon graduation, the young Eliot could not find his scientific niche, and with great and gentle understanding his father urged him to take his time and not rush into a career that did not fit. For a few months, Charles studied at Harvard's Bossey Institute, a nascent school of agriculture.

Fortuitously, on his son's behalf, the senior Eliot consulted his brother-in-law and successful Boston architect Robert Peabody (1845–1917), as well as his friend Frederick Law Olmsted (1822–1903). Out of these discussions came Olmsted's offer to permit young Charles to apprentice in landscape architecture in his office. The fit was perfect. Charles went from a basic and successful apprenticeship to a European tour of gardens, landscape design, public parkland, and a range of natural conservatories and libraries. His letters home and his meticulous and sharply observed notes impressed and pleased his father, who clearly projected the experience into a prototype of adaptation to a scientific career. Upon his return to Boston in 1893, Olmsted made Eliot a partner in the firm and steered him into a large and responsible work in the design of the Boston Fens and the development of Boston's Municipal Park System. At the peak of his career, during the final design of White Park in Concord, New Hampshire, young Charles contracted a rare case of meningitis and died. The senior Eliot over many years organized his son's personal and professional papers, and then wrote a moving and fascinating biography, *Charles Eliot: Landscape Architect* (1924). His son's singular career convinced Eliot of the power of designed environment as much on educational sites as on cities; the older Eliot worked with Frederick Law Olmsted to make landscape architecture (and later regional planning) a university-based career and a unit of Harvard's School of Applied Science (originally the Lawrence Scientific School, where the senior Eliot had taught).[28] By the end of the twentieth century, this unit had become the independent Harvard Graduate School of Design, one of the stellar consequences of Eliot's insistence on "scientific" reforms.

The elder Eliot's organizational abilities manifested themselves throughout his entire presidency. Eliot had characterized the new university president in 1869 as a "constitutional executive" not a dictator. His sense of his own role always involved the Harvard Corporation, which he had said was the heart of the university. In addition, the alumni-elected Board of Overseers, all thirty of them, provided a double check on the corporation's decisions and represented external influences and ideas. But the pattern in this complex edifice was increasingly to reduce the teaching responsibilities of the faculty, increase the endowment to cover such a change, and very gradually as the twentieth century approached to liberate the faculty's research talents. This particular priority, only faintly acknowledged in 1869, received accelerated attention when Johns Hopkins University in 1876 became primarily a graduate institution committed to generating new knowledge rather than collegiate teaching as its first priority.[29] Where Eliot had earlier on (and later also) highly valued Harvard-trained appointments, by the end of the nineteenth century, pressured by Johns Hopkins competition, he became more attracted to faculty of genuine promise and established reputations outside Harvard's orbit.

Emphatically the heart of Eliot's university was the corporation, but the public image rested with the newly organized Graduate School of Arts and Sciences in 1890. This new organizational unit had its dean, like the three professional schools (divinity, law, and medicine), but here Eliot himself presided, using the dean as a subordinate. Here Eliot ensured a melding of traditional and innovative subjects and where the full impact of his elective system—by 1886 a feature of all four undergraduate classes—had its distinctive characteristic effect. Not only did choosing electives signal the maturity of Harvard's student body, the system argued a new faculty freedom to pursue in smaller classes the specialized work that characterized their research. The twofold effect tended to blur graduate and collegiate forms of instruction and resisted the University of Chicago solution of dividing faculty into undergraduate and graduate layers. Unlike many Harvard alumni, Eliot did not fret about overspecialization but was concerned with the departmentalization of subjects. The departments tended to participate in larger councils in increasingly self-interested fashion, unwilling too often for Eliot's taste, to put the university's interests over the departments'. Like his instruction to his son, Eliot sought open discussions and critical debate in order that the university's larger purpose would continue to fit into both Boston and national society.

Eliot's organizational achievement appeared in concrete form with the reorganization of the physical campus, made especially dramatic with the erection of Sever Hall (1880). Originally designed as a classroom with a large lecture hall and art gallery on the top floor, the building became not only a breakthrough piece of architecture for the designer, Henry Hobson Richardson (1838–86), a Harvard graduate (class of 1859), but in the designer's eye a device for integrating the Harvard Yard buildings that had been constructed over two centuries. Sever Hall, considered one of Richardson's early masterpieces, used crimson brick to blend with the eighteenth-century buildings of the yard, which had not achieved a complete collegiate cloister. Richardson integrated not only the colonial traditions but here demonstrated his predominant, Romanesque style, especially in the central welcoming doorway facing its Cambridge neighbors on Quincy Street. The architect, like the school's president, had made a career out of innovative design experiments but also worked toward the integration of multiple traditions and practical uses. His beautifully proportioned yet varied use of window sets to establish horizontality combined with three-story bay towers emphasized variations within a basic monumental symmetry. The new order simultaneously reinvented the yard while accepting the interaction of learning and a larger industrializing society.[30] Sever Hall set in motion Harvard's response to the late nineteenth-century need for campus integrity and a graphic cohesion of its multiple objectives.

By contrast, at the end of his presidency Eliot oversaw the construction of Widener Library (1914) in an imposing monument in the new Beaux-Arts style. The Widener culminated Eliot's building record, which included thirty-five buildings, twenty-two of which were gifts of individuals who often preferred their own architect. Since at least seven times their "free choice" went to Robert S. Peabody, Eliot's distinguished brother-in-law, the president did not need to intervene.[31] Six of these buildings required subscription drives that tended to organize the alumni behind significant and tangible improvements. But the final contribution of Eliot's tenure was this new centralizing library design in a Beaux-Arts style. Its sheer size, so disproportionate to the other yard dormitories and classrooms, created the largest university library in the country and overwhelmed the Harvard Yard with an edifice devoted emphatically to research and scholarship. The building arose out of a donation from the mother of an alumnus, Harry Elkins Widener (class of 1907), who perished on the *Titanic*. Widener's noted personal library had always been intended for Harvard to upgrade the volumes in its predecessor, Gore Hall. For the library's design, the Philadelphia donor selected the Philadelphia architectural firm of Horace Trumbauer and Associates, who in turn selected their chief designer, Julian F. Abele (1881–1950), a graduate of the University of Pennsylvania and of Paris's L'École des Beaux-Arts. Abele, the first African American graduate of the University of Pennsylvania, applied the principles of the geometric Beaux-Arts style, its paring away of vernacular traditions, its expansive and elegant Renaissance classicism, its imposing insistence on public order, and its success in suborning individual to larger social interests.[32] If the new library clearly stated the prominence of learning on Harvard's landscape, its incongruity with its older, neighboring buildings testified that Eliot's organizational skills were not always dominant and indeed had waned considerably in the face of twentieth-century trends.

Harvard's own character took on a distinctive university form by the end of the century. It was in no small way a function of Eliot's design for precollegiate education and his work on the National Education Association's Committee of Ten. Eliot's own record in both precollegiate and university planning began in the 1870s and changed in intensity and purpose in the 1890s as he helped both preparatory and collegiate institutions to align their distinctive organizations in relation to each other. Harvard had distinguished itself with the public promotion of its "elective system." It had developed a policy structure via the president and fellows making policy decisions with the Board of Overseers providing both monitoring of those policies and linkages with the wider Boston society. Its very cohesiveness and Eliot's personal embodiment of "Brahmin" values kept the decision-making forces in close harmony. This cohesion enabled Harvard, unlike the more heterogeneous social context of other colleges and universities, to expect student "elections" of courses to function within a relatively manageable range of choices. The institution controlled the number and content of course offerings from which students could choose, which provided an indirect control on "free choice." By the 1880s Eliot had participated in sufficient educational organizations to feel confident in exporting the elective principle down this new organizational ladder to preparatory high schools and academies and thereby guarantee a continuous student flow to his university system.

In 1892 the National Education Association (NEA) sought to put some order in the range of secondary school curricula and turned to Charles Eliot, whose reputation for administration and design had achieved a national audience. Eliot went to work with alacrity to create a systemic curriculum for American secondary schools, one completely calibrated to his brand of university, focused on scholarship and privileging research at a truly advanced level. Eliot's role in this enterprise was both administrative and strategic. Ideologically Eliot's participation in New England associations like the New England Association for College and Preparatory Schools, as well as the American Institute of Instruction, had put him in a dialogue with college-educated schoolmen, like John Tetlow and Edwin Seaver. That success did not translate into immediate national action. The NEA had unevenly tried to use its annual conferences to discuss secondary and collegiate coordination. That organization had limped through the last years of the 1880s hampered by lack of resources, great separating distances from coast to coast, and a small number of days to reach face-to-face agreement. James H. Baker (1848–1925), a native of Maine and graduate of Bates College in Lewiston, had migrated to Denver where he served as principal of its public high school. Baker had badgered his NEA fellows to contribute their thoughts on a range of issues about systemic coordination between secondary and college instruction. He sought for his patchwork synthesis on "uniformity" a serious hearing at the NEA meeting in 1892 in Saratoga, New York. He invited Charles Eliot in particular to be present and, upon receiving his agreement, sent out select invitations to prominent and representative schoolmen from high schools, prep schools, colleges, and universities. Eliot, however, was the key presence and at the pivotal meeting proposed an ambitious plan of many nationwide conferences, orchestrated by an umbrella Committee of Ten. For the 1892 meeting, the NEA elected Baker president, and, back home in Denver, he moved from the high school principalship to the presidency of University of Colorado in Boulder, where he served for the next twenty-two years.[33]

Eliot, who would chair the NEA Committee of Ten, had lectured to the NEA at the 1892 conference "Undesirable and Desirable Uniformity in American Schools." He was adamant that one curriculum not be imposed on all. The obligation of systemic instruction was to cultivate rather than smother individual initiative and curiosity. But the very responsibility of dealing with groups of individuals suggested that there be some desirable uniformity, some way of assessing student progress and achievement. Among the nine individuals who accepted service on the Committee of Ten, six were university faculty or university presidents, all mindful of the need for more uniform admission standards. All had graduated from college; only one, James Mackenzie (1852–1931), had normal school experience.[34] Though James H. Baker began as a secondary schoolman, by the end of 1893 he led a university, leaving only three members representing the secondary educational level. Several of the nine had taught in both elementary and secondary schools. Only one of these, Oscar Robinson of Albany, New York, represented the American public high schools. The other two represented private college-preparatory schools: Lawrenceville in New Jersey and Tetlow's hybrid Boston's Girls' High and Latin School. The American educational system by 1892 had not achieved clear distinctions between "levels," which also varied regionally. The nine members' careers reflected the absence of clear career trajectories, like Baker's from high school to university presidency. Tetlow himself had also begun by teaching at the college level but ultimately committed to a high school career. Still, there was a collegiate bias, not only in actual numbers but also in the six members who graduated from New England colleges, including, of course, Eliot himself.

The collegiate weighting of the committee did not preclude a range of differences over curricular matters. However, all were united on the role of a new design to be determined by practicing schoolmen, like themselves. Although several, like William Torrey Harris (1835–1909), wanted a traditional classical mandate, most of the others desired a reexamination of Latin and Greek's dominance. There seemed to be tacit agreement that only by the modification of the classics would there be time and space for alternative subjects, especially history and modern languages (which meant French and German). Eliot worked hard to enhance the committee's power and influence and to expand the committee's data and expertise to do so. He used the NEA budget of $2,500 to mail questionnaires and to fund travel to regional conferences. He and his committee had developed nine subject focus groups with ten different members each. He provided them with largely technical questions concerning, for example, the hour parameters for instruction. Within this context, Eliot began to work out four programs: classical, Latin-scientific, modern languages, and English, which mixed the emphases on different subjects. No one curriculum would be imposed on any group of students; all student groups could fit their distinct talents into curricular preferences that would uncover their special gifts.[35]

The ninety individuals participating in the focus groups submitted to the Committee of Ten reports with surprising cohesion. Most gratifying to Eliot was the agreement that teaching should be the same for students whether they went to college or not. A well-disciplined mind was a social resource, whatever a person's subsequent career. Many schoolmen, including Eliot, were mindful of the small size of the college-age cohort in the 1890s. As Eliot was to state later, only 10 percent of graduates of elementary schools went on to high school, and only 10 percent of them went on to college. In 1900 under 3 percent of the United States' college-age cohort actually attended college. While these numbers meant college was a highly privileged experience, they also signified how selective both public and private high schools were. The high school would not become a mass institutional experience—with 50 percent of the high school age cohort in high school—until the 1930s. Therefore, Eliot's Committee of Ten report presented an elective schema that applied to a small minority of American youth. Even those who had little or no Latin necessarily came from families who could afford to have their adolescents remain outside the workforce and not become economic contributors to the family income. Still, many educators declared the multitract system a strategy against a single, regimenting caste system in America, a topic about which Eliot and his collegiate colleagues on the committee remained very circumspect.[36]

Eliot's important work as chair of the Committee of Ten concentrated on the elective principle: students have different talents and will pursue them if school instruction is not overly rigid and uniform. "Uniformity," he had famously pronounced, "is the curse of the American school."[37] The election he had in mind was not a classical training for college-oriented youth and "English" courses for those entering the workforce instead of advanced schooling. In his mind the elective groupings ideally concentrated on the power of learning, which schooling at all levels had in common. In fact, this important argument became Eliot's retort to critics who claimed the Committee of Ten was a thinly veiled apologia favoring collegiate-oriented students. In his earliest defense of the committee, Eliot addressed the American Institute of Instruction in 1894, claiming his committee's work was "education construction" rather than "educational reform." The collective aim was to commit all levels of education to their basic commonality. His speech, "The Unity of Educational Reform," sought to reduce the wide range of schools, educational levels, and pedagogies. "In this process of education construction, so new, so strange and so hopeful," Eliot argued, "I believe the chief principles and objects are the same from the kindergarten through the university."[38] Those principles—the individuation of instruction, power in action as the true end of education, the selection of studies, the appeal to permanent rather than temporary motives for controlling conduct, the specialization of teaching, and the right principles of organization—applied to all education worth the name. Distinction of size, numbers of students, and virtually all contextual pressures became secondary in the face of these unifying principles.

Eliot had articulated a new ideology of education that, unlike his antebellum predecessors, did not focus on inculcation of moral values but on inculcation of skills and a lifelong discipline. His ideal school increasingly took no explicit responsibility for class origins or subsequent career as a measure of institutional efficacy. Eliot had narrowed the range of the school's work, correctly, as he himself noted, to "school construction" rather than educational reform. The construction was to produce an individual of "self-control" who would lead a decently civic life. The school should not try to dictate the outcome of individual careers, since it could not. Indeed the school could not really engineer the fit of individual student and subject matter. What the school could do was to keep the subjects diverse, encourage a student to cultivate his proclivities, and try to keep the selection of career from occurring prematurely. The teacher's role was central here, but in this newly complex organization the superintendent and administrator provided, not guarantees, but an additional layer of monitoring for the student's adaptive process.

Eliot's new institutional ideology became primarily technical and practical; it left the substantive moral decisions to the individual student rather than the school. Eliot offered no measures for the success or accuracy of his new administrative stratagems. They would manifest themselves in the later careers and contributions of a school's graduates. Projecting such judgments into the future and emphasizing the basic unity of educational work gave Eliot the context for a new argument about education in a democracy. Popular education cannot be satisfied with reading, writing, and ciphering; it also cannot mean the education of everyone to the highest standard. Individuals differ in their circumstances, in their talents, and in their choices. Schooling should train up all, however, to understand that "the supreme attainment for any individual is vigor and the loveliness of character."[39] Part of this training involved a sense of the limited mastery of any individual in a single subject. Concomitantly the mark of an educated person would ideally be to recognize the mastery of others who have different training capacities. "Confidence in experts, and willingness to employ them and abide by their decisions, are among the best signs of intelligence in an educated individual or an educated community; and in any democracy which is to thrive, this respect and confidence must be felt strongly by a majority of the population."[40] True individuation rested, Eliot felt, on informed deference to a select group of one's fellows. His lifelong promotion of an elective system rested on his confidence in the stability of Boston and New England's social and cultural environments and in America's industrial leaders.

The actual margin of error in any elective system became thereby very limited. The locus of individuation lay within each individual and could not be standardized or rendered uniform or precisely measured (and only by the future success of graduates' careers). However, the school that promoted this new democratic ideology of process depended on the inculcation, not of moral or religious dogma, but of the confidence in the institutional enterprise and on the limited power of self-determined choice within an established framework. "Democratic education," Eliot concluded, "should also inculcate on every child the essential unity of a democratic community, in spite of the endless diversities of function, capacity, and achievement among the individuals who compose the community. . . . For unity is attainable, while equality of conditions is unnatural and unattainable. . . . This unity in freedom is the social goal of democracy, the supreme good of all ranks of society, of the highest no less than of the lowest." The result, he claimed, was a distinctive "democratic nobility."[41]

Eliot's ideology had inflated difference to mask the exploitative character of privilege. His oxymoron, democratic nobility, and his seemingly genteel defense of class advantage offered a powerful argument for colleges like Harvard and the new institutions like Johns Hopkins, Clark, and Chicago, which laid claim to the generic term "university" via an emphasis on research. All had the benefit of large initial endowments generally from men with minimal education but extraordinary business success.[42] All used the antebellum denominational college as a conceptual foil to measure their different orientation, in spite of the antebellum colleges' actual record in science, electives, and other innovations that the universities tried to possess for themselves.[43] Like Eliot, many of the forceful voices leading the new university model assumed very condescending attitudes toward the proliferating normal schools due to their successful inroads into the available student pool at the end of the century.[44] The new university leadership developed a remarkably unified network, which took their new evangelizing in behalf of science, research, and university instruction into the national arena. With speeches to large groups and small, then publishing them as articles in periodicals like the *Outlook*, *Atlantic Monthly*, and so on, which approached large public audiences, the new university men promoted their privileged vision as an American innovation that worked for the benefit of all.[45] Eliot's perception about the power of bureaucratic institutions soft-pedaled the layering and stratification of power and responsibility in both the university and the nation. He was confident that "pupils should be taught that what is virtue in one human being is virtue in any group of human beings, large or small—a village, a city, or a nation; that the ethical principles which should govern an empire are precisely the same as those which should govern an individual; and that selfishness, greed, falseness, brutality and ferocity are as hateful and degrading in a multitude as they are in a single savage."[46] Whatever those ethical principles were, Eliot had amplified them to a new level of abstraction. In the process, he had extended the power and aegis of the university to ensure their proper interpretation or interpretations. The unifying force of a new educated democratic elite not only created a new American corporation with national aspirations; it reinterpreted a privileged elite as the necessary democratizing element in a new industrial culture.

Besides the problems of class and power, Eliot's educational writings needed to address religious issues, especially the inherited commitment to nondenominationalism. This new elite of university presidents required something more than a rhetorical promise that the future would bear witness to the university's democratic modernization. Eliot's Unitarianism had dogged him from his earliest years. Many competitors in the smaller denominational college pressed him on the religious character of the new graduate. How could morality be transmitted without the special coherence of doctrinal dogma? If the modern university promoted nondenominational ethics, his critics asked, would the result be moral clarity or ambiguity? Eliot never distanced himself from religious study as a part of the university curriculum, yet the introduction of newer, more scientific courses necessary qualified the antebellum preeminence of the college president's course in moral philosophy. For many colleges the continuation of this unifying, capstone tradition increasingly became a distinctive badge of honor.[47] Eliot's response held to his pattern of organizational solutions to normative problems: reorganize the traditional place of religious study in the undergraduate curriculum; find the appropriate faculty member; urge that person to give a "practical" application to religious instruction, compatible with the hands-on laboratory work that distinguished university instruction.

Eliot did not have to search far, and in 1881 named his brother-in-law Francis Greenwood Peabody (1847–1936) professor of social ethics. The faculty position was an intellectual way station between the evangelical didacticism of the divinity school and the applied philosophy of Harvard's philosopher, William James.[48] Peabody had graduated from Harvard College (1869) and the divinity school (1872). He then went to Germany's University of Halle for further study, where he developed an inductive approach to human nature and ethical activity. Between his return to the United States in 1873 and his Harvard appointment (1881), Peabody served as minister of the First Parish Church (Unitarian) in Cambridge. His appointment as the Parkman Professor of Theology also involved a legitimating formal linkage to the divinity school. His first course, however, was open to undergraduates and entitled "Ethical Theories and Moral Reform."[49] In 1906 Harvard would consolidate its several courses in ethical problems into the Department of Social Ethics. Until his retirement in 1913, Peabody taught a large portion of the Harvard undergraduates. In addition to academic study, he encouraged his students successfully to volunteer their energy in actual city places and institutions, much like the contemporary social settlement workers in the pursuit of social reform. Peabody's successful publishing and teaching career, his attraction of outside philanthropy to the cause of social ethics and the creation of a Museum of Social Ethics, all informed a new religious idealism. Peabody embodied Eliot's ideal of ethical applications, interdisciplinary linkages to other departments, and student enthusiasm. Most of all, Peabody strengthened the image of religious instruction at Harvard without subscribing to overt denominational evangelizing. In retrospect, it was a holding action against the new university religion of science that in the early twentieth century would overwhelm older religious and ethical elements in the university's culture.[50]

The generic university Eliot sought did not in the end create a blueprint for other comparable institutions. He set his sights on research and teaching at an advanced level, but everywhere "advancement" was contingent upon a student's skills at entry and financial resources. His plans, however, did have some clear victories. Admissions tests fluctuated but gradually displaced the classics with other studies. Undergraduate instruction did become surrounded by new professional schools, most of which were quasi-autonomous and rarely welded into a coherent university spirit. Institutional growth and campus development often proceeded in an ad hoc fashion dependent upon philanthropic donations or alumni whims. Religious affiliations, never completely rejected, were also worn very lightly and, like Harvard, removed chapel attendance as a school requirement. In all these areas, Eliot's achievement by 1909, his last year as Harvard's president, marked features attached to any university, but nationwide the variations were so multiple that the real generic university lay in the minds of its beholders more than in actuality.[51] Eliot's lasting contribution to American higher education was the generic problem he posed for university and college leaders: exactly how did an increasingly selective school contribute to America's democratic tradition?

Whatever its limits, Eliot's ideology expressed a collage of assumptions about higher learning that stretched far beyond Eliot himself, beyond Harvard and New England. His assumptions about the benign impact of formal organization, the shaping force of individual choice, the ability of schools to train and screen a new leadership class, his intent that science become a disciplined process of inquiry, which reworked earlier notions of advanced education, became essential elements of late nineteenth-century academic culture (generational culture #4). The disparagement of denominational collegiate training helped advance this new mind-set, centered in the idea of a university, but also by its very insistence documented how forceful the denominational tradition continued to be even into the twentieth century. It was largely Charles W. Eliot and his fellow university presidents that projected the advantages of higher learning—its science, its special campus locus, and its systemic organization—on a society and a governmental structure that had not made educational advancement a social priority. Eliot's argument and his transformation of Harvard College into a university standard set a new agenda for his generation's distinctive academic culture from the later decades of the nineteenth century into the early years of the twentieth century.

CHAPTER SEVEN

Educated Women and the Inflation of Domesticity

In 1908 President Charles W. Eliot of Harvard University addressed the Association of Collegiate Alumnae (founded 1881). Here he had a chance to redress his 1869 inaugural stipulations that women would not be permitted to study at Harvard. Almost forty years had passed, and he had witnessed many changes, some of them—like the creation of women's colleges—nearly unprecedented at the time of his 1869 speech. To the female graduates who composed his audience, Eliot began with praise for their enhancement of social welfare. In his eyes this achievement, however, was an attribute of educated women giving domestic concerns their highest priority. He moved beyond his earlier sentiments and acknowledged women's ability to handle "men's studies." But this parity did not argue for coeducation or even for women competing with men in school or in the professions. Women's colleges, he insisted, should devote themselves exclusively to studies geared to women's greatest single occupation, child-rearing. "The one great occupation for women," Eliot intoned, "is the most important occupation there is in the world. It calls, and calls loudly, and often calls in vain, for carefully trained mental powers as well as great moral powers. . . . I look forward therefore to the future of higher education for women as a [preparation for] life, of family life, of household joy and good."[1] In spite of a century of argument and experimentation, and a historical record that documented women's intellectual and economic work beyond "domesticity," Eliot's words indicated the powerful resilience of America's educational leadership endorsing separate gender spheres.

In part, Eliot's conservative remarks rooted themselves in his preoccupation with the limits of schooling. In his eyes, colleges and universities, no less than other schools, were not primarily places of reform; they were rather "opportunities" for individuals to refine and improve their native talents. The new university structure held much promise but only with a particular brand of self-discipline, of not flying in the face of nature's dicta, of not responding to male and female needs as if they were the same. Still, another part of Eliot's argument lay with the implicit competitions set up by the record of women's higher education in the last third of the nineteenth century. While the college population had more than tripled in these years, the numbers of collegiate women had increased eightfold. In the first two decades of the twentieth century, this group would expand an additional sixfold, a large percentage of whom would be daughters of collegiate alumnae.[2] Women had rapidly achieved a critical mass, particularly in the state coeducational universities and had begun to provide an able cadre of female administrators, who understood personally the pros and cons that domestic values had upon higher education. In 1908 Eliot might well be seen as working to stem this advance by expanding "domesticity" modestly, to quasi-domestic work like teaching or nursing to collegiate women.

However, the Association of Collegiate Alumnae (ACA) was not an ideologically homogeneous body.[3] Its first generation of members (roughly 1881–1901) operated more forcefully than their successors as innovators and activists, but both generational groups contained women who worried overly that advanced study was inimical to women's health. The association had become controversial with the publication of Harvard Medical School faculty member Edward Clarke's (1820–77) 1873 book, *Sex in Education*, which purported to give the authority of medical science to the perception that book learning damaged women's health. Later G. Stanley Hall (1844–1924), a noted psychologist and president of Clark University in Worcester, Massachusetts, would actually argue that overly trained women set civilization on a course of race suicide. His evidence followed from documentation that educated women seemed to be producing fewer children than their less educated counterparts, a phenomenon that scholars had monitored and worried over for much of the nineteenth century.[4] Indirectly the ACA responded to issues of educating women by investing much of its energy into ranking female colleges and fund-raising to support capable women. They also sought to evade the criticism entirely by sending select individuals overseas to prestigious European universities.[5] The organization had the potential to be a voice for those demanding equalizing reforms that Eliot and his confreres held suspect.

The more conservative female leaders held sway, however, and the tempered tradition of idealized domesticity characterized the careers of even activist nineteenth-century women educators and writers. The first cohorts of pioneering women educators, notably, Zilpah Grant (1794–1874), Emma Willard (1839–98), Almira Phelps (1793–1884), Catharine Beecher (1800–1878), and Mary Lyon (1797–1849), achieved their deserved notoriety by advancing an academically rigorous model for female instruction. Their insistence on literature or "belles lettres," history, science, and the languages did not ignore drawing, music, manners, pronunciation, sewing, and other more domestic subjects. However, the inclusion of demanding intellectual studies associated with their schools—Ipswich Seminary, Troy Female Seminary, the Patapsco Institute, Hartford Female Seminary, and Mount Holyoke Seminary—established model institutions and, even more, informal networks that extended well beyond their immediate New England and Middle Atlantic regions.[6] These early schools, however, faced all the difficulties of fund-raising and student recruitment of their male counterparts. Even more, the majority of advanced educational institutions before the Civil War always cultivated local allegiances, whatever their larger aspirations. While their intellectual aspirations set them off from many competitor schools, their values alone were not sufficiently widespread to attract more than a select few.

The advances in the national economy shortly before and especially after the Civil War changed the context for a new growth and saw a changing sociological cohort of men and women with new views and social resources. Women entered "higher" educational institutions in greater proportions and set the context for a few new, well-endowed colleges for women, like Vassar (founded 1865), Smith (chartered 1871 and opened its doors 1875), and Wellesley (founded 1875).[7] However, these advantaged schools accounted for a very small percentage of educated-oriented women. In larger part, the reason for this expanding female pool of aspiring students had to do with a strategic shift in the demographic profile of women at mid-century. During the first half of the nineteenth century, families' life chances became modified by the new industrialization clashing with an inherited agricultural culture. All the children of large families could not be supported by family farms, and families without property had to consider older unmarried children as a liability to family resources. Families began to plan particularly for female children, expecting for them a basic education, then marriage. Without disrupting this traditional career pattern, by mid-century increasing years separated the completion of education (fourteen to fifteen) and a marriage contract (twenty-one to twenty-five). Industrial work often meant the departure of marriageable males for other communities or accommodated at the very least mobility patterns unfamiliar to localized farming cultures. The postponement of marriage and the possibilities of spinsterhood turned many families' attention toward additional education in the widening limbo years between grammar school instruction and marriage.[8] The aim was to enhance women's marriageable prospects or their economic self-sufficiency. Particularly teacher training became the foremost occupational training path for women (and many male college graduates) for most of the nineteenth century.

The majority of women self-consciously seeking additional instruction filled teaching-oriented female seminaries like Mount Holyoke (founded 1837) and after 1837 took advantage of teacher-training normal schools. Like Mount Holyoke, students at Bridgewater State Normal School (founded 1840) in Massachusetts, predominately women, ranged in age from sixteen to nineteen, and enrolled with far fewer mature (over twenty-one) students than male colleges in the middle of the nineteenth century.[9] Both the seminaries and the normal schools reflected the impact of industrial pressures on the female student pools. Until late in the nineteenth century, the normal schools and most female seminaries sought institutional linkages to the emerging city grammar schools and the few high schools rather than to women's colleges, since their students came from these schools and would return there to teach. The scholarly ideal as a preeminent educational goal rarely served to measure achievement or efficacy, except in a few rare exceptions like the graduates of Bryn Mawr in the later 1880s under M. Carey Thomas (1857–1935).[10] Bryn Mawr's record set an unusual pattern with 90 percent of its graduates working during their lives, 53 percent remaining unmarried, and 10 percent becoming academics.[11] No other school approached that pattern in the first two generations of women pursuing higher education.

The lives of Bryn Mawr students differed from those at other colleges or normal schools of the time, especially in their preparation in private institutes or academies.[12] There is probably no way to improve upon the estimate of Henry Barnard (later the first US commissioner of education and longtime editor of the *American Journal of Education*) that in 1850 there existed approximately six thousand academies in the United States enrolling a quarter of a million students, about 6 percent of the relevant youth cohort.[13] Into this catchall category went academies, institutes, seminaries, and sometimes colleges, both legally chartered and uncharted. In the cities one found the more improved and expensive types of the genre, where relatively elaborate advertisements specified the credentials and teaching plans of such schools.

In the nation's capital, shortly before the Civil War, Washington, DC's *National Intelligencer* promoted to its readers the Washington Female Institute.

Mrs. Eliza W. Smith, the principal, established her credentials, not with her education and training, but with her previous occupational experience, as principal of Mystic Hall Seminary in Massachusetts. She had brought with her two other Mystic Hall graduates, one teaching Latin, English grammar, dictation, and physiology, the other piano and calisthenics. She enlisted a local Protestant Episcopal minister to instruct her students in moral science and Latin classics. In addition, she arranged for two members of the local Columbia College (later George Washington University) to lecture on chemistry, natural philosophy, and anatomy, as well as modern languages. A second former principal from Goshen Female Seminary in Goshen, New York, joined the faculty to teach mathematics, natural philosophy, and chemistry. Ten additional individuals ensured instruction in music, singing, drawing, dancing, and painting as well as proficiency in foreign language (French, German, and Spanish). The school boasted a large gymnasium (ropes, ladders, vaults, and swings) plus horseback riding. "A cultivated mind and elevated morality," the advertisement chided, "will accomplish little with a feeble or weakly constitution." Tuition was an expensive $300 per year with $150 down, entitling students "to board and the comforts of a good home, such as furnished room, heat, light etc., including a bowling alley and library."[14] Smith, the principal, aged forty-four in 1860 and a widow, rented a home nearby, sheltering her five children (ages eight to twenty-three), one of her teachers, a cook, and three servants.[15] Smith embodied the entrepreneurial possibilities of teacher training and experience, particularly for women whose husbands for whatever reason were no longer the primary family provider.

Two major features of such female schools that endured and flourished consisted of an urban base and a translocal organization. After the Civil War, many of the academies founded for both males and females began to suffer in the competition with the public, tax-supported high schools, which numerically eclipsed their private counterparts sometime in the 1880s. Under threat, the private academies that survived became exclusive boarding schools, cultivating an alumni network with extensive geographical reach especially into the cities and thus remaining an important social force like the more prestigious women's colleges.[16] The histories of these new schools also showed that religious and denominational influences still played a part in many schools, however "nonsectarian" or "nondenominational."[17]

One example of this pattern can be found in the early history of Catholic education by religious sisters. On March 25, 1848, sponsored by a group of German investors, a group of Munich-based nuns belonging to the Poor

School Sisters of Notre Dame came to teach in Baltimore's Catholic schools. Three sisters arrived in Baltimore that year and immediately established three grammar schools. To staff these schools, the order created an academy, first, in Milwaukee (with its extensive German-speaking population) in 1851—Saint Mary's Institute—then in 1863 in Baltimore with a state charter one year later and the imprimatur of the city's Archbishop Martin Spaulding (1810–72). The first class consisted of twenty day students and six boarders in a new Aisquith Street building: the Institute of Notre Dame, which had actually developed with classes in the convent that began in 1848. By 1871 the school's expansion required an entirely new locus, out of the city but on the central avenue, Charles Street, and a thirty-three-acre campus, eventually to become nearly sixty acres opposite Johns Hopkins University.[18] It also required a new name—Notre Dame of Maryland Collegiate Institute for Young Ladies—and cost $220 for tuition and board. In 1873 the academy opened to sixty-three students (ages six to twenty), who originated from eight different states and the District of Columbia plus Cuba, Puerto Rico, Strasburg (Austria), and Prussia. The nineteen faculty members (one male teacher of Spanish) taught science, rhetoric, languages (German, French, and Spanish), mathematics, elocution, etymology, history, geography, music, drawing, and painting. By the end of the century, the School Sisters of Notre Dame had recruited over three thousand young women (many of them of Irish descent) into their work and had founded 265 schools in the United States and Canada.

As important for understanding the power of a translocal organization and its city network (especially using faculty from the newly formed Catholic University in Washington, DC; the University of Maryland; and neighboring Loyola College and Johns Hopkins University) is the transition of institute/academy to collegiate status. In 1895 the Notre Dame Collegiate Institute for Young Ladies became the first Roman Catholic college for women in America and reorganized its curriculum and career aspirations.[19] In this transition, the school successfully sought from the state a (1896) charter to grant collegiate degrees but resisted any aspiration for a university orbit. In the earlier period where instruction sought to prepare young women for college, the schools welcomed essentially all ages and previous states of schooling and channeled them into appropriate grades: primary (which began study of French or German), preparatory (ages ten to thirteen, studying the three Rs, geography, history, and general science), academic (ages fourteen to sixteen, pursuing grammar, geography, medieval and world history, botany, physiology, physics, algebra, elementary Latin, and one modern language), and collegiate (ages seventeen to nineteen or twenty, studying belles lettres, ancient history, zoology, plane geometry, botany, and physiology). A final senior-level department permitted the mastery of literature, logic, geology, solid geometry, trigonometry, civics, and economics.

It was this last echelon where education evolved into an operative collegiate curriculum, changing its name to the College of Notre Dame of Maryland, and subsequently offering three concentrations at the college level: regular, scientific, and literary, which led to three distinctive degrees: bachelors of arts, of science, and of literature. From 1895 the four-year course required twenty-four to twenty-five periods of forty-five minutes per week, of which twenty were prescribed and four to five were elective (one of which was Latin). The options for art and music shifted outside the formal curriculum. Laboratory work in chemistry and physics became axiomatic. After 1899, history extended beyond the earlier ancient focus to modern and American history. In 1902 the New York State Board of Regents gave its official approval to this curriculum, which at the turn of the century exceeded Vassar in the study hours for English, classics, modern languages, mathematics, chemistry, and physics (and, of course, church doctrine and church history).[20] In 1899, in the new wing of the central building, James Cardinal Gibbons (1834–1921) of Baltimore, a substantive supporter and frequent visitor to the school, conferred the first college degrees on six candidates.

The consistent feature of Notre Dame College's successive stages was its commitment to higher education teaching over any university aspirations for professional or research dimensions. It was a choice made by many liberal arts colleges generically in these years. Possibly through the counsel of James Cardinal Gibbons, Notre Dame's drive was twofold: a) a guarantee for able Catholic women to pursue their studies outside the often-present nineteenth-century anti-Catholic animus; and b) an effort to respond to the novel demands of the church's "modernism" movement. Many Catholic leaders worried that university research unfairly challenged biblical studies and introduced a democratic relativism that held Catholic didacticism suspect.[21] A possible third dimension lay with the educational opportunity the school offered to women of less affluent Catholic ethnicities.[22] All three considerations undergirded the emergent institutional culture that concentrated itself in Catholic religious practice and that became an endemic part of the college's esprit.

Catholics were not alone in creating schools that protected denominational values and cultivated the less affluent for special collegiate training programs. A denominational spirit permeated one of the most touted examples of female collegiate instruction, namely, at Oberlin Collegiate Institute. In 1833, out of both ideological conviction and economic necessity (to expand the student pool), Oberlin's founders explicitly named female students as particularly welcome and two years later made a similar overture to black students, the first such American institution to do so.[23] Women, however, were quickly segregated into separate facilities, were offered less rigorous studies, and were invited to support themselves by laundering collegians' clothes and sheets. An elaborate set of rules followed, proscribing times for gender-specific library study and indeed for all manner of attitudes and behavior when in mixed company, like church attendance, picnics, and so on. By midcentury even the niece of President Henry Fairchild (1815–89) would write to a cousin about her fears of going into an Oberlin straitjacket.[24] The college's denominational tradition and its reputation as a revival agency under its first two presidents—Rev. Asa Mahan (1799–1889) and noted preacher Charles Grandison Finney (1792–1875)—both had set an "educational" standard of piety over intellect at the school. Gradually the force of the university standards of research and seminar work in the 1880s pressed the issue of a college's shaping force on its society. The president's own leadership, that is, supporting a tolerance of Darwinian science as well as evangelical Protestantism, influenced faculty at colleges like Oberlin. The acceptance of the new science of evolution opened such collegiate communities to support its graduates attending German universities and those immersed in reformist politics. Gradually women found themselves caught up in these newer patterns and stretched their aspirations beyond domesticity. Even Oberlin's denominational origins and early commitments to "domesticity" for women students began to take second place to scientific inquiry and to responsible civic life.[25] Oberlin's early and constant commitment to the higher education of women has long served as a powerful icon of this much-debated value of the educated female.[26]

The secularization of the denominational teaching colleges, seminaries, and institutes did not come quickly or easily. Until the Civil War, such schools reflected more the tradition of antebellum academies than any of the college standards that would follow in the later decades of the century. The primary considerations were not educational but geographical and economic. Exactly how many families could tolerate youthful members' absence from the household economy, and how many could afford to permit their absence for two or more years, even apart from the dangers of travel to distant places? The sheer variety and versatility of the "academy" tradition resisted the kind of generic coherence that postwar colleges soon implied.

The response to multiple local needs and its easier survival in or near larger towns and cities with population concentrations were key features to any school's endurance. It is hardly surprising that an academy precedent often provided the necessary groundwork for their postwar upgrading into either boarding school or college status. Mount Holyoke Seminary, Notre Dame Collegiate Institute, and Oberlin Collegiate Institute succeeded in this conversion, where many more proprietary schools, like Washington Female Institute, did not.

Most of all the female seminaries and institutes of the antebellum period—whether Roman Catholic or Protestant—could hardly resist the powerful and ubiquitous force of evangelism that powered most reform movements, especially education before the Civil War. After the Civil War, the emergence of the independent women's college began to refocus the debates over women's intellectual capacity. These schools began to introduce a new demography and eventually a convincing record of achievement that altered the old academic culture. The key feature of this change involved a redefinition and expansion of older notions of domesticity. Mount Holyoke Seminary's institutional success, of course, had much to do with the presence of its founder, Mary Lyon. However, the founder had only a dozen years to set the foundation of her enterprise. Historian Helen Horowitz has argued persuasively that this foundation rested in the school's traditional commitment to an enlightened domesticity. The balance of piety and intellect did not ignore a strong sense of Christian service, to missionary work and to the training of less affluent women to teach women like themselves. These values at the outset and for much of the nineteenth century were reflected in the central building of the school, a large Georgian structure with a piazza on its second floor, making it resemble nothing so much as a hotel, an enlarged household. This residential arrangement, which housed faculty and students together, enabled close scrutiny of all students' educational and moral progress. If some students chaffed against the school's strictures, the majority clearly found, especially in retrospect, that the ordered environment contributed to the missionary and social services that Mount Holyoke trumpeted in its prized graduates.[27]

After the Civil War, this residential quality was not abandoned so much as inflated in the construction of Vassar College's asylum structures. The central building, designed by James Renwick (1818–95) following the mansard style, then (1860s) so prominent in the redesign of Paris, featured an imposing central building with extensive wings.[28] In the center the school housed the presidential offices; in its wings, student classrooms on the first floor;

and above, dormitories for students and resident faculty. The self-conscious sorting and hierarchical arrangement projected a protective rather than a residential environment, particularly important given the majority of young students who early on entered the preparatory (not abandoned until 1888) rather than the collegiate department. The lack of educational preparation necessitated greater support from the environment in shepherding students quickly into a demanding educational curriculum envisioned by its founder. Although he had through his advisors several connections to Mount Holyoke and continued Mary Lyon's domestic priorities, Matthew Vassar (1792–1868), the school founder and benefactor, had created his school anew, without a precedent seminary and without modeling on existing male colleges. In spite of hiring several strong, capable female faculty members like astronomer Maria Mitchell (1818–89), Vassar relied strategically on male help and sought expertise in the newer area of technical training. He hired John Raymond (1814–78), former principal of Brooklyn Polytechnic and Collegiate Institute, to preside over his experiment.[29]

Yet, Raymond's appointment did not signal a break with older traditions of female education at Vassar. Modified Mount Holyoke traditions of domesticity and the continued influence of religious instruction played an important role in the creation of two additional women's colleges, Wellesley (founded 1875) and Smith (founded 1871). Henry F. Durant (1822–81), a Harvard graduate and Boston lawyer, founded Wellesley after two wrenching personal experiences, first, the death of his son, and, second, an evangelical conversion to matters of religion. He turned his attention to education and served on the Mount Holyoke Seminary board. There he began to consider ways of using his wealth to refine and spread the evangelical and domestic values so central to early women's colleges. His thinking developed while he funded a library for Mount Holyoke. He ensured a feminine influence by putting his wife on the Wellesley Board and by wooing five of his first eight trustees from his fellow Mount Holyoke board members. Second, he began to appoint well-trained females to the faculty and to the presidency. The first president was Ada Howard (1829–1907), a Mount Holyoke graduate and former principal of the women's department of Knox College. Durant followed Vassar's model of a great central building, but at Wellesley the center held not the president's office but the library and chapel, intellect and piety in a more strenuous key. Here, however, Durant used a rambling Gothic style to project these evangelical Protestant values.[30]

Durant intended to sustain a prominent female presence and educational leadership at Wellesley. Smith College gave Mount Holyoke's residential domesticity a more communal interpretation. First, its dormitories resembled enlarged cottages, each of which housed a resident matron as well as a female faculty member. The school itself built no chapel or library, relying on the existing structures of its town, Northampton, Massachusetts. The strategy proposed to integrate more fully young women into the fabric and dynamics of the existing community rather than to create a distinctive society of its own on the municipal periphery. In addition, Sophia Smith (1796–1870), whose fortune created the school, had studied for a term at Catharine Beecher's Hartford Female Seminary.[31] But more strategically, she received advice from her pastor, Rev. John Morton Greene (1830–1919), an Amherst graduate (class of 1853), a Smith trustee (1875–1919), and the husband of a Mount Holyoke graduate (where he had also been a trustee, 1866–75).[32] He urged Smith to expend only half her fortune in the venture, holding the rest in reserve to avoid the overcommitment to building construction as exemplified by Matthew Vassar. Second, he advised strongly to appoint a male president and a strong male presence on the faculty to ensure intellectual standards. Greene was instrumental in the selection of Amherst College professor of English literature L. Clark Seelye (1837–1924) as president, where he served until 1908. Seelye, a graduate of Union College, had studied two years at the Universities of Berlin and Heidelberg.[33] The appointment, Greene and Smith hoped, would hold Smith's educational values close to those of nearby Amherst College, where Seelye's brother was its longtime president and had also served as a trustee of Mount Holyoke.[34] The centerpiece of the school became a church-like Gothic structure complete with clock tower, housing classrooms and a social hall (where chapel sessions were conducted every day but Sunday). More important, under Seelye's leadership, Smith College adopted a close approximation of the Amherst curriculum, with emphasis on ancient languages and higher mathematics.[35]

Smith became the first college to achieve educational offerings on a par with existing four-year male colleges. If its "cottage strategy" implemented the domestic values of Mount Holyoke Seminary, its teaching and curriculum—with no preparatory department—accelerated its progress to a substantive intellectual experience, an experience toward which Mount Holyoke and Notre Dame Collegiate Institute too were moving but would not achieve for several decades.

The key factors for Smith's status were extraordinary philanthropy and the close imitation of the Amherst College model.[36] But in its early years, Smith College remained protective about its students' moral as well as their intellectual well-being and appointed a head of the ladies department in imitation of Vassar's procedure. Smith's selection was Sarah Humphrey, the daughter of the late Amherst College president.[37] As dramatic as were the large sums that started Vassar, Smith, and Wellesley, the original funding actually seems to have inhibited further donations and resulted in all these schools tightening their belts for a number of years. For all of these schools, the recruitment of properly trained faculty and prepared students was as constant a problem as much as financing or the proper balance of piety and intellect as institutional values. For the women's college as a genre, few would function as the equivalent of the best male colleges until the 1890s.

The one great exception was Bryn Mawr College, founded as a Quaker institution in 1885 and modeled not on men's colleges but on the university goal of research. The intellectual conviction of its founder, Joseph W. Taylor (1810–80), an Ohio tanning magnate, eventually compelled him to modify his vigorous Quaker strictures on student and trustee recruitment. Taylor felt compelled by both the example of Quaker Haverford College (founded 1833) and the philanthropy of Quaker merchant Johns Hopkins (1795–1873) to the first research university (founded 1876) in the United States, to create a demanding collegiate school for women. He drew from the board of Johns Hopkins University for several trustees and paid visits to Mount Holyoke, Smith, and Wellesley for advice and insight. Taylor resisted the pressure to appoint a female president, though a Quaker raised candidate with a recent PhD from the University of Zurich—M. Carey Thomas (1857–1935)—was keenly interested. In spite of substantive gains in behalf of female education and the expansion of "domesticity," the fears of education's adverse impact on women continued to exert its power. Taylor opted for James Rhoads (1828–95), a Pennsylvania medical doctor and early Bryn Mawr trustee.[38] When Rhoads retired in 1894, M. Carey Thomas, who had been made college dean in 1885, succeeded him and presided there successfully until 1922.

M. Carey Thomas should generally be given credit for the high intellectual standards Bryn Mawr set. She had struggled with her own education and eventually won family support for a college education at Cornell University (class of 1877). Initially with the support of her family, several of whom sat on the Johns Hopkins Board of Trustees, she attended classes at Johns Hopkins but could not participate in seminar discussions or receive a degree. She then traveled to Europe and eventually settled in at the University of Zurich where she took a demanding schedule and achieved great academic distinction, including the PhD. The driving forces behind her were her own special sense of womanhood, several remarkable friends, and her adventurous reading.[39] Her personal drive and conscious distancing from a conventional marriage permitted her to pursue an intensive personal commitment to academic research and the life of the mind. Her example seems to have made its mark on Bryn Mawr graduates, some 39 percent of whom between 1889 and 1908 became teachers, 18 percent went into social work, 4 percent into the professions, and only 10 percent into no work at all. By comparison for the same period, Wellesley graduates sent 18 percent into teaching, 2 percent into college instruction, 3 percent into social work, 2 percent into the professions, and 65 percent into no work at all. In the same period, 53 percent of Bryn Mawr graduates never married, compared with Wellesley's 43 percent. Thirty-two percent of Bryn Mawr graduates who married had no children, compared to 23 percent for Wellesley.[40]

Thomas was instrumental in creating a different culture at her school by insisting on caps and gowns worn to class. She ultimately created a series of Gothic quadrangles with crenellated towers and stone enclosures, echoing the enclosed, medieval atmosphere of Oxford and Cambridge Universities in England. The architects were Philadelphians Walter Cope (1860–1902) and John Stewardson (1858–96), who in these same years designed analogous Gothic structures for Princeton, the University of Pennsylvania, and Washington University in Saint Louis, Missouri.[41] The architecture signaled a school quite different from those with a residential cottage structure or one with a protective asylum atmosphere. With no preparatory department and its own admissions exam, Bryn Mawr had clearly separated itself from the inherited tradition of domesticity in ways no comparable women's college had.

For all of their symbolic innovation, the women's colleges in the late nineteenth century actually taught fewer than 6 percent of the national cohort of college-aged women. Yet increasingly, since the Civil War, first hundreds, then thousands of women sought some form of advanced education. The workhorses of this experience, especially outside the eastern seaboard states, were the state universities, particularly those that benefited from the Morrill land-grant legislation of 1862. However, many of these institutions, often no larger than their denominational college competitors, were as financially strapped as most colleges for sufficient funds. The US Congress had funneled grants based on the federal distribution of western lands to select institutions. However, the financing of railroads, especially the soon to be completed (1869) first transcontinental railroad, not to mention the awarding of western lands in the aftermath of the Homestead Act (1862), meant that land values had dropped. State land-grant institutions that sought immediate cash for their grants often settled for a few cents on the dollar. The one institution that did not follow this pattern was Cornell University, largely due to the advice and insistence of its founder, and successful businessman, Ezra Cornell (1807–74). Though controversial, Cornell insisted that his bequest to establish a new institution would be contingent on the state awarding all of its land-grant monies to a single institution, his beneficiary. At the time he served in the New York state legislature and ingeniously steered enabling legislation to passage. He had substantive help and educational advice from a fellow legislator, Andrew D. White, who would become Cornell's first president. Equally ingenious, Cornell himself bought the undervalued New York land grants and held them until their value rose, with a tenfold gain for his university.[42]

Cornell's commitment to coeducation from the beginning became an important example for state universities nationwide. It was to Cornell that M. Carey Thomas went to study, along with several other strategic educational leaders of women's colleges. The creation of this new university, privately initiated but sustained by public money, became a special land-grant institution. Here Cornell's practical experience in construction and business became an interactive force with Andrew White's substantive education first at Yale, then in German universities.[43] It was Ezra Cornell who insisted that Cornell University be famously inclusive: "I would found an institution where any person can find instruction in any study."[44] Cornell was inclusive about the students as well, but momentarily was persuaded by White that coeducation would initially raise more issues about their school than it would settle. Particularly Cornell traveled to the East Coast to examine Harvard, Yale, and Brown, particularly their buildings. In spite of White's scholarly mastery of art and architecture, Cornell selected a workmanlike, if unimpressive, architecture purportedly imitating a Renaissance palazzo. He wanted lasting structures of stone from local quarries and sketched out a quadrangle plan, roundly criticized by Frederick Law Olmsted (too rigid and too short-sighted concerning future expansion or terrain) to no avail. Cornell seems to have been impressed by the example of sturdy and imposing Vassar, where he sent his eldest daughter in 1865 and where he imitated the only concession to stylish elegance, its mansard roof.[45] Durability took priority over questions of education, salary equity, or student composition.[46]

Coeducation at Cornell would quickly become an issue in the guise of Cornell friend and university trustee lumberman Henry Sage (1814–97). At the inauguration of the university, Sage quietly promised to pay for a women's dormitory, when White and Cornell thought the time propitious. In fact, he financed Sage College for Women ($267,000) within the Cornell aegis, and the school opened in 1874 with thirty female students.[47] The public debate that slowed Cornell's commitment to coeducation involved the familiar ones about intellectual demands taxing women's physical constitution, concerns about social interactions of the sexes, and the challenge of college instruction to the natural, domestic priorities of marriage and motherhood. However, once they had visited other coeducational schools, Cornell and White believed these fears exaggerated and that many schools found women's presence a civilizing effect on the male students. However, once coeducation began at Cornell, factions of both students and faculty worked to segregate extracurricular activities of the sexes, committee work, class publication, and elections.[48] Such biases gradually eroded in the face of the critical mass of coeducational institutions—30 percent of all colleges in 1870 were coeducational and 71 percent in 1900. These higher education institutions accounted for 3,044 women in 1870 and 19,959 in 1900, a sixfold increase. If one factors in the normal schools, whose offerings increasingly strengthened throughout the century, postsecondary women students numbered eighty-five thousand, an impressive 40 percent of the total collegiate population.[49] Comparatively women's colleges increased from a population of 9,572 in 1870 to 15,977 in 1900, a near doubling of this constituency.[50] Coeducation at the turn of the century appeared to be, if not the wave of the future, then a new cultural space in spite of the continuing drag of the domestic tradition.[51]

But even at Cornell, coeducation did not mean full integration of women, especially as the physical campus developed. Andrew White served as president of Cornell from 1867 to 1885 and trustee from 1866 to his death in 1918. The formative presence of Ezra Cornell prevented White from realizing many of his architectural and educational ambitions for the new school, but, gradually as Cornell's business obligations drew his attention elsewhere, White began to prevail. Henry Sage's donation of a building to house women collegians opened the way for White to indulge a more ornamental Gothic design in Cornell buildings as well as a campus landscape that capitalized on the hilly site of the school. White sought many European architects for the Sage College for Women but settled for Rev. Charles Babcock (1819–1913), the son-in-law of Richard Upjohn (1802–78), the distinguished architect of Trinity Church in Manhattan and leader in the American Gothic Revival. Babcock had worked with the Upjohn firm as an architect for a number of years but gravitated into a second career as Anglican minister. White offered him a professorship in architecture and the position of Sage College designer. Shortly he would also become pastor of Saint Paul's Church (1874–92) in Ithaca, while completing the plans for Sage College and several additional Cornell buildings. In retrospect, his impressive design for a self-contained building—classroom, dormitory, dining room, parlor, study halls, assembly—replete with bay windows for light and air and an imposing entryway topped by an inspirational tower was considered the real beginning of Cornell's campus aesthetic and an embodiment of Ruskinian ideals.[52] The Sage College building, distinctly set in a landscape of its own and apart from the existing quasi-quadrangle, had the capacity for 125 women but did not achieve that number for several decades.[53]

In spite of its segregated status and slow growth, Cornell's Sage College established the coeducational pattern for the land-grant institutions, especially the public state universities.[54] There women sought courses equivalent to those in men's studies and began the pursuit of journalism, music, and literature. Many of the institutions that had admitted women earlier, like Iowa in 1855, later ended that policy or permitted only women from the home state. Cornell opened its doors, soon after permitted female attendance at all classes, and, protectively and paternalistically, cared for their needs in a specifically designed facility. However, the richest and the poorest of the female collegiate pool were generally not contenders for Cornell University classes. Teaching careers still absorbed the majority of female graduates, who came from homes of middling businessmen and professionals. Many of them found cheaper lodging in Ithaca despite the inconveniences. Increasingly Cornell refused admittance to those needing additional preparation, to those younger than seventeen, and to those older than twenty-two, all features of the collegiate cohort to 1870.[55] With the proliferation of public high schools, coeducational and women's colleges could become increasingly selective as the end of the century approached, and they did.[56] Yet, for those women who could begin to consider careers beyond teaching or even careers alongside motherhood, more substantial family resources gave them an edge in enhancing their choices. It is also hardly surprising that, even with the rise of temperance, social settlement, and suffrage movements to attract college graduates, few female college graduates openly embraced values that later generations would recognize as feminist.

The state universities may have trailed the older colleges like Harvard, which transformed themselves by the end of the nineteenth century into universities with noted faculty, endowment, library holdings, and philanthropic success. But their commitment to coeducation proved to be a long-term resource, however hesitantly they began their service to all citizens. By the last third of the century, like Cornell, the research-oriented state universities, especially in the Midwest, had acquired a solid leadership committed to coeducation and, as important, steady and increasing support from their state legislatures (increasingly peopled by their graduates). The University of Michigan, operating as a university since 1841, did not admit its first female students until 1870 when the board of regents formally adopted the coeducation policy. In the fall of 1870, thirty-three entered: two in law, eighteen in medicine, and thirteen in the literary department.[57] By the early 1880s, with the student enrollment holding at 1,500, women's numbers rose gradually: one hundred in 1875, two hundred in 1885, and three hundred in 1888. From 1894 to 1918, women represented 40–48 percent of Michigan's undergraduate enrollment. President James B. Angell (1829–1916), who would preside over the school's university modernization from 1871 to 1909, quickly boasted that by 1882 Michigan's women graduates occupied six faculty positions on Wellesley's faculty including its president, Alice Freeman Palmer (1855–1902).[58] As Michigan modernized, its female graduates reflected features closely akin to their counterparts at Smith and Wellesley (and increasingly Bryn Mawr): 13 percent took MA degrees, 2 percent PhD degrees, 2 percent entered the professions of law and medicine, and 79 percent had no advanced study. Twenty-four percent entered the work of teaching, 2 percent entered college teaching, 66 percent had no occupation after graduation, and 53 percent married. At Wellesley in the same years (1889–1918), 17 percent took MA degrees, 2 percent won PhD degrees, 2 percent entered law or medicine, and 61 percent had no advanced study. Sixteen percent entered the work of teaching, 2 percent entered college teaching, 66 percent had no occupation after graduation, and 63 percent married.[59] As influential as singular educational leaders were, as potent as many alumnae considered their college élan, broader cultural and economic forces, including the reservations about women and domesticity, dominated the career worth of women's collegiate education, whether in women's colleges or coeducational universities.

By the end of the century, the cohort of well-educated female high school graduates had expanded sufficiently for all schools admitting women to become more selective. The critical mass of colleges and universities admitting women put to rest many of the earlier reservations of male-only institutions. But, like male-only schools, hierarchies and sorting devices began to emerge, rank ordering the intellectual standards of schools from proprietary institutes and technical training through private and public universities. The presence of women still affected this new ranking even as they gained ground in elite universities. Reluctantly even Harvard and Columbia had given and worked out arrangements that admitted women to their classes. In Harvard's case, President Eliot and others avoided any association with the female seminary or coeducational alternative. They sought an educational option that retained a segregated male culture, especially for Harvard's extracurricular activities. The solution was to legitimate an earlier experiment, promoted since 1873 by schoolmaster Arthur Gilman (1837–1909), brother of Johns Hopkins University's first president, and his wife, to pay select members of Harvard faculty outside their regular class schedules to tutor or lecture a small cadre of young women. The Gilmans' daughter was a member of the first class of twenty-seven, mostly part-timers.

Through the 1880s the experiment continued, powered by the resources of Elizabeth Cary Agassiz (1822–1907), the second wife of noted naturalist and Harvard professor Louis Agassiz (1807–73) and stepmother of copper magnate Alexander Agassiz (1835–1910). Elizabeth Agassiz became president of the informal organization, the Society for the Collegiate Instruction of Women (founded 1882), that would evolve into Radcliffe College, memorializing Harvard's first woman benefactor. In 1893 Radcliffe College opened, charging an expensive $400 for one year's tuition. Harvard's Corporation agreed to a tenuous link, following the model of Cambridge's Girton College.[60] Harvard would monitor the education and countersign the Radcliffe diploma, something different from awarding women a Harvard AB. Agassiz had also extracted from President Eliot permission for select women to take Harvard graduate courses. Massachusetts chartered Radcliffe College in 1894.[61] Elizabeth Agassiz considered the Harvard imprimatur decisive, the single factor that kept the arrangement from producing one more female seminary. However, many of her other ideas about educating women comported completely with those of the best seminary tradition: a) education was no impairment to women's health; b) education, while training many to teach, had a value of itself; c) domestic customs continued to be a high priority, not only through regular collegiate teas with her students but also in her own family responsibilities.[62]

Radcliffe's example as a coordinate college, permitting its own organization but with close alliance to a nearby male-only university, was particularly a city alternative. Parallel experience followed at Pembroke College (1891) in Rhode Island near Brown University, Sophie Newcomb College (1886) near Tulane University in New Orleans, and Trinity College (founded 1897) in Washington, DC, near Catholic University. The examples were important in the creation of Barnard College in Manhattan near Columbia University. In 1889 the wealthy Jewish philanthropist Annie Nathan Meyer (1867–1951) invoked Radcliffe's example and sought to use her resources to develop an analogous opportunity for women. Meyer enlisted a singular elite cadre of women philanthropists and created a classroom for instruction rather than a residence. She explicitly excluded normal school applicants and began hiring a separate faculty, though vetted by Columbia. This distancing from the Columbia operation nevertheless opened the way to the hiring of female faculty and kept a curriculum conservatively focused on the classics. The first dean of the college, Emily James Smith (1865–1944), was herself a Greek scholar, a graduate of Bryn Mawr, and formerly a student of both Girton College in Cambridge and the University of Chicago.[63]

Smith's and Meyer's intellectual visions led to other challenges to "egalitarian" higher education. Initially the high intellectual aspirations of Barnard did not clash with the new-formed (1887) Teachers College, which also addressed the ideals of collegiate women. However, Barnard's effort to monopolize undergraduate women's education at Columbia quickly led them to argue against Teachers College courses in liberal arts, especially for special students without college degrees. Stimulated by larger elite donors, Barnard's deans pressured Teachers College to become a distinctive professional, that is, postcollegiate, school. The strategy also concomitantly burnished Barnard's image of high intellectual standards commensurate with older women's colleges like Smith, Vassar, Wellesley, and Bryn Mawr. More importantly at issue were the social class dynamics of Barnard's elite aspirations and the Teachers College clientele of working-class women, a division that unfortunately began to separate out liberal arts and professional goals that earlier seminary and coeducational traditions had mixed together.[64] The division played through the early decades of the twentieth century as Barnard sought formal association with other women's colleges and their increasingly selective student body. Barnard had both elite students retaining their urban social circles as well as poorer students who could not afford to board away from home. Barnard's tuition in 1914 held at $150, while Mount Holyoke had risen to $425 per year.[65]

Barnard sustained its high standards hoping to shape their student body by admitting only women with strong, privileged preparations. But when poorer day students met these standards, particularly ones with Jewish and Catholic backgrounds, Barnard's longtime influential dean, Virginia Gildersleeve (1877–1965), responded. On the one hand, Gildersleeve lobbied internally for women's access to Columbia's other professional schools; on the other hand, externally, she was instrumental in organizing the Seven College Conference of Women's Colleges, an institutional grouping to buttress

Barnard's curricular and admissions standards.[66] It was also an effort to project the women's college as a genre not with local or regional roots but national (and international) educational and social prominence. Gildersleeve thereby glossed those ethnic portions of its student body that did not fit its inherited, elite image. The effort broke with one of Barnard's initial, inclusive impulses, driven forcefully by its principal Jewish philanthropists, Annie Nathan Meyer and Jacob Schiff (1847–1920).[67] Gildersleeve worked forcefully to construct dormitories to reduce the day student population. She arranged for a central building in the Beaux-Arts design of McKim, Mead and White to present a face to the city, one of monumental order and symmetry in an urbane, Renaissance style, a mask to the ideological and class divisions within.[68]

Barnard was not unique. In the early years of the twentieth century, women's colleges became progressively elitist and shifted away from their original, at times, inclusive impulses. The late nineteenth-century schools, even those protective of the traditional values of domesticity—and few could afford to disdain this tradition—differed in their commitments to domesticity. The early schools were primarily locally rooted enterprises, sometimes with one eye on a genuine commitment to cultivate natural female talent, with another eye on fiscal concerns for the continuance of the school. Most early schools began with strategic support from male educators, often fathers or brothers of talented women, who knew the social reservations against female intellect and careers to be limiting. Like Catharine Beecher,[69] many female educators were explicit in their efforts to view educated women as resources to the body politic rather than challenges to them. Not all female educators were from or oriented to the wealthy elite. After the disruptions of the Civil War, many educated widows founded schools to produce needed income. The entrepreneurial spirit and the traditional need of seminaries and institutes to be flexible to survive led to experimenting with other subjects, also taught at male institutions.

The preeminent driving force here was the role of the public school teacher, which created a quasi-domestic occupation for women and was powered still by a school committee's desire to control costs by paying women substantially less than their male counterparts. The expansion of the public schools had created a huge demand for new teachers and low-cost institutions to train them. By 1900 with sixteen thousand students in women's colleges, normal schools enrolled seventy-six thousand educated women.[70] Many normal schools in these last years of the century offered more than two years schooling and for the sake of qualified teachers had begun to offer college-level instruction. It was this potentially professional career that drove women's ambitions generally, much less than any curricular competition with male colleges at the increasingly selective women's colleges, which also sent their graduates into the public schoolroom, when they chose work over marriage.

The teaching role had a great deal to do with the expansion of domesticity, insofar as instruction made an ideal of an affective pedagogy, cultivated a cliché of female temperament, a supportive rather than a didactic approach to intellectual discipline. Domesticity had also become a rhetorical veneer for established collegiate subjects like home economics and occupations outside the home, like social work, as legitimate activities for educated women. This expansion beyond subjects like domestic crafts (sewing, food preparation, home decoration, etc.), to include educational administration, settlement work, nursing, and other nonfamilial work, actually inflated the meaning of "domesticity" beyond its antebellum connotations.[71] If many women seemed to pay a high price in having no families or smaller families to achieve their careers, advocates of a traditional domesticity dealt with the educated women as a manageable problem but not a crisis. In 1908 Charles Eliot's lecture to the Association of Collegiate Alumnae to keep educated women on a domestic track was, of course, a recognition of a widely held value, supported by conservative schoolmen like himself as well as many members of his distinguished audience. A minority of educated women, like M. Carey Thomas, disagreed but worked below the level of formal policy to achieve career advancement in individualized settings.[72]

Without formally confronting the cultural assumptions of "domesticity," educators, like M. Carey Thomas, quietly transformed the intellectual training of women in the last half of the nineteenth century. By the early decades of the twentieth century, a critical mass of female students had achieved an educational record that could not be denied. If individuals like President Charles Eliot of Harvard could patronize an older set of assumptions about women's capacity, the historical record documented a different intellectual trajectory entirely. Women actually reached a near parity with men in attendance at higher education institutions by World War I. The debates accompanying that expansion had inflated the older ideology of domesticity so substantively that the word had assumed a new meaning, one that set the context for, say, the legality of women's suffrage and many attendant (generational culture #4) cultural shifts.

CHAPTER EIGHT

The Academic Culture of Nineteenth-Century Collegians

The nineteenth-century denominational college as a widespread model became one of the casualties of the Civil War. Of course, such colleges proliferated after the Civil War and into the twentieth century. However, after the war they functioned in a different orbit, trying to compete with new university alternatives for students as well as for philanthropies benefiting from postwar industrial fortunes. Older colleges, while loath to shed their denominational origins, recognized the necessity to reach out beyond their regional and sectarian boundaries. The focus of the antebellum college on studies of mathematics, languages, rhetoric, and didactics, as well as general science and moral philosophy, seemed out of step with a society that relied less and less on oratory, public debate, and verbal suasion, even in the major professions of law, ministry, and medicine (not to mention teaching) and more on specialized knowledge. Where the antebellum student societies provided both nontheological libraries and a locus for debating skills, the postbellum college and university experimented with newly applied curricula. Through the 1870s and 1880s, many institutions of higher education experimented with various courses of study that mixed and matched classical, scientific, and practical studies, not unlike their university counterparts.

Such experimentation faced limits, practical as well as ideological. The older antebellum college adapted its curriculum to its resources and its student clientele. It took for granted that the end point would be a person of upright "character," to use the nineteenth century's own standard of educational achievement. Schoolmen publicly proclaimed "character" to be nondenominational as well as nonpolitical. Student bodies ranged in age from fourteen to twenty-five and faced close scrutiny from presidents and faculty who accepted the role of in loco parentis. For the younger members of the student body, such parental monitoring seemed obvious and acceptable; for the older members of the class, such watchfulness resulted not just in resentment but in outright rebellion. Not only were student rebellions frequent, they often caused such disruption that colleges temporarily closed to suppress them. After the Civil War, most colleges introduced admission policies that excluded both the very young and older students in their mid- to late twenties. Student bodies began to range more narrowly between ages seventeen and twenty-two, though in the West and nonurban areas the antebellum pattern continued. One major consequence of this change was the substantive reduction of student rebellions.

The shifts in curricula and student ages signaled more important transformations, particularly those of educational ideals, which set the context for a new student culture. In retrospect, there are few windows for viewing the actual impact of the curricular and organizational changes in the postwar period. However, one fictional source, the novel *Stover at Yale* (1911) by Owen Johnson (1879–1952),[1] depicted the (eastern and privileged) college experience from the student's eye view. The novel, drawing on the author's student years at Yale in the 1890s, opened with a prim profile of Dink Stover, fresh out of Lawrenceville (New Jersey) Preparatory Academy, taking the train to New Haven. His upscale clothes alone marked him a member of the affluent middle class, eager to engage the college experience. The first half of the novel recorded Stover's freshman year and has remarkably little to do with the intellectual values advanced by college and university leaders. Classroom work is clearly secondary to athletics and extracurricular activities. However, through these activities Stover gradually acclimated to a larger social and environmental coaching that Yale College supposedly engineered.

The Yale "system" implemented its values through its noncurricular activities like wrestling, crew, and most of all football, where Stover excelled.[2] On the gridiron Dink Stover had a conversion experience, "suddenly realizing the stern discipline of it all. . . . Directly, clearly visualized, he perceived for the first time, what he was to perceive in every day of his college career, that a standard had been fashioned to which irresistibly, subtly, he would have to conform, the standard that imposed itself upon him was bigger than his own."[3] That discipline was almost entirely extracurricular and experiential and contrasted with much of the official discourse of higher education leaders. These extracurricular attractions differed completely from the antebellum student societies, where intellectual values and rhetorical skills were uppermost. After football season, the author, Owen Johnson, observed: "He [Stover] had won his spurs and the right to lounge, and he looked forward eagerly to the rest of the year as a time for reading and the opening up of friendships of which he had dreamed." An upperclassman transmitted some corroborating, practical advice: "Now you've got to do a certain amount of studying here. Better do it in the first year and get in with the faculty. . . . And, Stover, it's easy enough when you know how. Play the game as others are playing it. It's a big game, and it will follow you through life. There it is; it's up to you."[4] This higher social standard requiring deference also contained a large component of individual initiative. The central problem of the book required a weaving together of this potential contradiction: self-initiative and adaptation to a larger commonweal.

The second remarkable feature of Stover's student culture was the subordination of intellectual values, a corollary of extracurricular athleticism. The power of the college's formal education supposedly combined intellectual and extracurricular work, but the actual teaching faculty and presidential leadership are barely visible in the narrative. The student body, its organizations, and its extracurricular sports seem to be primary in delivering the collegiate influence. Stover had taken exception to the sophomore societies as exclusivist, and for a time experienced a marginalization from his fellows. This separation set the context for his relationship with an older student, Tom Regan, who, it turns out later, was married and had to use his summers for work to pay for college. Stover's own summer labor—away from the college—with his friend introduced him to labor issues and union activity, which Owen Johnson makes clear, played little part in actual discussions at Yale itself. In addition, Stover meets Brockhurst, whom Johnson painted as a minor character, even though he edited the school paper, which attacked the business influence at Yale. But this time Stover is not swayed by his friend's example. Brockhurst's gadfly role represented the book's only intellectually driven figure and is branded by the author as an "impractical" and "visionary crank." Yale's academic culture in this fictional presentation seemed to engage, for example, only minimally in the vibrant debate over curricular experimentation, collegiate authority, and national politics that new university presidents actively promoted in the last two decades of the nineteenth century.

Stover's ability to thrive at Yale in spite of his opposition to "undemocratic" student societies nevertheless received the admiration of his fellows. Ultimately he is elected to the prestigious Skull and Bones Society, which oddly evaded his criticism of the exclusivist sophomore societies because Skull and Bones, he believed, rewarded merit and achievement. Stover's repatriation with his class through participation in the debating society purportedly realized the power of the student culture to insist on a compatibility of individual and social aims. Stover's individualism becomes a function of tailoring his aims with those of his college. The novelist explains that Stover's election effectively legitimated the college experience as a whole. The driving force propelling Stover was neither intellectual purpose nor ideological clarity but a quasi-Darwinian "savage magnetism" and natural superiority that his peers instinctively recognized.[5]

From the novel's point of view, the Yale student body with its cultural environment becomes the shaper of student character. Its forcefulness was not didactic but effectively indirect. The routine exposure to the strategic, collegiate influences trumped intellectual training and formal classroom instruction. Moreover, mature individual character was achieved not by resisting but by acclimating one's preferences to those of the social group, a notion of individuality that the twentieth century would reverse. In its way the academic culture that Owen Johnson depicted was not wholly alien to the goal of the antebellum college—the conception of an influential body of the faithful that produced an entity more than the sum of its parts. The result was not homogenization but a functioning unit with all of its members' idiosyncrasies intact. Here the older students and the rebellious few played minor roles, but still had their contributing parts to play. College leaders emerged from a natural process to which all participants gave their assent. The triumph that the fictional hero, Dink Stover, achieved without planning or deliberation represented one version of the Darwinian debate, the survival of the fittest. Stover's dominant "character" accepted rather than disrupted the collegiate culture. In what ways did these three features of late nineteenth-century academic culture—the natural compatibility of self-initiative and social purpose, the subordination of intellectual values, and the routine deference to singular leaders—connect to emergent assumptions about college/university distinctions?

The postwar colleges of the 1860s and 1870s continued for a time the older collegiate tradition of evangelizing youth to their adult responsibilities through a forceful "inculcation." The national turmoil of the 1860s, however, caused a momentary reduction of applicants until the 1880s when the actual averages for the better-known New England colleges—Amherst, Bowdoin, Dartmouth, Union, Williams, and Wesleyan—experienced a modest 2.8 percent increase.[6] When antebellum colleges pressed for more stringent discipline, students had revolted. At times, they resorted to nighttime bedlam; at other times, they harangued local newspapers; at still other times, they sought forms of "student government" that would relieve them of church worship obligations, close monitoring of extracurricular activities, or even deference to the dicta of a sitting president.[7] In the postbellum college of the late nineteenth century, however, power granted to student government within higher education institutions, extracurricular activities, and especially organized sports resulted in fewer rebellions. These newer activities, benefiting from a more homogeneous age grouping, led to one important object: an end to the tradition of in loco parentis that most schools inherited from the antebellum period. Other factors in reducing the need for faculty oversight included the influence of electives, physical science laboratories, and social science experimentation, which began to appear in many college offerings and recognized varied academic interests.

Faculty and student resistance to an older tradition of college leadership, especially presidents who were ordained ministers, achieved widespread notoriety in the decades after the Civil War.[8] The faculties were a significant force in reducing student supervision as they fought to redefine their own role in advanced study. The faculty's ideal, often nurtured abroad in German universities, for truly advanced research and teaching, urged many to direct their critical skills against their own institutions. At Wesleyan, Dartmouth, and Amherst Colleges, to name only a few, pitched battles were waged against presidents who considered their person and their office to represent the epitome of the institution's ideals.

By the end of the century, this postbellum turmoil had produced two new features in American higher education. First, a new brand of president, often (though not usually) not a minister, emerged as the head of the college. Even in colleges that elected ministers, their leaders were often of a distinctly liberal theological stripe, like William De Witt Hyde (1858–1917) of Bowdoin who had recently graduated from Andover Theological Seminary. More frequently, presidents like Bradford Raymond (1846–1914) of Wesleyan, Franklin Carter (1837–1919) of Williams, or William Jewett Tucker (1839–1926) of Dartmouth had less theologically driven educational experiences, a broad welcoming embrace for divergent modes of thought, and organizational and promotional values that included especially their urban alumni as part of their institutional community. This generational change in leadership and curricular policies translated quickly into an upsurge of enrollments in the last decade of the nineteenth century. Where higher education growth had increased no more than 2.8 percent after the Civil War, the six prominent

New England male colleges registered increases of 35.1 percent between 1890 and 1900.[9] Although many differences of scale remained, earlier distinctions between college and university became functionally less polarized as the century ended. Some colleges like Harvard became self-conscious universities in these years, while colleges like Dartmouth remained within the college genre, while nevertheless managing professional schools and new, advanced studies.

Perhaps most important was the role of the student body in colleges and universities. Rhetorically the college sought to project an image of a moral community, which ideally achieved an organic cohesion. The university necessarily grappled with this conceptual tradition and did so effectively, if uneasily, so long as its size bore some resemblance to its collegiate competition. Eventually size and concomitantly financial pressures provoked a breakdown of the college organization that fostered cohesiveness, especially the inability to house and feed growing numbers of youth. The problem of size had begun as early as the 1820s with the influx of poor students, ill-prepared educationally and unable to afford college residence halls.[10] While college rhetoric persisted in its images of communal harmony, functionally surviving colleges necessarily admitted enough (whatever their preparation) students to cover the institution's basic expenses.

This pattern led to a second strategic problem, especially for schools that sought to uphold an older denominational connection. Some schools became more denominational as they developed a national constituency. Until 1890, some colleges, like Wesleyan in Middletown, Connecticut, were able to maintain a predominantly Methodist commitment in the faculty and student body, no less than among donors and trustees. They reformed their original commitments by publicly embracing nondenominational values, while cultivating a stronger and wider Methodist network including ministerial conferences and secondary schools, at least region-wide. Functionally, in the decades after the Civil War, Wesleyan became more denominational and more organizationally conscious than before and also somewhat less reliant on local Middletown resources and more on Methodist resources in other regions.[11] Parallel developments occurred in the Baptist and Presbyterian denominations, no less than among Catholic, especially Jesuit, colleges. In the process, higher education institutions necessarily shed their nondenominational allegiances.

The influences that impacted both colleges and universities after the Civil War gradually began to differentiate the two genres of schooling, depending on how each institution committed itself to its traditional college or to new technical and professional subjects. But the Civil War had introduced another component that threatened some of the Republic's bedrock values, which stressed the larger social contribution of schools and colleges. Exactly how did classroom drill and recitations in the classics guarantee the upright moral character a republic expected of its citizens? Did a regimented pedagogy and rote learning plus recitation produce a discerning judgment in a school's graduates? Or did such a mechanized pedagogy undermine ethical training entirely? While the classics throughout the nineteenth century hovered under such critical scrutiny, the Civil War produced an additional layer of uncertainty about the Republican values of America's best schools. Until the Civil War, America's more educated political leaders reflexively prided themselves upon their abilities to debate their knottiest social and political issues and to explore areas of common ground in reaching compromises with parties of different views. Particularly among the Whig party, to which so many leading educators subscribed in the antebellum years, America's constitutional tradition provided the last best hope of settling issues short of violence and war.[12] The Constitution was the indisputable safety net for the republican order. However, the South had seceded, and the North had resorted to arms to insist on compliance to its more centralized, federal interpretation of the Constitution. The North, in other words, had gone to war to defend the Constitution, which was designed to prevent resorting to physical, indeed deadly, coercion. Ironically the North's victory at Appomattox brought out a substantive layer of anxiety that the Constitution itself was no longer a safety net. No longer were constitutional politics a guarantor of republican order. Without this incontestable constitutional protection—and the instruction in the classics that attempted its legitimacy—what values and what curricular methods could possibly fill the apparent void in schooling and produce a new kind of republican and civic order?[13]

After the war there were many other issues of training and funding to preoccupy America's educational leadership. But there was also intensive experimentation, particularly in the practical arts, agriculture, and the mechanical trades. The Morrill Act attempted to encourage these distinctively utilitarian subjects from 1862 and later with a second Morrill Act in 1890. New academic subjects with a more obvious connection to subsequent work and career—an echo of Francis Wayland's reform arguments—spurred a broader interest in substitutions for classical and literary training. Few were so bold to attack these older subjects and methods as worthless, but many were receptive to new experiments in scientific training. The last half of the century witnessed science draw even with the arts in shaping a liberal arts core in colleges and universities. By 1890 it had become axiomatic that the sciences had great substance and presence in any advanced training worth the name. Even literary scholars, trained in philology in German universities, caught the scientific spirit in traditionally nonscientific studies, like biblical study and the mastery of ancient languages. However, many Americans returned from Germany seemingly indifferent to the social class arrangements and state support for advanced work in Europe. They returned, however, with a great appreciation for disciplined, methodical approaches to issues for which the answers were as yet unknown. In a sense the greatest achievement of overseas study was not simply the example of European institutions operating at a truly advanced level; it was the embrace of a "scientific method" that seemed to operate independent of social context or historical tradition, opening the possibility for science to replace the Constitution as a civic panacea.[14]

Debates that began apart from a discourse on higher learning eventually had a substantive impact on the essence of a late nineteenth-century American academic culture, especially the reinterpretation of religion's relation to science. The comforting unity of religion and science of the antebellum period pervaded the antebellum college, whatever their particular denominational persuasion. The language of harmonious moral order appeared liberally in the exhortations of the typical, antebellum college president's senior course in moral philosophy, the capstone of the collegian's education.[15] This collegiate ideological unity struck antebellum faculty as compatible with and reinforcing the basic ideals of higher learning and of the Republic. The constitutional crisis posed by the Civil War—the Constitution's ideal being sustained by extraconstitutional force of arms—meant concomitantly that the presumed moral order carried no automatic guarantees of producing citizens of moral character. If the Constitution and America's evangelical Republicanism could not and did not forestall civil war, what social or intellectual values could serve as substitutes for this older religious and political tradition?

One possible answer to this cultural dilemma—scientific knowledge—did not appear in a flash with the publication in 1859 of Charles Darwin's *The Origin of the Species*. Darwin himself did not extrapolate in his work on the social or ethical implications of the "origin." His work began with recognition—axiomatic for most Americans and Europeans in the nineteenth century—that the universe followed the design of a Creator. However, after assuming a design, Darwin sought to explain the panoply of variation between and even within particular species. He argued that plant and animal life survived by ingenious adaptation to specific environments and endured by passing these adaptations on to succeeding generations of their kind. The species unable to adapt went out of existence, characterized by his famous phrase, "the survival of the fittest." Despite disclaimers, Darwin's work began to be seen as incompatible with religious-based beliefs in human origins. Darwinian life was a vigorous competition, at times seemingly ruthless, but eventually producing more complex and advanced forms of being. This process of "natural selection" at any given moment rested on the alternatives that an individual species faced in a limited environment, insofar as scientific observation was able to tell. Subsequent interpreters of Darwin's work—Herbert Spencer (1820–1903) in England and John Fiske (1842–1901) in America—would expand Darwin's argument to social arrangements and social selections and would undergird this extrapolation to make "progress" and "natural development" coincident with the divine will. According to Spencer, any effort of man to intervene in either the natural or the social process with a human design would threaten the larger order. In a famous 1882 New York review, Fiske's interpretation of man's evolution, offered to a broad audience of businessmen, journalists, clergy, and academics, received Spencer's immediate and personal imprimatur.[16]

Darwin's disciples, most notably Spencer and Fiske, had their counterparts in many social and educational venues. At Harvard, where both Louis Agassiz (1807–73) and John Fiske taught, there was intense probing of the consequences of Darwin's work for science, religion, and society. Agassiz wrote a spirited critique of *The Origin of the Species*, explaining among other charges that Darwin failed to document the cause of specie variation, that many fossilized species had no obvious or documentable antecedents, and that Darwin obscured his scientific observation with unproven theory. Unperturbed, Fiske attempted to calm the antievolutionary clergy by arguing evolution's compatibility with Christianity, how accessible the divine plan now was to both biologist and botanists, no less than to scholars seeking to make a science of social study. Both resistance and bridge building followed, but emphatically evolutionary arguments contributed three major features to the post–Civil War cultural crisis: 1) The role of individual species seems to acquire more responsibility for its life chances than before, and the divine role may have an initiating step but no longer one of constant and strategic intervention. *Religion,* in other words, experienced a reduced authority, and individualized choice appeared most creative in an "adaptive" mode. 2) *Science* no longer primarily followed a deferential role, collecting specimens for organization according to existing categories of matter, but actually discovered new knowledge about the process of change in all species and human social life. From the point of view of human knowledge, it mattered less that natural features did not conform to inherited religion-based expectations; more important, the interactive process between organism and environment determined the possibilities of both survival and natural order, both of which were more contingent than hitherto thought. 3) The *sociopolitical order* became the product of many self-interested adaptations rather than any particular human design, especially that of a constitutional order. For America, a Constitution, increasingly suspect in the postwar period, risked interfering with a more profound, natural order that man incompletely grasped. Organizational and institutional designs inferentially were counterproductive. For educational leaders, accepting Darwinian arguments meant, for example, that school organizations must necessarily be limited and self-restrictive, lest they inhibit and interfere with the all-important "choices" and "electives" that ultimately determined a student's worth and social value.

Historically, of course, colleges had expanded their organizational networks intradenominationally and professionally to a range of organizations. Universities had engaged in a process of merger with competitive organizations and professional schools. If the rhetoric of "social Darwinism" did not comport with the rise of monopolistic institutions, the implications of Darwinian science responded directly to the cultural crisis of the late nineteenth century. More than any other nation, America gave Darwin and his interpreters their most enthusiastic endorsement.[17] The full implications of "natural selection" insisted that no human order operated as efficiently as the order that was beyond human control. For a time corporation leaders could invoke the economics of laissez-faire and receive the legitimacy of Darwinian science; they could insist that federal and indeed state regulatory intervention risked damage to a complex interaction that at best could be understood after the fact. Darwinian science took the onus off political priorities to advance any regulatory legislation. The role of politics in the Gilded Age became the responsibility, not of the federal government, but (and only as a course of last resort) of state intervention when contesting parties had reached an impasse. The interpretation of Darwin provided a substitute for the confidence Americans once placed in constitutional politics and the evangelical moral order, so ubiquitous in the antebellum period. Significant decision making for a new America should not emerge from governmental legislatures but from the accumulated decision making of every citizen. No one person or institution should purport to speak or act for the social whole. The purpose of intelligent design was to adapt one's decisions and patterns closely to the perceived regimens of nature, represented by one's environment. From an educator's perspective, one strove to encourage students to adapt their priorities to those of the commonweal.

In the last decades of the nineteenth century, universities and colleges both extended their curricula to include more scientific instruction and to a course of elective studies. They incorporated other schools and networks, justified in the name of extended options to students. Most universities and many colleges could find faculty receptive to the Darwinian message or heresy, as fit the case. But now the great variations of ideologies and pedagogies within American higher education became less cause for concern. Each institution defined itself according to its resources and possibilities, which is to say its environment. This variety made it practically impossible to define "university" or "college." Ultimately the survival of the fittest, educational leaders intimated, would produce a more advanced tradition of research and professional instruction.

Some college leaders, however, were not willing to concede the charge of university reformers that the college was an atavism. They rose to defend the college in the era of the university. One of these was Rev. Noah Porter (1811–92), president of Yale College from 1871 to 1886, whose work shaped the Yale culture that novelist Owen Johnson had fictionally imagined in *Stover at Yale*. In 1871, the very year he assumed the presidency of Yale College, the Reverend Noah Porter published a spirited riposte to the gauntlet thrown down by university voices—Charles Eliot of Harvard, James B. Angell of Michigan, and Andrew White of Cornell. Porter's treatise, *The American College and the American Public*, reminded the critics of the American college that many of the "reforms" advocated after the Civil War—electives, science labs, practical studies, modern languages instead of "dead languages"—were familiar proposals before the war. Reputable schools like Brown University, Amherst, and Harvard itself, indulged many curricular experiments, usually at the expense of Latin and Greek, often in the name of "public demand." Citing President Francis Wayland of Brown, Porter chastened reformers who invoked the public will as the rationale for change: "The colleges, so far as I know, which have obeyed the suggestions of the public, have failed to find themselves sustained by the public."[18] Quick curricular experiments, in Porter's review, exonerated the classics, which generally had accommodated the physical sciences, mathematics, philosophy, and other subjects. The colleges had not calcified but rather continually responded to many influences that educational reformers unfairly claimed as their own.[19]

Porter's book also offered one of the most articulate defenses of the classics as the heart of collegiate discipline. Porter approved John Stuart Mill's (1806–73) preference for classical over modern language for its elemental yet elegant structure. Mastery of the classics rendered quick and efficient the command of modern languages. Far from dead, the classics put the reader into a realm of imagination and invention, indispensable to the refinement of intellectual discipline. But more important, Porter argued, "The man of the ancient world is a different being from the man of modern life. Stately, artificial, decided, clear in his opinions, positive and outspoken in his aims, objective in his life, positive and sharp in his diction, impetuous in his impulses, grand in his connection with the state, heroic in his virtues and almost in his vices, he stands forth in striking contrast with the man of modern times."[20] Judgment and analysis in our own times, Porter insisted, necessitated rooted comparisons. The engagement with Latin and Greek immersed the reader into the spirit of another age that shaped our later modern period. The grasp of the modern was impossible or superficial without genuine knowledge of ancient cultures. Modern languages quickened one's faculties but did not provide the depth and severer discipline of the classics, filled as they are with life's "germinant forces and their controlling principles."[21] Until the mind matured, trained on such forces and principles of language, other subjects—science, mathematics, and philosophy—are not possible but can only be instructed by way of studies that do not belong in higher learning. Here, Porter felt, is the danger of short-changing the classics by substituting subjects that would appear more relevant to students' later careers.

Moreover, the efficacy of colleges to impart knowledge and culture depended on the students' previous training and education. "If the colleges are to aim to become more positively refining and liberal in their culture," Porter explained, "they will need youths whose general as well as special training has been liberal and refined both at school and at home."[22] He was confident that the college had to be a limited institution and acquitted its duty by holding to a prescribed curriculum, privileging the classics. Porter rejected Eliot's version of the elective system, which made the classics optional, but he accepted that after a point students' interests diverged and electives could be admitted without compromising the college's distinctive duty to create intellectual discipline and nurture student enthusiasm. Would that produce a corps of graduates equipped to deal responsibly with the vicissitudes of American life?

Porter doubted that students of eighteen or nineteen years of age had the maturity to choose proper electives among a "smattering of studies" and was confident that the preferred curriculum cultivated for students of twenty to twenty-two guaranteed a different and better seasoning. Here he explicitly challenged "The New Education" arguments of Harvard's Charles W. Eliot.[23] Porter defended a close encounter of subjects through constant examination, particularly in the early years, rather than imparting information impersonally through lectures. However, he conceded that examination on basic information could lead to boredom for both student and teacher and urged teachers to keep interest high to avoid the student's indulgence of "cramming" or studying for class rank. The love of learning and "self-culture" needed to be the high standard for the American college. "Perhaps there is no point," Porter worried, "in which students err more seriously than in respect to the use of their leisure, the selection of private or special studies, the direction of their reading and the cultivation of facility in writing and speech."[24]

At the same time, Porter admitted, neither class studies nor faculty interactions encompassed the full experience of college life and instruction. The large community made up of one's fellows—especially in the enclosed and encapsulated residential schools—provided a valuable education. "The intellectual stimulus and education," Porter asserted, "which are furnished by the college community are of a kind which neither circumstances nor instructors can impart. They are eminently a self-education. Most of the efforts at self-improvement . . . fall in with the voluntary activities of awakening manhood and dawning responsibility. They train to the dignity and duty of self-culture."[25] The college system, Yale's president promised, echoing the central observation of *Stover at Yale*, promoted both individual character and the general culture; the college as a whole delivered "us from that gross vulgarity of taste and superficial conceit of knowledge to which it [a country like ours] is especially exposed."[26] Porter's Yale had uplifted the older evangelical model of college conversion to a social experience and justified the college as the moral leaven of culture. For him any college that converted itself into a university seeking advanced learning and research compromised its essence.

The crucial difference for Porter between a college and a university—a distinction he acknowledged was problematic—rested with the student bodies of each institution. The university presumed a trained and matured intellect capable of making decisions about training for life; a college assumed the immaturity of its students' minds and sought to bring those minds under a monitored and fraternal discipline. In Porter's conception universities only functioned at an advanced level if the college's work had been well done. Porter's articulation of the American college as the lynchpin of the educational system did not, however, consider that college dynamics at Yale during his administration could be displaced by extracurricular activity (as Stover's Yale experience testified). It was a time, one later observer remarked, "When the future and the past met together, and could not thus meet without awakening more or less of conflict."[27] Porter had assumed his office in 1871, just as the United States entered a period of severe economic recession and debate about the future course of the country. However, by the end of the decade, the economy boomed, and Yale received an unprecedented largesse from its alumni, and there was an accompanying change of power at Yale. The alumni received the trustee seats originally reserved for appointed state officials and elected their own alumni to the governing board. In addition, Yale built ten new buildings, particularly accentuating its expanding professional schools and its scientific departments: North Sheffield Hall, the Astronomical Laboratory, and the Peabody Museum of Natural History. In 1876 half the courses of the last two collegiate years became elective, the policy that Porter openly and regularly criticized at Harvard. But most of all, the student body expanded: from 755 in 1871 to 1,076 in 1886 (the year Porter resigned the Yale presidency). This expansion was largely outside the core academic department.[28] Porter's published defense of the generic college—popular enough to go into later editions—occurred at the very moment his own college moved into a university orbit and offered alternatives to training students into roles as responsible citizens and professionals.

From the generation of Porter to that of novelist Owen Johnson (class of 1899), there is unmistakably a value of unconscious natural selection in the work of Yale's collegiate education. If Porter overstated the role of classroom instruction and his faculty teaching abilities, Johnson clearly seconded Porter's perceived power of the extracurricular collegiate culture. In spite of Porter's insistence on the classics as the preferred disciplinary agent, supported by science and unsectarian Christian instruction, these values appeared nowhere in Owen Johnson's novel *Stover at Yale*, suggesting a substantive disconnect between Yale's student culture and its leaders' priorities. Porter's sense of the moral force of the collegiate community probably had greater resonance with the leaders of 563 schools of college/university grade in 1870. By 1900 America's colleges and universities had nearly doubled to 977 institutions, with a largely new faculty and student body and likely distanced from Porter's vision.[29] The university example put pressures on the colleges that were exploited and rejected by turns. But clearly the shaping of a university from a college core gained momentum and thereby compelled the colleges to sharpen their own self-definition. The college by 1900 insisted it was the prerequisite for university's professional and advanced training. Even university leaders began to accept that argument. In addition, the university found itself reorganizing and ultimately qualifying its elective system to put a liberal arts and science curriculum at the heart of its work. It is one of the ironies of this interaction that higher education leaders celebrated their expansion and soft-pedaled their centralization of institutional power. Their adoption of the evolutionary rhetoric and the assumptions of social Darwinism put the onus for academic change on the student's natural and instinctual abilities more than on the intellectual ideology of the school. That change came at the very moment they were creating an indispensable place for the life of the mind.

For the last decades of the nineteenth century and into the twentieth, efforts to redefine the college would be affected by the aggressive public role of university leaders.[30] Both college and university spokesmen began to cultivate a translocal dimension, that is, a metropolitan or regional mission, and for the very ambitious, especially for individuals and trustees who aspired to create an American university comparable to those in Europe, the expanded educational role took on national significance. This national aspiration grew rapidly after the Civil War, particularly after the Morrill Land Grant Act legitimated federal government support for new science and mechanical instruction on a par with older classical and scientific training. But the national goal became particularly poignant for universities that were beginning entirely anew, without the baggage of any collegiate inheritance or undergraduate culture. In 1875 Daniel Coit Gilman (1831–1908), the first president of Johns Hopkins University, approached the creation of the advanced research institution with precisely this attitude. "We should hope," he wrote to a university trustee (as well as former US senator from Maryland and US minister to Great Britain), Reverdy Johnson (1796–1876),[31] "that the Faculty soon to be chosen will be so catholic in spirit; so learned as to what has been discovered and so keen to explore new fields of research; so skillful as teachers; so cooperative as builders; and so comprehensive in the specialties to which they are devoted,—that pupils will flock to their instruction, first from Maryland and the states near to it,—but soon also from the remotest parts of the land."[32]

Gilman had come to his loftier educational aspiration through his own student and postgraduate experience. After his graduation from Yale (1852), he studied science at Harvard for a year, residing in the home of the eminent geologist and geographer Arnold Guyot (1807–84).[33] Gilman then traveled to Europe with his fellow classmate and lifelong friend Andrew D. White (1832–1918), who as president of Cornell University had recommended him to the Johns Hopkins trustees. The pair remained in Europe for two years, based in Saint Petersburg, Russia, at the American legation but traveling widely, visiting many capitals and examining their educational systems. Gilman supplied many documents to noted schoolman Henry Barnard (1811–1900) for that author's *National Education in Europe* (1854).[34] On his return Gilman joined the faculty of Yale's Sheffield Scientific School, where he served as librarian and teacher, and witnessed the in-fighting that the existence of an experimental scientific school fomented in those that tried to make collegiate training primarily classical and philosophical. Though his organizational abilities put him in line for the Yale presidency, the selection of Rev. Noah Porter with his classical tradition prompted Gilman to look elsewhere and accept the presidency of California's land-grant university at Berkeley in 1872. There he experienced the full critical brunt of trustees and editorialists who wanted colleges to be locally attuned and oriented to practical occupations rather than the research and national ideals he had hoped to institutionalize there. In spite of adverse pressures, he laid the foundation for an interaction between the public school system and university operations, a task he had earlier achieved with New Haven public schools and the Sheffield Scientific School. Soon thereafter, he left the time-consuming politics of public academia for Baltimore in 1875. Once again, he was hopeful that his energies would produce a true American university with the financial backing of city merchant, Johns Hopkins (1795–1873).

It is a commentary on the postbellum ferment in higher education that Johns Hopkins and his trustees were not in agreement about the nature of the university to be created. Hopkins himself had already funded a hospital in Baltimore and had become concerned about medical research in the treatment of cholera that plagued his own and other major seaport cities. His research was locally grounded. In contrast, his friend Reverdy Johnson Jr. had himself taken a law degree from University of Heidelberg, and held loftier notions, closer to Gilman's. Seven trustees were businessmen who held a range of ideas about the mission of higher education. One of them, the wealthy Baltimore and Ohio Railroad executive John Work Garrett (1820–84), quit the board when he perceived a majority wanted a school for something more than practical, immediate occupational training.[35] All the trustees experienced a sharp learning curve in their preparatory visits to other campuses as they sought a president for their new school. At Harvard, Charles Eliot had offered substantive advice but concluded with the qualified notion that Hopkins could not be anything but a local institution because of the state of public education in Maryland. The students were simply not sufficiently prepared for research work or for the "elective system," which marked for Eliot the epitome of a university's maturation.[36] Trustees were surprised at the efficacy of coeducation at Cornell but were unpersuaded by its president that female education belonged in a university's mission, a demurral underscored by Eliot. President James B. Angell (1829–1916) of Michigan, like Eliot, stressed the centrality of professional schools for any true university. Though favorable to medical and law schools, Hopkins's trustees resisted for many years creating such units. Eliot, White, and Angell (and also President Noah Porter of Yale) all agreed, however, that Daniel Coit Gilman was eminently qualified to become the Johns Hopkins president. They probably also concurred that the trustees were overambitious in their desire to create a university that would not only rival Europe's universities but would compare well with other American institutions.[37] Such debates were conducted with little reference to any student culture, which university presidents seemed to assume would naturally follow their public prospectus.

In their advice to the Hopkins's trustees, the three university presidents showed how varied still their conception of a "university" was in these formative years. Gilman was no exception. In spite of his exposure to the greatest of Europe's universities, his inaugural address stressed the university's teaching function, normally a collegiate responsibility. The ability to discover new knowledge via research, which would ultimately distinguish Hopkins as the first distinctively American university, did not appear self-consciously in Gilman's initial university definition.[38] Hopkins initially had no undergraduate student body. "Teaching" would rapidly segue into a chain of features, foreign to the antebellum college: electives, service, research, professional schools, departmental organization, and, above all, scientific training equal to that hitherto offered in classics, math, language, and literature. But the goal of character building, like the classics, had staying power; it continued in the basic rhetoric of higher education's aims, precisely because the new universities, even those that only aspired to research status, actually formed a minority of higher education institutions between the Civil War and World War I. These universities could not completely turn their backs on the progress of normal schools or colleges—especially for those who defined the university as a collage of college-dependent professional schools—any more than the colleges that had made their peace with older values of moral culture or liberal arts instruction could ignore the expansion of the research universities.

In the decades immediately after the Civil War, a small cadre of individuals, who were often Yale graduates with personal experience of the German universities, agreed that higher learning in America was not equivalent to its European counterparts. For the next two decades, they became self-conscious publicists, not only for the idea of a university, but for the disparagement of all other claimants to the status of higher education. Some approached the problem with great gentility. Daniel Coit Gilman was one who created a historical schema: a real university began after the first two stages in college development were over. The first stage, which committed schools to liberal culture structured primarily on the classics, no longer met "the requirements of the country."[39] The second stage, which added to collegiate work a cluster of professional schools, often directed by separate trustee boards, was also passé. In the present third stage, he argued, the country required something more comprehensive than the classical college and more integrated than a collage of professional and postgraduate schools. "We are not agreed," he admitted candidly, "to exactly what we want, and we are more at a loss as to how to get it."[40] Yet tentatively Gilman insisted that a new institution must be "tailored to the peculiarities of the country" and was not to follow German models uncritically. New funding was essential: for the West, publicly funded, land-grant institutions; for the East, gifts and legacies from men of wealth. Most of all, the new institutions would necessarily regard scientific teaching and research as an equal partner with a "love of letters." This new science, he insisted, must not be of a wholly technical sort but would encourage exploration of issues whose immediate worth is not obvious. The result would be not simply a definably "advanced" learning but a new educational standard that affected both academies and high schools. The result he sought would be a multifaceted, public but not egalitarian school system. If universities remained select and centralized, the apex of an organizational order, would America be able to challenge Europe? Gilman's schema demanded no repetition of the antebellum college student profile, prepared and unprepared together. Now a university must be advanced not only in its instruction and methodologies but also in its admission of the truly prepared.

By the 1890s Gilman's initial ambivalence about the university' design was gone. Between 1872 and 1892, the university presidents had simplified their public argument and increased their disparagement of old college instruction, which concentrated on the classics as a means of producing moral character. Josiah Royce (1855–1916), distinguished Harvard philosopher and an early PhD of Johns Hopkins University, intoned the mantra: universities require an exacting organization, their success must be measured by "the training of the nation's leaders who possessed an originating power, who could reach forward."[41] Royce, like other university spokesmen—including James B. Angell of Michigan, Charles R. Van Hise of Wisconsin, Andrew White of Cornell, G. Stanley Hall of Clark, and, of course, Charles Eliot of Harvard—all shed their caution and promoted an advanced, varied (and expensive) alternative to the American college.[42]

Seth Low (1850–1916), a second-generation university voice and president of Columbia University (1890–1901), noted that the new demands of systemic leadership in education required not a pedagogue but a manager. He explained how he rendered efficient a complex organization and delegated authority for an institution beyond the capacity of a single individual. He created a representative council for multifaceted discussion of deans and department chairs, regular faculty meeting (twice a month), a twelve-month calendar, pensions and sabbaticals for faculty, deans elected by faculty rather than appointed by the president, and all other means to ensure the value of economy in running the educational corporation.[43] Low had accepted election to Columbia's board of trustees in 1885 and had openly conceded to a fellow board member that he was in no way an academic but, equally important, realized that the new university was often not served by an academic as president. His explicit insight upon accepting the Columbia presidency was that his job was to remove confusion about his institution's priorities.[44] Among his other corporate priorities, Low sought an 1892 merger of Columbia with New York University, whose resources were one-fifth those of Columbia. His effort, advanced in principle by most university leaders, was to centralize the higher education system in New York City and reduce the expense of competition for funds, faculty, and students. Low received the backing of his board, which, in the late nineteenth and early twentieth century, was in the process of changing the trustee profile. The most obvious and helpful shifts on the board were a reduction of members of the clergy and an increase of bankers and businessmen. If his overture to New York University failed (its president Henry M. MacCracken [1840–1918] correctly feared total absorption and the elimination of higher learning alternatives for its urban middle-class students), Low's record made clear that mergers of university corporations satisfied analogous dynamics to the industrial mergers that distinguished other turn-of-the-century corporations.[45]

The corporate model reconfigured the duties of presidents, converting them into managers and money-raisers more than educators; the faculty grouped themselves into departments, which diminished their institutional loyalty to their employer. The internal changes were, at times, propelled by a new set of outside influences. More and more, the new professional associations—the American Historical Association (founded 1884), the American Mathematical Association (founded 1888), and so on—claimed a substantive allegiance and gave faculty members an independent vantage point for asserting academic autonomy. Of course, university benefactors continued their interventions, often to the point of breaching that very academic autonomy. Eventually such outside interference prompted the founding of a countervailing organization, the American Association of University Professors (founded 1915).[46] Important to both colleges and universities, alumni and benefactors played increasingly larger roles in shaping admission policies, hiring policies and curricular innovation. These organizational shifts tended to abandon the old collegiate ideal of moral harmony, which was reflected in the college president's course on moral philosophy in the senior year. This course intended to culminate a multiyear collegiate experience in relatively regimented instruction in the classroom and a more freewheeling, mutual training in the student extracurricular organizations. The president and faculty shifted themselves away from roles as substitute parents and recognized that the new close grouping of youth aged seventeen to twenty-one did not require the social monitoring of younger students.

New organizations attempted to solidify the advantages of collegiate changes. In 1915, 179 liberal arts colleges founded the Association of American Colleges (AAC).[47] As important to the AAC's curricular models were efforts to use extracurricular resources to maintain college cohesion and to insist on the college as the foundation of university work. Intercollegiate sports received forceful support from the rhetoric of Darwinian selection. However, in the last decades of the nineteenth century, few colleges gave official, institutional support to intercollegiate athletics. Most colleges in these years reluctantly changed in substantial ways, pushed by student-generated interests, particularly as student bodies increased. Dartmouth, for example, grew from three hundred students in 1890 to two thousand by 1910 and began to draw from all parts of the country. Colleges would not develop a generic sense of college or a collective identity like the "Ivy League" until after World War I. But ultimately, via intercollegiate athletics, many colleges developed regional and other collective entities. It was not until December 1936 that student editors from Columbia, Princeton, Dartmouth, Cornell, Harvard, Yale, and Pennsylvania simultaneously published an editorial—"The Time Is Now"—to create an Ivy League of intercollegiate sports. Though initially rejected, within three years the presidents of Harvard, Yale, and Princeton had signed an agreement that established mutual policies on scholastic ability, financial assistance, and recruitment from preparatory schools.[48]

The nineteenth-century debates over student life and curricular development affected both college and university priorities. By the end of the century, there was a profound cultural shift in American higher education as it concentrated on evolutionary science and corporate system. The change put collegiate instruction at the center of American higher education, making it the foundation for advanced work. Darwinian assumptions helped replace the earlier confidence in a constitutional process to achieve social stability and a civic order; instead, leaders of American higher learning put their confidence in a methodical process, whose end point was often uncertain. The reliance on empirical knowledge, however, seemed to provide a grounding for tentative agreement in many intellectual and political arenas. A new corporate mentalité affected colleges and universities no less than it did America's business and social life. In Stover's Yale, as well as in the new universities' professional work, one achieved maturity and individuation by accommodating and adapting to the priorities of relevant groups. The atmosphere and environment of a school, its special cohesive culture, provided an agency as instructive as formal classes. Owen Johnson's fictional Yale intended no criticism of his alma mater by marginalizing classroom instruction. His real intent was to underline the new *experience* of higher learning and to make the process of ingesting it a holistic social process. With such assumptions a new student culture meshed with large scientific and organizational expansions in American higher education—the distinctive campus, departmental disciplines, external professional associations, state and philanthropic fiscal regulation, and clearer divisions between collegiate instruction and university research—to produce a distinctive late nineteenth-century (generational culture #4) academic culture.

CHAPTER NINE

Progressive Ideology in American Higher Education

Of the 977 or more "colleges" and "universities" in turn-of-the-century America, commentators have noted that few could legitimately claim to be universities or even prestigious four-year colleges.[1] Contemporary commentators, often based in research universities, applied the standard of the most privileged institutions to all the rest and also applied a relatively static definition of higher education to competing schools. Most of these schools had originated in the nineteenth century and had experienced all the problems of funding and clientele that every school faced at its outset. The obvious problem for understanding these 977 schools was that no definition could fit all, and the creation of an elevated ranking worked to the advantage of the best funded of the lot. To evaluate the state of higher education at the end of the nineteenth century then, one should approach these 977 institutions historically rather than definitionally. First, though the concentration of higher education institutions was greatest in the northeastern United States, virtually all states and territories contained some institutions with a claim to collegiate or university status. Second, though not costly by twentieth-century standards, collegiate instruction required financial sacrifice, planning, and organization for any family sending its youth to any collegiate institution. In other words, colleges and universities had become calculating and selective in admissions, partly because they were viewed as an attractive asset for future employment by a rapidly growing middle class. One Harvard student had notably exclaimed to a faculty member, historian Henry Adams (1838–1918), that a Harvard degree would be worth money in Chicago.[2] Adams was likely as horrified by the student's crassness as he was about the inflated currency that the college degree had become. It mattered not where one finished in class rankings, so long as one walked away with a diploma in hand. These and other anti-intellectual and extracurricular collegiate dynamics made higher education a part of the national social dialogue by 1900 in a way it had not been at any point in the previous century.

The disparities between a university president's public rhetoric of educational aims and the realities of student life widened as colleges and universities expanded in the twentieth century. All institutions were subject to indigenous pressures and proposals, and presidents, strapped for funds, could rarely resist the pet projects of affluent alumni or donors. With donations coming more from businessmen rather than denominational organizations, many social commentators, like John Jay Chapman (1862–1933) and Upton Sinclair (1878–1968), popularized the perception that business interests controlled academia.[3] More to the point, a range of external influences had always pressured schools with "higher" aspirations. The real issue, impossible to gauge among the panoply of 977 schools, was at what point the integrity of instruction actually became corrupted from outsider support. Given the variety of institutions and their precarious financing, most educational leaders focused on institutional survival and fretted about educational excellence afterward. Such lapses in the midst of popularized Darwinian rhetoric made sheer survival a practical, widespread standard. Internally the canons of research or even a standard of advanced learning had not trickled down to undergraduates. Surprisingly the increased specialization of the academic professional reconfigured the faculty's sense of themselves and shifted their allegiance to their professional associations and their articulated standards of research and teaching. Colleges and universities were not only varied; they were layered with functions difficult to integrate. In spite of this difficulty, universities in the popular press were continually depicted as having coherence that actuality belied the reality.

This bureaucratic layering at once resulted in a series of institutional realignments: a narrower role for academics confined in departments, an expanded role for the president as manager of the parts, a masking of the actual role of trustees, and a largely indifferent attitude toward the educational impact upon students. Bureaucracies became subjects to discuss in their varied parts rather than holistically, that is, in their autonomous operations. The new position of dean of students, which began to appear in the early years of the century, presented schools with a choice: did bureaucratic officers ease students' progress through the system, interceding for them to administrators and teachers, or were they institutional enforcers of impersonal organizational priorities? Did the new deans become advocates for student needs hitherto ignored, or did they become representatives of established policies to which students must defer? Were administrators agents of students or presidents?[4] Similarly alumni officers, admission representatives, and guidance and personnel assistants, as well as the public relations efforts, were seldom seen as conflicted arms of the educational institution. Rather, each added office was viewed as a legitimate response to external needs noticed by a consuming public; each new bureaucratic office quickly became an attractive feature of higher education to ensure that the tuition charges bought a good deal more than any school's competitor. Imposing buildings and winning athletic teams also added to the luster surrounding higher education. The one feature that largely went unsung was the *intellectual* gains of a four-year collegiate experience.

The obvious casualty of a diversified, bureaucratic college/university was the inherited expectation of a holistic experience, a goal still advanced by many denominational schools reluctant to shed their religious allegiances. Within the largely Protestant aegis of American higher education, a congregational model still survived that resisted the multiple specializations, disciplines, services, and electives, which complicated an integrated, holistic model. A true college, many publics expected, should be an organic operation, functionally more than the sum of its parts. If it were no longer an obvious moral entity, an early twentieth-century college might claim to impart the basic value of a society and culture via its academic priorities. However, as colleges grew and took responsibility for several hundred students, all capable of transfer to competitive institutions, even educational leaders became increasingly less precise about their core educational experience. Educational spokesmen diluted institutional goals and indulged the language of practicality, utility, and culture, sometimes stressing one more than others, sometimes implying that the three could be crafted into a whole. The result was that after 1900 any effort to conceptualize college and university work became a progressively abstract exercise.[5]

Incontestably the rising importance of the city in American life drove the Progressive movement for reform and progress that began in the 1890s. The sheer density of urban populations had exacerbated all problems of the social order—education, health, safety, and so on—to a new scale. In many cases, particularly in the fiscally precarious urban universities, the quantity of students that schools needed to balance their accounts overwhelmed existing facilities. For example, early efforts to include female students to sustain a fiscally supportable student population ignored women's special needs and continued to build as if their students were only male.[6] At the end of the century, a number of universities like New York University and Columbia University in New York City simply chose to evade urban problems by relocating northward to University Heights in the Bronx and to Morningside Heights, respectively. The city not only quickly caught up to this strategy and built past higher education schools trying to evade urban problems. Higher education faculty and Progressive intellectuals soon recognized the need to engage rather than evade urban pressures and dysfunction as principles of modern life: modern solutions, they assumed, can never be static, one-size-fits-all responses. Some deference to students' abilities and aspirations, like jobs and after-schooling employment, needed attention. Progressives welcomed local agencies that invited internships or summer work that might well lead to careers and professional opportunities. If uncertainty and waste became concomitant features of innovation, then the ensuing insight or reform became thereby more realistic and practical than pat answers and quixotic schemes of social and political ideologues.[7] Progressive leaders made higher education more central to the social process than it had ever been. The new institutionalization at the turn of the century set the context for a thoroughgoing rethinking of the impact of higher learning on society as a whole.[8]

Within the discourse over higher education, university leaders had gingerly moved toward electives and other novelties in a competitive spirit. However, individuals who became important to higher learning were increasingly city-based industrialists or merchants like Robert C. Ogden (1836–1913),[9] men whose careers had little to do with traditional education and who engineered limits on both Progressive reform and the roles of university and college in Progressive work. (Seth Low of Columbia fit this pattern, becoming president of Columbia University and setting a precedent followed by others, like his successor Nicholas Murray Butler [1862–1947] and William Rainey Harper [1856–1906] of University of Chicago, who were appreciated and known for their management more than their educational acumen.) Instead, Ogden and his associates created conferences and foundations that cast a far wider aegis than the networks of even the most renowned colleges or universities. Following the example of the earlier Peabody Education Fund, Ogden began his educational philanthropy by organizing a trainful of wealthy associates to tour the underdeveloped colleges and universities of the South. Part investment, part educational fieldwork, part vacation, Ogden's initiative eventually formalized itself into two organizations: the Southern Education Board (founded 1901), whose mission was raising and distributing money to backward Southern institutions, and the Conference for Education in the South (founded 1898), a propaganda agency promoting public taxation for the separate education of black and white Southerners.[10]

Ogden's bedrock motivation was both economic and political more than educational. He controlled the extensive merchandising organization of John Wanamaker (1838–1922) in Philadelphia and managed the department store enterprise from New York after Wanamaker merged with A. T. Stewart in 1896. His vast retail experience in Philadelphia and New York made him aware of the South's economic underdevelopment. Like George Peabody, who also began as a dry-goods merchant, Ogden firmly believed that private initiatives, locally rooted in indigenous institutions, were the only solutions to the "failed efforts" of US Reconstruction. The Peabody Education Fund, which had begun with support to Southern public school systems, later had narrowed its strategy—to select teachers for university fellowships, then to creating a special normal school through an endowment to Peabody College for Teachers (later a unit of Vanderbilt University).[11] By contrast, Ogden would begin where the Peabody Fund ended, by targeting the gatekeeping institutions of the next generation's leaders: first at Hampton Institute, then Tuskegee Institute, and finally Columbia's Teachers College. Both Peabody and Ogden, although a generation apart, began with the defeated South as their central problem but shifted their attention to select higher education institutions to serve actively in the work of benevolent reform. Peabody and Ogden worked in behalf of a different institutional complex that embraced both Northern and Southern funders and administrators. They found ways, initially through commerce, then through cultural experiments, to reshape their nation.[12]

There is no question that Ogden's efforts stimulated money and organization that would not have occurred but for his initiative; it is also the case that Ogden's own historically driven assumptions accepted black Southerners as racially limited.[13] Ogden's ideology, however, infused his conservative, racial biases into a Progressive organizational network. His national goals, though city based, had focused upon the South as the strategic target of reform. These values also clarified the newfound, organized interaction between a capitalist economy and university instruction. His first order of business was to avoid overt racial division and to promote individuals, like Booker T. Washington (1856–1915), who would literally ride circuit through the South and the nation promoting a special view of gradual social evolution. His second order of business was to redress the South's financial plight through public taxation rather than through charity or federal support. He accepted research conclusions that established that the South's economy remained a shambles. In seven Southern states, the annual earning power of the individual farmer was $150, and the annual per capita wealth of the rural white population stood at $425. In 1898 the taxes generated in the South only reached the levels earlier achieved in 1860.[14] Consolidation of school systems, county supervision, and a minimal operation of schools for eight months depended on all Southerners being convinced of the merits of taxation. His argument for schooling both whites and blacks, however unequally money was distributed for their schooling, promised a new economy through improved farming knowledge and methods.

Ogden collaborated with Peabody Education Fund trustees and staffers—J. P. Morgan (1837–1913) was the fund's last chair; Daniel Coit Gilman, president of Johns Hopkins University, functioned as a longtime trustee; Southerners J. L. M. Curry and Wickliffe Rose (later the longtime president of Rockefeller's General Education Board [GEB]) had served as general agents of the Peabody Fund. Ogden financed over a dozen conferences in the South and worked closely with George Peabody's nephew, the investment banker George Foster Peabody (1852–1938), making him vice president and treasurer of the Southern Education Board. Ogden identified individual Southerners whose views coincided largely with his institutional ideology, and he selected board members for the Southern Education Board. This network not only inherited personnel and ideology from the Peabody Education Fund; it provided money for projects and incentives and, even more, brought together a progressive generation of Southern leaders to see their colleges and universities as broader agents of change. This younger cadre included, for example, in 1907, Edwin Alderman (1861–1931), president of the University of Virginia; Richmond College historian S. C. Mitchell (1861–1948), who was soon to be president of the University of South Carolina; Hollis B. Frissell (1851–1917), president of Hampton Institute; Philander P. Claxton (1862–1957), professor of education at the University of Tennessee and, from 1911 to 1921, Woodrow Wilson's US commissioner of education; Charles Dabney (1855–1945), president of the University of Tennessee and later president of the University of Cincinnati; Edgar Gardner Murphy (1869–1913), Southern Education Board secretary and publicist; Wallace Buttrick (1853–1926), secretary of the GEB; and Walter Hines Page (1855–1918), influential editor (*Atlantic Monthly*, among others) and Woodrow Wilson's ambassador to Great Britain. Formal dinners in New York only expanded this network of Northern financiers, merchants, publicists, and educators to include Southern university presidents.[15]

One of the immediate consequences of Ogden's "conferences" was a consolidation of observations about the South. These conferences had no direct coercive authority; but their indirect appropriation of older nineteenth-century voluntary methods—using the power of conversation and experience to "inculcate" new priorities for action—proved very effective to his city-based associates, grappling for both knowledge and approaches to America's perceived problems.[16] Ogden's meetings did lead directly in some cases to constructive action. In 1903 John D. Rockefeller Jr. (1874–1960), who had left Ogden's 1901 conference held in Winston-Salem, North Carolina, persuaded his father to create and fund ($1 million at the outset, to be spent over ten years) the GEB, one of the largest and most effective charitable foundations in American history.[17] Its first and longtime secretary was Wallace Buttrick, a former Baptist minister, who had once served the same management role during the later days of the Peabody Education Fund (1867–1914). The GEB began its work on the model of the Peabody Education Fund: support for select teachers in designated universities, subsidies to select county supervisors, and cooperation with state farm programs of the US Department of Agriculture. The board's modest contribution to black education singled out schools modeled on the agricultural, industrial, and teacher-training priorities of Hampton and Tuskegee Institutes.[18]

Gradually, however, the GEB widened its attention to the panoply of colleges and universities beyond the South and set itself the task of shaping a national system of higher education. On a larger scale, the GEB had mirrored the earlier experience of the Peabody Education Fund: their national goals had progressed from the reform of city and state systems, to the less expansive selection of key teachers and personnel, and finally more narrowly to the designation of a select school that it would endow and through which it would offer, not only a model curriculum, but a degree with career implications. The board began its quest in the South with a research survey that discovered a great unevenness of quality and financing throughout the region; beyond the diversity they discovered too many mediocre or poor colleges and universities. The board established a set of standards that privileged schools that were close to large populations and already commanded a clientele. In brief, they favored city-based institutions in and beyond the South. Over the next two decades, they distributed $60 million nationwide, primarily to school endowments, given on the organizational principle that a financially shaky school could not be a good school. Their initial priority of regional uplift had become a selective, elitist standard. Many of the board's contributions were matching grants, which gave a receiving institution the means to demonstrate its existing strengths and stretched the board's own dollars. By 1914 the board's matching grants of $10.5 million, they proudly boasted, had generated over $40 million for the fortunate recipients. By 1920 twenty institutions had received 75 percent of the board's largesse.[19]

The central figure of this systematic philanthropy was Frederick Gates (1853–1929), a young Baptist minister whose own educational training gave no indication of the seminal role he would play in the shaping of higher education in America. Like Rev. William Rainey Harper, who became the first president of the University of Chicago (founded 1890), Gates had grounded his career in the evangelical organizations of the Baptist missions. Harper excelled at the Chautauqua circuit of lectures; Gates had organized the American Baptist Mission Society to raise and funnel money to Baptist schools and missions, especially among the western tribes and Southern blacks. In the early planning of a "university," both men were thinking expansively, even nationally and beyond denominational boundaries; it would be, Harper once thought, "an educational trust" incorporating many colleges, all with a uniform organization. A university in the country's heartland, however, had not materialized due to the reluctance of Chicago's Baptist donors. This resistance forced Gates to seek new allies.[20] Once Gates had enlisted John D. Rockefeller Jr. and then his father, the initial plans for a new university in Chicago took on a more focused direction. First, Gates determined that the initial buildings would avoid mortgages but would adhere to a large plan, to be fleshed out as monies became available. Second, the leadership would be Baptist but would encourage the participation of other denominations. Third, the university would be governed by elected rather than appointed departmental chairmen. Finally, Rockefeller insisted his name not be put upon the institution, if for no other reason than to encourage a range of other donors. Harper received extensive autonomy in his decisions, most notably in his selection of an architect of Gothic structures and his penchant for committing to expansions before he had the money in hand. By the time of his resignation and early death in 1906, Harper had created a mountain of debt, exactly the opposite of his Baptist donors' advice.[21]

Despite Harper's actions, during the 1890s, Frederick Gates won Rockefeller's confidence and became the philanthropist's full-time advisor. It was Gates who suggested a mechanism for the distribution of Rockefeller's money via a general purpose foundation, ultimately resulting in the GEB of 1903. The GEB would eventually be the model for the Rockefeller Foundation, chartered in New York in 1913.[22] The GEB began to give thought, not simply to the improvement of Baptist interests, but also more expansively to the shaping of Chicago's and America's fortunes.[23] As Gates rose in Rockefeller's confidence and assumed executive authority for the magnate's organizations, his vision narrowed—the pattern of the Peabody Education Fund and the Southern Education Board—to the creation of a single institution, a university that would not compete and siphon students away from existing Baptist seminaries or colleges but would compare favorably with the expanding eastern universities. Gates's University of Chicago, he hoped, would become the progressive model of America's higher education institutions.

The particulars of the new university's development illuminate the features and assumptions of this generation's higher education culture as well as the twentieth-century American university.[24] Its founding arose from external interests beyond the city but nevertheless concentrated its focus on the city itself; its business ties guaranteed that it would be adaptable to the technical and commercial forces of the new metropolis; its design, however inchoate, intended an institution greater than a single college; and finally its serendipitous construction clearly documented that the university was still an experiment in practice and conception.[25] Rockefeller, the major funding presence, kept his distance from the enterprise by offering a grant of $600,000, to be matched by an additional $400,000 within a specified period. The match drew in a number of non-Baptist groups and solidified a Chicago elite, each member of which brought along their memberships in a range of cultural organizations. The trustees contained but one minister, the rest representing the city's many business interests. Still, historical commentary about the founding of the University of Chicago has overstated the centrality of three individuals, but their action was nevertheless strategically important: the financial founder, John D. Rockefeller; the entrepreneur and eventual Rockefeller agent, Frederick Gates; and the first president, William Rainey Harper. Rockefeller, a devoted Baptist congregant, had hesitated for years to invest substantively in Baptist colleges and universities, largely because of the failure of a previous University of Chicago and the impecunious nature of the denomination's schools.[26] When finally persuaded that a central institution of renown might enhance the fortunes of all its colleges, Rockefeller focused on a city institution. He was distracted from forthright action by several other formidable Baptist proposals, particularly those favoring a grand institution in New York City and another favoring Columbian College in Washington, DC (eventually George Washington University).

Harper and Gates in combination helped shift the donor's preference to Chicago, but Rockefeller's early donations targeted a "college" and his funding permitted the creation of little more than a liberal arts institution.

Rockefeller did not want to be the sole funder of the school and offered matching grants to entice other Baptist donors. The absence of a groundswell in favor of a flagship institution—the several dozen existing Baptist colleges all had their own sponsors—made Rockefeller very reluctant to commit funds comparable to those that founded Johns Hopkins, Clark, Stanford, or Catholic Universities, all founded in the same period with serious graduate-level aspirations. His substantial correspondence with many advisors eventually settled on William Rainey Harper as the potential leader of the new institution. Harper's substantive Yale commitments made him hesitate until Rockefeller added a million dollars to the new University of Chicago endowment and added a promise of more funding to win Harper's acceptance as the first president of the school—now elevated in the discussion to "university." Rockefeller's million set aside $700,000 for a graduate school endowment, but with the stipulation that none of the rest could be targeted for buildings.[27]

Harper was a powerful presence and, like his contemporary university presidents, was appreciated as much or more for his administrative abilities than his actual scholarship. Harper's plan was for a university with five divisions—the University Proper; University Extension; University Press; University Libraries, Laboratories, and Museums; and University Affiliations (which anticipated linkages with existing Baptist colleges and organizations). Harper named four executives, a head for each department, and academic ranks from professor, associate, assistant, instructor, docent, lecturer, reader, and fellow, each rank with a specified term of appointment.

The immediate pressure to open in 1892 with a full faculty and substantive student body made clear to Harper and others how inadequate his funding was. Chicago merchandiser Marshall Field (1834–1906) had donated a three-block site on the city's Midway for its locus, but lacking funds for buildings and faculty salaries, especially for the coveted professors already comfortably fixed in established institutions, left Harper uncompetitive. Marshall Field offered an additional $100,000 if Harper could raise a million dollars in ninety days. Harper and his associates achieved the number and began site planning for the Chicago campus. However, Harper had exhausted potential and friendly donors in this last frenetic campaign and had nowhere to turn for a salary budget, except the reluctant Rockefeller. Through Gates's intervention, Rockefeller added another million for faculty recruitment. Also unexpectedly a transplanted Chicagoan, William Ogden (1805–77), dedicated funds in his will for a graduate school of science. The Baptist Union Theological Seminary in nearby Morgan Park, where Harper had once taught, also joined the university as its school of divinity. Within the space of only twenty-one months, the University of Chicago had become an institution that had a seventeen-acre site, funds for ten buildings, a substantive endowment, and a 120-member faculty and operated a preparatory academy (using the old Baptist Union Theological Seminary's buildings), a college, two graduate schools, and a divinity school.[28]

Perhaps the most obvious sign of Harper's ambitions was its architecture. In spite of its Baptist origins, the university architect, Henry Ives Cobb (1859–1931), established a Gothic style for the earliest buildings.[29] His development of quadrangular blocks on the campus necessarily followed Harper's appreciation of Oxford University and its values of endurance, collegiality, tradition, and inspiring ornamentation.[30] This style pervaded the nineteen buildings constructed in the university's first decade, many of them exclusively built for specific sciences: anatomy, botany, chemistry, physiology, zoology, and the Ryerson Physical Laboratory, which Harper pronounced the most beautiful university building in the world.[31] By 1901, buildings for male students—dormitories, recreation, and eating commons—plus buildings for the professional schools, humanities, social sciences, geology, and geography as well as a library all lay in the future. If Harper had a plan, as several knowledgeable associates claimed, practical priorities determined the actual development of the university. Its Gothic style invited criticism for its association with monastic traditions of didacticism, royal sponsorship, and derivative historical dependence. Critics also found the Gothic icon strange for its seeming anti-utilitarian values, for its distancing from public needs and services that many university voices claimed as a primary goal. However, even after its original architect was dismissed, subsequent designers—Charles Coolidge (1858–1936), Dwight Heald Perkins (1867–1941), and James Gamble Rogers (1867–1947) remained within a Gothic motif.[32] The Gothic association with endurance and solidity—given the university leaders' sense of contingency and vulnerability—carried more weight than any apparent ideological inconsistency.

The Gothic image of the university seems stranger still for its appearance simultaneously with the 1893 Columbian Exposition. The dramatic introduction of the fair's Beaux-Arts style—monumental classical forms, axial landscapes, and its orderly accommodation of diverse building formats and locations—would influence major public buildings in all American cities for a generation. University of Chicago's Gothic architect, Henry Ives Cobb, trained not in Paris but at MIT, shifted to a Beaux-Arts style in his reconfiguration later of the American University in Washington, DC.[33] Chicago's Gothic design, however confined by its landholdings and sense of tradition, still insisted on its experimental modernity, by planning for a university complex—separate buildings for distinct sciences, laboratories, study halls, and dormitories, plus (eventually) a library. Its conception transcended the inherited tradition of the college campus and pressed on to think of its organism as a self-contained city, a "Gray City" adjacent to the Columbian Exposition's "White City."[34]

The absence of a library did not mean that Harper had backed away from a commitment to the Progressive model of a university. The center of the new university's urbane coherence lay with its embrace of science. Not only was Chicago's first building explicitly devoted to the physical sciences, the university's entire orientation sought to move beyond the American college's moral didacticism. Even its ordained minister-president, William Rainey Harper, like so many of his contemporary university leaders, sought to distance themselves from denominational litmus tests in their faculty hiring, trustee appointments, and public outreach. Their goal was not antidenominational, as much as an integration of inherited religious traditions with newfound, open-ended experimental inquiry.[35] For Harper's generation the search for individuals who could bridge the older moral and newer scientific standards comfortably remained very frustrating. Especially outside the natural sciences, in philosophy where ethics and the evidences of Christianity were decreasingly emphasized, faculty hiring signaled the university's priorities.

The full impact of Chicago's intellectual ferment of the first generation of American career academics can only be captured by examining the scholarship and careers of Harper's faculty hires. One of Harper's first hires in 1894 was a man who became central to modern education and a prominent democratic philosopher: John Dewey (1859–1952). Dewey's doctoral degree from Johns Hopkins (1884) and his early work on Hegelianism struck the correct chords of advanced thinking without openly affronting the tenets of established beliefs.[36] Dewey's decade-long service at the University of Chicago, however, not only took a sequence of surprising turns, his work set him on a course into the workings of the learning mind that would eventually set the boundaries of a distinctively American philosophy, pragmatism, but more importantly a broadly American way of thinking. In the seeds of his Chicago work lay the foundation of a singular intellectual revolution in American academic culture, which we now label Progressivism.[37]

Dewey's fascination with the learning process originated with observations of schoolchildren at play. Left alone, even very young children found ways of adapting themselves to their fellow players and their surroundings.

Often completely reinventing established rules of play, an entire group on the playground could reinvent complex protocols that arose and grew in a seemingly "natural" way. Dewey's amazement in the face of these reconstructions led him to infer the disruptive force of adult imposition and to substitute the foundations of Progressive education. Left to themselves, he observed, children progressed, however wastefully and erratically, by incorporating the talents of their fellows and the resources of their environment. The collective impact of such serendipitous progressions, he concluded, were far more rooted in democratic learning than any alternatives, especially those prepared, professional plans for the public classroom. For classroom education to teach with a comparable dynamic, everyday, natural experience had to enter the classroom. Teachers needed to begin "where the child was" and not presume a prejudged stage that actually may be beyond the teacher's or students' understanding. Dewey demanded freedom in the classroom for student interaction and, importantly, for teachers to experiment constantly. But how would school administrators judge the quality and extent of learning, if every classroom and school developed their own trajectories? Dewey would insist that his learning was not rudderless but actually adhered to a broader natural sequence that teachers and administrators would only grasp in retrospective assessments. The natural thread in all learning, he argued, inhered in every situation, however varied their outer appearances. In his 1916 book *Schools of Tomorrow*, Dewey offered a range of examples from a poor Alabama school where learning originated in a dirt bank to an affluent Chicago school designed by Frank Lloyd Wright and showcased children improvising ballet. Implicitly Dewey argued that the psychological patterns of education overrode the power of social class and contingent circumstances.

Dewey's thinking and writing in 1890s Chicago culminated in the publication of *The Child and the Curriculum* and *School and Society*, which guided his work in the university's School of Pedagogy. These accessible pamphlets gave no hint of the deep philosophical debates that underlie them. Their widely read argument seems to make the complicated process of instruction readily accessible to every citizen and parent. For Dewey, the unstructured interaction of child, parent, teacher, and social environment created an authority superior to those of professional schoolmen with their plans and tests. The process of learning, like the process of social change itself, improved, so the pragmatist Dewey's argument ran, by following out the lines of its own inner rationality, which rarely could be predicted ahead of time. Any directive or school authority could only be so for a brief and contingent period. Everything was subject to the scrutiny of participants. The one predictive feature was change itself, conducted ideally (with Dewey's Vermont origins in play) in a town-meeting dynamic, where every voice received considered attention.

Dewey's argument went beyond pedagogy and on to a redefinition of "science" itself. His "science" was something very different from the narrow, empirical meaning it would assume later in the twentieth century. In 1900 science purported to move away from the deductive morality of evangelical Protestantism, so dominant in nineteenth-century American culture. It sought a rationale for open-ended experimentation; it coached its adherents into a new comfort level with problems without obvious and certain answers; it sought a methodical, inferential, and inductive approach to both learning and social reform. If Dewey's science did not completely substitute for an inherited and holistic moral tradition, science's new meaning seemed to accept and encompass the diversity and ambiguity that modern urban life constantly presented to its citizens.

Dewey's definition of science was not without its critics, who operated from different philosophical and political assumptions. The limits of Dewey's emergent philosophy registered themselves most prominently in two events: first, the opinions of his fellow faculty member (and fellow Johns Hopkins doctorate) Edward Bemis (1860–1930), a political economist who supported labor in the Homestead strike and publicly critiqued the adverse and exploitative tactics of capitalism. His published opinions resulted in his 1895 firing by President Harper. The event had a chilling effect upon many, including Dewey, who at the time publicly did not resist such social censorship but privately acknowledged its destructive presence.[38] Second, Harper's treatment of Dewey's experimental Laboratory School in the Department of Pedagogy made it clear that not all environments were supportive and benign. When Harper summarily fired Dewey's wife, Alice, from the Laboratory School's principalship in 1904, Dewey resigned not only from the directorship of the school but also from the philosophy department. He quickly received and accepted an offer to teach philosophy at Columbia University and served on that faculty for the remainder of his career.[39] However completely Dewey's scientific arguments met the novelty of urban and national experience in America, its practical implementation did not always win converts or benign supporters to this new pragmatic way of thinking. Some interactions did not conclude with benign results.

Harper's imposed Gothic standard impacted adversely on another distinguished faculty member during the university's early years, one whose scholarly work, unique as it was, nevertheless illuminated the newer problems and assumptions of his academic generation. One of Harper's appointments was Thorstein Veblen (1857–1929), a sociologist and economist, who had studied at Johns Hopkins and held a PhD (1884) from Yale, where he had been a student of Noah Porter. Veblen had a different mind-set than Dewey, although both belonged to the new progressive wave. Veblen had developed a singular, almost European admiration of the research professor, and openly criticized the social outreach of colleges and universities as a distraction from serious faculty work. His years at Chicago (1892–1906) concentrated his criticism on one of Harper's prized creations, the Division for Extension Courses to bring university insight to current social problems and to advance modest business reforms. This overture to immediate and present issues, Thorstein Veblen argued, indulged a crass faddishness that pandered to moneyed interests primarily. The real raison d'être of any university, Veblen insisted, was the reverse of Harper's priorities, namely, knowledge and instruction first, and faculty researches second. Veblen felt Harper's intensive merger of university and mercantile priorities went beyond the mere corruption of higher learning; it underscored the power of the wealthiest and least productive members of a community. Unlike Dewey's finesse of social class stratification, Veblen drew upon the philological skills of his Yale graduate training and scrutinized closely the ordinary language and behavior of American institutional life. In his classic 1899 publication, *The Theory of the Leisure Class*, Veblen presented America's affluent elites as the exploitative parasites of the country's largesse. Their "conspicuous consumption" and indulgence of leisure effectively reversed Darwinian expectations of survival of the fittest. Rather, Veblen insisted class tensions only resulted in the exploitation of the less affluent and permitted the least fit to survive. Unlike Karl Marx, Veblen did not believe class tensions aroused consciousness and set the context for dramatic reform. In fact, he stated, most self-conscious reforms were generally doomed to defeat. The most constructive activity in behalf of a truly civil society involved a documentation of long-standing patterns of thought and behavior that would result ultimately in the realistic understanding of institutional interactions. For him scholarship was the key to reform. The study of such basic institutional forms led Veblen to create and edit the *Journal of Political Economy*, an enormously influential scholarly forum published by the University of Chicago Press.[40]

Veblen's reliance on the power of intellect—he called intelligence a "primitive hunger"—seemed at once both new and old-fashioned. Increasingly he cultivated the stance of the spectator, the outsider dispassionately apart from the dynamics he studied. In part, he was naturally different from many of his fellow first-generation career academics.[41] Wisconsin was his birthplace, in 1857, of parents who were first-generation farming immigrants from Norway. As a young man, he reveled in the Icelandic sagas and the social power of the Bunde. He attended the denominational Carleton College in neighboring Minnesota and after six years of study took his BA. He pursued graduate work in 1880–81 at Johns Hopkins University before enrolling at Yale where he took his PhD. He then returned to the family farm and was out of the academic world for seven years, until 1891 when he accepted—at age thirty-four, that is, late for a first appointment—an economics fellowship at Cornell with J. Laurence Laughlin. Almost immediately Laughlin became one of the prizes of William Rainey Harper's infamous raids on other universities. Veblen accompanied Laughlin to Chicago where he remained for more than a decade, editing his prestigious journal and writing his stinging critical tract on America's leisure class.

Veblen soon lashed out at his employer as well as capitalist America. He entitled the final chapter of *The Theory of the Leisure Class* "The Higher Learning as an Expression of Pecuniary Culture." Most of its observations and comment rested on the University of Chicago in its nascent years. His characterization of the "captains of erudition" matched that of the "captains of industry" whose self-indulgence and resistance to productive work disrupted both America's older tradition of a harmonious moral economy and the popularized versions of Darwinian progress. Veblen intended no apologia for either of these powerful modes of conceptualizing America's national agenda. Like John Dewey but with different assumptions, Veblen intended nothing less than an invigorated scientific argument about American ambition. The efficient engineer rather than Dewey's educator would later become Veblen's epitome of productive craft labor rather than self-centered businessmen who played to short-term goals and the veneer of success. Veblen's book parodied the academic tract, all the while reworking the meaning of his key terms, making "conspicuous consumption," for example, a primitive and predatory offense. Many of his characterizations—"vested interests," "savage culture," "idle curiosity"—contained multiple layers of meaning while maintaining the pretense of a technical idea. It was his university—Chicago—that, one assumes, he had primarily in mind for his argument that institutions regularly outlive their usefulness, suffer a lag far behind their espoused values, and badly needed the scrutiny of scientific study.[42]

The critical force of Veblen's arguments in his widely read books documented the historical transformation within the new university and the need for greater clarity in its purpose. Veblen and this influence were not entirely negative. For all of the barbed, satiric narration, so different from John Dewey's style, the two authors contributed substantively to a new respect for criticism, for the legitimacy of different opinions, for experimentation as a methodical, scientific way of life, for a wholesale reworking of the meaning of intellect. For both scholars, social and institutional outcomes were the new measure of progress. Henceforth for both writers, "success" was tentative, problematic, and ongoing. Both scholars concentrated on the possibilities of ordinary citizens, who held unsuspected power within their daily routines. The older moral didacticism no longer carried any special authority, which did not diminish religion as such but made denominational evangelism highly suspect as an intellectual power. Science went beyond orderly classification and now required empirical facts and evidence; it became refined by application and debate. Other academics would accept that definition and made experimentation the heart of all university work and gave rise to a range of new disciplines—economics, anthropology, political science, sociology, psychology—all once integrated in moral philosophy for the antebellum college and in philology in the German university. Cumulatively these new disciplines strove to redefine the scientific mantle and give voice to an entirely new academic culture in America.[43]

Veblen and Dewey were not representative figures of the first generation of career academics; however, their striving for new knowledge, a new way of conceptualizing learning as well as their concerns for the organizational devices for its transmission defined key features of the generation later labeled Progressives.[44] Their search for a new methodical approach to both learning and social development they called "science" and consciously sought to distance themselves from the deductive force of religious belief, so much a part of their cultural inheritance. They were not alone in these preoccupations, and their ideas were taken up by many other college and university locales. Veblen and Dewey represented a range of kindred spirits. What is historically distinct about this progressive, collective effort was the lack of encouragement from the business community at large—in spite of a handful of exceptional philanthropists—much less from governmental resources. There was no public clamor for a new university, much less a rationale for new knowledge.[45] In large part, the forceful drive for a new university culture arose from within academia itself, but its conscious outreach to nonacademic publics would determine its long-term success. If Veblen and Dewey positioned themselves on different sides of this issue, their preoccupation with the connection between research and social relevance kept this central issue of their profession forefront in the minds of all its practitioners.

Veblen's and Dewey's fellow progressive academics differed from their predecessors not only in their disciplinary training, in their engagement with new professional institutions, and in their scholarly discourses. The professional organizations, linking faculty members in a range of geographically distinct colleges and universities, became an alternative structure for higher education careers, once contained within a single institution: in 1876 the American Chemical Society, in 1883 the Modern Languages Association, in 1884 the American Historical Association, in 1892 the American Psychological Association, most of them with their own periodicals, established the future pattern for all the disciplines.

In these voluntary organizations, most importantly, scholars collectively developed the discourses and research problems that ideally guided university development. Veblen, of course, in these years could have belonged to several of these organizations given the psychological and anthropological strains in his economic scholarship. But his outsider role seemed to have kept him from them, particularly until in 1925 when he famously rejected the presidency of the American Economic Association "because they didn't offer it to me when I needed it." By contrast, Dewey was a joiner. Among his many associations one should include his membership in the National Academy of Sciences, the American Psychological Association (president 1899–1900), the American Philosophical Society (president 1905–6), corresponding member of the Institut de France, and a member of New York City's intellectually oriented Century Club. Dewey also was a founding member of the American Association of University Professors (1915), (and along with Veblen) the New School for Social Research in 1919, and the American Civil Liberties Union in 1920. Later he was active in the Progressive Education Association (honorary president, 1928) and the American Federation of Teachers and was a founding member of New York Teachers' Guild. All of these professional and social reform organizations provided linkages to fellow academics and created an alternative, extramural culture, initially quite distinct from that of their host institutions.

The presidents of the new universities set an analogous pattern of social outreach that actually extended to many nonuniversity organizations. President William Rainer Harper himself, for many years before and during his Chicago presidency, lectured to New York's Chautauqua Institute, was a member of the Chicago Board of Education and founding member of that city's Civic Federation. He joined both the prominent Union Club and Merchants' Club and served on their education committees, and he participated in the Chicago Association of Commerce and the Industrial Art League of Chicago and was a trustee on the Chicago Symphony Orchestra.[46] Such social and professional connections went far in engaging the informed leadership and philanthropists of the city but, more importantly, made the graphic connection between higher learning and civic service.

Harper was not alone among the new university leaders in cultivating such organizational matrices. They all worked their jobs with a new zest for extensive publications in both scholarly and nonscholarly venues, at the very moment when America experienced its first breakthroughs in mass publications. The result was a relatively distinctive genre of presidential biography and autobiography that overemphasized harsh, unsupportive childhoods (whatever the reality), chance encounters, hard work for meager educational training, occasional inspirational teachers or mentors, and final triumph into a productive, academic community. Thomas W. Goodspeed's *A History of the University of Chicago: The First Quarter Century* (1916) provided the hagiography for William Rainey Harper. G. Stanley Hall of Clark University, Andrew White of Cornell University, and Nicholas Murray Butler of Columbia University provided their own selective autobiographies to make their cases for a new presidential profile and to establish the generic model of educational manager.[47] The upshot was that later commentators of this university president type tended to credit them with greater scholarly accomplishment than the record deserved. Functionally this first generation of university presidents owed more in conception to the Emersonian aphorism that an "institution was the lengthened shadow of a man." They tended to inflate an older order of college president, purportedly a *primus inter pares*, presiding over a lively and energetic academic community. The academic credentials of these newer individuals actually were less important than how their careers reflected the geographically broader institutional matrix and "enlarged usefulness" within which the university now operated. The tension, of course, was the very issue Veblen made so central: to the extent that one admitted social and economic forces into the university for its survival, the greater the danger that academic priorities and research agendas would be pared and compromised Such tensions were a part of higher education's long history, but, near the end of the nineteenth century, they took center stage despite the attempts of their practitioners to ignore them.[48]

Harper may have had a plan for his new university, but many of his shaping decisions were decidedly improvised and pragmatic like the new academic mantra. The University of Chicago began with Rockefeller money, an initial sum of $600,000, which Harper persuaded the philanthropist to increase to $1 million. Harper's early appointments began with reputed scholars from Yale, where he himself served as professor of Semitic languages and literature. His rule of thumb was to pay heads of department no more than

$6,000 per annum (later raised to $7,000), and cannily he recruited to the Chicago faculty (with many concessions as to laboratory space, library purchases, and other accoutrements) nine presidents of other higher education institutions: Ezekiel G. Robinson of Brown (1815–94), George W. Northrup of Baptist Union Theological Seminary (1826–1900), Galusha Anderson of the Old University of Chicago and Denison (1832–1918), Albion W. Small of Colby (1854–1926), Thomas C. Chamberlin of Wisconsin (1843–1928), Franklin O. Johnson of Ottawa (Kansas) (1836–1916), Alice Freeman Palmer of Wellesley (1855–1902), Howard B. Grose of South Dakota (1851–1939), and John M. Coulter of Lake Forest (1851–1928).[49] All nine had solid administrative reputations and concomitantly extensive networks for advice and recruitment. But the group, more importantly, represented the successive academic cultures that influenced the early years of Chicago. Five of the former presidents were older than Harper, born between 1815 and 1836, and were ordained clergymen whose periodical work and pastoral publications reflected their evangelical heritages. All had substantive connections to Baptist-based theological seminaries, especially Rochester Theological Seminary (founded 1850).[50] Four—Chamberlin, Coulter, Small, and Palmer—represented a later generation born between 1843 and 1855—and held earned doctorates (Wisconsin, Michigan, Indiana, and Johns Hopkins, respectively). Their Chicago appointments followed teaching roles at small but distinguished liberal arts colleges (Beloit, Hanover, Colby, and Wellesley). The oldest and in 1892 the most distinguished of them was Thomas C. Chamberlin, whose presidential tenure at the University of Wisconsin not only reorganized the curriculum into a manageable (basic and advanced) elective system, but in his faculty appointments and promotions, he favored individuals with Johns Hopkins doctorates, recognizing the power of that institution's cutting-edge standards. Among those whose careers advanced under Chamberlin's leadership were historian Frederick Jackson Turner (1861–1932), medievalist Charles Homer Haskins (1870–1937), economist Richard Ely (1854–1943), and psychologist Joseph Jastrow (1863–1944). Most important, Chamberlin cultivated a strong extension division and summer school to emphasize the university's practical service to the state and its communities. Later commentators credit Chamberlin with setting the context for the "Wisconsin Idea," the formal institutionalization of research, instruction, and social reform.[51]

When the University of Chicago's doors opened in 1892, the faculty consisted of some seventy-seven individuals, not including the University Extension and the University Academy. Over 750 students had been admitted from thousands of applications, all of whom had received individual screenings, since a high school or comparable diploma was an insufficient entry credential. Within four years (1895) Chicago could boast 1,815 students, 127 more than enrolled in Harvard in 1886–87 and 570 more than Yale. While expanding rapidly, the early universities, like Chicago, achieved no major economic gains because of the increases by comparison with a number of established American colleges. Of course, few colleges or universities would have predicted the geometric expansion that lay ahead in the first generation of the twentieth century. It was not Harper's "genius" that inspired his public outreach—the University Extension—his stratified organization of faculty into professors, assistant professors, tutors, and readers or his four-quarter system to ensure his buildings brooked no fallow summer or vacation time. It was largely—given his "Gothic" roots—his ambition to send a national message that his urban-based institution strove for new, progressive goals.[52]

Harper's death in 1906, very suddenly, at age fifty, did not slow the institution's progressive agenda. Harper prided himself that no Chicago faculty had been hired with any knowledge of the faculty member's religious denomination. In spite of his personal ties to the Baptist church and his professional allegiances to biblical exegesis, Harper professed his determination to make Chicago nondenominational in terms of its welcome to both faculty and students of all persuasions. This rising diffidence toward organized religion would actually become a distinctive academic trait for most national research universities over the next several generations, a marked contrast to college academics even into the middle of the nineteenth century where piety and religious affiliation still played an important role in collegiate culture.[53] Still, Harper had weighted the theological department with a distinctive Baptist influence, but he did not do so with the trustees that he vetted with John D. Rockefeller and Marshall Field. Of the twenty-one trustees on the first board, only one, in addition to Harper himself, was an ordained minister, Rev. Alonzo K. Parker, pastor of Chicago's Central Baptist Church. The rest were men of singular achievement and involvement in civic organizations, whose careers centered on Chicago but had begun elsewhere, often in the eastern states. They were businessmen, bankers, editors, and lawyers. Harper was the sole academic and one of the few with a college degree. The trustees' average age was about forty-three, not much older than the thirty-five-year-old Harper. One of the trustees, Daniel Shorey, a lawyer, had a son, Paul Shorey, trained at Harvard with a PhD from the University of Munich (1884), in the first Department of Classics.[54] Harper's university persona in no way represented those of his faculty, his trustees, or the highly diverse student body, the way earlier liberal arts college were thought to encompass the institutional spirit in their president.

Whatever the new university was, its organization reflected less a harmonious culture than it did niches and layers of common intent. The Gothic architecture clearly overstated the school's institutional cohesion. If there was any area of consensus, it lay more with the quiet acceptance that higher learning did not culminate in the American collegiate tradition of disciplinary inculcation and character building. The new scientific purpose of advanced training sought a seemingly more authoritative method and system that most agreed had not yet been achieved in America.[55] All participants in the new enterprise accepted a new pragmatic attitude that accepted the essence of their work lay in the future, that it would be achieved incrementally, that it could not be realized without risk (and mortgages). Even more, Harper drove himself to create an institution that would modernize biblical interpretation in ways denominational seminaries could not, given their didactic mandates. Theological interpretation would benefit not by preexisting assumptions but rather by the ongoing, open-ended interpretation he envisioned with "scientific research."[56]

But this new pragmatic orientation did not emerge out of whole cloth and even individuals like Harper could be found to set it aside on occasion. One such episode occurred when Harper summarily fired Edward Bemis. The circumstances of this episode made clear how an emergent collegiality in the academic community could be summarily supplanted by presidential authority. It also clarified the limits of scholarly respect that had been touted in purportedly new standards of faculty hiring. Young Bemis—he was thirty-five in 1895, a tenured associate professor and a Johns Hopkins economist (PhD 1885)—had offered public criticism of capitalist monopolies in the area of utilities—water, gas, electricity, telephone, and even railways—which he argued should be publicly held as essential social resources. Bemis specifically offered public criticisms of the railroads practice during the Pullman strike, which Harper, although an explicit supporter of academic free inquiry, felt went beyond academic boundaries.[57] The contradiction may not have been lost on any of the university's constituencies, but certainly the trustees tolerated the problem as one might expect from men whose city fortunes rested unequivocally on Chicago's extensive railroad network.[58] Even for older, seasoned trustees like Elmer L. Corthell (1840–1916), a Civil War veteran and civil engineer whose life intertwined with large engineering ventures (both railroad and bridge construction) in the American West and internationally—Mexico, Argentina, and Brazil—the railroad disruptions at

Pullman could not compute with the broader national systems of commerce and transportation. Corthell personally participated in the design of railway accesses to Chicago, the essence of its claims to be the national hub, and would never have accepted characterizations of his university trusteeship as atavistic or antiprogressive in the Bemis unpleasantness.[59] The sheer force of the city's dynamics, expressed by the collective vision on the trustees, weighed against Bemis and his quasi-Populist affinities. With few individuals who had experienced little more than elementary school training, any appeal to a new, higher standard of intellectual tolerance had to appear presumptive, compared with the still tenuous state of Chicago's economic ambitions in America. Chicago as a self-consciously new American city was no match for notions of *Lehrfreiheit* and *Lernfreiheit* imported from prestigious German universities. Bemis's rejection showed that the new American university had not automatically achieved a new intellectual gravitas in the early years.[60] In virtually every instance of university building, the socioeconomic environment proved to be more of a force and influence than any putative German model or American paradigm of "university."[61] Chicago's contribution to this ongoing university discourse was a disturbingly ordered administrative and architectural visage, while coping with contextual forces of diversity from its faculty, its student body, and its progressive city.

The University of Chicago's early history exemplified not only a new corporate presence in American higher education; it made abundantly clear how the ongoing traditions from earlier in the century fared as they confronted unprecedented urban and industrial advances. Out of these interactions emerged a new intellectual ideology, pragmatism, and a distinctive Progressive energy in the institutions of higher learning. No longer were the administrators of such knowledge citadels mere monitors of scholarships and curricular innovations; they had become secular watchmen of their society's commonweal using science as their authority. Led by the University of Chicago's example, colleges and universities turned their attention to the role of intellectual discovery in proposing Progressive reforms of their host society. Ideally scientific insight was no longer a neutral resource for a professional elite; it was the basis upon which new ways of thinking guaranteed Progressive advancement in public areas well beyond American academia. The Progressive thrust of the urban university gave social reform a new power, and made social redesign and environmental change the basis of a new twentieth-century (generational culture #5) academic culture.

CHAPTER TEN

Academic Expertise in the National Interest

At the turn of the century, American college and university leaders could not anticipate the unprecedented increases in students, financing, and organization that the next generation would bring. The increased number of students alone would have propelled transformations, but the change of the college-age population actually in colleges shifted from 3 percent to more than 25 percent of the college-age cohort between 1900 and 1930. This change caused a substantive shift in both behavior and conception. At the turn of the century, there was no one clear definition of college or university, and each institution's priorities were powerfully driven by local or regional dynamics. Still, there was a prevalent general debate over higher education to which all institutions attended. Especially in the wake of the Depression of 1893, the greatest depression in American history to that point, higher education leaders remained especially sensitive to their own social and national claims: American democracy required different kinds of leaders in all walks of life. What precisely was the social responsibility of a university or college-educated person?

Higher education leaders publicized the need for advanced training in a democratic society no longer modeled on the local town meeting or the denominational congregation. In his essay "The Function of Education in a Democratic Society" (1897), Charles W. Eliot, the president of Harvard University, dismissed earlier claims that "a Yankee can turn his hand to anything" as "a mischievous delusion." Education needed to be tailored to specific services, for which universities provided training. The problematic feature was less a university's ability to develop such training but rather the public's recognition of this "expertise" once realized. "Confidence in experts, and willingness to employ them and abide by their decisions, are among the best signs of intelligence in an educated individual or an educated community, and in any democracy which is to thrive, this respect and confidence must be felt strongly by the majority of the population."[1] Eliot went on to insist on the oxymoronic idea of a "democratic nobility" to which individuals belonged by dint of their training rather than their social or inherited status. "Every person of the true quality, no matter what his station or vocation, is admitted of right to this simply democratic nobility which home, church and school unite in recruiting; and there are, consequently, more real nobles under the democratic form of government than under any other." Eliot's awkward argument was a self-conscious effort to reconcile democratic traditions with a privileged education. He offered the American public a legitimation of privilege and status, while denying traditional class stratifications. Explicitly he made no concessions to social inequity and downplayed the power of expert-producing institutions. In his institution, Harvard University, Eliot claimed that individuals, not institutions, determined when to leave formal training and that learning was lifelong, personally rather than institutionally determined. The granting of degrees should not be construed as the end of intellectual growth.[2] Universities influenced social arrangements only indirectly, through the careers of its graduates. It was thus very difficult to assess precisely the social impact of university work, since education's impact lay in the future. In this context university work needed to avoid reformist actions or association with political dynamics, both of which went beyond a given school's responsibility. The university ideal became a person trained to function above politics, someone who therefore had no need to engage self-interested matters.

This distancing of higher learning from the political environment created for Eliot a special authority for expertise. His gradualist assumptions about fundamental change enabled him to insist that no true university was capable of engineering social reform, much less social revolution. However, these ideas in the hands of a subsequent generation of experts became increasingly suspicious of the "neutrality" of university power. Thorstein Veblen, for example, had worried that the putative neutrality of the university obscured how deferential such institutions had become to the shaping influences of money and politics.[3] His question shifted Eliot's from how to legitimate intellectual privilege in a democracy to how to keep expertise from becoming complicit in society's destructive social propensities. Veblen worried, especially in his 1918 book *The Higher Learning in America*, that the captains of industry would woo the educated elite away from their defining craft of neutral research and intellectual priorities. For Veblen, a generation younger than Eliot, all institutional goals remained permanently problematic, in endless need of attuning, regularly experiencing a cultural lag between their purposes and social needs. The true contribution of the trained expert, he argued, was the reassertion of his investigative craft ("idle curiosity") and the high intellectual value of criticism.[4] The different viewpoints represented nothing less than a major cultural transformation (from generational culture #4 to #5) in higher learning, substituting university "expertise" for the earlier nineteenth-century collegiate goal of "moral character."

In most American universities at the turn of the century, aspects of these educational ideologies contended for dominance and shaped the discourse that defined a university or college. Expertise itself implied that the destiny of higher learning lay outside the walls of academe, shaping and reshaping social organizations.[5] Both Eliot and Veblen sought to give the place of expert training a special privilege, but the trajectory from Eliot to Veblen—from the expert as an apolitical neutral value to an embedded critical stance—suggested that the larger organizational network of higher learning (related professional associations and others) was becoming less and less neutral than alleged. Concomitantly universities and colleges were increasingly considered activist agents in the shaping of American society and culture (certainly by the general purpose foundations among others), not passive entities as Eliot had earlier conceived it. Precisely for that reason, more and more individuals turned to learning and research for legitimating applications of power and for using professional careers where ideas and investigation translated into constructive action.

By the early twentieth century, the focus on research and intellect that gave the new university a value beyond mere dissemination of information or character building drove many kinds of centralizing changes. One of the more important was the tendency of previously separate schools to come under the universities' wings. While some institutions like New York University boasted a law school from the 1830s, by 1900 seventy-one of one hundred American law schools, many of which began as proprietary enterprises, now had university affiliations.[6] Law schools willingly moved into the university structure, especially after the influential case method mode of instruction, which gave legal training a scientific cache, arose at Harvard via Christopher Columbus Langdell (1826–1906).[7] This approach examined actual legal decision making in order to document judicial patterns and to enhance a counsel's ability to predict probable outcomes in litigation. In effect, the new legal approach took the practice of law out of the circuit court and away from the nineteenth-century tradition of contentious courtroom debate and adjudication by a jury of one's peers. After the introduction of the case method, the measure of legal success became a standard of keeping litigation out of the courts altogether. Negotiation and settlement before courtroom appearance (where jury judgments often disrupted the predictions of legal or constitutional expectation) determined legal expertise.[8]

Similarly medical apprenticeship with practicing physicians gave way to more systematized formal training and eventually to internships in central city hospitals. These institutions replaced the local neighborhood clinic, which often served to separate contagious disease from the home. Until the end of the nineteenth century, the home had been the center for patient care, and generally, until the introduction of germ theory and controlled intervention, the physician relied only on time and laudanum for the patient's recovery. Germ theory, advanced in late nineteenth-century Germany by Dr. Robert Koch (1843–1910), did not make a regular appearance in American medical instruction until after 1900. Medical education and practice in the nineteenth century began to shift its strategic work from home care to larger hospitals and university research. Largely through the pioneering role of Dr. William H. Welch (1850–1934) at Johns Hopkins University, the hospital and science-based prescriptions replaced the local clinic and a physician's homemade concoctions.[9]

Other occupations aspired to professional status and turned to the university's sheltering arm and more centralized organizations. In science, practitioners increasingly distanced themselves from philosophical debates over the description and placement of specimens, so characteristic of the early nineteenth-century practice. Increasingly scientists cultivated empirical experimentation in controlled laboratories. The use of science as practiced by respected, antebellum scientists on the lyceum circuit, like Louis Agassiz (1807–73), as both dramatic demonstration and popular entertainment, gave way to closely and collegially monitored research. The meaning of science began to connote testing by replicable practice and published findings in refereed journals. There was more to the defining and protection of expertise. Virtually all such practitioners formed professional associations, like the American Association for the Advancement of Science (founded 1848), and committees of their university-trained peers to arbitrate disagreements.[10] Thereby the experts became the arbiters of disagreements rather than the public or governmental committees.

In similar fashion, education professionals worked to keep administrative jobs—principals, superintendents, commissioners—a male prerogative and sought to shape their training with as much "science" as their work would permit. They converted their normal schools into teachers' colleges, then into university-based schools of education, like New York University, which set a precedent in 1891 with the first program of graduate training in education. In search of professional status, educational leaders rejected the two-year curriculum of the normal schools, which were both locally driven and dominated by female students. Similarly aspirant experts in education worked to convert city school systems away from locally sensitive (and at times politically compromised) wards into citywide, elected boards of education, which favored city elites over ward leaders. They also kept discussion of professional standards public by way of the American Institute of Instruction (founded 1830) and later the National Education Association (founded 1857).[11]

Politics too felt the impact of the new "scientific" university. The cultivation of commissions to address problems that could be adjudicated and ameliorated with research-based policy proposals rather than by politics alone first began in Massachusetts with the Massachusetts Board of Railroad Commissioners (1869). Initially the board held no statutory powers of enforcement but relied on the nineteenth-century tradition of informed discussion and negotiation, strengthened only with the authority to publish its findings and implicitly to shame capitalists into more socially responsible behaviors. In spite of these institutional limitations, the Massachusetts Board under the decade-long leadership of Harvard-trained Charles Francis Adams (1835–1915) achieved a number of constructive modifications of coordination, safety, and accident prevention.[12] This largely voluntary, state model later would be adopted nationally with the passage of the 1890 Sherman Anti-Trust Act with its concomitant regulatory commissions. In 1903 President Theodore Roosevelt developed a parallel agency, the US Board of Corporations, not to mention his Pure Food and Drug Agency; in 1914 President Woodrow Wilson created the Federal Trade Commission and the Federal Reserve Board and strengthened the Interstate Commerce Commission, each of which based its activities on systemic, empirical information. Such regulatory commissions were led by appointed officials, mostly university trained, but answerable to elected politicians.[13]

City leaders too formed organizations to provide data for reform efficiencies. In New York City, the 1907 Bureau of Municipal Research attracted a small quality staff that included the historian and Columbia faculty member Charles Beard (1874–1948), who in 1921 was succeeded by Luther Gulick (1892–1993). Gulick studied at both Oberlin College and later New York University

Medical School where he took his advanced degree in 1889. The Bureau of Municipal Research recommendations resulted in a centralized budgetary system and financial planning for the city. It also initiated a number of social surveys that improved social services, especially in health and welfare.[14] Gradually the bureau's model, which reorganized in 1921 as the National Institute of Public Administration, influenced the work of many national advisory agencies of the New Deal and other large international bodies.

From the turn of the century, private American corporations began to establish their own research departments, as much a defensive function to protect patented products as it was from a genuine interest in new discoveries. American Telephone and Telegraph Company had recognized the need to form its own research nucleus as early as 1910 with the hiring of Frank Jewett (1879–1949), a PhD (physics) graduate of the University of Chicago. The corporation supported a research department from 1916 and formally incorporated its work in 1925 as Bell Telephone Laboratories with Jewett as its president (1925–40).[15] Independently, the railroad industry turned to science after disastrous public relations episodes over rates and safety in order to alter its public image of exploitation and mismanagement. In 1910 the industry's Executive Committee of Six—which included Daniel Willard (1861–1942), president of the B&O, and William C. Brown (1853–1924), president of New York Central—pooled the industry's resources to form the Bureau of Railway Economics, which sought to establish a statistical base for issues of rate regulation and safety and to leave behind a pattern of merely reacting to rather than actively preventing disasters. The Bureau's first general statistician was Frank H. Dixon (1869–1944), a Michigan PhD (economics) who served from 1910 to 1918, while simultaneously holding a faculty position at Dartmouth College.[16]

At the turn of the century, the transformation of the university was not simply a matter of new science and professional research discourses but even more of taking its place within a system of powerful, capitalist institutions.[17] Its effort to retain a special authoritative role in political and cultural priorities depended, as Eliot, Veblen, and others had routinely insisted, on its nonpolitical character. However, the pretense of remaining nonpolitical, while working full bore to shape and change the city, state, and national orientation, put the university in a very precarious situation. Universities as institutional entities could claim to have no political party allegiances but only so long as they grounded their recommendations and suggestions on factual data that seemed impartial, both in its collection and in its practical applications. As political conflicts deepened, including the rise of radicalism, the university's role in such things as regulation increased, making it difficult to maintain a reputation as nonpartisan.

At the University of Wisconsin, efforts on the part of its social scientists—economics, sociology, psychology, and so on—to research and write legislation based on new evidence led to the popular model of the "Wisconsin Idea" with faculty experts drafting legislation. Some felt the model served as the essence of the Progressivism for which the state and its native son Robert La Follette (1855–1925) became nationally renowned. Such famous university involvements in the political process did endanger the perception that universities were neutral and that science, even social science, could find purely objective solutions to social and political problems. There were many who suspected that the University of Wisconsin's very "activism" may well have threatened its tax-supported financing and government initiatives, which its critics felt bordered on the socialistic. However problematic the "Wisconsin Idea" was, the possibility of university autonomy became increasingly debatable, as the university claimed greater strategic significance in the shaping of social priorities and values.[18] By 1900 it was no longer possible realistically to claim, as Eliot had, that the university influenced American society only through its graduates; the university as an institution had become a strategic presence, producing findings with consequences for social application. But exactly how could the university remain a social, indeed a national, force, and yet resist any temptation to use scientific data to favor one group over another? Did the university's claim to be nonpolitical mean that it had no political role or ambition at all? The first voices in behalf of a new order of priorities and new scientific methodologies came from a mixed cadre of university presidents and philanthropic leaders who proposed to clarify national priorities and channel money discretely to a few model institutions. It is in this work that Charles W. Eliot (1834–1926) was more prescient than in his transformation of Harvard College into Harvard University. His post-university career (1909–26) drew on his service to the Carnegie Endowment for the Advancement of Teaching (where he had been chairman), the Rockefeller-funded GEB, and later the Carnegie Endowment for International Peace. Along with Columbia's President Nicholas Murray Butler (1862–1947), Eliot substantively assisted in the creation in 1900 of a system that would make university admissions seem truly meritocratic and ensure a public image of neutrality especially through the College Entrance Examination Board. All of these endeavors indirectly shaped American higher education for standardizing admission, regulating faculty careers with pensions, and legitimating research-based policy proposals.[19] On an unprecedented scale, higher education experts had thereby thrust themselves into strategic changes in American life.

From the perspective of the nineteenth century, the men who set the context for a new university were greatly different from those a twentieth-century university would produce. These individuals built on a nineteenth-century experience but took their experience to another level entirely. A later biographer of Henry Pritchett, one of the key role models of post–World War I academic builders, would see no loss in the suppression of nineteenth-century career patterns. Pritchett's biographer, Abraham Flexner (1856–1959), acknowledged that Henry Pritchett's collegiate institution, the Pritchett Institute (run by his father), had minimal classification of studies and a cavalier organization. Students graduated when they mastered their studies whether it took them two, four, or six years, effectively acknowledging that the school was both preparatory and collegiate. The annual tuition of $100 had to be paid in advance of the forty school weeks of study.[20] The contrast with such a retrospectively ragtag experience and the University of Munich, which Pritchett later attended, was likely very stark, but Pritchett's German doctorate put him in a singularly different category. In his subsequent appointment to the US Geodetic Survey, he experienced the full impact of the Spanish-American War, which siphoned off staff, ships, and resources. The changing political atmosphere compelled Pritchett to appeal successfully to President McKinley for restraint in making political rather than professional appointments to his unit. Pritchett tried hard to enforce a rule of scientific competency and apolitical distance at the very moment he worked to a new principle of applied science.[21]

Pritchett's political experience apparently apprenticed him well to deal with limited resources and tutored him in the possibilities of strategic, organizational change. He worked with Andrew Carnegie (1835–1919) and the early modest proposals of the Carnegie Foundation for the Advancement of Teaching. His work to ensure pensions for academic faculty demonstrated how modest shifts could achieve momentous reform. His faculty pension plan early on eliminated state and denominational institutions from participation with Carnegie support. At the outset Yale's congregational traditions, Princeton's Presbyterian allegiances, and the University of Chicago's specification of a Baptist president disqualified them from Carnegie pension support. Even so the Carnegie endowment, Pritchett realized, would generate a mere $500,000 for the 327 colleges and universities that qualified for Carnegie pensions. Those institutions that met Carnegie's qualification admitted only students who had successfully completed a four-year high school curriculum. At the moment of Pritchett's calculations, approved higher education institutions employed 6,207 faculty members worthy of pension support. Pritchett's first priorities required new systemic standards: how could one assess a four-year secondary curriculum filled with varied subjects and different levels of mastery? Exactly when should a college be characterized as denominational (mindful that his own Pritchett Institute claimed to be "Christian" but not denominational)? What constituted an adequate pension?[22]

Gradually Pritchett altered Carnegie's original idea for pensions, broadening the system to include state universities. Carnegie also saw his original endowment was insufficient and had the newly formed Carnegie Foundation (founded 1911) increase the pension fund capital. By 1917 Carnegie's pension fund amounted to $17 million, which still fell short of a proper pension for all qualified faculty. Pritchett helped shape a new organization, the Teachers Insurance and Annuity Association, in 1918, which funded pensions by joint contribution from both faculty and employer, an arrangement that satisfied Carnegie's original intent that the pension not be a charity. Twenty-five years later the fund introduced a new system affecting 956 college and universities. This mechanism accounted for over thirty-one thousand individual annuities and more than thirteen thousand insurance policies.[23] Carnegie's original pension plan had evolved under Pritchett's tutelage to become a rationalizing agent for American higher education.

Pritchett, a generation younger than both Carnegie and Charles W. Eliot, played a central role in the transformation of American philanthropy and higher education. Carnegie's original initiative, a pension system to reward altruistic academics (somewhat akin to his Hero Fund) became a shaping instrument under Pritchett's guidance. Not only must qualified institutions for the pension fund meet the Carnegie Foundation for the Advancement of Teaching's four years of high school requirement and no explicit denominational affiliation, Pritchett engineered further conditions, which revealed how varied the American college was in the early twentieth century. Colleges had to have at least six full-time professors and a regular curriculum of four years of liberal arts. Later he stipulated all qualifying institutions had to have reached an annual budget of $100,000 and demonstrate that politicians did not control their governing boards.[24] Carnegie's philanthropic organizations had moved considerably beyond the funding of libraries and church organs as well as rewards for altruistic individuals. An unforeseen consequence of these interventions in behalf of system building was the organization among small denominational colleges—the Association of

American Colleges (founded 1915)[25]—and the activation of the National Association of State Universities (founded 1887), both to open negotiations with the Carnegie Foundation for the Advancement of Teaching to find ways of gaining access to its philanthropic resources. These negotiations would further systematize America's postwar academic culture.

In the wake of Andrew Carnegie's 1919 death, Pritchett reintroduced a strategy that proved to be remarkably successful earlier: the survey. In 1910 the Carnegie Foundation for the Advancement of Teaching had published a report on medical schools. The report concluded that the studied medical schools fit into three categories: first, approved (based upon the operative standard set by present-day Johns Hopkins University Medical School); second, imperfect but remediable; and third, beyond salvage. Twenty percent of those in the latter category closed within two years, permitting the inference that public exposure (rather than known financial strains or pressure from state licensing boards) could produce redemptive effects in the social and educational arena.[26]

The report imposed a university standard on medical training, urged all such training institutions to operate within the university aegis, and be staffed by men of eminent biological and chemical training. At certain points the report shocked its readers with its scurrilous dismissal of some medical school's laboratory equipment as compactible in a cigar box, with indifferent use of disinfectant, descriptions of rank corpses, libraries without books, and faculty preoccupied with their private practices. The report made clear the high expenses of adequate medical training, not just medical equipment but multiple years devoted to its mastery. One immediate impact of the report was a fall in medical school enrollment and an increase in debates in state legislatures over support, lest some states host no medical school at all.[27] The long-term consequence of the report was both a funneling of new dollars ($91 million by 1936) of GEB money, not simply to American medical training, but rather to a select elite of medical schools. Seven institutions received two-thirds of this largesse.

Pritchett's agent for the Carnegie Foundation for the Advancement of Teaching's now famous *Bulletin Four* was Abraham Flexner, a graduate of Johns Hopkins and brother of Simon Flexner (1863–1946), protégé of Hopkins's distinguished Dr. William H. Welch and president of Rockefeller Institute for Medical Research. Abraham Flexner's own biographical profile followed the large contours of his fellow philanthropic reformers—men like Pritchett—and confirmed the generational pattern. Abraham Flexner was born in 1866 in Louisville, Kentucky, of immigrant Jewish parents and—age twenty—graduated from Johns Hopkins University after only two years of intensive classical study. The transformational impact of the Hopkins experience would be manifest later as he used the university's example in setting the standards for medical practice. Flexner then returned to his native state where he taught first in public high school, then from 1890 his own private secondary school, purportedly downplaying rules, records, and examinations, much like Pritchett's experience at the Pritchett Institute. From Louisville he sent occasional students to Harvard, prompting Charles W. Eliot's inquiry about a school with able graduates but well outside Harvard's watershed. After a brief exchange, Flexner left Kentucky and its rural culture for Cambridge, Massachusetts, and graduate study at Harvard. From there he went to the University of Berlin for psychology and philosophy but without taking a degree. In 1908, at age forty-two, he joined the staff of the Carnegie Foundation for the Advancement of Teaching. In his first assignment, he gave voice to his educational priorities, especially the necessity of disciplined instruction with very high standards and, however contradictory, the school's duty to accommodate the cultural values of the region or nation. Unspoken in his report was the assumption that an educational bureaucracy would produce a desired and predictable product. Flexner's research resulted in *Bulletin Four: Medical Education in the United States and Canada* (1910), and became known as the "Flexner Report." If its reformist impact was overstated then and later, there is little question that the document forecast a new institutional standard and a gravitation of all schooling within the shadow of the university and its scientific norms.[28]

In 1913 Flexner left the Carnegie Foundation for the Advancement of Teaching for the GEB. He labored there until 1928, taking a special interest in articulating the advanced standards of secondary education—*The Modern School* (1916) and *A Modern College* (1923), and, of course, his 1910 vision of the advanced medical school. Even more important than his argument for an integrated system of generic schools was Flexner's work with philanthropic professionals inside and outside the GEB. In the early years of the GEB's work, its attention addressed issues of the rural South, something that Flexner knew a good deal about. Their initial cooperation with the Slater Fund and the Peabody Education Fund explored many specific issues of Southern education. The GEB, like its sister foundations, sought to mend the regional divisions of the North and South and later the nation as a whole. They concentrated attention—as had the Third Republic in France in this same generational span[29]—on a teacher corps from which a national leadership might be drawn. At the very least, this impetus drew a cadre of professionals into philanthropic work, backed them with an endowment greater than that of most of America's colleges and universities combined, and urged them to make "feasible" (Flexner's specific characterization) the application of high standards to institutions and regions of low practice.[30]

Flexner's depiction of the quintessential philanthropic expert was a person who did not "invent" or "coerce." His claim was in its way innocuous and preposterous by turns. How was it possible to create new institutional machinery, a general purpose foundation, powered by uncommitted dollars, and aiming to improve an entire national system of education and culture, and not compel someone to do something they had not been doing? Flexner worked hard to keep his new university expert seemingly an ordinary citizen who simply went about his regular tasks. He wrote two biographies of exemplar experts after he retired, one of Daniel Coit Gilman, one of Henry Pritchett. Though these individuals were a generation apart in age, Flexner strove to make them professional kinsman, members of a single cohort. Indeed, though far from the truth for Gilman,[31] he claimed they achieved great advantage from working in areas without precedent, without the baggage of tradition. For Gilman, Flexner projected a figure gradually experienced, in one of the most traditionally laden colleges in America—Yale—and at the University of California, burdened with the political inheritances of the Morrill Land Grant Act. Flexner conceded that Gilman and Pritchett were "realists" and competent "executives" rather than men of original minds. Though he described the extensive and complicated organizational networks each expert created, Flexner found ways of insisting their careers benefited from finding the right man for the job and leaving him to his devices.[32] Somehow Flexner's expert had inherited the old nineteenth-century Emersonian assumption that a real institution was the lengthened shadow of a man. In practice, Flexner presented the expert as a new social type.

But the new institutional system Flexner and his generation produced was anything but the creation of singular individuals. Flexner himself noted how the Johns Hopkins trustees requested advice from many distinguished presidents of American universities: Harvard, Yale, Cornell, Pennsylvania, Virginia, and Michigan. They sought information from the principal universities abroad. Andrew White of Cornell had stressed the importance of collegiate training, especially technical training while not excluding traditional subjects; James Angell of Michigan stressed "practical subjects;" Charles Eliot underscored the need to move incrementally and support strong preparatory schools to enable students to be worthy of elective systems like that at Harvard. Flexner enjoyed the notion that three of the great leaders in higher education could not agree in the 1870s on how one should go about creating a university from the ground up. Certainly few put the entire onus of university work, as did Gilman, on high research standards. In part, the diversity of opinion followed from the fact that the "university" remained an inchoate category of schooling. In part, Flexner used this context to burnish Gilman's star and his focus on the retrospective distinctiveness of the American university. It was less Gilman's own loose definition of a university—"they provide advanced instruction. . . . They bring together books, apparatus, works of art . . . they encourage investigation and the publication of important researches; they confer degrees"[33]—than the fact that he resolutely insisted on it through his entire tenure of office.

Gilman's practical plan for a university foundation had proposed making connections to many existing institutions in Baltimore and Washington, like the Peabody Institute or the Smithsonian Institution. At the trustees' suggestion, Gilman had traveled for a year in Europe, meeting distinguished university leaders and research scholars. His hope to begin recruiting at the highest levels was quickly dashed, and he sought the more "feasible" ground of selecting younger men, trained at distinguished places by scholars of repute. In the end Gilman built slowly and carefully, successfully attracting a number of individuals whose long-term commitments would be to Johns Hopkins University. He strongly encouraged his early hires to create journals to publish their work and to reconfigure the parameters of their specialties. If he did not know at the outset, Gilman learned soon that the university energized itself centrifugally as the hub of professional networks. He also did his part, as did his fellow university presidents, promoting their efforts in the new mass magazines.[34] The culmination of all this administrative energy was not, as Flexner would have had it, the actual realization of an American type of university, but rather the proposal to a larger American public that the university could serve as a new national resource.

Flexner had made a number of substantive, piecemeal contributions to the typology of the American university. But his most substantive effort came at the end of the 1920s with his book *Universities: American, English, German* (1930) and his role as first director of a new research model, the Institute for Advanced Study (founded 1930), located at Princeton but a separate institution from that university. His *Universities*, based on Rhodes lectures he gave at All Souls College, Oxford University, in 1928, sought to put a permanent stamp upon a "modern university." He acknowledged that the social environment shaped the university and its form differed within distinct national cultures. There was, in other words, no single university definition, but all universities nevertheless had in common the extension (and not simply the conservation and dissemination) of knowledge, the training of individuals at a high level, and a critical attempt to set values upon the doings of men.[35] Flexner expected strong presidents to shape each version of the university into an "organic unity." The resulting institution would not become so completely a product of its society and culture that it could not with its research offer novel proposals to reform its society. Flexner was appreciative of the delicate path university leaders needed to pursue and, naming several—Lord R. B. Haldane (1856–1928), Friedrich Paulsen (1846–1908), Michael Foster (1836–1907)—acknowledged that the pivotal administrators of their respective national universities were generally not men of "original minds" themselves. His expert was an orchestrator of talent, a "pragmatic idealist," a master of the feasible.

Unlike Charles W. Eliot a generation earlier, Flexner's issue was not achieving sufficient "detachment" for university work but avoiding "triviality" in the questions and responses of researchers, overreaching in the effort to establish the worth of higher learning. His specific charge was that American universities in his era "cheapened, vulgarized and mechanized themselves."[36] The difference in conception implicitly acknowledged the growth of universities in size and subject matter. Universities were not only involved deeply in their societies and cultures, they were indicators of the very soul of their social weal. In the 1890s the university had emerged at a time when fewer than 3 percent of the college-age cohort experienced some form of higher learning; in the 1920s the share had mushroomed to 20 percent. Not only had universities added on professional schools and self-consciously service-oriented departments, they had only belatedly considered an integration of these subjects to their basic instruction. In addition, most universities worked diligently by 1920 to shed their preparatory classes and to concentrate on college students who held secondary school diplomas. This tendency secured a minimal baseline for collegiate instruction but often left the transition from college to advanced study to a range of factors. Exactly how did college, graduate school, and professional instruction interact? How could basic college training, especially in the face of popular elective systems, become foundational for the myriad specializations that awaited the college graduate?

To Flexner's chagrin the medical model would not serve other sectors where the knowledge base was often nonexistent or substantive. He worried overly about the business school, library science, teacher training, and social work. The task at hand was to credit the democratizing forces in the American university and still offer a standard of selection that produced important subjects, grounded students, and competent teachers. If the line at times was difficult to draw, Flexner was confident that the sheer quantification of credits toward a degree falsely equated, say, military drill with an engagement in calculus. The emergence of home study departments that permitted students away from campus to complete courses by correspondence, outside the collegiate walls or away from the campus itself, further diluted the university's purpose. Finally the admission for college credit of courses on "poultry raising," "advertising layout," "clothing decoration," "gymnastics and dancing for men," and so on, hardly required a formal standard to reject such subjects from the collegiate curriculum. Cooking, wrestling, and typewriting were manifestly not on a par with music, science, and literature.[37] When endowed institutions, somewhat protected from public fads, succumbed like Columbia and Chicago to such untoward levels of tolerance (epitomized by intercollegiate athletics), was it surprising that state universities like the University of Wisconsin followed suit? Even though other reputable schools had resisted these diluting trends, Flexner worried that their existence anywhere would not only raise questions about the nature of the university. The very clarity of education as an intellectual engagement and discipline would thereby be compromised.

After World War I, the expansion of students, advanced subjects, and bureaucratic organizations outstripped everyone's expectations. The companionable models and collegial approach to problems that Flexner experienced with both the Carnegie Endowment for the Advancement of Teaching and the GEB became understandably strained. In 1929 Flexner delivered the Rhodes lectures at Oxford University and laid the groundwork there for his 1930 book *Universities: American, English, German*. There Flexner offered a succinct synthesis of his reservations about higher education development. Each system reflected its cultural environment and with graphic and pointed examples; he insisted that the heart of any university was its graduate school and its research purpose. American universities proliferated abundantly, and he applauded the American public's generosity. However, the resources had been spread too thin, the leadership had not educated the donors about the universities' true priorities, and their teaching obligations overindulged many students who were not of university grade. Britain has equated higher education with its teaching colleges, and their governance by its fellows undermined the possibility of research as a university goal. Its distinguished research institutions like the Cavendish Laboratory operated independently of collegiate work. Britain's division of higher education goals into humanities for Oxford University and science for Cambridge University, plus the underfunded, government subsidies, offered at once a singular teaching model and a failure of university ambitions.

Germany's long commitment to a high research standard, Flexner felt, came at the price of social class sorting (drawing under 3 percent of their student body from the working class)—Gymnasium (a high humanistic standard), Oberrealschule (a stern scientific ideal), and the Realschule (a combination of the two)—at the preparatory level and a worrisome politicization of academic appointments. The coveted professorial posts became appointments by the centralized Ministry of Education, were highly selective (though, Flexner insisted, based on published research achievement), and resulted in lower levels of university work experiencing both wandering scholars and long delays to genuine research posts. So intense was the national commitment to *Wissenschaft* that the German university at times seemed indifferent to social problems—the opposite of America's penchant—or unmindful of professional needs—the British preoccupation.

The organizational concerns of Flexner's three-part study left implicit how the advantages of each system could influence or be accommodated by alternative national paradigms. Precisely how should each cultural expression make intellectual achievement a national priority? Or, in other words, how can the truly gifted, intellectual talent become both an academic expert and a national resource? In his own life—as Flexner explained repeatedly in his 1940 autobiography—"The one kind of specific grant that in the long run will pay is a grant given to a promising man for the enlargement of his educational and scientific experience without reference to any particular problem."[38] He claimed all his life, advising leaders and administering philanthropic grants, that he followed the example of Johns Hopkins University's first president, Daniel Coit Gilman: hire the man and let him go. Given the impact of Flexner, his generational cohort, and his great foundational resources on producing a new organizational culture through the interwar years, his highly idiosyncratic individualism in his autobiography seems entirely counterintuitive. Flexner's entire life was a long chain of study, fresh definitions, and new standards like his model school, which led to the creation of the influential laboratory Lincoln School at Columbia Teachers College (1917–40). His cooperation in the application of Carnegie points to determine the completion of high school and its differentiation from college work (about which he still chaffed in his 1930 book, *Universities*). But perhaps most of all his use of Johns Hopkins University, not only as an exemplar of early university work in America, but for its medical school under the tutelage of German-trained Dr. William H. Welch, which became the national standard in his 1910 report on American medical education.

If the heart of all these enterprises was less organization than the recognition of singular talent, exactly how was such recognition acquired and cultivated? For all the organizational detail and data in Flexner's writing, his recurring theme eventually came to a discussion of this inchoate insight. There is of course excessive romanticism in his description of colleagues like Wallace Buttrick, who naturally trafficked between Southern and Northern educational leaders, who could "sniff out" problems that wholly escaped even Flexner's discerning eye. All his foundation colleagues, for all their idiosyncrasies, were depicted as sharing mutual respect, vigorous critical exchange, complete candor, and ultimate collegial conviviality. They were even-tempered and self-contained, witty, urbane, learned. They had no patience with small things (no "retail" matters, as one was fond of saying) and were willing to take chances. They had created, Flexner implicitly argues in his autobiography, a culture of pragmatic operation.

Flexner's remarkable, indeed admirable, career touched on many issues about which, he fully conceded, he entered without requisite knowledge. But his confidence was always high in behalf of scientific and medical issues. There he applied the example of Johns Hopkins University Medical School. He worked to improve, of course, admission standards and attract students who had completed high school. But much more than that, he sought to convince university presidents, first, of the centrality of clinical professorships over mere lecture formats and, second, to eliminate the distracting demands of private medical practices for clinicians whose full attention should be the laboratory. Even more, Flexner shaped his modus operandi in persuading George Eastman (1854–1932) to reform the medical school of the University of Rochester or the precedent-setting transformation of the University of Iowa, a public, tax-supported institution, into the first front-ranked medical school in the Midwest. The key was not the introduction of matched grants; the key was creating a unit—centered on singular individuals and "geniuses"—that pressured all other units of a university and of a region. After the success at Iowa, Flexner successfully argued against analogous support for Iowa's competitor universities. Within ten years they had all found the resources to follow the Iowa model. "The $50,000,000 allocated by the Rockefeller Foundation early in the century to improve medical education in the United States," Flexner proudly boasted, "was spent in such a way as to bring forth between ten and fifteen times that sum." "This," he continued," was a lesson in democracy. Important in dollars alone, it was more important in teaching the American people to support . . . the teaching of medicine in a sound, effective fashion."[39] Every successful venture had, he assumed, a large, constructive ripple effect. The historical ripple effect of this generation's philanthropy was to shift the center of practical science from Europe to the United States.[40]

Like his mentor Daniel Coit Gilman, Abraham Flexner sought out genius by fieldwork, by travel, by consultation with "men of superior wisdom, culture and experience."[41] His autobiography is more than an account of successful forays. It is actually an apologia for his generation, a cohort of individuals whom few would have predicted—because of their unprepossessing origins, their meager educational preparations, and the lateness of their arrival at the threshold of expertise—would have become not only the shapers of American higher education but also the models of American pragmatic expertise. Flexner's convincing account of his life makes clear that he passed through multiple levels of social and political experience, discriminated among varied influences and powers, and resisted the reduction of his approach to any simplistic method. In his life and in his book, he quickly put antebellum Kentucky behind and overly admired others who arose far from the corridors of power to settle in comfortably and constructively to that life without ever donning a false sense of self-importance. Flexner always insisted on data, on new research for any task, which invariably had not been systemically studied before. He always circulated drafts to collegial scrutiny and talked through points of difference. He made his peace with the fact that such a process often returned final drafts quite unlike the original. If *Wissenschaft* was his goal, unpressured experimentation was his mantra. If at the end of his life he felt compelled to acknowledge that his scientific and medical penchants had neglected the humanities (and he might well have added the "social sciences") in university reform, he also argued vehemently that intellectual ideals must prevail over organizational and technical strategies. In the end, his twentieth-century achievement and the achievement of American higher education was less than his ambition. His assumption that such interventions rarely exploited the advantage of money or imposed an intrusive vision may now strike later generations as naive.[42] But in the process of striving, Flexner and his generation embedded or reinforced an emergent pragmatic ideology in the center of university machinery. This machinery belatedly came to accept its duty to promulgate rather than probe or question a benign pragmatic bias as a distinctive American ideology.

Flexner and his expert colleagues in the new general purpose foundations gave rise to a new social type in American higher learning. In their personal careers, they exemplified not simply the creation of new knowledge but advanced instruction with transformational power. But even more, their personal trajectories and their ideologies spread far and powerfully the acceptance of scientific research and its pragmatic applications. Their movement between and among colleges and universities set precedents for institutional modeling and cooperation and extended the meaning of higher learning to an organizational network beyond higher education institutions. Their expansive work made clear how interconnected were the leadership and faculty of American academic life, but also how bound academic life was with larger national enterprises. Cumulatively these new foundation experts, moving in and out of higher learning organizations, demonstrated how malleable and extensive were the activist ideas of turn-of-the century Progressive scholars. Their efforts to articulate expansive, pragmatic priorities for American higher education produced a self-consciously designed model for colleges and universities and advanced for the first time a broadly public appreciation of the American academic as a cultural resource. Their repositioning of higher learning, not just as a complex organizational matrix, but as a cultural resource for the nation set the context for higher education as an unprecedented cultural benefit (generational culture #5).

CHAPTER ELEVEN

The Other Captains of Erudition: From Science to General Education

The real achievement of American higher education by the turn of the twentieth century was a maturing ideology of pragmatic science rather than a clear conception of a generic "university." In spite of efforts to see the university take a "modern" form shortly before World War I, every institution that claimed to be a university had both general, as well as localized, indigenous features that compromised the name. Virtually all such schools faced problems of finance and recruitment; few of them, including Harvard, reached beyond their regional orbit to attract students.[1] Some like Princeton had begun to encourage organizational bridges to preparatory schools like Lawrenceville, and in the depressed years of the 1890s Charles Eliot even considered graduates of the Boston public high schools. Others, like New York University or Columbia, sought students through new programs with an occupational link, such as teaching or nursing. The very preoccupation of all higher education leaders with finance and recruitment emphasized how little at the turn of the century the "university" ideal appeared to the American public as necessary to a person's career or life chances. Despite a surge of enrollment that began in the 1890s, all of America's higher education institutions together accounted for only 2.3 percent of students in the college-age cohort (eighteen to twenty-four) in 1900.[2]

The outreach of the early university presidents—Eliot, Harper, White, Gilman, and others—turned to the public press to make the case for the university as a public resource. They made a case for which there was little overt public support. And university advocates for nearly a generation were individuals within the walls of academe, especially those gravitating to scientific methodology and research. But in 1900 there was great distance between claims for systematic study of society—even of pressing social and urban problems like typhoid and cholera, much less poverty and crime—and the actual demonstration that research could result in constructive change. Even "germ theory," the tracking of infections and the pathology of disease, which developed in Germany in the 1870s, did not become standard in medical training until after the turn of the century. Medical science was largely an exercise of trial and error with homegrown prescriptions rather than of predictable stages of infection and effective intervention. If new philanthropies like the Carnegie Foundation for the Advancement of Teaching held out the hope of connecting research and public service,[3] that hope rested on individuals trained in the university's new scientific methodology. Abraham Flexner became a major exemplar of the new expert, and to a large extent he represented an advance guard, operating outside the university but functionally within an academic orbit. Flexner's articulation of the ideology of expertise—mastery of special skills in investigating problems without the distractions of politics and self-interested pressures—articulated a pragmatic standard for academic thinking between World War I and World War II.

These academic experts (see chapter 10) quickly became highly self-conscious in the creation of a new, institutional matrix that would bring credibility to the university's larger worth. The new experts linked university, philanthropic foundations, and American social institutions. Their goal was to influence leaders, especially political leaders, to recognize that universities could help create policies of incontestable public benefit. The Depression of 1893 and the crisis of uncontrolled railroad competition made it clear that nineteenth-century democratic processes—especially those that modeled themselves on town-meeting deliberation and suspicion of federal government initiatives—would not survive in the twentieth century. But did an alternative of increased autocratic powers, like those legitimated in economic crisis or wartime, risk the very fabric of democracy? The new experts thought they had another alternative, a quasi-democratic alternative, by providing complicated knowledge to elected officials. Such privileged information, not really subject to debate but confirmed by empirical data and expert experience, legitimized possible life-and-death decision making without necessarily including or ignoring the interests of the public at large. Ironically the new ideology of expertise advanced a notion of public service, which would be achieved by research independent of public pressures.

There were variations to the "expertise" for increasing the status of the university. During the 1893 Depression, President Charles Van Hise (1857–

1918) of the University of Wisconsin sought to place university graduates in the state's civil service, to provide informed advice on a range of issues. His model may well have been the agricultural experiment stations that fed state farmers current information and best practices on crops and livestock. What if similar conduits could be created for legal insights, medical treatments, public health, education, and food standards among a range of other issues? Later commentators organized this new enthusiasm for academic research under the rubric the "Wisconsin Idea" and singled out several stellar faculty in economics—Richard Ely (1854–1943) and John R. Commons (1862–1945) especially—to advise state legislators. The university's central iconic building, Bascom Hall, and its one-mile separation from the state capitol down State Street, became a metaphorical embodiment of the "Wisconsin Idea." The emergent interaction of legislators and researchers would eventually evolve into the Progressive political machine of one of America's leading politicians, Senator Robert M. La Follette (1855–1925). Wisconsin's well-known Progressive tradition, according to La Follette, was unthinkable without the support of his fellow alums and the resource of the university faculty, especially in the period before and after World War I.[4]

The ideology of scientific research as a public resource, however, did not emerge full force from the universities at the turn of the century. Several dramatic endeavors soon convinced larger public and business corporations of the merit and financial advantage of research. Andrew Carnegie endowed the Carnegie Institute of Washington in 1902 with $10 million, an amount that equaled the endowment of Harvard University and exceeded the total amount committed to research by all of America's universities and colleges.[5] Outside the universities, corporations, especially those that benefited from the surge of mergers at the end of the nineteenth century, began to create their own research departments and drew upon university graduates in relevant scientific areas. In business, research evolved idiosyncratically, though in retrospect very rapidly. The prolific inventor Charles F. Kettering (1876–1958) began in a most unprepossessing manner, but his career clarified why the relation between corporate need and university training would grow closer in the interwar years. Largely due to eyesight problems, he did not graduate from Ohio State University (founded 1870) until he was in his mid-twenties. He distinguished himself in electrical engineering and went to work for six years after his university training for National Cash Register Company. There he invented an electric motor for cash registers among many other devices and continued the pursuit of other electrical problems during his leisure hours. In his early thirties, he left National Cash Register to form his own company, Delco, with a product that would revolutionize the auto business, the electrical ignition for autos, a self-starting device that eliminated the hand crank, a nemesis especially for women drivers. Working out the wrinkles of that discovery led Kettering to examine the automobile's entire electrical system, lighting seals, solenoids, battery duration, and so on. In a few short years, he personally held one hundred patents on related devices and had made Delco an extraordinary technical and fiscal success. Kettering had caught the eye of William Durant (1861–1948), head of United Motors, an umbrella company of multiple automotive suppliers. Kettering had also befriended Alfred P. Sloan (1875–1966), who was soon to become the head of a new corporate model and a central force in the national economy, General Motors. After World War I, Sloan's General Motors not only purchased Delco but several other Kettering companies and made Kettering chief of General Motors' new Research Division, a position he held until the end of his life.[6] Kettering participated not only in the revolution of the American corporation; he founded the Kettering Foundation to capitalize new inventions and promote talent; he and Alfred P. Sloan, in addition, created the Sloan Kettering Institute (founded 1945) for cancer research.[7]

Kettering's generation rose to prominence after the Civil War and, after that conflict, with its extensive demands for mass-produced goods for winning the war, made clear the limits of civil and mechanical engineering's ad hoc apprenticeship methods. The rapidly expanding knowledge in both chemical and electrical engineering set the context for more systematic training in engineering departments allied to universities. Kettering's own mixed theoretical and trial-and-error preparation for his stunning inventive career reflected the transitional dynamics of the end of the nineteenth century. General Motors' purchase of his primary company, Delco, occurred at a most propitious moment. Kettering had created a number of companies to research and produce several key inventions, one of them an airplane company with aviation pioneer and fellow Dayton resident Orville Wright (1871–1948). During World War I, his effort to move laterally from auto to airplane production actually immersed him in novel problems of weight, thrust, and uplift that both thrilled and exhausted him. His business acumen was no match for his technical genius. Alfred Sloan, in effect, removed organizational burdens from Kettering's shoulders at precisely the moment when they might have consumed him entirely. His new position as chief of research for General Motors left him free to cultivate his inventive prowess without worry about the production costs. Unlike so many other inventors of his generation and later, Kettering thus had the full control of his insights rather than having them co-opted and developed by corporate capitalists.[8] In this regard Kettering became an exemplar not only of invention but also of the modern corporate edifice. His career spurred the empirical science arm of the new American university, and embodied an alternative "Captain of Erudition," alongside the scientific experts of the new research universities.

Kettering's experience illuminated another major feature of the research university's expansion. Especially in the interwar period, engineering and business schools became important units of postgraduate instruction in higher education. Their dominance over the humanities and social sciences was largely a function of the large number of university graduates who went into careers in industry rather than in higher education. The expansion of industry from the late nineteenth century onward absorbed virtually all the graduates that universities could produce. In the engineering field, especially after World War I, two-thirds of engineers became corporate managers within fifteen years of graduation.[9] Kettering, like his fellow manager Alfred Sloan—who earlier had directed Hyatt Roller Bearing Company before it was taken over by General Motors—quickly contacted his fellow MIT graduate Pierre S. DuPont (1870–1954). The DuPont Company had used World War I to solidify its diversification from gunpowder production—its mainstay since the American Revolution—into paints, synthetic fiber, glues, and a host of related products, all central to the new automobile production. Pierre DuPont invested substantively in General Motors and for a time served as the chairman of its board of trustees. By the early 1920, General Motors, DuPont, Goodyear, and General Electric had executive officers who two decades earlier were all students at MIT. Unlike corporations before the war, corporations after the war separated founding owners from strategic managers, so complex had these organizations become especially in key, monopolistic industries. Part of that development and one of the measures of corporate sophistication involved the creation of their own research departments and their recruitment of university graduates to staff them. By the mid-1920s, Westinghouse, General Electric, Kodak, American Telephone and Telegraph, and DuPont had pioneered in-house research as an essential part of the apparatus of the modern corporation.[10]

One reason the universities began to cultivate research after World War I had to do, not only with these expanding careers in industrial research, but with the institutional linkages between industry and scientific research created by World War I. The war experience went far to demonstrate to the American public what the universities could do; the universities concomitantly saw the opportunity for postgraduate occupations and careers in American industry. On April 16, 1916, officers of the National Academy of Sciences met with President Woodrow Wilson to offer the service of the scientific community to the war effort. George Ellery Hale (1868–1938), director of the Mount Wilson Observatory, and William H. Welch (1850–1934), the medical seer at Johns Hopkins Medical School, formed a committee in response to the president's enthusiastic support. They assembled a group of highly distinguished scientists—Princeton and Woods Hole Institute biologist Edwin G. Conklin (1863–1952); director of Rockefeller Institute for Medical Research Simon Flexner (1863–1946); University of Chicago physicist Robert A. Millikan (1868–1953); and California Institute of Technology chemist Alfred A. Noyes (1866–1936) to form the National Research Council (NRC). The NRC responded quickly to the threats of German submarine warfare, noxious gas attack, intelligence and psychological testing, among other war-related issues. The NRC's efficacy prompted President Wilson in 1918, several months before the armistice, to establish the group as a permanent quasi-governmental agency. Subsequently the NRC adopted a formal charter, committing them "to stimulate research in the mathematical, physical and biological sciences, and in the application of these sciences to engineering, agriculture, medicine and the other useful arts, with the object of increasing knowledge, strengthening the national defense, and of contributing in other ways to the public welfare."[11] The NRC became an umbrella organization for the most prestigious scientific societies in the United States (110 in the 1960s) and a powerful voice in behalf of the scientific expert in strategic policy-making councils for all of the twentieth century.[12] The organization was also instrumental in urging a prior claim on government, philanthropic, and corporate research funding to select universities.

The power of scientific rhetoric impacted disciplines outside the physical sciences. In 1923 a cadre of leaders of previously formed professional societies, like the American Historical Association (1884) and the American Economic Association (1885), gathered informally to coalesce their ranks and provided a formal linkage to the federal government and its research priorities. They established the Social Science Research Council (SSRC) and were joined by individual scholars who sought to cultivate a more self-conscious scientific aura in the disciplines of political science and sociology. In the interwar years, they worked to give their research an even more vigorous empiricism, a preference for factual accumulation rather than theoretical musings. By empirical research most of the practicing scholars simply meant close observation and replicable data. The connotations of science with "prediction" and probability projections lay one generation in the future, raising a bar that many humanistic disciplines like English and history had difficulty achieving. Initially the SSRC sought to focus interdisciplinary scrutiny on problems of human migration that seemed to elude the traditional disciplinary approaches. They also committed themselves less to full-blown investigations than to "preliminary studies" by which they would study a discourse and identify areas and issues meriting serious, long-term investigative study. Finally they sought to firm up scientific practice by gaining financial support for predoctoral and postdoctoral support for such research, often under the mentorship of a member in good standing.[13] The long-term fiscal sponsorship, however, did not come from government but modestly from private foundations. However, other learned societies—the American Anthropological Association, the American Psychological Association, and the American Statistical Association—joined the SSRC, hopeful that these contacts would lead to greater influence and national stature for their research. The first SSRC president was University of Chicago political theorist Charles E. Merriam (1874–1953), who at the time was also president of the American Political Science Association, and brother of the paleontologist John Merriam (1869–1945), first president of the NRC and longtime president of the Carnegie Institute of Washington (1920–38).[14] These linkages and expectations make clear the relatively small leadership pool in these early social science bodies as well as their expectations of funding below that of the physical sciences.

These new national organizations, like the NSC and the SSRC, began very modestly and their actual achievements were neither stellar nor as dramatic as later achievements, but they were a part of a trend that some feared would displace the humanities entirely. However, they represented recognition on the part of scholars, industry leaders, and government officials that a new organizational matrix had emerged and accelerated as a product of World War I, which had come to employ scientific knowledge as a defense resource. Their vision anticipated and helped create the functional commitment to scientific research a generation before academic and elected politicians began to see the advantages of cultivating scientific experts. By the end of the interwar period, when the larger public and its leaders came to appreciate the attractions of "science," the word had come to mean something more than a careful observation and organization of data. It began to carry expansive connotations of predictable action on behalf of constructive change without overt political conflict or suspicion of capitalist self-interests, a major intensification of the meaning of pragmatic science.

The mantel of science descended on colleges as well as established universities at the turn of the century. Efforts to improve or reform an older denominational tradition seemed to lead ineluctably to a transformation of the scientific curriculum. Washington University in Saint Louis (founded 1853)[15] became a case in point, when, struggling under its denominational and manual labor inheritances, the school became a favorite of wealthy businessman Robert S. Brookings (1850–1932) in the 1890s. The school had begun as Eliot Seminary, founded by William Greenleaf Eliot (1811–87), the grandfather of poet T. S. Eliot (1888–1965). Brookings was in his forties at the time of his purchase of a new 170-acre campus for the college on the west side of Saint Louis.[16] He had distinguished himself as a leading dry-goods merchant in the city and had made a fortune in the creation of Cupples Station, a major railroad warehouse. He had experimented with stock-sharing options for employees and other progressive strategies for reducing employer-employee tensions, so ubiquitous during the depression years of the 1890s. A nervous breakdown had resulted in the liquidation of his business assets and his shifting of his interest to education where he thought he could institutionalize his insights about training a new business and political leadership. He became president of Washington University in November 1895.[17]

Brookings had worked for nearly a decade at Washington University, when the Carnegie Endowment for the Advancement of teaching published its Flexner Report. The report argued the need to close the school's medical department. At first outraged, then more businesslike, Brookings contacted the Carnegie Endowment president Henry Pritchett (1857–1939), also a native Missourian. Their interchange and friendly meeting persuaded Brookings of the correctness of the Flexner recommendation and his commitment to a new medical school curriculum and staffing. Pritchett's admiration for Brookings prompted him to introduce him to Andrew Carnegie, whose own self-made career gave the two men much in common and formed the basis of a tight friendship. This connection led to Brookings's appointment to the board of trustees of the Smithsonian, the National Civic Federation, and the Carnegie Foundation itself. Brookings began to publicize his long-held ideas about the need for expert training for government managers and won Rockefeller Foundation support for the creation of an Institute for Government Research in 1916. Brookings also became involved with the Wilson administration and set the context for his appointment to the War Industries Board, once war had been declared. Brookings worked on the controversial price-fixing sector, which convinced him more than ever of the need for a new and special cadre of government experts in the modern national and international economy.[18]

Independently Brookings created a graduate school at Washington University in Saint Louis with an eye to training congressional staffers. The faculty would teach at both the university and the newly created, Carnegie-funded Institute for Economics, based in Washington, DC. The loquacious Brookings worried in *New York Times* editorials that the "economic slavery" of workers was a central national problem. Its remedy, in part, he argued was the appointment of workers to corporate boards, though he was quick to distance his proposals from socialism. He drew on an older set of nineteenth-century assumptions that capitalist and labor had the same common interests. Many of his notions, especially employee presence on policy-making boards, found receptive ears among Herbert Hoover (1874–1964) and many of the experts Hoover assembled in his postwar economic councils.[19] Like increasing numbers of social scientists, Brookings believed that research-based policies contributed more to the national well-being than the patronage-built engines of government that so often controlled the allocation of natural resources. If he was less sensitive to the actual political pressures that shaped social reforms, it was no more than a blind spot of his generation's "progressive" assumptions. In 1927 he established the Brookings Institution, which provided experts and influence on public policy from that year to the present. This organization was not alone in creating a new cultural home for academically trained individuals; it served as a model for many later "think tanks," however politically aligned.[20] Its seminal service in its early years was to advocate the utility of research, once thought too detached and arcane. His work did much to foster in American higher education a decisive brand of expert knowledge for current social and political decision making.

The new matrix of industry, government, and higher education achieved its clearest expression in the research departments, bureaus, and institutes of the interwar period. Universities with graduate programs may initially have had a favored position in associating with such bridging organizations but virtually all the "other captains of erudition" who fostered universities had themselves studied at small, especially midwestern colleges, before entering graduate school or German universities for their advanced work. Harold G. Moulton (1883–1956), who became the first and long-term president of the Brookings Institution, started his higher learning at Albion College in his native Michigan and supported himself in graduate study at the University of Chicago by teaching in the Evanston Academy.[21] The extraordinary Merriam brothers both attended Lenox College in Hopkinton, Iowa, when its students numbered about 125 and the school operated under the aegis of the Presbyterian Synod.[22] Henry Pritchett would move from his father's proprietary Pritchett College in Glasgow, Missouri, to a PhD from Munich to the presidency of MIT and later the Carnegie Foundation for the Advancement of Teaching.[23] Many institutions only tangentially related to science or research nevertheless became implicated in this vortex through the professional careers of their students. Leaders of such small colleges, no less than those of aspiring new universities, sensed the new winds and within their resources and capabilities responded with curriculum offerings and advisements to maintain their claim to "higher learning."[24]

By the end of World War I, the terms "college" and "university" came into common parlance as if they were generically distinct concepts. Indeed intellectually they were distinct; but functionally colleges were held to standards that were thought to apply across the higher education spectrum. However, they could not maintain the scientific facilities of the universities nor could they support university research and publication patterns of the larger institutions. Nor did they have the resources to cultivate the foundations, the research institutes, or the expert bureaus of state and federal government. Still, they had to deal with the accrediting agencies that monitored the progress of higher education institutions and that publicized their findings, especially, say, the percentage of faculty holding doctorates, faculty-student ratios, and size of endowments. Usually these extra-academic monitoring institutions had little statutory power to enforce academic standards, but the cold light of public knowledge was a powerful incentive for colleges and universities to get their houses in order. Nowhere was their transformational power more evident than in the delineation of high school from college or from college to professional schools within a university orbit.

The plight of Catholic colleges in 1900 serves as a paradigmatic example of how both internal academic pressures and external supervisory forces operated in the early years of the twentieth century. Their early twentieth-century history also illuminated the force of internal and external dynamics that sometimes interfered with higher education modernization. Neither the *Catholic Directory* nor the US Commissioner of Education's Report for 1900 agreed even on the sheer number of Catholic colleges and universities in the United States. The directory listed ten Catholic universities, 178 colleges for boys (which clearly included "academies" and "preparatory" schools), 109 seminaries (formally differentiated from "colleges" by the Third Plenary Council of Baltimore in 1884), and 662 "academies for girls" (which probably included the College of Notre Dame in Maryland, which had conferred baccalaureate degrees since 1899). The US commissioner only recognized sixty-two Catholic universities and colleges for men or for both sexes.[25] Half of these institutions were sponsored by local (usually urban) dioceses and were under the aegis of the local bishop, who took responsibility for financing, staffing, and sustaining such schools. Independent religious orders dominated the nondiocese institutions, many of them Jesuit sponsored, officially answerable to their provincial in Rome and by extension the pope. Often two institutions functioned in the same local and were competitive, diluting both resources and talent.

Jesuit institutions had followed a basic curriculum since the end of the sixteenth century, the *Ratio Studiorum*, which stretched over seven years and showcased science, belles lettres, philosophy, theology, and the classics plus history and a few other subjects as electives. They encompassed both preparatory and advanced studies over the seven years and, however successful for students lasting the full time, clashed increasingly with the American system. The Jesuit tradition stressed extempore discussion, disputation, rhetorical skills, and ideally the ability to reason, values once enshrined in small American liberal arts colleges. However, by the end of the nineteenth century, many academic values became subordinated to numerical and bureaucratic standards, like the number of hours taken in a subject over a specified number of years. Catholic higher education also harbored a distinctive, defensive disposition toward America's dominant Protestant culture and was self-consciously aware of the ethnic (Irish and German especially) character of their student body.[26] In 1900, too, Catholic leadership worried overly about the one major phenomenon that might warrant accommodation to the dynamics of modern America: more second- and third-generation immigrant Catholics attended non-Catholic colleges and universities than they did Catholic institutions.[27]

In 1900 Washington, DC, there were two major Catholic universities, one a pontifically chartered school and one a Jesuit college. The first was Catholic University, founded in 1887 and opened in 1889, and was originally conceived like Johns Hopkins University as an exclusively graduate institution; the second, the oldest Catholic institution of higher education in the United States, Georgetown University, founded by Jesuit-trained Bishop John Carroll in 1789. In the 1890s both institutions faced critical decisions about their academic standards and their futures. Both found themselves confounded by the presence of the other and complicated further (probably uniquely in the American experience) by uninformed interference from Rome. At the end of the nineteenth century, both were well aware of the concerted and effective effort of the National Education Association to formulate a national standard for high school. Georgetown was probably the larger beneficiary of this change, since some of its leaders were already working to differentiate its "college students" enrolled in the preparatory classes from college-ready students. Georgetown's president (1888–98), Rev. Joseph Havens Richards, SJ (1851–98), a Harvard-trained son of a convert, elevated admissions standards and reduced the "preparatory" component of the school. In the eyes of many, he thereby risked the fiscal security of the school by reducing the levels of enrollment needed to sustain its operations.[28] The reform of admission to "university" level was the first of a decade's worth of decisions Richards made to compete with experiments occurring nationwide.

Richards also extended a welcome in 1889 to Catholic University's head, Bishop John J. Keane (1839–1918), an extraordinarily progressive and enlightened leader, who had the imprimatur of a still more progressive and enlightened clergyman, James Cardinal Gibbons (1834–1921) of Baltimore, one of the formidable voices for a national Catholic university.[29] Left alone Richards and Keane would clearly have worked out a rapprochement supporting university standards. Indeed there had been talk of a merger, capitalizing on Georgetown's long tradition, and a commitment to the *Ratio Studiorum* to join Catholic University's professional training, concentrated, though it was early on in philosophy and theology, with large numbers of priests and nuns in its core student body. Georgetown's ultimate goal was "intellectual excellence" and friendlier understanding with Americans of other religious faiths.[30]

It was this twofold ambition—intellectual discipline and outreach to a non-Catholic establishment—that caused sharp reactions from conservative prelates in America and in Rome. The emphasis on renewed intellectual discipline (a modified *Ratio*), it was alleged, challenged and subordinated the role of faith itself. In addition, rapprochement with America's secular culture, it was alleged, threatened the power of Catholic dogma and put Catholic theology on a par with Protestant doctrine. The reactionary epithet was "Americanism," and ultimately it put extraordinary pressure on Georgetown's Richards (who was regularly criticized in private, back-channel messages to Rome)[31] and resulted in the 1896 firing of Bishop Keane as head of Catholic University. Regularly cited in the litany of criticisms against Keane was his delivery of the Dudleian lecture at Harvard University (October 1890), an event that took place in Appleton Chapel, with Keane in full episcopal regalia and imparting a final blessing to his audience, which included non-Catholics.[32]

The interference of the Holy See and the shuffling of mediocre talent by the Jesuit provincials between and among the several leading Jesuits colleges—Boston College, Fordham College, and Loyola College of Baltimore—served to brake the progress of Catholics toward a "university" vision. These more conservative elements prevailed throughout the interwar period in asserting a preference for fiscal stability and traditional instruction over intellectual excellence, for accommodating the largest number of immigrant students through the Catholic collegiate mill, and for professing primary commitment to spiritual over secular values. Still, at Georgetown, Richards was able to modify the seven-year *Ratio Studiorum* curriculum into a more American, four-year collegiate format and to reduce the emphasis upon classics to make room for other subjects. If he had laid a new and thoughtful foundation, Richards nevertheless was not succeeded by individuals who shared his vision. Successive twentieth-century presidents of Georgetown for the most part did not enjoy Richards's long tenure, and introduced a succession of shifting priorities. In the interwar period, for example, the only limit on Georgetown awarding scholarships to athletes and becoming (like Notre Dame) a football power were the visiting committees of the Middle States Accrediting Committee (founded 1892), which criticized the practice. Before World War II, the only reforms in behalf of intellectual or "university" values at Georgetown were those insisted upon by these impartial, outside regulators.[33] There were, of course, in every liberal arts college, Catholic colleges included, individuals and pockets of excellence that thrived in spite of institutional priorities. But overall, local pressures and those from Rome intruded and diminished progressive reforms in Catholic colleges until after World War II. Until then, the larger discourses on the social power of the natural sciences and the new university made little headway in the American Catholic colleges.

The number of Catholics attending non-Catholic colleges and universities suggests that the "immigrant constituency" was far readier to adapt to American patterns and traditions than the leaders of their advanced institutions. Even as educators like Georgetown's Richards shortened the classics and emphasized the sciences in order to compete with successful non-Catholic schools, he had difficulty justifying changes of the *Ratio* to fellow Jesuits and other Catholic authorities. These internal pressures accompanied forceful external pressures on the adaptation of the Jesuits' centuries-old reputation of *Ratio* success. Richards faced a second front in his war for scientific specialists in Catholic and Jesuit circles. In 1893 Harvard University published a list of colleges whose graduates would be readily admitted without examination to its law school. The new list of some sixty-nine colleges contained no Catholic colleges or universities. Subsequent public discussion found Harvard's president, Charles Eliot, explicitly differentiating Catholic curricula from that of "Protestant or undenominational colleges."

The difference, Eliot went on, lay with the influence of the Jesuit tradition and the fact that Catholic schools of higher education were led by priests. Eliot's reply prompted Richards to write Eliot directly, objecting that Eliot's differentiation was misplaced and offered materials to that effect. In reply, Eliot conceded that Georgetown graduates would henceforth be included on his list along with graduates of Boston College and the College of Holy Cross. Richards countered that all twenty-four Jesuit colleges in the United States in 1893 followed roughly the same curriculum and deserved inclusion. Eliot demurred, but the next year included Notre Dame and in 1909 Manhattan College but no other Catholic colleges.[34]

Then and later many Catholic commentators were quick to accuse Eliot and Harvard of bigotry. However, Eliot had cultivated many religious persuasions on the Harvard campus, including Catholics. In fact, the number of Catholics in the undergraduate student body had been rising sharply to above three hundred at the time of the law school controversy, and these individuals were not enrolled in any "preparatory" classes but were fully vetted collegians. Eliot did not use the fact of conferring an honorary degree on Catholic University's rector in 1890, nor did he mention his invitation for Bishop Keane to reside in Eliot's home during his Cambridge sojourn. More likely, the actual transitions and "modernization" that Richards had initiated at Georgetown had not fully matured. Also, as Eliot noticed to Richards, his list of colleges reflected the institutions that recent law applicants to Harvard had attended, and Georgetown graduates had not recently been among them. Eliot's Catholic and non-Catholic critics worried exceedingly that electives and courses celebrating the scientific method both in the social and physical sciences undermined the ethical and moral teachings for which denominational instruction had always been noted. If modernity demanded the demotion of denominational apologetics, the civilizing force of the humanities should still hold a substantive place in the higher education curriculum, a situation that recent study has argued, waned considerably in the first half of the twentieth century.[35]

The Eliot-Richards controversy over law school admissions documented a small but illuminating feature of the emergence of research and scientific method in turn-of-the-century higher education. The physical sciences received a cultural recognition and fiscal surge that would carry through the entire century; the social sciences coveted the surge and jettisoned much in their disciplinary traditions that did not lend itself to a definable scientific empiricism; the humanities, by definition unable to quantify its contribution to "arts and sciences," initially became a diminished sector of higher education, until humanists themselves reengaged their own historical tradition and began to advance their own humanistic perspectives independent of scientific standards.

The tension between religion and natural science in higher education was an issue even in universities where the nature of the university and the importance of science were enthusiastically discussed. How the tension was resolved set the context for many schools concerning the nature of their twentieth-century modernization. Charles W. Eliot at Harvard took several decades to register the argument that nonsectarianism nevertheless respected piety and religious instruction (including morning chapel prayers). His remarks at the 1876 Johns Hopkins University inauguration of Daniel Coit Gilman insisted that scholarship filled men with "humility and awe, by bringing them on every hand face to face with inscrutable mystery and infinite power. The whole work of a university is uplifting, refining and spiritualizing." Eliot predicted that nonsectarian Johns Hopkins would be, like Harvard, a seat of piety as well as learning.[36] He defended this delicate distinction in open debate with President James McCosh of Princeton, among many Protestant clergymen who saw Eliot's background as a chemist, his endorsement of electives over a required curriculum, and his enthusiasm for scientific method to be antithetical to the shaping of moral character.[37] The tensions between religion and a new empirical science at the scores of Catholic colleges and universities had their counterparts, even in non-Catholic institutions, thought to be advancing a new and modern brand of intellectual training.[38]

Humanists, historically quickened whenever marginalized, did not take long to develop a substantive response to the new enthusiasm for the scientific method. Few responses were outright hostile to "science" but were more concerned about overemphasis on it. One of the key humanist responses came from Charles Eliot's Harvard University successor, Abbott Lawrence Lowell (1856–1943).[39] Lowell was a graduate of Harvard College and of its law school (class of 1880). He had a modest career in legal practice and a productive stint as a legal scholar, publishing books on trusts and government. After a successful lectureship at his alma mater, he was offered and accepted a full professorship in government, even though he did not hold the now expected doctorate in the subject. In 1909 he succeeded Charles Eliot as Harvard president and almost immediately moved against the completion of a bachelor's degree in three years. This three-year option became possible because the "elective system" permitted some individuals to take courses distinguished for their lack of rigor. Unlike Eliot, Lowell thought the elective system only worked with mature individuals. Without monitoring or coaching, he argued, a school would lose the ability to shape not only an instinct for scholarship but also a sense of communal responsibility. Returning to some older academic values, he believed that part of any reputable school's focus on "character" required a broad command of the established sectors of knowledge rather than overspecializing in courses that one found interesting.[40] Lowell's response was not a rejection of Eliot's scheme but, according to his biographer, a fulfillment of the foundation that Eliot laid. Lowell put forward a system of concentrations, that is, subject majors and distributions, to ensure exposure to distinctive ways of knowing.[41] This exposure to multiple disciplines ideally would restore the humanities to a substantive place in the collegiate curriculum.

Lowell evinced also a greater concern for undergraduate college instruction and the humanities than Eliot and had done so without ignoring the place of professional training in the new university. During Lowell's tenure Harvard instituted Schools of Architecture, Education, Business Administration, and Public Health. But more characteristic of his personal priorities was his acceptance of Edward S. Harkness's (1874–1940) philanthropy[42] to create Harvard's House System. Several buildings became a locus for undergraduates, not simply dorms but residences with libraries, a dining room, and tutors' suites. The "House" mimicked the Oxford-Cambridge colleges as a place for intensive yet informal learning as well as living. Resident and nonresident faculty members became parts of this enlarged "family" intended to root students in the fabric of the university and prevent their getting lost in the larger, impersonal bureaucracy of the institution. Harkness had earlier offered his plan and his money to Yale, his own alma mater, but Yale refused. Harvard's acceptance made Yale reconsider and reopen negotiations with Harkness, whose father had joined John D. Rockefeller in the creation of Standard Oil and had become the second largest shareholder of that firm.[43] The House System enabled Harvard and Yale to reshape its undergraduate culture, to focus and challenge students without removing entirely the sense either of election or of responsible, faculty counseling. The House System gave a new legitimacy to informal talk, extempore inquiry, multifaceted perspectives, and collegiality between students and faculty. All these features reinforced fundamental humanistic values without ever throwing down a gauntlet to either Harvard's or Yale's preoccupation with "scientific method" or postcollegiate education.

Lowell represented the collegiate reaction to an earlier generation's preoccupation with science and its facilities as the heart of university work. He was not alone in devising organizational outlets for nonscientific instruction, but his support of the House System at Harvard put the undergraduate college at the center of the university more dramatically than any other effort in the interwar period. Lowell consistently labored to instill a new sense of scholarly discipline in higher education via comprehensive examinations, regulation of student electives, the introduction of tutors, and, perhaps above all, his personal funding of the Harvard Fellows program, an effort to support gifted individuals in scholarship outside the graduate degree apparatus.[44] His work made many institutions reevaluate the college's role in the university.[45] At the very least, Lowell set in motion a thought process—especially for institutions that had nowhere near the Harvard resources[46]—that refined both the university and the college as generically distinct entities. This reaffirmation of undergraduate instruction, especially in humanistic studies, was sufficiently seminal to warrant the characterization "the other captains of erudition," to a new generation of educational leaders, as diverse as Charles Kettering; John and Charles Merriam; Robert Millikan; Rev. J. Haven Richards, SJ; Alexander Meiklejohn; and Abbott Lawrence Lowell. Their work, as refiners and implementers of a new higher education ideal, was equivalent and perhaps even more important than the vision and foundation laid down by the earlier generation of university presidents and proselytizers.

As important as the new complex instructional infrastructure was in higher education—the foundation programs, the industrial laboratories, the research councils, the interdisciplinary institutes, and the reenergized and focused college curriculum—the greatest contribution of the interwar generation of educational statesmen came in the 1930s with a debate between Robert M. Hutchins (1899–1977), the young and dynamic president of the University of Chicago,[47] and the premier philosophical voice of the early twentieth century, John Dewey, a Columbia University faculty member and renowned public intellectual. The issue over the very meaning of higher education arose because pressures external to institutions of higher education seemed to have overridden the original purposes of providing instruction. For sake of guaranteeing funding and thereby survival, Hutchins charged, American higher education created a range of studies whose end result created careers and employment rather than an enhancement of intellect. The problem for Hutchins was to restore the intellectual priorities that advanced training once promised. The problem, of course, was not new, but one that attested to the prominence of higher education in public consciousness and prestige employment.[48] In his eyes, the tailoring of instruction to putatively "professional" values had actually become little more than vocational training, narrowly specialized tutoring that belied the long-standing development of a liberal mind: sensitive, inquiring, adaptable to a range of problems and circumstances. Hutchins drew substantively on his own earlier years at Oberlin College and his long-standing admiration for the Amherst experiment of Alexander Meiklejohn (1872–1964).[49]

Hutchins adopted a number of key Meiklejohn ideas including a prescribed curriculum, particularly centering on enduring works by Aristotle and Saint Thomas Aquinas, an emphasis on Socratic dialogue, comprehensive exams rather than a calculation of credit hours, and early admission to college (especially for gifted high school seniors). The intensive give and take of rational debate, he felt, was far preferable to many elective courses, which he considered vocational or even "custodial." Like Meiklejohn, he criticized the distractions of fraternities and organized athletics and in 1939 eliminated college football from the University of Chicago, alienating many alumni and donors. His emphasis on Great Books, which remained seminal across multiple centuries and cultures, led to his critique of empirical science in the social sciences, especially in their effort to address current public and policy issues. Instead, he strove to increase the exposure of students to history, geography, and literature, which, in Hutchins's mind, disciplined the intellectual faculties, the central work of collegiate instruction.

There were many variations on the critique of "practical subjects" and many critics of Hutchins's experiments. His critics quickly agreed that the problematic role of intellectual training in higher education merited serious discussion, and they credited him with prodding leaders to scrutinize schools that seemed to be more "service station" than cultural resource. They also conceded that student electives may have diluted many core subjects and disciplines. The sheer number of courses may have led to "confusion" over the relative worth of subjects, since manifestly some courses were not the equal of others in the shaping of an enlightened mind. Critics like Harry D. Gideonse (1901–85)[50] insisted that the passing of an older collegiate tradition focused on "character" undermined the assumption that "truth to a finite man is never single, complete and static. It is rather multiple, fractional, and evolving."[51] He pounced on Hutchins's admiration for Aristotle and Saint Thomas Aquinas, metaphysical voices serving earlier university models, to insist Hutchins's argument moved the conception of the university back to a rational absolutism and to a "monastic withdrawal" into "discarded metaphysics." Gideonse went on to insist that in Hutchins's own generation many institutions were experimenting with a variety of scientific and humanistic methods that enriched human knowledge. He could not see how institutional and curricular coherence would do anything but undermine the gains of the twentieth century.

There were still more basic confrontations with Hutchins's views. His own determination to create an environment for learning led him to identify a series of authors, ultimately a collection of Great Books, that to him exemplified a higher echelon of intellectual expression. He recruited a special cadre of individuals, several of them distinguished philosophers like Scott Buchanan (1895–1968), Richard McKeon (1900–1985),[52] and Mortimer Adler (1902–2001), to articulate an exemplary mode of metaphysical inquiry. This exercise served as a red flag to the philosopher John Dewey, whose life work made metaphysical first principles the antithesis of the democratic experience. Indeed any effort to project the essence of knowledge as contained in a finite group of books struck Dewey as an undemocratic imposition of one person's version of truth on all others. Wasn't the essence of democracy itself, Dewey argued, a collective deployment of experience from many quite diverse individuals and a collaborative effort to reach a temporary accord? This "scientific" method of induction, Dewey argued, was the precise counterpoint to the didacticism of earlier denominational colleges and to the European tyrannies America had sought to resist for all of its history. The result was a debilitating hierarchy of knowledge and an aloofness of teacher over student that, he felt, American pragmatism had already proven counterproductive. At the very least, Dewey charged, Hutchins's remedy for the subordination of intellect to a definable canon sacrificed a respect for freedom more characteristic of the fascism arising elsewhere in the world.[53]

The ease with which Hutchins's critics characterized his argument with the terms of fascism, atavism, and authoritarianism documented how thoroughly the ideology of pragmatism had suffused American higher education by the 1930s. Hutchins's book selections also seemed indifferent to the American environment by including only three books by American authors: *The Federalist* Papers, *Moby-Dick* by Herman Melville, and William James's *The Principles of Psychology*. His association with philosopher Mortimer Adler, an explicit critic of pragmatic philosophy, raised questions about his university vision. Was he trying to imitate a medieval model of a university integrated by philosophy as the Queen of the Sciences? These apparent reorientations to the past flew in the face of the University of Chicago's generation-long buildup of the social sciences, especially in anthropology (Edward Sapir [1884–1939]) and sociology (Robert Park [1869–1944], Ernest Burgess [1886–1966], and Robert Redfield [1897–1958]). This work had appeared so promising because of the social science orientation to the city of Chicago itself and the university's effort to study urban dynamics as a means of addressing seemingly intractable social policy problems. The focus, even of the philosophy department with scholars like George Herbert Mead (1869–1931), worked to strengthen the ties between the university and the city and to make the university a bastion for refining and elevating issues of modern social relations. What could Adler's and Hutchins's emphasis on great thinkers of the past contribute to the solution of America's urban and national dilemmas?[54]

Hutchins's own confidence in his powers of persuasion predisposed him to Adler's insistence on the power of dialectical reasoning to achieve an alternate university standard. Both men had come from very different backgrounds—Hutchins's Protestant evangelical upbringing in the Midwest, Adler's largely self-taught mastery of great literary and intellectual masterpieces plus his work translating them for public education in New York City's People's Institute.[55] Yet both had come to their primary respect for the power of time-honored ideas. Also their iconoclastic temperaments made them reflexively skeptical of research that argued for immediate functional consequences. In that context, much of the social science work at Chicago (and for Adler earlier at Columbia University) struck them as a lowering of the university standard. Adler had worked through his own point of view after study at Columbia with John Dewey but more importantly through a group of stellar individuals who were central to Columbia's curricular commitment to Western civilization as a core study—Jacques Barzun (1907–2012), James Harvey Robinson (1863–1936), Will (1885–1981) and Ariel (1898–1981) Durant, and most of all Everett Dean Martin (1880–1941), director of the People's Institute from 1916 to 1934. A number of these individuals and others like Alvin Johnson (1874–1971) would be instrumental in the creation and development of the New School for Social Research (founded 1919), a highly experimental effort of the 1920s in both social science research and social philosophy.[56] Their informal meetings in New York City living rooms did as much or more than their formal work in institutions of higher learning. These gatherings thrived on the power of extempore discussion, each individual drawing on a lifetime of reading and knowledge and eager to sustain that dynamic in mutual exchanges.

Adler and Hutchins shared a passion for converting informed discourse at a very high, interdisciplinary level into the center of university work. Not unlike the work of A. Lawrence Lowell at Harvard, they sought a more focused curriculum, a reduction of bureaucratic requirements, and a system of comprehensive examinations. Hutchins would eventually distinguish the University of Chicago by trying to shorten the time to an undergraduate degree to three years. Often he encouraged the admission of high school seniors directly into freshman collegiate classes. But perhaps most singularly, Hutchins and Adler worked to establish at Chicago a college degree based on the great thinkers and books of the West: Homer, Plato, Aristotle, the Bible, Saint Thomas Aquinas, Goethe's *Faust*, Shakespeare, and John Stuart Mill. Their ambition was to train individuals in a habit of probing mankind's essential issues of truth and moral authority rather than—in their view—the more mundane solutions to immediate social problems. Their critique of academia's pragmatic bent was that it lowered men's sights and ambitions. Emphatically the Great Books injected a new imaginative esprit into undergraduate instruction and checked the rampant march of specialization, vocationalism, and empiricism. Hutchins and Adler modeled their approach in a highly visible freshman seminar that eventually continued for two-hours per week over two years. Eventually Hutchins would expand the model downward to the university high school and upward into the law school and other collegiate divisions as well as to the extension school. Eventually ad hoc groups from coast to coast adopted a dialectic approach to the Great Books, which were published by the University of Chicago's newly acquired *Encyclopaedia Britannica* and entitled *The Great Books of the Western World*.[57]

The Great Books curriculum became the centerpiece of Hutchins's proposal for a commitment to "general education" at the university level. He sought to break the lockstep sequence between high schools and college, to enable individuals to proceed at their own pace, to offer a comprehensive examination when students felt ready, and above all, to defend both students and faculty from the pressures of "vocationalism." Without rejecting entirely graduate education and advanced scientific research,[58] Hutchins created a separate teaching faculty, whose skills—like his own—rested on rhetorical virtuosity and the Socratic method of collective inquiry. Hutchins began the implementation of his ideas from his appointment as president of the University of Chicago until his resignation twenty-two years later. His insistence on the primacy of intellectual training as the central work of the university became a national mantra in behalf of humanistically leaning "general education" and against the faddish introduction of courses to satisfy current public concerns or donor's whims. He characterized universities that pandered to such pressures as "filling stations." If his reforms did not continue after his presidency, during his long tenure the University of Chicago became renowned for its alternate view of a university standard and firmly lionized the primacy of humanistic education in the modern university. It was this intellectual heart of undergraduate instruction that lay the foundation for later, advanced graduate and professional instruction.

The ease with which Hutchins's critics could label him "conservative," "elitist," "undemocratic," and worse documents the prevalence of a pragmatic bias in American higher education.[59] Such characterizations continued even in Hutchins's postpresidential career as director of a Ford Foundation project, the Fund for the Advancement of Education, and later the Center for the Study of Democratic Institutions in Santa Barbara, California. Pragmatists' remarks about Hutchins's arrogance stemmed from his belief that truth was not endlessly pliable nor was it primarily stimulated by contextual or experiential forces. His critics thought his insistence on a moral core indicated a throwback to the influence of evangelical colleges like Oberlin. Actually Hutchins implicitly engaged one of the core problems of modern philosophy: whether the essence of truth lay within man or outside in the external environment. Dewey's pragmatism insisted that truth was external, contingent, and temporary, always changing as men adapted to unforeseen problems and resources. By contrast, Hutchins perceived such a course as rudderless, unable to discriminate between fundamental and trivial priorities. Hutchins's impatience with pragmatism rested in his implicit recognition that its insistence on change did not itself change and masked an unexamined set of absolutist assumptions about first principles, namely, a metaphysics. Dewey's putative rejection of absolutes, Hutchins argued, did not make his pragmatism synonymous with "democracy," since it could not be inclusive of all viewpoints. Hutchins, like other Dewey critics, argued the impossibility of treating all viewpoints with equal comprehension and respect, and therefore pragmatists misled their followers with the equation of pragmatism and democracy. The perils of pragmatic accommodation should have been clear not only then but later, when Hutchins among a small handful of presidents resisted the anticommunist charges of Senator Joseph McCarthy, rejecting any tolerance of loyalty oaths as undemocratic and defending freedom of inquiry in principle. When asked if communism was taught at University of Chicago, Hutchins supposedly replied, "yes, and cancer at the medical school."[60]

Hutchins reveled in controversy and disputation as a primary method of intellectual training and worked hard to be consistent in pointing out pragmatism's limitations. His self-confident insistence on humanistic values that could not be compromised, lest an individual or a society lose its bearings, struck many as preposterous idealism.[61] In spite of his critics, Hutchins worked hard to keep the University of Chicago as one major institution of higher education that defended "the single-minded pursuit of intellectual virtues."[62] His promotion of Aristotle and Saint Thomas Aquinas, particularly, permitted him to chide Catholic colleges and universities for failing to celebrate their own intellectual traditions.[63] In response, some wag could offer a loaded observation: Hutchins was using Jewish professors to teach Catholic doctrine to atheistic students with Protestant evangelical preaching methods. In spite of such disparagements, Hutchins probably did more than any other single individual of his generation to center a distinctive collegiate experience at the heart of university work. His example encouraged many others in less dramatic ways to prevent further erosion of the college's core curriculum and to foster a widespread reexamination of the meaning of both general education and university work.

Despite Hutchins's seeming success in defending the humanities at the center of undergraduate instruction, the ensuing pressures against a humanistic core continued into the remaining decades of the twentieth century. In the postwar period, the expansive presence of the federal government and public money would provide an extensive increase in support for applied scientific work, especially as it related to pragmatic problem solving. In addition, since the early years of the Depression, other forces worked to increase the role of practical training in the colleges. Policies developed to ensure that the high school became a mass institution for the first time. Professional educators and union leaders saw opportunities to argue keeping high school students in high school to avoid competition in the workforce with heads of households with families. About 1933 one-half of the US high school age cohort entered secondary education for the first time and the implications for a student surge at the college level sometime afterward were clear. World War II delayed this consequence, but the postwar period, supported by the GI Bill, ensured that the number of the next generation's university students would substantially exceed those before the war.

So, new money for research, public pressure against yet with staunch defenders of humanistic instruction, and a quantitatively different and larger student body with a great range of preparations compelled all schools of higher education to scramble to respond by the late 1940s and 1950s. A contributing factor to the impact of the Depression and World War II was the retirement of the first generation of career academics during the 1930s. In this transformational process, Hutchins's arguments were not so much ignored as bypassed until such time as later voices resurrected his arguments and his distinguished contribution to the maturation of American higher education. The generation of college leaders after that of the founding university presidents, roughly those born in the 1870s and 1880s, represented a different cohort of higher education activists. If some like Robert Brookings and Abbott Lawrence Lowell were older and others like Hutchins were younger, they all distinguished themselves for their investment in special features of their contentious academic culture. In particular, their work was more notable for refining inherited structures and ideologies. If they contributed to a sharpened sense of both "university" and "college," they also contributed substantially to organizational bridges to the wider, social world via institutes, foundational partnerships, governmental bureaus, and corporate laboratories. All of these bridges had intramural implications in curricular programs, interdisciplinary combinations, and original coursework. The distinctive features of university and collegiate achievement that strike one today as commonplace and familiar appeared during this generation's watch as new. They introduced useful innovations while assuming they were continuing the work of the earlier university presidents whose mission was to proselytize systematically for the centrality of higher education.

Especially during the interwar years, it was this later generation of educational leaders—the other captains of erudition—who developed and matured that early vision, and in the case of Hutchins and others transformed and clarified academic purpose in ways their predecessors would probably have not understood. The interwar voices for higher learning were all driven by an early, small liberal college experience and expanded many of the graduate and professional layers of university work. At the same time, they focused and reworked the collegiate foundation of advanced study. The righteous pragmatists like John Dewey and his followers distorted their more metaphysically prone arguments, falsely contending Hutchins's priorities were undemocratic, elitist, and indeed corroded. But in this contentious environment, the pragmatists' own principles had become widely accepted as a measure of higher learning's worth. If it was now axiomatic that American higher education accommodated multiple ideologies, it would soon become equally obvious that not all ideologies could be equally valued. The very proliferation of new organizations—foundations, institutes, research laboratories, professional associations, and so on—that this interwar generation worked so hard and so creatively to build contained inherent problems that its pragmatic culture had not addressed.[64]

In response to the university's expanding organization, inside and outside its walls, the interwar years witnessed a tightening and recommitment to collegiate standards. The rise of the university and its multiple constituencies reflexively compelled college leaders to reaffirm the work of basic instruction and the college's central place in the process of higher learning. Lowell's and Hutchins's careers labored hard to insist that the college contribution to knowledge differed dramatically from that of advanced, professional training. Without resorting to a reprise of denominational didactics, Hutchins particularly sketched out curricular goals that resisted both empirical primacy and utilitarian applications. His insistence on the Great Books attempted to reserve a place for enduring works of the imagination as well as artistic and aesthetic conceptions that transcended manageable and documentable responses to human problems. The backlash of criticism in behalf of pragmatic instruction documented how widespread pragmatic, educational goals had become since the early decades of the twentieth century. The uncritical acceptance of pragmatic assumptions also made clear to the defenders of a humanistic tradition how difficult it was to critique embedded cultural assumptions.

CHAPTER TWELVE

From the Liberal Core to an International Discourse

From the vantage point of post–World War II, the American university before World War I looked so different from the nineteenth-century college that commentators were wont to insist that an academic revolution had occurred by the first decade of the twentieth century. Substantive changes had happened, but the transformation of American higher education actually occurred, not just in the older, but also in many relatively new institutions, like the University of Chicago and Johns Hopkins University, which had only recently adopted high intellectual standards and a new orientation to science. These changes in the ideal of research had come into prominence in academia largely through the experience of individuals who had studied overseas at German research universities. In all, about nine thousand Americans had traveled to Germany for study during the nineteenth century.[1] Many of them did not complete their doctoral degrees there, and large numbers went into professions other than higher education. Still, the pursuit of disciplined inquiry at a very high level set new standards, and American higher education evolved beyond the dissemination of basic knowledge. At the end of the nineteenth century, the new standard for a university was research and the creation of original knowledge.

At the beginning of the new century, no longer was the college president's course in moral philosophy the preeminent and summarizing experience of one's college years. No longer were pulpits and tutorial rooms sufficient for the kind of inquiry required in the modern world. Required chapel and close association with specific denominations continued apace for the majority of American colleges, but, for institutions that aspired to a genuine higher learning, the inculcation of moral doctrine appeared as so much indoctrination, the opposite of unfettered inquiry into the knotty questions of society and nature. While denominational colleges continued to flourish and grapple with new twentieth-century scientific standards promoted at select universities, newer institutional linkages and associations of higher education institutions made incremental headway with their new educational ideals. Faculty roles reflected these organizational matrices, dividing their allegiances between two camps: one for their own institution, another for their professional area of specialization. Faculty positions became ranked, departmentalized, and broadly sectored into the physical sciences, the social sciences, and the humanities, each with their own distinctive trans-institutional discourses. On some campuses, these three divisions were given distinct and separate buildings. The university president answered to an increasingly active board of trustees and to alumni groups. Fund-raising became one of the preeminent, constant duties of academic leadership. In a word, a new organizational complex, inside and outside institutional walls, had emerged out of a shift in educational ideology. The resulting shift over two generations, roughly from 1890 to 1940, however, was something less than a revolution.

The much vaunted German influence had a strategic but not dominant role in influencing this transformation. Its simultaneous arrival at the time of early twentieth-century changes in higher education made it seem more important than it actually was to later historical interpreters. Americans returning from study at German universities did bring back a new sense of intellectual discipline plus the accompanying organizational instruments: the laboratory, the seminar, the scholarly journal, and the great lecture hall. The upshot was a selective borrowing from German practice rather than an uncritical imitation. Americans who wrote about their experiences later generally ignored the highly class-bound German social structure that reinforced the German university. They had little comment upon the historical deference to the state paid by often highly privileged, "independent" German scholars, the centralized government funding, and government-appointed professorships.[2] In the early 1900s, commentators rarely suspected how such a structure could become corrupted by demagogic, political changes or political policing. Few Americans sustained or expanded their German academic contacts after returning to America, and many let their German fluency grow stale once back in the United States. The German influence was not entirely technical in its American applications, but the driving force of the German *Geist* and the spiritual connotations of German science did not survive the Atlantic crossing.[3] Ultimately the German influence upon the emergent American university was a smaller and narrower version of the original.

World War I provided the ultimate test of German influence upon their American students. The vast majority of American students, once back home, had favored American patriotic rhetoric, especially appeals to self-discipline and laissez-faire, something challenged by eminent German professors.[4] The Americans disappointed many German politicians who thought German-trained American faculty provided a cultivated elite that might sympathize with German war aims. Few German-trained scholars went so far as John Burgess of Columbia University to point out British hypocrisy (with its extensive empire) in criticizing Germany's imperial aggression. Fewer still held with Burgess that Germany was the model state of Europe and the avant-garde of Western civilization, largely for its alleged preference for trade (rather than the military) to lead its fellow states.[5] Instead, most American academics set aside any notion of German intellectual superiority—*Lehrfreiheit*—or the necessity for academic autonomy in the face of wartime patriotism. For faculty as well as for the general public, patriotic motives and national conformity trumped any effort to put German military incursions in a favorable light. The absence of open debate and unfettered inquiry in wartime also documented the temper of the American university genre through the first third of the twentieth century.

The new research emphasis of the American university, reinforced by the German example, did not expunge the older value of teaching or pedagogy inherited from the nineteenth-century denominational college. The place of undergraduate instruction and teaching revived in the early twentieth century and reasserted itself in the new university, especially in the humanistic sector. In the University of Chicago and elsewhere, the college became the foundational basis for later professional studies. The emphasis on teaching also remained a powerful force in both old and new colleges, even those that began to distance themselves from their denominational origins. Both values—research and teaching—became components of faculty leverage in the new bargaining relationships between presidents and deans as well as between deans and their faculty. Neither value had dominant autonomy in the "advanced" institutions of higher education nor did they have clear devices of integration. This uneasy state within higher education—teaching responsibilities at one's home institution versus research obligations to a larger discourse—resulted in the creation of a special new association in 1915, the American Association of University Professors, which tentatively—the founders refused to take up issues of salary and equitable recompense—offered an independent monitoring process for intramural disputes.[6] In Germany academic autonomy was a function of one's appointed position at state-funded universities; in the United States increasingly outspoken academics who entered the political fray did not automatically legitimate a point of view or escape reprisals. The American Association of University Professors came into being ideally to identify the relative expertise and special authority of academic viewpoints and to adjudicate disputes.

American academics' indifference to German appreciation of knowledge for its own sake reinforced indigenous American pragmatic assumptions that advanced knowledge should contribute more directly to both social and cultural values. Wartime service of academics, like John Dewey's role in support of the Committee on Public Information, softened any intimation that ivory-tower researchers had lost touch with immediate, pressing issues. Their wartime work gave many academics a new sense of using their hard-won knowledge for the public good. Pragmatic assumptions that wed research with public service—formally linked earlier at the University of Wisconsin with the "Wisconsin Idea"—legitimated university research as well as lowered research sights to attend to immediate, technical problems. During the 1920s and later, this indigenous pragmatism and problem-solving service tradition overrode for many the vestiges of "German" (or British) influence in this generation's academic culture.[7]

The post–World War I resurgence of core liberal arts courses in American higher education argued more strongly for a British rather than a German influence in the interwar years. After the allied victory, the strengthened ties between Great Britain and the United States internationally set the context for a new appreciation of the collegiate ideal as a basic element of the university experience. The established British model of the college as the teaching engine of any university, the basic liberal arts appreciation for interpretive skills (over factual acquisition or specialized knowledge), the enduring insistence on character building, the elevation of higher learning above day-to-day, especially urban routines, and the manly shaping force of physical sport received new admiration. From 1902 onward, the newly founded Rhodes Scholars program captured the élan and the power of the British collegiate ideal within the rhetorical claims of a new university.[8]

Despite the reemphasis on older collegiate ideals, the real novelty of the American university came from the postwar experience of the state university, its embrace of "service" and vocational subjects and the cultivation of the new university-level professions: social work, business, accounting, engineering, nursing, teaching, and so on. The easing of standards for admissions and the exponential rise in student numbers at state institutions contrasted sharply with what many older institutions—Harvard, Yale, Princeton, and so on—introduced, namely, capping enrollments to ensure a new exclusivity. The manufacture of an "Ivy League" tradition and a fictive heritage of intellectual excellence sought an opposite value: an educational aristocracy masking as a national resource. Princeton, for example, coined a new motto—"In the Nation's Service"—as they consciously limited the enrollment of Jews, Catholics, and African Americans.[9] In contrast, with critical masses of state legislators with state university degrees, state universities began receiving for the first time regular fiscal support. They now intoned the inheritance of the Morrill Land Grant Act of 1862, the legal precedent for publicly supported universities. But, until the interwar period, few state universities excelled the small denominational colleges that were their principal competition. After World War I, state universities worked diligently to offer higher education opportunities for larger numbers of students. They opened their admission doors and embraced an inclusive, democratic ideal for the first time. This expansion was not simply one to raise funds or enhance enrollment but also to offer curricula that enabled graduates to compete well in the American labor market. Perhaps most important of all, commentators considered the new state university model of higher education a check against a single national educational standard. The postwar emphasis stressed an engine of diversity attuned to the state and regional hosts of publicly supported higher education.[10]

This sensitivity to local and regional needs departed from the German ideal of comprehensive mastery of a single subject. Rather, state universities (as well as some of their elite competitors) cultivated an exposure to multiple areas that, some thought, trivialized and compromised any standards of higher learning. Such divisions of opinion about basic disciplines could be found throughout American academic offerings in these years. In the field of history, for example, some insisted the discipline remain true to its humanistic heritage and savor the power of knowing multiple cultures and societies; others thought that modern history needed to embrace the social sciences from which sociology, anthropology, political sciences, and economics had broken off in the last years of the nineteenth century. History needed to establish and disseminate the incontrovertible facts and documentable data of historical change: dates, names, events. Interpretation elevated discussion into the problematic world of the subjective and away from history's social science associations. Contentious debate could be curtailed and at times completely avoided, if commentary rested on the bedrock of facts that no belief system could deny. Neither alternative—history as a humanistic study or history as a social science—achieved the autonomy of German scholarship nor did either variation advance the American goal of useful skills and practical applications.

By comparison with its German counterpart—socially stratified, state supported, and epitomized by an authoritative, elite professoriate—the American university in the interwar period was a mixture of competing models.

Progressives in higher education expected that the unity of purpose and knowledge would emerge in the future and worked methodically without overt worry about ideological or definitional unity. Humanists who sought such conceptual clarity gave support to new courses in Western civilization (especially now that the United States had become through wartime the standard bearer of the West). In effect, such courses became devices by which "Western civilization" took on new, twentieth-century meanings and claims.[11] The defeat of Germany as a predatory nation further distanced scholars from Germany's earlier esteemed and respected place. American academics in wartime often set aside their critical viewpoints—some like John Dewey himself working for the US government's propaganda arm—and afterward gained public esteem by seeming to ally their patriotic and academic priorities. They achieved a new public status by effectively subordinating critical thought to patriotic action, however much philosophically they insisted that thought and action were interactively dependent.[12] The World War I experience distanced many academics with German degrees from their educational and professional roots of rationality and discipline. Their ambivalence about the role of critical thought often led contradictorily to heightened statements of patriotism and oversimplified accusations against Germany as simply inherently military, predatory, and evil. For some participants, the psychic costs of such uncritical simplifications lasted well beyond the armistice.[13]

The war also permitted an expansion of America's indigenous, service tradition in higher education. Universities offered leaves of absence to faculty with special skills favored by the federal government; they promised rapid graduation to students whose majors were in demand, especially in mechanical and electrical engineering; but most of all, they saw in the war an opportunity to deliver tangibly on the promise of higher learning as a broad social and national resource. For institutions that hesitated in the pell-mell rush to patriotic support, the backlash would be quick and dangerous. An attack on the University of Wisconsin—due to the state's large German-American population, the antiwar sentiments of its US senator Robert M. La Follette, and its critical Progressive tradition—invited charges not simply of being unpatriotic but of approaching treason. President Charles R. Van Hise (1857–1918), the principal articulator of the "Wisconsin Idea," orchestrated an extensive and long-term campaign to dispel such charges, addressing state representatives, the nation, and especially President Woodrow Wilson.[14]

The First World War narrowed the priorities of the physical and social sciences by using the federal imprimatur and philanthropic funding to accomplish specific war-directed priorities. The government support of the newly founded NRC appeared to physicists like Robert Millikan (1868–1953) as an unprecedented advantage. From his vantage point at the Throop Institute of Technology (eventually the California Institute of Technology), Millikan joined astronomer George Ellery Hale (1868–1938)[15] in his ambitious efforts to create a new scientific research center in California. Millikan served during the war as vice chairman of the NRC and allied scientific research to federal government needs.[16] In psychology the NRC supported the work of Robert Yerkes (1876–1956)[17] on "mental testing," which sought to establish grades for emotional capabilities and defects, first applied to 1 million army recruits, and then for other strategic occupations.[18] His wartime work with NRC led to Rockefeller Foundation funding, which in turn served his pioneering creation of the Laboratory of Primate Biology at Yale University after the war.

The social sciences and the humanities viewed the war also as an opportunity and tailored their research projects and curricular reforms accordingly. At many institutions the new courses in Western civilization resulted in expanded interests in the languages of allied countries: French, Italian, and Spanish.[19] Supporters noted the dividend for such instruction might well be careers in the State Department and commercial positions overseas. For veterans—professors and students—returning to campus from the war, much of the older curriculum now struck them as antiquated and out of touch with the dangers and realities they had recently faced. They worked diligently to adapt higher education curricula to a modern world.

However, two distinctive developments put brakes on the upgrading of the collegiate and university curriculum. The first was the sheer national expansion of the student body. Before 1900 no more than 4 percent of the college-age population was in college, representing about 238,000 undergraduates. By 1920 the percentage had doubled, reaching 12 percent during the 1930s and 18 percent by 1940.[20] The best colleges and universities had eliminated their "preparatory" departments but still admitted many students who were not ready for rigorous study at advanced levels. The largest surge occurred in the state universities, which balanced with great difficulty their traditional liberal arts programs with the introduction of many new, untraditional courses.

A second feature of academic culture in the 1920s resulted from the expanding enrollment rather than a consequence of wartime priorities. Extracurricular organizations—fraternities, sororities, theater groups, student newspapers, and especially the athletic programs—grew exponentially. In many institutions the accolades accorded winning football teams were too attractive to administrators and loyal alumni to resist investing rising percentages of their operating budgets into athletic programs. Stanford University, for example, was not alone in its reputation as offering a four-year, country-club interlude before engaging the realities of career and family. Stanford's public reputation gave little hint of the transformation it would undergo during World War II and the research powerhouse and intellectual bastion that it would become in the second half of the twentieth century.[21]

The conceptual confusions of the American university, its insecurity as a regional or national resource, and the sheer variety of its applicants, in retrospect, became the precise context for its transformation in the middle and second half of the twentieth century. Demographic expansion and the construction spree of the 1920s stopped sharply with the Depression, surprising many educational leaders who had expected a wholesale transformation of American higher education. But below the surface of these obvious changes was another, far more profound and long-lasting one, which might well have not occurred but for the American university's internal disarray and lack of a functional, national model.

This great change began in the early 1930s and led to a special kind of German influence. The rise of Hitler and Nazism in this period set in motion a series of purges in German universities that benefited American higher education extraordinarily. This purge of scholars who were critical of the Nazi regime or who were perceived to be hostile by dint of religion or of "racial purity," forced many academics, especially Jewish scholars, into exile. Many of the most esteemed German scholars had little or no reputation in the United States and received offers of academic appointments at institutions without research traditions.[22] The problem of language became a major impediment to their teaching and to any larger academic impact, but even more problematic for them was the absence of public deference and esteem Germany accorded its scholars. The barriers of limited English and of social indifference to researchers in general made the émigrés' transition both awkward and disconcerting. Even more, the theoretical orientation and underpinnings of German academic discourses clashed with the American university's service tradition and focus on practical research for pressing social problems.

The reception accorded Europe's refugee scholars provided a telling difference between the two national traditions of higher education. American universities of the interwar period, in great need of credentialed scholars as teachers, welcomed their European counterparts with only perfunctory regard for their actual scholarship.[23] Refugees in the physical sciences and mathematics generally assimilated better than scholars reliant on language or international recognition. Blueprints, as historian Lewis Coser insisted, have no language, and mathematics has no vernacular.[24] A fine example of this observation occurred with the career of Richard Courant (1888–1972). He was born in Silesia but followed a peripatetic schooling due to his father's shifting business interests: from Lublinitz to Glatz to Breslau. In this latter city, he attended Kaiser Wilhelm Gymnasium, which evaluated him as "less than satisfactory" in mathematics.[25] At age fourteen, nevertheless, he began to tutor students in mathematics to offset to the family's declining fortunes. In 1904 the family moved to Berlin, leaving him to support himself and his studies at the University of Breslau.

Three years later Courant shifted, first, to the University of Zurich, and then made a strategic and fortunate relocation to the University of Göttingen. There he flourished, exploring the interrelations of mathematics and physics, which would occupy him for the rest of his life. He completed his doctorate in 1910, taught at Göttingen until it was time for his military service. An early war wound proved fortuitous, and he returned in 1918 to the university, where he was instrumental in the creation of its Mathematics Institute. In 1933 he was expelled from his professorship due to the German Civil Service Law forbidding Jewish teachers from holding such positions. In 1934 he went briefly to Cambridge, England, and then to America and New York University. There he was poorly paid and found his faculty colleagues as poorly prepared as the students. Still, he survived by cultivating a mastery of institutional operations and by his administrative acumen. He also brought to the university a range of visiting lecturers, which prompted New York University to encourage his creation of a graduate center and to offer him a professorship. From 1936 to his death in 1972, Courant modeled the New York University facility on the old Göttingen Institute (dissolved by Nazi purges) and created a world-class institute, later in 1964 named after him—"the Courant Institute of Mathematical Sciences."[26]

Courant's successful career trajectory resulted from his previous administrative experience at a major comparable facility in Germany, his own publications and reputation, and no small amount of personal ingenuity, all of which overcame the provincialism of his host institution and its spare academic standing in the 1930s and 1940s. The presence of an international scholar in the midst of a commuter university with vocationally oriented students might appear an anomaly but actually was precisely the verdant ground for Courant and his vision. Malleable students, indifferent colleagues, ambitious administrators, and modest amounts of seed money became the ingredients by which Courant transformed the insularity of multiple departments with his insistence on interdisciplinary interactions with competent, outside mathematical scholars. The model would not fit every discipline or university, but New York University's receptivity to Courant, whom they gradually understood to be a superlative academic resource, overcame their usual short-sighted, tuition-driven priorities.[27]

Mathematics also proved to be a bridge to a major advance in the social sciences. A promising young Viennese student, Paul Lazarsfeld (1901–76), received a degree in applied mathematics from the University of Vienna and immediately began teaching in a gymnasium. His personal interests in the flagging socialist student movement led him into psychology, not then a formal university subject. However the social psychology of Alfred Adler (1870–1937) sparked his fascination with the social origins of the mind. In 1923 Charlotte (1893–1974) and Karl (1879–1963) Buehler received appointments to the university and organized a psychology department or institute, and Lazarsfeld attended their seminars and soon was invited to teach a course in statistics.[28] Gradually he began to offer a separate course in social and applied psychology (while still teaching at the gymnasium). This niche permitted him to develop contract work connecting psychological insights to current economic and social problems. In 1933, on a Rockefeller Fellowship, Lazarsfeld came to the United States where he visited several psychological centers. The following year the Conservative Party of Austria overthrew the government, outlawed socialism, and imprisoned his family. Lazarsfeld received the message from Austria: don't come home. The Rockefeller Foundation extended his fellowship another year and, through the guidance of Robert S. Lynd (1892–1970),[29] a Columbia sociologist, Lazarsfeld obtained a position at the University of Newark. In 1937 he became associated with the Rockefeller-funded Office of Radio Research, where he developed mathematical schemas to assess the reach of radio beams in order to calculate the efficacy of radio advertisements.[30] The office transferred to Columbia University, and in 1940 he received an appointment as professor of sociology, where he remained for the rest of his career, pioneering the basic field of polling and statistical analysis of social patterns.

Lazarsfeld's work specifically drew upon European interests in social stratification, especially on the diverse individual aspirations of middle-class versus working-class employees. Following Max Weber, he became interested in the shaping influence of religion in occupation choices. In addition, Emile Durkheim's (1858–1917) scholarship, focusing on social and structural entities—village, town, class, and so on—rather than personality traits, introduced a significant new dimension into both psychological and sociological discussions. Lazarsfeld made the most of it, seeking ways of challenging and also overlapping with American behaviorism. The point of Lazarsfeld's scholarship was the cultivation of a theory that integrated multiple vantage points, the seeking of a new cohesion out of diversified data, both structural/objective and situational/subjective. Even more important was his acquisition at the Buehler Institute in Vienna of the skills to create a research institute, first at the University of Newark, then later, at Columbia, the esteemed Bureau for Applied Social Research (1941–72). While formalizing many of Lazarsfeld's personal research interests, the bureau became a home for maverick scholars like C. Wright Mills (1916–62) and promising young scholars like Robert K. Merton (1910–2003), both major figures later in American sociological discourses.

The bureau also became a pioneer in university satellite units funded by outside entities like the federal government, American corporations, and business interests.[31] This development made the bureau a model for market survey research, monitored by Columbia to ensure its work was "consistent with the purposes of the university." A constant drumroll of criticism within Columbia for accepting this outside support prompted Lazarsfeld to assert that the bureau succeeded "in spite of Columbia" not because of its sheltering arm.[32] The controversy, however, could not deny the interdisciplinary impact of the bureau in influencing Columbia faculty like historian Lee Benson (*The Concept of Jacksonian Democracy: New York as a Test Case* [1961]) and later indirectly Lazarsfeld's Harvard son-in-law, Bernard Bailyn (b. 1922), with his statistical analysis *New England Merchants in the Seventeenth Century* (1955). Lazarsfeld and Merton contributed directly to the founding of the Center for Advanced Study in Behavioral Sciences at Stanford University (though formally independent of Stanford University), sponsored by funds from the Ford Foundation, and which served as a successor to the bureau from the early 1950s.[33] Lazarsfeld's fortunate career, as he admitted himself, came from his youth and the absence of ingrained German academic rituals and expectations. His earlier socialist commitments, always a backdrop in his later work, nevertheless concentrated on the role of quantified data in establishing existing and projected social preferences. His willingness to compete with the American academics and the pragmatic discourses of his adopted country, particularly in applied research, also ensured him a receptive audience.

By contrast, older, seasoned German refugee scholars looked in vain for niches that replicated the social standing and cultural respect that their native country accorded academics. Max Horkheimer (1895–1973), a native of

Stuttgart, Germany, initially worked in the family factory, but, after World War I, he enrolled in the University of Munich, studying philosophy and psychology. Later he moved to the University of Frankfort where he took his doctorate (1925) and taught. He met there his lifelong friend Theodor Adorno (1903–69)[34] and initiated a highly fruitful academic collaboration. In 1930 Frankfurt's Institute for Social Research appointed Horkheimer director, and, in the same year, he assumed the professorial chair of social philosophy at Frankfurt. In this position he created the influential *Zeitschrift fur Sozialforschung*, which he edited for many years. This institutional and journalistic base provided the environment for a critical collaboration of Marxist scholars who labeled their work "critical theory," a sharply interpreted critique of modern bourgeois society. In 1933 the Nazi regime closed the institute and revoked Horkheimer's license to teach. However, he had anticipated this oppression and moved much of his operation and resources, first to Switzerland, then to the United States.[35]

Horkheimer's Jewish background shaped his view as an outsider even in his native country. But this distancing from his host culture continued in America, where he continued to publish his journal in German, reducing much of its impact on his English-speaking audience. Columbia University's president, Nicholas Murray Butler (1862–1947), a politically conservative administrator but one who had studied in Germany, welcomed Horkheimer and his associates and helped establish them on Morningside Drive, with loose ties between Horkheimer's transplanted Frankfort Institute and Columbia University. The Depression plus a depletion of his organization's funds due to poor realty investments began to take their toll on the institute in the 1930s. Once war was declared, Horkheimer applied for citizenship (granted 1940), shifted his journal's title to English—*Studies in Philosophy and Social Science*—and softened the sharp edges of his Marxist and structural analyses of modern society. In 1950 the institute published one of its most famous studies, *The Authoritarian Personality* by Theodor Adorno, which reflected the cohesive ideology of the institute and Horkheimer's leadership. This ideology employed a Marxist framework but introduced many historical variables to reduce any simplistic deterministic dynamic in social affairs. Though hardly center stage in American social science, Horkheimer's institute provided a forum and a forceful, theoretical alternative that influenced a range of subsequent scholars. Horkheimer himself returned to Germany in 1949, re-created his institute on his native soil, and ended his career as rector of the University of Frankfort.[36]

Another story of setbacks and eventual success characterized the career of Alexander Gerschenkron (1904–78), who formally may be called an economist but whose theoretical and cultural stance differentiated his "economics" from that of his American colleagues. Gerschenkron was born in Odessa, Russia, and journeyed through Hungary to the University of Vienna, where he took his doctorate in 1928, which showed the influence of the university's less doctrinaire Marxist criticism. Like the Austrian Marxist school, Gerschenkron insisted on the power of ideas, political processes, and institutions in shaping historical consequences. His Russian background in Germany, not to mention his Jewish inheritance, precluded prestigious appointments early in his career. He held subordinate positions in several research agencies, but notably the Austrian Business Cycle Research Institute, led by Oskar Morgenstern (1902–77). This agency put him in contact with American scholars—notably Charles Gulick (1896–1984) of the University of California, Berkeley—who would aid his later career.[37]

In 1938 when Hitler invaded Austria, Gerschenkron escaped to Switzerland, then to the United States. His contacts rather than his published record gained him research positions for a decade, until the publication of *Bread and Democracy in Germany* (1943), which established the model for interest group analysis, a framework that swept American sociology and political analysis. He worked for the Federal Reserve Board in Washington, DC, from 1944 to 1948, in which year he accepted an appointment at Harvard University. There he taught economic history and Soviet studies. Eventually he created Harvard's Economic History Workshop, which published a limited but influential set of papers that gave economics a broad political and cultural context. Gerschenkron's institutional base was not as extensive or as long-lived as Horkheimer's, but it quickly became an important influence in the American discourse for its theoretical and interdisciplinary dimensions.[38] One of Gerschenkron's major contributions was his fascination with and interpretation of economic "backwardness," which in a comparative context, was found to contain many advantages over more "advanced" economies: the ability to capitalize on other's inventions, the possibility of progressing exponentially rather than incrementally, the edge afforded by capital-intensive over labor-intensive industry, and so on.[39] Even "backward" economies had much to teach if one inserted them in a historical and comparative context. His framework concentrated on the strategic, contingent factors of socio-economic change and cultivated a pluralistic interpretation of the past, without abandoning his original Marxist point of view.

The introduction of subjective and idiosyncratic dynamics in social science analysis and blending it with structural Marxist determinants remained an ambition in many disciplines, but never more so than in the field of psychoanalysis, as many scholars sought to work beyond the Freudian dicta.

Sigmund Freud (1856–1939) had come to the United States for a conference at Clark University in 1909. But, it is fair to say, his *Interpretation of Dreams* (1899) had not been a central focus of psychotic research and practice until late in the interwar years. In America psychoanalysis was not a field of study until the work of Karen Horney (1885–1952), the German-born daughter of a Norwegian sea captain. Horney took advantage of the new (1900) access to German higher education by women. She studied medicine, first at the University of Freiberg, then Göttingen, and finally Berlin, from which she took her MD in 1913. Subsequently she served residencies in several neurological institutes in Berlin and in 1915 wrote her thesis, "Post-Traumatic Psychoses."[40] Suffering her own bouts of depression, Horney underwent psychoanalysis with Karl Abraham (1877–1925), one of Freud's foremost students in Berlin. Her dissatisfaction with Freudian methods, developed in a long string of papers, led her to emphasize the power of sociocultural factors over organic and innate influences on mental anxiety. She began to shape her own understanding of neurosis by arguing that it was a continuous process rather than an episodic event of the unconscious. Her work at the Berlin Psychoanalytic Clinic and Institute (1919–30) produced a very different appreciation for feminine anxieties and further moved her from the Freudian orbit.

In 1930 Horney accepted an appointment at the Chicago Institute for Psychoanalysis, which was directed by Franz Alexander (1891–1964), a Berlin colleague. Differences between the two compelled Horney to relocate to Brooklyn where she took teaching positions at the New School for Social Research and the New York Psychoanalytic Institute. In this period she wrote two important works that solidified her reputation: *The Neurotic Personality in Our Time* (1932) and *New Ways in Psychoanalysis* (1939). In 1941 she resigned from the institute and founded—with Clara Thompson (1893–1958), Erich Fromm (1900–1980), and Harry Stack Sullivan (1892–1949)—the American Association for the Advancement of Psychoanalysis and its teaching arm, the American Institute for Psychoanalysis. She also accepted a teaching position at the New York Medical College and founded a journal, the *American Journal of Psychoanalysis,* which she edited until her death in 1952. In 1950 she published her summary argument, *Neurosis and Human Growth*.[41] As her career pattern indicates, Horney's work operated from a university base but in association with institutes that were somewhat removed from university research. Educators and other professionals adopted many psychoanalytic concepts in the interwar period, but its heyday as a professional practice would come after World War II, especially in the 1960s and 1970s. Only then would established medical departments make faculty appointments explicitly in psychoanalysis, a practice that existed in Europe before World War I, at least for subscribers to the Freudian orthodoxy.

In addition to post-Freudian psychoanalysis, European scholars brought a new authority to social psychology. Kurt Lewin (1890–1947), in particular, came to the United States after establishing an important presence at the University of Berlin where he had taken his doctorate. He had served there as lecturer and associate professor of psychology in that institution's Psychological Institute. The influence of his mentor, Carl Stumpf (1848–1936), impressed upon Lewin the Gestalt theory of psychology. This theory attempted a holistic approach to perception and behavioral change rather than breaking down all ingredients into the lowest, measurable parts. Lewin came to the United States in 1933 in reaction to Nazi oppression and brought with him an impressive publication record and the experience of a year's teaching as visiting scholar at Stanford. His reputation and connections with scholars like Stanford's Lewis Terman (1877–1956) did not, however, open doors for Lewin to America's prestigious universities. His first teaching appointment put him in Cornell University's Department of Home Economics and then at the University of Iowa in the Child Welfare Research Station (1935–44). From this improbable starting point, Lewin created a new generation of social psychologists and a journal, *Human Relations*. In these venues he advanced his research into "force fields," "action research," "industrial psychology," and, most importantly, "sensitivity training" in his now famous T-groups.[42] Only late in his career did he receive institutional recognition from MIT and its Center for Group Dynamics plus his National Training Laboratories at Bethel, Maine. His fellow psychologists have credited Lewin with modifying psychological drives connected to one's past and shifting psychology toward the immediate pressures of one's environment to account for personality development. Posthumously the American Psychological Association would honor him as one of the important psychologists of the twentieth century.[43]

Other scholars and professionals found initial or lasting careers outside the most prestigious American universities. Gunnar Johansen (1906–91), the distinguished pianist, left his native Copenhagen at an early age for study in Berlin. He toured Europe in his late teens winning considerable reputation for his piano virtuosity and interpretive insight. In the early thirties, he removed to California, where he both composed his own works and prepared a recital repertoire, which he performed at many cities and universities. In 1939 he offered his recital on the history of piano music at the University of Wisconsin, which offered him an appointment as the first musician-in-residence at an American university. He was subsequently offered other appointments but remained in Madison, saying, on one occasion, that he remained "because they gave me shelter when I needed it." His prodigious body of his own compositions and his lifelong fascination with the work of Ferruccio Busoni (1866–1924) was part and parcel of a performing, cultural niche he created on the Madison campus. He often joined another distinguished refugee, Rudolf Kolisch (1896–1978), for free performances in the old university chapel.[44]

Similarly many later distinguished careers had prosaic starting points but eventually established challenging research areas for their American colleagues. Hans Morgenthau (1904–80) arrived in the United States with a fascination for literature and philosophy that he studied at the University of Frankfurt. However, he shifted to law at the University of Munich and developed a preoccupation with Bismarckian *realpolitik* that informed his later writing on international relations. In 1931 he was appointed acting president of the Labor Law Court, a recognition of his published books and articles on labor law. When the Nazis came to power, Morgenthau moved first to Switzerland, then to Madrid, and finally arrived in the New York in 1937. His mastery of Germanic law was minimally attractive to the common law traditions of US law. He initially found part-time teaching posts (at night and paid by the hour) in political science at Brooklyn College (founded 1930), itself a new educational entity on the metropolitan scene. In 1939 he took a position teaching American law, which he had studied informally, at the University of Kansas City. Ultimately he passed the American bar exam in 1943, the same year he accepted a visiting professorship in political science at the University of Chicago, whose faculty were not immediately congenial to Morgenthau's more theoretical (rather than a case-by-case) approach to his subject. He remained at Chicago until 1968, taking postretirement positions at the City University of New York and the New School for Social Research.[45]

Morgenthau was unusual in finishing his career at the New School; many, many refugee scholars arrived there hopeful that the New School's understanding of international scholarship would become an entrée to an American career. The New School began in 1919 with a primary orientation in adult education. The founding scholars, the distinguished historians Charles Beard (1874–1948) and James Harvey Robinson (1863–1936), with the fiscal backing of Dorothy Straight (1887–1968), sought education without the bureaucratic trappings of degrees, departments, and so on. The New School's original brownstones on Twenty-Second and Twenty-Third Streets in Manhattan had provided classrooms, a library, and apartments for Robinson, Thorstein Veblen (1857–1929), the philosopher Horace Kallen (1882–1974), and the historian Harry Elmer Barnes (1889–1968). By 1922 fiscal pressures pressed the school to reorganize and hire a second-generation Danish émigré, Alvin Johnson (1874–1971), who would direct the facility for the next forty years. Among Johnson's most important achievements was his editing of *The Encyclopedia of the Social Sciences,* which took him to Europe to meet renowned scholars and to ensure that the work would move beyond the parochial boundaries of much American scholarship. Even before the Nazis came to power, Johnson had conceived of a "University in Exile" for many scholars, especially Jewish scholars, driven out of Europe by National Socialism. His selection of an initial core of a dozen individuals rapidly expanded, providing in a remarkably short period the academic talent to inaugurate a graduate school in the social sciences.[46] Many early New School scholars like Sidney Hook (1902–89) and Max Lerner (1902–92) groused about the "Germanizing" of the faculty but were as likely to be affronted more by the very different methodological approaches and theoretical questions that the refugee scholars brought from Germany.[47] For several decades many of the most outstanding German refugees would thrive in this unusual environment, and from this base the real German influence would emanate into the broader American intellectual discourses.

Émigré German scholars did not overtly challenge or surprise certain select university disciplines. One of these was art history, where European scholarship was renowned and appreciated, especially in art history bastions like Princeton University and New York University's Institute of Fine Arts. Leading art historians, especially Erwin Panofsky (1892–1968), drew upon their association with the Warburg Institute[48] and its distinguished library. Scholars here, like Panofsky, attempted to go beyond mere iconographic analysis—the description of artifacts in paintings, the adherence to painterly methods and forms, the authentication of relevant dates of creation, and so on—into a study of symbolic meanings that illuminated historical and philosophical contexts. Panofsky called such analysis iconology and achieved an international reputation with it, even before the rise of German Nazism. He came to the United States in 1931 at the invitation of New York University's Richard Offner (1889–1965), with the imprimatur of Walter W. S. Cook (1888–1962), himself a reputed medieval art historian and director of the Institute of Fine Arts.[49] Panofsky then shuttled between this institution and the University of Hamburg for several years. In 1935 he accepted an appointment to the Institute for Advanced Study at Princeton but kept his New York University ties and teaching commitments. Through his intervention a number of distinguished refugee scholars came to both Princeton and New York University. More important, of the estimated eighty to one hundred art historians who came to the United States in the 1930s, Panofsky helped place many of them in universities in the South, the Midwest, and the West Coast, in many cases creating art departments where none had existed before. In many of these institutions, Panofsky and the Warburg Institute (which moved to London in 1935) worked to bring art history into the mainstream of cultural and social development. They made works of art, not simply items of connoisseurship, but windows into the historical fabric of a period. They particularly emphasized those symbolic aspects about which the artist may not have been fully conscious, as intensively familiar to his moment as they were.[50] New York University's Cook and his colleague, Offner, certainly were aware of this scholarly development, but without the influx of refugee scholars, Panofsky alone could never have engineered the transformation of his field in so short a time or on such a national scale.[51]

In so many instances, however prosaic their beginnings, refugee scholars created institutional niches, originated forums and scholarly journals, and developed interdisciplinary linkages with fellow refugees and with their American colleagues. There was an entrepreneurial spirit to the most successful of these arrivistes and, one suspects, a recognition by them that America had become their new homeland, rather than a way station before their return to Germany. Many of the refugees eventually gravitated, especially after World War II, to America's more prestigious universities: psychologist Erik Erikson (1902–94) at Harvard and Roman Jakobson (1896–1982) in linguistics at Harvard and MIT; the scholar of comparative literature Rene Wellek (1903–95)[52] and historian Hajo Holborn (1902–69) at Yale; the sociologist Hans Gerth (1908–79) and the historian George Mosse (1918–99) at the University of Wisconsin; the historian Hans Baron (1900–1988) and the child psychologist Bruno Bettelheim (1903–90) at Chicago; philosopher Herbert Marcuse (1898–1979) at Brandies University; the political theorist Hannah Arendt (1906–75) at Princeton; and cultural historian Paul O. Kristeller (1905–99) at Columbia, among scores of others. Even in areas where German refugees' scholarship did not introduce new dimensions, their presence provided a needed international prestige in many fields where it had not existed before. Their impact on a successive generation of American scholars had much to do with the surge of cutting-edge scholarship that followed World War II and catapulted American universities into an acclaimed, global renown.

The proliferation of new specializations in the physical sciences, the social sciences, and the humanities in the interwar period was dramatized through the joint work of mathematicians and physicists fleeing Germany. Many of them, like the early Budapest mathematics prodigy John von Neumann (1903–57),[53] always fascinated by the interface between mathematics and physical dynamics, quickly found traditional forms of differential and integral equations and the theory of analytic functions wholly inadequate for the problems they faced.[54] His association with Albert Einstein (1879–1955) at the Institute for Advanced Study in the mid-thirties and his collaboration with Austrian economist Oskar Morgenstern, in *Theory of Games and Economic Behavior* (1944), reveal a small sample of his discoveries. Particularly important was his recognition of the enormous sequences of calculations for some of his problems, which led him directly into the basic layout of the modern computer. He also participated—along with Danish physicist Niels Bohr (1885–1962), Italian scientist Enrico Fermi (1901–54), Hungarian chemist Leo Szilard (1898–1964), and many others—in the development of fission theory and in the work of the Manhattan Project at Los Alamos, New Mexico, which produced the atomic bomb.[55] The rapid social and academic assimilation of these scientists and their paradigmatic work on highly successful scientific research confirmed not only the relevance of university investigation but concomitantly—one of the dramatic features of academic culture in the twentieth century—the enthusiastic fiscal endorsement of it by the federal government.

One might note also the peripatetic character of academic careers, evidenced by but not exclusively practiced by émigré scholars. From the interwar period onward, academic careers combining study, teaching, and research in several institutions became the norm. Allegiance to a single institution or imitation of the German model of one chair per subject in a university was not the American model. The proliferation of research universities made it possible for disciplines and especially collaborative, interdisciplinary scholarship to develop independent research groups that often went beyond any single university organization or institutional loyalty.[56]

The seeds of another important postwar shift arose in the interwar years in the African American colleges and universities, and they illuminate the serendipitous reception of European scholarship in America's pragmatic academic culture. The impact on intellectuals of European scholarship became the starting point for a cultural breakthrough in the career of W. E. B. DuBois (1868–1963), Massachusetts born and Harvard trained—that institution's first African American PhD—but powerfully influenced by his years of study at the University of Berlin or more formally at the Friedrich-Wilhelm III Universitat.[57] This institution, founded in 1809, still carried the nimbus of its founding rector, Johann Gottlieb Fichte (1762–1814), who made clear that his institution had the responsibility of restoring the German nation in the wake of Napoleon's defeat. The interconnection between university, culture, and political leadership were also explicit and continuous in the lectures of Georg W. F. Hegel (1770–1831) and the historical discipline exemplified by Leopold von Ranke (1795–1886), the teacher of Max Weber (1864–1920).[58] From university lectures and travels, DuBois merged his studies in history, sociology, and politics and began to see interactions between the role of race and multiple world cultures.

DuBois's career in the United States was peripatetic, shifting from academic positions and research publications to activism with the nascent National Association for the Advancement of Colored People and as editor of that organization's influential publication, the *Crisis*. DuBois also visited many black colleges and universities, at times simply sitting and talking with students in dormitory sessions as well as offering formal lectures. One young woman at Atlanta University remembered that "we'd sit on the floors and sit in chairs whatever and just listen to him talk. Well, now you can imagine my surprise. Here's this man talking about things, going to Europe and going to Russia and doing things in this country and doing things in that country . . . and I didn't even know where these countries were. I sat there really in a state of absolute unbelief that this man knew so much about everything. And he, he never let us forget that we had a right, and we shouldn't let color prevent us from having set goals for ourselves, and that we should work toward those. He believed that there were opportunities, but that we needed the appropriate education to be able to do those things."[59] This same epiphany recurred countless times in DuBois's long career, and his writings set the stage for breaking down the gap between black college graduates and America's social expectations for them. DuBois preached a different kind of higher education, one that went beyond race, beyond Booker T. Washington's deferential pragmatism, beyond the familiar collegiate complacency of the interwar years.[60]

DuBois argued for an independent intellectual discipline in higher learning and emphasized the importance of ideas in social activism. He followed the lead of many nineteenth-century missionaries trying to inculcate a basic liberal arts curriculum and critical thinking. He rejected Booker T. Washington's Tuskegee Institute model, which he thought often masked a vocational veneer to placate Southern biases and philanthropic expectations.[61] His own scholarship, especially *Black Reconstruction in America* and *The Philadelphia*

Negro, attempted an empirical documentation of the achievement of black culture in America. He urged college graduates not only to pursue leadership over money in their careers but also to go beyond racial barriers to address problems faced by all Americans. His historically informed perspectives galvanized a series of new organizations including the Urban League and later the Student Nonviolent Coordinating Committee. Out of these DuBois-influenced organizations arose a new standard of social criticism in the 1920s and 1930s backed by protest and invocations of traditional forms of social justice.[62] Subsequently this model of democratic change would influence larger protest movements in the 1960s and 1970s and offer a new ideal of higher learning and social action.[63] His death on August 27, 1963, was one of the announcements made by leaders of the March on Washington.

The real impact of German learning on DuBois and other Americans was appreciated after their actual experience of German learning at the time. Others have written about the sense of release and freedom many Americans experienced initially once in Germany,[64] but few have tracked how these lines of influence played out in their subsequent scholarship once they returned to America. The high research standard was the most obvious consequence, but the self-conscious *theoretical* basis of much European social analysis was foreign to Americans. Their pre-European training remained a formidable influence on their newfound German disciplines. Any examination of German-trained American scholarship, once the Americans returned home, must recognize the interaction between their German models and their American audience needs to account for the American suspicions of theoretical interpretation as deterministic, deductive, and constricting. One actual impact was that German émigré scholars in America during the interwar period often took many years for their scholarship to make its way into the American discourses. One astute scholar has noted that the German example in America was often one of "storage,"[65] of banking ideas and publications until a later time when, under different stresses than those presented by the Depression, scholars could mull over the possibilities of borrowing and imitating European precedents.

There was no coherent drum roll of European influence associated with the émigré scholars. Their scholarship itself was a work in progress when National Socialism disrupted so much work and compelled it to a vagabond destiny. Some of the eventual consequences of this disruption—one thinks of Max Horkheimer's postwar welcome back to the University of Berlin and the reestablishment of his institute there, fully funded and comfortably endowed[66]—meant that the American storage of some scholarship had to wait a generation or more for recognition. But for others European insight remained embedded or thrived in wayside shelters, awaiting post–World War II discovery. It should also be noted that this "storage" experience also meant that the émigré scholars in American would eventually transform and challenge American scholarship in substantial ways, however irregular, however late. The initial American resistance to European scholarship eventually gave way in the post–World War II period to a different intellectual discourse. The introduction of qualitatively different points of view, the essence of critical perspective, and a new respect for the theoretical underpinnings of all scholarship has to be one of the lasting benefits provided in these years to American academic traditions.

The expansion of pragmatic assumptions by mid-twentieth-century America, in academia no less than the society at large, helps explain the cultural barriers faced by émigré scholars during the interwar period. The émigrés' strategic presence and continuing influence in their fields would likely never have happened had their crossing to American not occurred in the wake of the 1920s expansion of collegiate populations and the 1930s economic constrictions. These tumultuous decades left the American academic establishment confused once more about its basic priorities and indifferent for a time to the insights of European scholars. The dynamics of World War II compelled a refocus and a rediscovery of scholarship that America had for too long marginalized or compartmentalized. But for the leaven of European theoretical research, it is difficult to see how the force of American pragmatic assumptions would have received the critical scrutiny it did in the post–World War II period. It is also difficult to see how indigenous American forces could have transformed American postwar scholarship in so short a period without the challenge of scholarship that demanded a different set of issues and interdisciplinary organizations.

CHAPTER THIRTEEN

Federal Policy and the Postwar University

In the post–World War II period, the American university had broken with many of the structures and academic patterns that operated since 1910. In 1910, the universities shaped academic careers; in the post–World War I period, scholarship, especially collaborative, interdisciplinary, scientific scholarship, made disciplines and their trans-university organizations the driving force for new knowledge and discourses.[1] Universities appointed presidents less for their own academic achievements and more for their pragmatic organizational skills. Universities rewarded scholarly achievement over teaching excellence and forfeited to smaller liberal arts colleges the primary reputation for teaching. Individual scholars within the university might devote themselves to teaching but paid heavily for that priority in salary and prestige. Colleges and universities shifted the ways they were managed and funded. Entire staffs, for example, devoted themselves to the cultivation of both alumni and nonalumni donors, which, above all now, included the federal government itself. These broad differences of organization and scope make an important, emphatic point that the university, so difficult to define at any point in time, was now an entity understood mainly by its history and by its peculiar aggregation of structural units.

In spite of these developments, many commentators still offered definitions of the American university and made higher learning a subject of debate in public forums. Similarly World War I had emphatically registered the necessity of cultivating intellectual resources, as the equivalent of economic or military resources, in the defense of American national interests. The leading university presidents had become early in the century both powerful presences in their budding institutions but also popular advocates in behalf of research and intellect as an American (they would have said "democratic") resource. By 1930 the institutions, which had sheltered the first generation of full-time academics, were beginning to retire their first professionally trained cohort and hand over the reins of power to their protégés. At this very moment, political and social upheavals elsewhere in the world would send a surge of distinguished yet culturally different scholars to American colleges and universities. The ensuing ferment in scholarly debate, not to mention controversies over actual staffing of higher education institutions with accomplished personnel, catapulted the American university into another orbit entirely. Two generic responses to the public debate and institutional competitions resulted in the creation of the Ivy League (and the Seven Sisters consortium), which would become highly selective institutions with specified admission ceilings; at the same time, state universities, now substantively supported fiscally for the first time by their state legislatures (with many alumni in legislative offices), embarked on a more inclusive and explicitly democratic option, to provide a welcoming opportunity in higher education for ever larger percentages of the college-age cohort. In 1910 under 5 percent of college-age youth attended American higher education institutions; in 1950 almost 18 percent. By 1970 75 percent of college-age youth attended public institutions, a shift from 2.5 million students in 1950 to 8.8 million. By 1970 public universities would produce three-quarters of America's doctoral degrees and regularly appear on most "ten best" lists. Exactly how did this quantitative revolution come about, and what has its impact been on the American society that higher education purports to advance (and not just "serve")?[2]

The academic changes after World War II had deep roots in the interwar history of American higher education. The Depression experience set the context for a deep-seated cultural change in the nation as a whole. Franklin D. Roosevelt, a fiscally conservative Democrat, embarked on a national scheme of experiments that replicated the successful public works programs he initiated as governor of New York in the 1920s. An alphabet soup of federal agencies attempted to address the economic crisis and succeeded, not so much in eliminating but moderately reducing the sharp edges of the economic downturn. More importantly, the nation endorsed his experimentations and thereby shifted away from a long-standing fear of federal initiatives on the social fabric of the country. Until that moment, for the most part, Americans had subscribed to the axiom that that government governed best that governed least. Most efforts at reform had seemed to prefer local, certainly not more than state, prerogatives. The federal government embarking on a wide range of pragmatic (yet never systemic) interventions required a fundamental shift in social and cultural assumptions. It was a transformation that happened quickly but not completely. Even Roosevelt himself was not so confident of his newfound Keynesian strategies of government borrowing and spending. In 1937 he tried to return the nation to a balanced budget, which sent the American economy into a recession. What began as an experiment, his New Deal reforms, ended as a fundamental principle of a new Democratic ideology: the government legitimately played a major activist role in the shaping of the economy and American life.[3]

In the context of this New Deal effort, Americans relaxed much of their inherited suspicions of centralized government power. Many still worried about the possibilities of governmental abuse at the federal level and openly taunted New Deal initiatives as latent socialism. Others thought they detected the latent abuses of centralized power that they associated with National Socialism on the German model, a 1930s nemesis that would soon enough become a mortal enemy. Indeed for all the modest gains of the New Deal, it was the wartime economy after Pearl Harbor that restored the American economy and returned the American labor force to full employment. After the country declared war on Germany and Japan, congressional leaders reminded themselves of the experience of the First World War, which ended with economic and labor crises. Even while they prosecuted the Second World War, congressmen sought ways to avoid a repetition of the last war's aftermath. Their greatest fears were a repeat of postwar inflation, large-scale unemployment due to returning veterans demanding their old jobs, and the resulting violent labor actions. With the cessation of military contracts at war's end, Congress worried overly about immediate unemployment (estimated at 8–9 million jobs) as well as the time lag for retooling and retraining for a peacetime economy, as a million veterans a month began to arrive home from overseas.[4]

History provided American leaders with little solace. Congressmen were well aware that World War I required 30 percent of the national economy to support 4 million men in arms. By contrast, World War II would require 70 percent of the national economy and would support 11 million individuals in the war effort. American politicians reminded each other that only Great Britain and America had avoided major government overthrows in the interwar period, which had been fueled by disgruntled veterans. The cautionary tales of Russia, Italy, Germany, and France underscored America's own close encounter with the 1932 March on Washington by a "Bonus Army" of veterans seeking the promised but unpaid World War I bonus. Congress was mindful that social upheavals in other countries were directly related to the unrest of jobless veterans, many still in possession of their arms.

The deliberations that began during World War II took on a defensive and narrowly economic turn. There was little thought given to a holistic domestic recovery affecting all citizens.[5] Here was an immediate and present need to stifle predictable social upheaval, and the problem was how to use the nation's resources to stall the inevitable. The question at hand was how to funnel money into veterans' pockets, and one of the gradually emerging solutions was through higher education. If some thought that finally the moment had arrived where the United States would formulate a national educational policy, even for higher education, they were sadly mistaken. A number of distinguished educators concurred with the often prescient president of the University of Chicago Robert M. Hutchins (1899–1977), who declared publicly: "Colleges and university will find themselves converted into educational hobo jungles. And veterans, unable to get work and equally unable to resist putting pressure on the colleges and universities, will find themselves educational hobos. . . . Education is not a device for coping with mass unemployment."[6] Similar worries kept the National Education Association and the American Council on Education from participating actively in shaping strategies for distributing these new federal funds.

Neither political nor educational leaders, however, were the dominant influence on one of the profoundly democratic pieces of twentieth-century legislation: the Serviceman's Readjustment Act of 1944, known familiarly as the GI Bill. It was the American Legion, formed in the aftermath of World War I, which continued to lobby for resources for homecoming veterans and their transition to civilian life. This new 1944 legislation arose out of the legion's sense that it had failed in its earlier venture. After World War I, veterans received sixty dollars and a train ticket to their hometown. Disabled veterans did somewhat better with educational benefits: tuition, fees, books, and a subsistence allowance ($90–$145) for rehabilitative and professional training. However, economic dislocations resulted immediately in breadlines for millions of veterans, who were unable to compete with the new technologies and work skills of the postwar industrialization. The legion studied the experience of Great Britain, which after World War I had offered government grants to many of their veterans, as did some American states (Wisconsin, California, New York, Minnesota, Oregon, and North Dakota).

The American Legion also fretted about the differences in the military cohorts of the two wars. In World War I, the educational levels of soldiers were relatively low. Only 20 percent had gone beyond grade school, while fewer than 5 percent had attended college. By contrast, 57 percent of World War II enlistees had completed one year of high school, a much higher portion than draftees.[7] These statistics argued that whatever "benefits" the US congress offered would have to include postsecondary education. Still, neither legion advocacy nor deliberating politicians fathomed the change they were setting in motion. They ended by offering benefits without regard to religion, class, gender, or race, even though all of those factors, especially race, would dramatically affect eventual outcomes. Most Americans in the 1940s, including the veterans of World War II, belonged to the working class and very few of them ever anticipated the possibility of higher education, homeownership, or middle-class careers. The GI Bill made all of those amenities suddenly and improbably possible.[8]

The support of college tuition was but one portion of the GI Bill, but it was one that received considerable publicity in the nation's newspapers. If some university leaders worried about a dilution of academic standards with an influx of irregularly prepared veterans, others welcomed veterans to their empty wartime classrooms. Others enthused about the bill's stipulations supporting construction of academic buildings. There was continued worry about the dilution of academic standards. It was not until years later that scholars discovered veterans actually had enhanced the academic quality of most of the campuses they attended. Some 2.2 million veterans took advantage of the opportunity to attend college, an option a majority never considered before the war. In 1947, at the peak of this veteran influx, 51 percent of college enrollees were veterans. They sensed a limited time frame for completion of their studies and for fiscal support. One consequence of that pressure plus the maturity of the veterans was an indifference to fraternities as frivolous distractions. Veterans came to study subjects that in the near term enhanced their career prospects, but they also took courses that began to make sense of the world they had discovered outside their own country. They committed themselves to the social sciences, especially political science, as well as the physical sciences and business. Veterans were intensely serious students. They also provided a bulwark against the emergent red-baiting that would flourish in the early 1950s after their college studies had ended. The GI Bill struck them, as one insightful study has it, as a powerful recompense for their military sacrifices, one that solidified the new civic patterns of the New Deal and supported a constructive interventionist role for the federal government.[9]

The GI Bill's higher education stimulus also had a ripple effect elsewhere in the American educational system. Over 2 million veterans went to college on the GI Bill, but 7.8 million used the bill for some brand of educational advantage. Vocational training was particularly popular among veterans, since it provided skills that elevated them into the middle class. The GI Bill smoothed the transition, even for those who would have returned to college anyway. Federal support permitted them to attend class full-time during the day, for example, rather than part-time at night. The bill sent many veterans into better schools than they would have attended had they remained in their original communities. Ninety percent of those using the bill came originally from low- or moderate-income families, and the bill generally ensured a social class advance beyond these original circumstances. It was also no small gain that the GI Bill broke down entrenched college quotas against Jewish and Catholic students and occasionally even for black students.[10] However black veterans were more likely to use noncollegiate vocational education programs or the college programs at traditionally black universities. While many white veterans moved after graduation into suburban homes and voluntary civic organizations, black GI Bill veterans—Hosea Williams (1926–2000), Medgar Evers (1925–63), Harry Belafonte (b. 1927), and others—often channeled their energies into nascent civil rights organizations. The full impact of the GI Bill came, they believed, not with themselves but with their children and grandchildren.[11]

The GI Bill, which originally had expected only 20 percent of veterans to benefit, surprised its creators by supporting over half the returning veterans. The congressional shapers of the original legislation actually delivered on one of their major objectives—$14.5 billion of federal money of which $3.9 billion went to tuition for schooling—the stimulation of the American economy and forestalling worrisome economic crises during the 1940s. The bill's other provisions for higher education construction and for home ownership confirmed in the public's mind the beneficial possibilities of federal policy activism and fiscal stimuli in domestic life. The implementation of the bill and the veterans' own response spread the bill's impact and made it one of the most inclusive and democratic pieces of legislation in the twentieth century. However, few noticed at the time or indeed afterward how serendipitous and surprising the bill's impact was. Retrospectively, the bill's impact should *not* be considered the product of responsible policy making. The bill did not segue into a discussion of a national federal policy in education, nor did it displace a long-standing American tradition, the prevailing local and state responsibilities for American public education.

The GI Bill did mark the point from which postwar changes in American higher education can be measured. It solidified the New Deal's transformative impact and legitimated a permanent role for federal government initiatives in setting the nation's social priorities. More than that, it bears repeating, the GI Bill set in motion an expansion of the middle class and new opportunities for many working-class veterans. Equally important, the GI Bill was the stimulus for the accelerating expansion of American higher education in the last half of the twentieth century and a substantive challenge to the hitherto prominent role of the selective college and university. The GI Bill became a model for channeling taxpayer's dollars into the public university to make it a more inclusive and more democratic institution than it had ever been. Although it was never its creators' intention, the bill became the starting point for a profound transformative dynamic in American academic traditions, the baseline for a distinct generational culture.[12]

The GI Bill enhanced social expectations dramatically for all Americans and made them regard—as Robert Hutchins cautioned them not to do—higher education as a new passport into a range of desirable careers. The bill also stabilized college and university budgets for both the 1940s and 1950s and made those institutions avidly solicitous for state and federal funding, willing at times to sacrifice intellectual autonomy for institutional expansion. Especially during the McCarthy era amid accusations of unpatriotic and communist behavior, the targeted academics' own institutions often did the work of interrogation and firing. Universities felt they could not survive any perception that "academic freedom" protected ideologues hostile to American values.[13] The reactionary roles that many educational leaders thus cultivated related directly to the Department of Defense's expanded funding for scientific research in American higher education.[14]

There was much more than the GI Bill that transformed the universities and the public conception of higher education in these years. During the war the American military, especially the Office of Naval Research, had liberally funded many university research projects and, in the postwar period, these research institutions sought to maintain this pattern. Predictably wartime technical research was privileged. Institutions like MIT (especially its radiation laboratory with its applications of radar), the California Institute of Technology, Harvard University, and the University of Chicago (so central to the development of the atomic chain reaction with the Manhattan Project) received substantive funding. In the 1920s federal support had amounted to $20 million; by 1938 university research had received over $200 million from federal sources. In the postwar period, roughly $20 million annually went to two hundred select universities, increasingly going to smaller projects but still under the wartime-like veil of security and secrecy. In 1950 the formation of the National Science Foundation (NSF) took over from the Office of Naval Research distribution of university research grants but had to compete for university research talent with the Atomic Energy Commission and the National Institutes of Health.[15]

Despite that, during the 1950s university research had become a big business, and federal funding created a special layering and rank order in American higher education. Research universities—approximately two hundred of them—shifted from basic to (formerly suspect) applied research and were still able to occupy the peak of the American higher education pyramid. From a close-knit and like-minded group of scientists who had become university administrators—Vannevar Bush (1890–1974), director of the Carnegie Institute of Washington; James B. Conant (1893–1978), president of Harvard University; Karl Compton (1887–1954), president of MIT; Frank Jewett (1879–1949), director of Bell Labs; Richard C. Tolman (1881–1948), dean of California Institute of Technology; and others—the relationship between scientific research and the federal government was forged with minimal bureaucracy. After the war the successes of this group—accustomed to secrecy and minimal public debate—could not be sustained. Some, like Vannevar Bush, sought to solidify the wartime gains in peacetime for private universities and federal funding. Failing that, he sought a device for scientists to determine scientific over political priorities, prompted especially by President Harry S. Truman's intervention and use of the atomic bomb. University leaders generally supported new strategies to guarantee federal funding in peacetime, on the grounds that responses to future crises would favor an intellectually prepared nation.[16] Wartime victory vastly inflated the expectations for scientific researchers in peacetime, but it did not clarify who would set the final priorities.

The postwar strategies for federal scientific support not only created a special status for institutions receiving such funds; they also began to break down wartime academic collegiality into distinctive public and private beneficiaries. The MIT and the California Institute of Technology became major university recipients of federal dollars, so much so that during the 1940s and afterward they operated almost as a separate echelon. New agencies, like the Atomic Energy Commission and the National Institutes of Health, began to funnel money, both to select government labs—most notably the Livermore Laboratory in California for its cyclotron research and its work on the hydrogen bomb, so pivotal in the early days of the Cold War—and to preferred universities. Among these universities a few were public institutions, which had cultivated a research ambition before World War II: Michigan, Wisconsin, California, Illinois, and Minnesota.[17] Unlike the private universities with their larger endowments, the public universities could rarely support research centers or collaborative efforts without government dollars. There was always a precarious dimension to public universities welcoming any large research endeavors for fear of being dragged into future, fiscal obligations and left with expensive unfunded operations that would drain money. Even in private institutions, like Harvard in the late 1940s, its president and wartime federal science advisor, James B. Conant, sought to distance the funding of scientific research from political dynamics that academics could not influence or control.

Such concerns led to a major shift in federal-academic relations. Conant's vocal resistance to the "Super," the hydrogen bomb (where he joined Robert J. Oppenheimer [1904–67]), began a federal government shift to a younger, more empathetic group of research scientists. Despite the reservations of individuals like Conant, federal dollars had their attractions. For the private universities, philanthropic support had fallen during the Depression and would not reach pre-Depression levels until the mid-1950s. So government support with its largely short-term and often military-related objectives began a political penetration of American higher education. This shift only accelerated with McCarthyism's narrowly defined standard of patriotism and the subsequent intimidation of many critical academics and scientists.[18]

Cumulatively these federal incursions led to a new academic culture. In the 1950s the presence of federal support for scientific research, most especially in the physical sciences, represented a qualitative shift in American academic culture. Federal funding was not simply an additional and benign enhancement of university work. First, it challenged the hitherto transparent approach to research projects, since much of the military-related research had to remain secret. Some universities, like Conant's Harvard, initially rejected the change in tradition and worried that applied research would eliminate basic research.[19] Others—MIT and the University of California, Berkeley—from the outset considered adherence to an ethos of secrecy the price of survival. This broad-scale acceptance of federal dollars was not pain free, causing significant changes within universities, especially a newly stratified and fragmented faculty. Universities welcoming federal dollars initially covered the costs of overhead themselves, compelling some to complain about necessary budget shifts for laboratory space and replacement teaching personnel. Budgetary planning also become a regular casualty of this putative largesse, since federal awards often went to individual researchers rather than to institutions, and unanticipated changes disrupted a university's best-laid plans. If a researcher left for another university and took his funding with him, the original host university could be left in the breach. For much of this research, universities lost monitoring control and felt that their research component had begun to undermine other higher education priorities. Salaries for federally funded researchers, for example, became dramatically higher than faculty elsewhere in the institution. If the NSF belatedly began to fund some social science research, a university that treasured its humanities could do little but plead with private foundations for support.

The novelty of this abundant federal funding prompted a range of responses. MIT went with alacrity to the source and—depending on one's perspective—ignored traditional university obligations to nonscientific sectors and cultivated its Research Laboratory of Electronics as if it were a patriotic undertaking, especially as the Cold War began to heat up. Its longtime director (1952–61), Jerome Wiesner (1915–94), eventually served as MIT president from 1971 to 1980, more than doubling its budget and sparking the creation of over sixty electronic firms, often with MIT faculty as advisors or executives. Not all of the basic research initiatives connected directly to Defense Department objectives. Belatedly MIT's preoccupation with military communication segued into a Department of Linguistics, a context for Noam Chomsky's (b. 1928) breakthrough work on syntax and language patterns. Incrementally MIT's Department of Social Sciences aggressively cultivated empirical data collecting. This work gave the social sciences a coveted empirical authority and also reconnected the university with the technical aspirations of its land-grant origins.[20]

By contrast, the University of California, Berkeley, began to use its extensive federal funds for its deservedly famous cyclotron and the Livermore Laboratory directed by E. O. Lawrence (1901–58), a 1939 Novel laureate. For a time Lawrence's radiation lab operated in its own orbit, wooing Glenn Seaborg (1912–99), a Berkeley PhD noted for his discovery of plutonium, from the University of Chicago. Seaborg came and brought his entire lab and his assistants, making Berkeley the international center for atomic physics.[21] In the process, these separate labs often created tensions in regular science departments because they could not secure regular faculty appointments for their staffers. Berkeley, however, created its own university-wide Office of Research and began to support research in the social sciences especially, tempering somewhat the imbalances caused by federal scientific funding.

In the postwar period, a new generation of administrators clearly sensed they were operating in a new and different culture. When he took over the Berkeley chancellorship in 1952, Clark Kerr (1911–2003) undertook a wholesale restoration of institutional morale. He set a standard for all departments to become nationally ranked at sixth or better in their subject disciplines and made appointments accordingly. Where they fell below that standard, Kerr found support, concentrating on three or four departments annually. He also ignored the custom of state-supported universities and insisted Berkeley's student body be national and not just Californian. His 1960 academic plan succeeded by 1965, bolstered by an ambitious building plan, a doubling of student enrollments, and a generally bullish national economy. His successor, Glenn Seaborg, created a Committee of Humanities to ensure they were not left behind. The upshot was that the University of California, Berkeley, became itself a paradigm for the new multidisciplinary research university, as indeed it became a model for statewide university systems.[22]

A third model of response to the new academic culture—beyond the special science labs and the state system of higher education—was Yale University. In 1950 A. Whitney Griswold (1906–63) became Yale's president and faced the dilemma of privileging the graduate school and research or else the undergraduate program and teaching. Griswold's response initially focused on the undergraduate liberal arts curriculum. He closed down the respectable graduate programs in nursing and education to signal his priorities. Yale's best departments were small, and its weakest were exactly those required to attract federal dollars—physics, economics, chemistry and sociology. Though its 1946 endowment of $116 million was second only to Harvard, much of it was restricted and gave small leeway for new expensive upgrades or experimental curricular departures from tradition. Like many of Yale's prep-school-trained students, Griswold had a personal aversion to the sciences. He also worried overly about a deterioration of standards, often manifested as the inability to write and speak or, in a word, the eclipse of the liberal arts.[23] In response, some independent department chairs cultivated un-Griswoldian strategies. One, the physics department, successfully solicited the Atomic Energy Commission for a reactor around which Yale could build a larger professional staff; another, in the economics department, hired superlative recent doctorates and negotiated ahead of time a fund for resisting raids from competitive institutions. Griswold tolerated the new scientific emphasis only so long as his beloved liberal arts remained central. He too opposed conducting any research for outside constituencies, and only research institutes that snugly fit into existing departments would survive his tenure.[24] Federally supported research became the magnet on the compass of ambitious higher education institutions, whatever their varied responses.[25]

This postwar transformation of academic culture produced a different historical pattern from the one that was familiar in the first half of the twentieth century. The new culture continued select features of earlier history, but it had a dramatic response pattern to pressures "from above"—especially to the federal funding and its sometime indifference to institutional priorities—but also "from below"—from dynamics that changed substantively the way a university, even older universities, operated within its walls. As historian Margaret O'Mara has well argued, the postwar universities became "cities of knowledge," new technological products, interacting with political hierarchies, funneling immense capital outlays and producing excessive competitions for faculty and new projects.[26] Select universities had imitators, as if the model was exportable to any institution. The American university's original approach to research—operating in the overstated ideal of "objectivity"—moved into a political and self-interested orbit. The shift privileged a select cadre of universities that could guarantee scientific excellence, supported by their wartime records.

Two areas especially favored by federal funders were schools in suburban locations, benefiting from earlier federal legislations like the GI Bill and projects for national defense.[27] For reasons of security, from President Harry S. Truman's tenure onward, the defense intelligence establishment cultivated "decentralization" of the nation's technical and intellectual resources. Areas outside cities, unlike the skyscraper cities of Detroit, Chicago, and New York, had the additional advantage of land for expansive new building rather than densely crowded, expensive city-based sites. Second, universities in geographical areas welcoming to the new technical industries were thought to have special advantages. The West, for example, had reflected this asset during the war, along with its proximity to the Pacific theater.[28] Such local and contextual features, often more powerful than federal funding or policy objectives, shaped the new postwar university. Analysts, then and now, hesitated to assume that any university could become a research or scientific "city of knowledge" even with the right leadership and enough money. However, as some universities enjoyed a new postwar prominence, their success became envied by other institutions. The result was a competition for federal resources that introduced a false standard, since only a few institutions had distinguished themselves in disciplines across the board. To the extent that other universities with limited means still aspired to national reputation in research, the post–World War II American academic culture adopted a rhetorical coherence that was belied by their actual accomplishment. In the heady postwar rush for federal dollars, many institutions inflated their distinctive identities and soft-pedaled criticism about political influence over scientific research.[29] Older values of pursuing research wherever it may lead became suborned to putatively scientific polls that established annually a shortlist of "best" universities and colleges. Exaggerated public images and rhetorical competitions became an important feature of the new academic culture.

During the 1950s federal funding generally continued its wartime pattern, funneling from the Pentagon and Atomic Energy Commission 76 percent of the funds for academic research. Most of this research was programmatic and favored the select universities of the wartime period and often their leadership, who had continued their tenures into peacetime. The one lone voice came from the NSF, founded in 1950, to support the growth of scientific personnel, to develop a national science policy, and, maybe most importantly, to defend the value of basic research. However, its close university ties in the early 1950s raised skeptical eyes among Senator Joseph McCarthy and his supporters. Congress initially funded the agency well below its stated ceiling of $15 million, which it did not reach until 1964.[30] Its budget kept its voice small in the "big science" discourse (in 1965 the National Institutes of Health's budget was three times that of NSF in spite of its budget increases); NSF's constricted power made a national science policy a quixotic goal, but its drum roll in behalf of basic science research gradually had an effect by the end of the 1950s.

In the late 1950s, international events accelerated the new changes in academia. On October 4, 1957, Russia launched an orbiting satellite they named Sputnik (Russian for "satellite") and arrested international attention. The Russians clearly manifested an unsuspected scientific competence, which had been initially registered in 1949 with the detonation of a hydrogen bomb, an advance American policy makers predicted would not occur for a generation. Sputnik's impact immediately upon the US Congress produced the 1958 National Aeronautical and Space Administration (NASA) and a charged atmosphere of rehabilitating America's supposedly laggard scientific research program. To some extent, Sputnik implicitly legitimated those voices that had called all along for basic research over the short-terms gains of programmatic applications. Two major consequences were the program of graduate fellowships in science and quasi-scientific areas after passage of the National Defense Education Act of 1958, which expanded university infrastructure (rather than support sciences that commanded existing university facilities). NASA's $5 billion budget supported a large academic expansion and resulted in the tripling of basic research. This shift received substantive support from the newly created Presidential Scientific Advisory Board (PSAB), headed by James Killian (1904–88), president of MIT.

Two consequences of these new organizations and voices became clear with the PSAB's report in 1960 under the leadership of Glenn Seaborg, then chancellor of the University of California, Berkeley, and soon to be chair of the Atomic Energy Commission (1961–71). The report not only developed the new ideology on behalf of basic scientific research; equally important, it linked such research to the public preoccupation with national security. Seaborg made clear that science was not a crisis resource but a permanent national investment. A commitment to basic research meant going beyond mere funding of projects to guarantee far-sighted graduate training. Basic research meant the production of resources to confront new and unforeseen challenges. Such training embellished the national welfare, the report argued, not just in matters of defense but also in matters of health and well-being. Finally, Seaborg noted the nation's universities were at present unable to finance such cohesive priorities. Timely arriving with the election of John F. Kennedy, Seaborg's report became the touchstone of political debate and expansive science funding in the 1960s. In effect, support for research involved the entire academic establishment, a point not lost on political sensibilities like those of Lyndon B. Johnson and others who wanted this new investment to be distributed beyond existing geographical concentrations. Between 1958 and 1964, federal funding increased from $456 million to $1.2 billion, with basic research receiving the lion's share.[31] In the 1960s this increase would peak and decline due to other congressional priorities, but the surge of money, talent, and an expansive university community in the research orbit endured and solidified the postwar revolutionary gains. The PSAB was summarily terminated in 1972 after the reelection of Richard Nixon (1913–94).

During the 1960s the small cadre of well-funded research universities expanded into a far larger group. In part, this increase came about because the Atomic Energy Commission with its expanding budget supported a wider array of institutions, often helping them to expand scientific research and targeting universities that could do so by adding resources of their own. In 1964 the Atomic Energy Commission supported 514 research contracts to 150 colleges and universities.[32] In addition, NASA, with its highly focused mission, had come late to research funding and began to seek out institutions that had missed the first wave of federal funding. The Georgia Institute of Technology, the University of Maryland, Rice University, and Texas Agricultural and Mechanics University all benefited. NASA's institutional support between 1962 and 1971 amounted to $225 million.[33] The Department of Defense, which had reduced its wartime contract support through the early

1950s, accelerated its funding after Sputnik. Its Advanced Research Projects Agency attempted to coordinate research among all the services and shifted its priorities once it became the Department of Defense Research and Engineering. Most of all, this offer produced something the individual services—so short-term and military oriented—could not: it established exploratory technical projects, some long-term, outside narrowly defensive parameters. Perhaps most important was its support for early computer development to advance the field of artificial intelligence.[34]

In the late 1960s, the Department of Defense, increasingly sensitive to universities that had become hostile to Reserve Officers' Training Corps programs and secret military research, began to cultivate new institutions like Indiana, Northwestern, Ohio State, Duke, and New York Universities,[35] which had not been favored in the 1950s. Before it ended in 1971, the Department of Defense's Project Hindsight spread $95 million across one hundred universities that began to cultivate special scientific niches of their own. The continuing campus protests against the Vietnam War ultimately had their effect on Department of Defense research, which declined by 50 percent between 1969 and 1975.[36] Still, the infrastructure funding of the later 1950s and 1960s and the increase of researchers and students in the same period—in the 1960s undergraduates increased by almost 200 percent and graduate students by 147 percent[37]—weathered the 1970s downturn of federal support and maintained the expanded levels within the new, federally funded academic infrastructure.

A prime example of the postwar university was Stanford, which until World War I had been distinguished for its athletic programs and country-club atmosphere. During the war, many of its leading scientists gravitated to defense research, at Harvard and MIT. But some early work at Stanford in innovative electronics began to attract federal dollars. One of the leading voices for cultivating federal money was Stanford graduate Frederick Terman (1900–1982). Terman, a student of Vannevar Bush and a wartime researcher at Harvard's radio research lab, had worked his way through the university structure at Stanford, serving as chair of the electrical engineering department, then as dean of engineering, and provost of the university from 1955 to 1965. After the war he used his wartime contacts to strengthen the field of applied science. Here he was less circumspect about business-academic relations. He worked closely with Stanford graduates and businessmen to promote the undeveloped areas of Palo Alto and to create a welcoming environment for science with commercial applications. The location was ideal in climate and beauty to take advantage of emergent Cold War concerns about the necessity of decentralizing America's economic and scientific centers. For reasons of strategic security, the federal government under both Presidents Truman and Eisenhower pushed to use federal dollars to promote suburbanization. It is widely recognized that Truman's 1944 GI Bill and Eisenhower's 1957 Highway Act did much to foster this decentralization. But the security mantra washed over into other areas like scientific innovation.

Terman's special contribution was to take advantage of both top-down federal pressures as well as local circumstances. Leland Stanford, the university's founder, had stipulated that his gift to the new institution's nine thousand acres could be leased but never sold. After the war the undeveloped portion of this largesse became a tax liability as legislators considered taxing portions as farmland, and the university trustees sought ways of reducing their tax obligation. Even though Stanford was a nonprofit institution and hence outside the regular tax structure, all of its land was not tax exempt. By 1951 Terman's willingness to cultivate science- and research-oriented businesses resulted in the creation of a distinctive Stanford Research Park. There businesses could set up offices that linked directly to university research. Their consultants and part-time staffers were often Stanford faculty. Successful scientific discoveries brought both profits to their satellite firms and donations to the sponsoring university. The design of a special landscape for Stanford land development centered on a suburban model. Land surrounding research buildings as well as attractive, individual residences mandated 60 percent of the area remain open space. The rising values of these homes and workplaces evolved into an increasingly exclusive enclave that altered the class diversity of earlier suburban paradigms.[38] By the end of the 1960s, Stanford Research Park generated millions per year for the Palo Alto community and the university.[39] These dynamics at Stanford subsequently produced Silicon Valley, the global center of a new scientific culture. It also became the base of a political ideology that used centralized government support to foster a new entrepreneurial esprit.[40] Among the many successful entrepreneurs to rise out of the Stanford Research Park was the Hewlett-Packard Corporation (founded 1937), makers of oscillators early on but later an international company producing computers, electronic testing equipment, data storage, networking hardware, and information delivery services.

Federal dollars alone did not create the new university culture but rather a historic pairing of both national and local dynamics.[41] The upshot was more than mere university expansion. Stanford had become the major engine for land development and economic growth in a strategic region, not to mention a major player in the national defense strategy. Stanford's private status afforded easy adaptation and maneuverability due to private funds and a large endowment, while the University of California, Berkeley, had to answer more publicly to its trustees and constituents. Berkeley was also strapped by land constrictions as well as ideological reservations about potential complicity with the federal government and business interests. Berkeley trustees and some faculty continued to worry about the independence of scientific inquiry when short-term expectations, if not profits, were so closely involved. The new postwar academic culture made clear how muted and small the inherited distinctions of public and private models of higher education had become. The postwar changes also underscored how favored the Sunbelt had become over the Rust Belt regions. The Sunbelt universities had space for expansion and offered carte blanche to build new buildings, especially designed for the demands of unprecedented research, whereas the older universities, especially those in diverse eastern and midwestern areas and densely populated cities, required expensive rehabilitation and reconfiguration, not to mention tense relations with surrounding, often low-income neighborhoods.[42] Not every aspirant for university research status could compete with the Stanford model; but those that approached the standard emphasized select, technical specializations and simultaneously enabled some faculty groups to enjoy more unequal, academic privileges.

The transformation of academic culture in the 1960s distinguished itself with new federal money, stratified faculty echelons, close association with for-profit satellite businesses, aggressive recruiting of noted faculty, inflated claims of academic distinction, often uncritical deference to short-term pragmatic goals, or, in a word, a mimicry of the American corporate world. These features confirmed many of the traditions of the postwar patterns of American higher education. However, politics played an intermediary role of no insubstantial portions. Postwar academic priorities began to be influenced by the shifting political constituencies of the South (fearing federal coercion in matters of civil rights) toward Republican priorities (which resisted federal activism in all matters of social welfare). The Democratic penchant tried to sustain aspects of the New Deal that had gone unrealized because of the war. They became divided among several issues, preferring, say, federal financial support to Catholic parochial schools, to center-city underprivileged public schooling versus money to college students facing rising tuition costs. The election of John F. Kennedy, whose only initial educational ideas connected vaguely to support for parochial education, brought into play rivalries among the professional educators: educational experts usually from the Ivy League worried about an entrenched bureaucratic mentality in state offices of education, while others, notably Francis Keppel (1916–90), US commissioner of education (1962–65), felt that substantive federal money could only be apportioned by state officials familiar with the peculiarities of their regions.[43]

Kennedy's response was to appoint a task force in 1962 headed by Frederick Hovde (1908–83), a distinguished electrical engineer (like so many postwar university leaders) and president of Purdue University. This independent body sought to integrate many disparate ideas into an omnibus education bill addressing both elementary and higher education rather than apportioning legislation according to particular constituencies. The task force sought, in effect, to articulate a national educational policy beyond the squabbling factions. It tried to take advantage of the Kennedy élan as well as the momentum of postwar federal successes with the 1944 GI Bill and the 1957 Highway Act models, which had enhanced both the national economy and the life chances of many Americans. The Hovde task force succeeded in exposing both the ongoing power of special political constituencies and the improbability of a national educational consensus. Still, the task force set in motion dynamics that would accelerate political give-and-take negotiations and ultimately set the context for to the 1965 Elementary and Secondary Education Act (ESEA) plus the Higher Education Act. Together this legislation produced a patchwork foundation for educational development in the next decades. Subsequent task forces—President Lyndon B. Johnson created 135 in his first year of office[44]—became less public if not downright secret, remained small, and were sparsely staffed.

The later task force headed by John Gardner (1912–2002), then (1955–65) the president of the Carnegie Foundation, was the one that learned from the Hovde group's errors and carried forward a new educational vision.[45] Gardner's work, which would result in the 1965 ESEA, had important implications for federal support for higher education. The task force advanced three possible mechanisms for implementing a national educational policy, fashioned out of existing contentious competitions. First, Gardiner proposed university-based community extension programs that would become Title I of ESEA; second, he recommended supplementary educational centers, which were realized in ESEA's Title III; third, he urged fifteen to twenty national educational laboratories, modeled on four existing structures at the Universities of Oregon, Pittsburgh, Wisconsin, and Harvard University.[46] Title II of the eventual legislation targeted "impacted areas" using "supplemental" money, which ensured that most school districts and parochial schools received support for "instructional materials." Functionally Title II funds more often went to middle- and upper-class districts than to the impacted urban districts that were their original target.

The ESEA legislation gave a large stimulus to higher education to devise ideas and mechanisms to improve elementary and secondary instruction. The accompanying Higher Education Act of 1965 provided still more. With special lobbying from the American Council on Education, its Title I focused special attention on private, urban universities and shifted funding away from traditional land-grant public institutions, which often privileged the agricultural and rural components of state institutions; Title II favored libraries and, though the funds were not large, many constituencies benefited; Title III allocated support to private, traditional black colleges, a central feature of Commissioner Keppel's special agenda; Title IV offered substantive student financial assistance, largely through loans with low interest rates and a ten-year repayment schedule. Title V intended to establish a National Teachers Corps with a presence in every local school, something that was especially feared by conservative Southerners and Republicans. The $3 billion allocated by Congress raised calls for a wholesale reorganization of the Department of Education, which many felt was outdated.[47] The eventual result created a department with distinct functions—elementary, secondary, higher education, vocational education, and research—rather than multiple programs for particular constituencies, so favored by congressional committees.

By the early 1970s, the combination of task forces and a reorganized Department of Health, Education, and Welfare stood to benefit from Lyndon Johnson's Great Society programs. In spite of Republican resistance, Democratic congressional majorities sustained the policy dynamics of the Great Society. From 1955 to 1974, the number of college students in the United States rose from 2.5 to 8.8 million. The age cohort attending college expanded from 17.8 to 33.5 percent. Black student numbers increased from 95,000 to 814,000, and women students expanded from one-third to one-half of the college population. College faculty rose from 266,000 to 633,000, and awarded degrees went from 58,000 at the master's level to 278,000, while doctoral degrees went from 8,800 to 33,000. Most dramatically, the 400 community colleges in 1955 became 973 by 1974 with concomitant increases in students (325,000 to 3.4 million) and student populations (from 800 students on the average school to 3,700). This extraordinary accomplishment was not attributable to President Johnson or any one person. Myriad individuals were involved, many of them from universities.

At the same time, the universities had become bastions of resistance to President Johnson's Vietnam War policy, and Johnson was facing mounting hostility to his domestic agenda, which he himself had begun to curtail to shift funds to support his increasingly unpopular war. Still, his ubiquitous, domestic advisor, Joseph Califano (b. 1931), worked both publicly and behind the scenes to brace the Great Society's entire reformist agenda: the Model Cities program, his antitobacco crusade, his reshaping of the Department of Transportation, and the staunch defense of a new educational policy. From the earliest four Johnson task forces, Califano created eleven, with thirty-four additional task forces to ensure interagency coordination. His close work with the Office of Management and Budget guaranteed sufficient start-up funds for all his programs. Califano followed Johnson's political penchant for "the camel's nose," getting the animal nose under the tent, that is, passing the essential legislation for start-up programs, then letting subsequent congresses explain to their constituents why increases were improvident.[48] Inevitably the university-based antiwar movement expanded into the middle class, whose radicalization ironically did more to temper the Great Society's advances than any organized political opposition.

After the fall of Saigon and the election of President Jimmy Carter, Joseph Califano accepted one more assignment in an effort to achieve the Great Society's educational goals. In 1977 he became Secretary of Health, Education and Welfare and worked assiduously to reinstate the momentum of his 1960s domestic initiatives. His advocacy for women in college athletics, his support for equal opportunity measures and equal access for the handicapped, his antismoking campaigns, and his reorganization of student loan priorities, all capitalized on his earlier experience. But perhaps most of all, his effort to clarify the nation's own educational policy resulted in one of his highest achievements, the invigoration of the National Institute of Education (founded 1972) and the appointment of educational historian Patricia A. Graham (b. 1935) to direct it.[49] The National Institute of Education was originally intended to set the national research agenda with both articulating problems and generating empirical data, which, it was hoped, would temper the political influences on education. The organization suffered from early growing pains and had difficulty early on (and after Graham left) resisting political influences. Graham's leadership and her ability to recognize solid talent within the institute's staff created an effective example of relatively impartial research in behalf of seemingly intractable issues. The major beneficiaries of her tenure were primarily women and minorities in higher education, not to mention empowering a new cadre of educational experts, largely university based, in the shaping of the national discourse on education.[50] The institute's ambitious ideal of long-term research projects became foreshortened and downsized with its subsequent appointments by Republican President Ronald Reagan.

The new postwar university was primarily a technically scientific corporation, favored by federal dollars but still with considerable independence from many political pressures. Its relative independence was largely a function of geography and history, where it was located and when a given institution embraced the pragmatic demands of both federal government and the commercial applications of its scientific inventions. Two institutions—Harvard University and MIT—exemplified a new research model largely through the leadership of James B. Conant at Harvard and Vannevar Bush at MIT. Their cochairing of the wartime Manhattan Project and its incontestable success in using science for atomic weaponry welded in the public mind the values of science and national defense. The two institutions supported in myriad ways the corridor of scientific research institutions outside Boston on Route 128. The force of their federally funded scientific engineering became so formidable that few institutions could presume to compete in any comparable orbit.[51] Yet other institutions would compete, like Stanford University, which would in a few short decades convert itself from a country-club ambience to one of America's premier research universities. Stanford's case is instructive, as historian Margaret O'Mara has made clear, because its transformation was so self-conscious as to clarify the key elements of the new postwar genre of the modern university.[52] Federal dollars were historically strategic; the uncritical embrace of pragmatic science (and the willingness early on to devalue the humanities and social sciences) was also a major ingredient. But as important were the Cold War tensions of the 1950s and 1960s, which made concentrations of industries, resources, and talent problematic. Centralized cities, for example, exposed the nation to great vulnerability from atomic attack. Far preferable was a decentralization of population, professional skills, and production machinery. In this context the shift toward a new suburban culture that distributed a nation's resources widely underlies many federal policies on taxation, highway construction, building codes, automobile design, and so on.[53]

Still, the federal government in its pursuit of decentralized scientific capacities and research production operated as if "science" was a constant and that federal investment would override other considerations.[54] At the University of Pennsylvania, for example, its own inherited traditions provided curbs on its competition for federal support. Penn's academic inheritance made it more circumspect about close connections to for-profit industries and potential benefactors. In addition, its science leaned toward medicine, health, and biology rather than physics and engineering. Perhaps, most of all, Penn thrived in the city of Philadelphia, not in the city's suburbs. Although it claimed 1754 as its founding date, the oldest building on the twentieth-century campus was constructed in the 1880s. Only in the early years of the twentieth century had Pennsylvania nourished its "Ivy League" status and its educational commitments. Even using the Great Society's urban renewal money, Penn could not create faculty or student facilities to comport with middle-class standards (at least not until the 1990s). In fact, the surrounding housing sheltered a substantive African American population in the 1950s and 1960s, a population seldom cultivated to that point by the university. Penn's geography, demography, and its own academic history compelled it to lag behind Stanford's golden model.[55]

Similarly the Georgia Institute of Technology, an emphatic engineering school, could not embellish its tradition or its local elites to shape it into a facility attractive to federal dollars. Its science was considered a regional resource; its services catered to local industries of textiles, cotton, and lumber; its powerful state politicians, Senator Richard Russell (1897–1971) and Congressman Carl Vinson (1883–1981)—respectively heads of the Senate and House Armed Services Committees—worried overly about Atlanta's own "progressivism" in the area of race relations rather than the possibility of using Georgia Tech as an economic engine of modernization in the South. In addition, where modernization occurred, it provided corridors from central Atlanta to outlying suburbs like Buckhead, ensuring a largely commuting faculty and student body. When the city elected its first black mayor, Maynard Jackson (1938–2003), in 1973, the city leadership shifted attention away from issues of higher education, which had never cultivated its African American population. By the time Georgia elites and politicians realized the possibilities of Georgia Tech in a larger social and economic context, their competitors had stolen a three-decade march on them.[56]

The new postwar university was a product of historic timing that combined large amounts of federal dollars, driven by the Cold War and decentralizing values of a rapidly suburbanizing nation. Their internal institutional traditions plus the dynamics of their locales played strategic roles. The most successful of these universities, and increasingly there were fewer and fewer in the upper echelons of the genre, became powerful economic and political entities in their own right, extending influences far beyond their formal, academic boundaries. Academic careers that once sequenced government service, industrial advice, and scientific research, now often combined all three simultaneously, leaving the college's and university's once vaunted values of teaching and cultural transmission to others. The postwar university was incontestably a more powerful entity than its predecessors, and their leaders felt less obligated to their inheritances. Science contained such connotations of the "future" and masked older roles of the humanities, historic debate, and multiple ways of seeing, that even primarily undergraduate instruction felt its impact. Parental pressures for "useable knowledge" greatly marginalized the force of the liberal arts as a foundational, intellectual experience. University budgets reflected this shift and disingenuously invoked "market forces," as if some uncontrollable regulator determined the policies of modern universities. The legacy of the postwar university was a new pecking order of institutions, one in which newcomers remained seriously disadvantaged in the pursuit of fiscal resources to maintain the status quo. The universities that emerged out of World War II and followed Stanford's lead continued into the twenty-first century to affirm their entrepreneurial model; they have thereby made "science" a self-legitimating endeavor, an authority without subordination to "nonscientific" evaluation or judgment. Thomas Kuhn's 1962 argument that "science" itself changes and takes on different meanings in distinct historical eras has minimal traction in most current public debates.[57] The consequence is that, given the gaps between science and, say, the humanities in today's academic culture, the metaphysical foundations of science in the present go largely undiscussed, as if only empirical truth is worthy of the designation "science" and public admiration.

By the last third of the twentieth century, higher education had effectively cultivated a roughly scientific standard that was admired and imitated by the two hundred wealthiest institutions of higher learning in America. These institutions became the preeminent voices for the several thousand institutions that claimed postsecondary status. Incontestably the new change agent for a postwar university model was the presence and funding of the federal government, and its intervention into academic affairs formed a more utilitarian bond between research and funding agents than ever before. In addition, the most privileged of the new research universities assumed a global dimension more influential than at any time in the history of higher education. However, local dynamics continued to have their force and many nonscientific disciplines found shelter in the enlarged shadow of the expanded colleges and universities. But the intensive stratification of higher education institutions and its concomitant impact of the life chances of their students raised new issues of higher learning as an American and democratic resource. For all the beneficial gains of the GI Bill and its successors, particularly the Great Society's educational legislation, the new postwar academic culture (generational culture #7)—driven by federal dollars, globally distinguished, intensively utilitarian, and increasingly privileging an elitist caste—made the meaning of a college diploma and a university degree as historically problematic as they had ever been.

CHAPTER FOURTEEN

Clark Kerr: The Unapologetic Pragmatist

The uncritical embrace of science by both academics and the public in the post–World War II period contained a large element of the irrational.[1] Scientists' sheer delivery of a dramatic and climactic victory over powerful enemies in World War II via brainpower exercised such an indelible impression on the American and the global psyche that every institution of higher learning in the United States would seek reorganizations that might make them attractive to the federal Treasury.[2] Certainly for institutions cultivating science and technology in the interwar period, their timing was propitious, and they often led with their physical science proposals but sometimes extended the aura of scientific authority to the social sciences and to a lesser extent to the humanities. American universities abandoned any pretense of an inherited corporate or ideological order, not that their earlier efforts to define the university or insist on its generic boundaries had resulted in such coherence for most of their earlier history.[3] Their fundamental sense of cohesion, academics confidently assumed, lay in the pragmatic process of search and discovery, of mediating and managing external forces rather than adhering to a coherent set of educational principles. If greater unifications were to occur, they lay ahead in future development. The dynamic legitimacy of experimentation in many applied fields, often without coordination and with wasteful duplication, nevertheless, flowed like a magic elixir in the post–World War II period.

Before World War II, most public systems of higher education grappled with the knotty problem of democratic access to higher education while also maintaining a high quality of instruction. Admitting a majority of high school graduates to higher learning seemed a powerful and distinctive American ideal, especially at public institutions that had employed the successful GI Bill of 1944. However, the dilution of resources—both human and fiscal—to achieve this goal of democratic access tended to distract talented faculty from the essential research function of a modern university. In California, which had become the largest public higher education system in the United States shortly after World War I, the dilemma took on the form of institutional competition. For two decades in the interwar period, the University of California, Berkeley, in particular, resisted the state's public colleges' efforts to cultivate any research capacity, even in areas of education and engineering where the key research universities were not particularly energetic. The major research institutions at Berkeley and Los Angeles fended off state college incursions by allying with the many local junior colleges (fifty-five in 1947),[4] to argue that California met both democratic and academically excellent goals. The universities would admit, generally, 12–15 percent of the ablest high school grads, and the state colleges and junior colleges would provide the safety net for less prepared students.

The California State College system (created in 1935 with the conversion of the state's teachers' colleges) offered a four-year program and celebrated its primary commitment to teaching rather than research. Almost immediately the state colleges moved their curriculum beyond teacher training and toward the more traditional liberal arts. For a time that was not a problem, but then, during the interwar period, institutional expansions and the geometric rise in college and university applicants after World War II put the major research institutions in a special bind. Either they had to concede research capacity to their competitors for the pool of able students and state support, or they had to expand their own capacity and risk becoming unwieldy. At times some university leaders contemplated absorbing the state college system in its entirety to preserve the universities' distinctive research function. While educational leaders fretted over these alternatives, lawmakers—some self-interested in behalf of their constituents' economic priorities, some reflecting responsibly on the role of education in the state's economic health—regularly proposed the creation of new state colleges and even additional major universities in various areas of the state. This unregulated expansion of the three-tiered California system threatened both the state's financial resources and the high quality university instruction that Californians had produced in the first half of the twentieth century.[5]

In 1930 Robert Sproul (1891–1975), a native Californian and a 1913 graduate of the University of California, Berkeley, in civil engineering, had become president of the University of California system. Though not an academic, he had distinguished himself as Berkeley's comptroller and unofficial lobbyist with the state legislature. His personal history, his powerful memory, and his oratorical skills stood him in excellent stead for his new position. He defended the university's research superiority steadfastly to every constituency and made it the major talking point for his claims on the state's treasury. His political acumen helped greatly in turning back many different proposals for state college incursions into "university" territory. His success was sufficiently complete that the California State Board of Education that ran the colleges had difficulty expanding the curriculum. They were limited to traditional college instruction and sophisticated vocational problems for students not pursuing advanced degree training.[6] By the post–World War II period, Sproul seemed indifferent to the student increases (121,000 students in 1940 that were expected to become 250,000 by 1960) and to educational demands that would be created by industrial growth (California employment increased 40 percent between 1947 and 1957).[7] Many in the press and commercial world found his perceived intransigence against college expansion "elitist" and, of course, implicitly questioned his university assumptions, especially consigning colleges to a secondary status.

Sproul's longtime tenure (1930–58) at the head of the University of California system unraveled in the wake of his administrative pragmatism. His ability to maneuver within a system that had first emerged during the Progressive years (1911–17) of Governor Hiram Johnson (1866–1945)[8] appeared increasingly antiquated in the context of postwar population and student increases, which lawmakers felt required a modernized centralization of higher education administration. Of course, lawmakers, worried about state allocations, began to clamor for system-wide proposals, complete with comparative figures that showed how different institutional levels functioned. Were the private universities, as the University of Southern California claimed,[9] more efficient than the state universities that somewhat complacently expected incremental budget increases every year? In the absence of clear statistical comparisons, which the university's board of regents and the state board of education did not provide, lawmakers began their own analyses of "wasteful duplication" in the tripartite layers of the California system of higher education. Sproul seemed helpless to deal with these new critiques, even before the GI Bill and later the launching of the Soviet satellite Sputnik made the stellar system of California higher education appear to be falling behind America's Cold War competitor.[10]

California lawmakers had worried from time to time about the allegiances of California's academics. A number of episodes through the institution's history had given citizens some concerns about the relative expertise of researchers as they commented publicly on knotty political issues. While veterans on the GI Bill formed a majority of students on California's postwar campuses, the rumblings about leftish professors remained in check. By 1948 most veterans had finished their college and university training, at the very moment when Senator Joseph McCarthy (1908–57) of Wisconsin worried an anxious public about traitors in responsible public roles. California legislators set up their own investigating committee and leveled charges at university academics, including Robert Oppenheimer (1904–67), the director of the Manhattan Project, which had produced the atomic bomb. Sproul sought to control the damage to the university's image by proposing successfully to the board of regents a loyalty oath that all faculty would take eschewing communism. The move caused a major furor among faculty who felt the loyalty oath was an impingement on academic freedom. The widespread public debate on this issue did little to enhance the university's pioneering image and caused the board of regents consternation about Sproul's leadership. Still more, thirty-one academics were dismissed from the university system for refusing to take the oath.[11]

In the wake of the loyalty oath controversy, the Regents of the University of California appointed chancellors at its two major research universities, ostensibly to assist Sproul in handling wide-ranging administrative issues. At the University of California, Los Angeles, their appointee was Raymond B. Allen (1902–86), former president of the University of Washington, where he had supported faculty firing for purportedly communist affiliations. For Berkeley their choice was Clark Kerr (1911–2003), an economist and successful labor negotiator who had over five hundred negotiations to his credit including the 1946 West Coast shipping strike.[12] In the loyalty oath controversy, Kerr had signed the pledge but acknowledged its threat to academic freedom. During Sproul's remaining years as president of the University of California system, Kerr worked in a decidedly secondary status, using his time to shape a coordinating plan for the tripartite system. In Sproul's view such work, far from the day-to-day interactions he loved, seemed innocuous and of little moment to his office. However, in this work, a different kind of pragmatic initiative laid the groundwork for a new administrative leadership, one that shortly the board of regents would prefer to Sproul's own.

Initially, Kerr became Sproul's successor by continuing his predecessor's association of research with genuine university work but also by gaining political allies and rejecting Sproul's resistance to new and expanded roles for the state colleges. In his time as Berkeley's chancellor, Kerr recognized three things that Sproul did not: a) things could not continue as they had been, due to their wartime and postwar influx of federal money;[13] b) every higher education institution and indeed every region and constituency clamored for state funds; and c) a new pragmatic criterion for state allocations must be both a systemic and a collaborative process. Kerr's ingenuity in forming alliances and dealing with adversaries arose from his labor negotiation experience: every player in the game had to have a voice, but not every player would realize his ideal ambitions. Kerr began neither as democrat nor elitist but as an administrator who was determined to produce a new and transparent criterion for California's postsecondary schools. Historian John Aubrey Douglass has meticulously documented this arduous process: the pragmatic give and take, the failure and missteps, as well as the ultimate, cliff-hanging conclusion that produced the 1960 California Master Plan for Higher Education, arguably Kerr's masterpiece, though he would undoubtedly be the first to acknowledge the multiple players in the production. Such an end product—hard-bargained, surprising, clumsy, serendipitously designed, and collectively shaped—was precisely the essence of a Kerr achievement.[14]

One individual, whom Kerr would undoubtedly have recognized as seminal, was the chair of the Master Plan Committee, Occidental president Arthur G. Coons (1900–68). Coons was well versed in the nationally recognized (1947) Truman Commission on Higher Education, which notably drew from its experience with the GI Bill and promoted the value of equal opportunity for all able high school graduates to attend college. This goal the Master Plan Committee advanced in spite of its own projections of enormous increases in higher education populations in California over the next decade. The committee had predicted 4.6 million by 1960, much lower than the actual 5.5 million of 1966 and 6.5 million of 1967.[15] Coons accepted the major proposals of the Truman Commission and applied them in his service on Dwight Eisenhower's 1956 President's Commission on Education beyond the High School. This commission notably addressed ways of financing the projected increases in the nation's student population. Coons steadfastly resisted complete federal government support for public higher education and argued any assistance must extend to both public and private schools.[16] Coons used the arguments of the 1955 legislation proposed by the California Scholarship Plan to assist able students at both public and private institutions. He recognized that private schools relieved a substantive portion of the public school burden, thereby reducing the costs of public school buildings and services.[17] He also argued that this strategy was not a narrow proposal but rather one that considered all the resources of the state. His expansive statesmanship amid a swirl of political self-interests appeared to many a policy-making model of its kind.[18]

In the end, the University of California, Berkeley, retained the research prominence Sproul and Kerr always sought and avoided the demands to expand its undergraduate offerings. The state colleges acquired long-sought master's but not doctoral programs. Most importantly, the state college tier (with nineteen institutions in 1972) also won its own board of trustees. This step liberated the colleges from a perceived second-class status and enabled them to lobby for their own academic and fiscal priorities. The third tier, the junior colleges, received a new portion of state largesse and no longer had to peg its expansion to local resources. Moreover, they received a significant inflow of construction money to accommodate their expanded postwar enrollments. A Coordinating Council was formally assigned responsibility for rationalizing the budget proposals of the three-tier system, controlling, economizing, and prioritizing the state's higher education resources as lawmakers had demanded for decades. The council had responsibility for future development, both for policy and planning. Most important of all, the moment the Master Plan became formally accepted, all aspects of the tripartite system began to change with each of the tiers testing the bounds of their new demarcations.[19]

There is no contesting the political achievement of California's Master Plan and its influence on virtually all other state systems,[20] which in the postwar period suffered analogous pressures but often did not achieve either a comparable plan or a functioning blend of democracy and academic excellence. If subsequently the California Idea did not play out as envisioned, the plan itself became a formidable agent in the shaping of American higher education in the latter half of the twentieth century. To take one example, North Carolina's Research Triangle Park, founded in 1959 and developed by a cohort of businessmen, politicians, and educational leaders like William C. Friday (1920–2012), the longest serving university president of the twentieth century, created a sixteen-unit system of higher education, driven by indigenous forces but aided by the national "multiversity" discourse. The ultimate achievement, centering on the North Carolina State University, the University of North Carolina at Chapel Hill, and Duke University—a mix of public and private entities—produced in two generations the educational jewel of the South and an economic transformation of the state and region. North Carolina did not follow California's example but provided its own locally driven variant of the multiversity.[21]

In this new postwar discourse, Kerr exercised a less collaborative role and more of a highly personal imprint. In 1963 he offered his own views of American higher learning and projected its future with his Edwin L. Godkin

Lectures at Harvard University. Subsequently the lectures became the widely read book *The Uses of the University* (1963). His lectures underscored the new role of the federal government, which indirectly had shaped the California Master Plan. In 1960 alone, he reported, the federal government spent $1.5 billion on education, a hundredfold increase in twenty years. He did not press the point, but the money was unevenly distributed. Only a few federal agencies, especially the Department of Defense, the NSF, the Atomic Energy Commission, the Department of Agriculture, and the National Aeronautics and Space Administration, were the main patrons. The list also favored the demarcation of knowledge: the physical and biological sciences, the health sciences and engineering.[22] Moreover, 57 percent of all federal dollars went to six universities; twenty universities received 79 percent.[23]

Despite Kerr's reputation as an inclusive labor negotiator before the war and his triumph of delegating power to the select branches of the California system, his democratic sensibility extended to few distinguished universities outside those receiving federal support. In fact, Kerr's intonation of his most famous idea—the multiversity—a "descriptive" term that, in Kerr's eyes, drew heavily on his California example. The university, he argued, was a smorgasbord supporting both excellence and instruction of all aspirant students. The federal government with its selective funding had nevertheless created a new elite within this confusing array. The pretense of a complex organization, so varied from region to region, from place to place, masked a distinct pecking order that included both new and established institutions.[24] The new multiversity became so many things to so many people that, in Kerr's terms, "it must of necessity be at war with itself." The multiversity's contradictory features were less important than its diverse services to its state and nation.

Kerr's argument about a multiversity did not address how contradictory and competitive elements in a university would be sorted out with a roughly equitable distribution of resources. The university might develop without planning, he said, but it was not "directionless," that is, the consequences were not entirely unpredictable.[25] The university's chief administrator was no longer the institution's central figure, as in the nineteenth century; that person was now a stoic pawn—"mediator" was his actual term[26]—of social forces, trustee priorities, student demands, and funders' imperatives. The effective service of Kerr's notion, multiversity, was its opaqueness, its resistance to any single definition or internal cohesion. He made a virtue of the indefinable character of the institution (while making numerous historically distinct claims for it, especially its priority of research over its teaching) and permitted himself great enthusiasm for things as they were. His "multiversity" also accorded him the luxury of rejecting older, alternative models—"the day of the monarchs [Benjamin Jowett of Oxford, Benjamin Wheeler of Berkeley, Nicholas Murray Butler of Columbia] has passed"[27]—which put great pressure on schools with fewer resources than Berkeley outside his academic model. In a sense, his resistance to any single definition of the university underscored how powerful the postwar universities had become and how aggressively these new "federal mutants" would work to succeed in the postwar competition.

The Uses of the University hardly discussed specific curricular subjects or research issues despite the rapid substantive advances of the previous two decades. This omission was actually a clue, evidence of how detached the curriculum had become from the ideological aims of university administrators. The collage of departments, institutes, research and development centers, and other organizations that Kerr described made clear not only how dominant pragmatic, administrative values had become in higher education, but also how well he had traced the latitude accorded to faculty researchers if funding could be found for their work. If he misstated this fragmentation as autonomy, Kerr's views about multiple academic niches made a historic point. New departures in knowledge or even wholesale indifference appeared to contribute similarly and benignly to the institution that had no organic nature. But few critics (until later) sought to ask Kerr whether his "diversity" had limits or destructive downsides.[28] Even more, how would "mediation" and "adaptation" lead a university in constructive directions, and who should monitor the initiative? Were all novel departures gains for the overall university structure? Historically the production of the 1960 Master Plan, for example, shows how forceful and central Kerr's own role was and how far his administrative aegis went beyond mediation and adaptation.

These issues of pragmatic accommodation over educational priorities helped focus Kerr's attention on the distinctive, historical assumptions of his generation: his basic overconfidence in internal equity and his apolitical worry about external pressures. He achieved his complacent equilibrium by a rejection of past university models and indeed of any inherited patterns of decision making. *The Uses of the University* was a singularly ahistorical and anti-intellectual apologia for a new state system of higher learning.[29] The book explicitly embraced (1) a democratic inclusiveness that embellished the older and very different land-grant tradition, (2) a new service orientation without forfeiting claims to research excellence, (3) a heuristic linkage of teaching and research, (4) a recognition of external federal interests without undue worry about their disruptive consequences, and (5) a rhetorical defense of the university as a unique resource in the modern world. Comprehensiveness seemed to inform his notion of the multiversity. However, listing the issues and engaging them constructively were two different things and were usually left to the resources and talents of very different administrators. Nationwide, all institutions of higher learning instinctively recognized the problems of managing conflicting pressures, but very few had the resources of Kerr's California system to address them or to keep them from appearing damaging. Kerr offered not a description of a new genre of higher education but a thin gloss on a single institution, the University of California, Berkeley.

Kerr's listing of the multiversity's features sparked a vigorous national discussion, a singular achievement, and appeared to position him as the architect of a new model of higher education. His descriptive rather than analytic approach to the multiversity in part explained the welcome reception to these ideas in the postwar period.[30] But his outlook and pragmatic distance from the theoretical and historical energy of, say, wartime German academic émigrés, which so enlivened a range of academic disciplines, was remarkable and telling. Kerr's argument attempted to operate outside theory and definition entirely, as if administrative implementation was an activity without ideology. His book merely described present-day features of American higher education; it did not propose to offer a futuristic vision, a set of priorities for constructive change. Rather, with the language of "complexity" and "adaptation," Kerr sought to assure his readers that university work was a national resource and positioned to face a range of challenges. By contrast, the interwar émigrés often experienced a distinct marginalization in American academic culture precisely because of their theoretical and ideological stances. Their sense of risk and limitation, the need to prioritize their basic values, so reinforced by Nazi oppression, contrasted with the embedded, buoyant pragmatism in America's higher education institutions.[31]

In his lectures Kerr well represented a can-do pragmatism that represented the high point of this brand of American academic culture. The ubiquitous sense of positive change in both university administration and scholarly discourses helped explain the slow penetration of cutting-edge European perspectives into American higher education after the war. Kerr's pragmatic ideology pervaded not only public conceptions of the university but also much of the scholarship the universities produced. The Cold War exacerbated some of the key features of Kerr's ideology, especially the new rapprochement between federal financial support and the university research establishment. Kerr's inference that the relationship was not problematic but manifestly productive went far toward resisting any intimations of a socialist paradigm, that is, government-supported social services. Cold War anxieties and a public rhetoric of military competition with the Soviets also gave rise to widespread acceptance of technical research as the epitome of modernism. The inequality of resource allocation among engineering, electrical, and chemical research, on the one hand, and the social sciences and the humanities, on the other, caused almost no comment among higher education leaders. The new institutional elites and favored scientific consortia seemed to pose no threat or contradiction either to America's tradition of democratic inclusiveness and equal opportunity.[32]

Such problematic features could be found well beyond Kerr's own work and in many higher education niches to the end of the twentieth century. These ideological stances of university administrators would be reflected in the assumptions of American scholarship in these years. In the wake of Kerr's popular book, another influential work of prodigious scholarship but derivative conceptualization would ultimately become *The Emergence of the American University* (1965), the product of a Berkeley doctoral dissertation. Its author, Laurence Veysey (1933–2004), rested his case for the university's "emergence" on a dozen elite institutions, whose longevity and post–World War II stature were incontestable. No matter that there were at the time of its publication over two thousand institutions of higher learning in America; no matter that the "university-builders"—Charles W. Eliot, Daniel Coit Gilman, Andrew White, William Rainey Harper, and so on—were not themselves clear about the organizations they were creating, overstated the university's clarity, and masked how problematic the historic university in America actually was. For Veysey, like Kerr, ideas remained remarkably literal and effective when implemented. Throughout his study, ideas and applications remained the dichotomous methodology of his inquiry. Ideas that did not pan out illuminated nothing. Institutions that universities sought to ignore—normal schools, denominational colleges, female seminaries, endowed academies, and so on—contributed not at all to the university's "emergence."[33] Veysey's moment of "emergence"—"1910"—witnessed a kind of amalgamation of the three deductive models that his twelve distinguished universities represented. Certainly at no point did Veysey treat them as political or ideological competitors.[34]

What was important to Veysey was the arbitrary delineation of three categories of higher education—utility (especially state universities), research (especially the innovative Johns Hopkins University), and liberal culture (represented by Harvard University under Charles W. Eliot). Veysey's theme was the turn-of-the-century blend of all three with their concomitant contradictions into a newly generic "university." His massive data bank organized itself into these varied categories, displaying many insightful patterns the author characterized as "middle-level." There would be no overarching explanation of which of the three traditions was the more socially or historically important or when they became so. There would be no 1910 definition of the historical American university, except as an implicit hybrid of its inheritance. If the result was a diversified amalgam, so be it. Ideas, by implication, were to be evaluated not by their newly organic composition but by their outcomes, even if side by side with competitive or contradictory educational values. The framework of Veysey's history operated snugly within the slipstream of Kerr's own pragmatic ideology.

Despite the hat-tipping to "new money," the "German influence," and a determination to avoid the (exaggerated) pitfalls suffered by colleges in the nineteenth century, Veysey did not assess the relative role of "outside" forces over the intramural dynamics of the American university. Each institution's soul arose from its founders' energies and public presence, which was historically formidable in both articles and speaking engagements. Veysey never puzzled about this departure from precedent by university leaders. He accepted their confidence in their vision as completely as he took for granted the significance of the "university" in 1910. No matter that at the time less than 5 percent of the youth cohort was in college and one did not need college training to enter the professions or sustain an influential career. Exactly when did the university become a significant national institution? How novel was the institution in 1910, and in the name of which "university" rhetoric did it advance most profoundly? None of these historical questions appear in the book, which functionally became little more than a defensive apologia in behalf of Veysey's arbitrary categories. Were all the university builders completely satisfied with their fellow builders' "university ideas" or indeed with the 1910 amalgam?[35]

Veysey was no more concerned with the incomplete interaction of actual ideologies in his 1910 university than Kerr was with Berkeley or the multiversity in 1963.[36] The secondary role of ideas, the dominance of administrative patterns to explain the institution, the unproblematic character of key interpretive notions (especially the university), the facile differentiation between past and present, the expectation that external forces would be consistently benign, and, most of all, the depoliticization of an institution that one wished to assert was nationally significant—all could be found in both Veysey's study and Kerr's lectures. Both texts celebrate key components of pragmatic ideology—diversity, fragmentation of viewpoints, the irrelevance of paradoxical visions. Both Kerr and Veysey resist interpretive definition. Neither author accepted the full force of history nor acknowledged how time bound their perceptions were and would continue to be. It seems to be the putative absorption of contesting traditions that gives the university its centrality in both treatments.[37] So long as the university's operation continued to function, all other issues seemed manageable or "middle-level." This overprivileging of pragmatic continuance permitted especially Kerr the luxury of concluding virtually all his essays and lectures on an upbeat note of myopic optimism.

Yet both Kerr and Veysey, a generation apart themselves, testified to the dominance and continuity of a pragmatic ideology at the heart of the American university. Institutions became mechanisms, not of contesting discourses or exploratory experiments, but rather as arbiters of ideas that survive and prevail.[38] Their relevant contexts are implied in their structure and workings and need not be critically explicated for one to understand them. Universities, like their rhetorical priorities, remain uncomplicated, literal expressions of their intent at given moments in time. One need only organize them rather than probe them for deeper or latent meanings.[39] Many established assumptions of American pragmatic ideology received frontal challenges from the recent German émigrés' scholarship, particularly in the social sciences and the humanities. It took another generation for those approaches to make themselves felt. During that generational lag, the physical sciences surged ahead in both financial support and public acclaim, often outstripping the very analytic standards of ethical practice and humanistic limits that the nonphysical disciplines provided at their best. In a sense, the immediate post–World War II period witnessed a separation of science and culture not only in the university but in the society that now the university influenced so significantly. It would take the wrenching upheaval of the 1960s for both science and culture to be recognized as historical, changing phenomena themselves, not the transcendent, predictive authorities that their practitioners often presented them to be.[40]

Clark Kerr's long-term legacy was the creation of a research university model largely supported by federal government resources. His own stellar, postwar university set the context for a new academic elite endowed through federal grants that offered them autonomy and professional mobility unheard of before World War II. Kerr created such respect for scientific research that later publics would have great difficulty perceiving science as culturally conditioned, even when in the service of a narrowly focused national security state. The university had become a model of activities that ranged far beyond its particular origins to achieve economic advantages not only for its region but, ideally, for the nation as a whole. Governor Ronald Reagan's firing of Kerr did not tarnish Kerr's model for his admirers. His apocryphal quip to explain his departure via Reagan's fiat was signature Kerr: "I leave this job as I entered it: fired with enthusiasm!"[41] His multiversity remained a new feature of the late twentieth-century American educational landscape, technically advanced, intellectually innovative, politically neutral in its advance of the public good. For the rest of the century, alternative educational models—critical student protests, open ideological debate, teacher training and interdisciplinary innovations, politically informed policy discussion—were often made to appear as extreme and parochial versions of the California model. Kerr's California university system settled in the American mind as an incontestable standard, until the early twenty-first century when California politicians, like politicians in many states nationwide, withheld public resources, drove away talented faculty and students, and made clear that the multiversity for all its virtues was a contingent, historical structure at the mercy of multiple, conflicting ideologies.[42]

Kerr's historical contribution was to demonstrate how firmly entrenched were pragmatic assumptions, not only in academic discourses but in the national debates over pressing issues. Scholars and pundits alike kept their focus on empirical outcomes and downplayed bolder imaginative and ethical ambitions. Ideas, especially critical ideas that projected long-term consequences, quickly were treated as distractions or fanciful concoctions, grist for the science fiction of entertainment cinema or leisure reading. The gap between actual policy making and, say, historical or philosophical analysis had widened substantially in the postwar period. Kerr's career and his advocacy of the "multiversity" showed how uncritical academic values had become toward pragmatic thought and behavior. During the 1960s and afterward, it would take more than countercultural ideas and behavior to modify, if not turn, this pragmatic wave (generational culture #7) into genuinely innovative directions.

CHAPTER FIFTEEN

Challenging Pragmatism

For much of the twentieth century, university leaders and faculty functioned within a pragmatic paradigm.[1] They assumed their work was experimental rather than ideological (as if the two were antithetical). They presumed, as did philosophical pragmatism, that they were not constricted by inherited first principles but rather worked forward to changing mores, a process that would be legitimated by public recognition and peer approval. They also took for granted a general public collegiality that supposedly gave their work a democratic character. The academics' influence on the larger society operated incrementally, playing out in applications of insights and interpretations that entered a larger public discourse. The sheer variety of disciplines and expertises that had emerged since World War I seemed to make implausible any facile characterization or metaphysical imperative of higher learning. As the tradition of "academic freedom" of the early twentieth century implied, researchers always saw themselves following out their own line of inquiry without initially fretting about the consequences or impact of their work upon the body politic. Their pragmatic assumptions about continual testing and modification of results seldom registered as an ideology all its own. The ubiquity of this mind-set pervaded virtually all levels of higher education. Most researchers took significant comfort in the seeming tolerance of diversity, enshrined in Clark Kerr's metaphor of "multiversity." At the coining of the term "multiversity," few worried that the university had ceased to become a critical gadfly of its society's priorities. By the publication of Kerr's *The Uses of the University*, the culture of American academia had become coincident with the dominant values of American society.

Like most major cultural shifts, the mid-1960s challenges to pragmatism in the United States did not begin in a moment nor did they contain a middle and an end. It was primarily a process with many precedents; it contained many surprising, unruly consequences, including resistance and backlash arguments, and a set of influences that have not yet terminated. Only in retrospect might one point to sparks of revolutionary change before 1950, say, the dramatic teaching techniques of Alexander Meiklejohn, Abraham Flexner's cultural critique of the American university in the post–World War I period, the satirical warnings of Veblen's "captains of erudition," or the visionary courage of Robert Hutchins at the University of Chicago. Yet in the larger narrative of American higher education's history, all these breakthrough moments were treated as minor aberrations, measures of the essential soundness of the academic core. Retrospectively they appeared to point to something else entirely, namely, manageable problems within increasingly powerful institutions, strategically necessary to both the American economy and professional careers. One major assumption of the early critics was that the central device for schooling American brainpower, national ingenuity, and an inherent ability to tinker and self-correct the body politic was in danger of losing its way.[2]

Indirectly a national change began in the wake of the 1950s and 1960s civil rights movement and nonviolent protest embedded in African American sit-ins. The TV coverage of the public abuse of the protestors, the water cannons, the police clubbing unarmed citizens, and attack dogs menacing those who objected to systemic social abuse set a context for a debate in leading universities that went beyond the Southern context. The graphic depiction of Southern physical oppression galvanized the idealistic instincts of a new academic generation also spurred on by the rhetoric of America's postwar president, John F. Kennedy (1917–63). In some sense Kennedy's own slow response to civil rights petitions produced a void for reformist action and expanded civil rights initiatives into a new national imperative, which was dramatically displayed in the 1963 March on Washington and Martin Luther King's (1929–68) galvanizing "I Have a Dream" speech.

Students at Kerr's University of California, Berkeley, chastened by its early 1950s loyalty oath controversy, cultivated their free speech alternatives on Berkeley's Bancroft Way. Among other issues students recruited individuals for a 1964 Mississippi Freedom Project, which sought to register black voters during the summer of 1964. By the start of fall 1964 classes, many veterans of the summer Freedom Project had returned to campus demoralized by the fact that only 1,200 or so blacks had actually registered. More importantly, they were dispirited by the violence that they had experienced: three individuals murdered, thirty-five shootings, one thousand arrests, and thirty house burnings. The efforts of some Berkeley students to capitalize on the violence to question and agitate for a national response resulted in the closing of Bancroft Way to petitions and fund-raising. These measures implicitly put a dramatic curb to free speech at the California system's showcase university. Student resistance followed immediately as did pressure from the state legislature for university leaders to quell academic disorder.[3]

The turmoil at Berkeley had its counterparts elsewhere. At the University of Michigan, Tom Hayden (1939–2016), a native of the Detroit suburb Royal Oak and raised in a Roman Catholic household, had come to the university on a tennis scholarship. Initially without a self-conscious political viewpoint, he selected English as a major and edited the school newspaper. After graduation in 1957, he continued his journalism work both in the university's graduate school and in his reporting of the Student Nonviolent Coordinating Committee's (SNCC) registration efforts in the South. His witness of the beatings that followed transformed and focused his energies. He quickly went beyond his civil rights reportage to a probing of the root causes of civil unrest and the impact of American institutions. He became disenchanted with the liberal expectation that empirical reportage and public criticism would result in constructive social change. A 1961 Ann Arbor conference created a national SNCC Executive Committee with representatives from universities across the nation and with Hayden as its executive secretary. Out of this organization came the Port Huron Statement, which yoked together a range of issues from civil rights to nuclear terror, all of which clashed with the middle-class life and education of Hayden himself and so many of his fellow students. The Port Huron Statement, which shaped the Students for a Democratic Society (SDS), specifically rejected the liberal leadership of the university and the nation as well as its attendant pragmatic style.[4]

Hayden honed his viewpoint with graduate research into the writings of C. Wright Mills (1916–62), an outspoken sociologist whose own work owed much to the University of Wisconsin émigré Hans Gerth (1908–78). Gerth and Mills had translated the writings of Max Weber into English and made sociological theory an essential component in the academic discourse.[5] Mills, a native of Texas and a graduate of University of Texas at Austin, had gone to the University of Wisconsin–Madison, where he encountered the work of cutting-edge scholars of social institutions. However, the American reception of European sociology, with its self-conscious theoretic and historical components, was lukewarm and resisted Mills's critique of their empirical orientation and preference for mathematical schemas. Ever flinty about his perceived outsider status, Mills's writings attracted Tom Hayden for precisely that reason. Even more, Mills's doctoral dissertation, published posthumously (1964) as *Sociology and Pragmatism: The Higher Learning in America* (echoing Veblen's classic work *The Higher Learning in America*) offered a powerful philosophical critique of America's leading pragmatic thinkers, especially Charles Peirce (1839–1914), William James (1842–1910), and above all John Dewey (1859–1952). Mills worried that the pragmatists' deference to external contexts alone eventually would lead to a confirmation of the status quo rather than reformist change. He never went so far as to reaffirm the necessity for metaphysical ideals and a coherent ideology to check this problem, remaining effectively a pragmatist for all his critics' charges of "radical" ideas. Still, he treated pragmatic philosophers less as a distinct American philosophical school and more as "stylists" of social thought.[6] Mills went forward exploring the theories of Marxism, while Hayden sought something more substantive, a new moral purpose to ground social critiques of American social class patterns. Mills went on to write his famous trilogy of American Society—*The New Men of Power: America's Labor Leaders* (1948), *White Collar: The American Middle Class* (1951), and *The Power Elite* (1956)—and Hayden relied on Mills's influence in his coauthorship of the Port Huron Statement and the presidency of the SDS, which lasted for much of the 1960s.[7]

For all Hayden's admiration of Mills, his graduate critique of his mentor proved prescient. Hayden wanted to get beyond the traditional sociologist capitalist-labor polarities to understand the need for social activism and explore the deep roots of American racism. Hayden rejected, as Mills had not, the expectation that social change would arise out of an intellectual leadership. Rather, Hayden pursued the possibilities of mass action, treating the American middle class as less homogeneous than his mentor and more capable of embracing multiple grassroots initiatives. Mills's Weberian preference for strategic institutions and thoughtful agitators winning ever larger audiences seemed to Hayden to ignore the real power of class prejudices, which were resistant to rational argument. How far one could push strategies of coercion in behalf of social justice became highly problematic for him, when, late in the 1960s, black power advocates rejected white followers as complicitous with establishment oppression. Splinter groups of SDS, like the Weathermen, took up bank robbery, kidnapping, and even murder as modes of rejecting the power elite. At the end of the 1960s, Hayden found himself at the 1968 Democratic Convention in Chicago and was arrested with the famous Chicago Seven in the wake of dramatic urban riots. Ultimately his version of "radicalism" rejected violence as his subsequent career in the California legislature and Democratic Party politics bore witness.[8]

On many campuses across America, student activism grew apace in the 1960s. Some would channel their idealistic energies into the newly formed Peace Corps, which injected a substantive international dimension into the meaning of social reform. Others took a more traditional course into politics itself and offered public support to Lyndon's Johnson's Great Society program, especially his War on Poverty. However, a countercurrent began after Johnson's election when his administration sought, not only a completion of New Deal domestic policies, but also an expansion of an overseas presence in Southeast Asia. Johnson's escalation of troops to Vietnam at the end of 1964 took a dramatic turn with the bombing of North Vietnam in February of 1965. Immediately student organizations rallied, connected with each other nationwide, and began to hold extensive, multiday sessions on the war, its rationale, past US foreign excursions, the political apparatus for national commitments to war, and broad public sentiment about such a military exercise. They called these session "teach-ins," a variant on the student civil rights exercises known as sit-ins. Within a month the teach-ins had galvanized student energies, drew upon their apprenticeship skills in both civil rights and campus organizing, and quickly shaped a broad consensus opposing the president's wartime priorities. The teach-ins also drew upon faculty expertise in politics (how long could America be committed to war without a formal declaration ratified by the Senate?), economics (how much would this overseas outlay drain from domestic social programs, so enthusiastically passed by Congress?), and geography (where is Vietnam, and how was its fate functionally connected to America's overseas priorities?). Both university students and faculty recognized how basic course knowledge could be brought to bear on present-day questions, a consideration often obscured by ordinary curricular requirements.[9] There was an open, self-consciously voiced sentiment that "real university education" must have both authoritative factual backing and progressive social implications. Where was this standard for relevant knowledge in the routine course offerings of the American university?

A graphic example of this dilemma arose on April 1, 1965, at the University of Wisconsin when an all-day teach-in promised to extend into the night in a packed auditorium. Members of the faculty, students, and citizens from the general public sought a deep immersion in the multifaceted debate over Vietnam. Both information and interpretive perspectives became focal points of lectures and discussions. Germaine Bree (1907–2001), a member of the university's Institute for Humanities, offered a powerful contrast in moral commitment by comparing the different ideologies of Albert Camus (1913–60) and Jean-Paul Sartre (1905–80).[10] Like so many in the audience, the two French writers faced a problem during and after World War II: exactly how to redress patterns of violence and social injustice that seemed beyond their control. For Sartre who judged his free choice to be a conscious embrace of one of the forces of history—in his case the proletariat over the bourgeoisie—the process of commitment opted for an alliance with an objective protagonist whose eventual outcomes could not be foreseen but to which everything must be sacrificed. For Bree the process of achieving an ongoing commitment trumped Sartre's actual record in the French Resistance, his atheism, and his communist sympathies. For Camus similar historical forces—ideological movements, national war machines, authoritarian social systems—should never be permitted to cancel the overriding human sentiment of one human for his fellows, even in situations where "redress" or even "resistance" seemed quixotic, impossible, and even ineffectual. Commitment in behalf of one's fellows always created leverage, an independent moral sphere, the possibility of shaping rather than deferring to historical forces. Here too Camus's work with the French Resistance and his antireligious proclivities took second place. These two very different brands of individual commitment—historically or humanistically driven—Bree elaborated in a sophisticated analysis, worthy of any lecture in an advanced undergraduate or graduate class. But, if once a matter of scholarly specialization, now these issues had become a matter of pressing immanence. Bree's audience, intently seeking both knowledge of Vietnamese history and US State Department policy, was in the process of rethinking their own citizens' commitment to "American values," no longer clearly understood and which for some time to come remained problematic. Most arresting for her audience, Bree had offered not just a key debate in the history of existentialism but a demonstration of moral discovery outside any religious tradition. An enrapt audience listened in respectful silence as Bree demonstrated the connection between scholarship and issues of utmost national, international, and ethical concerns.

Following Bree's University of Wisconsin presentation, William Appleman Williams (1921–90) of the history department rose and was immediately challenged by a veteran of the army officer corps and a graduate of West Point to demonstrate his patriotic (not just his academic) credentials. Williams matched this challenge not only by invoking his own schooling at the US Naval Academy but his military service in World War II. But he quickly segued into a concise reprise of his scholarship in diplomatic history over a number of years, especially his influential book *The Tragedy of American Diplomacy*

(1959). Williams argued that America's domestic and foreign policy initiatives were always closely allied. From the articulation of the 1823 Monroe Doctrine, America embarked on a distinctly and proudly democratic approach to both foreign and domestic sectors. By the end of the nineteenth century, particularly with the presentation of the 1899–1900 Open Door Notes, America had seemed to update the earlier policies' tripartite objectives: a) noncolonization by Europe in the Western Hemisphere; b) noninterference by America in European affairs; and 3) nonintervention of any party in the internal affairs of independent New World nations. Secretary of State John Hay (1838–1905) and President William McKinley (1843–1901) sought to use the Open Door policy to prevent the partitioning of China and leave the United States an opening to Asian trade, thought to be essential for American economic interests. While the formal language of the Open Door resembled earlier diplomatic priorities, Williams sensed the meaning of the Monroe Doctrine language had changed from a defensive and democratic posture to an aggressive and exploitative imperialistic orientation. American foreign policy, he argued, no longer protected the integrity of independent nations (including that of the United States) but had become an arm of industrial capitalism in the marketing of goods overseas. Since the turn of the twentieth century, and including the present incursion into Vietnam, America had consistently used the language of self-determination to exploit the resources of other countries, expanding domestic and international class stratification. America's imperialistic history had become the weakness and tragedy rather than the strength and virtue of the American system.[11]

Such controversial and debatable viewpoints played themselves out weeks and days later, not only at the Madison campus, but also at many other colleges and universities nationwide. The students' immediate perceptions of the links between academic scholarship and immediate political action were patent. What followed in the short-term was an enthusiasm and intellectual energy that surprised the entire American academic community. For some students, whose first exposure to many of the arguments was at the teach-ins, the experience was both surprising and formative. Many resorted to the library to mull over the confrontation with deeply held assumptions, especially America's democratic traditions. Had they imbibed them too uncritically? What exactly did the critics of teach-ins' participants have to say, and how credible was their criticism? Other students threw themselves into organizing their fellow students and the broader university community. Protest actions by students, walking Madison's State Street, a symbolic mile connecting the university with the state capitol, became increasingly sophisticated.

Often antiwar marches began with quick instruction in how to protect oneself in the face of police batons and at times police dogs. Increasingly participants, especially Quaker families, not affiliated with the university, swelled the students ranks, opening the possibility—soon realized—that initial student actions could eventually result in a broader radicalization of America's middle class. When Lyndon Johnson discovered in February 1968 that his war policies were opposed by the CBS commentator Walter Cronkite (1916–2009), he apocryphally remarked, "If I have lost Walter Cronkite, I have lost middle America."[12]

The intellectual ferment in the student bodies across the nation waffled between a chain of protests versus a public dialogue, airing the pros and cons of the Vietnam policy. Most faculty members counseled the continued discussion and felt the importance of gaining the ears of power, which also underscored the complicity of pragmatic values in both government and academic sides of the debate. Some faculty felt they paid a "heavy price" for joining student protests and even resisted the teach-in characterization for fear of association with the sit-ins and civil disobedience.[13] Still, as events developed and the possibility of a national teach-in materialized, faculty began to sense the possibilities of expanding their classroom influence to a mass audience with national TV exposure, a very heady possibility. Some students, however, demurred and felt marginalized by the faculty interventions and began to insist on the educational and political merits of protest alone as both criticism and sheer resistance. No one has an accurate count of the number of teach-ins or the quantity of participation but clearly American higher education at every level had experienced something very surprising, beginning in March of 1965 at Ann Arbor, Michigan, and peaking in May at University of California, Berkeley, with thirty-five thousand students continuing a discussion for thirty-six hours. Beyond the increasing power of a national discourse and a counterargument to established policy, student activism had introduced a different cultural mind-set, the essential context for substantive academic change.

As the spring semester closed in 1965, students left their campuses, and the strategy of protest alone lost its temporary backers. In this interim, faculty began to press the government for a national debate over all aspects of the Vietnam policy. Lyndon Johnson's voice for the government view became his national security advisor, McGeorge Bundy (1919–96), a former faculty member and dean at Harvard University. Bundy objected to the critics' selection of his debating antagonist, Hans Morgenthau (1904–80) of the University of Chicago. Bundy asked if Morgenthau was truly representative of the critical academic voices. After sparring on this and other technical points, a national debate was arranged for May 1965. At the critical juncture, Bundy did not show and instead offered a letter of apology.[14] He was replaced by Asian expert Robert Scalapino (1919–2011) of the University of California, Berkeley. This national debate occurred before a Washington, DC, audience of five thousand, with more than one hundred thousand people at one hundred university campuses joined by radio hookups.[15] Subsequently, after additional faculty appeals, a nationally televised debate was held. There Bundy defended the policy of Vietnam in America's national interest. He argued that Vietnam's resistance had global implications, to demonstrate an Asian alternative to Chinese communism, thought by many to be invincible. In reply, Morgenthau insisted that American policy was indefensible since the Diem regime was an American construct and the people of South Vietnam did not support its leadership, and that the policy did not fit the facts of the case—the United States was not liberating Vietnam or protecting its integrity. There was, he insisted, no policy at all, and it could not in conscience be defended.

Two points become especially clear about post–World War II American academic culture with this exchange. First, both sides argued for the empirical merits of their case but drew different interpretations from the same set of facts. Second, the authoritative point of view rested less on actual facts than on the perceived expertise of each disputant. Bundy represented the US government with its vast resources of special intelligence, data gathering, and privileged information. His critics offered a public critique that related foreign policy not only to America's past but also to a wide range of issues beyond foreign policy including civil rights, discrimination in the military, unemployment, and so on. To be fair, Bundy never shielded his views with the invocation of special intelligence unavailable to a wider public. However, government-sponsored "truth teams" sent out to universities in the wake of the national teach-ins turned his argument into a mantra, in effect, arguing, "Trust us; we know what we are doing better than anyone else." The public impact was largely one of backlash, expecting rational argument and getting paternalism and arrogance in return. The public also witnessed an increasing governmental indifference to the widening public dissent, which ultimately held the potential of undermining representative government. The truth teams also underscored the perception that with heightened escalation of the war, the government also raised the barriers between itself and the American people. The teach-ins had not only offered a powerful counterargument to the government; they had implicitly opened the question of moral values: how does one differentiate between conflicting fact-based viewpoints, both of which claimed to be authoritative?[16] Wasn't there a normative standard for adjudicating the two expertises? What were the moral commitments of a citizen in the face of tarnished authorities? At the very least, the limits of pragmatism, often considered synonymous with American democratic procedure, began to alarm the public consciousness.[17]

For the university's part, events from the early teach-ins at Michigan and Wisconsin through the national teach-in in the fall of 1965 began to expand the old notion of academic freedom. Once a function of speaking from the mastery of a body of knowledge, academic freedom came to mean a larger public acceptance of ideas only if they were subjected to open verification and an acceptable process of rational inquiry. Criticism itself, once treated gingerly as acceptable only as a civil exchange among equals, could now tolerate an open confrontation. The vaunted middle ground, which pragmatists generally assumed would always exist, became narrow or was nonexistent. Protest itself (without alternative "solutions") often drew attention to problems that had gone ignored or were masked by willful deception and propaganda. In the face of no obvious solution, "dissent" came to be viewed as a legitimate, public resource.[18]

The revolutionary impact of the college and university teach-ins, short-lived as they were, lay in their opening up of broad public questions about the nature of academic autonomy. The very enthusiasm for the teach-ins implicitly reminded many—students and faculty alike—that classroom instruction was neither detached nor arcane knowledge. It was also not exclusively the only means of transmitting higher learning. What exactly was any university's responsibility to its larger public? Moreover, students themselves insisted their role was neither inconsequential nor utterly deferential but ideally should play a part in shaping institutional priorities and should participate more substantively in the formal decision-making apparatus of a university. The very integration of so many university disciplines during the teach-ins argued strongly for interdisciplinary collaboration and for transnational, global, and comparative perspectives. Actually the proliferation of higher education's specialized discourses called attention to the parochial nature of much academic scholarship, so removed from the issues of the day.[19] In the aftermath of the teach-ins, university leadership took on a defensive posture with the appointment of lawyers as heads of leading academic institutions: Kingman Brewster (1919–88) at Yale, Robben Fleming (1916–2010) at Michigan, Derek Bok (b. 1930) at Harvard. Such appointments led to the suspicion among many students that the university structure was itself an impediment to student activism and constructive social reform, not to mention a useful higher learning.

The teach-ins did not begin by probing fundamental questions but originated as a voluntary, practical device to inform the university community about a faraway place and American foreign policy. However, in the end the protest, debates, and confrontations that followed raised the question of legitimacy between and among civil authorities. The debate over technicalities and facts could not settle or assuage issues that fundamentally were normative and moral. Different opinions over strategies in a national conflict rested on questions of values and their interpretive applications. The dilemma of values for assessing seemingly legitimate, pragmatic stances raised an issue many considered settled generations ago: universities did not indoctrinate moral perspectives. Rather, they generally claimed to set aside subjective biases and produce trustworthy objective knowledge that would stand in spite of political biases. How could universities veer from their inherited objective tradition to engage and train moral judgment? How must students or wider publics react when faced with diametrically opposed views among established authoritative voices? What did it mean to be a student or a citizen? The questions themselves illuminated the narrow empirical frame within which much education had operated for much of the twentieth century. The uncritical celebration of science and pragmatism had led on the part of both government and its critics to an escalation of righteousness and arrogance about their own viewpoints.[20] Did science and pragmatism after all contain moral imperatives that were not being acknowledged? Did this long-standing insistence on "objectivity" help explain the limited tradition of sustained dissent within the twentieth-century university? Gradually some began to notice that the allocation of university resources had resulted in the marginalization of the humanities, where moral and aesthetic values as well as refined critical thinking were traditionally thought to be housed and protected. Exactly how could one institutionalize a pedagogy that sought the understanding of points of view not one's own? Didn't the insistence, in the national teach-in and in post–World War II academic culture, that one find "representative" voices and that one strike a "balance" among differences always produce workable alternatives? Shouldn't one strive for "objective" knowledge, which always leaned toward one side more than another? Gradually, in response to such questions, new possibilities arose, namely, that in different contexts, what is representative, balanced, or objective often depended on many masked (historical) factors and manipulated environments.

The ultimate inheritance of the teach-ins was the revelation of graphic limits to "authoritative knowledge" and the need for a nationwide initiation of a qualitatively different discourse on a range of issues. Its full implications have yet to be spelled out but implicitly the challenge to the rooted tradition of pragmatic inquiry began there in earnest: It was now possible by way of protest to raise objections without having a clear substitute for a solution; all knowledge contained latent political dimensions and could not claim special authority, like objectivity, for feigning apolitical interests;[21] relevant knowledge had always harbored political and ideological connotations; researchers should now set an older mode of inquiry into a different perspective and should acknowledge its distinct limitations.[22] Implicit in this newer epistemology was recognition that the nature of expertise, especially scientific authorities, always contained limitations. Often academic experts had insisted that mastery of a body of knowledge rested largely on descriptive or technical reportage. However, important as facts are, normative assumptions have always operated as the real drivers of inquiry. Most values—even those of pragmatism or science itself—cannot be legitimated by empirical facts alone; they carry their metaphysical trappings like shadows. The values of "open-ended" inquiry, of balance and representativeness, rest on historical, grounded assumptions and on time-bound parameters rather than established or empirical patterns of behavior. Factual knowledge is not alone automatically and naturally superior to other kinds of knowledge. Sometimes innocent questions, arising from genuine puzzlement—like the teach-ins' famous query, Why are we in Vietnam anyway?—overrode efforts to provide only information and required a different level of commentary. The questions of nonacademic publics during the teach-ins had at times outshone those of careerist and informed scholars. These teach-in issues, spreading from university to a wider national discourse, illuminated a larger trajectory that has not yet ended but which initiated a seismic shift in America's academic culture in the second half of the twentieth century.

The teach-ins thus prodded universities themselves to reconsider their public role and to see their organizational activism, at times, to be a crucial integer in a national issue or debate. The insularity of the American research university was not so much a casualty of student activism in the 1960s as it was an old problem viewed in a new light. It was still possible after the teach-ins to retreat into seminar, laboratories, and classrooms, but it was no longer possible to ignore the social forces that pressed on academic walls. Finally the revolutionary nature of the teach-ins was to initiate thinking about the nature of academic power itself, especially the role of dissent and protest about any established canon. However, the process of graduate training, the pecking order and stratification of higher education institutions, and the politics of promotion and tenure, all contributed mightily to a mentality that resisted the gadfly, the critic, the innovator. If nothing else, the teach-ins illuminated the ubiquitous benefit of the dissenter at crucial stages of higher learning. For the moment the critical mind and the examined life were now thought to pervade any academic culture worth the name.[23]

The mitotic cells of change represented by the teach-ins did not, of course, result in immediate or obvious transformations. But over time, it set the context for a range of institutional and curricular changes that would not have occurred without them. Not least of these changes was the reconsideration of core curricula over individualized instruction and programs. Aspects of the traditional humanities, especially in philology, religion, and philosophy, themselves much degraded by the pressures of multiple generations of pragmatic priorities, experienced a rejuvenation and legitimacy as a part of the basic liberal arts accorded to a genuine educated person.[24] To be sure, in America's two dozen Jesuit colleges and universities scholars like Étienne Gilson (1884–1978), Jacques Maritain (1882–1973), and John Courtney Murray, SJ (1904–67) had not been sidelined in their own universities, but such scholars were largely marginalized in the public and private universities where the narrow philosophical visions of logical positivism and reflexive antipathies to religious belief held sway.[25] There is also no denying that, especially in state universities, utilitarian pressures set in motion many highly technical and career-oriented programs that supported an older pragmatic tradition. At times these utilitarian pressures affected even religiously affiliated colleges that protected their long-standing moral tradition of inquiry. But the reconsideration of moral and ethical instruction, too often wrongly equated with propaganda and oppressive didacticism, as a viable higher education course of studies represented a serious, cultural change and a new stage of research interests.[26]

A number of scholars began to consider how new bridges might span an older pragmatism, which determined truth by the practical consequences of actions rather than by the invocation of absolute values, and a new humanistic stance, a moral ethos that was difficult to consider before the 1960s.[27] The teach-ins had propelled forward a new framework for judging actions, one that did not rely solely on empirical data. This consideration explicitly sought alternative ways of knowing and perspectives that, up until that time, had not participated in mainstream discourses. This shift drew upon the seismic vibrations of the civil rights and the feminist movements to insist on a more inclusive university disposition toward African Americans, Jews, Catholics, women, and new immigrant minorities benefiting from the 1965 Immigration and Naturalization Act.[28] To be sure, inclusion of these groups had been constructively assisted by the earlier GI Bill but sustaining their numbers had been difficult until the 1960s. Universities with departments of American studies began to reflect America's own self-conscious global role and expanded their research to Latin America, Africa, and Asia. Contributing to this departure were the late twentieth-century interdisciplinary programs that took up "the Atlantic World" in reconsiderations of America's colonial past. Scholars reexamined the scholarship on nations and increasingly found national borders to be artificially restrictive in considering historical events and policy impacts. By the 1990s much historic research about "national pasts" developed an expansive global thrust and incorporated study of transnational migrations, which adopted pioneering computerized methodologies and an appreciation of demography.[29] New professional organizations like the Social Science History Association (founded 1975) specifically encouraged and sustained a commitment to interdisciplinary programs as well as collaboration between and among international colleagues.[30]

The post-teach-ins values of inclusion, transparency, and progressive social transformation influenced the research university model of intensive specialization and attempted to rethink their place in the curriculum. Renewed efforts to establish core curricula and honors programs at universities that hitherto had emphasized individualized selection over even distribution requirements tried to address the hyperspecialization in almost every field. The older interwar programs that had attempted a restrictive (i.e., paternalistic) distribution of cultural subjects—literature, philosophy, and the other liberal arts—had no real attraction in the post-1960s period. Here the issue was a genuine reconfiguration of a course of studies to examine the place of Western thought in a larger global context. This broadened sweep, it was thought, would provide a more realistic inclusion of many racial, ethnic, and low-income groups, up until now excluded from higher education instruction; it would also get beyond disciplinary boundaries, to promote complex methodologies that enabled many disciplines to engage hitherto elusive research issues. Much of the new breakthrough research that would follow may have come out of traditional departments and disciplinary specializations, but the product of their work lapped over into many other multidisciplined discourses.[31]

The reorganization that followed from energized traditional departments and new topic-oriented programs also accommodated sheer numerical increases in student, faculty, and administrative expansions. In 2000 35 percent of the American college-age cohort studied in institutions of higher learning, compared with fewer than 3 percent for most of the nineteenth century. Between 1950 and 1970, that college-age cohort had increased fivefold, which translated in raw numbers for undergraduates from 2 to 9 million individuals.[32] This incontestable fact of the American college and university serving a near-mass population and willy-nilly becoming numerically more democratic set the context for a new brand of general education. Ironically, the expansion of graduate instruction spiked in these years (184,000 full-time faculty in 1963 became 331,000 in 1968, a majority below the age of forty), resulting in "revolution," as the widely read 1969 study *The Academic Revolution* by Christopher Jencks (b. 1936) and David Riesman (1909–2002) insisted. Their "revolution," however, consisted of a new emphasis on meritocracy. Actually the teach-ins' momentum had already gone beyond earlier meritocratic considerations and made the Jencks and Riesman version of "revolution" a problem in need of reexamination itself.[33] Before the 1960s, the American university had created a vibrant meritocracy committed to advancing knowledge and uplifting its democratic society. This new phenomenon, however, was clearer in its goals than it was in its execution. The critique of Jencks' and Riesman's "revolution" followed from the quantitative and qualitative changes of the 1960s, in which the humanities experienced solid increases, at least until the mid-1970s.[34] But in the process a new climate, receptive to a critique of empirical pragmatism and mere instrumentalism, expanded the discourses in several disciplines.[35] Still, the distinguished MIT linguist Noam Chomsky offered his summary judgment: "Big changes took place in the whole culture in the 1960s, and the university was in many ways involved in it. There were major changes in attitudes toward everything, and these changes affected the entire society: in personal relations, in attitudes toward women, toward the environment, respect for other cultures—across the board there has been a very substantial change."[36]

The 1960s initiated a shift from an earlier generation's appreciation of synthesis for more analytic scholarship, and the ensuing history of scholarship in several of these disciplines helps clarify their own cultural changes. No better example of this trend could be found than in the scholarly discourse over American history. In 1944 Merle Curti (1897–1997) won the Pulitzer Prize for History for his ambitious compendium *The Growth of American Thought*. That work and Crane Brinton's (1898–68) *The Anatomy of Revolution* (1938) jointly created the field of intellectual history in the United States. Both books attempted to synthesize forceful ideas in history but attempted to set them in their specific social contexts, in order to treat ideas as influential forces shaping human events. The emphasis on social context also gave rise to the new specialization of social history. Social historians greatly expanded historical scholarship beyond its long-standing and familiar work in political and military history, not to mention biography. Curti at the University of Wisconsin and Brinton at Harvard attempted to train students to think of groups and organizations bonded by ideas and committed to social action. The profession as a whole legitimated these innovations when each historian was elected to the presidency of the American Historical Association.

The ensuing generation invigorated this emphasis on social context and developed a methodology of intellectual and institutional interaction to explain historical change. Herbert Gutman (1928–85) grew up with left-leaning parents in the industrial city of Paterson, New Jersey, and developed a consuming commitment to understand radical social change. He arrived at the University of Wisconsin to pursue his interests in labor unions with his liberal mentor, Howard Beale (1898–1983), and the equally Progressive Merle Curti. His master's thesis on the Panic of 1873 left him particularly unsatisfied, since most of the labor actions he studied were exercises in failure. He often admitted that he had no intention of committing his life to the depressing study of failed idealism. However, his research had opened up a new avenue of possibility that he channeled into his 1959 doctoral dissertation: the question of how groups with minimal resources could galvanize their ambitions to resist the daunting and largely unforgiving forces of American capitalism. This question took his scholarship deeper into the social fabric of labor communities, where he actually found workers using their religious (especially Protestant) traditions of mutual support to legitimate resistance. Gutman's work drew the notice of British historian E. P. Thompson (1924–93) whose seminal study, *The Making of the English Working Class*, explored similar themes. In 1976 Gutman gathered a number of his essays into *Work, Culture and Society in Industrializing America*, and the following year published *The Black Family in Slavery and Freedom*.[37]

Gutman's intellectual interests were hardly unique in the 1960s, but his work and career especially illuminated a new research orientation that came to be called the "new social history." The new social history focused on a range of social groups that hitherto had received short shrift in the major American history textbooks: workers, immigrants, women, families, schools and teachers, and children, or, in a word, the building blocks of the American community. Not only could such communities (many of them in their pre–Civil War stages) be studied by a single researcher, the 1960s had introduced a new resource, computing methods for gathering census statistics and enabling the reconstruction of families, neighborhoods, and towns. Scholars could actually reconstruct with numerical precision the distinct groupings and the social class stratification of a particular society whose members had hitherto been largely undocumented. If initially the prominent studies focused on social groupings in the 1850s to the 1880s (before small towns and cities became too large for a single scholar), the methodologies of approach and analysis became routine yet highly innovative.

A new set of premises arose, engaged other disciplines, and quickly became canonical in its claims for new knowledge and methodologies:[38] a) significant change did not always proceed from the top down but also arose from the bottom up; b) important demographic changes often occurred with ordinary people voting with their feet and migrating to different places; c) churches and schools, or indeed temporary voluntary associations, hitherto thought to be less consequential than the structured agencies of the government or the military, actually had informal power that lasted beyond general expectations; d) the role of leaders cannot be fairly judged until set in the broader social context of their historical moment; and e) often oppressed groups do not merely acquiesce or remain wholly passive but rather take distinct initiatives on their own behalf, constructing vibrant institutions and possibilities, unimagined by different ethnic or social classes. The histories of communities, social groups, and organizations that scholars of the 1960s and 1970s reconstructed compelled a wholesale retelling of the American story and produced at its best textbooks like *A People and a Nation,* which began in the 1970s and by 2007 had gone through eight editions, each continuously revised by taking into account the new scholarship.[39]

It takes little imagination to grasp how profoundly the 1960s civil rights movements, the sit-ins in Greensboro, North Carolina, and elsewhere, the Southern violence against nonviolent protesters and voter registration, then more expansively the student free speech movement at many university campuses especially Berkeley, the antiwar protests, the Black Panther movements, and the criminal activity of the Weathermen, all played through a national challenge to familiar assumptions about America's role at home and abroad. Initially both the civil rights and the antiwar movements began with no clear expectation of altering the established powers of government or the military, but these protests had such an educational effect on the populace as a whole, reinforced by the ubiquity of television networks. Many middle-class individuals, with or without children in the universities, experienced the hostility of some Americans toward others that they clearly never thought possible in an America still prideful about the triumph over Nazism in World War II. Viewing electric prods, fire hoses, and dogs used against their fellow citizens, many of whom explicitly voiced their nonviolent intentions, began a rapid process of radicalizing the American middle class (without whom the protesting students would have had little lasting effect). The possibilities of protest, spurring gadfly candidates like Senator Eugene McCarthy (1916–2005) against President Johnson and the State Department policy, made ordinary citizens reexamine their democratic commitments. The ensuing protest movements of feminists and environmentalists crossed political party lines and confirmed new assumptions about the historic force of ordinary citizen initiatives. It would have been impossible for academic scholars to have missed these developments; of course, how they acted in their wake did not follow a predictable pattern.

Through the 1980s and 1990s, the new social history underwent many mutations and changed inherited scholarly methodologies. Not the least of these involved oral history, which recognized that every citizen possessed a dramatic narrative. Often these experiences had gone unrecorded in the familiar venues of newspapers and historical archives. However, historians with tape recorders and video cameras quickly cultivated these ordinary sources of information, which an earlier generation of scholars thought too subjective and hence untrustworthy. Now, however, with official government experts offering testimony that was so clearly self-interested and biased, historians began to assume all documents contained historical limitations, oral testimony no less than testimony under oath or sanctioned by official institutions. All documents, many historians argued, were documents for something; they required only astute questioning and analysis to extract from them insights of significance. Similarly historians began to see historical values embedded in evidence other than documents, in artifacts, in architecture, in artwork, in the familiar utensils of daily life, in the range of nonverbal evidence, so long treasured by their archeological and anthropological colleagues. Historians began to collect and photograph "the material culture of daily life" as graphic data that often connected to and embellished print sources. Some academics began to discover the pedagogical powers of the camera, the digital recorder, and the computer. Historical documentaries followed that not only gathered empirical evidence but often the subjective arguments of participants. In the process an older tradition of scholarship, overconfident about the authority of empirical evidence, had to make way for newer bodies of evidence.[40]

Students and teachers alike became sensitive to the powers of the new media both in gathering data and in graphic communication. Such interdisciplinary methodologies began to influence both scholarship and university instruction. In the early 1980s, one sector of the American history establishment initiated a special field, public history,[41] that employed the entire range of techniques—statistical quantification, documentary presentation, media pedagogy, dramatic narrative, image and artifact analysis—and with a special appreciation of students' roles as teachers as well as the instructional power of ordinary people. Out of this energized approach to social history came a range of novel products that drew upon the latest scholarship but kept the public audience in focus: exhibits, dramatizations, film documentaries, and websites. The interaction between expert and public became the field's innovative focus and drew its energies from its 1960s rediscovery via the new social history of "the ordinary citizen."[42] Implicitly historical research that focused on nonacademic audiences inevitably called into question the professional historians' insistence upon "objectivity" in their scholarship. That debate, which had continued through the 1970s and 1980s, tended to disparage the original work, sources, and methods that public history introduced. But the new scholarship of public history sustained its own innovations because it welcomed the values of greater inclusiveness and imagination in research and teaching and because it rejected the shortcomings of the older, "objective" scholarship that had been circumscribed by the 1960s revolution.[43]

Such sectors of the American historical profession sharpened the general sense of a 1960s academic revolution and explored many new areas of inquiry well into the twenty-first century. If others continued to use new techniques and methodologies to follow a pre-1960 preference for military and political history and to produce textbooks accordingly, their scholarship only documented the flexibility of the profession and especially its educational commitments to an intelligent reading public. Both older and newer generations of historians were conscious of a distinctive "public" role for their work. They looked askance at scholarship that introduced arcane terms and language that distanced them from an intelligent reading public. The profession as a whole respected the discourse of an informed public and resisted infusing obscurantist terms that supposedly argued their special expertise.[44] If some historians worked to have their professional approach become a more scientific standard, especially with the use of computers and "hard data," few indulged technical terms that broke an informed train of thought. Historians by and large used the language of the newspaper-reading public and, as the twentieth century went on, found ways to discuss the historic role of the public as a seminal agent of change as well as a new source of factual data. They wished ordinary people to find themselves and their traditions more readily in the authoritative textbooks of their moment. Still, elements within the profession, especially those accepting history as a social science, felt their scholarship should be more useful, more attractive to the corridors of power and elected officials, more sought after by the shapers of public policy. At one candid moment at a conference of historians and policy makers, one policy expert simply exclaimed: "Historians bleed too much," that is, they savor context and the factual details leading up to a decision, when policy makers are bent on reducing risk and arriving at predictable knowledge.[45] In spite of both sides seeking useful scholarly insights and interweaving the facts of a case, the gap between the two viewpoints remained substantive. Policy makers always sought predictable even replicable results, while historians shaped "context" and interpreted the unique features of an event or pattern.

In the discipline of philosophy, pragmatism, stemming from the writing of John Dewey and William James that criticized any invocation of metaphysical first principles, tended to undergird most academic assumptions until after World War II. An undercurrent of positivism—authoritative knowledge that involved only sensory and measurable phenomenon—had always interacted with pragmatism in the theories of testing that followed from the work of Edward L. Thorndike (1874–1949). After World War II, positivism energized itself in a most practical way with the expansion of educational testing in many forms. Thorndike's maxim, that everything that existed existed in some amount and could be measured, influenced not only philosophers but psychologists as well.[46] Stimulus-response research attempted to connect measurable behaviors with the intellectual priorities and capacities of individuals and played itself through a battery of formal tests that purported to make concrete the hitherto mysterious capacities of the human mind.[47] Pragmatism itself began to take a backseat in both philosophical and psychological discourses in the immediate post–World War II period. The analytic philosophy of Ludwig Wittgenstein (1889–1951) and A. J. Ayer (1910–89) abetted this shift toward a more "scientific" foundation and catapulted American psychologists like B. F. Skinner (1904–90) to the national fore.[48] However, educational administrators, often content with the burden of judgment that testing removed from their shoulders, nevertheless remained in a broadly pragmatic trajectory. Roughly speaking, pragmatism had come to mean a loose intellectual framework that resisted certitude and moralizing, endorsed contingency, change, and ongoing experimentation as permanent expectations and a reliance on knowledge that was democratically acceptable.[49] Pragmatic philosophy, however, served to maintain a questioning probe into American academic assumptions that has lasted into the twenty-first century. Was truth merely the physical consequence of action, or did this seeming indifference to ethical and imaginative insight omit considerations essential to culture and human aspiration? Pragmatism may still have informed the American philosophical discourse and more broadly have characterized the nation's distinctive train of thought, its ubiquitous academic organizational mode and its political rationale,[50] but after the 1960s its dominance could be challenged more easily than ever before.[51]

After the 1960s, pragmatism's claims to ideological neutrality became particularly circumspect. Philosophers like John Dewey, who lived long and wrote extensively, labored to make pragmatism not only a democratic philosophy but also a practical methodology for solving social issues and problems. Dewey had rejected the positing of first principles, or metaphysics, on the empirical grounds that they could not be convincingly demonstrated. Such absolute truths always seemed, in Dewey's view, to degenerate into someone's self-interests and hence became politically elitist. Such truths succeeded, he felt, only in being coercively imposed upon others rather than operating for a larger social good. Instead, Dewey substituted a process of experimental behavior, temporarily legitimated by any given social group and always susceptible of improvement. The process rested on each individual's participation and tolerance of contingency. Differences of opinion and wasteful false starts were merely the price of a democratic process that guaranteed, not truth, but momentarily-agreed-upon priorities. Dewey premised that each participant's experience would maintain an ongoing corrective and keep the process from distracting and destructive abstractions (like Descartes's *cogito, ergo sum*). Participation kept both learning and progress active (not passive as in Locke's *tabula rasa*). Experience, personal and particular rather than universal, Dewey consistently averred, kept the process creative and benign. Dewey resisted admitting that his uncritical commitment to change, to social activism, to the primacy of experience, was in any way a commitment to absolute principles themselves.[52] However both within academia and in the nation at large, as in the 1960s debates, the public faced versions of pragmatism that seemed so diametrically opposed to each other, that pragmatism appeared to be a rhetorical veneer masking conflicting ideologies, each with their own nonnegotiable absolute truths.

Surprisingly, humanistic disciplines like English literature might have given pragmatists like Dewey the close reading that operated as their forte. But the search for a bedrock starting point or foundation for academic inquiry never preoccupied the literary discourse. Instead, from the late nineteenth century to the interwar period of the twentieth century, the standard courses for an English major remained relatively similar, grounded as they were in the mastery of multiple languages, followed by their application to literary works via philological analysis. The singular features, especially of graduate studies in English, were its detachment from the lecture and instructional obligations newly minted doctoral candidates confronted. Their early career obligations were with sweeping surveys of substantive periods. In the Depression years, the discursive historical background and cultural framework of a text began to shift to a preoccupation with the text itself as a self-contained entity. The close reading of the so-called New Critics—Allen Tate (1899–1979), Cleanth Brooks (1906–94), Robert Penn Warren (1905–89), and others—did not dominate the literature field so much as energize novel approaches to the subject.[53] When joined with the expanding American studies field—interdisciplinary approaches using philosophy, history, English, and the arts—the postwar field of literary studies consciously connected scholarship and everyday life.[54] The impact of the 1960s welcomed not only women in significant numbers but also feminist studies alongside Latino, Asian, and black literary works, to respond to the new undergraduate groupings. However, as in the field of history, the specialized, "integrated" studies available at both the undergraduate and graduate level fragmented and overspecialized further the humanistic fields that earlier had purportedly sought consensus of interpretation or methodology.

For all the expansion of the applied sciences and social sciences in academic spheres in the last decades of the twentieth century, the humanities remain not only resolute but also vibrant in their ingenuity and energetic probing of new scholarship and discourses. Such innovations testify not only to the health of the humanities but the necessity for their representation in any modern university. It is out of the humanities that multiple theories of learning arise, putting in perspective the more homogeneous assumptions of empirical science. For example, M. H. Abrams (1912–2015),[55] a distinguished Harvard scholar of an older literary school, has taken an alternative view and has observed that the current analysis has underscored in energizing ways an expansive field of representation—literature. That field with its range of high and low modes of construction—cartoons, film, pornography, streetside communication, and so on—has served as a context for once again showcasing distinctive works of literature. Beyond the criticism of their elitism, oppression, and sexism, the range of newly considered works set themselves apart from other forms of representation and communication. At some not too distant point in the future, these eminent products of human ingenuity will have reaffirmed, Abrams feels, their special contribution to seeing ourselves as others see us, with all the constructive differentiation of experience and perspective that literature has always presented to human curiosity. Enduring works of literature will leave the reader questioning and probing in matters that connect one person to his fellow beings. In this sense, the scholarship of the early twenty-first century will represent another in a long chain of innovative approaches that will return us in another vernacular to a different consciousness that we will nevertheless recognize.[56] The upshot of post-1960s innovation in the literature discourse has been substantial, almost as substantive and discordant as that of the history discourse. This consequence, if Abrams is correct, seems to demonstrate that the essential core of the humanities becomes both intensively adaptive and especially creative when it finds itself in crisis.[57]

The discourse of political science emerged from the 1960s still grappling with its ongoing worry about how scientific were its methodologies and how substantively the field had contributed to an understanding of democracy. Some of its leading voices fretted that in the first half of the twentieth century, political scientists had produced no "findings" of lasting import. Their work—statistical graphs, survey research, content analysis, and mathematical models—tended to provide substantive verification for processes that were generally known by an informed public. Its reporting function was no small contribution but not the prized insights and experts of its sister colleagues in economics and psychology. Its most astute practitioners also became concerned, even before the challenges of the sixties, that their own democratic assumptions had been too uncritically benign.[58] The sixties confronted the complacency of the field's assumptions about democratic organizations, their uncritical acceptance of elite leadership, their seeming indifference to issues of race, gender, and marginalized groups, and, above all, their biases against the unpredictable course of democratic politics. Their inherited preoccupation with an authoritative scientific methodology kept them resistant not only to the normative theories of continental scholars but also to the challenges from student critics of the sixties.[59]

Still, however much the political science field itself remained in denial and treated the rebellion of the sixties as an aberration, younger members of the profession opened their scholarly research to new questions and topics. First, they began to see their work serving as a voice for suppressed minorities. Second, they began circumspection about the rigid rationality of their scientific method, acknowledging, as in the work of James March (b. 1928) of Stanford and others,[60] the serendipitous organizational shifts that their "rational" structures often ignored. This new political sensibility extended also to the aberrant nature of political party development and interest groups, whose histories regularly breached their espoused priorities. The political science model of science, shadowing the replicable processes of natural science, often distorted the actual working of ordinary politics. This new assumption gave a welcoming authority to groups officially *outside* the political framework but whose gadfly activity nevertheless influenced the process. Of course, not all political scientists subscribed to the new trends, and the field remained a conversation with "separate tables." But groups who had experienced the 1960s protests (not to mention those who had witnessed the threats of overseas totalitarian regimes) entered political science with a distinct shift in determination, one resolved to compel their research to raise larger issues and to engage the current political realm and civil society more aggressively than their forebears.

The distinguished political scientist Ira Katznelson (b. 1944) put it this way: "By confronting a more senior generation, they [radical scholars] forced revisions to existing approaches, deepening their research and depth. By exploring new themes and ways of working, they directly altered the character of their fields. By way of these extensions, they created intellectual space for subsequent insurgencies. . . . None of this would have been possible without the charged challenges of the sixties."[61] The upshot of political science changes since the sixties has concentrated on scholarship that has been more intensely social (extending to labor, race, gender, and varieties of collective action) than formally structural, more international (engaging both imperialism and decolonization) than strictly oriented to traditional American politics, and more normative in ways that qualify their inherited pragmatic, scientific methodologies. Although these changes occurred within the profession and were implemented by a seeming "loyal opposition," the reworking of the pragmatic methodology was quietly transformative. In other words, like most substantive changes, the academic shifts of the 1960s had an extended life in spite of countercurrents and were not over by any definition at the end of the century.

The case of the economics discourse represents a substantive countercurrent to its sister disciplines in the social sciences. Before World War II, the power of John Maynard Keynes's (1883–1946) *The General Theory of Employment, Interest and Money* (1936), his magnum opus, became increasingly canonical in both undergraduate and graduate instruction, particularly through the textbook of Paul Samuelson (1915–2009), *Economics: An Introductory Analysis* (1948), which popularized Keynesianism. Part and parcel of this orientation was an appreciation of the history of economic theory and a descriptive immersion in the debates of the past. In the course of wartime dynamics, Keynesianism became preoccupied with three major principles:

1) the rationality of the labor market; 2) the expectation of purposeful behavior, both on the part of self-interested consumers and profit-oriented organizations; and 3) the striving for equilibrium between employee and employer satisfaction. By and large, economists accepted the simplicity of these basic assumptions for the benefit of both collaborative discussion and for the increasing possibilities of quantifying data and giving their findings a numerical legitimacy.[62] In the postwar period, quantification received a substantial boost from practitioners desirous of sustaining economists' claims to science. Still later, the introduction of computerization and the promise of governmental subsidy in "hard" data collection, economics took a sharper turn toward mathematics and model building.[63] During the student protests of the 1960s, the economics profession reflected an academic resistance to student protest and proceeded with its rapprochement toward mathematics and, especially at the graduate level, additional mathematical courses to achieve technical mastery of the economic models. These additional requirements marginalized courses in economic history and its traditional concerns for the actual operations of economic institutions over time.

For students aspiring to nonacademic careers in finance, banking, and organizational administration, the mathematical models of academic economists increasingly seemed detached from the actual worlds of financial exchange. Many doctoral graduates, whose careers began in undergraduate education, found themselves ill equipped in teaching positions either to translate the significance of their graduate mathematical models to entry-level courses in economics or to teach more traditional courses in economic history, money and banking, and so on. Many found it challenging even to instruct students in the theoretical differences between Keynesianism and the Chicago monetarist school. For graduates of elite liberal arts colleges, nonacademic employers became increasingly concerned with the absence among economics majors of problem-solving and communication skills.[64] Some of the economic doctoral candidates at the end of the twentieth century gradually began to take up issues of comparative economics, analyzing differences between modern nation-states and underdeveloped countries. Similarly they began to challenge the simplicities of the canonical assumptions, especially about "equilibrium" when economic structures globally began to reflect dramatic disruptions. All of the quantifiable givens of an early postwar generation received critical comment, drawing especially from historical examples to suggest, say, that employer and employees did not always opt for choices in their own self-interests or that environmental factors often drastically altered seemingly rational choices. In a relatively minor fashion, some of the key priorities of the sixties began to creep into the economics discourse but not, according to one observer, enough to shift the principal graduate programs in economics from their longtime mathematical focus. Liberal arts colleges, staffed by such professionally trained university PhDs, faced an agonizing choice of educating a multifaceted body of undergraduates in "real world" exchanges or to train the professionally bound elect in mathematical models.[65]

The ferment in the late twentieth-century academic discourses developed two layers, at least in the principal social sciences and humanities. Several, like economics notably, have sustained a commitment to produce scientifically precise knowledge and have willingly preferred their research training to any outreach to broader social or normative national concerns. Other disciplines, notably history and English, have cultivated research innovation precisely with their eyes on previously marginalized groups and organizations. The one option has produced a coherent focus aware of the need to expand its traditional boundaries; the other, multifaceted strands of inquiry whose mutual relevance and import is often hard to establish. In both disciplines there have been efforts to energize older pragmatic traditions yet to honor a degree of divergent experimentation without clear understanding of where they would lead, much less how they would invigorate the sociocultural whole.[66] Hovering below all these discussions is the knotty issue of what knowledge is most trustworthy and how is it to be established. But one needs to emphasize that departments and disciplines, however tradition bound, nevertheless maintain themselves at the very center of university work and change by their very posing of such essential questions.

One of the central inheritances of the 1960s is the recognized ease with which scientific data could be made to serve sharply political ends. The recurring problem with the pro-scientific discourses rests with an older maxim about their "results" transcending ideology and political bias. Part of the inferences of the 1960s rests with a determination to grasp how ideological their own priorities of scientific research are. The "objective" attack on ideology—a central mantra of old-style pragmatism—and its attendant rejection of metaphysical principles were a self-imposed and constricting pattern of thought. Thomas Kuhn seems to have been closer to the mark by noting every generation develops its distinctive paradigm and time-bound first principles, which contain unexamined assumptions that resist empirical proof.[67] Dewey's assumption that his pragmatic thought and the social process systematically produced benign results became in a post-1960s framework an abstract romanticism of the democratic process. His approach ignored how complete a metaphysical aura he invested in the concepts of change and experience themselves. The recognition of the 1960s students that State Department ideologies embraced an unexamined self-interestedness was the first step toward a reinterpretation of pragmatism's own indulgent myopia, its expectation that ongoing interaction of individuals led ineluctably to benign democratic progress. Subsequent university research that sought a reengagement with values and norms, not to mention ethics and moral limits, was a necessary step toward an improved twenty-first-century academic culture.[68]

The 1960s student resistance, first to the Vietnam War, then more broadly to American values, as well as a subsequent generation of younger faculty in the post-1960s American universities, did not engineer a wholesale change in the span of a single career. What they did achieve, while their professional research wrestled with their pragmatic inheritance, was a revolutionary shift of priorities. In varying ways virtually all areas of the social sciences and humanities cultivated new departures and a range of creative intellectual innovations. This ferment has for its implicit goal, not a single truth or credo, but a new recognition that empirical science, as progressive as it is and as fundamental and it has been and will be to university work, does not exhaust the approaches to trustworthy knowledge.[69] Instead, a new respect for poetic insight, artistic expression, religious belief, and the centrality of subjective conscience presumes significant limitations on the discoveries of America's scientific establishment. The university, as both shelter and garden for all these approaches, has assumed in the post-1960s world a yet more difficult challenge, how to orchestrate all these brands of knowing into a coherent and mutually supportive whole. Nothing less will satisfy the necessities for our land, our time, and our culture.

The open-ended nature of this final culture (still generational culture #7) nevertheless affords several summary observations about the history of American higher education. First, centrality of faculty presence in all academic cultures leads us to expect that future changes will originate with this sector of higher learning. Faculty may be spurred by students' voluntary organizations as they were in the nineteenth-century literary societies or in the twentieth-century teach-ins, but the regular, multidecade length of faculty careers will make them the arbiters of permanent change. Second, this observation also implies that however forceful external influences have been and will be, the dominant agents of change in academic culture will arise from the faculty's disciplines and discourses that mediate and interpret external forces on academic traditions, which is to say, predominantly from "below" rather than from "above," that is, from administrative fiat, trustee recommendations, or short-term, for-profit schemes servicing forceful donors. Third, faculty and departmental discourses, which have seldom been "ivory towers," however distanced their research and writings sometimes seems to be from pressing issues of the moment, will continue their monitoring and borrowing from other colleagues' work and continue to be influenced by the scholarship of their fellows, inside and outside their own departments. Any changes that propose to bypass or sideline faculty members only ensure a disconnect between the structures of higher education and the larger culture, a scenario for failure. Fourth, the central research and teaching of higher education inevitably grounds itself in the arts and sciences curriculum, where questions of ultimate value have their staunchest presence. Without roots in the multiple approaches to knowledge, colleges and universities lose their reason for being. If at times, especially in the recent past, the physical sciences appear to lord it over their less empirical disciplines, the humanities begin to reassert their fundamental purposes, which is one of the reasons for this chapter offering thumbnail glimpses of humanities and social sciences shouldering their authority against the pragmatic assumptions of the prevailing culture. If our own cultural moment documents an important instance of cultural shift, it behooves us all to recognize the change for what it is and, if possible, to join the discourse in a critical but constructive fashion. Finally, one might underscore a central methodological feature of this study: the central role of faculty and their ideas could never have been established by studying faculty alone. One of the major assumptions of this study's approach is that one must cast a wider net beyond the halls of academe in order to understand the essence of America's academic cultures.

Notes

INTRODUCTION

1. Paul H. Mattingly, Konrad H. Jarausch, John Craig, Joseph F. Kett, and James Turner, "Universities in Europe: North American Perspectives on European Historiography," *History of Education* 37, no. 3 (May 2008): 469–90.

2. William R. Taylor, "On the Dangers of Theory without History," *International Labor and Working-Class History*, no. 37 (Spring 1990): 29–31.

CHAPTER ONE

1. Samuel Eliot Morison, "Precedence at Harvard College in the 17th Century," *Proceedings of the American Antiquarian Society* (1932): 377–415. As Harvard approached its three hundredth anniversary (1936), its distinguished historian, Samuel Eliot Morison, began his researches into his alma mater. The above essay went to extensive lengths to explain the rank order of seventeenth-century students and rejected rank by social standing. However, so many exceptions to the principle of ranking arose, that Morison very tentatively offered an explanation of "merit" which he also quickly modified. He noted that rank often coincided with social standing, precisely because the few students involved (before 1650 Harvard classes consisted of under ten students, and before 1660 under twenty) came from families with resources to prepare them better than their fellows. Morison's seventeenth-century scholarship, often interpretively strained, nevertheless strove to make the precedent colonial college much more than it ever was in practice. John R. Thelin's *A History of American Higher Education* (Baltimore: Johns Hopkins University Press, 2004), chap. 1, sensibly talks about the early colleges' twentieth-century celebrations and their newfound roots to set a context for the "colonial seventeenth-century college." Many of the seventeenth-century stories of America's first colleges involve twentieth-century assumptions, full of ahistorical notions about higher learning.

2. Database of historian James McLachlan, who shared with the author (February 16, 2012) tables 1 and 2, which are printed here with permission. My thanks to Professor McLachlan for a close reading of the first two chapters of this study.

3. James A. Henretta, *Evolution and Revolution: American Society, 1600–1820* (Lexington, MA: D. C. Heath, 1987), 103–4.

4. Richard Hofstadter, *America at 1750: A Social Portrait* (New York: Vintage, 1971); Patricia Bonomi, *Under the Cope of Heaven: Religion, Society and Politics in Colonial America* (New York:

Oxford University Press, 1986), chap. 5; see also Henretta, *Evolution and Revolution*, 104–9; J. David Hoeveler, *Creating the American Mind: Intellect and Politics in the Colonial Colleges* (New York: Rowman and Littlefield, 2002).

5. Sidney Ahlstrom, *A Religious History of the American People* (New Haven, CT: Yale University Press, 1972), calls Whitefield "a tremendous engine of transformation in all the colonies" (281) and later "the Grand Itinerant" (283).

6. Stephen Nissenbaum, ed., *The Great Awakening at Yale College* (Belmont, CA: Wadsworth, 1969), 25; see also Gary Nash, *The Urban Crucible: Social Change, Political Consciousness and the Origins of the American Revolution* (Cambridge, MA: Harvard University Press, 1979), chap. 8.

7. Ahlstrom, *A Religious History*, 283.

8. Benjamin Franklin, *Autobiography and Other Writings* (New York: Signet, 1961), 119–20.

9. Nissenbaum, *Great Awakening at Yale*, 23. Louis L. Tucker, *Puritan Protagonist: Thomas Clap of Yale College* (Chapel Hill: University of North Carolina Press, 1962.); James E. Scanlon, "American College Presidents in the Eighteenth Century," *History of Education Quarterly* 11, no. 1 (Spring 1971): 72–77.

10. Edwin S. Gaustad, *The Great Awakening in New England* (New York: Harper, 1957); C. C. Goen, *Revivalism and Separatism in New England, 1740–1800* (New Haven, CT: Yale University Press, 1962).

11. *George Whitefield's Journals* (London: Banner of Truth Trust, 1960): Tennant, 16–17, 347; Davenport, 489, 516–17n; Buell, pastor of First Presbyterian Church at East Hampton, Long Island, NY, 516–17; Pemberton, who served as pastor of the First Presbyterian Church of New York City, 1727–53, 259–60, 528. In actual fact, many of these itinerants had begun their work before Whitefield galvanized public attention. See Douglas Sloan, *The Great Awakening and American Education* (New York: Teachers College Press, 1973).

12. *Whitefield's Journals*, 371.

13. One might note that in this same period Oxford University produced fewer graduates than its American counterparts. The reason lay with the rising costs of university education, indifference to poorer students, and a falling off of career opportunities for educated men. Lawrence Stone, "Size and Composition of Oxford Student Body, 1580–1910," in *The University in Society*, vol. 1 (Princeton, NJ: Princeton University Press, 1974), 42–50.

14. Robert Sklar, "The Great Awakening and Colonial Politics: Connecticut's the Minds of Men," *Bulletin of the Connecticut Historical Society* 28 (1963): 81–95.

15. Nissenbaum, *Great Awakening at Yale*, 254–58. Cf. Howard Miller, *The Revolutionary College: American Presbyterian Higher Education, 1707–1837* (New York: New York University Press, 1976), 101; James McLachlan, *Princetonians: A Biographical Dictionary* (Princeton, NJ: Princeton University Press, 1976).

16. Brooks Mather Kelly, *Yale: A History* (New Haven, CT: Yale University Press, 1974), 55; George W. Pierson, *The Founding of Yale: The Legend of the Forty Folios* (New Haven, CT: Yale University Press, 1988); Kathryn M. Moore, "The War with the Tutors: Student-Faculty Conflict at Harvard and Yale, 1745–1771," *History of Education Quarterly* 18, no. 2 (Summer 1978): 115–27.

17. Nissenbaum, *Great Awakening at Yale*, chap. 8.

18. Too many accounts synthesized by Frederick Rudolph's *The American College and University* (New York: Vintage Books, 1962) affected that text's oversimplified version of a complex Calvinist inheritance, one that drew on the scholarship of Samuel Eliot Morison and never mentioned a single item from the extraordinary opus of Perry Miller; Nissenbaum, *Great Awakening at Yale*, chap. 8.

19. Nissenbaum, *Great Awakening at Yale*, 28–34.

20. Ibid.

21. Ibid., 254. Collegiate status at Yale was fixed by the rector at the end of a student's first year and was a social rather than an academic designation. A student's class designation in the eighteenth century more often was the year of entry rather than the year of graduation.

22. Ibid., 208–16.

23. Actually the charge of Arminianism became so difficult to define because it was a charge made by revivalists against the established colleges as well as college leaders against the itinerants. Cf. Thomas J. Wertenbacker, *Princeton, 1746–1896* (Princeton, NJ: Princeton University Press, 1946), 26.

24. Perry Miller, *Errand into the Wilderness* (New York: Harper, 1956); Nissenbaum, *Great Awakening at Yale*, 142.

25. Christopher M. Jedry, *The World of John Cleaveland: Family and Community in Eighteenth-Century New England* (New York: W. W. Norton, 1979), 29. More often the ministerial-oriented graduates came from relatively modest, even rural, backgrounds and had fathers who were farmers or local officeholders rather than ministers themselves; also they tended to be older students, 30 percent of whom were over twenty between 1702 and 1750. See also Richard Warch, *School of the Prophets: Yale College, 1701–1740* (New Haven, CT: Yale University Press, 1973).

26. Nissenbaum, *Great Awakening at Yale*, 133.

27. Ibid., 70.

28. Ibid., 103.

29. Howard Miller, *The Revolutionary College: American Presbyterian Higher Education, 1707–1837* (New York: New York University Press, 1976), chap. 3; Perry Miller, *Errand into the Wilderness* (Cambridge, MA: Harvard University Press, 1964).

30. The older studies of Princeton, like Varnum Collins, *Princeton* (New York: Oxford University Press, 1914), stress the natural evolution of the school within an expanding and progressively nationalistic context. The stress for the Varnum Collins' s text stemmed from the 1896 conversion of the College of New Jersey into Princeton University and the new-named college's motto, "In the Nation's Service." Consequently for Collins the denominational dynamics of both the eighteenth-century college and the society are subordinated to the social and political events of the American Revolution. More recent studies, like Howard Miller's superb *The Revolutionary College: American Presbyterian Higher Education, 1707–1837* (New York: New York University Press, 1976), and Mark A. Noll's *Princeton and the Republic, 1768–1822* (Princeton, NJ: Princeton University Press, 1989), probe the Great Awakening's distinctive and disruptive impact on college founding, trying to explain the religious and millennial expectations of the eighteenth-century college. See also Ahlstrom, *A Religious History*, 289.

31. Wilson Smith, ed., *Theories of Education in Early America, 1655–1819* (New York: Bobbs Merrill Company, 1973), 145.

32. Thelin, *American Higher Education*, 14–15.

33. Ahlstrom, *A Religious History*, 376. Brown was chartered in 1764, opened in 1765, and graduated its first class of seven in 1769. The next year it moved its location from Warren to Providence. These dates are often confused in histories of Brown's "founding," but 1764 is usually given as the correct starting moment. William G. McLoughlin, *New England Dissent, 1630–1833: The Baptists and the Separation of Church and State* (Cambridge, MA: Harvard University Press, 1971), vol. 1, chap. 27; see also Walter C. Bronson, *The History of Brown University, 1764–1914* (Providence, RI: Brown University, 1914).

34. Richard McCormick, *Rutgers: A Bicentennial History* (1966); Thomas Frusciano, "Rutgers, the State University of New Jersey," in *Encyclopedia of New Jersey* (New Brunswick, NJ: Rutgers University Press, 2005), 709.

35. The university has insisted on several founding dates but grounds its origins definitively in 1755 and the award of a charter for the "College, Academy and Charitable School of Philadelphia." The instigators of this event were several groups of Philadelphians, sometimes craftsmen, sometimes, merchants, but, according to institutional lore, all stemmed from Benjamin Franklin, who drew upon his deist biases and the city's Quaker influences to assure a conscious nonsectarianism alongside a distinctly secular and work-oriented curriculum. However, the building that

housed the school was a large structure, erected in 1740–42 to shelter the preaching of Rev. George Whitefield. This event gave the university in some quarters to claim 1740 as its founding date. Edward Potts Cheyney, *A History of the University of Pennsylvania, 1740–1940* (Philadelphia: University of Pennsylvania Press, 1940), chaps. 1–3; Martin Meyerson and Dilys Pegler Winegrand, *Gladly Learn and Gladly Teach: Franklin and His Heirs at the University of Pennsylvania, 1740–1976* (Philadelphia: University of Pennsylvania Press, 1978), chap. 2. A statue of the famous itinerant—George Whitefield—stands today in the university's quadrangle to memorialize his connection to the school's origins; Edmund Morgan, *Benjamin Franklin* (New Haven, CT: Yale University Press, 2002), 21–22.

36. Douglas Sloan, *The Scottish Enlightenment and the American College Ideal* (New York: Teachers College Press, 1971), 42–60; Jurgen Herbst, *From Crisis to Crisis: American College Government, 1636–1819* (Cambridge, MA: Harvard University Press, 1982), chap. 6.

37. Sloan, *Scottish Enlightenment*, 42–60.

38. Ibid.

39. Richard Bushman, *From Puritan to Yankee: Character and Social Order in Connecticut, 1690–1765* (New York: W. W. Norton, 1967), 243–45.

40. Tucker, *Puritan Protagonist*, 76.

41. Jurgen Herbst, "The Eighteenth-Century Split between Private and Public Higher Education in the United States," *History of Education Quarterly* 15, no. 3 (Fall 1975): 273–80.

42. Tucker, *Puritan Protagonist*, chaps. 4 and 5.

43. Quoted in Joann M. Kusk, "Fund-Raising in Colonial Colleges, 1745-1770" (1989), New York University Archives, 5. See also Margaret W. Masson, "Pessimism Surpassed: New Colleges as Bastions against Barbarism in North America," *Studies in Eighteenth-Century Culture* 8 (1979): 69–86; Beverley McAnear, "The Raising of Funds by the Colonial Colleges," *Mississippi Valley Historical Review* 38, no. 4 (March, 1952): 591–612. Benefactions (over half from British donors) and lotteries paid for extraordinary expenses, like buildings and libraries. Operational costs required horseback circuitry. Equally formidable an impediment to college entrance was cost. David Humphrey estimated that only one in ten New Yorkers could afford King's College's tuition (£200 to £350 for four years), ensuring effectively that only professionals, more affluent businessmen, and large landholders (rather than farmers) were the real target group of recruitment rhetoric. David Humphrey, *From King's College to Columbia, 1746–1800* (New York: Columbia University Press, 1976), 94–98.

44. McAnear, "The Raising of Funds," 598. The sole exception was Queen's College, founded by the Dutch, which sought a separation from the Amsterdam classis. They petitioned and received a charter from England in 1766 but fell out of favor when they resisted merger with either the College of New Jersey or King's College in New York. Dutch evangelicals thus could raise money in neither Holland nor England. See Kusk, "Fund-Raising in Colonial Colleges," 13.

45. This perception took institutional form in 1808 when the first seminary for ministerial instruction was founded in Andover, Massachusetts. "Andover Theological Seminary," in *Cyclopedia of Education*, ed. Paul Monroe (New York: Macmillan, 1911), 1:121.

46. Phyllis Vine, "Another Look at Eighteenth-Century Colleges," *History of Education Quarterly* 18, no. 1 (Spring 1978): 61–69; William D. Carrell, "America College Professors, 1750–1800," *History of Education Quarterly* 8, no. 3 (Fall 1968): 289–305, 358–74.

47. Perry Miller, *Jonathan Edwards* (New York: William Sloan Associates, 1949). Miller particularly emphasizes Edwards's fascination with the writings of John Locke and the possibilities of science.

48. Princeton seems to have been the most successful cultivator of these "feeder" networks, establishing in a remarkably short period, a chain of Presbyterian academies, especially in the South. Cf. Miller, *The Revolutionary College*. Douglas Sloan in his introductory remarks to *The Great Awakening and American Education* (26) estimated that the academies founded by New Light revivalists,

especially in the Middle and Southern Colonies, would number more than fifty by the end of the Revolutionary War, a number of them evolving into colleges themselves; Donald R. Come, "The Influence of Princeton on Higher Education in the South before 1825," *William and Mary Quarterly*, 3rd ser., 2 (1945): 359–96.

49. Peter D. Hall, *The Organization of American Culture, 1700–1900: Private Institutions, Elites and the Origins of American Nationality* (New York: New York University Press, 1984), esp. chaps. 1–3; Alan Heimert and Perry Miller, eds., *The Great Awakening* (Indianapolis: Bobbs-Merrill, 1967); Phyllis Vine, "The Social Function of Eighteenth-Century Higher Education," *History of Education Quarterly* 16, no. 4 (Winter 1976): 409–24.

50. David D. Hall, "Religion and Society: Problems and Reconsiderations," in *Colonial British America: Essays on the New History of the Early Modern Era*, ed. Jack P. Greene and J. R. Pole (Baltimore: Johns Hopkins University Press, 1984), 325–26.

CHAPTER TWO

1. James McLachlan, "Education," in *Scotland and the Americas, 1600–1800* (Providence, RI: John Carter Brown Library, Brown University, 1995), 65–75. This study of the 818 college or university migrants to the American colonies found that 26 percent (213) went to New England, while 74 percent (605) went into the Chesapeake. The statistics here represent the entire cohort rather than a sample; James McLachlan Archives; Morison, *The Founding of Harvard College*, 92–100, reports no fewer than thirty-five Cambridge emigrants to America had formal connections to Emmanuel College (founded 1584), whose statutes were imitated when graduates like Harvard president Henry Dunster needed a model to draw upon.

2. Samuel Eliot Morison, *Three Centuries of Harvard University* (Cambridge, MA: Harvard University Press, 1936); William Haller, *The Rise of Puritanism* (New York: Columbia University Press, 1938), chap. 1.

3. David Hackett Fischer, *Albion's Seed: Four British Folkways in America* (New York: Oxford University Press, 1989), 326. Fischer states, "Rates of mortality may have been twice as high in tidewater Virginia as in rural Massachusetts, and higher also than in many parts of England during the seventeenth century."

4. Courtlandt Canby, "A Note upon the Influence of Oxford University upon William and Mary College in the Eighteenth Century," *William and Mary Quarterly*, 2nd ser., 21 (July 1941): 243–47.

5. Robert Emmett Curran, SJ, *The Bicentennial of Georgetown University*, vol. 1, *From Academy to University, 1789–1889* (Washington, DC: Georgetown University Press, 1993), 5; Geoffrey Holt, SJ, *St. Omers and Bruges Colleges, 1593–1773* (London: Catholic Record Society, 1979); Paul H. Mattingly, "A Maryland Jesuit in Eighteenth-Century Europe," *Maryland Historical Magazine* (Summer 2012): 1–14.

6. James McLachlan, "Education," in *Scotland and the Americas, 1600–1800*, exhibition catalog (Providence, RI: John Carter Brown Library, 1995), 65–76.

7. Ibid.; see also Fischer, *Albion's Seed*, esp. "The South of England to Virginia," 207–418; Carole Shammas, "English-Born and Creole Elites in Turn-of-the-Century Virginia," in *The Chesapeake in the Seventeenth Century*, ed. Thad Tate and David Ammerman (New York: Norton, 1979), 274–96.

8. Bernard Bailyn, "Politics and Social Structure in Virginia," in *Shaping Southern Society: The Colonial Experience*, ed. Timothy H. Breen (New York: Oxford University Press, 1976), 193–214.

9. Jack Greene and J. R. Pole, eds., *Colonial British America: Essays in the New History of the Early Modern Era* (Baltimore: Johns Hopkins University Press, 1984), 142–43, 148–50; John J. McCusker and Russell R. Menard, eds., *The Economy of British America* (Chapel Hill: University of North Carolina Press, 1985), esp. chap. 10, "The Growth of Population"; Gloria Main, *Tobacco Colony* (Princeton, NJ: Princeton University Press, 1982).

10. McLachlan, *Scotland and the Americas*, 66.

11. John Rainbolt, "The Absence of Towns in Seventeenth-Century Virginia," *Journal of Southern History* 35 (1969): 343–60; Carville Earle and Ronald Hoffman, "Stable Crops and Urban Development in the Eighteenth-Century South," *Perspectives in American History* 10 (1976): 77–78.

12. Sydney E. Ahlstrom, *A Religious History of the American People* (New Haven, CT: Yale University Press, 1972), 188–92, notes that the legislative assembly, the House of Burgesses, created (and often poorly supported) parishes, which were managed by a lay vestry, usually of substantive landowners. "Libraries," in *Encyclopedia of Southern Culture*, ed. Charles Reagan Wilson and William Ferris (Chapel Hill: University of North Carolina Press, 1989), 255–57. For both the seventeenth and eighteenth centuries, libraries were more important than colleges in the intellectual life of the Southern Colonies. The libraries of William Byrd of Westover, John Mercer, and Robert Carter of Nomini Hall set the model for the intellectually ambitious landholder. In eighteenth-century Georgia, Rev. George Whitefield's Bethesda Orphanage concentrated on the creation of an important library that its founder hoped would become a college. Cf. Joseph F. Kett and Patricia A. McClung, "Book Culture in Post-Revolutionary Virginia," *Proceedings of the American Antiquarian Society* 94, pt. 1 (1984): 97–147.

13. Louis Wright and Marion Tinling, eds., *The Great American Gentleman: The Secret Diary of William Byrd of Westover in Virginia, 1709–1712* (New York: Capricorn Books, 1963); cf. Lawrence Cremin, *American Education: The Colonial Experience, 1607–1783* (New York: Harper and Row, 1970), 1:393. Byrd was sent to England at an early age where he attended a grammar school in Essex and afterward Middle Temple before a brief business training in Holland. His education ended in 1704, at age thirty, with the death of his father and his return to his Virginia responsibilities. *The Great American Gentleman*, 3–4.

14. Cremin, *American Education*, chap. 11; Fischer, *Albion's Seed*, 344–49.

15. Fischer, *Albion's Seed*, 344–49; William Byrd matter-of-factly reported the infusion of £500 from Queen Anne in June 1709. Cf. Wright and Tinling, *The Great American Gentleman*, 28.

16. Cremin, *American Education*, 342–43; John Calam, *Parsons and Pedagogues* (New York: Columbia University Press, 1971).

17. McLachlan, *Scotland and the Americas*, 67. These clergymen divided into 115 Episcopalians and twenty-three Presbyterians. Scottish migrants to the Chesapeake resisted the high mortality patterns more quickly than their English counterparts. The average age of death for Scottish migrants after 1700 was sixty-seven; for the English, fifty-four. Though a minority, the Scots were longer lived and hence influential beyond their numbers. See also Douglas Sloan, *The Scottish Enlightenment and the American College Ideal* (New York: Teachers College Press, 1971), and Richard B. Sher and Jeffrey R. Smitten, eds., *Scotland and America in the Age of Enlightenment* (Princeton, NJ: Princeton University Press, 1990).

18. David C. Humphrey, "British Influences on Eighteenth-Century American Education," *History of Education Quarterly* 13 (Spring 1973): 65–72.

19. David Hackett Fischer and James C Kelly, *Bound Away: Virginia and the Westward Movement* (Charlottesville: University of Virginia Press, 2000), chap. 1, "Migration to Virginia." The study argued persuasively that in Virginia Governor William Berkeley recruited many second sons of the British aristocracy in the period 1650–70 who for a time applied British values (social stratification, political arrogance, personal display) to their coastal estates and operations.

20. Rhys Isaac, *The Transformation of Virginia, 1740–1790* (Chapel Hill: University of North Carolina Press, 1982), 194–98.

21. James Turner, *Philology: The Forgotten Origins of the Modern Humanities* (Princeton, NJ: Princeton University Press, 2014), 85–88; Hugh Kearney, "Locke and the Politics of Education," *History of Education Quarterly* 12 (Spring 1972): 107–15; see also Kearney's *Scholars and Gentlemen: Universities and Society in Pre-Industrial Britain* (Ithaca, NY: Cornell University Press, 1970). Many members of the Royal Society held degrees from Oxford.

22. Cremin, *American Education*, 229, 232; John Lawson and Harold Silver, *A Social History of Education in England* (London: Methuen, 1973), 125, 132. Gresham enrolled no students, awarded no degrees, and made its lectures available free to the public. From the beginning it considered itself both an institution of higher learning and a challenge to the established colleges and universities of England.

23. Park Rouse, *James Blair of Virginia* (Chapel Hill: University of North Carolina Press, 1971).

24. David C. Humphrey, "Colonial Colleges and English Dissenting Academies: A Study in Transatlantic Culture," *History of Education Quarterly* 12 (Spring 1972): 184–97.

25. Nicholas Phillipson, "Commerce and Culture: Edinburgh, Edinburgh University and the Scottish Enlightenment," in *The University and the City: From Medieval Origins to the Present*, ed. Thomas Bender (New York: Oxford University Press, 1988), 100–16; Sloan, *The Scottish Enlightenment*.

26. McLachlan, *Scotland and the Americas*, 68–69. The Penal Laws put great pressure on colonial Catholics in the matter of higher education, no less than in office holding, arms bearing, etc. By comparison, during the colonial period, 14 percent (forty-four) of European-trained Americans attended Oxford and 17 percent (fifty-five) studied at Cambridge. The Scottish bias seems to have been affected largely by Glasgow's dominance of the tobacco trade in the same period, an example, as McLachlan says, of intellect following commerce. Scottish universities also had an international reputation for their medical instruction.

27. Fischer and Kelly, *Bound Away*, chap. 2, "Migration in Virginia."

28. Brubacher, *Higher Education in Transition*; Hofstadter, *Academic Freedom in the Age of the College*, 75–77; Wertenbacker, *Princeton*, 81–89; http://en.wikipedia.org/wiki/Dissenting_academies.

29. Humphrey, "Colonial Colleges"; see also Lawson and Silver, *Social History of Education in England*, 132. The concrete attraction of the dissenting academies for the American colleges was alternative sources of revenue and books. On the very gradual emergence of Locke's and Newton's teaching within the sleeve of older (and contradictory) modes of instruction, see the very perceptive analysis of Edmund P. Morgan, *The Gentle Puritan: A Life of Ezra Stiles, 1727–1795* (New Haven, CT: Yale University Press, 1962), 48–57.

30. Cf. chapter 1.

31. Keith Thomas, *Religion and the Decline of Magic (New York: Scribner's, 1971)*; see also chapter 1 of this study.

32. Jurgen Herbst, "The First Three American Colleges: Schools of the Reformation," *Perspectives in American History* 8 (1974): 7–52; Lawrence Stone, "The Educational Revolution in England, 1560–1640)," *Past and Present*, no. 28 (July 1964).

33. Herbst, "First Three American Colleges," 28. During her reign, Elizabeth I created Trinity College, Dublin (1592), which was given degree-granting privileges in the hopes of making it the center of a full-fledged university. Earlier in 1582 Edinburgh College in Scotland was created but without degree-granting privileges, a nuance the institution functionally ignored, like its counterparts in the American colonies.

34. See Michael Heyd, "The Geneva Academy in the Eighteenth Century: A Calvinist Seminary or a Civic University," 79–99, and Anthony Grafton, "Civic Humanism and Scientific Scholarship at Lieden," 59–78, both in *The University and the City*, ed. Thomas Bender (New York: Oxford, 1986); see also Alan Karp, "John Calvin and the Geneva Academy: Roots of the Board of Trustees," *History of Higher Education Annual* 5 (1985): 3–41.

35. Herbst, "The First Three American Colleges," 40–45. In New England the source and control of collegiate funds came from public money; in Virginia the British Crown became the primary funder of William and Mary College. However, both variations remained not corporations but rather colony-wide trusts that were governed by boards of trustees. As such, Herbst argues, their organizational roots are grounded on Reformation blueprints rather than on medieval, royal, or local/city models. See the complementary argument in A. Bailey Cutts, "The Educational

Influence of Aberdeen in Seventeenth-Century Virginia," *William and Mary Quarterly*, 2nd ser., 15 (July 1935): 229–49.

36. Frederick Rudolph, *Curriculum: A History of the American Undergraduate Curriculum since 1636* (San Francisco: Jossey Bass, 1977).

37. Thomas Bender makes the intriguing point that the force of the European city, especially in the cases of Leiden, Geneva, and Edinburgh, during the Enlightenment was the primary reason for their transformations from earlier forms of schooling into serious university life. *The University and the City*, 6.

38. Benjamin Franklin, *Autobiography* (New York: A Signet Classic, 1961), 72–75.

39. Isaac, *The Transformation of Virginia*, 285–95.

40. Robert D. Heslep, *Thomas Jefferson and Education* (New York: Random House, 1969), 33.

41. *The Life and Selected Writings of Thomas Jefferson*, ed. Adrienne Koch and William Peden (New York: Modern Library, 1944), 4–5.

42. Ibid., 5.

43. See Letter to Thomas Jefferson Randolph, Washington, DC, November 24, 1808, in *Crusade against Ignorance: Thomas Jefferson on Education*, ed. Gordon Lee (New York: Teachers College Press, 1961), 156; in Europe these informal instructions went back more than a century. Peter Burke, *A Social History of Knowledge: From Gutenberg to Diderot* (Cambridge: Polity Press, 2000), 47–48.

44. Daniel Boorstin, *The Mysterious Science of the Law* (Cambridge, MA: Harvard University Press, 1941). Jefferson himself worried about Blackstone's Tory propensities and in his correspondence recommended Sir Edward Coke's *Commentary on Littleton* and his Whiggish interpretations of the English common law. Honeywell, *Jefferson*, 122.

45. Letter to John Bannister, Paris, October 15, 1785, in Lee, *Crusade against Ignorance*, 107.

46. Ibid., 109. This insistence on college-training at home had become a commonplace for those who despaired of family or church regulating the apprenticeship to republican leadership. See Phyllis Vine, "The Social Function of Eighteenth-Century Higher Education," *History of Education Quarterly* 16, no. 4 (Winter 1976): 409–24.

47. David Robson, *Educating Republicans: The College in the Era of the American Revolution, 1750–1800* (Westport, CT: Greenwood Press, 1985), 106–11.

48. James Maury, "On the Education Appropriate for a Virginia Gentleman (1762)," in *Education in the United States: A Documentary History*, vol. 1, ed. Sol Cohen (New York: Random House, 1974), 453–57.

49. Jack P. Greene, "Foundations of Political Power in the Virginia House of Burgesses, 1720–1776," in Breen, *Shaping Southern Society*, 219–20. Greene notes that only two went to Oxford and one to Cambridge, while two or three went to Edinburgh University; Christopher Hill, "The Inns of Court," *History of Education Quarterly* 12, no. 4 (Winter 1972): 543–50.

50. This political responsibility of the Chesapeake planter not only provided a visible social service, which the public judged; it permitted planters inside information on land and shipping transactions. The rise in wealth and power, though grounded in landholding, did not come primarily from crop profits but from a planter's lending and investments. Thus, the "useful education" of history and law, which commentators recommended to college builders, necessarily was an integral part of Chesapeake husbandry and enterprise. Cf. Aubrey Land, "Economic Base and Social Structure: The Northern Chesapeake in the Eighteenth Century," in Breen, *Shaping Southern Society*, 232–46.

51. Lee, *Crusade against Ignorance*, 83–97.

52. Roy J. Honeywell, *The Educational Work of Thomas Jefferson* (Cambridge, MA: Harvard University Press, 1931 [reprint 1964]), xvi. Honeywell notes Jefferson's shifting references—sometimes ten, sometimes more—to the actual number of school districts, which he (Honeywell) puts at twenty. Of course, these twenty would be at public expense, but the affluent gentry could still

send their sons only by paying tuition. See also Roy J. Honeywell, "A Note on the Educational Work of Thomas Jefferson," *History of Education Quarterly* 9, no. 1 (Spring 1969): 64–72.

53. Rhys Isaac, "Evangelical Revolt: The Nature of the Baptists' Challenge to the Traditional Order in Virginia, 1765 to 1775," *William and Mary Quarterly*, 3rd ser., 31 (1974): 345–68.

54. Ahlstrom, *A Religious History*, 320–24, 371–79.

55. Lee, *Crusade against Ignorance*, 145.

56. Jennings Wagoner, "Constraint and Variety in Virginia Higher Education," *History of Education Quarterly* 25 (1985): 184; Honeywell, *Jefferson*, 125–26.

57. Lee, *Crusade against Ignorance*, 148.

58. James E. Scanlon, *Randolph-Macon College: A Southern History* (Charlottesville: University of Virginia Press, 1983), 20.

59. Honeywell, *Jefferson*, 128.

60. Ibid., 135. The UVA charter dated from 1819, and its doors opened in 1825.

61. Ibid., 110–11. His inability to receive students properly prepared in Latin grieved him severely and rendered dysfunctional the many books in the classical languages he had already purchased for the university library.

62. Ibid., 132. The university's only caveat was that all "graduates" had to have mastered Latin.

63. Paul V. Turner, *Campus* (Cambridge, MA: MIT Press, 1984), 76–87; Honeywell, *Jefferson*, 79; Garry Wills, *Mr. Jefferson's University* (Washington, DC: National Geographic, 2002), 71, 77, 93.

64. Letter of TJ to Littleton Waller Tazewell, January 5, 1805, quoted in Jennings Waggoner, "Honor and Dishonor at Mr. Jefferson's University: The Antebellum Years," *History of Education Quarterly* 26, no. 2 (Summer 1986):157. For a thoroughgoing discussion of the "republican biases" in late eighteenth-century collegiate curriculum, see Robson, *Educating Republicans*, chap 3.

65. Andover Theological Seminary, often considered the first in the country, emerged in 1808; Princeton Theological Seminary was founded in 1812. Mark Noll, *Princeton and the Republic, 1768–1822* (Princeton, NJ: Princeton University Press, 1989), 255–56. There were other forces, too, like Unitarianism, that explain the rise of the seminaries. However, they could be collectively grouped under the notion of "secularism" for which Jefferson became a potent metaphor. See also Merrill Peterson, *The Jeffersonian Image in the American Mind* (New York: Oxford University Press, 1962), 241–43.

66. Cf. "Report of the Commissioners Appointed to Fix the Suite of the University of Virginia" (1818), in Lee, *Crusade against Ignorance*, 119.

67. Jurgen Herbst, *From Crisis to Crisis: American College Government, 1636–1819* (Cambridge, MA: Harvard University Press, 1982), 244–53.

68. Curran, *Georgetown University*, vol. 1. See also Robson, *Educating Republicans*, which curiously omits any discussion of Georgetown (founded 1789).

69. Merle Borrowman, "The False Dawn of the State University," *History of Education Quarterly* 1, no. 2 (June 1961): 6–22; Allen Nevins, *The State Universities and Democracy* (Urbana: University of Illinois Press, 1962). One should note that the University of Vermont, created in 1791, was the only experiment outside the South to attempt a state-supported institution.

70. Edmund Morgan, *The Gentle Puritan: The Life of Ezra Stiles, 1727–1795* (New Haven, CT: Yale University Press, 1962), 363.

71. Robson, *Educating Republicans*, 202–3.

72. Ibid., 91–93.

73. Ibid., 152.

74. This pattern pertained also to denominational colleges in the South in both the eighteenth and nineteenth centuries. See Robert Polk Thompson, "Colleges in the Revolutionary South: The Shaping of a Tradition," *History of Education Quarterly* 10, no. 4 (Winter 1970): 399–412.

75. Jurgen Herbst, "The American Revolution and the American University," *Perspectives in American History* 10 (1976): 279–354; John F. Roche, *The Colonial Colleges in the War for American Independence* (Millwood, NY: Associated Faculty Press, 1986).

76. Wagoner, "Honor and Dishonor at Mr. Jefferson's University," 154–79; Virginius Dabney, *Mr. Jefferson's University: A History* (Charlottesville: University Press of Virginia, 1981).

CHAPTER THREE

1. The author wishes to express his thanks to James E. Scanlon and Roger Geiger for especially close and face-saving critiques of this essay in earlier drafts. Two anonymous readers of the *History of Higher Education Annual* also contributed substantively to the published version in vol. 17 (1997): 73–96. The current essay is substantially different and revised from the previously published version.

2. James McLachlan, "The American College in the Nineteenth Century: Towards a Reappraisal," *Teachers College Record* 80, no. 2 (December 1978): 287–306.

3. Harvey Graff, *The Literacy Myth: Literacy and Social Structure in the Nineteenth-Century City* (New York: Academic Press, 1979).

4. Colin Burke, *American Collegiate Populations: A Test of the Traditional View* (New York: New York University Press, 1982), 14. Burke puts the number at 241 colleges, which included some seventy institutions operating at a preparatory level, hence the discrepancy between Burke's and McLachlan's figures. The difference underscores the mercurial meaning of "college" in these years.

5. Ibid., 19.

6. Daniel Boorstin, "Culture with Many Capitals: The Booster College," in *The Americans: The National Experience* (New York: Vintage Books. 1965), 152–61.

7. Perry Miller, *The Life of the Mind in America: From the Revolution to the Civil War* (New York: Harcourt Brace and World, 1965), 40–43. Miller argues that this "voluntary principle" set the context for a new brand of nationality that embraced denominational diversity and individual freedom as bastions against didactic European institutions, both religious and political. A generation of informal organizations—from camp meetings to fraternal societies—carried a message of mutual social improvement without dogmatism. See also R. Jackson Lears, "Mass Culture and Its Critics," in *Encyclopedia of American Social History*, vol. 3 (New York: Charles Scribner's Sons, 1993), 1599, discussing the special role Alexis de Tocqueville assigned to "voluntary associations" in antebellum America.

8. Ralph Waldo Emerson captured the ideological heart of this concept in his 1841 essay "Self-Reliance," his most often cited writing (and the most misunderstood). Gay Wilson Allen, *Waldo Emerson* (New York: Penguin Books, 1981), 360–70.

9. Sidney Ahlstrom, *A Religious History of the American People* (New Haven, CT: Yale University Press, 1972), 513–14; Charles Lippy, "Religion," in *Encyclopedia of American Society History*, vol. 1 (New York: Charles Scribner's Sons, 1993), 516–17; Paul Conkin, *The Uneasy Center: Reformed Christianity in Antebellum America* (Chapel Hill: University of North Carolina Press, 1995), 139–41. Conkin notes that the Congregationalists and Presbyterians dominated college founding in this period and exceeded those of the Baptists and Methodists. Still, in these years the denominations cultivated an organized interdenominationalism that aspired to a national presence, a goal that was modified by 1850 as Roman Catholics became the dominant minority and succeeded in creating a number of permanent colleges. Jay Dolan, *The American Catholic Experience* (New York: Doubleday, 1984), 249–50.

10. Wilson Smith, *Professors and Public Ethics: Studies of Northern Moral Philosophers before the Civil War* (Ithaca, NY: Cornell University Press, 1956), 77–80; Daniel Walker Howe, *The Political Culture of the American Whigs* (Chicago: University of Chicago Press, 1979), 218. Howe's fine study talks very little about the college surge in this period, but his exploration of a new institutional sensibility nevertheless applies to this burst of college founding.

11. Jonathan Messerli, *Horace Mann* (New York: Alfred Knopf, 1971); Cremin, *American Education*, 133–43.

12. Cf. Gregory H. Singleton, "Protestant Voluntary Organizations and the Shaping of Victorian America," in *Victorian America*, ed. Daniel Walker Howe (Philadelphia: University of Pennsylvania Press, 1976), 47–58; Paul H. Mattingly *The Classless Profession: American Schoolmen in the Nineteenth Century* (New York: New York University Press, 1975), esp. chap. 3. Key materials for this book are preserved in Paul Mattingly Collection on the American Institute of Instruction, Special Collections, Monroe C. Gutman Library, Harvard Graduate School of Education.

13. David Allmendinger, *Paupers and Scholars: The Transformation of Student Life in Nineteenth-Century New England* (New York: St. Martin's Press, 1975), studied the then backcountry colleges of Williams, Amherst, Bowdoin, Dartmouth, Waterville, etc., and found many of their students varied in ages and were often poor, having to earn their way through college. For them accessibility to schooling trumped denominational allegiances.

14. Cf. Jack C. Lane, "The Yale Report of 1828 and Liberal Education: A Neorepublican Manifesto," *History of Education Quarterly* 27, no. 3 (Fall 1987): 325–38. Constructively, this article contributes to a rejection of early interpretations that made the report a conservative atavism, but it overstates the historical agency of the report on both American colleges and American culture.

15. The word "university" derives from the Latin *universitas*, which refers to a group or guild of individuals committed to the transfer and advancement of knowledge. Although such instruction occurred in monastic organizations since the sixth century, the word "university" generally originates with the 1088 founding of the University of Bologna due to its legal charter, *Constitutio Habita*. It is the oldest, continually operating university independent of king, emperor, or religious sponsorship. The University of Paris (ca. 1150) arose out of a cathedral school, one of the few universities to do so. A number of European universities began with regal sponsorship, like Charles University in Prague, founded by King Charles IV in 1348. Oxford University originated from schooling in the eleventh century but generally puts its official date at 1167 when King Henry II banned English students from attending the University of Paris. Oxford and Cambridge (1209) are privately governed but "public" institutions with substantial government funding over the years. Most scholars agree with Walter Ruegg that the "university," in spite of variations, is primarily a European organization. Hilde de Ridder-Symoens, ed., *A History of the University in Europe*, vol. 1, Universities in the Middle Ages (Cambridge: Cambridge University Press 1992), xix; http://en.wikipedia.org/wiki/university.

16. *National Intelligencer*, September 9, 1835. For a collegiate history that should serve as a model of the historical genre, see Robert Emmett Curran, SJ, *The Bicentennial History of Georgetown University*, vol. 1, *From Academy to University, 1789–1889* (Washington, DC: Georgetown University Press, 1993). The college had been founded in 1789 as the first Roman Catholic College in America and operated until 1815 without a charter. For the first several decades of the nineteenth-century, non-Catholic students variously comprised one-quarter to one-third of the student body.

17. Thomas Bender, Peter D. Hall, Thomas Haskell, and Paul H. Mattingly, "Institutionalization and Education in the Nineteenth and Twentieth Centuries," *History of Education Quarterly* 20, no. 4 (Winter 1980): 449–72.

18. *National Intelligencer*, July 10, 1833. Due to stipulations in Girard's will as well as trustee interpretation of it, Girard College did not begin its actual operation until January 1848, when it admitted one hundred orphans. Within little more than a year, its students numbered about three hundred. Most of these were assigned to a "preparatory" department (ages six to ten) while plans were afoot for intermediate (ages ten to fourteen) and collegiate departments (ages fourteen to eighteen). Cf. Henry W. Arey, *The Girard College and Its Founder* (Philadelphia: C. Sherman, 1854).

19. See Daniel Walker Howe, *The Political Culture of the American Whigs* (Chicago: University of Chicago Press, 1979), esp. 182–84. Of course, de Tocqueville remarked extensively on the ubiquitous voluntary associations in *Democracy in America*, considering them major devices for countering divisive party organization in a democracy.

20. Burke, *American Collegiate Populations*, 43–50, discusses antebellum endowments, stressing that most colleges thought themselves fortunate to have endowments whose interest covered

the president's salary (usually averaging between $1,500 and $2,000). See also Merle Curti and Roderick Nash, *Philanthropy and the Shaping of American Higher Education* (New Brunswick, NJ: Rutgers University Press, 1965). Girard fully expected his legacy would pay building costs as well as operational expenses. The will has been, in part, anthologized in Edgar Knight and Clifton Hall, eds., *Readings in American Educational History* (New York: Appleton Century Crofts, 1951), 247–55.

21. Bray Hammond, *Banking and Politics in the Jacksonian Era* (Princeton, NJ: Princeton University Press, 1957). The connotations of endurance and power were short-lived for the bank, which was vetoed by President Jackson in 1832 and which only survived until 1836. In spite of its failure, the bank served antebellum orators as a metaphor of centralized institutional power and aristocracy for well over a generation afterward. See also Arthur M. Schlesinger Jr., *The Age of Jackson* (Boston: Little Brown, 1945), 91.

22. Cf. Louis Romano, "Manual and Industrial Education at Girard College, 1831–1865: An Era of American Educational Experimentation" (unpublished PhD diss., New York University, 1975), chap 3.

23. Cf. Burke, *American Collegiate Populations*, esp. chap. 1. Until Colin Burke's pathbreaking book, the conventional wisdom of Frederick Rudolph's *The American College and University* followed Donald Tewkesbury's argument that early nineteenth-century colleges experienced an extraordinary pattern of "failure." Tewkesbury made his calculations based on the number of college charters awarded by state legislatures, without ever reflecting on how promotional and political such exercises were. In terms of colleges *actually founded and operative*—Burke's methodology—antebellum colleges experienced surprisingly little failure, however erratic their funding and administration. But these contextual features of varied resources meant that the "college" was not a functional, generic school even in the antebellum era. See also Natalie Naylor's insightful "The Ante-Bellum College Movement: A Reappraisal of Tewksbury's Founding of American Colleges and Universities," *History of Education Quarterly* 13, no. 3 (Fall 1973): 261–74.

24. "Girard College," in *Cyclopedia of Education*, ed. Paul Monroe (New York: Macmillan, 1913), 3:113. Girard College gradually assumed features more common to other colleges after the Civil War. The process by which its organization grew beyond service to youth between ages six and ten and reworded Stephen Girard's original will is detailed in Romano, "Girard College." See also Cheesman Herrick, *History of Girard College* (Philadelphia: Girard College, 1927).

25. *National Intelligencer*, July 10, 1833. In Girard's will he explicitly proclaimed the civic sweep of his educational goals: "I would have them . . . by every proper means a pure attachment to our republican institutions, and to the sacred rights of conscience, as guaranteed by our happy constitution, shall be formed and fostered in the minds of the scholars." "Girard College and Its Founder," *American Journal of Education* 27 (Hartford, 1897): 593–616.

26. *National Intelligencer*, July 10, 1833. Peter Hall makes the essential argument about the place of trusts in college development, a major tenet of antebellum Whig politics as well as the nemesis of their Jacksonian opponents. See Hall, *Organization of American Culture*, chap. 6.

27. Girard explicitly charged the college "to instill into the minds of the scholars the *purest principles of morality*, so that, on their entrance into active life, they may, *from inclination and habit*, evince *benevolence towards their fellow creatures*, and *a love of truth, sobriety and industry*, adopting at the same time such religious tenets as their *matured reason* may enable them to prefer." Cf. Knight and Hall, *Readings*, 254.

28. Howe, *Political Culture of the American Whigs*, 181–84; see also Hall, *Organization of American Culture*, chap. 8. Put very simply, Jacksonian republicanism in the antebellum period favored publicly supported and locally rooted institutions, hence Jackson's antipathy to the Bank of the United States. The Whig republican tradition regularly stressed a translocal, if not national perspective, which accommodated a range of institutional genres, from the Bank of the United States to nascent bureaucracies like Horace Mann's Massachusetts public school system.

29. Perry Miller, "The Voluntary Principle," in *The Life of the Mind in America* (New York: Harcourt Brace and World, 1965), 40–43. For the broader educational co-option of the evangelical tra-

dition, see Mattingly, *The Classless Profession*, and David Tyack and Elizabeth Hansot, *Managers of Virtue: Public School Leadership in America, 1820–1980* (New York: Basic Books, 1982).

30. Mark A. Noll, *Princeton and the Republic, 1768–1822* (Princeton, NJ: Princeton University Press, 1989).

31. Daniel Boorstin, *The Americans: The National Experience* (New York: Vintage Books, 1965), chap. 20, "Culture with Many Capitals: The Booster College."

32. Allmendinger, *Paupers and Scholars*.

33. Rudolph, *American College and University*, chaps. 5–10.

34. Roy J. Honeywell, *The Educational Writings of Thomas Jefferson* (Cambridge, MA: Harvard University Press, 1931), esp. chap. 2.

35. This differentiation offered only the advantage of declaring an alternative to the traditional term "college" that Dartmouth had used. In the antebellum period, "college" and "university" appeared to contain no real differences of structure or meaning.

36. John Whitehead, *The Separation of College and State* (New Haven, CT: Yale University Press, 1973), chap. 2; Jean Edward Smith, *John Marshall: Definer of a Nation* (New York: Henry Holt, 1996), 433–38; "Dartmouth College Case," in *Cyclopedia of Education*, ed. Paul Monroe (New York: Macmillan, 1912), 2:252.

37. Rudolph, *American College and University*, 211.

38. Cf. Ronald Story, *The Forging of an Aristocracy* (Middletown, CT: Wesleyan University Press, 1980), 148–49; Codman Hislop, *Eliphalet Nott* (Middletown, CT: Wesleyan University Press, 1971), 201–2. I am obliged to Roger Geiger for noticing these Dartmouth College case connections.

39. Burke, *American Collegiate Populations*, 41.

40. Peter D. Hall, "The Spirit of the Ordinance of 1787: Organizational Values, Voluntary Associations and Higher Education in Ohio, 1803–1830," in *"Schools and the Means of Education Shall Forever Be Encouraged": A History of Education in the Old Northwest, 1787–1880*, ed. Paul H. Mattingly and Edward W. Stevens Jr. (Athens: Ohio University Libraries, 1987), 97–114.

41. Steven Novak, "The College in the Dartmouth College Case: A Reinterpretation," *New England Quarterly* 47, no. 4 (December 1974): 550–63. The article insists the case was fundamentally a religious debate, which the Federalist trustees (and traditional evangelism) won. Novak's defense of "pietistic" did stretch beyond his denominational meaning to include both individuals like Girard and Jefferson. Both of these individuals claimed a "moral discipline" in their versions of essential education, however different their meanings of "piety."

42. Girard's will took more than a decade to be realized due to financial and interpretive problems. In virtually all of the major issues, the college's priorities gravitated ever more deeply into an explicitly Whig tradition. The first president, Alexander Dallas Bache, was sent to Europe to study educational precedents and returned to publish a powerful Whig-leaning report, *Education in Europe* (1839). Similarly when Girard trustees sought additional educational advice, they turned to Francis Lieber, whose *A Manual of Political Ethics* (1838) had a shaping influence on Whig institutional assumptions. Bache and Lieber went on to distinguished scholarly careers and were instrumental members of the Lazzaroni who successfully promoted the creation of the Smithsonian Institution and the American Social Science Association. Cf. Romano, "Girard College," chap. 2; also Howe, *Political Culture of the American Whigs*, 86–87; Thomas Haskell, *The Emergence of Professional Social Science* (Urbana: University of Illinois Press, 1977), esp. 70–74.

43. John Whitehead and Jurgen Herbst, "How to Think about the Dartmouth College Case," *History of Education Quarterly* 26, no. 3 (Fall 1986): 334.

44. Howe, *Political Culture of the American Whigs*.

45. David Potts, *Wesleyan University, 1831–1910* (New Haven, CT: Yale University Press, 1992); Curran, *Georgetown University*. See note 2 above. For the efficacy of Catholic collegiate training of Protestants, see Alexis de Tocqueville's reported 1831 conversation with Benjamin Latrobe in J. P. Meyer, ed., *Alexis de Tocqueville: Journey to America* (New Haven, CT: Yale University Press, 1962), 78.

46. See chapter 5.

47. Many of such institutions reflected the history of the Troy Female Seminary, so well presented in Anne Firor Scott, "The Ever Widening Circle: The Diffusion of Feminist Values from the Troy Female Seminary, 1822–1872," *History of Education Quarterly* 19, no. 1 (Spring, 1979): 3–46. Many of these comparable dynamics endured beyond the antebellum period. See W. Bruce Leslie, "Localism, Denominationalism and Institutional Strategies in Urbanizing America: Three Pennsylvania Colleges, 1870–1915," *History of Education Quarterly* 17, no. 3 (Fall 1977): 235–56.

48. Potts, *Wesleyan,* 127; see Nancy Beadie, *Education and the Creation of Capital in the Early American Republic* (New York: Cambridge University Press, 2010), chap. 16.

49. Scanlon, *Randolph-Macon College,* chap 2. Later Trinity College, now Duke University, commandeered Randolph-Macon's North Carolina constituency, further reducing its geographical aegis.

50. Theodore Jones, *New York University* (New York: New York University Press, 1933). For most of the nineteenth century, New York University's student population remained the size of comparable colleges. In spite of initial plans to orient itself to the city, the school quickly reverted to the orbit of the Calvinist Dutch Reformed denomination, an alternative to Anglican Columbia. See also Thomas Frusciano and Marilyn Pettit, *New York University and the City* (New Brunswick, NJ: Rutgers University Press, 1997).

51. Letter of George Ticknor to Thomas Jefferson, March 28, 1825, cited in *American Higher Education: A Documentary History,* vol. 1, ed. Richard Hofstadter and Wilson Smith (Chicago: University of Chicago Press, 1961), 268. "These [New England] colleges," Ticknor confided to Jefferson, "are now very numerous and under one pretext or another, are constantly becoming more so. Competition, therefore, is growing more and more active among them, and all are endeavoring to find new and better modes of instruction with which to contend against their rivals."

52. Natalie Naylor, "The Theological Seminary in the Configuration of American Higher Education: The Ante-Bellum Years," *History of Education Quarterly* 17 (Spring 1977): 17–30.

53. Allmendinger, *Paupers and Scholars*; Mattingly, *The Classless Profession,* esp. chap. 2; Howard Miller, *The Revolutionary College* (New York: New York University Press, 1976), 218–33.

54. Howard Miller, *The Revolutionary College,* 125ff, includes in Princeton's loose voluntary network, largely fostered by its graduates or members of the Presbyterian denomination, Liberty Hall (1774; now Washington and Lee University) and Hampden-Sydney (1776) in Virginia; Dickinson College (1783) in Pennsylvania; Transylvania Seminary (1794), Centre College (1819), and Kentucky Academy (early 1780s) in Kentucky; and Cumberland College (1823) in Tennessee. Miller persuasively argues that denominational proselytizing forced a break from an older late eighteenth-century conception of religious harmony toward a tolerance of religious competition, which characterized the antebellum period.

55. Burke, *American Collegiate Populations,* 35; Nancy Beadie and Kim Tolley, eds., *Chartered Schools: Two Hundred Years of Independent Academies in the United States, 1727–1925* (New York: Routledge Falmer, 2002).

56. Miller, *The Revolutionary College,* 249; Sidney E. Ahlstrom, *A Religious History of the American People* (New Haven, CT: Yale University Press, 1972), 462.

57. *Who Was Who in America: Historical Volume* (Chicago: Marquis, 1967), 104. The western schools of the Presbyterian network tended to be more consciously and aggressively denominational, but the generic character of academy work takes on a peculiarly historical character. Although chartered as Jefferson College in 1802, Baird's alma mater was long known as Canonsburg Academy but retained a theological department recognized by the Virginia Synod of the Presbyterian Church. H. Miller, *The Revolutionary College,* 250. See P. Miller, *The Life of the Mind in America,* for Baird's contribution to the nineteenth-century meaning of "voluntarism" (40–43); Ahlstrom, *A Religious History,* 859, uses Baird's writing to demonstrate how ingeniously American evangelicals adapted their religious style—"the activity, the bustle and the lay support of the churches"—to a larger American ethos. My thanks to Peter Wosh of New York University for drawing attention to Baird.

58. In the antebellum period, primary education and collegiate instruction were equally pressing issues, often promoted by the same individuals. See Mattingly, *The Classless Profession*; Timothy Smith, "Protestant Schooling and American Nationality," *Journal of American History* 53 (March 1967): 679–95; David Tyack, *Managers of Virtue* (New York: Basic Books, 1982); Clifford Griffin, *Their Brothers' Keepers: Moral Stewardship in the United States* (New Brunswick, NJ: Rutgers University Press, 1960).

59. James Findlay, "The SPCTEW and Western Colleges: Religion and Higher Education in Mid-Nineteenth-Century America," *History of Education Quarterly* 17 (Spring 1977): 39. Among the colleges that received SPCTEW aid were Lane Theological Seminary as well as Marietta and Western Reserve Colleges in Ohio, Wabash College in Indiana, and Illinois College in Illinois. After the Civil War, the organization also supported black Wilberforce College in Ohio.

60. Peter Wosh, *Spreading the Word* (New York: Cornell University Press, 1994), 73–88; Anne Boylan, *Sunday School* (New Haven, CT: Yale University Press, 1988).

61. Roger L. Geiger, "The Era of Multipurpose Colleges in American Higher education, 1850–1890," *History of Higher Education Annual* 15 (1995): 64ff. In this essay Geiger provides extensive documentation on the number and variety of college founding in this and the later nineteenth century. His "multipurpose" formula, however, obscures what, if anything, these multipurposed institutions had in common, culturally or historically. This essay prodded me to ask whether the prevalence of the classical curriculum or of evangelical influences didn't document deeper, structural continuities amidst the colleges' multipurposes. And also, exactly how did such shared patterns connect to the "market revolution" or political influences of the antebellum period?

62. James Scanlon, *Randolph-Macon College: A Southern History* (Charlottesville: University Press of Virginia, 1983), 33. Scanlon has claimed that thirty-four of these schools were Methodist colleges, rapidly gaining on the Presbyterians with forty-nine and ahead of the Baptists with twenty-five, the Congregationalists with twenty-one, the Episcopalians with eleven, and the Roman Catholics with fourteen; see also Jennings W. Wagoner, "Constraint and Variety in Virginia Higher Education," *History of Education Quarterly* 25 (Spring–Summer 1985): 181–93.

63. Wosh, *Spreading the Word*, chap. 3.

64. Scanlon, *Randolph-Macon College*, chap. 2.

65. Burke, *American Collegiate Populations*, 194–200.

66. Ibid., 38.

67. One needs to qualify the putative democratic interpretations of popular accessibility by noting that college tuition nationwide had shifted from one-third of a skilled laborer's annual wage in 1800 to two-thirds by 1860. Ibid., 50.

68. Cf. John Barnard, *From Evangelicalism to Progressivism at Oberlin College, 1866–1917* (Columbus: Ohio State University Press, 1969), 17–18. Cf. Robert Fletcher, *A History of Oberlin College* (Oberlin, OH: Oberlin College, 1943), 2 vols. Until the end of the century, these patterns only widened, and the costs of college attendance—travel to the institution, boarding in adjacent towns, food and accessories—greatly exceeded tuition fees. Still, in the 1870s Oberlin charged thirty dollars for a year's collegiate instruction, when Yale reportedly mandated ninety dollars, Brown and Amherst seventy-five dollars, and Dartmouth sixty dollars. Cf. W. C. Bronson, *A History of Brown University, 1764–1914* (Providence, RI: Brown University Press, 1914), 368.

69. James McLachlan, *American Boarding Schools* (New York: Charles Scribner's Sons, 1969) chaps. 1–4.

70. Burke, *American Collegiate Populations*, 37–38. Burke estimated that the cutoff point in dollars was about $2,600 for communities planning a "college." If communities could not command amounts above that, it was less likely that a "college" would ensue. For enrollment figures cited here, see ibid., 49. Nancy Beadie and Kim Tolley, eds., *Chartered Schools: Two Hundred Years of Independent Academies in the United States, 1727–1925* (New York: Routledge Falmer, 2002).

71. Claude Fuess, *Amherst: The Story of a New England College* (New York: Little Brown, 1935), chaps. 3 and 12, esp. 127. Hitchcock did hold a (1820) degree from Yale but in the theological

department (Yale Theological Seminary was not founded until 1822). He built his reputation via instruction in natural history at Amherst for ten years before assuming its presidency. But his reputation ranged beyond Amherst village because of his scientific textbooks, used equally by academies and colleges, and his spirited defense of the antebellum academy. Cf. *Who Was Who in American History: Historical Volume* (Chicago: Marquis, 1967), 323. See also Theodore Sizer, ed., *The Age of the Academies* (New York: Teachers College Press, 1964), which includes Hitchcock's forceful 1845 address, "The American Academic System Defended," itself a dedication of a new academy at Williston, Massachusetts. See also "Edward Hitchcock," in *Dictionary of American Biography*, vol. 5, ed. Dumas Malone (New York: Charles Scribner's Sons, 1932), 70.

72. William R. Taylor, *Cavalier and Yankee: The Old South and the American National Character* (New York: George Braziller, 1961), argues that between 1830 and 1860 the intrastate traffic and nationally oriented trade between the two sections developed definitive cultural mythologies that forced a new, more sectional and regional sense of difference between North and South; William R. Taylor, "Toward a Definition of Orthodoxy: The Patrician South and the Common Schools," *Harvard Educational Review* 36 (Fall 1966): 412–26; see also Michael Sugrue, "We Desired Our Future Rulers to Be Educated Men: South Carolina College, the Defense of Slavery, and the Development of Secessionist Politics," *History of Higher Education Annual* 14 (1994): 39–72; E. Merton Coulter, *College Life in the Old South* (Athens: University of Georgia Press, 1979; 1st ed., 1928). Of course, in some states, like Virginia, slave-owner dominance prevented taxation for public schooling earlier than states like Georgia.

73. Yale College had 325 enrolled college students in the year the report was published. In addition, there were another 149 students—"resident graduates"—studying medicine, law, and theology. The size and differentiated units give "Yale College" a "university" complexion during this period.

74. Allmendinger, *Paupers and Scholars*. It may well have been this feature that compelled the authors of the Yale Report to acknowledge the merits of "partial education" for those unable to complete a "thorough" course of collegiate study. See "Original Papers in Relation to a Course of Liberal Education," *American Journal of Science and Arts* 15 (January 1829): 312. "The Yale Report" has become a convenient scholars' reference to this essay, written in 1828 and published in 1829.

75. The Yale Report noted that its charter permitted admission to youth no younger than fourteen but occasionally dispensed with the rule. "Original Papers in Relation to a Course of Liberal Education," 317.

76. Notable efforts to explain how an older evangelical rhetoric translated into specific actions are Wilson Smith, *Professors and Public Ethics* (Ithaca, NY: Cornell University Press, 1956); Richard J. Carwardine, *Evangelicals and Politics in Antebellum America* (New Haven, CT: Yale University Press, 1993); and more recently, Conkin, *The Uneasy Center*. For an insightful commentary on important theoretical aspects of institutionalization, see W. W. Powell and Paul DiMaggio, *The New Institutionalism in Organizational Analysis* (Chicago: University of Chicago Press, 1991).

77. Stephen Novak, *The Rights of Youth: American Colleges and Student Revolt, 1798–1815* (Cambridge, MA: Harvard University Press, 1977).

78. "Original Papers in Relation to a Course of Liberal Education," 308–9.

79. Quoted in Melvin I. Urofsky, "Reforms and Response: The Yale Report of 1828," *History of Education Quarterly* 5, no. 1 (Spring 1965): 57.

80. Yale graduate, Rev. Lyman Beecher, illustrates the point with his *A Plea for Colleges* (Cincinnati, OH, 1836). Beecher's career as a widely admired missionary model for this antebellum generation receives an insightful treatment in Donald M Scott, *From Office to Profession: The New England Ministry, 1750–1850* (Philadelphia: University of Pennsylvania Press, 1978), 69–75.

81. Brooks Mather Kelley, *Yale: A History* (New Haven, CT: Yale University Press, 1974).

82. Ibid., chaps 10 and 11.

83. Urofsky, "The Yale Report of 1828," 62. Urofsky, misquoting George Schmidt, claimed that four-fifths of the colleges in operation in 1840 were led by either Yale (thirty-six) or Princeton (twenty-two) grads. These schools did impress Schmidt with the number of their graduates in college presidencies, but his study offered no four-fifths specification. Schmidt used an undiscussed sample of seventy-five colleges, leading Urofsky to his erroneous calculation of four-fifths or fifty-eight graduates of Princeton and Yale. However, the seventy-five did not represent the total of antebellum colleges. See George Schmidt, *The Old Time College President* (New York: Columbia University Press, 1930), 96, 146. My thanks to Roger Geiger for initiating this correction. Even where the Yale Report was not explicitly endorsed nor operated as a part of the loose voluntary network out of Yale, the classics were defended for their special pedagogical role. Wilbur Fisk, a graduate of Baptist Brown and first president of Methodist Wesleyan University, as well as his Southern counterpart, Stephen Olin, a graduate of Congregational Middlebury and first president of Methodist Randolph-Macon, both echoed sentiments of the Yale Report and endorsed the classics in the inaugural speeches at their respective colleges. Cf. Scanlon, *Randolph-Macon College*, 55–57. See also Frederick Rudolph, *Curriculum: A History of the American Undergraduate Course of Study since 1636* (San Francisco: Jossey-Bass, 1977), 65–75. But again, like their counterparts, their ability to deliver on the blueprint was a function of dynamics often beyond their control.

84. Lawrence Cremin, *American Education: The National Experience* (New York: Harper and Row, 1980), 405–9.

85. Frederick Rudolph, *American College and University*, 131–35. More persuasive are the insightful arguments of Peter Hall in "Institutionalization and Education in the Nineteenth and Twentieth Centuries," *History of Education Quarterly* 20, no. 4 (Winter 1980): 461–63, or of Louise Stevenson, *Scholarly Means to Evangelical Ends: The New Haven Scholars and the Transformation of Higher Learning in America, 1830–1890* (Baltimore: Johns Hopkins University Press, 1986), which argues the creative force of nineteenth-century evangelical culture.

86. Roger L. Geiger, "The Era of Multipurpose Colleges in American Higher Education, 1850–1890," *History of Higher Education Annual* 15 (1995): 51–92.

CHAPTER FOUR

1. Richard Hofstadter, *Academic Freedom in the Age of the College* (New York: Columbia University Press, 1955).

2. David F. Allmendinger Jr., *Paupers and Scholars: The Transformation of Student Life in Nineteenth-Century New England* (New York: St. Martin's Press, 1975).

3. Rev. Francis Wayland, "Introductory Discourse," in *Lectures and Proceedings of the American Institute of Instruction*, vol. 1 (Boston: Hilliard, Gray, Little and Wilkins, 1830): 2–23.

4. Francis Wayland, "A Discourse Delivered at the Dedication of Manning Hall, the Chapel and Library of Brown University, February 4, 1835," cited in William Smith and Richard Hofstadter, eds., *American Higher Education: A Documentary History* (Chicago: University of Chicago Press, 1961), 1:242–43.

5. See Joseph Blau, introduction to Francis Wayland's *The Elements of Moral Science* (Cambridge, MA: Harvard University Press, 1963); also Donald Fleming, *Science and Technology in Providence, 1760–1914* (Providence, RI: Brown University, 1952). One important exception to the patterned treatment is the still insightful analysis Wilson Smith, *Professors and Public Ethics: Studies of Northern Moral Philosophers before the Civil War* (Ithaca, NY: Cornell University Press, 1956), chap. 7.

6. Fleming, *Science and Technology*, 31–43; Lawrence A. Cremin, *American Education: The National Experience, 1783–1876* (New York: Harper and Row, 1980), esp. chap. 8, "Prudent Learning." See also David Walker Howe, "The History of Education as Cultural History," *History of Education Quarterly* 22 (Summer 1982): 205–14. Cremin and Howe both underscore the point of widespread

benefits at collegiate reform for much of the nineteenth century, a counterpoint to an earlier school of scholarship that emphasized the retrograde quality of collegiate instruction.

7. Roger Rasmussen, "Eliphalet Nott," in *Biographical Dictionary of American Educators*, ed. John Ohles (Westport, CT: Greenwood Press, 1977), 2:957–58; Codman Hislop, *Eliphalet Nott* (Middletown, CT: Wesleyan University Press, 1971). In addition to the creative presidency of Francis Wayland, Nott inspired the similarly reformist and scientifically receptive work of Henry Tappan (Union, 1825) as the first president of the University of Michigan in 1852. Tappan's influence continued into the shaping of many state universities of the nineteenth century.

8. Henry Barnard, "The South Atlantic States in 1833, as Seen by a New Englander," ed. Bernard Steiner, *Maryland Historical Magazine* 13 (September 1918): 289. See also Stanley M. Guralnick, *Science and the Antebellum College* (Philadelphia: American Philosophical Society, 1975); Thomas Bender, "Science and the Culture of American Communities: The Nineteenth Century," *History of Education Quarterly* 16, no. 1 (Spring 1976): 63–77.

9. Francis Wayland, "Introductory Discourse," in *American Institute of Instruction*, 22–23; see also Douglas Sloan, *Faith and Knowledge: Mainline Protestantism and American Higher Education* (Louisville, KY: Westminster John Knox Press, 1994).

10. Not only did Wayland implement the cheap but good educational value at Brown, he made it a broader tenet of his deservedly famous essay (1842), *Thoughts on the Present Collegiate System in the United States* (New York: Arno Press, 1969).

11. Francis Wayland, *Thoughts on the Present Collegiate System in the United States* (Boston: Gould, Kendall and Lincoln, 1842), chap. 3. See also Allmendinger, *Paupers and Scholars*.

12. Wayland, *Thoughts*, 52–53. See also "Francis Wayland," in *Wikipedia*, http://en.wikipedia.org/wiki/Francis_Wayland.

13. In his formative years, Abraham Lincoln read avidly and appreciatively Wayland's books, and Wayland reciprocated by voting for Fremont in 1856 and Lincoln in 1860. Daniel Walker Howe, *The Political Culture of the American Whigs* (Chicago: University of Chicago Press, 1979), 270.

14. Paul H. Mattingly, *The Classless Profession: American Schoolmen in the Nineteenth Century* (New York: New York University Press, 1975); Theodore Crane, "Francis Wayland: Political Economist as Educator," *Rhode Island History* 21, no. 3 (July 1962): 82ff.; Albert S. Weston, "Francis Wayland," in *Biographical Dictionary of American Educators*, ed. John Ohles (Westport, CT: Greenwood Press, 1978), 3:1360.

15. Edward Stevens's important study *The Grammar of the Machine: Technical Literacy and Early Industrial Expansion in the United States* (New Haven, CT: Yale University Press, 1995), argued forcefully that this "grammar" provided the bridge where both theoretical science and mechanical practice met, sweeping along many institutes, seminaries, and colleges into its distinctive conceptual vortex. See also Brooke Hindle, *Emulation and Invention* (New York: New York University Press, 1981).

16. Alexis de Tocqueville, *Democracy in America* (New York: Vintage Books, 1958; 1st ed., 1835 [English trans.,) 1840]), vol. 2, 2nd bk., chap. 7, 123–28; variations on his theory of civil associations appear frequently in his notebooks. See J. P. Meyer, ed., *Journey to America: Alexis de Tocqueville* (New Haven, CT: Yale University Press, 1952), 214–16. Peter D. Hall well argues that early voluntary associations differed dramatically from later versions. He insists the mythology of a linear connection between their distinct historical formats has impeded a clear understanding of their special organizational contribution to American life. Peter D. Hall, *Inventing the Nonprofit Sector* (Baltimore: Johns Hopkins University Press, 1992), chap. 1. Daniel Calhoun, *The Intelligence of a People* (Princeton, NJ: Princeton University Press, 1973), makes a spirited argument for the qualitative shift of intelligence toward practicality and away from abstraction in the late antebellum period. Implicitly this new intelligence represented one component of new, supportive attitudes toward voluntary organizations that made them complementary to institutional organization rather than the predictable start of a self-interested cabal.

17. Wayland, *Thoughts*, 43–62.

18. Walter Bronson, *A History of Brown University* (Providence, RI: Brown University Press, 1914), 218–28; "Nicholas Brown [1769–1841]," in *Who Was Who in American History: Historical Volume* (Chicago: Marquis, 1967), 147. His 1804 gift ($5,000) of a chair in oratory and belles lettres occasioned the change of name from Rhode Island College to Brown University.

19. Wayland, *Thoughts*, 41.

20. Other colleges like Harvard put their 1845 tuition at seventy-five dollars and generally estimated colleges expenses doubled tuition charges. Harvard's college expenses would reach an estimated $400 by the Civil War. Harvard kept its admissions policies selective and held their student body to about fifty students in the antebellum period. The school catered increasingly to wealthier Bostonians. Ronald Story, "Harvard Students, the Boston Elite and the New England Preparatory System, 1800–1876," *History of Education Quarterly* 15 (Fall 1975): 282. See also Robert A. McCaughey, "The Transformation of American Academic Life, 1821–1892," *Perspectives in American History* 8 (1974): 239–332.

21. Wayland, *Thoughts*, 41.

22. Ibid., 62.

23. Ibid., 53. See also Peter D. Hall, "Resolving the Dilemmas of Democratic Governance: The Historical Development of Trusteeship in American, 1636–1996," in *Philanthropic Foundations: New Scholarship, New Possibilities*, ed. Ellen C. Lagemann (Bloomington: Indiana University Press, 1999), esp. 10–17.

24. Wayland, *Thoughts*, 62–67. Allmendinger, *Paupers and Scholars*, esp. 118–22, argues compellingly that Wayland abandoned all but minimal faculty supervision and replaced it with a combination of intramural regulations, which, in combination with family monitoring, would introduce a new internalized discipline in every student. The result, Allmendinger insisted, was a new collegiate order, different from both the expensive, quadrangle culture of England and the looser, more intellectually focused Scottish model; David B. Potts, "Students and the Social History of American Higher Education," *History of Education Quarterly* 15, no. 3 (Fall 1975): 317–27.

25. Bronson, *Brown University*.

26. Burke, *American Collegiate Populations*, 61.

27. Andrew White, *Autobiography* (New York: Century, 1905), 1:256–57. Andrew White claimed to have heard this advice from Wayland and immediately set his sights on the West, accepting a first academic assignment at the University of Michigan, the start of a long and distinguished academic and diplomatic career.

28. Fleming, *Science and Technology*, 35ff. Brown University's benefactors had invested substantively in the textile factories powered by water, but enhanced their enterprise dramatically with the invention of Providence resident George Corliss of a steam engine that halved the waste of power of its predecessors. In addition, the Providence firm of Brown and Sharpe, especially noted for its clocks and calipers, the symbolic metaphor for scientific precision, set a context for disseminating scientific knowledge in the city; Jon Roberts and James Turner, *The Sacred and Secular University* (Princeton, NJ: Princeton University Press, 2000).

29. Bronson, *Brown University*, 289. Rhode Island students made up roughly one-quarter of Brown students in the first half of the nineteenth century. The majority came from Massachusetts.

30. Ibid.

31. Burke, *American Collegiate Populations*.

32. Ibid.

33. Francis Wayland, *Report to the Corporation of Brown University, on Changes in the System of Collegiate Education, Read March 28, 1850* (Providence, RI, 1850).

34. Bronson, *Brown University*, 323. Parallel experiments occurred in the same period at Harvard under President Josiah Quincy, only to be checked by his successor, Edward Everett. Josiah Quincy, *Remarks on the Nature and Probable Effects of Introducing the Voluntary System in the Studies of Greek and Latin* (Cambridge, MA: John Owen, 1841).

35. Fleming, *Science and Technology*, 40ff.

36. The lecture circuit proved to be a powerful, popular competitor with colleges for higher learning. See Donald M. Scott, "The Popular Lecture and the Creation of a Public in Mid-Nineteenth-Century America," *Journal of American History* 66 (March 1980): 791–809; also "Print and the Lecture System, 1840–1860," in *Printing and Society in Early America*, ed. William Joyce et al. (Worcester, MA, 1983), 278–99; Mary Kupiec Cayton, "The Making of an American Prophet: Emerson, His Audiences and the Creation of the Culture Industry in Nineteenth-Century America," *American Historical Review* 92 (June 1987): 597–620. Peter Wosh, "Going Postal," *American Archivist* 61 (Spring 1998): 220–39, presents the emergent communication "system" of the antebellum period—a national postal system, the enthusiasm for the telegraph, the lecture circuit, and in general the broad flow of organized, public information that competed with the college's effort to dominate the transfer of knowledge.

37. This intellectual superstructure Wayland configured in two important discourses before the American Institute of Instruction, twenty-five years apart. See "Introductory Discourse" (1830) and his reprise in 1854, "Introductory Discourse," in *Lectures and Proceedings of the American Institute of Instruction* (Boston: Ticknor and Fields, 1955), esp. 21–28.

38. David B. Potts, "'College Enthusiasm!' as Public Response, 1800–1860," *Harvard Educational Review* 47, no. 1 (1977): 28–42.

39. Wayland's fund-raising campaign after 1850 drew in $128,000 and remained a stabilizing factor in spite of the failure of his educational design. Providence donors accounted for $98,000, but the rest came from a wider outreach to Boston, New York, and Philadelphia. Theodore R. Crane, "Francis Wayland: Political Economist as Educator," *Rhode Island History* 21, no. 4 (October 1962): 116. Wayland considered that his fellow Baptists in this strategic drive had abandoned the institution!

40. Bender, "Science and the Culture of American Communities," 63–77; Sally Kohlstadt, "Reassessing Science in Antebellum America," *American Quarterly* 29, no. 4 (Autumn 1977): 444–53; Stanley M. Guralnick, "Sources of Misconceptions on the Role of Science in the Nineteenth-Century American College," *Isis* 65, no. 3 (September 1974): 352–68; George Daniels, *American Science in the Age of Jackson* (New York: Columbia University Press, 1968); David F. Allmendinger, *Ruffin: Family and Reform in the Old South* (New York: Oxford University Press, 1990), shows the central role of agricultural societies in the dissemination of science; Neil Harris, *Humbug: The Art of P. T. Barnum* (Chicago: University of Chicago Press, 1981), shows the fluctuating line between genuine public curiosity about scientific matters and sheer showmanship.

41. Fleming, *Science and Technology*, 41–42.

42. Thomas S. Harding, *College Literary Societies: Their Contribution to Higher Education in the United States, 1815–1876* (New York: Pageant Press International, 1971), esp. chaps. 8 and 9; James McLachlan, "The Choice of Hercules: American Student Societies in the Early 19th Century," in *The University in Society*, vol. 2, *Europe, Scotland and the United States from the 16th to the 19th Century*, ed. Lawrence Stone (Princeton, NJ: Princeton University Press, 1974), 449–94.

43. Jonathan Messerli, *Horace Mann: A Biography* (New York: Alfred Knopf, 1971), 46–48. Horace Mann, eventually to be one of the most forceful educators of the century, would serve as the first superintendent of public schools in Massachusetts and later (after an interlude as an abolitionist congressman) as president of Antioch College in Ohio. In his collegiate days at Brown (class of 1819), he belonged to the United Brothers, a literary society that managed 1,400 volumes in Mann's time and that grew to four thousand by 1840. See also McLachlan, "The Choice of Hercules: American Student Societies in the Early 19th Century," 449–94.

44. Smith, *Professors and Public Ethics*. See also D. H. Meyer, *The Instructed Conscience: The Shaping of the American National Ethic* (Philadelphia: University of Pennsylvania Press, 1972). See also Timothy Dwight, *Memories of Yale Life and Men* (New York: Dodd Mead, 1903), 62–66; D. H. Meyer, "Conservative Federalists and the Liberal Arts: Two Old-Time College Presidents," *History of Education Quarterly* 16, no. 2 (Summer 1976): 229–34.

45. Daniel Boorstin's "The Booster College" argues that this communal impetus was the primary agent. Conveniently his argument ignores the expansive aspirations of antebellum leaders who experienced the instabilities and disruptions of communal support alone.

46. The sensitivity to criticism by European travelers, few of whom credited American colleges with European university levels of instruction, reflects one more aspect of collegiate longing in the antebellum period. P. A. Siljestrom's *Educational Institutions of the United States* (Sweden, 1853) offered such a fair-minded and discriminating set of distinctions to warrant its American popularity. From his perspective America's "system" aspired to an integrated and graded educational mechanism, from common school to academy and on to college, encompassing democratic aims that he contrasted favorably to the multiple class-oriented systems of Europe.

47. It is not an accident that Wayland was a graduate of Union, a trustee of West Point, and a president of Brown University. For all their differences, these institutions linked themselves cohesively and ideologically with the threads of adapting tradition and the classics to new economic and scientific arrangements.

48. Mattingly, *The Classless Profession*; Edward W. Stevens Jr., *The Grammar of the Machine: Technical Literacy and Early Industrial Expansion in the United States* (New Haven, CT: Yale University Press, 1995), esp. chap. 6; Allan Horlick, *Country Boys and Merchant Princes* (Lewisburg, PA: Bucknell University Press, 1975); Bruce Sinclair, *Philadelphia's Philosopher Mechanics: A History of the Franklin Institute, 1824–1865* (Baltimore: Johns Hopkins University Press, 1974); Thomas Frusciano et al., *New York University and the City* (New Brunswick, NJ: Rutgers University Press, 1997); and also Louise Stevenson, "Preparing for Public Life: The College Students at New York University, 1832–1881," in *The University and the City*, ed. Thomas Bender (New York: Oxford University Press, 1988), 150–77; Geoffrey Hellman, *Smithsonian: Octopus on the Mall* (Philadelphia: J. B. Lippincott, 1967).

49. See Roy Porter, "The Scientific Revolution and Universities," in *Universities in Early Modern Europe*, vol. 2, ed. Hilde de Ridder-Symoens (Cambridge: Cambridge University Press, 1996), chap. 13.

50. Roger Geiger, "The Rise and Fall of Useful Knowledge: Higher Education for Science, Agriculture and the Mechanic Arts, 1850–1875," *History of Higher Education Annual* 18 (1998): 47–65.

51. Ibid. See Robert V. Bruce, *The Launching of Modern American Science* (Ithaca, NY: Cornell University Press, 1987), 84–85; Scott Montgomery, *Minds for the Making: The Role of Science in American Education, 1750–1990* (New York: Guilford Press, 1994), esp. chaps. 4 and 5.

52. Caroline Winterer, "The Humanist Revolution in America, 1820–1860: Classical Antiquity in the Colleges," *History of Higher Education Annual* 18 (1998): 111–29. This article argues persuasively that the classics were a necessary ingredient of the collegiate preoccupation with republican ideals. Importantly, after 1830 classical instruction shifted from Latin grammar to a more contextualized and sophisticated pedagogy, emphasizing Greek and the innovations of German humanistic scholarship via literature and history. The philological study of Periclean Athens as a model of republicanism also indirectly subtracted from the classics' earlier preoccupation with biblical studies, especially of the New Testament, and by extension a traditional moralized conception of the antebellum college.

53. Carl Diehl, "Innocents Abroad: American Students in German Universities, 1810–1870," *History of Education Quarterly* 16, no. 3 (Fall 1976): 321–41.

54. Rudolph, *American College and University*, 108–9. One can find a different and more persuasive argument in Louise Stevenson, *Scholarly Means to Evangelical Ends: The New Haven Scholars and the Transformation of Higher Learning in America, 1830–1890* (Baltimore: Johns Hopkins University Press, 1986).

55. Noah Porter, *American Colleges and the American Public* (New York: Charles Scribner's Sons, 1878; 1st ed., 1870); Dwight, *Memories of Yale Life and Men*, 342–53. See also Peter D. Hall, "'Noah Porter Writ Large': Reflections on the Modernization of American Education and Its Critics, 1886–1916," *History of Higher Education Annual* 16 (1996): 39–70.

56. Richard D. Brown, *Knowledge Is Power: The Diffusion of Information in Early America, 1700–1865* (New York: Oxford University Press, 1989).

57. Harding, *College Literary Societies*, 34.

58. Marilyn Tobias, *Old Dartmouth on Trial: The Transformation of the Academic Community in Nineteenth-Century America* (New York: New York University Press, 1982), chap. 2; "Samuel Colcord Bartlett," in *Who Was Who in American History* (Chicago: Marquis, 1967),112.

59. Tobias, *Old Dartmouth on Trial*, chap. 2; Martin Finkelstein, "From Tutor to Specialized Scholar: Academic Professionalization in Eighteenth- and Nineteenth-Century America," *History of Higher Education Annual* 3 (1983): 99–121.

60. Tobias, *Old Dartmouth on Trial*, chap. 3. David F. Allmendinger Jr., "New England Students and the Revolution in Higher Education, 1800–1900," *History of Education Quarterly* 11, no. 4 (Winter 1971): 381–89.

61. Tobias, *Old Dartmouth on Trial*, apps. 10, 12, and 14.

62. Burke, *American Collegiate Populations*; Ronald Story, *The Forging of an Aristocracy: Harvard and the Boston Upper Class, 1800–1870* (Middletown, CT: Wesleyan University Press, 1980); W. Bruce Leslie, *Gentlemen and Scholars: College and Community in the "Age of the University," 1865–1917* (State College: Pennsylvania State University Press, 1992); John Barnard, *From Evangelism to Progressivism at Oberlin College, 1866–1917* (Columbus: Ohio State University Press, 1969); David B. Potts, "American Colleges in the Nineteenth Century," *History of Education Quarterly* 11 (1971): 363–80.

63. Hugh Hawkins, *Banding Together: The Rise of National Associations in American Higher Education, 1887–1950* (Baltimore: Johns Hopkins University Press, 1992).

64. Roger Geiger, *The History of American Higher Education: Learning and Culture from the Founding to World War II* (Princeton, NJ: Princeton University Press, 2015), 376, notes that Union College in 1882 and Hamilton College in 1884 had similar "trials" and dynamics.

65. George Peterson, *The American College in the Age of the University* (Amherst, MA: Amherst College Press, 1964); Thomas Le Duc, *Piety and Intellect at Amherst College, 1865–1912* (New York: Columbia University Press, 1946).

CHAPTER FIVE

1. Paul V. Turner, *Campus: An American Planning Tradition* (Cambridge, MA: MIT Press), 1984), 4.

2. John Barnard, *From Evangelicalism to Progressivism at Oberlin College, 1866–1917* (Columbus: Ohio State University Press, 1969)

3. See the speech of Justin S. Morrill, "On the Bill Granting Lands for Agricultural Colleges," in the House of Representatives, April 20, 1958, in the Papers of Justin S. Morrill, Library of Congress. Morrill began his speech identifying a national problem of soil exhaustion and, with a new national need, a clearinghouse of scientific data to redress the problem: "It is one of the political maxims of the writer already quoted [Adam Smith] everywhere accredited, that national wealth is greatly increased or diminished by the more or less skill, dexterity, and judgment, with which labor is generally applied. As legislators, we can have no subject before us of higher universal importance."

4. New York University, originally on the city's fringe, quickly became merely the eastern and southern border of Washington Square in America's largest metropolis. In response, Samuel F. B. Morse, artist and faculty member (and later inventor of the telegraph), painted the university's Main Building in 1836, setting it into a fictive Tuscan landscape. Nothing more forcefully connoted higher education's general ambivalence about its necessary urban ties and its rural, idyllic aspirations. Thomas J. Frusciano and Marilyn Pettit, *New York University and the City* (New Brunswick, NJ: Rutgers University Press, 1997), 35. The most ambitious work connecting architecture and

collegiate goals is Helen Horowitz, *Alma Mater* (New York: Alfred Knopf, 1984), which addresses the distinctive post–Civil War model of women's colleges.

5. Roy Rosenzweig and Elizabeth Blackmar, *The Park and the People* (Ithaca, NY: Cornell University Press, 1992).

6. Olmsted's prewar *New York Times* reportage of travels in Britain—*Walks and Talks of an American Farmer in England* (1852)—and then in the South—*A Journey in the Seaboard Slave States* (1856)—secured his reputation as a sensitive voice and acute observer, not just of social conditions but of cultural terrain: geography, dialect, manners. His private antislavery Whig sentiments did not keep him from the hope that his writings would persuade the South that slavery corrupted civilization. Frederick Law Olmsted, *The Slave States before the Civil War*, ed. Harvey Wish (New York: Capricorn, 1959), 7; Paul H. Mattingly, "The Olmsted Legacy," www.visithistoricalelizabethnj.org/essay.htm.

7. Laura Wood Roper, *FLO: A Biography of Frederick Law Olmsted* (Baltimore: Johns Hopkins University Press, 1973). See also Charles Beveridge and Paul Roicheleau, *Frederick Law Olmsted: Designing the American Landscape* (New York: Rizzoli, 1995), esp. chap. 5, "Academic Campuses and Residential Institutions." Also Wytold Rybczinski, *A Clearing in the Distance: Frederick Law Olmsted and America in the 19th Century* (New York: Touchstone Books, 1999); Albert Fein, *Frederick Law Olmsted and the American Environmental Tradition* (New York: George Braziler, 1972).

8. Rosenzweig and Blackmar, *The Park and the People*.

9. The distinguished Olmsted scholar David Schuyler assures me (Letter of April 12, 2000, to author, Lancaster, PA) that there is no correspondence between Olmsted and Morrill in the early years of the Civil War. Their formal relationship, well documented, came in the early 1870s with Olmsted's work on the design of the US Capitol grounds. However, Olmsted's widely read 1866 article on campus landscape had to be known to Morrill in the early years of land-grant college formation.

10. Joseph F. Kett, *The Pursuit of Knowledge under Difficulties: From Self-Improvement to Adult Education in America, 1750–1990* (Stanford, CA: Stanford University Press, 1994), chap. 4; Coy F. Cross II, *Justin Smith Morrill: Father of the Land-Grant Colleges* (East Lansing: Michigan State University Press, 1999), chap. 5; Daniel W. Lang, "The People's College, the Mechanics' Mutual Protection and the Agricultural College Act," *History of Education Quarterly* 18, no. 3 (Fall 1978): 295–321.

11. Within the aegis of the two land-grant measures Congress in 1894 combined twenty-nine tribal colleges into this category, raising the total number of "land-grant schools" to 104. By 1997, 3 million students had attended these schools, which have awarded over 20 million degrees, including one-third of all master's degrees and half of all doctorates in the United States. Cross, *Morrill*, 88. Although known for his economic positions on the tariff, the currency and taxes, Morrill labored constantly to increase federal support for these schools throughout his career. See speeches like "National Colleges," delivered December 5, 1872; "The Educational Fund," delivered April 26, 1876; and "On the Education Bill," delivered December 15, 1880, all in the US Senate, in the Papers of Justin S. Morrill, Library of Congress.

12. Morrill became Vermont's US Senator in 1866 and later would chair the Committee on Buildings and Grounds (1869–77) for the US Capitol. In 1873 he arranged for Olmsted to redesign the grounds, improving on the original design by Olmsted's friend, A. J. Davis (1803–92). William G. Andrews, "Frederick Law Olmsted," *American National Biography*, vol. 15 (New York: Oxford University Press, 1999), 882–84. See Morrill's speech "The Capitol and Its Grounds," March 31, 1879, in the Paper of Justin S. Morrill, Library of Congress.

13. David Schuyler, *The New Urban Landscape: The Redefinition of City Form in Nineteenth-Century America* (Baltimore: Johns Hopkins University Press, 1986), pt. 2; Geoffrey Blodgett, "Frederick Law Olmsted: Landscape Architecture as Conservative Reform," *Journal of American History* 62 (March 1976): 869–89.

14. George Frederickson, *The Inner Civil War: Northern Intellectuals and the Crisis of the Union* (New York: Harper and Row, 1965), esp. chap. 7, 98–112.

15. Peter D. Hall, *The Culture of Organization* (New York: New York University Press, 1982). The Quartermaster Corps was responsible for the procurement and distribution of most military goods and services throughout the war. Thomas Scott, in fact, was second-in-command there during the war and clearly mastered this apprenticeship by fire.

16. Ibid., 227.

17. Cross, *Morrill*, 67; Roper, *FLO*, 159, 167. Of course, there were others who came to similar conclusions and actually had also studied German and English school models for remedying the situation. Several of these individuals formed the faculties at Rensselaer Polytechnic, Sheffield Scientific School at Yale, and the Lawrence Scientific Institute at Harvard. William B. Parker, *The Life and Services of Justin Smith Morrill* (Boston: Houghton Mifflin 1924), 273. Cf. Winton Solberg, *The University of Illinois, 1867–1894* (Urbana: University of Illinois Press, 1968), 32–40, for precedent intellectual and institutional traditions in science that led to the land-grant idea.

18. Terry Reynolds, "The Education of Engineers in America before the Morrill Act of 1862," *History of Education Quarterly* 32, no. 4 (Winter 1992): 459–82. See also Stephen Ambrose, *Duty, Honor, Country: A History of West Point* (Baltimore: Johns Hopkins University Press, 1966), esp. chap. 3, 38–61.

19. Edward W. Stevens Jr., *The Grammar of the Machine: Technical Literacy and Early Industrial Expansion in America* (New Haven, CT: Yale University Press, 1995), 170–75.

20. Cross, *Morrill*, chap. 5.

21. Justin S. Morrill, "National Colleges," Senate speech, delivered December 5, 1772, in the Papers of Justin S. Morrill, Library of Congress.

22. In fact, this ordinance had resulted in several important petitions from Ohio (1802), Tennessee (1806), Indiana (1816), and elsewhere to create universities. By 1862 the federal government had already allocated substantial acres of public lands for education. The 1862 Land Grant Act alone committed more than 11 million additional acres. Paul H. Mattingly and Edward W. Stevens Jr., eds., "*. . . Schools and the Means of Education Shall Forever Be Encouraged": A History of Education in the Old Northwest, 1787–1880* (Athens: Ohio University Libraries, 1987).

23. Frederick Rudolph, *The American College and University* (New York: Vintage Books, 1962), 250–51. See also Allen Nevins, *The State Universities and Democracy* (Urbana: University of Illinois Press, 1962); Earle Ross, *Democracy's College: The Land Grant Movement in the Formative Stage* (Ames: Iowa State College Press, 1942).

24. Edward Danforth Eddy Jr., *Colleges for Our Land and Time: The Land-Grant Idea in American Education* (New York: Harper, 1956). In 1872, Hampton Institute managed to receive one-third of Virginia's allotment of Morrill land-grant funds, freeing it from denominational dependence upon the American Missionary Association. Robert F. Engs, *Freedom's First Generation: Black Hampton, Virginia, 1861–1890* (Philadelphia: University of Pennsylvania Press, 1979), 148; Samuel H. Shannon, "Land Grant College Legislation and Black Tennesseans: A Case Study in the Politics of Education," *History of Education Quarterly* 22, no. 2 (Summer 1982): 139–57.

25. Nevins, *State Universities and Democracy*, 37. A Pennsylvania educator in the 1860s offered the $47,000 figure, assuming most of it went to faculty salaries at $1,500 per year.

26. Cross, *Morrill*, 86; James Anderson's authoritative *The Education of Blacks in the South, 1860–1935* (Chapel Hill: University of North Carolina Press, 1988), 113, 238, notes the presence of sixteen black land-grant schools by 1915 but argues their minimal significance until after the 1920s.

27. Actually seventeen schools, benefiting from land-grant resources, were founded before 1862. Nevins, *State Universities and Democracy*, 26.

28. In an 1876 speech to the US Senate, Morrill explicitly promised that land-grant colleges would contribute to "the intellectual stamina of our country." "The Educational Fund" (April 26, 1876), in the Papers of Justin S. Morrill, Library of Congress.

29. Nevins, *State Universities and Democracy*, 56.

30. Edward Stevens, *The Grammar of the Machine*; David F. Allmendinger Jr., *Ruffin* (New York: Oxford University Press, 1990), esp. chap. 5; Steven Conn, *Museums and American Intellectual Life, 1876–1926* (Chicago: University of Chicago Press, 1998), esp. chap. 2.

31. Charles E. Rosenberg, "Rationalization and Reality in Shaping American Agricultural Research, 1875–1914," in *The Sciences in the American Context: New Perspectives*, ed. Nathan Reingold (Washington, DC: Smithsonian Institution Press, 1979), 143–63; also Charles E. Rosenberg's *No Other Gods: On Science and American Social Thought* (Baltimore: Johns Hopkins University Press, 1976).

32. Rybczynski, *A Clearing in the Distance*, 256.

33. Roper, *FLO*, 280–81.

34. John Aubrey Douglass, *The California Idea and American Higher Education* (Stanford, CA: Stanford University Press, 2000), chap. 1.

35. On this point Olmsted certainly agreed with Cornell's Andrew White, who had prepared for an academic career in art history and architecture. During his tenure White called for multiple integrating campus plans to "create," he insisted, "an atmosphere that would make students something more than machines." Kermit Carlyle Parsons, *The Cornell Campus* (New York: Cornell University Press, 1968), 20.

36. Turner, *Campus*, 141. Olmsted's recommendations were often not followed in the form he specified, leading him to publish his influential essay "A Few Things to Be Thought of before Proceeding to Plan Buildings for the National Agricultural Colleges" (1866), reproduced in *The Papers of Frederick Law Olmsted*, ed. David Schuyler et al., vol. 6 (Baltimore: Johns Hopkins University Press, 1992), 130–50.

37. Schuyler, *Olmsted Papers*, 6:142.

38. Dona Brown, *Inventing New England: Regional Tourism in the Nineteenth Century* (Washington, DC: Smithsonian Press, 1995), makes a persuasive argument that tourism in New England after 1830s cultivated images of cohesive towns where formerly village life had actually produced scattered communities. The idealized village green was a nineteenth-century product of the newly emergent tourist industry that fostered a fictive New England cohesion.

39. Schuyler, *Olmsted Papers*, 6:142–44. *The Nation* followed up the October 1866 article with a review of Olmsted's published report in their December 27, 1866, issue. See also John Aubrey Douglass, "Creating a Fourth Branch of State Government: The University of California and the Constitutional Convention of 1879," *History of Education Quarterly* 32, no. 1 (Spring 1992): 31–72, which explores the legislative debates and political pressures over land-grant college values. Olmsted's problems in California involved more than his disagreements with the trustees.

40. Turner, *Campus*. Turner's superb book identifies a number of other schools that benefited from Olmsted's drawings and advice. Olmsted's firm, carried on by his son Frederick Law Olmsted Jr.—a major presence in twentieth-century design and urban planning—specifically listed 150 schools and universities among their clients, until the son's retirement in 1949. See also Susan Klaus, "Frederick Law Olmsted, Jr.," in *American National Biography* (New York: Oxford University Press, 1999), 16:700–702.

41. Turner, *Campus*. Actually Jefferson's architectural influence in university design did not impact the nineteenth century substantially. See Merrill Peterson, *The Jeffersonian Image in the American Mind* (New York: Oxford University Press, 1959), 395–99.

42. See "National Colleges," his Senate speech of December 5, 1872, in the Papers of Justin S. Morrill, Library of Congress.

43. John Brubacher and Willis Rudy, *Higher Education in Transition* (New York: Harper and Row, 1968; 1st ed., 1958), 65, 419. Farmers' organized pressure produced different language in the Second Morrill Act of 1890, restricting funds to courses in agriculture, mechanics, English, mathematics, science, and economics, "with special reference to their applications in the industries of life." For a close case analysis of the original dynamics of the 1862 law, see Daniel Lang, "The

People's College, the Mechanics Mutual Protection and the Agricultural College Act," *History of Education Quarterly* 18 (Fall 1978): 295–321.

44. Rudolph, *Curriculum,* 116–34. For a corrective to the usual presidential hagiography, see David F. Allmendinger Jr., "Strong Men of the Academic Revolution," *History of Education Quarterly* 13 (Winter 1973): 415–25. Actually the new land-grant college presidents regularly worried about older institutions' political influence in the scramble for limited governmental funds. President W. S. Clark (1826–86) of Massachusetts Agricultural College wrote Justin Morrill: "I take the liberty of asking you to protect us. No member of Congress from Massachusetts has ever visited our college or knows much about it, and as many of them have eastern connections which might lead them to favor measures which would make it possible for Harvard College or other interested parties to seize upon what belongs rightly to us." Letter of W. S. Clark to Justin S. Morrill, February 23, 1871, in the Papers of Justin S. Morrill, Library of Congress.

45. Solberg, *University of Illinois,* 92–95. See also David Schuyler, "Frederick Law Olmsted and the Origins of Modern Campus Design," *Planning for Higher Education* 25 (Winter 1996–97): 1–10.

46. John Kersey, *John Milton Gregory* (Urbana: University of Illinois Press, 1968).

47. Solberg, *University of Illinois,* chaps. 3 and 4. See Gregory's speeches to the American Institute of Instruction, especially, just before his Illinois presidency, "The Problem of Education," in *Lectures and Proceedings of the American Institute of Instruction,* vol. 34 (Boston: Ticknor and Fields, 1964), 1–36. Gregory reprised this argument at an 1874 Institute meeting during his presidency: "The Real Problem of Modern Education," [summarized] in *Lectures and Proceedings of the American Institute of Instruction* (Boston: A. I. I., 1875), xxviii–xxix. In the next centennial year, the Institute gave its formal endorsement to the government-sponsored land-grant system.

48. In his 1872 address "National Colleges," Morrill made the connection explicitly: "It absorbs the labor of a whole lifetime to become an expert in a single pursuit. If that labor is diffused over too wide an extent, it vanishes before the blaze of day. Not that a man may not love art and politics, literature and science, and diverse human interests, often with profit, but that the highest individual perfection and supremacy is rarely reached save when the main effort is made in one direction." In the Papers of Justin S. Morrill, Library of Congress.

49. See, for example, William Rothstein, *American Physicians in the Nineteenth Century* (Baltimore: Johns Hopkins University Press, 1972), and William R. Johnson, *Schooled Lawyers* (New York: New York University Press, 1978). See also Johnson's essay "Profession in Process: Doctors and Teachers in American Culture," *History of Education Quarterly* 15 (Summer 1975): 185–99.

50. See Andrew White, *Autobiography* (New York: Century, 1905), 1:318, and his portrait of Ezra Cornell as a public figure for his time. For all his commitment to the public good, White never employed the language of democracy to describe this generation's ideal.

51. Theodore Crane, "The Modern American University and Regional Service," *History of Education Quarterly* 22, no. 4 (Winter 1982): 479–90.

52. Hofstadter and Smith, *American Higher Education: A Documentary History* 2:549. Cornell did better with its land grants than many other institutions. Ezra Cornell, whose money had originally created the institution, bought the land scrip and held it until prices rose, garnering about five dollars per acre (when most other institutions received but one dollar per acre). "Cornell University, Ithaca, NY," in *Cyclopedia of Education,* ed. Paul Monroe (New York: Macmillan, 1911), 1:206.

53. Kermit Carlyle Parson, *The Cornell Campus: A History of Its Planning and Development* (Ithaca, NY: Cornell University Press, 1968), 20–23 and chap. 6; Rudolph, *Curriculum,* 116–29.

54. Merle E. Curti and Frederick Carstensen, *The University of Wisconsin: A History,* vol. 1 (Madison: University of Wisconsin Press, 1949), 360–63, 345–48; see also Ray Allen Billington, *Frederick Jackson Turner: Historian, Scholar, Teacher* (New York: Oxford University Press, 1973). Turner's mentor, William Allen, did not offer the first university course in American history, an honor usually accorded Andrew White, who taught it at the University of Michigan (1857–67) also after study at German universities.

55. Nevins, *State Universities*, 28–35.

56. This figure exaggerates the actual situation, since in 1860 the best secondary preparation for higher learning came from academy graduates. These schools, the most prestigious of which were concentrated in the East, were formerly private in charging tuition but public in terms of their goals and actual services. After the war they would gradually blend with the public high schools—literally merging while keeping both private and public traditions as in Saint Johnsbury (VT) Academy—or become expensive boarding schools, like Groton or Phillips Andover Academies. James McLachlan, *American Boarding Schools* (New York: Charles Scribner's Sons, 1970).

57. Ibid., 41. White conceded the difficulty caused by Ezra Cornell's advertisement in the *New York Tribune*, promising any student could work his way through the college by devoting half his time on manual labor, constructing its buildings. The resulting opening class of 412 contained many unprepared and unskilled youth. Careful culling could result in tiny student bodies: University of California's first class numbered twenty-six, Illinois fifty, Missouri twenty-six, and even these contained a portion of "ill-prepared" students. Nevins, *State Universities and Democracy*, 41–42. By comparison MIT opened in 1867 with 175 students, rose to 348 in 1872–73, then following the Panic of 1873 fell off precipitously to 188 in 1878–79. Samuel C. Prescott, *When MIT Was Boston Tech* (Cambridge, MA: MIT Press, 1953), 65, 90. Similarly the University of Wisconsin in 1865 had 290 of its 331 students in the preparatory, special, or normal (teacher-training) classes. The university also suffered wide enrollment swings. It experienced a rise and fall, from 1866–67 with 304 students to nearly 500 in 1870, back to 316 in 1876–77. Wisconsin would not approach 500 students again for another decade. The unprepared students went to the preparatory department, which was not abolished until 1880. Curti and Carstensen, *Wisconsin*, 364–65.

58. Allen Bogue and Robert Taylor, eds., *The University of Wisconsin: One Hundred and Twenty-Five Years* (Madison: University of Wisconsin Pres, 1975), 28–29. The university generally is thought to have come of age under the leadership of La Follette's 1879 classmate Charles Van Hise, once a student and later professor of metallurgy and geology, who became president in 1903 and served until his death in 1918. See also Robert M. La Follette, *La Follette's Autobiography: A Personal Narrative of Political Experiences* (Madison: University of Wisconsin Press, 1968; 1st ed., 1911).

59. Roger L. Williams, *The Origins of Federal Support for Higher Education: George W. Atherton and the Land-Grant College Movement* (University Park: Pennsylvania State University Press, 1991). This important book makes clear that Atherton too had his cohort, which included major players like Henry Alvord (1844–1904), president of the University of Maryland (1887–92); and Henry Goodell (1839–1905), president of the University of Massachusetts (1886–1905), both of whom, like Atherton, served as officers in the Civil War. See also Hugh Hawkins, *Banding Together: The Rise of National Associations in American Higher Education, 1887–1950* (Baltimore: Johns Hopkins University Press, 1992), 26–28, 34.

60. Quoted in Nevins, *State University and Democracy*, 90–91.

61. Schools listed as clients in Olmsted Associates twentieth-century promotional literature included Bryn Mawr College; University of Chicago; Columbia University; Cornell College in Mount Vernon, OH; Groton School; Harvard Medical School; Johns Hopkins University; Lawrenceville (NJ) School; Mount Holyoke College; Smith College; Leland Stanford University; Phillips Academy, Andover, MA; Williams College; Eastern Kentucky Normal School in Richmond; Lafayette College, Easton, PA; Western Maryland College in Westminster; and Northwestern University. See Letter of John C. Olmsted to Bruce Payne [Director of Summer School, University of Virginia], Charlottesville, VA, May 10, 1911, in the Papers of Olmsted Associates, Library of Congress. Olmsted's tradition continued through the person of Beatrix Farrand, who, with Olmsted and Charles Eliot, was a founding member of the American Association for Landscape Design. Her asymmetrical configurations, her respect for the contours of land rather than imposing her designs, her preferences for restructuring landscapes with trees and flowering shrubs more than formal flower beds, all comported with Olmsted's precedent. Her work at Princeton and Yale represented long-term

commitments to simplified designs, using lawn and accenting ivy and wisteria, and put her on mark on the landscape tradition. Jane Brown, *Beatrix: The Gardening Life of Beatrix Farrand, 1872–1959* (New York: Viking, 1995); Diana Balmori, Diane Kostal McGuire, and Eleanor M. McPeck, *Beatrix Farrand's American Landscapes: Her Gardens and Campuses* (Sagaponack, NY: Sagapress, 1985).

62. Curti and Carstensen, *Wisconsin*, 422. While much land-grant college scholarship has projected images of "cow colleges" and other agricultural icons, engineering and the "mechanics" side of the land-grant equation was the prevalent choice of graduates later in the century. Williams, *Origins of Federal Support*, 240; J. David Hoeveler Jr., "Higher Education in the Midwest: Community and Culture," *History of Education Quarterly* 14, no. 3 (Fall 1973): 391–402.

CHAPTER SIX

1. David F. Allmendinger Jr., "Strong Men of the Academic Revolution," *History of Education Quarterly* 13, no. 4 (Winter 1973): 415–25; Hugh Hawkins, "University Identity: The Teaching and Research Functions," in *The Organization of Knowledge in Modern America, 1860–1920*, ed. Alexandra Oleson and John Voss (Baltimore: Johns Hopkins University Press, 1979), 285–319. Hawkins stresses the range of relationships between teaching and research among the early university leaders but with organizational priorities paramount for them all; Laurence Veysey, *The Emergence of the American University* (Chicago: University of Chicago Press, 1965).

2. See Clark Kerr's paean to Eliot in his foreword to Seymour Martin Lipset and David Riesman, *Education and Politics at Harvard* (New York: McGraw Hill, 1975). The relevant chapter in Kerr's study also burnishes Eliot's image: "The Golden Age of Eliot."

3. The earliest reference to this metaphor, Boston Brahmin, appeared in the 1861 novel *Elsie Venner*, by Oliver Wendell Holmes, at the time a professor of medicine at Harvard University and regular contributor to the *Atlantic Monthly*, an influential journal of opinion.

4. Ronald Story, *The Forging of an Aristocracy: Harvard and the Boston Upper Class, 1800–1870* (Middletown, CT: Wesleyan University Press, 1980), chaps. 1–3. The families of Bowditch, Story, Nichols, Saunders, and Ward, for example, moved from Salem, into the network of Brahminesque organizations and reconstituted the Boston elite by the first third of the nineteenth century.

5. Charles W. Eliot, *Charles Eliot: Landscape Architect* (Cambridge, MA: Harvard University Press, 1924).

6. Hugh Hawkins, *Between Harvard and America: The Educational Achievement of Charles W. Eliot* (New York: Oxford University Press, 1972).

7. Story, *The Forging of an Aristocracy*, chap. 4; see also Robert McCaughey, "The Transformation of American Academic Life: Harvard University, 1821–1892," *Perspectives in American History* 8 (1974): 239–332.

8. Hawkins, *Between Harvard and America*, 95.

9. Charles Krug, ed., *Charles W. Eliot and Popular Education* (New York: Teachers College Press, 1961), "The New Education," 32.

10. Carl Diehl, *Americans and German Scholarship, 1770–1870* (New Haven, CT: Yale University Press, 1978), chap. 5. This important study argues that the much-touted German university model played less of a shaping role than hitherto thought. Before 1870 most Americans studied classical philology but did not practice it once they returned. Many, like George Bancroft and Edward Everett, achieved fame outside academia entirely, that is, in American politics. The German impact rested largely on respect for research and scholarship in general as an educational and national ideal. A second generation of German-trained Americans absorbed, not German values and the class-bound structure of its universities, but more the technical features of research—the seminar and laboratory—and channeled them into professional careers unavailable to their predecessors. See also Edward Shils and John Roberts, "The Diffusion of European Models Outside Europe," in

A History of the University in Europe, ed. Walter Ruegg (Cambridge: Cambridge University Press, 2004), 3:164–75, for a persuasive analysis of German university features that did not attract an American audience.

11. Krug, "The New Education," in *Charles W. Eliot and Popular Education*, 46.

12. Peter D. Hall, *The Organization of American Culture, 1700–1900: Private Institutions, Elites and the Origins of American Nationality* (New York: New York University Press, 1984), 217–19.

13. Gen. Joshua Chamberlin. ed., *Universities and Their Sons* (Boston: R. Herndon, 1899), 2:522

14. "Editorial," *National Journal of Education* 12 (November 18, 1880): 344; "Who-Where-What," *Journal of Education* 55 (February 27, 1902): 137; "Educational Intelligence," *Journal of Education* 60 (July 14, 1904): 80.

15. John Tetlow, "Some Aspects of the Higher Education for Women," *Lectures and Proceedings of the American Institute of Instruction*, vol. 53 (Boston: AII, 1882): 95–124; John Tetlow, "The College and Non-Classical High Schools," *Lectures and Proceedings of the American Institute of Instruction*, vol. 66 (Boston: AII, 1896): 3–28; "Educational Intelligence," *Journal of Education* 33 (February 26, 1891): 141. Among the other founders of the New England Association of Colleges and Preparatory Schools were Tetlow's fellow Brown graduates and friends, R. G. Huling and W. C. Collar, mentioned in this 1902 article; "Who-Where-What," *Journal of Education* 55 (February 27, 1902): 142; "John Tetlow," *Journal of Education* 72 (November 24, 1910): 518; *Historical Catalogue of Brown University* (Providence, RI: 1902), 277. On select points Tetlow can be found taking exception to Eliot's views toward women's education. He also worried about students committing to careers too early in their studies.

16. Eliot, "The New Departure," in Krug, *Charles W. Eliot and Popular Education*, 38.

17. Story, *The Forging of an Aristocracy*, 97–108; see also David F. Allmendinger Jr., *Paupers and Scholars: The Transformation of Student Life in Nineteenth-Century New England* (New York: St. Martin's Press, 1975), especially Harvard's ability to reduce early the number of poor and mature (twenty-three and older) students by mid-nineteenth century, unlike the hinterland colleges of Amherst, Williams, Colby, Dartmouth, etc.; see also James McLachlan, *American Boarding Schools* (New York: Charles Scribner's Sons, 1970), which traces these schools from their more public, antebellum achievement to their postbellum wealth, privacy, and exclusivity.

18. Henry James, *Charles W. Eliot*, vol. 1 (Cambridge, MA: Riverside Press, 1930), 198; also Story, *The Forging of an Aristocracy*, chap. 8. The 1866 law mandated that each year at commencement Harvard alumni elect five members for six-year tenures.

19. Charles W. Eliot, *Educational Reform: Essays and Address* (New York: Arno Press; 1st ed., 1898), 1–3.

20. Eliot, *Educational Reform*, 20. Eliot used the word "democratic" only once in this speech, to insist that "The College is intensely American in affection and intensely democratic in temper."

21. Ibid., 31.

22. Hawkins, *Between Harvard and America*, 59.

23. Abraham Flexner's now famous 1910 report for the Carnegie Endowment for the Advancement of Teaching stimulated much discussion over the quality of medical training. His ideal followed Eliot's to make a college the prerequisite for entrance to medical school.

24. William R. Johnson, *Schooled Lawyers* (New York: New York University Press, 1978), 103–5; Robert Stevens, "Two Cheers for 1870: The American Law School," *Perspectives in American History* 5 (1971): 435–41; James Willard Hurst, "Changing Responsibilities of the Law School, 1868–1968," *Wisconsin Law Review* (1968): 336–44; Arthur E. Sutherland, *The Law at Harvard: A History of Ideas and Men, 1817–1967* (Cambridge, MA: Harvard University Press, 1967).

25. Paul H. Mattingly, *The Classless Profession: American Schoolmen in the Nineteenth Century* (New York: New York University Press, 1975), 173–74. In the early nineteenth century, one-twentieth of college graduates went into the work of teaching; by the end of the century, one-quarter went into teaching, 5 percent more than any other professional; Arthur Powell, "The Education of Educators

at Harvard, 1891–1912," in *Social Sciences at Harvard, 1860–1920: From Inculcation to the Open Mind*, ed. Paul Buck (Cambridge, MA: Harvard University Press, 1965), 223–74. Powell notes (263) that for a generation Harvard's commitment lagged, measured by its educational budget in 1912—$10,250 against Columbia's ($156,750), Chicago's ($30,516), Missouri's ($20,800), and California's ($16,000).

26. Albert W. Winship, "The Harvard Normal," *Journal of Education* 33 (May 21, 1891): 328; Arthur Powell, *An Uncertain Profession: Harvard and the Search for Educational Authority* (Cambridge, MA: Harvard University Press, 1980), esp. chap. 3; Paul H. Mattingly, review of Powell's *An Uncertain Profession, Teachers College Record* 83, no. 3 (Spring 1982): 477–83.

27. Powell, *An Uncertain Profession*. Hanus deferred to Eliot's priorities and became more influential as an educational expert in the reorganization of Boston's schools than in his instructional message. These lectures did not mutate into the Graduate School of Education until 1920, after Eliot's departure from the Harvard presidency. Hanus's overweening deference can be measured by his memorial remarks after Eliot's death in Paul Hanus, *Adventuring in Education* (Cambridge, MA: Harvard University Press, 1937), 102–4. Hanus had come to Eliot's attention in Denver, while visiting his son Samuel Eliot, pastor of the Denver Unitarian Church, of which Hanus was a trustee. At the time (1890–91), Hanus was principal of a Denver high school and president of the Colorado State Teachers Association.

28. Eliot, *Charles Eliot: Landscape Architect*; James Ropes, "Harvard University," in *Cyclopedia of Education*, ed. Paul Monroe (New York: Macmillan, 1912), 3:231; Keith N. Morgan, "Charles Eliot (1859–1897) Landscape Architect," in *Pioneers of American Landscape Design*, ed. Charles Birnbaum and Robin Karson (New York: McGraw-Hill, 2000), 107–9.

29. Hawkins, *Between Harvard and America*, 65. Charles C. Bishop, "Teaching at Johns Hopkins: The First Generation," *History of Education Quarterly* 27, no. 4 (Winter, 1987): 499–515, argues that teaching and research became mutually reinforcing goals in Johns Hopkins University's early years.

30. Bainbridge Bunting, *Harvard: An Architectural History* (Cambridge, MA: Harvard University Press, 1985), esp. chap. 4; Margaret Henderson Floyd, *Henry Hobson Richardson: A Genius for Architecture* (New York: Monocelli Press, 1997), 210–18; James F. O'Gorman, *H. H. Richardson: Architectural Forms for an American Society* (Chicago: University of Chicago Press, 1987), 42–44.

31. Bunting, *Harvard*, chap. 5.

32. Wayne Andrews, *Architecture, Ambition and Americans* (New York: Free Press, 1964; 1st ed., 1947), 194–204; http://www.harvard.edu/widener/about/history.html. Dell Upton, *Architecture in the United States* (New York: Oxford University Press, 1998), 273, points out that Abele further distinguished himself later with the (ca. 1925) design of Duke University's campus and Duke Chapel for which Trumbauer and Associates were the principal architects. See Paul Turner, *Campus: An American Planning Tradition* (Cambridge, MA: MIT Press, 1984), 204, 252–53; Arthur Drexler, ed., *The Architecture of the Ecole des Beaux Arts* (New York: Museum of Modern Art, 1977).

33. Edward Krug, *The Shaping of the American High School, 1880–1920* (Madison: University of Wisconsin Press, 1969), chap. 2. "James Hutchins Baker," in *Who Was Who in America*, vol. 1 (Chicago: Marquis, 1968), 48. Baker became the university's third president and in 1892 presided over a fifteen-year-old "university" with sixty-six students. At his retirement in 1914, the students numbered over a thousand, and his school had gone far to imitate Eliot's generic university with a graduate department, law school, and college of engineering and arranged for Denver to teach medical, dental, and pharmaceutical students.

34. Samuel A. Farmerie, "James Mackenzie," in *Biographical Dictionary of American Educators*, ed. John Ohles (Westport, CT: Greenwood Press, 1978), 2:837–38.

35. Krug, *The Shaping of the American High School*, 61–62.

36. Edward Krug, introduction to *Charles W. Eliot and Popular Education* (New York: Teachers College Press, 1961), 14.

37. Charles W. Eliot, "Shortening and Enriching the Grammar School Course [1892]," in Krug, *Charles W. Eliot*, 55.

38. Charles Eliot, "The Unity of Educational Reform [1894]," in *Educational Reform* (New York: Arno Press, 1969; 1st ed., 1898), 317.

39. Charles W. Eliot, "The Function of Education in a Democracy [1897]," in Krug, *Charles W. Eliot*, 107.

40. Ibid., 111.

41. Ibid., 113–14.

42. Merle Curti and Roderick Nash, *Philanthropy and the Shaping of American Higher Education* (New Brunswick, NJ: Rutgers University Press, 1965).

43. See the scholarly revisions of Richard Hofstadter and Walter Metzger's *The Development of Academic Freedom in the Age of the College and University* (New York: Columbia University Press, 1955), and Daniel Boorstin, "Universities in a Republic of Letters," *Perspectives in American History* 1 (1967): 369–79; James Axtell, "The Death of the Liberal Arts College," *History of Education Quarterly* 11 (1971): 339–52; James McLachlan, "The American College in the Nineteenth Century," *Teachers College Record* 80 (December 1978): 287–306.

44. Paul H. Mattingly, "Academic and Professional School Careers, 1840–1900," *Teachers College Record* 81, no. 2 (Winter 1981): 219–33. The biographical profiles that document the career patterns of nineteenth-century schoolmen in this scholarship were donated to Harvard University. Consult Paul Mattingly Collection on the American Institute of Instruction, Special Collections, Monroe C. Gutman Library, Harvard Graduate School of Education.

45. Hugh Hawkins, "The University Builders Observe the Colleges," *History of Education Quarterly* 11, no. 4 (Winter 1971): 353–62.

46. Eliot, "The Function of Education in a Democracy," in Krug, *Charles W. Eliot*, 107.

47. Wilson Smith, *Professors and Public Ethics: Studies of Northern Moral Philosophers before the Civil War* (Ithaca, NY: Cornell University Press, 1956); George Peterson, *The New England College in the Age of the University* (Amherst, MA: Amherst College Press, 1964).

48. David B. Potts, "Social Ethics at Harvard: A Study in Academic Activism," in Buck, *Social Sciences at Harvard, 1860–1920*, 93ff.

49. Ibid.; Merle Curti, *Human Nature in American Thought* (Madison: University of Wisconsin Press, 1980).

50. James Turner, *Without God, Without Creed: The Origins of Unbelief in America* (Baltimore: Johns Hopkins University Press, 1985); by the same author and Jon Roberts, *The Sacred and the Secular University* (Princeton, NJ: Princeton University Press, 2000); George Marsden, *The Soul of the University* (New York: Oxford University Press, 1994); Julie Reuben, *The Making of the Modern University: Intellectual Transformation and the Marginalization of Morality* (Chicago: University of Chicago Press, 1996); David Hollinger, "Inquiry and Uplift: Late Nineteenth-Century American Academics and the Moral Efficiency of Scientific Practice," in *The Authority of Experts*, ed. Thomas Haskell (Bloomington: Indiana University Press, 1984).

51. Paul H. Mattingly, "Structures over Time: Institutional History," in *Historical Inquiry in Education: A Research Agenda* (Washington, DC: American Educational Research Association, 1983), 34–55. Eliot's model was particularly and self-consciously rejected by Southern higher education. See Joseph Stetar, "In Search of a Direction: Southern Higher Education after the Civil War," *History of Education Quarterly* 25, no. 3 (Fall 1985): 341–67.

CHAPTER SEVEN

1. Charles W. Eliot, "Address to the Association for Collegiate Alumnae" (1908), in "Higher Education for Women," *Harper's Bazaar* (June 1908): 519–22.

2. Colin B. Burke, *American Collegiate Populations* (New York: New York University Press, 1982), 213–19. The author argued that most institutions in the last half of the nineteenth century inflated

their enrollments. Whenever possible, they established "growth" by adding women students (often up to 40 percent of the student body), summer school students, and professionals (postgraduates). The national figures for higher education did grow in these years, with a special spurt in the depression-bound 1890s.

3. M. Carey Thomas used the twenty-three colleges that belonged to the ACA as one of her key integers to determine the top fifty-eight US colleges or universities. Of the fifty-eight she deemed first-rate, she reported proudly that thirty-seven admitted women. The other relevant integers required such institutions enroll more than three hundred students and have an endowment of $500,000 or better. Seven, including Bryn Mawr, were exclusively female colleges. M. Carey Thomas, *Education of Women* (Albany, NY, 1900), 11–12.

4. Roberta Frankfort, *Collegiate Women: Domesticity and Career in Turn-of-the-Century America* (New York: New York University Press, 1977); Anne Firor Scott, "The Ever-Widening Circle: The Diffusion of Feminist Values from Troy Female Seminary, 1822–1872," *History of Education Quarterly* 19 (Spring 1979): 3–25; Sue Zschoche, "Dr. Clarke Revisited: Science, True Womanhood and Female Collegiate Education," *History of Education Quarterly* 29, no. 4 (Winter 1989): 545–69.

5. Thomas Woody, *A History of Women's Education in the United States* (New York: Science Press, 1929) 2:191–93. Woody's own historical construct receives a perceptive treatment in Maxine Schwartz Seller's "A History of Women's Education in the United States: Thomas Woody's Classic—Sixty Years Later," *History of Education Quarterly* 29, no. 1 (Spring 1989): 95–108.

6. Scott, "The Ever Widening Circle," particularly notes the reach into the South and the Mississippi valley, which paralleled the Southern networks of Princeton and the midwestern arc of the Yale Bands. See Kathryn Kish Sklar, *Catharine Beecher: A Study in American Domesticity* (New Haven, CT: Yale University Press, 1973), 72–77; Eunice Caldwell Cowles, *The Power of Christian Benevolence Illustrated in The Life and Labors of Mary Lyon* (New York: American Tract Society, 1858); Lucy F. Townsend, "Female Seminaries," in *Historical Dictionary of American Education*, ed. Richard Altenbaugh (Westport, CT: Greenwood Press, 1999), 139–40.

7. Horowitz, *Alma Mater*. For many years after its founding, Vassar put the majority of its estimated 350 students in its "preparatory" class, which was not abolished until 1888; its actual collegiate student body remained quite small. The result was that early Vassar functioned more like America's private academies or seminaries than like a college, though these categories were often functionally interchangeable. Robert Church and Michael Sedlak, *Education in the United States* (New York: Free Press, 1976), 34–36; Theodore Sizer, ed., *The Age of the Academies* (New York: Teachers College Press, 1964), 1–48.

8. David F. Allmendinger Jr., "Mt. Holyoke Students Encounter the Need for Life-Planning, 1837–1850," *History of Education Quarterly* 19 (Spring 1979): 27–46. Mary Lyon at Mount Holyoke Female Seminary notably worried about young women of little means. "The wealthy," she insisted, "can provide for themselves" (33). Lyon sought out ordinary citizens rather an a few wealthy donors, raising $27,000 from one thousand subscribers in ninety distinct communities. Merle Curti and Roderick Nash, *Philanthropy and the Shaping of American Higher Education* (New Brunswick, NJ: Rutgers University Press, 1965), 90; Kathryn Kish Sklar, "The Founding of Mt. Holyoke Female Seminary: A Case Study in Educational Change," in *The Women of America: Original Essays and Documents*, ed. Carol Berkin and Mary Beth Norton (Boston: Houghton Mifflin, 1979); Margaret A. Nash, "'A Salutary Rivalry': The Growth of Higher Education for Women in Oxford, Ohio, 1855–1867," *History of Higher Education Annual* 16 (1996): 21–38.

9. Mattingly, *The Classless Profession*, 154–55. Corroborating statistics about the first generation of normal school students can be found in Jurgen Herbst, *And Sadly Teach* (Madison: University of Wisconsin Press, 1989), chap. 3; Christine Ogren, *The American State Normal School* (New York: Palgrave Macmillan, 2005).

10. Frankfort, *Collegiate Women* (New York: New York University Press, 1977); Helen L. Horowitz, *The Power and Passion of M. Carey Thomas* (New York: Alfred A Knopf, 1994); Barbara R. Peltzman, "Mar-

tha Carey Thomas," in *Biographical Dictionary of American Educators*, ed. John Ohles (Westport, CT: Greenwood Press, 1978), 3:1286–87. Mount Holyoke Seminary only gained college status in 1893.

11. Helen L. Horowitz, "Academic Women," *History of Education Quarterly* 20 (Fall 1980): 339.

12. Frankfort, *Collegiate Women*, 50. In its first decade of operation 73–78 percent of Bryn Mawr students attended private prep schools beforehand. M. Carey Thomas herself had gone to a private Howland Institute before her college training.

13. Henry Barnard, ed., "Educational Statistics of the United States in 1850," *American Journal of Education* 1 (1855): 368.

14. "Washington Female Institute," *National Intelligencer*, February 20, 1860 (repeated March 10, 1860). During the same year, comparable instruction could be arranged at the Academy of the Visitation, one of the oldest Roman Catholic preparatory schools in the country, for $200, which included board, tuition, stationery, and doctor's fees (July 17, 1860). Similarly well-regarded schools like the Virginia Female Institute or Saint Timothy's in Catonsville, Maryland, outside Baltimore, charged $200 and $250, respectively.

15. US Federal Census, District of Columbia, [July 9,] 1860 (1st Ward), Roll M653-102, 403. All of these features—classical preparation like college-oriented preparatory schools, legitimation via experiential credentials, city clienteles, appropriation of collegiate (male) faculty—contrasted markedly with comparable schools, especially in the South, featuring Christian motherhood and teaching careers. Cf. Amy Friendlander, "A More Perfect Christian Womanhood: Higher Learning for a New South," in *Education and the Rise of the New South*, ed. Ronald Goodenow and Arthur O. White (Boston: G. K. Hall, 1981), 72–91.

16. James McLachlan, *American Boarding Schools* (New York: Charles Scribner's Sons, 1969). Of course, colleges in the throes of modernization and adaptation to a new national economy had a parallel experience. See Marilyn Tobias, *Old Dartmouth on Trial: The Transformation of the Academic Community in Nineteenth-Century America* (New York: New York University Press, 1982).

17. Nancy Beadie and Kim Tolley, "A School for Every Purpose: An Introduction to the History of Academies in the United States," in *Chartered School: Two Hundred Years of Independent Academies in the United States, 1727–1925* (New York: Routledge Falmer, 2002), 3–16.

18. Anne Scarborough Philbin, *The Past and the Promised* (Baltimore: Alumnae Association of the College of Notre Dame of Maryland, 1959), chap. 2.

19. Sr. Mary David, SSND, *The College of Notre Dame of Maryland, 1895–1945* (New York: Declan X. McMullen, 1947), chap. 2, esp. 46 for the ages of students.

20. David, *College of Notre Dame*, 57–61.

21. Philip Gleason, *Contending with Modernity: Catholic Higher Education in the United States* (New York: Oxford University Press, 1995), introduction.

22. Mother Grace Dammann, RSCJ, "The American Catholic College for Women," in *Essays on Catholic Education in the United States*, ed. Roy J. Deferrari (Washington, DC: Catholic University of American Press, 1942), 173–84; Sr. Mary M. Bowler, *A History of Catholic Colleges for Women in the United States of America* (Washington, DC: Catholic University of America Press, 1933), chap. 3.

23. "Oberlin College," in *Cyclopedia of Education*, ed. Paul Monroe (New York: Macmillan, 1913), 4:522. Four women entered the freshman course in 1837 and three graduated in 1841, thought to be the first female collegiate graduates in the United States receiving degrees equal to men's colleges. In 1911–12 Oberlin's collegiate student body numbered 998 while three hundred studied in its noncollegiate (preparatory) grouping. It changed its name to Oberlin College in 1850, although its 1833 state charter permitted the awarding of college degrees. Scholars have generally accepted Oberlin's claim to be the first collegiate experience for women, but there are many other contenders for this definitional prize. See Mabel Newcomer, *A Century of Higher Education for American Women* (New York: Harper and Bros., 1959), 12–14.

24. John Barnard, *From Evangelism to Progressivism at Oberlin College, 1866–1917* (Columbus: Ohio State University Press, 1969), chap. 1, esp. 24–25.

25. Ibid. Actually by 1865, in spite of many women entering the preparatory courses, only seventy-nine Oberlin females had completed the college course and received the BA degree. This pattern held for other coeducational college, like Antioch, which was founded in 1853 and shaped by its first president Horace Mann along lines he pioneered with the early Massachusetts normal schools. Mann's view of coeducation did not extend to social interchanges of the sexes outside the classroom. John Rury and Glenn Harper, "The Trouble with Coeducation: Mann and Women at Antioch, 1853–1860," *History of Education Quarterly* 26, no. 4 (Winter 1986): 481–502; see also Elizabeth K. Adams [Smith College professor], "Higher Education of Women: A Historical Sketch," in *Cyclopedia of Education*, ed. Paul Monroe (New York: Macmillan, 1913), 5:795–811. David Potts has well argued that after the Civil War most denominational colleges became more corporate in their organization and expanded their denominational networks in spite of rhetoric favoring non-denominationalism: "American Colleges in the Nineteenth Century: From Localism to Denominationalism," *History of Education Quarterly* 11 (Winter 1971): 363–80.

26. James C. Albisetti, "American Women's Colleges through European Eyes, 1865–1914," *History of Education Quarterly* 32, no. 4 (Winter 1992): 439–58. This article explores the initially favorable impression of early Oberlin by overseas visitors. Eventually the tenor of opinion shifts, especially away from the single-sex model in Europe for fear of offering women second-rate instruction. Even when European schools admitted women, they did not necessarily cultivate female scholars on their faculty for many years, seemingly to harbor conflicting values.

27. Helen L. Horowitz, *Alma Mater*, chap. 1; Elizabeth Alden Green, *Mary Lyon and Mount Holyoke: Opening the Gates* (Hanover, NH: University Press of New England, 1979), chap. 6.

28. "James Renwick," in *Who Was Who in American History: Historical Volume* (Chicago: Marquis, 1967), 509. Renwick, a graduate of Columbia College, trained as an engineer on Erie RR projects and the construction of the Croton Aqueduct. His early career favored a Gothic style in his design of many New York City churches, like Grace Church on Broadway and later Saint Patrick's. Before his Vassar design, he achieved a considerable reputation for his Smithsonian Institution (1848), the smallpox asylum on Ward's Island, and the lunatic asylum on Blackwell's Island, both in New York City's East River. These large public asylums set the context for Vassar's buildings rather than his design for New York Free Academy (1848), later City College of New York. Paul Turner, *Campus: An American Planning Tradition* (Cambridge, MA: MIT Press, 1985), 117, 133.

29. Newcomer, *Higher Education for American Women*, 21–24. Vassar initially put up $400,000 but added subsequent amounts to total about $1 million, generally thought to be equivalent to Henry Durant's philanthropy to Wellesley and considerably more than Sophia Smith's donation to her college. See also Lynn Gordon, *Women and Higher Education in the Progressive Era* (New Haven, CT: Yale University Press, 1990), chap. 4.

30. Horowitz, *Alma Mater*, chap. 3; Patricia Palmieri, "Here Was Fellowship: A Social Portrait of Academic Women at Wellesley College, 1895–1920," *History of Education Quarterly* 23 (Summer 1983): 195–214. This last article makes a spirited and convincing case that Wellesley recruited a stellar group of intellectually and collegially oriented women. However, Palmieri's "community" does not include students whose postgraduate careers did not vary much from the record of other women's colleges in terms of percentage of individuals who work, who marry, and who have professional careers. See Roberta Frankfort, *Collegiate Women*, for a more provocative and historical interpretation, one that argues that more intellectually oriented Bryn Mawr reengaged and transformed the genteel domestic tradition in the early years of the twentieth century. See also Mary Ann Dzuback, "Women and Social Research at Bryn Mawr College, 1915–1940," *History of Education Quarterly* 33, no. 4 (Winter 1993): 579–608, for subsequent intellectual developments.

31. Curti, *Philanthropy*, 285.

32. Robert L Fletcher, ed., *Amherst College: Biographical Record of the Graduates and Non-Graduates* (Amherst, MA: Trustees of Amherst College, 1939), 89.

33. "College Notes," *Journal of Education* 68 (September 24, 1908): 695–96.

34. Horowitz, *Alma Mater*, chap. 5. Julius Hawley Seelye, himself a graduate of Amherst, had studied in Germany at the University of Halle and Auburn Theological Seminary, before accepting in 1858 a teaching position at Amherst, where he served as president from 1876 to 1890. He was a trustee of Mount Holyoke from 1872 to 1895. Fletcher, *Amherst College*, 76–77.

35. Rev. L. Clark Seelye, "The Higher Education of Women: Its Perils and Its Benefits," *Lectures and Proceedings of the American Institute of Instruction*, vol. 59 (Boston: AII, 1888): 69–86.

36. Curti, *Philanthropy*, chap. 5. Until Vassar's gift of $800,000 to begin that school and Smith's $400,000, no American college (excepting Stephen Girard's $2 million 1830s bequest) had received more than $100,000 before the Civil War. Durant paid an estimated $1 million to create Wellesley. The largest philanthropy went to Sophie Newcomb College in New Orleans, which began with a $100,000 bequest in 1886, eventually mushrooming to $3.5 million. Newcomb distinguished itself early on with an Arts and Crafts emphasis that centered on pottery making and the creation of a distinctive niche of professional artistry for many of its graduates. http://www.newcomb.tulane.edu/new_hist.html. See also Gordon, *Women and Higher Education*, chap. 5.

37. Horowitz, *Alma Mater*, 78.

38. "James Rhoads," in *Who Was Who in American History: Historical Volume* (Chicago: Marquis, 1967), 510; Cynthia Farr Brown, "'Putting a Woman in Sole Power': The Presidential Succession at Bryn Mawr, 1892–1894," *History of Higher Education Annual* 8 (1988): 79–97.

39. Helen L. Horowitz, "'Nous Autres': Reading, Passion and the Creation of M. Carey Thomas," *Journal of American History* 79, no. 1 (June 1992): 68–95. The adventurous reading focused on Dante Gabriel Rossetti, Algernon Charles Swinburne, and Theophile Gautier, but also included European travel and museums, discouraged by her Quaker traditions; Laurence Veysey, "Martha Carey Thomas," *Notable American Women*, ed. Edward T. James et al. (Cambridge, MA: Harvard University Press, 1971), 3:446–50.

40. Frankfort, *Collegiate Women*, chap. 5. A good summary of scholarship on this issue can be found in Barbara Sicherman, "College and Careers: Historical Perspectives on the Lives and Work Patterns of Women College Graduates," in *Woman and Higher Education in American History*, ed. John Mack Faragher and Florence Howe (New York: Norton, 1988), 130–64.

41. Turner, *Campus*, 223–25; Cornelia Meigs, *What Makes a College: A History of Bryn Mawr* (New York: Macmillan, 1956). One of Walter Cope's relatives, Francis Cope, served on the college's first board of trustees and another relative, Julia Cope, was a member of the first class. 58–59.

42. Curti, *Philanthropy*, 121–24. The difference has been estimated at $600,000 if cashed upon receipt. The ultimate payoff for Cornell amounted to nearly $5 million.

43. Nancy Beadie, "From Academy to University in New York State: The Genesee Institutions and the Importance of Capital to the Success of an Idea, 1848–1871," *History of Higher Education Annual* 14 (1994): 13–38.

44. Morris Bishop, *A History of Cornell* (Ithaca, NY: Cornell University Press, 1962); "Cornell University, Ithaca, NY," in *Cyclopedia of Education*, ed. Paul Monroe (New York: Macmillan, 1912), 2:206–7; Daniel Lang, "The People's College, The Mechanics' Mutual Protection and the Agricultural College Act," *History of Education Quarterly* 18, no. 3 (Fall 1978): 295–321.

45. Kermit Carlyle Parsons, *The Cornell Campus: A History of Its Planning and Development* (Ithaca, NY: Cornell University Press, 1968), 1–35. For all the detail about the school's origins and his praises for Ezra Cornell, White omits Olmsted from his two-volume autobiography of this founding moment. Andrew White, *Autobiography* (New York: Century, 1905).

46. James Morgan Hart, *German Universities* (New York: G. P. Putnam's Sons, 1874), discussed the "American" university and found it wanting, compared to the German universities of his experience (Göttingen JUD 1864). The overinvestment in buildings, Hart found, was particularly inhibiting and prevalent at Cornell, which had hired him into its early faculty (1868–72) to teach modern languages. "James Morgan Hart," in *Who Was Who in American History*, vol. 1 (Chicago: Marquis, 1968), 529. An excellent analysis of the putative German influence on American higher

education can be found in James Turner and Paul Bernard, "The 'German Model' and the Graduate School: The University of Michigan and the Origin Myth of the American University," *History of Higher Education Annual* 13 (1993): 69–98.

47. Curti, *Philanthropy*, 103; Bishop, *Cornell*, 146–49.

48. Woody, *Women's Education in the United States*, 248–49.

49. Burke, *American Collegiate Populations*, 215–16,

50. Woody, *Women's Education in the United States*, 252.

51. David F. Allmendinger Jr., "History and the Usefulness of Women's Education," *History of Education Quarterly* 19 (Spring 1979): 117–24; Rosalind Rosenberg, "The Academic Prism: The New View of American Women," in *Women of America: A History*, ed. Carol R. Berkin and Mary Beth Norton (Boston: Houghton Mifflin, 1979), 318–41.

52. Montgomery Schuyler, "The Architecture of American Colleges," *Architectural Record* 30, no. 6 (December 1911): 566. In this postwar period, other central college and university structures, like Healy Building at Georgetown University (architects were Viennese émigrés John L. Smithmeyer and Paul Pelz, who later designed the Library of Congress), bear close resemblances to Babcock's design.

53. Charlotte W. Conable, *Women at Cornell: The Myth of Equal Education* (Ithaca, NY: Cornell University Press, 1977); Barbara Solomon, *In the Company of Educated Women* (New Haven, CT: Yale University Press, 1985), 51–52.

54. Solomon, *In the Company of Educated Women*, 51–53. The author notes that state universities were slow to notice that the Morrill Land Grant Act did not exclude "women" from its legislative language, opening a wedge in the argument against women.

55. Sarah Gordon, "Smith College Students: The First Ten Classes, 1879–1888," *History of Education Quarterly* 15 (Summer 1975): 147–67.

56. These age and social class patterns differed markedly in the first British women's colleges at the same period, where admission was largely a function of privileged class and where cultural biases against children of businessmen and tradesmen reduced their ranks considerably. Joyce S. Pederson, "The Reform of Women's Secondary and Higher Education: Institutional Change and Social Values in Mid and Late Victorian England," *History of Education Quarterly* 19, no. 1 (Spring 1979): 61–91; Martha Vicinus, *Independent Women: Work and Community for Single Women, 1850–1920* (Chicago: University of Chicago Press, 1985).

57. Howard H. Peckham, *The Making of the University of Michigan, 1817–1967* (Ann Arbor: University of Michigan Press, 1967), 65; "University of Michigan," in *Cyclopedia of Education*, ed. Paul Monroe (New York: Macmillan, 1913), 4:216–17; for the pioneering role of Michigan, see Susan R Richardson, "Research Note: State Higher Education Database, 1870–1965," *History of Higher Education Annual* 22 (2002): 109–30.

58. Peckham, *University of Michigan*, 82. *Historical Catalogue of Brown University* (Providence, RI: Brown University, 1905), 216. One might note that Ada Comstock, the influential dean of women at Smith, was a graduate of the University of Minnesota, and Mary Woolley, president of Mount Holyoke, was an 1894 graduate of Brown University. Prestigious women's colleges owed much to coeducational universities. In the academic year 1889–90, the University of Michigan became the largest university in the country with an enrollment of 2,153 (Peckham, *University of Michigan*, 85), momentarily edging out Harvard.

59. Frankfort, *Collegiate Women*, chap. 5 and appendix.

60. John Lawson and Harold Silver, *A Social History of Education in England* (London: Methuen, 1973), 307, 343. In 1869 a Girls College at Hinton was founded and five years later moved to Cambridge as Girton College, setting the precedent for Newnham College at Cambridge and Somerville and Lady Margaret Hall at Oxford in the 1870s. University authorities admitted women to degrees but not to full equality for another seventy years.

61. Hugh Hawkins, "Elizabeth Cabot Cary Agassiz," in *Notable American Women*, vol. 1 (Cambridge, MA: Harvard University Press, 1971), 22–25; Barbara Solomon, *In the Company of Educated Women* (New Haven, CT: Yale University Press, 1985), chap. 6.

62. Doris Malkmus, "Small Towns, Small Sects and Coeducation in Midwestern Colleges, 1853–1861," *History of Higher Education Annual* 22 (2002): 33-65, suggests that this "eastern" seminary model contrasted with a "western" variant, where local developers and denominational organizations played more central roles.

63. Annette K. Baxter, "Emily James Smith Putnam," *Notable American Women*, vol. 3 (Cambridge, MA: Harvard University Press, 1971), 106–8; John Thelin, *A History of American Higher Education* (Baltimore: Johns Hopkins University Press, 2004), 182–86. Most early deans faced the dilemma of either representing student interests to their presidents or defending school policy to students. Jana Nidiffer, *Pioneering Deans of Women: More than Wise and Pious Matrons* (New York: Teachers College Press, 2000).

64. Merle Borrowman, *The Liberal and the Technical in Teacher Education* (New York: Teachers College Press, 1956); Bette Weneck, "Social and Cultural Stratification in Women's Higher Education: Barnard College and Teachers College, 1898–1912," *History of Education Quarterly* 31, no. 1 (Spring 1991): 1–25; Horowitz, *Alma Mater*, chap. 10.

65. Carole B. Shmurak and Bonnie Shandler, "'Castle of Science': Mount Holyoke College and the Preparation of Women in Chemistry, 1837–1941," *History of Education Quarterly* 32, no. 3 (Fall 1992): 315–42, make clear two important points: a) the physical sciences drew equal to studies in the old seminary evangelical tradition after the 1880s, and b) seminary collegiality did not impede the engagement of science or scientific careers at Mount Holyoke.

66. Anne Baxter, "Virginia Crocheron Gildersleeve," *Notable American Women: The Modern Period* (Cambridge, MA: Harvard University Press, 1980): 273–75. Gildersleeve was Barnard's dean from 1911 to 1947.

67. Horowitz, *Alma Mater*, 258–61. Meyer served as a trustee from the school's founding in 1889 to 1951 and was much chagrined that when its original building, Students' Hall, was renamed, the name chosen was Barnard Hall rather than Schiff Hall after its donor. Lynn Gordon, "Annie Nathan Meyer and Barnard College: Mission and Identity in Women's Higher Education, 1889–1950," *History of Education Quarterly* 26, no. 4 (Winter 1986): 503–22.

68. Gordon, "Annie Nathan Meyer."

69. Donald M. Scott, "Women and Education," *History of Education Quarterly* 15, no. 2 (Summer 1975): 213–17.

70. Burke, *American Collegiate Populations*, 216.

71. The very careers considered for educated women made little mention of farmwork and the medial trades of lower-class city women, which always required not only physical energy but also organizational and dexterous skills possessed by a majority of working women. The omission of this majority of working women underscored the class assumptions of people debating "women's education."

72. Thelin, *American Higher Education*, 142–45; Margaret Rossiter, *Women Scientists in America: Struggles and Strategies to 1940* (Baltimore: Johns Hopkins University Press, 1982); Geraldine J. Clifford, *Lone Voyagers: Academic Women in Coeducational Institutions, 1870–1937* (New York: Feminist Press at the City University of New York, 1989).

CHAPTER EIGHT

1. For a discussion of the small literature of reminiscences and fictions of college life, see Roger Geiger with Julie Ann Bubolz, "College as It Was in the Mid-Nineteenth Century," *History of Higher Education Annual* 16 (1996): 105–15; John Thelin, *A History of American Higher Education* (Baltimore: Johns Hopkins University Press, 2004), 64–67.

2. Joseph F. Kett, *Rites of Passage: Adolescence in America 1790 to the Present* (New York: Basic Books, 1977), 174–82; Ronald A. Smith, *Sports and Freedom: The Rise of Big-Time College Athletics* (New York: Oxford University Press, 1988), makes clear that the embedded mythology of college

sports as character shapers completely masked the extent to which colleges, especially Yale, recruited professional players, overpaid their coaches, and created funds for the special cultivation of favored athletes from the mid-nineteenth century onward.

3. Owen Johnson, *Stover at Yale* (New York: Collier Books, 1968).

4. Ibid., 22. See also John R. Thelin, *A History of American Higher Education* (Baltimore: Johns Hopkins University Press, 2004), 163–68.

5. It is perhaps not too much of a stretch to find the connection between athletics and social Darwinism reinforced via Walter Camp, Yale athletic promoter and coach, married to the sister of William Graham Sumner, Yale's most forceful voice endorsing Darwinian precepts of physical struggle and survival of the fittest. "Walter Camp," in *Who Was Who in American History*, vol. 2 (Chicago: Marquis, 1968), 186–87.

6. George E. Peterson, *The New England College in the Age of the University* (Amherst, MA: Amherst College Press, 1964), 147.

7. Ibid., 145–47. See James Turner, "Secularization or Sacralization: Speculations on Some Religious Origins of the Secular Humanities Curriculum, 1850–1900," in *The Secularization of the Academy*, ed. George M. Marsden and Bradley J. Longfield (New York: Oxford University Press, 1992), 74–106; Alexander Urbiel, "Student Government," in *Historical Dictionary of American Education*, ed. Richard Altenbaugh (Westport, CT: Greenwood Press, 1999), 353–55.

8. Marilyn Tobias, *Old Dartmouth on Trial: The Transformation of the Academic Community in Nineteenth-Century America* (New York: New York University Press, 1982), 112–13, chap. 2.

9. Peterson, *The New England College*, 147. Colin B. Burke's study, *American Collegiate Populations* (New York: New York University Press, 1982), 215–24, argues persuasively that enrollment figures for the postbellum period have been largely inflated and were probably lower than cited here. There were modest increases—below 2 percent of the white males between twenty and twenty-four—between 1860 and 1880 with a surge appearing in the 1890s.

10. David F. Allmendinger Jr., "New England Students and the Revolution in Higher Education, 1800–1900," *History of Education Quarterly* 11 (Winter 1971): 381–89; see also David Potts, "Students and the Social History of American Higher Education," *History of Education Quarterly* 15 (Fall 1975): 317–27.

11. David Potts, "American Colleges in the Nineteenth Century: From Localism to Denominationalism," *History of Education Quarterly* 11 (Winter 1971): 363–80, David Potts, *Wesleyan University, 1831–1910: Collegiate Enterprise in New England* (New Haven, CT: Yale University Press, 1992), esp. chap. 4.

12. Daniel Walker Howe, *The Political Culture of the American Whigs* (Chicago: University of Chicago Press, 1979).

13. Peter D. Hall, *The Organization of American Culture, 1700–1900: Private Institutions, Elites and the Origins of American Nationality* (New York: New York University Press, 1982), 215–19.

14. Carl Diehl, *Americans and German Scholarship, 1770–1870* (New Haven, CT: Yale University Press, 1978). More recently scholars have questioned the extensive German influence on American higher education. See James Turner and Paul Bernard, "The Prussian Road to University? German Models and the University of Michigan, 1837–c. 1895," *Rackham Reports* (1988–89): 7–52.

15. Wilson Smith, *Professors and Public Ethics* (Ithaca, NY: Cornell University Press, 1956).

16. R. J. Wilson, *Darwinism and the American Intellectual* (Homewood, IL: Dorsey Press, 1967), 44–45; Richard Hofstadter, *Social Darwinism in American Thought* (Boston: Beacon Press, 1955; 1st ed., 1944), 15; Cynthia E. Russett, *Darwin in America: The Intellectual Response, 1865–1912* (San Francisco: W. H. Freeman, 1976), 50–55.

17. Hofstadter, *Social Darwinism*, chap. 2.

18. Noah Porter, *The American Colleges and the American Public*, 2nd ed. (New York: Charles Scriber's Sons, 1878; 1st ed., 1871), 15; George Leveque, "Noah Porter Revisited," *History of Higher Education Annual* 27 (2007): 29–66.

19. Many university scholars of the twentieth century have accepted the nineteenth-century university leaders as accurate in their criticism of the "restrictiveness" of the American college. The political competition of the late nineteenth century—before the generic character of university or college solidified—became an uncritical university apologia. Richard Hofstadter's judgment (*Academic Freedom in the Age of the College* [New York: Columbia University Press, 1955]) of the nineteenth-century college as retrograde exemplifies the problem. Revision of this ahistoricism commenced with James Axtell, "The Death of the Liberal Arts College," *History of Education Quarterly* 11 (Winter 1971): 339–52, and went further still with James McLachlan (a student of Hofstadter), "The American College in the Nineteenth Century: Towards a Reappraisal," *Teachers College Record* 80 (December 1978): 287–306. One of the casualties of defining modernism in the university as anticlassical was the Jesuit alternative (*Ratio Studiorum*), dismissed both by Porter, a potential ally, and subsequent historians. See Kathleen A. Mahoney and Caroline Winterer, "The Problem of the Past in the Modern University: Catholics and Classicists, 1860–1900," *History of Education Quarterly* 42, no. 4 (Winter 2002): 515–43.

20. Porter, *American Colleges*, 48–49.

21. Ibid., 52.

22. Ibid., 77.

23. Ibid., chap. 3, esp., 115.

24. Ibid., 153.

25. Ibid., 173–74.

26. Ibid., 180.

27. Timothy Dwight, *Memories of Yale Life and Men, 1845–1899* (New York: Dodd Mead, 1903), 367. Dwight's praise of Porter's predecessor and candid assessment of his limitations likely reflected Dwight's own university predilections, which he exercised once he became Yale's president (1886–90). However, Louise Stevenson, *Scholarly Means to Evangelical Ends: The New Haven Scholars and the Transformation of Higher Learning in America, 1830–1890* (Baltimore: Johns Hopkins University Press, 1986), makes clear that Porter belonged to a cadre of influential faculty recruited by his predecessor Theodore Dwight Woolsey. He was not a lone voice of conservative reaction, the usual interpretation of his Yale tenure. For a revisionist analysis of Porter, see Peter D. Hall, "'Noah Porter Writ Large': Reflections on the Modernization of American Education and Its Critics, 1866–1916," *History of Higher Education Annual* 16 (1996): 39–70.

28. Dwight, *Memories*, 346–48.

29. *Historical Statistics of the United States*, pt. 1 (Washington, DC: Bureau of the Census, 1975), 383; Bruce Leslie, *Gentlemen and Scholars: College and Community in the "Age of the University," 1865–1917* (University Park: Pennsylvania State University Press, 1992), makes clear that small denominational colleges kept abreast of educational and scientific advances in this period. Variously they distanced and strengthened denominational ties but appreciated faculty with German training and alumni with urban connections. In other words, colleges and universities experienced similar dynamics. Many of Leslie's points received earlier treatment in Marilyn Tobias's *Old Dartmouth on Trial* and Peterson's study. A recent essay that adds detail to Peterson's treatment of Amherst's division is J. M. Opal, "The Making of the Victorian Campus: Teacher and Student at Amherst College, 1850–1880," *History of Education Quarterly* 42, no. 3 (Fall 2002): 342–67.

30. Kett, *Rites of Passage*, chap. 7.

31. "Reverdy Johnson," in *Who Was Who in America: Historical Volume* (Chicago: Marquis, 1967), 351.

32. Hugh Hawkins, *Pioneer: A History of the Johns Hopkins University, 1874–1889* (Ithaca, NY: Cornell University Press, 1960), 23; D. G. Hart, "Faith and Learning in the Age of the University: The Academic Ministry of Daniel Coit Gilman," in *The Secularization of the Academy*, ed. George M. Marsden and Bradley J. Longfield (New York: Oxford University Press, 1992), 107–45. Hart's work stressed Gilman's use of Darwinian evolution to meld science and religion, a linkage ignored in some Gilman biographies and a linkage that makes Gilman's modern university an extension of

the old evangelical college. See also David Hollinger. "Inquiry and Uplift: Late Nineteenth-Century American Academics and the Moral Efficacy of Scientific Practice," in *The Authority of Experts*, ed. Thomas Haskell (Bloomington: Indiana University Press, 1984), 142–56.

33. "Daniel Coit Gilman," in *Cyclopedia of Education*, ed. Paul Monroe (New York: Macmillan, 1916), 3:111; Abraham Flexner, *Daniel Coit Gilman: Creator of the American Type of University* (New York: Harcourt Brace, 1946).

34. Edith Nye MacMullen, *In the Cause of True Education: Henry Barnard and Nineteenth-Century School Reform* (New Haven, CT: Yale University Press, 1991), 196–97. For many of Gilman's letters to Barnard, see the Henry Barnard Papers, New York University Archives.

35. Hawkins, *Pioneer*, 4–5.

36. Ibid., 10, 13.

37. Henry James, *Charles W. Eliot* (Boston: Houghton Mifflin, 1930), 2:5. At Gilman's twenty-fifth anniversary, Eliot paid handsome acknowledgment to the competitive dynamics set up by Johns Hopkins example. Eliot and Gilman had many years to discuss these dynamics, since they both summered every year between 1885 and 1907 in Northeast Harbor, Maine, where Eliot had a summer home.

38. Ibid., chap. 4.

39. Daniel C. Gilman, "On the Growth of American Colleges and Their Present Tendency to the Study of Science," *Lectures and Proceedings of the American Institute of Instruction*, vol. 42 (Boston: AII, 1872): 96–115.

40. Ibid., 99. This lecture was offered several times, the first while Gilman still served as a faculty member of Yale's Sheffield Scientific School—a land-grant recipient—and later to the new leadership of Cornell University, also a land-grant recipient.

41. Josiah Royce, "Present Ideals of University Life," *Scribner's Magazine* 10 (September 1891): 383ff.

42. Charles R. Van Hise, "Inaugural Address [at the University of Wisconsin]," *Science* 20 (1904): 194-205; Daniel Coit Gilman, "Higher Education in the United States" [address at Chicago's Columbian Exposition, 1893], reprinted in *University Problems in the United States* (New York: Arno Press, 1969), 287–310.

43. Seth Low, "Higher Education in the United States," *Educational Review* 5 (January 1893): 1–16.

44. G. Allan Conway, "Columbia and New York Universities Consolidated: A Study in Urban and Social Consciousness" (unpublished PhD diss., New York University, 1974), 99ff.; Thomas Frusciano and Marilyn Pettit, *New York University and the City* (New Brunswick, NJ: Rutgers University Press, 1997), 128–29.

45. Robert McCaughey, *Stand, Columbia: A History of Columbia University in the City of New York* (New York: Columbia University Press, 2003), 177–90. Low's involvement of the faculty in significant decision making raised the authority of faculty above both that of administrators and students, inviting a sneer from his successor, Nicholas Murray Butler: "Low had a New York (or Brooklyn) commercial mind. He would have been good running a steamship company or a manufacturing firm" (179).

46. Christopher J. Lucas, *American Higher Education: A History* (New York: St. Martin's Griffin, 1994), 197–99; Walter Metzger, *Academic Freedom in the Age of the University* (New York: Columbia University Press, 1955), chap. 5.

47. http://www.aacu.org/About/timeline/index.cfm.

48. John Thelin, *The Cultivation of Ivy: A Saga of the College in America* (Cambridge, MA: Schenckman, 1976), 25–28. For an informative essay on the changing uses of sport at black colleges, see Patrick B. Miller, "To 'Bring the Race along Rapidly': Sport, Student Culture and Educational Mission at Historically Black Colleges during the Interwar Years," *History of Education Quarterly* 35, no. 2 (Summer 1995): 111–33.

CHAPTER NINE

1. *Historical Statistics in the United States: Colonial Times to 1970* (Washington, DC: US Bureau of the Census, 1975), pt. 1, 383.

2. Henry Adams, *The Education of Henry Adams* (Boston: Houghton Mifflin, 1918), 305–6.

3. Christopher Lucas, *American Higher Education: A History* (New York: St. Martin's Press, 1994), 191–94.

4. Pamela Nelson, "Women and the University in the 1920s: The Early Career of Dorothy McSparran Arnold at NYU" (1988), New York University Archives, Public History Program RG 20.9—Activities, Box 4, Folder 11.

5. Paul H. Mattingly, "Institutional History: Structures over Time," *Historical Research in Education: A Research Agenda*, ed. John Hardin Best (Washington, DC: AERA, 1983), 34–55. Laurence Veysey's influential book, *The Emergence of the American University* (Chicago: University of Chicago Press, 1965), artificially categorizes his material by separating the values of research, utility, and culture and ends his study in 1910 with an intimation that any university worth the name embraced all three. In fact, most colleges and universities had mixed these values all along and would do so in the future. John Thelin's excellent synthesis, *A History of American Higher Education* (Baltimore: Johns Hopkins University Press, 2004), concurs. Edwin Slosson's *Great American Universities* (New York, 1910), often used to identify America's fourteen truly great institutions, actually studied the irregularities of their management and the precariousness of their claims to be "best" on any number of standards.

6. Thomas Frusciano and Marilyn Pettit, *The University and the City* (New Brunswick, NJ: Rutgers University Press, 1998).

7. Morton White, *Social Thought in America: The Revolt against Formalism* (Boston: Beacon Press, 1970).

8. Thomas Bender, Peter D. Hall, Thomas L. Haskell, and Paul H. Mattingly, "Institutionalization and Education in the Nineteenth and Twentieth Centuries," *History of Education Quarterly* 20, no. 4 (Winter 1980): 449–72. Peter Hall has argued that turn-of-the-century patterns of allying men's clubs, the chamber of commerce, professional groups, and corporations in the Lehigh valley transformed not only economic opportunity there (and elsewhere) but enabled Muhlenberg College and other nearby institutions to become incontestable parts of the regional culture. See Karel Lee Kibler Hall and Peter Dobkin Hall, *Lehigh Valley: An Illustrated History* (Woodland Hills, CA: Windsor Publications, 1982), 116.

9. http://american-education.org/1445-ogden-robert-curtis-1836-1913.html.

10. "To the Conference Friends," in Box 18: Education in the South, 1914–16, in Robert C. Ogden Papers, Library of Congress. See also Ogden's prickly defense of these organizations to the critical Oswald Garrison Villard (owner of the *New York Evening Post*), March 11, 1905, also in Robert C. Ogden Papers, Library of Congress.

11. Franklin Parker, *George Peabody: A Biography* (Nashville: Vanderbilt University Press, 1971); Paul Conklin, *Gone with the Ivy: A Biography of Vanderbilt University* (Knoxville: University of Tennessee Press, 1985), 126–27, also chap. 8. Also J. L. M. Curry, *Peabody Education Fund* (New York: Negro Universities Press, 1969; 1st ed., 1898).

12. Phillip Whitwell Wilson, *An Unofficial Statesman: Robert C. Ogden* (Garden City, NY: Doubleday and Sons, 1924); Robert H. Bremner, *The Public Good: Philanthropy and Welfare in the Civil War Era* (New York: Alfred Knopf, 1980), 185–90.

13. James D. Anderson, *The Education of Black Americans in the South* (Chapel Hill: University of North Carolina Press, 1988); Robert F. Engs, *Educating the Disfranchised and Disinherited: Samuel Chapman Armstrong and Hampton Institute, 1839–1893* (Knoxville: University of Tennessee Press, 1999).

14. Correspondence on these matters was intensive, with many shared and circulated letters between and among these individuals. Often the discussion took a very detailed political turn

concerning local and state issues in Southern cities and states. See, for example, Edgar Gardner Murphy to Wallace Buttrick, November 14, 1907, Box 10 "Special Correspondence Oct–Nov 1907," in the Robert Ogden Papers, Library of Congress.

15. "List of Guests at dinner in Honor of the Southern Education Board and the General Education Board, Thursday, January 8, 1903, Waldorf Astoria New York, given by Robert C. Ogden," Subject File, Box 17 "Education of the South, 1903," Robert C. Ogden Papers, Library of Congress. The seating chart contains 152 names and reads like a who's who of New York's power elite.

16. Paul H. Mattingly, "The Guarantees of Voluntary Associations," in *The Classless Profession: American Schoolmen in the Nineteenth Century* (New York: New York University Press, 1975), 117–33; Gregory H. Stapleton, "Protestant Voluntary Organizations and the Shaping of Victorian American," in *Victorian America*, ed. Daniel Walker Howe (Philadelphia: University of Pennsylvania Press, 1976), 47–58.

17. Merle Curti and Roderick Nash, *Philanthropy and the Shaping of American Higher Education* (New Brunswick, NJ: Rutgers University Press, 1965), 215–17; J. William Hess, "General Education Board," in *Foundations*, ed. Harold M. Keele and Joseph C. Kiger (Westport, CT: Greenwood Press, 1984), 146–53.

18. Hess, "General Education Board," 148–49.

19. Curti, *Philanthropy*, 217.

20. Stephen Diner, *A City and Its Universities: Public Policy in Chicago, 1892–1919* (Chapel Hill: University of North Carolina Press, 1980), 15, chap. 3.

21. Richard J. Storr, *Harper's University: The Beginnings* (Chicago: University of Chicago Press, 1966), 11–34.

22. Raymond Fosdick, *Adventure in Giving: The Story of the General Education Board* (New York: Harper and Row, 1962); Kenneth W. Rose, "Frederick Taylor Gates," *American National Biography*, http://www.anb.org/articles/10/10-00618.html. Gates experienced a very erratic and disconnected college preparation in Missouri and Kansas, entered New York's Rochester University as a junior in 1875, and graduated there two years later. In 1880 he received a divinity degree from Rochester Seminary.

23. Daniel A. Wren, "American Business Philanthropy and Higher Education in the Nineteenth Century," *Business History Review* 57 (Autumn 1983): 321–46.

24. Diner, *A City and Its Universities*, 15; Thomas W. Goodspeed, *A History of the University of Chicago: The First Quarter Century* (Chicago: University of Chicago Press, 1972; 1st ed., 1916), chap. 3.

25. Storr, *Harper's University*, chap. 3. Rockefeller had added an additional million dollars to attach a college and graduate studies to an existing divinity school and to woo William Rainey Harper from his Yale professorship into the University of Chicago presidency.

26. George E. Vincent, "The University of Chicago," in *Cyclopedia of Education*, ed. Paul Monroe (New York: Macmillan, 1911), 1:603–7.

27. Goodspeed, *University of Chicago*; Storr, *Harper's University*.

28. Goodspeed, *University of Chicago*, chap. 6.

29. Edward W. Wolner, *Architecture, Institutions and the Making of the Modern Metropolis* (Chicago: University of Chicago Press, 2011).

30. Jean F. Block, *The Uses of Gothic: Planning and Building the Campus of the University of Chicago* (Chicago: University of Chicago Library, 1983), chap. 8. One might note other colleges in this same period, like Bryn Mawr, employed Gothic architecture to signal its advanced aspirations.

31. Ibid., 45. Numerically the humanities faculty numbered about half the first faculty, while the physical sciences composed about one-third, with the rest in the social sciences. Storr, *Harper's University: The Beginnings* (Chicago: University of Chicago Press, 1966), 75ff.

32. Coolidge continued his Gothic designs at a number of other schools like Vanderbilt, Western Reserve, Stanford, Yale, and Harvard; Perkins worked with the university but is better known

for the forty public schools he completed for Chicago including his masterpiece, the Carl Schurz High School; Rogers flourished in the 1920s and 1930s using Gothic designs at Yale (Harkness Tower, Sterling Library), Columbia (Butler Library), Tulane, and New York University (School of Education).

33. Paul Turner, *Campus* (Cambridge, MA: MIT Press, 1984), chap. 5, "The University as City Beautiful"; "Henry Ives Cobb," in *Who Was Who in American History*, vol. 1 (Chicago: Marquis, 1968), 234. Turner makes clear that the Beaux-Arts model would far surpass the Gothic in its twentieth-century influences, noting particularly the campus designs of Columbia and New York Universities, as well as Stanford White's influential redesign of Jefferson's University of Virginia after its disastrous 1895 fire.

34. James Gilbert, *Perfect Cities: Chicago's Utopias of 1893* (Chicago: University of Chicago Press, 1991).

35. Julie Reuben, *The Making of the Modern University* (Chicago: University of Chicago Press, 1996), esp. chaps. 2, 4, and 5.

36. Neil Coughlan, *Young John Dewey* (Chicago: University of Chicago Press, 1975).

37. Robert Westbrook, *John Dewey and American Democracy* (Ithaca, NY: Cornell University Press, 1991); Helen Horowitz, *Culture and the City: Cultural Philanthropy in Chicago from the 1880s to 1917* (Louisville: University of Kentucky Press, 1976); Daniel Rogers, "In Search of Progressivism," *Reviews on American History* (1972): 113–32; Stephen Diner, *A Very Different Age: Americans of the Progressive Era* (New York: Hill and Wang, 1998).

38. Westbrook, *John Dewey*, 91. Dewey observed the irony of a moral censorship but free social expression at state-supported University of Michigan. At Chicago, led by a Baptist president and Baptist money, there was free moral expression and social censorship concerning capitalism.

39. Westbrook, *John Dewey*, chap. 5, "No Mean City." See also Louis Menand, "The Real John Dewey," *New York Review of Books* 39, no. 12 (June 25, 1992): 50–54. Dewey claimed Harper's action toward his wife was not the sole reason but was a precipitating event at the end of a long history of offending decisions. See also George Dykhuisen, *The Life and Mind of John Dewey* (Carbondale: Southern Illinois University Press, 1973), 112–14; Andrew Feiffer, *The Chicago Pragmatists and American Progressivism* (Ithaca, NY: Cornell University Press, 1993).

40. "Thorstein Veblen," in *Who Was Who in American History: Historical Volume* (Chicago: Marquis, 1968), 1276; http://en.wikipedia.org/wiki/Thorstein_Veblen.

41. Until the post–Civil War period, most permanent academics had little formal training for their college subjects, other than training—usually apprenticeships—for the traditional professions, especially the ministry. After the Civil War, especially at the older or prominent colleges and universities, some disciplinary training—notably at German universities—was considered ideal. Martin J. Finkelstein, *The American Academic Profession* (Columbus: Ohio State University Press, 1962), chap. 2; Carl Diehl, *Americans and German Scholarship, 1770–1870* (New Haven, CT: Yale University Press, 1978); Laurence Veysey, *The Emergence of the American University* (Chicago: University of Chicago Press, 1965); Robert McGaughey, "The Transformation of American Academic Life: Harvard University, 1821–1892," *Perspectives in American History* 8 (1974): 237–332.

42. Max Lerner, ed., introduction to *The Portable Veblen* (New York: Viking Press, 1977), 1–49; David Riesman, *Thorstein Veblen: A Critical Interpretation* (New York: Charles Scribner's Sons, 1953); C. Wright Mills, introduction to Thorstein Veblen, *The Theory of the Leisure Class* (New York: New American Library, 1953), vi–xix.

43. Walter Ruegg, ed., *The History of the University in Europe, 1800–1945* (Cambridge: Cambridge University Press, 2004), vol. 3, chap. 10; James Turner with Jon H. Roberts, *The Sacred and Secular University* (Princeton, NJ: Princeton University Press, 2000); see also James Turner, *The Liberal Education of Charles Eliot Norton* (Baltimore: Johns Hopkins University Press, 1999), 340; James Turner, *Philology: The Forgotten Origins of the Modern Humanities* (Princeton, NJ: Princeton University Press, 2014), 270–73.

44. Daniel Rogers, "In Search of Progressivism," *Reviews on American History* (1972): 113–32; Stephen Diner, *A Very Different Age: Americans of the Progressive Era* (New York: Hill and Wang, 1998); Robin F. Bachin, "University of Chicago," in *The Encyclopedia of Chicago*, ed. James R. Grossman, Ann Durkin Keating, and Janice L. Rieff (Chicago: University of Chicago Press, 2004), 846.

45. Roundtable on "The History of the University in Europe, 1800–1945," at Social Science History Association meeting, Portland, OR, November 4, 2005: Paul H. Mattingly, Konrad Jarausch, Joseph F. Kett, John Craig, and James Turner, published as "Universities in Europe: North American Perspectives on European Historiography," *History of Education* (England) 37, no. 3 (May 2008): 469–90.

46. Diner, *A City and Its Universities*, 17.

47. David Allmendinger, "Strong Men of the Academic Revolution," *History of Education Quarterly* 13 no. 4 (Winter 1973): 415–25; Mark Beach, "President's Eye-View of the History of Higher Education," *History of Education Quarterly* 12, no. 4 (Winter 1972): 575–87. The authors underscore how powerfully these accounts have shaped the later histories of American higher education, which have deferred uncritically to these presidential voices.

48. Nicholas Murray Butler, "University Administration in the United States," *Educational Review* 41 (April 1911): 325–44; E. Benjamin Andrews, "The Organization of the University and the Distribution of Authority Therein," *Proceedings of the National Association of State Universities* 5 (1907): 114–21; Andrew S. Draper, "The University Presidency," *Atlantic Monthly* 97 (1906): 34–43; Henry M. MacCracken, "The Metropolitan University," speech delivered to Nineteenth Century Club, April 12, 1892. Student culture, research agendas, the pressing issues of distinct disciplines, and faculty lives especially apart from higher education rarely appeared as relevant portions of these accounts or, until recently, the ensuing histories. Mattingly, "Structures over Time: Institutional History," 34–55.

49. Goodspeed, *A History of the University of Chicago*, 203.

50. Ibid. The author of the first history of the University of Chicago, Thomas W. Goodspeed, was himself a graduate of the Rochester Theological Seminary, an ordained Baptist minister, secretary to the University of Chicago Board of Trustees from 1890 to 1913 and eventually a trustee himself from 1906 to 1913. From 1894 he also served as a trustee to Chicago's Baptist Union Theological Seminary where Harper himself had studied. *Who Was Who in American History*, vol. 1 (Chicago: Marquis, 1968), 468.

51. Merle Curti and Vernon Carstensen, "The University of Wisconsin to 1925," in *The University of Wisconsin: One Hundred and Twenty-Five Years*, ed. Allan Bogue and Robert Taylor (Madison: University of Wisconsin Press, 1975), 23–25. The youngest member of the older evangelical group of university presidents, Franklin Johnson, did earn a doctorate from the University of Jena (1869), received after his work at Colgate Theological Seminary and his ordination. Laurence Veysey, *The Emergence of the American University* (Chicago: University of Chicago Press, 1965). The influence of the "Wisconsin Idea" was both historical and geographical, and its influence extended even to California. John Aubrey Douglass, *The California Idea and American Higher Education* (Stanford, CA: Stanford University Press, 2007), 83.

52. Storr, *Harper's University*, chap. 11; Michael Lee, "Higher Criticism and Higher Education at the University of Chicago: William Rainey Harper's Vision of Religion in the Research University," *History of Education Quarterly* 48, no. 4 (November 2008): 508–33.

53. Harper was not alone here. Another singular example arose in the 1893 transition at Dartmouth between the presidencies of Josiah Bartlett and William Jewett Tucker. Cf. Marilyn Tobias, *Old Dartmouth on Trial: The Transformation of the American Academic Community in Nineteenth-Century America* (New York: New York University Press, 1982).

54. "Paul Shorey," in *Who Was Who in American History*, vol. 1 (Chicago: Marquis, 1968), 1121.

55. Storr, *Harper's University*, 71–78.

56. Lee, "Higher Criticism and Higher Education at the University of Chicago," 508–33.

57. Diner, *A City and Its Universities*, 47–48. Parallel episodes occurred during the 1890s at Indiana University, University of Wisconsin, Brown University, Marietta College, Lawrence College, North Dakota Agricultural College, Syracuse University, Kansas State Agricultural College, Northwestern University, and Stanford University. Walter Metzger, *Academic Freedom in the Age of the University* (New York: Columbia University Press, 1955; 1966, paperback ed.), 146–47; Storr, *Harper's University*, 83–85.

58. Harold E. Bergquist Jr., "The Edward W. Bemis Controversy at the University of Chicago," *American Association of University Professors Bulletin* 58, no. 4 (December 1972): 384.

59. "Elmer Lawrence Corthell," in *Who Was Who in America*, vol. 1 (Chicago: Marquis, 1968), 263. The Bemis episode was one of many that eventually led to the founding of the American Association of University Professors, which was to serve as a bulwark against arbitrary interference with the new standards of academic inquiry. See Walter Metzger, *Academic Freedom in the Age of the University* (New York: Columbia University Press, 1955), chap. 5.

60. Douglas Sloan, "Cultural Uplift and Social Reform in Nineteenth-Century Urban America," *History of Education Quarterly* 19, no. 3 (Fall 1979): 361–72; Willard J. Pugh, "A 'Curious Working of Cross Purposes' in the Founding of the University of Chicago," *History of Higher Education Annual* 15 (1995): 93–126.

61. William Cronon, *Nature's Metropolis: Chicago and the Great West* (New York: W. W. Norton, 1991), talks little about the impact of the economic market and railroading on the University of Chicago. His book actually stops just short of the events I have discussed here. But the book is definitive in its exploration of the environmental and economic patterns that led to the founding of the University of Chicago.

CHAPTER TEN

1. Edward Krug, ed., *Charles W. Eliot and Popular Education* (New York: Teachers College Press, 1961), 111.

2. University leaders like David Starr Jordan, president of Stanford University, echoed Eliot's basic arguments. See his *The Voice of the Scholar* (1889), cited in Christopher Lucas, *American Higher Education: A History* (New York: St. Martin's Griffin, 1994), 170.

3. David Riesman, *Thorstein Veblen: A Critical Interpretation* (New York: Charles Scribner's Sons, 1975; 1st ed., 1953); C. Wright Mills, "Introduction to the Mentor Edition," in Thorstein Veblen, *The Theory of the Leisure Class* (New York: New American Library, 1953), vi–xix.

4. Thorstein Veblen, *The Higher Learning in America* (1918).

5. Thomas L. Haskell, eds., *The Authority of Experts: Studies in History and Theory* (Bloomington: Indiana University Press, 1984), esp. ix–xxxix.

6. Ronald Brown, ed., *The Law School Papers of Benjamin Butler: New York University School of Law in the 1830s* (Westport, CT: Greenwood Press, 1987); John S. Brubacher and Willis Rudy, *Higher Education in Transition* (New York: Harper and Row, 1968; 1st ed., 1958), 209–10.

7. Robert Stevens, "Two Cheers for 1870: The American Law School," *Perspectives in American History* 5 (1971): 405–548; Bruce A. Kimball, "The Proliferation of Case Method Teaching in American Law Schools: Mr. Langdell's Emblematic 'Abomination,' 1890–1915," *History of Education Quarterly* 46, no. 2 (Summer 2006): 192–247.

8. William R. Johnson, *Schooled Lawyers: A Study in the Clash of Professional Cultures* (New York: New York University Press, 1978); J. Willard Hurst, "Legal Elements in United States History," *Perspectives in American History* 5 (1971): 3–92; Laura Kalman, *Legal Realism at Yale, 1927–1960* (Chapel Hill: University of North Carolina Press, 1986); Frederic Cople Jaher, "The Education of American Lawyers," *History of Education Quarterly* 21 (Spring 1981): 105–13; Morton J. Horowitz, *The Transformation of American Law, 1780–1860* (Cambridge, MA: Harvard University Press,

1977); Gerald Gawalt, ed., *The New High Priests: Lawyers in Post-Civil War America* (Westport, CT: Greenwood Press, 1984).

9. Paul Starr, *The Transformation of American Medicine* (New York: Basic Books, 1982); Charles Rosenberg and Morris Vogel, eds., *The Therapeutic Revolution* (Philadelphia: University of Pennsylvania Press, 1979); Joseph F. Kett, *The Formation of the American Medical Profession* (New Haven, CT: Yale University Press, 1968); William Rothstein, *American Physicians in the Nineteenth Century* (Baltimore: Johns Hopkins University Press, 1972); David Rosner, *A Once Charitable Enterprise: Hospitals and Health Care in Brooklyn and New York, 1885–1915* (Princeton, NJ: Princeton University Press, 1982).

10. George Daniels, *American Science in the Age of Jackson* (New York: Columbia University Press, 1968); Edward Lurie, *Louis Agassiz: A Life in Science* (Chicago: University of Chicago Press, 1960); Nathan Rheingold, *The Sciences in the American Context: New Perspectives* (Washington, DC: Smithsonian Institution Press, 1979); Sally G. Kohlstadt, *The Formation of the American Scientific Community: The American Association for the Advancement of Science, 1848–1860* (Urbana: University of Illinois Press, 1976); Thomas L. Haskell, *The Emergence of Professional Social Science: The American Social Science Association and the Nineteenth-Century Crisis of Authority* (Urbana: University of Illinois Press, 1977).

11. Paul H. Mattingly, *The Classless Profession: American Schoolmen in the Nineteenth Century* (New York: New York University Press, 1975); Christine A. Ogren, *The American State Normal School* (New York: Palgrave Macmillan 2005); Merle Borrowman, *The Liberal and Technical in Teacher Education* (New York: Teachers College Press, 1956); Willard Elsbree, *The American Teacher* (New York: American Book, 1939); Colin Burke, *American Collegiate Populations* (New York: New York University Press, 1982); Thomas Frusciano and Marilyn Pettit, *New York University and the City* (New Brunswick, NJ: Rutgers University Press, 1997).

12. Thomas K. McCraw, *Prophets of Regulation* (Cambridge, MA: Harvard University Press, 1984), esp. chaps. 1 and 3; Stephen Skowronek, *Building a New American State: The Expansion of National Administrative Capacities, 1877–1920* (New York: Cambridge University Press, 1982).

13. John Milton Cooper Jr., *The Warrior and the Priest: Woodrow Wilson and Theodore Roosevelt* (Cambridge, MA: Harvard University Press, 1983).

14. Bernard Hirschhorn, "Institute of Public Administration," in *Encyclopedia of New York City* ed. Kenneth Jackson (New Haven, CT: Yale University Press, 1995), 589; Jane S. Dahlberg, *The New York Bureau of Municipal Research: Pioneer in Government Administration* (New York: New York University Press, 1966); Phillip J. Gambaccini, "Institute for Public Administration," in *Research Institutions and Learned Societies*, ed. Joseph C. Kiger (Westport, CT: Greenwood Press, 1982), 302–6; "Luther Halsey Gulick," in *Who Was Who in American History*, vol. 1 (Chicago: Marquis, 1968), 494; Clarke A. Chambers, *Paul U. Kellogg and the Survey* (Minneapolis: University of Minnesota Press, 1971); James Allen Smith, *The Idea Brokers: Think Tanks and the Rise of the New Policy Elite* (New York: Free Press, 1991), 40–45, 49–51.

15. David F. Noble, *America by Design: Science, Technology and the Rise of Corporate Capitalism* (New York: Alfred Knopf, 1977), esp. 115–16.

16. "Frank Haigh Dixon," in *Who Was Who in American History*, vol. 2 (Chicago: Marquis, 1977), 157; Albro Martin, *Enterprise Denied: Origins of the Decline of American Railroads, 1897–1917* (New York: Columbia University Press, 1971), 255–59.

17. Magali Sarfatti Larsen, "The Production of Expertise and the Constitution of Expert Power," in *The Authority of Experts*, ed. Thomas Haskell (Bloomington: Indiana University Press, 1984), 28–80.

18. Edward A. Purcell Jr., "Service Intellectuals and the Politics of 'Science,'" *History of Education Quarterly* 15, no. 1 (Spring 1975): 97–110; Robin Content, "The Emergence of the American Professor," *History of Education Quarterly* 13, no. 3 (Fall 1973): 431–34.

19. Hugh Hawkins, *Between Harvard and America: The Educational Achievement of Charles W. Eliot* (New York: Oxford University Press, 1972), 177–78, 290–99; Nicholas Leman, *The Big Test: The Secret History of American Meritocracy* (New York: Farrar Straus Giroux, 1999).

20. Abraham Flexner, *Henry S. Pritchett* (New York: Columbia University Press, 1943), 14–15.

21. Ibid., 52.

22. Ibid.; see also Henry Pritchett to Clyde Furst [President of Carnegie Foundation], September 17, 1929, Santa Barbara, CA, in Henry Pritchett Papers, Box 3, "Carnegie Foundation for the Advancement of Teaching," Library of Congress; Ellen C. Lagemann, *Private Power for the Public Good: A History of the Carnegie Foundation for the Advancement of Teaching* (Middletown, CT: Wesleyan University Press, 1983).

23. Ibid., 98–100.

24. Hugh Hawkins, *Banding Together: The Rise of National Associations in American Higher Education, 1887–1950* (Baltimore: Johns Hopkins University Press, 1992), 107–9; Ellen Condliffe Lagemann, *The Politics of Knowledge: The Carnegie Corporation, Philanthropy and Public Policy* (Chicago: University of Chicago Press, 1989), 120; Thelin, *American Higher Education*, 145–46.

25. In 1995 this organization renamed itself the American Association of Colleges and Universities.

26. Paul Starr, *The Social Transformation of American Medicine* (New York: Basic Books, 1982), 118–26; Stephen C. Wheatley, *The Politics of Philanthropy: Abraham Flexner and Medical Education* (Madison: University of Wisconsin Press, 1988).

27. Starr, *American Medicine*, 120–23.

28. Abraham Flexner, *I Remember* (New York: Simon and Schuster, 1940); Thomas Bonner, *Iconoclast: Abraham Flexner and a Life in Learning* (Baltimore: Johns Hopkins University Press, 2002); Maurice Vance, "Abraham Flexner," in *Encyclopedia of American Biography*, ed. John Garrity (New York: Harper and Row, 1974), 364–65; Michael Schudson, "The Flexner Report and the Reed Report: Notes on the History of Professional Education in the United States," *Social Science Quarterly* 55, no. 2 (December 1974): 347–61.

29. Frances A. Kelleher, "Gender, State Policy, and Professional Politics: Primary School Teachers in France, 1880–1920" (unpublished PhD diss., New York University, 1988); Joan W Scott, "Socialization in Two Villages," *History of Education Quarterly* 13, no. 1 (Spring 1973); Paul Vogt, "Schools and Colonizing of the French Countryside," *History of Education Quarterly* 18 (Winter 1978).

30. Abraham Flexner, *Henry Pritchett*, 95; J. William Hess, "General Education Board," in *Foundations*, ed. Harold M. Keele and Joseph C. Kiger (Westport, CT: Greenwood Press, 1984), 146–53; Raymond Fosdick, *Adventure in Giving: The Story of the General Education Board* (New York: Harper and Row, 1962); Abraham Flexner, *Abraham Flexner: An Autobiography* (New York: Simon and Schuster, 1960; first published in 1940 as *I Remember*), 289.

31. Flexner conveniently ignored Gilman's affinity with the old-time college, defended by his Yale mentor and president, Rev. Noah Porter, as well as Porter's assumptions that moral instruction and science were not antagonists, any more than were the college and the university. Speaking of his colleague at Yale's Sheffield Scientific School, James Dwight Dana, Gilman had written about his own ideal of academic expert: "He was not a man who enjoyed cant phrases or who was eager to express his most sacred thoughts or display his emotions. Nor was he tenacious of denominational tenets, or inclined to philosophical and ecclesiastical discussions.... He was not only a man without guile—he was a man of strong convictions, definite principles and devout aspirations." See also D. H Meyer, *The Instructed Conscience: The Shaping of the American National Ethic* (Philadelphia: University of Pennsylvania Press, 1972).

32. Flexner, *Pritchett*, 106; Abraham Flexner, *Daniel Coit Gilman: Creator of the American Type of University* (New York: Harcourt Brace, 1946), 53.

33. Flexner, *Gilman*, chap. 3, 62. The research dimension of the early Johns Hopkins University has recently come under scrutiny as an overstatement of Gilman's teaching priorities. See Charles C. Bishop, "Teaching at Johns Hopkins: The First Generation," *History of Education Quarterly* 27, no. 4 (Winter 1987): 499–515.

34. David F. Allmendinger, "Strong Men of the Academic Revolution," *History of Education Quarterly* 13, no. 4 (Winter, 1973): 415–25.

35. Abraham Flexner, *Universities: American, English, German* (New York: Oxford University Press, 1968; 1st ed., 1930), 8.

36. Ibid., 44.

37. Ibid., 56.

38. Flexner, *Flexner*, 207.

39. Ibid., 277.

40. Robert Kohler, *Partners in Science: Foundations and National Scientists, 1900–1945* (Chicago: University of Chicago Press, 1991); Robert Kohler, "Science, Foundations and American Universities in the 1920s," *Osiris*, 2nd ser., 3 (1987): 135–64.

41. Flexner, *Flexner*, 108.

42. Larsen, "The Production of Expertise and the Constitution of Expert Power," 28–80; David C. Hammack, "Foundations in the American Polity, 1900–1950," in *Philanthropic Foundations: New Scholarship, New Possibilities*, ed. Ellen C. Lagemann (Bloomington: Indiana University Press, 1999), 43–68; Peter D. Hall, *Inventing the Non-Profit Sector* (Baltimore: Johns Hopkins University Press, 1992); Barry D. Karl and Stanley N. Katz, "The American Private Philanthropic Foundation and the Public Sphere, 1890–1930," *Minerva* (1981): 236–70; James H. Madison, "John D. Rockefeller's GEB and the Rural School Problem in the Midwest, 1900–1930," *History of Education Quarterly* 24 (Summer 1984): 181–200; Judith Sealander, *Private Wealth and Public Life: Foundation Philanthropy and the Reshaping of American Social Policy from the Progressive Era to the New Deal* (Baltimore: Johns Hopkins University Press, 1997); Guy Alchon, *The Invisible Hand of Planning: Capitalism, Social Science and the State in the 1920s* (Princeton, NJ: Princeton University Press, 1985).

CHAPTER ELEVEN

1. Ronald Story, *The Forging of an Aristocracy: Harvard and the Boston Upper Class, 1800–1870* (Middletown, CT: Wesleyan University Press, 1980), chaps. 1–3.

2. *Historical Statistics of the United States: Colonial Times to 1970* (Washington, DC: US Bureau of the Census, 1976), 383.

3. Ellen C. Lagemann, *Private Power for the Public Good: A History of the Carnegie Foundation for the Advancement of Teaching* (Middletown, CT: Wesleyan University Press, 1983), 44–55.

4. John Thelin, *A History of American Higher Education* (Baltimore: Johns Hopkins University Press, 2004), 137–38; Merle Curti and Vernon Carstensen, "The University of Wisconsin to 1925," in *The University of Wisconsin: One Hundred and Twenty-Five Years*, ed. Allen Bogue and Robert Taylor (Madison: University of Wisconsin Press, 1975), 28; Robert La Follette, *LaFollette's Autobiography: A Personal Narrative of Political Experiences* (Madison: University of Wisconsin Press, 1960; 1st ed., 1911), 14; Patricia A. Graham, *Community and Class in American Education, 1865–1918* (New York: John Wiley and Sons, 1974), 211–21.

5. Ellen C. Lagemann, *The Politics of Knowledge: The Carnegie Corporation, Philanthropy and Public Policy* (Chicago: University of Chicago Press, 1989), 3–11; David O. Levine, *The American College and the Culture of Aspiration, 1915–1940* (Ithaca, NY: Cornell University Press, 1986), 50.

6. Stuart W. Leslie, *Boss Kettering: Wizard of General Motors* (New York: Columbia University Press, 1983).

7. Ibid., 319–22.

8. David F. Noble, *America by Design: Science, Technology and the Rise of Corporate Capitalism* (New York: Alfred Knopf, 1977).

9. Ibid.

10. John Rae, "The Application of Science to Industry," in *The Organization of Knowledge in Modern America, 1860–1920*, ed. Alexandra Oleson and John Voss (Baltimore: John Hopkins University Press, 1979), 258–56. In their early stages, "research" combined with a defensive, patent strategy that broke down inventions into many multiple parts and made any patent challenge an expensive and long-term proposition. Cf. Noble, *America By Design*, chap. 6; Leonard S. Reich, *The Making of America Industrial Research* (New York: Cambridge University Press, 1985).

11. Joseph Kiger, ed., "The National Academy of Sciences," in *Research Institutions and Learned Societies* (Westport, CT: Greenwood Press, 1982), 362–63; A. Hunter Dupree, "The National Academy of Sciences and the American Definition of Science," in Oleson and Voss, *The Organization of Knowledge*, 342–63; Hugh Hawkins, *Banding Together: The Rise of National Associations in America Higher Education, 1887–1950* (Baltimore: Johns Hopkins University Pres, 1992).

12. Kiger, *Research Institutions*, 363; President Wilson's public imprimatur did not fund the NRC, but paved the way for private funding from the Carnegie and Rockefeller Foundations. Robert H. Kargon, *The Rise of Robert Millikan: Portrait of a Life in American Science* (Ithaca, NY: Cornell University Press, 1982), chap. 4.

13. Kenneth Prewit (former president of SSRC), www.ssrc.org/inside/about/brief_history_of_the_council; Dorothy Ross, "Development of the Social Sciences," in Olsen and Voss, *The Organization of Knowledge*, 107–38.

14. Barry D. Karl, *Charles E. Merriam and the Study of Politics* (Chicago: University of Chicago Press, 1974).

15. http://wustl.edu/about/facts/history.

16. David F. Houston, "Washington University, St. Louis, Mo.," in *Cyclopedia of Education*, ed. Paul Monroe (New York: Macmillan, 1913), 5:754–55.

17. Candace O'Connor, *Beginning a Great Work: Washington University in St. Louis, 1853–2003* (St. Paul, MN: Litho, 2003), 76–77.

18. Donald D. Critchlow, *The Brookings Institution, 1916–1952: Expertise and the Public Interest in a Democratic Society* (DeKalb: Northern Illinois University Pres, 1985), chap. 3; William J. Lanquette, "The Brookings Institution," in *Research Institutions and Learned Societies*, ed. Joseph C. Kiger (Westport, CT: Greenwood Press, 1982), 168–71; Robert D. Cuff, *The War Industries Board: Business-Government Relations during World War I* (Baltimore: Johns Hopkins University Press, 1973), chap. 8.

19. Barry D. Karl, "Presidential Planning and Social Science Research: Mr. Hoover's Experts," *Perspectives in American History* 3 (1969): 347–409.

20. James Allen Smith, *The Idea Brokers: Think Tanks and the Rise of the New Policy Elite* (New York: Free Press, 1991), chap. 4.

21. "Harold G. Moulton," in *Who's Who in American History*, vol. 4 (Chicago: Marquis, 1968), 685.

22. "Lenox College," in *Cyclopedia of Education*, ed. Paul Monroe (New York: Macmillan, 1913), 4:678.

23. "Henry S. Pritchett," in *Who's Who in American History*, vol. 1 (Chicago: Marquis, 1968), 998.

24. James Axtell, "The Death of the Liberal Arts College," *History of Education Quarterly* 11 (Winter 1971): 339–52; George E. Peterson, *The New England College in the Age of the University* (Amherst, MA: Amherst College Press, 1964).

25. Philip Gleason, *Contending with Modernity: Catholic Higher Education in the Twentieth Century* (New York: Oxford University Press, 1995), 3.

26. Jay Dolan, *The American Catholic Experience* (Garden City, NY: Doubleday, 1985), 443–45.

27. Robert Hassenger, ed., *The Shape of Catholic Higher Education* (Chicago: University of Chicago Press, 1967).

28. For a fascinating discussion of the role of Catholic converts in America's religious culture, see Patrick Allit, *Catholic Converts: British and American Intellectuals Turn to Rome* (Ithaca, NY: Cornell University Press, 1997).

29. John Tracy Ellis, *The Life of James Cardinal Gibbons* (Milwaukee: Bruce, 1963).

30. Joseph T. Durkin, SJ, *Georgetown University: The Middle Years, 1840–1900* (Washington, DC: Georgetown University Press, 1963), chap. 12.

31. Robert Emmett Curran, *A History of Georgetown University*, 3 vols. (Washington, DC: Georgetown University Press, 2010), esp. vol. 2.

32. Ellis, *James Cardinal Gibbons*, 142. The prominent opposition to Americanism was led by Bishop Bernard McQuaid of Rochester, New York, Rev. Michael Corrigan of New York City, and Rev. Frederick X. Katzer of Green Bay, Wisconsin.

33. Curran, *Georgetown*.

34. Kathleen A. Mahoney, *Catholic Higher Education in Protestant America: The Jesuits and Harvard in the Age of the University* (Baltimore: Johns Hopkins University Press, 2003), 35–37.

35. Julie Reuben, *The Making of the Modern University: Intellectual Transformation and the Marginalization of Morality* (Chicago: University of Chicago Press, 1996); George Marsden, *The Soul of the University: Protestant Establishment and Established Nonbelief* (New York: Oxford University Press, 1994).

36. Hugh Hawkins, "Charles W. Eliot, University Reform, and Religious Faith in America, 1869–1909," *Journal of American History* 51 (September 1964): 199–211.

37. J. David Hoeveler, *James McCosh and the Scottish Intellectual Tradition* (Princeton, NJ: Princeton University Press, 1981), 135–37.

38. Hugh Hawkins, "The University Builders Observe the Colleges," *History of Education Quarterly* 11 (Winter 1971): 353–62.

39. http://en.wikipedia.org/wiki/Abbott_Lawrence_Lowell.

40. Henry A. Youmans, *Abbott Lawrence Lowell, 1856–1943* (Cambridge, MA: Harvard University Press, 1948), chap. 5.

41. Ibid., 65.

42. http//en.wikipedia/Edward_Harkness. Harkness was one of the largest stockholders in John Rockefeller's Standard Oil Company, of which his father was one of the original investors. His many philanthropies included his own alma maters, Phillips Exeter and Yale, along with many schools supported by the Commonwealth Fund, which he created. The architect for Harkness's many projects was his Yale classmate, James Gamble Rogers.

43. http://en.wikipedia.org/wiki/Edward_Harkness. One might also note the entire cohort of Standard Oil executives who imitated John D. Rockefeller's philanthropic pattern. Henry Folger (1857–1930) created the Folger Shakespearean Library in Washington, DC. See http://enwikipedia.org/wiki/Henry_Clay_Folger; William R. Kenan Jr. (1872–1965) used his fortune to fund more than eighty-five academic chairs at a number of colleges and universities including Johns Hopkins, Yale, Rochester, New York University, Syracuse, etc. See http://en.wikipedia.org/wiki/William_R_Kenan_Jr. Henry Flagler (1830–1913), the developer of Miami Beach and South Florida, let his oil fortune be channeled into a number of cultural enterprises including the Flagler Museum and Flagler College in Florida. See http://en.wikipedia.org/wiki/Henry_Flagler.

44. Harold Wechsler, "The Discriminating Ivy League," *History of Education Quarterly* 22, no. 1 (Spring 1982): 103–10. Wechsler notes that Lowell's educational values did not challenge the contextual prejudices of the New England elite and countenanced serious anti-Semitic biases in Harvard's admissions policy. See also Marcia Synnott, *The Half-Opened Door: Discrimination and Admissions at Harvard, Yale and Princeton, 1900–1970* (Westport, CT: Greenwood Press, 1979).

45. One might cite Alexander Meiklejohn's (1872–1964) Amherst College reforms or later his Experimental College work at the University of Wisconsin. Alexander Meiklejohn, *The Experimental College*, ed. John Walker Powell (Cabin John, MD; Washington, DC: Seven Locks Press, 1981; 1st ed., 1932); Allen C. Bogue and Robert Taylor, eds., *The University of Wisconsin: One Hundred and Twenty-Five Years* (Madison: University of Wisconsin Press, 1975), 40; Thelin, *American Higher Education*, 237–38; Robert T. Brennan, "The Making of a Liberal College: Alexander Meiklejohn at Amherst," *History of Education Quarterly* 28, no. 4 (Winter 1988): 569–97.

46. Daniel Bell's now classic *The Reforming of General Education* (New York: Columbia University Press, 1966), though focused on the problems of post–World War II, contains much historical information about these issues of the interwar period.

47. Benjamin McArthur, "A Gamble on Youth: Robert M. Hutchins, the University of Chicago and the Politics of Presidential Selection," *History of Education Quarterly* 30, no. 2 (Summer 1990): 161–86.

48. Robert M. Hutchins, *The Higher Learning in America* (Chicago: University of Chicago Press, 1936); Walter H. Hill, ed., *Learning and Living: Proceedings of an Anniversary Celebration in Honor of Alexander Meiklejohn* (Chicago: n.p., 1942), 3–4. At this conference Hutchins insisted that Meiklejohn "set about to make Amherst conform to the ideal he held before her. . . . There is no more brilliant passage in the history of American education than those twelve years."

49. http://education.stateuniversity.com/pages/2215/Meiklejohn_Alexander-1872-1964/html. Meiklejohn earned his doctorate in philosophy at Cornell (1897) and joined the faculty at Brown where he served as dean from 1901 to 1912. There he alienated alumni by downplaying athletics and other "distractions" from collegiate learning, like electives. His insistence on a focused curriculum continued when he became president of Amherst (1913–23) and later at the University of Wisconsin's Experimental College (1927–32), which famously boasted a prescribed, two-year curriculum, concentrating first on fifth century BC Athens and in the second year on nineteenth- and twentieth-century American history. Intensive classroom discussion and extracurricular tutorials made a lasting impression on all participants but flew in the face of standard testing, tensions that eventually closed the school. Its legacy involved many Experimental Colleges throughout the United States, especially in the Great Books curricula of Saint John's College, Annapolis; Joseph Tussman's Experimental College at University of California, Berkeley; and the Great Books program at the University of Chicago.

50. John F. Ohles, "Harry David Gideonse," in *Biographical Dictionary of American Educators* (Westport, CT: Greenwood Press, 1978), 2:507–8. Gideonse served on the University of Chicago's economics faculty (1930–38) in early Hutchins years. He later was longtime president (1939–66) of Brooklyn College and from 1966 to 1976 president of the New School of Social Research in New York City. See his *New York Times* obituary (March 14, 1985).

51. Harry D. Gideonse, *The Higher Learning in a Democracy* (New York: Holt Rinehart and Winston, 1937), quoted in Richard Hofstadter and Wilson Smith, eds., *American Higher Education: A Documentary History* (Chicago: University of Chicago Press, 1961), 948.

52. "Richard McKeon," in *Wikipedia*, http://en.wikipedia.org/wiki/Richard_McKeon.

53. John Dewey, "President Hutchins' Proposals to Remake Higher Education," *Social Frontier* 3 (January 1937): 103–4, quoted in Hofstadter and Wilson, *American Higher Education*, 2:949–53; Benjamin McArthur, "Revisiting Hutchins and *The Higher Learning in America*," *History of Higher Education Annual* 7 (1987): 8–28.

54. Harry S. Ashmore, *Unseasonable Truths: The Life of Robert Maynard Hutchins* (Boston: Little Brown, 1989); Mary Ann Dzuback, *Robert M. Hutchins: Portrait of an Educator* (Chicago: University of Chicago Press, 1991), chap. 4; Edward S. Shils, ed., *Remembering the University of Chicago: Teachers, Scientists, and Scholars* (Chicago: University of Chicago Press, 1991).

55. Dzuback, *Hutchins*, chap. 5; Joseph F. Kett, *The Pursuit of Knowledge under Difficulties* (Stanford, CA: Stanford University Press, 1994), 336–44; Peter Buckley, "The People's Institute," in *Encyclopedia of New York City*, ed. Kenneth Jackson (New Haven, CT: Yale University Press, 1995), 281–82. The People's Institute (1898–1934) attempted to provide a kind of higher learning for the working class in association with the Cooper Union.

56. Peter M. Rutkoff and William B. Scott, *New School: A History of the New School for Social Research* (New York: Free Press, 1986); Kett, *The Pursuit of Knowledge*, 336–44; Dzuback, *Hutchins*, chaps. 4, 5; Buckley, "The People's Institute," 281–82.

57. Dzuback, *Hutchins*, 102; James T. Kloppenberg, "The Place of Value in a Culture of Facts," in *The Humanities and the Dynamics of Inclusion since World War II*, ed. David A. Hollinger (Baltimore: Johns Hopkins University Press, 2006), 126–58.

58. "Robert M Hutchins, Long a Leader in Educational Change, Dies at 78" *New York Times*, May 16, 1977, 1, 48. Hutchins not only cultivated atomic research during World War II, he was instrumental in supporting the university's successful work in hiring the strategic scientists who conducted the first atomic chain reaction there in 1942. He was also a prodigious fund-raiser in behalf of Chicago's science establishment, producing $86 million during his tenure (president, 1929–45; chancellor, 1945–51).

59. The pragmatic bias is evident even in the scholarship on the Hutchins-Dewey controversy. See R. Freedman Butts, *The College Charts Its Course* (New York: McGraw Hill, 1939), chap. 16.

60. Thelin, *American Higher Education*, 276; Ellen W. Schrecker, *No Ivory Tower: McCarthyism and the Universities* (New York: Oxford University Press, 1986), 112–13, 337.

61. Scott Heller, "Quixote in Chicago," *New York Times Book Review* Sunday, March 1, 1992.

62. Robert M. Hutchins, *The Higher Learning in America* (Chicago: University of Chicago Press, 1936), 32.

63. Phillip Gleason, *Contending with Modernity: Catholic Higher Education in the Twentieth Century* (New York: Oxford University Press, 1995), 246–47.

64. David C. Hammack, "Foundations in the American Polity, 1900–1950," in *Philanthropic Foundation: New Scholarship, New Possibilities*, ed. Ellen C. Lagemann (Bloomington and Indianapolis: Indiana University Press, 1999), 43–68; Merle E. Curti and Roderick Nash, *Philanthropy and the Shaping of American Higher Education* (New Brunswick, NJ: Rutgers University Press, 1965); Donald Fisher, *Fundamental Development of the Social Sciences: Rockefeller Philanthropy and the United State Social Science Research Council* (Ann Arbor: University of Michigan Press, 1993); Roger Geiger, "After the Emergence: Voluntary Support and the Building of American Research Universities," *History of Education Quarterly* 25, no. 3 (Fall 1985): 369–81; Peter D. Hall, "Philanthropy as Investment," *History of Education Quarterly* 22, no. 2 (Summer 1982): 185–203.

CHAPTER TWELVE

1. Carol Gruber, *Mars and Minerva: World War I and the Uses of Higher Learning in America* (Baton Rouge: Louisiana State University Press, 1975), 17.

2. Daniel T. Rodgers, *Atlantic Crossings: Social Politics in a Progressive Era* (Cambridge, MA: Harvard University Press, 1998), chap. 3; Sterling Fishman, "German Mandarins and Weimar Culture," *History of Education Quarterly* 10 (Fall 1970): 381–85; Fritz Ringer, *The Decline of the German Mandarins: The German Academic Community, 1890–1933* (Cambridge, MA: Harvard University Press, 1969).

3. Gruber, *Mars and Minerva*, 20–21; Walter Metzger, "The German Contribution to the American Theory of Academic Freedom," *American Association of University Professors Bulletin* 41 (Summer 1955): 214–30; Charles E. McClelland, "German Universities and American Scholars," *History of Education Quarterly* 20 (Summer 1980): 229–32; Carl Diehl, *Americans and German Scholarship, 1770–1870* (New Haven, CT: Yale University Press, 1978).

4. Rogers, *Atlantic Crossings*, chap. 3.

5. Gruber, *Mars and Minerva*, 47–49. John Burgess, *Reminiscences of an American Scholar* (New York: Columbia University Press, 1934), concludes with an obsequious genuflection to German culture and states it in the wake of his filling the first Roosevelt Professorship at the University of Berlin (1906–7). Nicholas Murray Butler, Columbia's president, a German-university-trained sympathizer also, glossed his role in the final chapter of Burgess's *Reminiscences* (which effectively concluded in 1907). Robert A. McCaughey, *Stand, Columbia: A History of Columbia University in the City of New York, 1754–2004* (New York: Columbia University Press, 2003), 246.

6. Walter Metzger, *Academic Freedom in the Age of the University* (New York: Columbia University Press, 1961; 1st ed., 1955), chap. 5.

7. Christopher Lasch, *The New Radicalism in America, 1889–1963: The Intellectual as a Social Type* (New York: Alfred Knopf, 1965), chap. 6. Dewey's participation caused no small crisis for his version of pragmatism and set in motion a critical countercurrent that continued through the century (see esp. chapter 15 of this book, "Challenging Pragmatism"). See also Paul Bourke, "Philosophy and Social Criticism: John Dewey 1910–1920," *History of Education Quarterly* 15, no. 1 (Spring 1975): 3–16.

8. http://en.wikipedia.org/wiki/Rhodes_Scholars.

9. Marcia Synnott, *The Half-Opened Door: Discrimination and Admissions at Harvard, Yale and Princeton, 1900–1970* (Westport, CT: Greenwood Press, 1979); Harold S. Wechsler, *The Qualified Student: A History of Selective College Admission in America* (New York: John Wiley, 1977); James Axtell, *The Making of Princeton University* (Princeton, NJ: Princeton University Press, 2006), chap. 3.

10. Ellwood P. Cubberley and Edward C. Elliott, "National Government of the United States and Education," in *Cyclopedia of Education*, ed. Paul Monroe (New York: Macmillan, 1913), 4:380.

11. Daniel Bell, *The Reforming of General Education* (New York: Columbia University Press, 1965).

12. Merle E. Curti, *An American Paradox: The Conflict of Thought and Action* (New Brunswick, NJ: Rutgers University Press, 1956).

13. Gruber insists that the majority of participants were unaffected. However, philosopher John Dewey struggled with the problem of anticipatory judgment outside metaphysics. In his postwar book *Art and Experience* (1934), Dewey sought an aesthetic that would be compatible with his pragmatic instrumentalism while avoiding the perspectives that traditional philosophy gave to "first principles," a conceptual resource to fend against the perils of his wartime participation. See Robert B. Westbrook, *John Dewey and American Democracy* (Ithaca, NY: Cornell University Press, 1991), 387–402; Lasch, *The New Radicalism in America*, esp. chaps. 3, 6, and 9; Edward A Purcell, *The Crisis of Democratic Theory: Scientific Naturalism and the Problem of Value* (Lexington: University Press of Kentucky, 1973); Bourke, "Philosophy and Social Criticism:" 3–16.

14. Gruber, *Mars and Minerva*, 103–5; Merle Curti and Vernon Carstensen, "The University of Wisconsin to 1925," in *The University of Wisconsin*, ed. Allen G. Bogue and Robert Taylor (Madison: University of Wisconsin Press, 1975), 3–37; Rogers, *Atlantic Crossings*, 103–11.

15. http://en.wikipedia.org/wiki/George_Ellery_Hale.

16. Robert H. Kargon, *The Rise of Robert Millikan* (Ithaca, NY: Cornell University Press, 1982), esp. chap. 4.

17. http://en.wikipedia.org/wiki/Robert_Yerkes.

18. Joel Spring, "Psychologists and the War: The Meaning of Intelligence in the Alpha and Beta Tests," *History of Education Quarterly* 12 (Spring 1972): 3–15; Daniel Kevles, "Testing the Army's Intelligence: Psychologists and the Military in World War I," *Journal of American History* 55 (December 1968): 565–81.

19. Bell, *The Reforming of General Education.*

20. Christopher J. Lucas, *American Higher Education: A History* (New York: St. Martin's Griffin, 1994), 204.

21. Margaret P. O'Mara, *Cities of Knowledge: Cold War Science and the Search for the Next Silicon Valley* (Princeton, NJ: Princeton University Press, 2005), 99–103; Rebecca S. Lowen, *Creating the Cold War University: The Transformation of Stanford* (Berkeley: University of California Press, 1997); Stuart W. Leslie, *The Cold War and American Science: The Military-Industrial Complex at MIT and Stanford* (Berkeley: University of California Press, 1997).

22. http://archives.nypl.org/mss/922. A small but strategic effort to respond to the émigré crisis occurred in 1932 with the creation of the Emergency Committee in Aid of Displaced Foreign Scholars, financed initially by the Carnegie and Rockefeller Foundations. The key individuals were Columbia president Nicholas Murray Butler, former secretary of state Elihu Root, and especially CCNY professor Stephen P. Duggan (1870–1950), who directed the organization until it closed in

1945. His right-hand man was Edward R. Murrow from 1932 to 1937. The organization estimated that it helped 335 scholars relocate to the United States.

23. Laurence Veysey, "From Germany to America," *History of Education Quarterly* 13, no. 4 (Winter 1973): 401–7; Donald Fleming and Bernard Bailyn, eds., *The Intellectual Migration: Europe and America, 1930–1960* (Cambridge, MA: Harvard University Press, 1969).

24. Lewis A. Coser, *Refugee Scholars in America: Their Impact and Their Experiences* (New Haven, CT: Yale University Press, 1984), 6; Laura Fermi, *Illustrious Immigrants: The Intellectual Migration from Europe, 1930–41* (Chicago: University of Chicago Press, 1968).

25. http://www-groups.dcs.st-and.uk/~history/Biographies/Courant.html.

26. Ibid. See also http://en.wikipedia.org/wiki/Richard_Courant.

27. Thomas Frusciano et al., *New York University and the City* (New Brunswick, NJ: Rutgers University Press, 1997), 224.

28. Paul F. Lazarsfeld, "An Episode in the History of Social Research," *Perspectives in American History* 2 (1968): 270–74.

29. http://en.wikipedia.org/wiki/Robert_Staughton_Lynd.

30. Paul F. Lazarsfeld, conversation with author, National Academy of Education meeting, Columbia University, 1975; "Dr. Paul Lazarfeld Dies; Sociologist at Columbia," *New York Times*, September 1, 1976.

31. McCaughey, *Stand, Columbia*, 372–75.

32. Ibid., 374.

33. "Center for Advanced Study in the Behavioral Sciences," in *Research Institutions and Learned Societies*, ed. Joseph C. Kiger (Westport, CT: Greenwood Press, 1982), 179–82.

34. Martin Jay, *Permanent Exiles: Essays on the Intellectual Migration from Germany to America* (New York: Columbia University Press, 1985), chap. 3; http://en.wikipedia.org/wiki/Theodor_Adorno.

35. Martin Jay, *The Dialectical Imagination: A History of the Frankfurt School and the Institute for Social Research, 1923–50* (Boston: Little Brown, 1973); Coser, *Refugee Scholars*, 90–97; Martin Jay, "Urban Flights: The Institute of Social Research between Frankfurt and New York," in *The University and the City: From Medieval Origins to the Present*, ed. Thomas Bender (New York: Oxford University Press, 1988), 231–48.

36. Jay, *The Dialectical Imagination*; Charles E. McClelland, "The Frankfurt School," *History of Education Quarterly* 13, no. 4 (Winter 1973): 513–17.

37. https://en.wikipedia.org/wiki/Alexander_Gerschenkron.

38. One major American participant in the Gerschenkron circle was Thomas C. Cochran (1902–99), whose *The Age of Enterprise: A Social History of Industrial America* (New York: Harper, 1962), was a standard text in legions of American history courses for at least two decades after its publication. The book, coauthored with William Miller, was a synthetic tour de force, a forte of Cochran's generation. Cochran, a New York University graduate and for twenty-five years chairman of New York University's history department, served as both president of the American Historical Association and the Organization of American Historians.

39. Ibid.

40. Jack L. Rubins, "Karen Danielsen Horney," in *Notable American Women: The Modern Period*, ed. Barbara Sicherman and Carol Hurd Green (Cambridge, MA: Harvard University Press, 1980), 351–54.

41. Coser, *Refugee Scholars*, 76–82.

42. http://en.wikipedia.org/wiki/Kurt_Lewin.

43. Coser, *Refugee Scholars*, 22–27.

44. Gunnar Johansen, conversation with author, Blue Mounds, WI, 1967; "Gunnar Johansen, 85, a Pianist," *New York Times*, May 28, 1991; http://www.bach-cantatas.com/Bio/Johansen-Gunnar.htm. Before his emigration, Kolisch had an extraordinary European reputation, founding

the Vienna String Quartet (informally known as the Kolisch Quartet) and showcasing the works of Béla Bartók and Arnold Schoenberg, his brother-in-law.

45. Coser, *Refugee Scholars*, 219–23.

46. Ibid., 102–9.

47. Peter M. Rutkoff and William B. Scott, *New School* (New York: Free Press, 1986); see also Nathan Glazer, "New School," *New York Times Book Review*, August 31, 1986, 6–7; the accusation of "Germanizing" the American university was more slur than insight, since accusers generally knew little of the transformation of the German university. Cf. Konrad Jarausch, "The Social Transformation of the University: The Case of Prussia, 1865–1914, *Journal of Social History* 12, no. 4 (Summer 1979): 609–36.

48. The Warburg Institute originated with the art interests and library of Aby Warburg (1866–1929), a student of Renaissance art and culture. Later his collection became associated with the University of Hamburg, until 1933 when the rise of Nazism prompted its relocation to London. In 1944 it became associated with the University of London where it remains today. http://en.wikipedia/wiki/Warburg_Institute.

49. http://www.dictionarypfarthistorians.org/cookw.htm.

50. Coser, *Refugee Scholars*, 255–60.

51. Colin Eisler, "*Kunstgeschichte* American Style: A Study in Migration," *Perspectives in American History* 2 (1968): 544–629.

52. Robert M. Thomas Jr., "Rene Wellek, 92, a Professor of Comparative Literature, Dies," *New York Times*, November 16, 1995, B16.

53. http://en.wikipedia.org/wiki/John_von_Neumann.

54. S. Ulam, H. W. Kuhn, A. W. Tucker, and Claude E. Shannon, "John von Neumann, 1903–1957," *Perspectives in American History* 2 (1968): 235–69. The novelty of the new methodological approaches—with a tolerance of heuristic insight, contradiction, and organizational complexity in the pursuit of "science"—might have been captured by Neumann's deathbed embrace of Roman Catholicism, which shocked many of his colleagues and indeed his family. "John von Neumann," *New York Times*, February, 10, 1957.

55. Fermi, *Illustrious Immigrants*, chap. 7; Leo Szilard, "Reminiscences," *Perspectives in American History* 2 (1968): 94–151; in the same volume, see Charles Weiner, "A New Site for the Seminar: The Refugees and American Physics in the Thirties," 190–228.

56. Edward Shils, "The Order of Learning in the United States from 1865 to 1920," *Minerva* 16, no. 2 (Summer 1978): 159–95.

57. David Levering Lewis, *W. E. B. Du Bois: Biography of a Race, 1869–1919* (New York: Henry Holt, 1993), 130–46.

58. Ibid., 140–41; W. E. B. DuBois, *Dusk of Dawn: An Essay toward an Autobiography of a Race Concept* (New York: Schocken Books, 1940), 46ff.

59. Nida E. Thomas, interview with author, Historical Society, Elizabeth, NJ, August 15, 2001.

60. Ronald M. Johnson, "Higher Education and the Black Experience," *History of Education Quarterly* 14, no. 3 (Fall 1974): 419–25; Paula Fass, *The Damned and the Beautiful: American Youth in the 1920s* (New York: Oxford University Press, 1977), 360ff.

61. James McPherson, *The Abolitionist Legacy: From Reconstruction to the NAACP* (Princeton, NJ: Princeton University Press, 1975); Raymond Wolters, "The Puritan Ethic and Black Education," *History of Education Quarterly* 17, no. 1 (Spring 1977): 63–73; Kwame Anthony Appiah, "Battling with DuBois," *New York Review of Books* 58, no. 20 (December 22, 2011): 81–85.

62. Raymond Wolters, *The New Negro on Campus: Black College Rebellions of the 1920s* (Princeton, NJ: Princeton University Press, 1975); Vincent Franklin, "W. E. B. DuBois and the Education of Black Folk," *History of Education Quarterly* 16, no. 1 (Spring 1976): 111–18; Henry A. Bullock, "The Black College and the New Black Awareness," *Daedalus* 100 (Summer 1971): 573–602; C. Eric Lincoln, "The Negro Colleges and Cultural Change," *Daedalus* 100 (Summer 1971): 603–29.

63. Vincent P. Franklin, "What Ever Happened to the College-Bred Negro?" *History of Education Quarterly* 24, no. 3 (Fall 1984): 411–18; Clayborne Carson, *In Struggle: SNCC and the Black Awakening of the 1960s* (Cambridge, MA: Harvard University Press, 1981); Rayford W. Logan, *Howard University: The First Hundred Years, 1867–1967* (New York: New York University Press, 1969), 140, 580; Joe M. Richardson, *A History of Fisk University, 1865–1946* (Tuscaloosa: University of Alabama Press, 1980; Ralph L. Pearson, "Reflections on Black Colleges: The Historical Perspective of Charles S. Johnson," *History of Education Quarterly* 23, no. 1 (Spring 1983): 55–68.

64. Rodgers, *Atlantic Crossings*, 84–89; Lewis, *W. E. B. Du Bois*, 130–31.

65. Jay, *Permanent Exiles*, xii.

66. Jay, *The Dialectical Imagination*, epilogue.

CHAPTER THIRTEEN

1. Daniel Bell, *The Reforming of General Education: The Columbia Experience in Its National Setting* (Garden City, NY: Anchor Books, 1968). Bell's study is a classic account of the forming of an important interdisciplinary model, Columba's course in Western Civilization in the 1920s and afterward. Harvey J. Graff, *Undisciplining Knowledge: Interdisciplinarity in the Twentieth Century* (Baltimore: Johns Hopkins University Press, 2015); Jerry A. Jacobs, *In Defense of Disciplines: Interdisciplinarity and Specialization in the Research University* (Chicago: University of Chicago Press, 2013).

2. Christopher Jencks and David Riesman, *The Academic Revolution* (Garden City, NY: Doubleday, 1968); John R. Thelin has astutely noted that one feature of this revolution has been the rhetorical inflation of academic expectations and a masking of historical realities: "Expectations and Reality in American Higher Education," *NEA Higher Education Journal* (Fall 2007): 59–70.

3. Mary Beth Norton et al., *A People and a Nation*, 7th ed. (Boston: Houghton Mifflin, 2005), chap. 25, 686ff.

4. Ibid., chaps. 27 and 28.

5. Ira Katznelson, "Was the Great Society a Lost Opportunity?," in *The Rise and Fall of the New Deal Order, 1930–1980*, ed. Steve Fraser and Gary Gerstle (Princeton, NJ: Princeton University Press, 1980), chap. 7; J. M. Stephen Peeps, "A B.A. for the G.I. . . . Why?," *History of Education Quarterly* 24, no. 4 (Winter 1984): 513–24.

6. Robert M. Hutchins (1944), cited in Suzanne Mettler, *Soldiers to Citizens: The G.I. Bill and the Making of the Greatest Generation* (New York: Oxford University Press, 2005), 64.

7. Mettler, *Soldiers to Citizens*, 28.

8. Ibid. Mettler notes that 65 percent of veterans were Protestant, 24 percent Catholic, and 7 percent Jewish; 19 percent grew up in cities, 18 percent in medium sized town, 33 percent in small towns or cities, and 18 percent on farms. Almost all had experienced the hard times of the Depression, and 44 percent had unemployed fathers. Twenty-four percent had mothers working outside the home. Seventy-seven percent of veterans experienced some form of unemployment before the war that affected the family income and frequently disrupted any educational possibility. See also, Ira Katznelson, *When Affirmative Action Was White* (New York: W. W. Norton, 2005), 125–40; Lizabeth Cohen, *A Consumer's Republic: The Politics of Mass Consumption in Postwar America* (New York: Vintage, 2003), 137–44; David Kennedy, *Freedom from Fear* (New York: Oxford University Press, 2001).

9. Mettler, *Soldiers to Citizens*, chaps. 3 and 7, esp. 131.

10. Ibid., chap. 3; see also James Axtell, *The Making of Princeton University* (New York: Princeton University Press, 2006), 142–44.

11. Mettler, *Soldiers to Citizens*, chaps. 7 and 8.

12. Daniel A. Clark, "'The Two Joes Meet—Joe College, Joe Veteran': The G.I. Bill College Education and Postwar American Culture," *History of Education Quarterly* 38, no. 2 (Summer

1998):165–89; John Hardin Best, "The Revolution of Markets and Management: Toward a History of American Higher Education," *History of Education Quarterly* 28, no. 2 (Summer 1988): 177–89; George Keller, *Academic Strategy: The Management Revolution in American Higher Education* (Baltimore: Johns Hopkins University Press, 1983).

13. Ellen Schrecker, *No Ivory Tower: McCarthyism and the Universities* (New York: Oxford University Press, 1986.)

14. Margaret O'Mara, *Cities of Knowledge: Cold War Science and the Search for the Next Silicon Valley* (Princeton, NJ: Princeton University Press, 2005), 52–53.

15. Roger L. Geiger, *Research and Relevant Knowledge* (New York: Oxford University Press, 1993), chap. 1: Otto N. Larsen, *Milestones and Millstones: Social Science at the National Science Foundation, 1945–1991* (New Brunswick, NJ: Transaction Publishers, 1992).

16. Geiger, *Research and Relevant Knowledge*, 18.

17. Ibid., chap. 2.

18. Stuart Leslie, *The Cold War and American Science* (New York: Columbia University Press, 1993). See also Donald Wilson, "Academic Paragons," *Science* 262, no. 5134 (October 29, 1993): 771. The National Institutes of Health budget reached $60 million in 1951, somewhat less than half of the total federal support to scientific research at that time.

19. Geiger, *Research and Relevant Knowledge*, chap. 2.

20. Ibid., chap. 3; https://en.wikipedia.org/Noam_Chomsky; in Massachusetts the two institutions that received land-grant status were MIT in the eastern portion of the state and the University of Massachusetts near Amherst in the western portion.

21. Glenn T. Seaborg with Ray Colvig, *Chancellor at Berkeley* (Berkeley, CA: Institute of Government Studies Press, 1994).

22. Ibid. See chapter 15, "Clark Kerr: The Unapologetic Pragmatist," for more detail on this development.

23. A. Whitney Griswold, *Essays on Education* (New Haven, CT: Yale University Press, 1954).

24. Geiger, *Research and Relevant Knowledge*, chap. 3.

25. One should note that even major players like James B. Conant, president of Harvard, treated postwar federal funding as a novelty working within a traditional academic framework rather than a transformational force. The one slight reference to it in his substantive autobiography makes the point. He acknowledges that federal funding has created a "new climate of opinion" and accepts that private and public universities will compete for federal support. James B. Conant, *My Several Lives: Memoirs of a Social Inventor* (New York: Harper and Row, 1970), 179.

26. O'Mara, *Cities of Knowledge*, chap. 1.

27. Kenneth Jackson, *Crabgrass Frontier: The Suburbanization of the United States* (New York: Oxford University Press, 1965); Paul H. Mattingly, "The Suburban Canon over Time," in *Suburban Discipline*, ed. Peter Lang (Princeton, NJ: Princeton Architectural Press, 1997), 38–51.

28. Mattingly, "Suburban Canon," 38–51; Paul H. Mattingly, "Cities of Knowledge," *History of Education Quarterly* 46, no. 1 (Spring 2006):100–105.

29. See Colin Burke, *Information and Intrigue: From Index Cards to Dewey Decimals to Alger Hiss* (Cambridge, MA: MIT Press, 2014), for a highly illuminating practitioner's view of the new scientific and federal funding organizations before 1950.

30. Geiger, *Research and Relevant Knowledge*, chap. 6.

31. Ibid.

32. Ibid., 187.

33. Ibid., chap. 6.

34. Ibid.

35. Ibid., 204.

36. Ibid.

37. Ibid., chap. 7.

38. Paul H. Mattingly, *Suburban Landscapes: Culture and Politics in a New York Metropolitan Culture* (Baltimore: Johns Hopkins University Press, 2001); by the same author, "The Middle Class in the Suburbs," in *Encyclopedia of American Urban History*, ed. David Goldfield (Thousand Oaks, CA: Sage Publications, 2007), 472–75.

39. O'Mara, *Cities of Knowledge*, chap. 3. Varian Associates signed the first lease in 1951, but Hewlett-Packard would become known as the preeminent success story of the venture. In 2001 the Hewlett Foundation made a gift of $400 million, the largest in Stanford's history to that date. See also Rebecca S. Lowen, *Creating the Cold War University: The Transformation of Stanford* (Los Angeles: University of California Press, 1997).

40. Dawn Levy, "Biography Revisits Fred Terman's Roles in Engineering, Stanford, Silicon Valley," *Stanford Report*, November 3, 2004, http://news.stanford.edu/news/2004/november3/Terman-1103.html.

41. Rebecca S. Lowen, "Transforming the University: Administrators, Physicists and Industrial and Federal Patronage at Stanford, 1935–49," *History of Education Quarterly* 31, no. 3 (Fall 1991): 365–88. Lowen argues that internal dynamics were as forceful in changing Stanford as federal dollars.

42. O'Mara, *Cities of Knowledge*, chap. 3.

43. Hugh Davis Graham, *The Uncertain Triumph: Federal Education Policy in the Kennedy and Johnson Years* (Chapel Hill: University of North Carolina Press, 1984), chaps. 1–3; http://en.wikipedia.org/wiki/Francis-Keppel.

44. Graham, *The Uncertain Triumph*, introduction.

45. Gardner would subsequently become Secretary of the reorganized Department of Health, Education, and Welfare from 1965 to 1968. He is best known for his creation and support of Medicare and after government service the founding of Common Cause, a grassroots lobby staffed heavily by volunteers. Cf. Ellen C. Lagemann, *Private Power for the Public Good: A History of the Carnegie Foundation for the Advancement of Teaching* (Middletown CT: Wesleyan University Press, 1983), 126–27; see also J. Craig Jenkins and Abigail Halcli, "Grass-Rooting the System: The Development and Impact of Social Movement Philanthropy," in *Philanthropic Foundations*, ed. Ellen Lagemann (Bloomington: Indiana University Press, 1999), chap. 10; Peter D. Hall, *Inventing the Non-Profit Sector and Other Essays on Philanthropy, Voluntarism and Nonprofit Organizations* (Baltimore: Johns Hopkins University Press. 1992).

46. Graham, *The Uncertain Triumph*, chap. 3.

47. Ibid.

48. Ibid.

49. http://en.wikipedia.org/wiki/Joseph_A_Califano; http://www.gse.harvard.edu/facultyresearch/profiles/profile/shtml?vp; James Allen Smith, *The Idea Brokers: Think Tanks and the Rise of the New Policy Elite* (New York: Free Press, 1991), 151–52.

50. Paul H. Mattingly and Marilyn Tobias, "Race, Gender and Equity Policy," *History of Education Quarterly* 19, no. 4 (Winter 1999): 397–426; Lee Sproul, Stephen Weiner, and David Wolf, *Organizing an Anarchy: Belief, Bureaucracy and Politics in the National Institute of Education* (Chicago: University of Chicago Press, 1978); John Brademas and Lynne Browne, *The Politics of Education: Conflict and Consensus on Capitol Hill* (Norman: University of Oklahoma Press, 1987); Carl Kaestle and Marshall Smith, "The Federal Role in Elementary and Secondary Education," *Harvard Educational Review* 52, no. 2 (November 1982): 384–408; Arthur Wise, "The Taming of the National Institute of Education," *Phi Delta Kappan* (September 1976): 62–65; Phillip B. Zodhiates, "Bureaucrats and Politics: The National Institute of Education and Educational Research under Reagan" (unpublished doctoral diss., Harvard University, 1988); Maris Vinovskis, "The Changing Role of the Federal Government in Educational Research and Statistics," *History of Education Quarterly* 36, no. 2 (Summer 1996): 111–28.

51. Robert M. Rosenzweig, *The Political University: Policy, Politics, and Presidential Leadership in the American Research University* (Baltimore: Johns Hopkins University Press, 1998).

52. O'Mara, *Cities of Knowledge*, chap. 3.

53. Kenneth Jackson, *Crabgrass Frontier* (New York: Oxford University Press, 1986).

54. Hamilton Cravens, ed., *The Social Sciences Go to Washington: The Politics of Knowledge in the Post Modern Age* (New Brunswick, NJ: Rutgers University Press, 2004).

55. O'Mara, *Cities of Knowledge*, chap. 4.

56. Ibid., chap. 5.

57. Thomas Kuhn, *The Structure of Scientific Revolutions* (Chicago: University of Chicago Press, 1962). Kuhn's argument that science as progress by accumulation of accepted facts was part of a historic paradigm rather than an unchanging value. Over time, several paradigms of "science"—notably from Ptolemy to Copernicus—have emerged and dramatically altered "scientific" methods.

CHAPTER FOURTEEN

1. An earlier draft of this essay appeared in *Social Science History* 36, no. 4 (Winter 2012): 481–97, one contribution to several essays recognizing the fiftieth anniversary publication of Clark Kerr's *The Uses of the University*.

2. Hugh Davis Graham, *The Uncertain Triumph: Federal Education Policy in the Kennedy and Johnson Years* (Chapel Hill: University of North Carolina Press, 1984).

3. John Aubrey Douglass, *The California Idea and American Higher Education* (Stanford, CA: Stanford University Press, 2000), 265, notes, "Of the approximately seventeen states during the late 1950s and 1960s that modified their public and private systems to promote coordination and control costs, most looked toward reducing the autonomy of their public higher education institutions." They did so by creating "super boards" to which state legislatures could respond, especially on issues of budget, administrative appointments, and institutional expansion. It is questionable whether this simplification really "centralized" activity or created more chaos below the veneer of order.

4. Ibid., 192.

5. Ibid., chaps. 4 and 5; Kevin Starr, *Golden Dreams: California in an Age of Abundance, 1950–1963* (New York: Oxford University Press, 2009), chap. 8, "The Cold War Campus."

6. Starr, *Golden Dreams*, chap. 8; Barbara R. Peltzman, "Robert Gordon Sproul," in *Biographical Dictionary of American Educators*, vol. 3, ed. John Ohles (Westport, CT: Greenwood Press, 1978), 1226.

7. Douglass, *The California Idea*, chap. 8.

8. "Hiram Warren Johnson," in *Who Was Who in American History*, vol. 2 (Chicago: Marquis, 1975), 284.

9. It should be noted that the University of Southern California was but one of many strong, independent schools in the state, including the California Institute of Technology and Stanford University as well as liberal arts colleges like Pomona, Occidental, Claremont Men's, Harvey Mudd, and Scripps and the Jesuit schools, Loyola Marymount in Los Angeles, University of San Francisco, and the University of Santa Clara. Their presence and efficacy helps explain Kerr's cooperation with them in creating the California Scholarship Plan, which provided support to any California institution, public or private, awarding a full tuition voucher to any talented high school senior.

10. Douglass, *The California Idea*, chap. 7.

11. Ibid.; see also Ellen Schrecker, *No Ivory Tower: McCarthyism and the Universities* (New York: Oxford University Press, 1986), 121–25. Schrecker makes the crucial point that the thirty-one professors dismissed were understood by the university's own investigations to be noncommunists. They had objected to the oath's interference with academic integrity, as did so many American universities nationwide, which subsequently hired many of them. Ultimately by 1956 the thirty-one were exonerated and offered their back pay. Inside and outside California, many were alarmed

by how quickly the "loyalty" issue shifted away from charges of communism and inflated into extralegal arenas.

12. Douglass, *The California Idea*, chap. 9.

13. Starr, *Golden Dreams*, chap. 8. The postwar period witnessed a major economic shift in California from mining and agriculture to aviation, electronics, and aerospace. During the Korean War, the state experienced a 140 percent increase in employment in the aircraft industry alone. By 1959 Department of Defense spending on aerospace reached $228 billion, and one-quarter of all its contracts went to California. This work was research oriented, and the universities felt the impact of this support through the rest of the century.

14. Douglass, *The California Idea*, chap. 9.

15. Arthur G. Coons, *Crises in California Higher Education* (Los Angles: Ritchie, 1968), 12; "Arthur Gardiner Coons," in *Who Was Who in American History*, vol. 5 (Chicago: Marquis, 1973),149.

16. Coons, *California Higher Education*, chaps. 1 and 2.

17. Ibid., 26–27.

18. Ibid., chaps. 4–6.

19. Karen Arenson, "On Campus: Reflections of the Man Who Engineered California's State University System," *New York Times*, February 17, 1999. After the fact, Kerr himself began to propose additions to the major agenda that included greater attention to ethics!

20. Grace Hechinger, "Clark Kerr: Leading Educator and Former Head of California's Universities Dies at 92," *New York Times*, December 2, 2003. To be fair, Sproul's administrative tenure had produced a multicampus system, which became synonymous with Kerr's later idea, "multiversity." However, the two notions differed insofar as a single campus could become a multiversity, like University of California, Berkeley, or UCLA. Kerr's contribution was less serving as the architect of the system than it was offering a distinctive postwar rationale for the phenomenon.

21. William A. Link, *William Friday: Power, Purpose and American Higher Education* (Chapel Hill: University of North Carolina Press, 1997), 199, 208–9. Friday, who had a strong working relationship with Kerr on the Carnegie Commission on Higher Education, sent a contingent to visit California and to study its experience. See also Coons, *Crises*, 87.

22. Clark Kerr, *The Uses of the University* (New York: Harper and Row, 1963); Thelin, *A History of American Higher Education* (Baltimore: Johns Hopkins University Press, 2004), 278.

23. Thelin, *American Higher Education*; Roger Geiger, *Research and Relevant Knowledge: American Research Universities since World War II* (New York: Oxford University Press, 1993), esp. chaps. 1 and 2.

24. In the Fall 1964 special issue of *Daedalus*, titled "The Contemporary University," Kerr noted that the federal government invested $1.5 billion in higher education in 1960. "About one-third of this $1.5 billion was for university-affiliated research centers; about one-third for project research within universities; and about one-third for other things, such as residence hall loans, scholarships and teaching programs. This last third was expended at colleges as well as universities, but the first two-thirds almost exclusively at universities, and at relatively few of them." Quoted in Clark Kerr. "Prologue-Transformations," in *The Great Transformation in Higher Education, 1960–1980* (Albany: State University of New York Press, 1991), 123. Later in the same essay, Kerr adds: "Expenditures have been largely restricted to the physical and biomedical sciences, and to engineering, with only about 3 percent for the social sciences and hardly any support for the humanities" (124). This differentiation prompted no call for redress nor was it characterized as an inequity or a crisis.

25. Kerr, *The Uses of the University*, 122–24.

26. Ibid., 37. Kerr explicitly says that a modern university administrator "has no new bold 'vision of the end.'" See John Aubrey Douglass's review of Kerr's autobiography, *The Gold and the Blue: A Personal Memoir of the University of California, 1949–67*, in *History of Education Quarterly* 43, no. 1 (Spring 2003): 143–48.

27. Kerr, *The Uses of the University*, 32–33.

28. A year before Kerr's book, Paul Goodman asked in *A Community of Scholars* (New York: Random House, 1962) where the intellectual community had gone. Page Smith later sharpened the point in *Killing the Spirit: Higher Education in America* (New York: Penguin, 1990).

29. Kerr makes these implications specific in a later essay, "Prologue-Transformations," xv: "I have never read what I considered a fully objective account of events in which I have participated, either by an outside observer or by a participant. I have consequently developed a certain skepticism about all histories. History is an art and not an exact science, and an art of passion as well as analysis. One should write, as one should read, with realization of the limitations of all histories."

30. Henry David Aiken, "Enter the Multiversity," in *The Predicament of the University* (Bloomington: Indiana University Press, 1971), 113–23. Even astute historians of higher education became euphoric more than analytic or historical in the face of Kerr's abstract and contradictory multiversity argument. See Sheldon Rothblatt, "Clark Kerr and the Pursuit of Excellence in the Modern University," *Minerva* 33, no. 3 (1995): 265–77, as well as Jonathan Cole, *The Great American University* (New York: Public Affairs, 2009), 134–44.

31. Lewis A. Coser, *Refugee Scholars in America* (New Haven, CT: Yale University Press, 1984); Donald Fleming and Bernard Bailyn, eds., *The Intellectual Migration: Europe and America, 1930–1960* (Cambridge, MA: Charles Warren Center for Studies in American History, 1968); Daniel Kevles, *The Physicists: The History of a Scientific Community in Modern America* (New York: Alfred Knopf, 1978).

32. Andre Schiffrin, ed., *The Cold War and the University* (New York: New Press, 1997); Christopher Simpson, *Universities and Empire: Money and Politics in the Social Sciences during the Cold War* (New York: New Press, 1998). The latter book explores the adverse impact of federal support on the social sciences, especially in their models of capitalist development and management of Third World insurgencies, as in Ghana and Chile.

33. See Helen Lefkowitz Horowitz, "In the Wake of Laurence Veysey: Re-Examining the Liberal Arts College," *History of Education Quarterly* 45, no. 3 (Fall 2005): 420–26.

34. Laurence Veysey, *The Emergence of the American University* (Chicago: University of Chicago Press, 1965). Both Kerr and Veysey would likely have resisted the charge that their writings were ideological at all.

35. Julie Reuben, *The Making of the Modern University: Intellectual Transformation and the Marginalization of Morality* (Chicago: University of Chicago Press, 1996), makes the case for a less facile polarization than Veysey's, one in which "religion" and "morality" were not eliminated, so much as experienced reconfigurations. See also Mark Schwehn, "A 'Dying Light' or a Newborn Enlightenment: Religion and Higher Education in the Twenty-First Century," *History of Education Quarterly* 45, no. 3 (Fall 2005): 454–60.

36. Ruth S. Lowen, "The More Things Change: Money, Power and the Professoriate," *History of Education Quarterly* 45, no. 3 (Fall 2005): 438–45.

37. Christopher Loss, "Bureaucratic Tyranny: 'The Price of Structure' in the American University," *History of Education Quarterly* 45, no. 3 (Fall 2005): 446–53.

38. Paul H. Mattingly, "Structures over Time: Institutional History," in *Historical Inquiry in Education: A Research Agenda*, ed. John Hardin Best (Washington, DC: American Educational Research Association, 1983), 34–55.

39. Not surprisingly, these ideological assumptions played themselves out in Clark Kerr's post-Berkeley career at the Carnegie Commission on Higher Education. See Lewis B. Mayhew, *The Carnegie Commission on Higher Education* (San Francisco: Jossey Bass, 1973). See also Kerr's 1975 essay ("In Transit: What We Might Learn from the Climacteric," in *The Great Transformation*), 132, where his "reflections apply more particularly to research-oriented institutions than to others." His primary concern was the loss of public confidence in education, something exacerbated by the "student unrest" of the 1960s. Universities, he strongly urged, must cultivate "better contacts with the public."

40. C. P. Snow, *Two Cultures and the Scientific Revolution* (Cambridge: Cambridge University Press, 1960), offered this book as a development of a 1959 lecture, "The Two Cultures," which expressed a concern about a division that undermined the possibility of settling large national and global problems. It was widely discussed in the very period of the 1960s.

41. Cole, *The Great American University*, 138.

42. Craig Calhoun, "The Public Mission of the Research University," in *Knowledge Matters: The Public Mission of the Research University*, ed. Diana Rhoten and Craig Calhoun (New York: Columbia University Press, 2011), 1–33.

CHAPTER FIFTEEN

1. In its most simplistic form, pragmatism is a theory that measures worth/truth by its practical applications. Historically there are many versions of the theory, but all subscribe to the assumption that metaphysical principles/ absolutes distract inquiry from the authority of experience and engaging actual outcomes as experimental inquiry. https://en.wikipedia.org/wiki/Pragmatism.

2. Sheldon S. Wolin and John H. Schaar, "A Special Supplement: Berkeley and the Fate of the Multiversity," *New York Review of Books* 4, no. 3 (March 11, 1965): 15–18.

3. The literature on these events is extensive. Document collections include Michael V. Miller and Susan Gilmore, eds., *Revolution at Berkeley: The Crisis in American Education* (New York: Dell, 1965); Seymour Martin Lipset and Sheldon S. Wolin, eds. *The Berkeley Student Revolt: Facts and Interpretations* (New York: Doubleday Anchor, 1965). See also the quantitative analysis of Seymour Martin Lipset, *Rebellion in the University* (Chicago: University of Chicago Press, 1971).

4. Terry Anderson, *The Movement and the Sixties* (New York: Oxford University Press, 1965), chap. 1; David Farber, ed., *The Sixties: From Memory to History* (Chapel Hill: University of North Carolina Press, 1994).

5. Gerth himself was a student of noted social theorist and London émigré Karl Mannheim. Collectively their work reshaped much of the academic discussion of social progress, ideology, and institutional structures in the 1930s. Cf. Peter Novick, *That Noble Dream: The "Objectivity Question" and the American Historical Profession* (Cambridge: Cambridge University Press, 1988), 159–61. Nobuko Gerth, "Hans H. Gerth and C. Wright Mills: Partnership and Partisanship," *International Journal of Politics, Culture and Society* 7, no. 1 (1993): 133–54. Mills would also find academic shelter, once at Columbia University, not in the mainstream sociology department but in émigré Paul Lazarsfeld's Bureau of Applied Social Research. See Jonathan Sterne, "C. Wright Mills, the Bureau for Applied Social Research and the Meaning of Critical Sociology," *Cultural Studies, Critical Methodologies* 5, no. 1 (2005): 65–94.

6. C. Wright Mills, *Sociology and Pragmatism: The Higher Learning in America* (New York: Oxford University Press, 1964), esp. the introduction by Irving L. Horowitz; see also Rick Tilman, "The Intellectual Pedigree of C. Wright Mills," *Western Political Quarterly* 32, no. 4 (December 1979): 478–96. Also Henry Aiken, "C. Wright Mills and the Pragmatists," *New York Review of Books* 4, no. 3 (March 11, 1965):8–10.

7. http://en.wikipedia.org/wiki/C._Wright_Mills. In 2006 Tom Hayden published his MA thesis, *Radical Nomad: C. Wright Mills and His Times* (Boulder, CO: Paradigm Publishers, 2006). See the helpful review by Neil McLaughlin, in the *Canadian Journal of Sociology* online (March–April 2007), http://www.cjsonline.ca/reviews/radicalnomad.html.

8. Hayden's successors as SDS presidents, Todd Gitlin (1963–64) and Carl Oglesby (1965–66), also resisted uses of violence, insisted on persuasion, and subsequently had academic careers. Margalit Fox, "Carl Oglesby, 76, Antiwar Leaders in 1960s," *New York Times*, September 14, 2011.

9. Lee Lowenfish, "Students and Academic Unrest," *History of Education Quarterly* 13, no. 2 (Summer 1973): 195–200.

10. Germaine Bree, "Sartre and Camus: Two Concepts of Commitment," in *The Teach-Ins: Reports, Opinions, Documents*, ed. Louise Menashe and Ronald Radosh (New York: Frederick A. Praeger Publishers, 1967), 246–55.

11. William Appleman Williams, "Our Leaders Are Following the Wrong Rainbow," in Menashe and Radosh, *The Teach-Ins*, 45–53; Binoy Kampmark, "William A. Williams' Tragedy Fifty Years On," *Historical Journal* 53, no. 3 (2010): 783–94. Kampmark attributes some of Williams's interests in the theoretical process of social change to the influence of émigré scholar Hans Gerth while Williams was at the University of Wisconsin. Cf. Eleanor Hakim, "The Tragedy of Hans Gerth," in *History and the New Left: Madison, Wisconsin, 1950–1970*, ed. Paul Buhle (Philadelphia: Temple University Press, 1990), 252–63.

12. http://en.wikipedia.org/wiki/Walter_Cronkite.

13. Joan Wallach Scott, "The Teach-In: A National Movement or the End of an Affair?," in Menashe and Radosh, *The Teach-Ins*, 190–93.

14. Bundy's career epitomized the academic who moved easily in and out of government, in and out of the Foundation sector. Bundy would later head the Ford Foundation (1966–79) after he left the Johnson administration. After a controversial tenure there, he returned to academia and the history department of New York University, where he wrote a notable book on American nuclear policy. In 1965, however, Bundy, national advisor to President Johnson, became the flash point for a number of letters pointedly criticizing the administration's Vietnam policy and asking for a national debate. In a conversation with the author while both served on the history faculty at New York University, Bundy claimed he had wanted to honor his commitment to the debate with Morgenthau, but President Johnson insisted he represent the United States during its Santo Domingo incursion in summer 1965.

15. Douglas Martin, "Robert A. Scalapino, a Scholar of Asian Politics, Dies at 92," *New York Times*, November 12, 2011, A28.

16. This issue would develop into questions of national integrity, when many of the government's arguments proved false, not the least of which were those manipulated to achieve the Tonkin Gulf Resolution, which evaded the constitutional mandate for a Senate confirmation of any war declaration. These issues ultimately impacted the place of the humanities in American higher education. See Martin Jay, "The Ambivalent Virtues of Mendacity: How Europeans Taught (Some of Us) to Learn to Love the Lies of Politics," in Hollinger, *The Humanities and the Dynamics of Inclusion*, 107–25.

17. David Hollinger, "The Problem of Pragmatism in American History," *Journal of American History* 67 (1982): 88–107. Hollinger argues the ubiquity of pragmatism in the broad American discourse, both in academic and government policy circles, until 1980. Then he perceived a falling away from pragmatism's basic tenants. However, he later conceded pragmatism's enduing influence. David Hollinger, *In the American Province: Studies in the History and Historiography of Ideas* (Bloomington: Indiana University Press, 1985).

18. Kenneth J. Heineman, *Campus Wars: The Peace Movement at American State Universities in the Vietnam Era* (New York: New York University Press, 1993); Helen L. Horowitz, "The 1960s and the Transformation of Campus Cultures," *History of Education Quarterly* 26, no. 1 (Spring 1986): 1–38; Lynn Gordon, "In the Shadow of SDS: Writing the History of Twentieth-Century College Students," *History of Education Quarterly* 26, no. 1 (Spring 1986): 131–39; Kirkpatrick Sale, *SDS* (New York: Vintage Books, 1973). As these studies show, after the 1960s, students became a regular research target of social scientists in ways that they had never been before.

19. Thomas Bender and Carl Schorske, eds., *American Academic Culture in Transition* (Princeton, NJ: Princeton University Press, 1997); Peter Novick makes the important point that until after World War II the social sciences and the humanities at the college and university level achieved advancement more by teaching very heavy loads than by scholarship. This teaching tradition set a context by which American academics often failed to appreciate the high quality of scholarly work done by incoming émigré scholars in the interwar period. See Novick, *That Noble Dream*, 174–80.

20. The award-winning book *Fire in the Lake: The Vietnamese and the Americans in Vietnam* (1972) by Frances Fitzgerald demonstrated in exhaustive detail how the American and Vietnamese cultures never engaged each other, spent years talking past one another, and steadfastly refused to engage and understand the other. For Fitzgerald, the real tragedy of American involvement was its inability to grasp the limits of its own cultural assumptions. A parallel awakening about cultural intransigence was beginning at the same time in American academia.

21. Jon Wiener, *Professors, Politics and Pop* (London: Verso, 1991); Sigmund Diamond, *Compromised Campuses: The Collaboration of Universities and the Intelligence Communities, 1945–1955* (New York: Oxford University Press, 1992); James Gilbert, "The American University: Community, Oasis or Mummy?," *History of Education Quarterly* 10, no. 3 (Fall 1970): 367–74.

22. Peter Novick makes clear that analogous questions had begun a generation earlier among a cadre of historians, including Carl Becker and Charles Beard, questioning the possibility of "objective" knowledge. However, while much admired in select circles, their views were not taken up by their fellow professionals nor widely shared among the reading public. Novick, *That Noble Dream*, esp. chap. 9.

23. For a compelling discussion of the twentieth-century taproot of this issue, see James T. Kloppenberg, "The Place of Value in a Culture of Facts," in Hollinger, *The Humanities and the Dynamics of Inclusion*, 126–58; also James Gilbert, *Redeeming Culture: American Religion in an Age of Science* (Chicago: University of Chicago Press, 1997). One of the main concerns of Jonathan Cole's *The Great American University* (New York: New Press, 2009) is the early twenty-first-century efforts to curb faculty members' critical independence.

24. For the problematic role of ethics in John Dewey's thought, see Robert Westbrook, "Dewey's Truth," *History of Education Quarterly* 20, no. 3 (Fall 1980): 345–53, as well as his larger study, *John Dewey and American Democracy* (Ithaca, NY: Cornell University Press, 1993); Clarence J. Karier, "Liberalism and the Quest for Orderly Change," *History of Education Quarterly* 12, no. 1 (Spring 1972): 57–80. Without this broader debate, it would be unlikely that before 1980 studies would have emerged like Julie Ruben, *The Making of the Modern University: Intellectual Transformation and the Marginalization of Morality* (Chicago: University of Chicago Press, 1996), or discourses on the subject like George Marsden and Bradley J. Longfield, eds., *The Secularization of the Academy* (New York: Oxford University Press, 1992). In spite of twenty-first-century declines in the amount of required reading for class and hours spent writing for class and, most importantly, the absence of progress in critical thinking, the humanities students outperformed majors in business, communications, and other new subjects on the Collegiate Learning Assessment. Cf. Anthony Grafton, "Our Universities: Why They Are Failing," *New York Review of Books* 58, no. 18 (November 24, 2011): 38–42.

25. John McGreevey, "Catholics, Catholicism and the Humanities since World War II," in Hollinger, *The Humanities and the Dynamics of Inclusion*, 189–216. Catholic scholars generated their own internal debate with John Tracy Ellis's landmark 1955 essay, "American Catholics and the Intellectual Life" (*Thought* 30:351–88). In these same years, the Vatican actually contributed greatly to the confusion by silencing John Courtney Murray, SJ, on matters where he was a distinguished expert, the all-important relations of church and state. Such suppressions encouraged many important non-Catholic scholars from seeing Catholicism as anything but doctrinaire and conformist, attitudes that began to change in earnest in the 1970s and 1980s, in the wake of Catholic participation in the new social protests and in university participation at both the student and faculty levels. Individually some distinguished non-Catholic scholars with Catholic roots—Pulitzer Prize winners Garrett Mattingly (1900–1962) and Merle Curti (1897–1997), for example—used their liberal values to probe the Catholic caricature, found it wanting and welcomed Catholic graduate students at non-Catholic universities. See also Phillip Gleason, *Contending with Modernity: Catholic Higher Education in the Twentieth Century* (New York: Oxford University Press, 1995); William P. Leahy, SJ, *Adapting to America: Catholics, Jesuits and Higher Education in the Twentieth Century* (Washington, DC: Georgetown University Press, 1991); Robert E. Sullivan, ed., *Higher Learning and Catholic*

Traditions (Notre Dame, IN: Notre Dame University Press, 2001). For the deeper twentieth-century roots of these issues, see Gilbert, *Redeeming Culture*; James Hennessey, SJ, "Jesuit Higher Education," *History of Education Quarterly* 25, no. 3 (Fall 1985): 391–97; Robert Cross, "Recent Histories of U.S. Catholic Education," *History of Education Quarterly* 14, no. 1 (Spring 1974): 125–30.

26. John H. Roberts and James Turner, *The Sacred and Secular University* (Princeton, NJ: Princeton University Press, 2000); George Marsden, *The Soul of the American University: From Establishment to Established Nonbelief* (Oxford: Oxford University Press, 1994); Hollinger, *The Humanities and the Dynamics of Inclusion.* See also Patrick Allitt, *Catholic Converts: British and American Catholics Turn to Rome* (Ithaca, NY: Cornell University Press, 1997), chap. 11. The career of Berkeley sociologist of religion Robert Bellah, expands this point. www.en.wikipedia.org/wiki/Robert_Neeley_Bellah.

27. James Kloppenberg, "Pragmatism: A Old Name for Some New Ways of Thinking," *Journal of American History* 83, no. 1 (June 1996): 100–38.

28. Hugh Davis Graham, *The Uncertain Triumph* (Chapel Hill: University of North Carolina Press, 1984); Carol Lasser, ed., *Educating Men and Women Together: Coeducation in a Changing World* (Urbana: University of Illinois Press, 1987); John Hardin Best, "The Revolution of Markets and Management: Toward a History of American Higher Education since 1945," *History of Education Quarterly* 28, no. 2 (Summer 1988): 177–89.

29. Joan W. Scott and Debra Keates, eds., *Schools of Thought: Twenty-Five Years of Interpretive Social Science* (Princeton, NJ: Princeton University Press, 2001).

30. http://www.ssha.org/about-the-ssha-history. For the pros and cons of these programs, see Jerry A. Jacobs, *In Defense of Disciplines: Interdisciplinarity and Specialization in the Research University* (Chicago: University of Chicago Press, 2013).

31. See John Guillory, "Who's Afraid of Marcel Proust? The Failure of General Education in the American University," in Hollinger, *The Humanities and the Dynamics of Inclusion*, 25–49; Thomas Erlich, ed., *Civic Responsibility and Higher Education* (Phoenix: Oryx Press, 2000); Francis Oakley, *Community of Learning: The American College and the Liberal Arts Tradition* (New York: Oxford University Press, 1992).

32. Roger L. Geiger, "Demography and Curriculum: The Humanities in American Higher Education from the 1950s through the 1980s," in Hollinger, *The Humanities and the Dynamics of Inclusion*, 50.

33. In his 1992 Presidential Address to the History of Education Society, James D. Anderson makes a powerful case that meritocracy arguments were used to sustain patterns of racial discrimination in American higher education: "Race Meritocracy and the American Academy during the Immediate Post–World War II Era," *History of Education Quarterly* 33, no. 2 (Summer 1993): 151–75.

34. Andrew Schiffrin, ed., *The Cold War and the University: Toward an Intellectual History of the Postwar Years* (New York: New Press, 1997).

35. Douglas Sloan, "Knowledge, Values and Educational History: 'Once More into the Breach Dear Friends,'" *History of Education Quarterly* 25, no. 1 (Summer–Fall 1985): 1–19; several books that pressed critiques of narrow scientific instrumentalism became widely read as they might not have been a few years before, especially Thomas Kuhn, *The Structure of Scientific Revolutions* (Chicago: University of Chicago Press, 1962), and Michael Polanyi, *The Tacit Revolution* (Garden City, NY: Doubleday, 1966); Karl Popper, *The Open Society and Its Enemies (London: Routledge, 1945),* which elaborated his earlier arguments about the meaning and limits of modern science. See also Thomas Bender, "Politics, Intellect and the American University," in Bender and Schorske, *American Academic Culture in Transition*, 43–44.

36. Schiffrin, ed., *The Cold War and the University*, 187.

37. http://en.wikipedia.org/wiki/Herbert_Gutman. See Joseph F. Kett, "The Black Family under Slavery," *History of Education Quarterly* 17, no. 4 (Winter 1977): 455–60.

38. While earlier American history acted as a major player in the interdisciplinary efforts of postwar American studies, more often its real interdisciplinary successes occurred *within* the

history discipline itself. See Jacobs, *In Defense of Disciplines*, 26; Leila Zenderland, "Constructing American Studies: Culture, Identity, and the Expansion of the Humanities," in Hollinger, *The Humanities and the Dynamics of Inclusion*, 273–313.

39. Mary Beth Norton, David M. Katzman, Paul D. Escott, Howard P. Chudacoff, Thomas G. Patterson, and William M. Tuttle Jr. were the primary, original authors through 1998. *A People and a Nation: A History of the United States* (Boson: Houghton Mifflin Co., 1998).

40. Among many examples one might cite Studs Terkel's Pulitzer Prize-winning oral histories of World War II, *The Good War* (1945), and his 1970 examination of the Great Depression, *Hard Times*. His opus and media career greatly influenced many later histories like Debra Bernhardt and Rachel Bernstein, *Ordinary People, Extraordinary Lives* (New York: New York University Press, 2000).

41. Paul H. Mattingly and Rachel Bernstein, "The Pedagogy of Public History," *Journal of American Ethnic History* 18, no. 1 (Fall 1998): 77–92. Cf. http://dlib.nyu.edu/findingaids/html/archives/publhist/html.

42. To take one ongoing example, see http://www.visithistoricalelizabethnj. org.

43. Ron Grele, "Whose Public? Whose History? What Is the Goal of a Public Historian?," *Public Historian* 3 (Winter 1981), and assorted essays in these years in this journal; Novick, *That Noble Dream*, 512–21. Stellar public history programs at University of California, Santa Barbara; University of Massachusetts, Amherst; University of South Carolina at Charleston; and Arizona State University—all public institutions—and entrepreneurial, private urban schools like New York University and Temple University provided the models for the field.

44. Hayden White, "The Burden of History," *History and Theory* 5, no. 2 (1966): 111–34.

45. David J. Rothman and Stanton Wheeler, eds., *Social History and Social Policy* (New York: Academic Press, 1981), chap. 1.

46. Geraldine Clifford, *The Sane Positivist: Edward Lee Thorndike* (Middletown, CT: Wesleyan University Press, 1970).

47. Nicholas Leman, *The Big Test: The Secret History of the American Meritocracy* (New York: Farrar Straus and Giroux, 1999).

48. Hilary Putnam, "A Half Century of Philosophy, Viewed from Within," in Bender and Schorske, *American Academic Culture*, 193–226. Analytic philosophy gravitated away from both the history of philosophy and political theory, a distancing that became off-putting for students interested in "the big questions" brought to the fore by the events of the 1960s. See Rogers M. Smith, "Still Blowing in the Wind: The American Quest for a Democratic, Scientific Political Science," in Bender and Schorske, *American Academic Culture*, 272–73.

49. David Hollinger, "The Problem of Pragmatism in American History," *Journal of American History* 67 (1982): 88–107; Alexander Neuhaus, "Trends in Recent American Philosophy," in Bender and Schorske, *American Academic Culture*, 227–41, where the author argues that analytic philosophy dominates the major departments of philosophy in present-day America and where the philosophy discourse, unlike the literary or linguistic discourses, remains relatively cohesive and without fissures and dichotomies.

50. Henry Steele Commager, *The American Mind* (New Haven, CT: Yale University Press, 1950), where he notably declared, "Being pragmatic is essentially being American."

51. James Kloppenberg, "Pragmatism: An Old Name for Some New Ways of Thinking?," *Journal of American History* 83, no. 1 (June 1996): 100–38. This article strives hard to insist that pragmatism requires reaffirmation and remains highly attractive to professional practitioners in the American academic culture.

52. Ibid. See also Richard Rorty, "Dewey's Metaphysics," *Consequences of Pragmatism* (Minneapolis: University of Minnesota Press, 1982), chap. 5.

53. M. H. Abrams, "The Transformation of English Studies, 1930-1995," in Bender and Schorske, *American Academic Culture*, 123–49.

54. Jacobs, *In Defense of Disciplines*, chap. 8. Jacobs argues persuasively that American studies achieved a kind of coherent interdisciplinary model until the 1960s. Even in its less coherent decades (1970–1990s), its interdisciplinarity was less a panacea and solution to the problem of academic overspecialization than a phenomenon based on close interactions with the traditional disciplines of English and history.

55. https://en.wikipedia.org/wiki/M_H_Abrams. Abrams was the son of eastern European Jewish immigrants, who connected his life and work to an appreciation of an older scholarship not necessarily rooted in the American pragmatic experience.

56. Ibid.

57. Martha C. Nussbaum, *Not for Profit: Why Democracy Needs the Humanities* (Princeton, NJ: Princeton University Pres, 2010).

58. Charles Lindblom, "Political Science in the 1940s and 1950s," in Bender and Schorske, *American Academic Culture*, 243–70.

59. Rogers M. Smith, "Still Blowing in the Wind: The American Quest for Democratic, Scientific Political Science," in Bender and Schorske, *American Academic Culture*, 271–305; Carl E. Schorske, "The New Rigorism in the Human Sciences," in Bender and Schorske, *American Academic Culture*, 316.

60. James G. March and Johan P. Olsen, *Rediscovering Institutions* (New York: Free Press, 1989); and by the same authors, "The New Institutionalism: Organizational Factors in American," *American Political Science Review* 78 (1984).

61. Ira Katznelson, "From the Street to the Lecture Hall: The 1960s," in Bender and Schorske, *American Academic Culture*, 338, 344; see also by the same author, "The Subtle Politics of Developing Emergency," in Schiffrin, *The Cold War and the University*, 233–58.

62. David M. Kreps, "Economics—The Current Position," in Bender and Schorske, *American Academic Culture*, 89.

63. Robert M. Solow, "How Did Economics Get That Way and What Way Did It Get?," in Bender and Schorske, *American Academic Culture*, 57–76.

64. William Barber, "Reconfigurations in American Academic Economics," in Bender and Schorske, *American Academic Culture*, 105–21.

65. Ibid. See Howard Zinn, "The Politics of History in the Era of the Cold War: Repression and Resistance," in Schiffrin, *The Cold War and the University*, 35–72. In the same volume, see Richard Ohmann, "English and the Cold War," 73–105.

66. Richard Rorty, *Philosophy and the Mirror of Nature* (Princeton, NJ: Princeton University Press, 1979), represented a philosophical reengagement with Deweyan pragmatism, cognizant of the issues in several of the professional discourses.

67. Thomas Kuhn, *The Structure of Scientific Revolutions* (Chicago: University of Chicago Press, 1962).

68. More recently, the probe of empirical science and the rethinking of teleology, initiated by thinkers like Thomas Nagel, exemplify the ongoing creativity of this scholarship. Thomas Nagel, "A Philosopher Defends Religion," *New York Review of Books* 59, no. 14 (September 27, 2012): 62–63; H. Allen Orr, "Awaiting a New Darwin," *New York Review of Books* 60, no. 2 (February 2013): 26–28.

69. Tamar Lewin, "Colleges Slower to Branch Out," *New York Times*, January 12, 2012, A6.

Index